EXPLORATIONS AND SURVEYS FOR A RAILROAD ROUTE FROM THE MISSISSIPPI RIVER TO THE PACIFIC OCEAN.

WAR DEPARTMENT.

REPORT

ON THE

BOTANY OF THE EXPEDITION:

BY

JOHN TORREY AND ASA GRAY.

ROUTE ON THE FORTY-FIRST PARALLEL OF NORTH LATITUDE, UNDER THE COMMAND OF LIEUT. E. G. BECKWITH, THIRD ARTILLERY;

AND

ROUTE NEAR THE THIRTY-EIGHTH AND THIRTY-NINTH PARALLELS OF NORTH LATITUDE, UNDER THE COMMAND OF CAPT. J. W. GUNNISON, CORPS OF TOPOGRAPHICAL ENGINEERS.

CONTENTS.

PART I.

PART II.

BOTANICAL REPORT.

Botanical Report, by JOHN TORREY *and* ASA GRAY, *upon the Collections made by Captain* GUNNISON, *Topographical Engineers, in* 1853, *and by Lieutenant* E. G. BECKWITH, *Third Artillery, in* 1854.

I.—Plants collected by Mr. James A. Snyder, under the direction of Lieutenant E. G. Beckwith, U. S. A., in an expedition made under his charge from Great Salt Lake, Utah Territory, directly west to the Sacramento valley, in California, in the months of May, June, and July, 1854.

II.—Plants collected by Mr. F. Creutzfeldt, under the direction of Captain J. W. Gunnison, U. S. A., in charge of explorations for a railroad from Fort Leavenworth, *via* the Kansas, Arkansas, and Huerfano rivers, the Sangre de Cristo Pass, San Luis valley, Coochetopa Pass, Grand and Green rivers, and thence into the Great Basin, in the vicinity of the Sevier or Nicollet lake. The collection was made from early in June to late in October, 1853.

PART I.

Plants collected by Mr. JAMES A. SNYDER, *under the direction of Lieutenant* E. G. BECKWITH, *U. S. Army, in an expedition made under his charge from Great Salt lake, directly west, to the Sacramento valley, in California, in the months of May, June, and July,* 1854.

AQUILEGIA CANADENSIS, *Linn.; Torrey and Gray, Fl.* 1, *p.* 29. In a cañon east of the Sierra Nevada; June 17. Few phanerogamous plants of this country have so great a geographical range as has this species, (including the A. formosa, *Fischer,*) namely: from Hudson's Bay to Florida and New Mexico, and from Unalaschka to California.

DELPHINIUM MENZIESII, *DC. Syst.* 1, *p.* 355; *Hook. Fl. Bor.-Amer.* 1, *p.* 25. Near Great Salt Lake. Also, in a valley of the Sierra Nevada; with an incomplete specimen of what may be a white-flowered variety; May and June.

ESCHSCHOLTZIA CALIFORNICA, *Cham. and Nees, Flor. Phys. Berol. p.* 73, *t.* 15, *non Lindl.* Sierra Nevada; June 25.

TURRITIS RETROFRACTA, *Hook. Fl. Bor.-Amer.* 1, *p.* 41. Summit of a mountain in the Great Basin east of the Sierra Nevada. In flower only; June 1.

ERYSIMUM ASPERUM, *DC.; Torr. and Gray, Fl.* 1, *p.* 95. Mountains near Great Salt Lake; May.

SPRAGUEA UMBELLATA, *Torr. Pl. Fremont, in Smithson. Contrib. p.* 4, *t.* 1. Summit of Noble's Pass, Sierra Nevada; July 3. The specimens of this interesting Portulacaceous genus accord with those of Col. Fremont, who alone has gathered the plant hitherto; but being younger, the corollas are more conspicuous, and the scarious sepals not so large.

LEWISIA REDIVIVA, *Pursh, Fl.* 1, *p.* 368; *Hook. and Arn. Bot. Beech. p.* 334, *t.* 86. On the Sierra Nevada; June 25.

SIDALCEA MALVÆFLORA, *Gray, Pl. Wright.* 1, *p.* 16. Mountains east of the Sierra Nevada; June 14.

VIOLA BECKWITHII, (n. sp.): subcaulescent; ascending stems abbreviated; cauline leaves biternately or pedately parted, decurrent on the margined petiole, the lobes or segments oblong-linear, hirsute-puberulent; stipules minute, scarious, entire; sepals linear, obtuse, ciliolate; lower petal barely saccate at the base, purple, with yellow claws, the two upper shorter and deep violet. On the slope of a mountain between Great Salt Lake and the Sierra Nevada;

June 1. A well-marked species; with the foliage somewhat like that of V. delphinifolia, *Nutt.*; but the primary divisions compoundly divided in a ternate or pinnatisect manner; and there is a distinct stem, although it is only an inch long in the specimen. Lobes of the leaves half an inch or less in length. Stipules very small and inconspicuous, except those of the lowest and subradical leaves, which are larger. Peduncles 2 inches, naked. Petals half an inch long. Style short, clavate, minutely bearded at the gibbous summit; the stigma lateral.

TRIFOLIUM ALTISSIMUM, *Dougl. in Hook. Fl. Bor.-Am.* 1, *p.* 130, *t.* 48. On the Sierra Nevada; June 22.

ASTRAGALUS (PHACA) PURSHII, *Dougl. in Hook. Fl. Bor.-Am.* 1, *p.* 152. Phaca mollissima, *Nutt. in Torr. and Gray, Fl.* 1, *p.* 350; *Torr. in Stansbury's Rep. p.* 385, *t.* 3, *figs.* 4 and 5. Near Humboldt river; in fruit. In reuniting Phaca to Astragalus, the name given by Douglas to this species is to be restored, both on account of its priority, and because there is already an Astragalus mollissimus.

ASTRAGALUS (PHACA) UTAHENSIS: caespitose, very softly and densely white-tomentose; stems short and depressed; leaflets 6–9 pairs, broadly obovate or nearly orbicular; stipules lanceolate, subulate-pointed, free; peduncles equalling or exceeding the leaves, subcapitately 3–6-flowered; bracts setaceous, twice the length of the pedicels; teeth of calyx subulate, much shorter than the cylindrical tube; corolla violet-purple; legumes extremely woolly, sessile, oblong, pointed, incurved, strictly one-celled. Phaca mollissima β. Utahensis, *Torr. in Stansb. Rep. p.* 385, *t.* 2. Near Lone Rock, south of Great Salt Lake. In flower; May. Although closely allied to the preceding, this may safely be considered as a distinct species; and so Dr. Torrey was inclined to regard it. A. Purshii, besides its oblong and often acute or acutish leaflets, has the foliage and calyx, &c., clothed with villous or shaggy hairs, so that Hooker describes it as "hirsutissimus," and the flowers are said by Douglas to be yellow, meaning doubtless ochroleucous, except a purple tip to the keel. The present plant is white, with a soft and matted tomentum, and the corolla is violet-purple. The mature pods, (here described chiefly from a fruiting plant gathered by Captain Stansbury, which is doubtless a form of the species, though with shorter peduncles,) after detaching the thick mass of wool in which they are imbedded, are found to be narrower, but otherwise similar to those of the preceding. In the figure above cited, the tube of the calyx is mostly represented quite too short. It is really of the same elongated form as in A. Purshii, but the teeth are not so setaceous.

ASTRAGALUS (HOMALOBUS?) BECKWITHII, (n. sp.): glabrous or nearly so, low, perennial; stems branched from the base, ascending; stipules triangular-lanceolate, nearly free; petioles slender; leaflets 6–9 pairs, small, oval-orbicular, rather scattered; peduncles about the length of the leaves, 7–8-flowered; bracts subulate, small; calyx oblong-campanulate, sparsely and minutely black-haired; the aristiform-subulate teeth nearly as long as the tube; corolla ochroleucous, incurved, the oblong vexillum deeply emarginate; ovary linear, stipitate. On the Cedar Mountains, west of Lone Rock, and south of Great Salt Lake; May; in flower. The slender stems, with the peduncles that terminate them, are only 4 inches long in the specimen, and not exceeding the radical leaves; but as they go on to branch they doubtless attain a considerably greater height in the season. Leaflets 2½ or 3 lines long, slightly petiolulate, rather fleshy in texture, veinless, glabrous, except some minute hairs on the midrib and margins when first developed. Flowers crowded on very short pedicels; tube of the calyx 3 lines long; corolla 9 lines long, abruptly curved near the obtuse tip of the keel, which is much shorter than the wings and vexillum; ovary glabrous, more or less compressed, many-ovuled, neither suture at all introflexed, raised on a stipe which is soon about as long as the tube of the calyx. The fruit, unfortunately, is still unknown; but the plant is evidently one not before described.

ASTRAGALUS DIPHYSUS, *Gray, Pl. Fendl. p.* 34? Southwest of Great Salt Lake; May. In flower only, and not to be accurately determined.

LUPINUS AFFINIS, *Agardh, Syn. Lup. p.* 20; *Torr. and Gray, Fl. p.* 376. Agate Pass of the Quartz Mountains; June 1.

LUPINUS DECUMBENS, var. ARGOPHYLLUS, *Gray, Pl. Fendl. p.* 38. Utah, in a cañon; May 29. Flowers yellow and white. This is the same as Fendler's No. 167, and is very likely Pursh's L. argenteus. L. laxiflorus, perhaps, runs into it. The calyx is conspicuously saccate-spurred on the upper side.

ROSA GYMNOCARPA, *Nutt. in Torr. and Gray, Fl.* 1, *p.* 461. On the Sierra Nevada; July.

ŒNOTHERA MARGINATA, *Nutt. in Torr. and Gray, Fl.* 1, *p.* 500. On the summit of the Humboldt Mountains, Utah; May.

ŒNOTHERA (CHYLISMIA) CLAVÆFORMIS, *Torr. in Frem. Rep. 2d Exped. p.* 314. At the foot of the Sierra Nevada, on the eastern side; June. What appears to be a cinereous and somewhat hairy, more caulescent, and branching variety of this, was gathered by Coulter: No. 180 of his California collection.

ŒNOTHERA (SPHÆROSTIGMA) ALYSSOIDES, *Hook. and Arn. Bot. Beech. p.* 394; *Hook. Ic. Pl. t.* 339. Near Humboldt river; June. Flowers white.

ŒNOTHERA (PRIMULOPSIS) TANACETIFOLIA (n. sp.): stemless, perennial? minutely pubescent; leaves lanceolate in outline, interruptedly pinnately parted into very numerous small segments, some of them minute and oval or oblong, the others linear; all sinuate-toothed or pinnatifid; tube of the calyx shorter than the leaves, filiform, dilated at the summit; the segments lanceolate, shorter than the obovate petals and the style; anthers oblong, much shorter than the moderately unequal filaments; stigma discoid, entire. On the higher parts of the Sierra Nevada; June 18. Root apparently thick and perennial. Leaves 3 or 4 inches long, including the short petiole, 5 to 8 lines wide, finely dissected. Tube of the calyx 2 inches or more in length; the segments half an inch long. Petals bright yellow, nearly an inch long. Stigma broad and flat. Fruit not seen.

ŒNOTHERA (GODETIA) RUBICUNDA, *Lindl. Bot. Reg. t.* 1856. In the Sierra Nevada; June.

PEUCEDANUM NUDICAULE, *Nutt. in Torr. and Gray, Fl.* 1, *p.* 627, var. ELLIPTICUM. Minutely and softly pubescent; fruit narrowly elliptical, nearly three times as long as broad, the winged margin as wide as the disk. Round Valley, near the sources of the Sacramento, in the Sierra Nevada; June 27. Intermediate between P. nudicaule and P. macrocarpum, having exactly the foliage of the former and the fruit of the latter. The roots of this species are used as food by the natives.

PEUCEDANUM TRITERNATUM, *Nutt. in Torr. and Gray, Fl. l. c.* Seseli biternatum, *Pursh, Fl.* 1, *p.* 197; *Hook. Fl. Bor.-Amer.* 1, *p.* 304, *t.* 94. Sierra Nevada. The roots of this plant, in a dried state, were brought home by Lieutenant Beckwith. They are about the size of "peanuts," and are collected very largely by the Indians. When dried they are hard but brittle, and have a mild sweet taste. They afford a good proportion of the food of some tribes. Besides a large quantity of starch, they contain much other nutritious matter.

CYMOPTERUS MONTANUS, *Nutt. in Torr. and Gray, Fl.* 1, *p.* 624; *Gray, Pl. Fendl. p.* 67. Summit of the Goshoot Mountain, Central Utah. In the solitary specimen which the collection contained, the flowers are in a singular abnormal condition. The upper part of the ovary is furnished with ten spongy wings, which extend beyond the flower. The stamens are reduced to rudiments. The teeth of the calyx are normal. Instead of five petals there are only two or three, and these are of an unusual form. The styles are conspicuous, but seem to be destitute of stigmas.

CHÆNACTIS STEVIOIDES, *Hook. and Arn. Bot. Beech. p.* 371. Foot of the Sierra Nevada, on the eastern side; June.

LAYIA GLANDULOSA, *Hook. and Arn. Bot. Beech. p.* 358. Eastern side of the Sierra Nevada; June. Rays white.

TETRADYMIA GLABRATA (n. sp.): shrubby, divaricately branched, unarmed, young branchlets, and foliage loosely clothed with floccose white wool, which is soon deciduous; leaves subulate or acerose, rather fleshy; the primary ones erect (none of them converted into spines); the secondary ones crowded in axillary fasciales, glabrous; scales of the tomentose-canescent involucre and flowers four; hairs of the achenium much shorter than the barbellate-denticulate bristles of the pappus. On the Sierra Nevada, June 16. This is distinguished from T. Nuttallii by the acerose, terete, or angled and fleshy leaves, mostly mucronate or pointed, and glabrous, or soon glabrate: from T. spinosa (which it resembles in the secondary leaves) by the fewer flowers and involucral scales, the hairs of the ovarium much shorter than the pappus, &c.; and from both of the entire want of spines. It belongs to Tetradymia proper.

DODECATHEON INTEGRIFOLIUM, *Hook. Fl. Bor.-Am.* 2, *p.* 118; *and Bot. Mag. t.* 3622. In a cañon between Salt Lake and the Sierra Nevada; May.

PHLOX CANESCENS (n. sp.): dwarf, very much branched, and densely caespitose, tomentose when young, and canescent; leaves acerose, imbricated, at length recurved-spreading, not rigid, very woolly towards the base, the lower ones marcescent; flowers sessile; teeth of the calyx similar to the leaves, and fully as long as the woolly tube; tube of the corolla much longer than the calyx and the cuneiform obovate retuse lobes. P. Hoodii, *Torr. in Stansb. Exped. p.* 304. On the Cedar Mountains, south of the Great Salt Lake. This species (of which badly preserved specimens were also gathered by Colonel Fremont, in his second expedition) is allied to P. Hoodii and P. Douglasii. From the former it is distinguished by its more slender leaves and calyx-lobes, and much longer corolla; from the latter (which has longer calyx-teeth than is shown in Hooker's figure) it is distinguished by its woolliness, its less rigid foliage, longer calyx-lobes, and smaller corolla, but with the tube proportionally longer. The ovules are solitary in each cell. The limb of the corolla appears to be white; its tube yellowish.

GILIA PULCHELLA, *Dougl. in Hook. Fl. Bor.–Amer.* 2, *p.* 74. At the foot of the Humboldt Mountains, on the eastern side; May.

PHACELIA INTEGRIFOLIA, *Torr. in Am. Lyc. Nat. Hist. N. Y.* 2, *p.* 222, *t.* 3. Valley of Humboldt River, Utah; June 8.

PHACELIA HUMILIS (n. sp.): annual, low, much branched from the base; leaves oblong, spatulate or lanceolate, all simple and entire, indistinctly veined, minutely hirsute-pubescent like the branches, and glandular dotted; racemes densely-flowered; segments of the calyx linear, obtuse, hispid, a little shorter than the (deep violet-colored) corolla; stamens exerted. Near the summit of the Sierra Nevada, California; June. A well-marked species, three or four inches high, somewhat cinereous, with a fine pubescence, except the inflorescence, and especially the calyx, which is hispid with rigid white hairs. Leaves an inch or less in length, short-petioled. Corolla short, when expanded three lines in diameter; the base biplicate between the stamens. Filaments sparingly hispid above. Style glabrous. Ovules two in each cell. Capsule 2–3-seeded. This can hardly be the P. canescens of Nuttall, in Pl. Gambell., which accords better with some states of P. circinata.

SCROPHULARIA NODOSA, *Linn.; Benth. Pl. Hartweg. no.* 1877. Foot of the Sierra Nevada; June. The leaves are smaller, much truncate at the base, and more laciniate-toothed than the plant of the Atlantic States.

COLLINSIA PARVIFLORA, *Dougl. in Lindl. Bot. Reg. t.* 1802. Foot of the Humboldt Mountains; May.

PENTSTEMON SPECIOSUS, *Dougl. in Lindl. Bot. Reg. t.* 1270. Mountains in the western part of Utah; June.

PENTSTEMON HETEROPHYLLUS, *Lindl. Bot. Reg, t.* 1899? Sierra Nevada, California, on the summit of the mountains; June. Two forms, if not species, have been merged by Hooker and

Arnott under P. heterophyllus. The present single specimen resembles the var. α, in the narrow and marginless sepals, and in the smaller flowers; but the peduncles are principally three-flowered. Not improbably it belongs to an entirely different species.

PENTSTEMON HETERANDRUM (n. sp.): glabrous; stem slender, virgate; leaves lanceolate or oblong-linear, obtuse, callose-serrulate, obtuse or subauriculate at the base; panicle spicate, interrupted; cymes subsessile, several-flowered; calyx puberulous, the segments ovate-lanceolate; corolla (nearly white) infundibuliform, slightly gibbous above, with 5 short subequal lobes, in æstivation various; stamens glabrous, straightish, of nearly equal length, all antheriferous, or the fifth without an anther. Sierra Nevada, California; June 30. Flower white, with pink lines half an inch in length. Cauline leaves an inch long, and 3 lines wide; the floral ones successively reduced to small bracts. Anthers glabrous; the cells distinct, moderately diverging. Stigma minute and simple. Ovary, &c., apparently as in Pentstemon. Fruit not seen. Two peculiarities are to be noticed in this remarkable plant, either of which would have been sufficient to exclude it from Pentstemon, but both prove to be inconstant in the species. One of these relates to the stamens, which, in the flowers examined, were perhaps more frequently completely *pentandrous* than otherwise; the fifth (posterior) filament being similar to the others, and bearing either an exactly similar anther, or sometimes one with rather smaller cells, and with the filament or connective prolonged into a short and blunt apical appendage, as shown in figures 9 and 10. In some flowers, however, this anther was found to be reduced to a single and rather imperfect cell, and a bare rudiment of the second cell, as in fig. 11; in others again, (as in fig. 12 and fig. 6,) the fifth stamen is wholly destitute of any trace of anther, as in Pentstemon universally, with this exception, if such it be. It is also to be noted that the stamens of this plant are nearly equal in length, at least when all five are antheriferous, and that they are inserted into the very base of the corolla. The remaining peculiarity relates to the æstivation of the corolla; in which, although some of the flower-buds plainly have the two posterior lobes, or one of them, exterior to the others, in the manner of the Antirrhinideæ generally, (this being, indeed, the only absolute character of that suborder), as shown in figures 3 and 4; yet, in quite as many instances we find the lateral lobes exterior in the bud, and covering the two posterior as well as the anterior, (as is represented in figure 2), in the manner of the Rhinanthideæ: a new and striking instance of the instability of the modes of æstivation of the corolla, and one not altogether unexpected, since Mr. H. T. Clark, a former pupil of Dr. Gray, and an acute and zealous naturalist, showed him several years ago that both modes occur in Mimulus ringens, M. moschatus, &c.

MIMULUS LUTEUS, *Linn.* In the Sierra Nevada; June.

CASTILLEJA HISPIDA, *Benth. in Hook. Fl. Bor.-Amer.* 2, *p.* 105. Cedar Mountains, south of Great Salt Lake; May.

CASTILLEJA PALLIDA, *Kunth.* Foot of the Humboldt Mountains, on the eastern side; May.

AUDIBERTIA INCANA, *Benth. in Bot. Reg. t.* 1469; *and in DC. Prodr.* 12, *p.* 359. On the Sierra Nevada; June 20. Flowers blue.

MONARDELLA ODORATISSIMA, *Benth. Lab. p.* 332; *and in DC. Prodr.* 12, *p.* 190. β. GLABRIUSCULA; nearly glabrous; branches slender; leaves oblong-lanceolate, narrowed to a petiole at the base, rather acute; heads terminal; bracts ovate, (colored,) shorter than the calyx, rather acute; teeth of the calyx ovate-lanceolate, acute, unarmed. Sierra Nevada; July 8. Differs from M. odoratissima in its larger and conspicuously petiolate leaves, and in the narrower acutish bracts, &c. Flowers rose-colored.

Most of the species of this genus have the narrow lobes of the corolla sacculate at the apex; a character which seems to have escaped the notice of Mr. Bentham.

MERTENSIA OBLONGIFOLIA, *G. Don, Syst. Gard.* 4, *p.* 372; *DC. Prodr.* 10, *p.* 92. Pulmonaria oblongifolia, *Nutt. in Journ. Acad. Phil.* 7. *p.* 13. Pass in Humboldt Mountains; May 23. Flowers blue. This species was found also in various parts of Utah, by Colonel Fremont.

ERITRICHIUM GLOMERATUM, *DC. Prodr.* 10, *p.* 131. Myosotis glomerata, *Nutt. Gen.* 1, *p.* 112; *Hook. Fl. Bor.-Amer.* 2, *p.* 82, *t.* 162. Summit of Humboldt Mountains; May 27.

ECHINOSPERMUM FLORIBUNDUM, *Lehm. Pug.* 2, *p.* 24; *Hook. Fl. Bor.-Amer.* 2, *p.* 84 *t.* 164; *DC. Prodr.* 10, *p.* 143. Summit of Humboldt Mountains; May 27. Corolla white, finely veined with blue.

GRAYIA POLYGALOIDES, *Hook. and Arn. in Hook. Ic. t.* 271 *and* 388; *Bot. Beech. p.* 387. G. spinosa, *Moq. in DC. Prodr.* 13, *pars* 2, *p.* 119. Chenopodium (?) spinosum, *Hook. Fl. Bor.-Amer.* 2, *p.* 127. Eastern base of the Sierra Nevada; June 15, (in fruit.) This shrub is called *Greasewood* by the hunters.

EUROTIA LANATA, *Moq. Chenop. p.* 81; *and in DC. Prodr.* 13, *pars* 2, *p.* 121. Diotis lanata, *Pursh, Fl.* 2, *p.* 602; *Nutt. Gen.* 2, *p.* 206. Eastern base of the Sierra Nevada; June 15. Flowers monoecious and dioecious. Sepals of ♂ ovate, or rather acute. Moquin (l. c.) asks whether the ♀ flowers are not bibracteate and destitute of a calyx. This is no doubt their true structure, and is the view taken of them by Ledebour, (*Fl. Ross.* 3, *p.* 737.)

ERIOGONUM OVALIFOLIUM, *Nutt. in Journ. Acad. Sc. Phil.* 7, *p.* 51, *t.* 8, *fig.* 1. Eucycla ovalifolia, *Nutt. l. c.* (*n. ser.*) 1, *p.* 166. Eastern base of the Sierra Nevada; June 15. In our solitary specimen there is but a single scape, which is about seven inches high. The leaves are broader than in Nuttall's plant. The filaments are scarcely one-third the length of the sepals, and woolly.

ERIOGONUM CERNUUM, *Nutt. in Journ. Acad. Sc. Phil.* (*new ser.*) 1, *p.* 162, *β.* PURPURASCENS. Eastern base of the Sierra Nevada; June 16. Leaves sometimes almost reniform-orbicular. Scape sparingly and trichotomously branching an inch or two above the base. Peduncles purplish, and involucres glandularly pubescent. Sepals deep rose-color, with pale margins, the exterior ones somewhat retuse, much longer and broader than the inner ones. Filaments shorter than the inner sepals, glabrous. Achenium with a long acuminate point. Embryo curved, the radicle elongated, erect. Differs from the ordinary form of E. cernuum, which is much more branched, and has white flowers.

RUMEX VENOSUS, *Pursh, Fl.* 2, *p.* 733; *Nutt. Gen.* 1, *p.* 240; *Hook. Fl. Bor.-Amer.* 2, *p.* 130, *t.* 174. Mountains in Central Utah, May 12.

AMIANTHIUM NUTTALLII, *Gray, in Ann. Lyc. N. York*, 4, *p.* 123. Helonias augustifolia, *Nutt. in Trans. Amer. Phil. Soc.* (*n. ser.*) 5, *p.* 154. Amiantanthus Nuttallii, *Kunth*, 4, *p.* 181. Foot of Oquirrh Mountain, south end of the Great Salt Lake; May 6.

SISYRINCHIUM GRANDIFLORUM, *Dougl. in Bot. Reg. t.* 1364; *Bot. Mag. t.* 3509; *Hook. Fl. Bor.-Am.* 2. *p.* 207. Pass of Humboldt Mountain; May 23.

IRIS LONGIPETALA, *Herbert in Hook. and Arn. Bot. Beech. p.* 395. Fort of Humboldt Mountains on the east side; May 28.

CAMASSIA ESCULENTA, *Lindl. Bot. Mag. t.* 1486; *Kunth. Enum.* 4, *p.* 347; *Torr. and Gray in Whipple's Report, ined.* Phalangium Quamash, *Pursh, Fl.* 1, *p.* 226. Near the summit of the Sierra Nevada; June 18.

CALOCHORTUS NUTTALLII: stem 2-flowered; leaves very narrowly linear; petals obovate-cuneate, rounded at the summit (white, but yellow at the base), with an oblong dense tuft of hairs on the claw; and just above this a purple spot, with a few scattered hairs. C. luteus, *Nutt. in Journ. Acad. Philad.* 7, *p.* 51, *not of Dougl.* Summit of Noble's Pass, Sierra Nevada; July 3. We have little doubt of this being Nuttall's C. luteus, as it agrees exactly with his description, and with an imperfect but original specimen of that plant, except that the flower, according to Snyder, is white. Mr. N. was uncertain of the color of the flower in his specimen, for he says they are "apparently sulphur yellow." They are, indeed, yellow at the base even in the dried plant, and Mr. Nuttall supposed they were wholly of that color in the fresh state. The marking and other characters of the petals are unlike those of Douglas's C. luteus; and as his plant was first discovered, and probably first described, the name must be retained for it. Besides, the name given to it by Mr. Nuttall is inappropriate, if, as we feel pretty confident, the flower of his plant is white.

BRODIÆA GRANDIFLORA, *J. E. Smith in Linn. Trans.* 10, *p.* 3; *Kunth, Enum.* 4, *p.* 471. Scape glabrous; umbel, few-(8–12-) flowered; the rays usually 2–4 times longer than the flowers; abortive stamens linear, emarginate, and often also mucronate; cells of the ovary about 10-ovuled. Madelin Pass of the Sierra Nevada; June 26.

BRODIÆA PARVIFLORA, n. sp.: scape roughish; umbel, many-(15–20-) flowered; pedicels shorter than the flower; sterile stamens ovate-lanceolate, rather acute, entire; cells of the ovary 6–8-ovuled. With the preceding; June 26. Bulb ovate, sometimes more than an inch in diameter. Leaves all radical or nearly so, rather shorter than the scape, about two lines wide, smooth. Scape scarcely larger than a crow-quill, the upper part somewhat flexuous, terete, scabrous with very minute points. Umbel about an inch and a half in diameter; pedicels unequal, most of them scarcely half the length of the flowers. Involucrate bracts, 4–8, colored, about as long as the pedicels, the outer ones ovate and acuminate. Flowers about half an inch long, pale purple, the tube somewhat inflated; segments erect, ovate, rather acute. Fertile stamens 3, inserted at the upper part of the tube of the perianth, opposite the inner segments; anthers linear-oblong, acute at each end. Style filiform; stigma dilated, 3-lobed, the lobes fimbrillate-papillose. We have long had specimens of this plant, collected by Colonel Fremont on Prevost's Fork of the Utah; and others brought from the valley of the Sacramento by Dr. Stillman. It is easily distinguished from B. grandiflora by the characters given above.

PTERIS AQUILINA, *Linn.; Torr. Fl. N. York*, 2, *p.* 488. On the Sierra Nevada.

PART II.

Plants collected by Mr. F. CREUTZFELDT, *under the direction of Captain* J. W. GUNNISON, *U. S. Army, in charge of explorations for a railroad from Fort Leavenworth, by the way of the Kansas and Arkansas rivers, to Bent's Fort; thence by the Huerfano river and Sangre de Cristo Pass to the valley of San Luis; thence west from that valley to Grand and Green rivers; thence into the Great Basin, Utah, to the vicinity of the Sevier or Nicollet lake. The collection was commenced at Westport, in Missouri, in June,* 1853, *and finished late in October.*

[The Rocky mountain ranges were entered early in August. The Sierra Blanca, in which the Sangre de Cristo and Roubideau's passes are found, forms the eastern range of the Rocky mountains, and (at the head of San Luis valley, New Mexico) unites with the next western range, which is known as the Sierra San Juan or Sahwatch chain. This sierra, in turn, is joined around the head of Grand river to Elk mountain, and this again to the Roan mountains, the latter being only separated from the former by Blue river, which breaks through in a cañon; and the Roan mountains themselves are separated from the Wahsatch mountains only by the entirely similar cañon passage of Green river, which also breaks through the great east and west connecting range known as the Uinta mountains. All of these ranges, some more or less parallel, while others form cross and connecting chains, constitute properly the great mountain formation of the continent, to which the name of Rocky mountains is applied; the former names applying only to the subdivisions of this great feature.]

ANEMONE VIRGINIANA, *Linn.* Prairies beyond Westport, in Kansas Territory.

CLEMATIS PITCHERI, *Torr. and Gray, Fl.* 1, *p.* 10. Prairies between Westport and Cottonwood Creek.

THALICTRUM CORNUTI, *Linn.* Beyond Westport, in Kansas.

RANUNCULUS DIVARICATUS, *Schrank; Gray, Pl. Wright*, 2, *p.* 8. Kansas.

DELPHINIUM AZUREUM, *Michx.* Beyond Westport.

MENISPERMUM CANADENSE, *Linn.* With the preceding.

ARGEMONE MEXICANA, *Linn.* var. ALBIFLORA, *DC.* Walnut Creek.

THELYPODIUM INTEGRIFOLIUM, *Endl. in Walp. Repert.* 1, *p.* 172. Pachypodium integrifolium, *Nutt.; Hook. and Arn. Bot. Beech. pp.* 321 *and* 74. Coochetopa, Sierra San Juan. In flower. "Flowers reddish purple."

THELYPODIUM WRIGHTII, *Gray, Pl. Wright,* 1, *p.* 7 *and* 2, *p.* 12. In the Rocky Mountains. The specimens resemble Wright's No. 845.

CLEOME LUTEA, *Hook. Fl. Bor.-Am.* 1, *p.* 70, *t.* 25. C. aurea, *Nutt. in Torr. and Gray, Fl.* 1, *p.* 122. Sand-banks of Green River, Utah.

PARNASSIA PARVIFLORA, *DC. Prodr.* 1, *p.* 320; *Hook. Fl. Bor.-Am.* 1, *p.* 82, *t.* 27. Rocky Mountains, in the valley of the Grand River; August. This accords with specimens from the northwest coast, and with Hooker's figure (which is not cited in Torr. and Gray, Fl.) but is still more delicate and slender. The filiform scape is five or six inches long; the petals three lines long; the radical leaves less than half an inch long, but abrupt at the base, shorter than their petiole.

SILENE STELLATA, *Ait.* Upper Arkansas.

ARENARIA FENDLERI, *Gray, Pl. Fendl. p.* 13. Rocky Mountains, near the head of the Rio Grande; August. Resembling Fendler's plant, but not so tall.

PARONYCHIA JAMESII, *Torr. and Gray, Fl.* 1, *p.* 170. Plains near Fort Atkinson.

CALLIRRHÖE INVOLUCRATA, *Gray, Pl. Fendl. p.* 16. Prairies near Bluff Creek.

SIDALCEA MALVÆFLORA, *Gray, Pl. Wright.* 1, *p.* 16. Utah Creek; August.

SIDALCEA CANDIDA, *Gray, Pl. Fendl. p.* 24. In the Rocky Mountains, east of the Rio Grande; August. In flower.

SPHÆRALCEA ANGUSTIFOLIA, *Cav.* var. S. STELLATA, *Torr. and Gray, Fl.* Sandy banks of the Arkansas, near the Rocky Mountains.

CEANOTHUS AMERICANUS, *Linn.* Beyond Westport, near the Arkansas River.

POLYGALA ALBA, *Nutt.* Beyond Walnut Creek; July.

PSORALEA OBTUSILOBA, *Torr. and Gray, Fl.* 1, *p.* 300. Kansas; June.

AMORPHA CANESCENS, *Nutt. Gen.* 2, *p.* 92. Between Westport and Bent's Fort.

DALEA LAXIFLORA, *Pursh, Fl.* 2, *p.* 741. Near Walnut Creek; July.

PETALOSTEMON VIOLACEUM, *Michx. Fl.* 2, *p.* 50, t. 37. With the preceding.

PETALOSTEMON CANDIDUM, *Michx. l. c.* With the preceding species.

OXYTROPIS LAMBERTI, *Pursh, Fl.* 2, *p.* 740. Two varieties: one with pale, and the other with violet purple flowers. Rocky Mountains.

ASTRAGALUS ADSURGENS, *Pall.; Hook. Fl. Bor.-Am.* 1, *p.* 149. Rocky Mountains; August.

BAPTISIA LEUCANTHA, *Torr. and Gray, Fl.* 1, *p.* 385. Arkansas River; June.

HOFFMANSEGGIA JAMESII, *Torr. and Gray, Fl.* 1, *p.* 393. Near Fort Atkinson; July.

SCHRANKIA UNCINATA, *Willd.; Torr. and Gray, Fl.* 1, *p.* 400. Upper Arkansas.

RUBUS DELICIOSUS, *Torr. in Am. Lyc. Nat. Hist. N. York,* 2, *p.* 196. Rocky Mountains. Leaves only.

ŒNOTHERA SPECIOSA, *Nutt. in Journ. Acad. Philad.* 2, *p.* 119. Beyond Westport.

ŒNOTHERA SERRULATA, *Nutt.* var. DOUGLASSII, *Torr. and Gray, Fl.* 1, *p.* 502. Beyond Walnut Creek.

STENOSIPHON VIRGATUS, *Spach, Onagr. p.* 64.

GAURA SINUATA, *Nutt.* Near Fort Atkinson.

GAURA COCCINEA, *Nutt. Gen.* 1, *p.* 249. Walnut Creek.

EPILOBIUM ANGUSTIFOLIUM, *Linn.* Common in the Rocky Mountains.

LYTHRUM ALATUM, *Pursh; Torr. and Gray, Fl.* 1, *p.* 481. From Westport to Walnut Creek.

MENTZELIA (BARTONIA) NUDA, *Torr. and Gray, Fl.* 1, *p.* 534. Near Fort Atkinson; July.

CRYPTOTÆNIA CANADENSE, *DC. Prodr.* 4, *p.* 119. Beyond Westport; June.

THASPIUM CORDATUM, *Torr. and Gray, Fl.* 1, *p.* 615. Near Westport; June.

CONIOSELINUM CANADENSIS, *Torr. and Gray, Fl.* 1, *p.* 619. In the Rocky Mountains; August. In flower only.

GALIUM CONCINNUM, *Torr. and Gray, Fl.* 2, *p.* 23. Beyond Westport, Arkansas River; June.

GALIUM BOREALE, *Linn.* In the Rocky Mountains; August.

OLDENLANDIA ANGUSTIFOLIA, *Gray, Pl. Wright.* 2, *p.* 68. Beyond Westport; June.

BRICKELLIA GRANDIFLORA, *Nutt. in Trans. Amer. Phil. Soc.* (*n. ser.*) 7, *p.* 287. Rocky Mountains; August.

ASTER MULTIFLORUS, *Ait.* Utah Creek; August.

MACHÆRANTHERA TANACETIFOLIA, *Nees; Gray, Pl. Wright, 1, p.* 90. Fort Atkinson.

ERIGERON GLABELLUM, *Nutt. Gen.* 2, *p.* 147; *Torr. and Gray, Fl.* 2, *p.* 173. Utah Creek; August.

TOWNSENDIA FENDLERII, *Gray, Pl. Fendl. p.* 70. Valleys in the Rocky Mountains; August.

COREOPSIS PALMATA, *Nutt. Gen.* 2, *p.* 180. Arkansas River.

GAILLARDIA PULCHELLA, *Foug.; Torr. and Gray, Fl.* 2, *p.* 366. Beyond Walnut Creek; July.

ACTINELLA LANATA, *Nutt. Trans. Amer. Phil. Soc.* 7, *p.* 380. White River Mountains, Utah; October. The leaves are nearly smooth, and strongly punctate; awn of the pappus half as long as the scale. Seems about intermediate between this species and *A. Torreyana*, Nutt.

ARTEMISIA FILIFOLIA, *Torr. in Ann. Lyc. N. York*, 2, *p.* 211. Sand-banks of Green River, Utah; October.

ARTEMISIA DISCOLOR, *Dougl.; Besser; DC. Prodr.* 6, *p.* 109. Roubideau's Pass, Rocky Mountains; Sierra Blanca.

ANTENNARIA LUZULOIDES, *Torr. and Gray, Fl.* 2, *p.* 430. Higher parts of the Rocky Mountains; August.

CACALIA TUBEROSA, *Nutt. Gen.* 2, *p.* 138. Beyond Westport; June.

TETRADYMIA INERMIS, *Nutt. in Trans. Amer. Phil. Soc. l. c. p.* 415. Rocky Mountains; August.

LOBELIA LEPTOSTACHYS, *Alph. DC. Prodr.* 7, *p.* 376. Prairie near Westport.

LYSIMACHIA CILIATA, *Ait.* West from Westport, Arkansas River.

ASCLEPIAS PURPURASCENS, *Linn.* With the preceding.

ASCLEPIAS VERTICILLATA, *Linn.; β. Torr. in Nicollet's Report, p.* 154. Fort Atkinson. This is a dwarf variety, being often not more than 3–6 inches high.

ASCLEPIAS TUBEROSA, *Linn.* Beyond Westport, Arkansas River.

APOCYNUM CANNABINUM, *Linn.* Beyond Westport and Walnut Creek; June, July.

EUSTOMA RUSSELIANUM, *Don; Griseb. in DC. Prodr.* 9, *p.* 51. Near Fort Atkinson; July.

GENTIANA AFFINIS, *Grisebach, in Hook. Fl. Bor.-Am.* 2, *p.* 56. In the mountains, near Utah Creek; January.

IPOMÆA LEPTOPHYLLA, *Torr. in Frem. 1st Report, p.* 94, *and in Emory's Rep. p.* 148, *t.* 11. Walnut Creek; July. Dr. James was mistaken in supposing this handsome species to be an annual. It has a large perennial root, which has endured for four or five years in the Botanic Garden at Cambridge.

PHLOX ARISTATA, *Michx.* 1, *p.* 144. West from Westport, Kansas; June.

GILIA PULCHELLA, *Dougl. in Hook. Fl. Bor.-Am.* 2, *p.* 74. Rocky Mountains; August.

Polemonium pulcherrimum, *Hook. Bot. Mag. t.* 2979. Rocky Mountains; August.

Gilia pinnatifida, *Nutt. in Herb. Acad. Philad.?* In the Rocky Mountains, near the head of the Rio Grande; August. If this be a variety of Nuttall's plant (which is Fendler's No. 655) it is remarkable for its much less lobed leaves; those of the branches being mostly entire.

Gilia Gunnisoni, (n. sp.): annual; stem paniculately much branched from the base, nearly glabrous, as are the leaves; the latter alternate and scattered, subulate-filiform, all entire, mucronate; the crowded bracts viscid-puberulent (like the branchlets), subulate, with the dilated lower portion viscidly villous-ciliate, mostly shorter than the flowers, which are capitate-clustered at the summit of the branchlets; teeth of the calyx pungently pointed, a little shorter than the tube of the salver-shaped white corolla; stamens inserted in the sinuses of the corolla, rather shorter than its obovate lobes; ovules 2 or 3 in each cell. Sand-banks of Green River, Utah; October. Root slender, evidently annual; the stems or branches 6 or 8 inches high. Leaves all alternate, slender; the cauline and rameal scattered, filiform; the lower nearly an inch long; the upper gradually reduced to small subulate bracts. Calyx somewhat pubescent. Corolla 3 to 4 lines long, the limb rather shorter than the tube; style pubescent below.

Martynia proboscidea, *Glox.* Near Walnut Creek; July.

Dipteracanthus ciliosus, *N. ab E. in DC. Prodr.* 11, *p.* 122. Beyond Westport; June.

Dianthera pedunculosa, *Linn.* (Rhytiglossa pedunculosa, *N. ab E.*) Kansas, beyond Westport; June.

Pentstemon Cobæa, *Nutt.; Hook. Bot. Mag. t.* 3465. Prairie between Westport and Bluff Creek; June.

Pentstemon Digitalis, *Nutt.; Hook. Bot. Mag. t.* 2587. With the foregoing.

Orthocarpus luteus, *Nutt. Gen.* 2, *p.* 57. Utah Creek; August.

Castilleja purpurea, *Don.* Valleys of the Rocky Mountains; August.

Monarda fistulosa, *Linn.*; *Benth. in DC. Prodr.* 12, *p.* 361. Damp valleys of the Rocky Mountains.

Monarda aristata, *Nutt. in Trans. Amer. Phil. Soc.* (*n. ser.*) 5, *p.* 186; *Benth. l. c.* Roubideau's Pass; August. The specimens are evidently annual.

Eritrichium glomeratum, *DC. Prodr.* 10, *p.* 131. Myosotis glomerata, *Nutt. Gen.* 2, *p.* 112; *Hook. Fl. Bor.-Am.* 2, *p.* 80, *t.* 162. Declivities of the Rocky Mountains; August. A very rough form of the plant; flowers white, conspicuous.

Solanum triflorum, *Nutt. Gen.* 1, *p.* 128; *Dunal in DC. Prodr.* 13, *part* 1, *p.* 45. Near the Rocky Mountains; August. Leaves narrower and with fewer teeth on the lobes than usual. Stem branching from the base, and prostrate. Flowers pale blue.

Abronia fragrans, *Nutt. in Herb. Hook.; Hook. Kew. Jour. Bot.* 5, *p.* 261. Rocky Mountains; August. This is in Wright's (1711) and several other collections, as well as in Geyer's; but no character of it has yet been published. It is distinguished from A. mellifera by its pure white "porcelain-colored" flowers, scarcely winged fruit, and especially by the involucre, composed of very large, broadly ovate, scarious and white leaflets.

Oxybaphus augustifolius, *Torr. in Ann. Lyc. New York,* 2, *p.* 237; *Sweet; Choisy in DC. Prodr.* 13, *pars* 1, *p.* 433; var. linearis. Fort Atkinson, Arkansas river, and Roubideau's Pass, Sierra Blanca, Rocky Mountains.

Euphorbia marginata, *Pursh, Fl.* 2, *p.* 607. New Fort Massachusetts, San Luis Valley; August.

Polygonum lapathifolium, *Linn; var.:* leaves narrowly lanceolate, roughly pubescent on the veins underneath and on the margin; sheaths slightly hairy, ciliate with short hairs; peduncles glandularly pubescent and hispid. Between Westport and the Rocky Mountains; July.

ERIOGONUM ANNUUM, *Nutt. in Amer. Phil. Trans. (n. ser.) 5, p.* 164; *Benth. Eriog. in Linn. Trans.* 17, *p.* 414. Sandy river valleys, near Fort Atkinson, Arkansas river; July.

ERIOGONUM ALATUM, *Torr. in DC. Prodr.* 15, (*ined.*) *and in Sitgreaves's Rep. p.* 168, *t.* 8. Near the Rocky Mountains, on hill-sides; August. Plant 2-3 feet high. There is some mistake about E. alatum, in *Hook. Jour. Bot. and Kew. Gard. Misc. for September*, 1853. That species is not enumerated in Fremont's reports, and was described for the first time in the report of Captain Sitgreaves, which was not published till the summer of 1853. But specimens of the plant were distributed from Fremont's and other collections, with the manuscript name.

ERIOGONUM JAMESII, *Benth. in DC. Prodr.* 14, (*ined;*) *Torr. in Sitgreaves's Rep. p.* 168. E. sericeum, *Torr. in Ann. Lyc. N. York*, 2, *p.* 241, (*excl. syn.*) On the Sierra San Juan; September. This plant possesses considerable astringency, and is used as a remedy for diarrhœa by the hunters and Indians.

ERIOGONUM CERNUUM, *Nutt. in Jour. Acad. Phil.* (*n. ser.*) 1, *p.* 162; *Torr. in Sitgreaves's Rep. l. c.* This species in its early state has radical leaves only, which are clothed with a white tomentum, and the scape is sparingly branched. Later in the season the lower part of the stem or caudex, below the primary leaves, elongates and repeatedly forks, producing a tuft of leaves at every principal division, thus converting the scape into a leafy stem. Western side of the Sierra San Juan; September. Sepals white, often with a deep rose-colored midrib.

ERIOGONUM EFFUSUM, *Nutt. l. c.* β. LEPTOPHYLLUM, *Torr. in Sitgreaves's Rep. p.* 168, *t.* 10. Declivities of the Rocky Mountains; August.

Var.? FOLIOSUM: branches at first woolly, but at length nearly glabrous, leafy; leaves crowded, linear, revolute when old, nearly glabrous; cymes small, the rays diverging, very short, compound; involucre campanulate, few-flowered, glabrous, acutely 5-toothed; exterior sepals obovate, emarginate, interior similar in form, but one-third smaller. High prairies, San Luis valley; August.

ERIOGONUM LEPTOCLADON (n. sp.): stems slender, moderately branching, the internodes elongated, clothed with a deciduous woolly pubescence, nearly naked above; leaves lanceolate-linear, woolly, like the stem; inflorescence loosely paniculate, the ultimate divisions somewhat racemose; involucre campanulate, woolly, 5-toothed, smaller than the flowers; calyx campanulate; sepals somewhat equal, very obtuse, and slightly emarginate; filaments as long as the sepals, hairy nearly to the summit. Sandy soil on Green river; October. A shrub, about two feet high; the branches dichotomous, or sometimes trichotomous, of a greenish hue when the wool is detached; the ultimate divisions short, and not cymose. Involucre scarcely a line and a half long, few-(6-10-)flowered. Bracteoles linear, minutely glandular on the margin. Perianth glabrous, obtuse at the base. Achenium with a long glabrous beak. Embryo curved, the cotyledons orbicular; radicle enlongated. Allied to *E. effusum*, but much more slender, and differs also in the inflorescence.

ERIOGONUM CORYMBOSUM, *Benth. in DC. Prodr.* 14, (*ined.*) β. DIVARICATUM: shrubby and much branched, clothed with a dense white tomentum; leaves oblong lanceolate, on very short petioles, undulate on the margin, approximated; cymes large and widely spreading, the primary and secondary divisions trichotomous, the ultimate dichotomous; involucre oblong-companulate, obtusely 5-toothed; flowers (middle-sized) glabrous; exterior sepals broadly obovate, emarginate, the inner narrower and rather shorter; bracteole spatulate-linear; filaments hairy towards the base; ovary attenuated, glabrous; styles very long and exserted. Near springs on Green river; October. About a foot and a half high; leaves about three-fourths of an inch long, and nearly half that breadth. Perhaps a distinct species from *E. corymbosum* of Bentham, which, however, was founded on a specimen in Dr. Torrey's herbarium, collected by Colonel Fremont, very near where Lieutenant Beckwith's plant was found.

Eriogonum umbellatum, *Torr. in Annal. Lyc. N. York*, 2, *p.* 241*; and in Sitgreaves's Rep. t.* 12; *not of Benth.* Near the Rocky Mountains.

Quercus imbricaria, *Willd. Spec.* 4, *p.* 428; *Michx. f. Sylv.* 1, *p.* 69, *t.* 15. Upper Arkansas. A handsome tree from 35 to 45 feet high, with a trunk sometimes 18 inches in diameter.

Quercus alba, *Linn.; Michx. f. Sylv.* 1, *p.* 17, *t.* 1. *β?* Gunnisonii: shrubby; leaves oblong, somewhat coriaceous, smooth above, minutely pubescent underneath, pinnatifidly lobed, the lobes nearly equal, entire, semi-ovate, obtuse; fruit on a long peduncle; cup hemispherical; scales oblong, flattish, with a short, abrupt, discolored acumination; gland ovate. On declivities of mountains. Coochetopa Pass, Sierra San Juan. A shrub 6–10 feet high. Acorns less than half as large as in Q. alba.

Abies taxifolia, *Lamb. Pin.* 2, *t.* 47. Roubideau's Pass. A handsome tree growing from 35 to 40 feet high, and 12 to 16 inches in diameter. The specimens are without cones. The leaves are from an inch and a quarter to nearly two inches long, very slender and glaucous on both sides.

Pinus (undetermined); apparently between P. flexilis of James and P. Strobus. Highest places in the Coochetopa. Leaves in fives, about an inch and a half long, besmeared with a clear colorless balsam. This is the same pine that Col. Fremont collected on his first expedition, and is noticed in the Botanical Appendix to his Report, 1843, p. 97. For want of the cones, it cannot be satisfactorily determined. Perhaps it belongs to that section of the genus which includes P. edulis, *Engelm.* and P. monophylla, *Torr.*

Pinus Sabiniana, *Dougl. Mssc.; Lamb. Pin.* (*ed.* 2), 2, *p.* 146, *t.* 80; *Endl. Syn. Conif. p.* 159. Valley of the Sacramento. One of the cones brought home by Lieut. Beckwith measured 9 inches in height, by 21 inches in circumference.

Juniperus Virginiana, *Linn.; Michx. f. Syl.* 2, *p.* 354, *t.* 155; *Endl. Synops. Conif. p.* 27. Coochetopa. A small tree, not exceeding 15 feet in height.

Juniperus communis, *Linn.; Endl. l. c.* Prostrate under and around trees. Roubideau's Pass.

Tradescantia Virginica, *Linn.; Bot. Mag. t.* 105; *Kunth., Enum.* 4, *p.* 81. Prairies, Upper Arkansas; June.

Platanthera leucophæa, *Gray, Bot. N. States, p.* 472. Orchis leucophæa, *Nutt. in Trans. Amer. Phil. Soc.* (*n. ser.*) 5, *p.* 161. Prairies near Westport.

Melanthium Virginicum, *Linn.; Torr. Fl. N. York*, 2, *p.* 116. Zygadenus Virginicus, *Kunth, Enum.* 4, *p.* 195. Prairies, Upper Arkansas; July.

Zygadenus glaucus, *Nutt. in Jour. Acad. Phil.* 7, *p.* 56. Z. chloranthus. *Richards. Append. to Frankl. Narr. p.* 12; *Hook. Fl. Bor.-Am.* 2, *p.* 177. Anticlea glauca, *Kunth, Enum.* 4, *p.* 192. Roubideau's Pass, Sierra Blanca.

Sagittaria variabilis, *Engelm. in Gray's Bot. N. States, p.* 461. S. sagittifolia of most American botanists. In water, Upper Arkansas.

Heteranthera limosa, *Vahl, Enum.* 2, *p.* 44; *Kunth, Enum.* 4, *p.* 122. Leptanthus ovalis, *Michx. Fl.* 1, *p.* 25, *t.* 5, *f.* 1. Wet places, Westport, &c., Arkansas river. Corolla usually blue, but a white-flowered variety was found with the common form.

Calochortus venustus, *Benth. in Hort. Trans.* (*n. s.*) 1, *p.* 412, *t.* 15, *f.* 2, *var?*: sepals erect; petals obovate, bearded and without a spot below the middle, purple at the base. Grows under trees on high mountains. Utah. Stem 2–3-flowered. Leaves grass-like, about two lines wide. Flowers nearly 3 inches in diameter. Sepals lanceolate, striate with purple veins externally. Petals nearly twice as long as the sepals, the upper half white, pale yellowish-green lower down, where the inside is bearded with longish gland-tipped hairs, which are dark purple at the base. Near the base the hairs are more numerous, and form a transverse tuft; at the very bottom the claw is dark purple. Differs from *C. venustus* in its much narrower and less bearded petals, and in wanting the red spot above the middle.

Allium cernuum, *Roth; Kunth, Enum.* 4, *p.* 435. Roubideau's Pass. Differs from the description of A. cernuum, in the ovary being 6-toothed, or rather with 3 short processes, each of which is 2-lobed.

Carex vulpinoidea, *Michx. Fl.* 2, *p.* 69; *Torr. Fl. N. York* 2, *p.* 376. C. multiflora, *Muhl. in Willd. Spec.* 4, *p.* 233; *Schk. Car. t. Lll. f.* 154. Between Westport and Bent's Fort.

Scirpus lineatus, *Michx. Fl.* 1, *p.* 32; *Torr. Cyp. p.* 332. In thickets, Upper Arkansas.

S. lacustris, *Linn.; Muhl. Gram. p.* 32; *Torr. Cyp. p.* 221. Bluff Creek.

Cyperus filiculmis, *Vahl, Enum.* 2, *p.* 328; *Torr. Cyp. p.* 267. C. mariscoides, *Elliott, Sk.* 1, *p.* 67. Prairies near Fort Atkinson.

Bouteloua curtipendula, *Torr. in Emory's Report, p.* 153. B. racemosa, *Torr. Fl. N. York* 2, *p.* 449; *not of Lag.* Chloris curtipendula, *Michx. Fl.* 1, *p.* 59. Atheropogon apludoides, *Muhl. Gram. p.* 287. Prairies, Upper Arkansas.

Chondrosium oligostachyum, *Torr. in Marcy's Report, p.* 300. Atheropogon oligostachyum, *Nutt. Gen.* 1, *p.* 78. Eutriana? oligostachya, *Kunth, Enum.* 1, *p.* 96, *and* 2, *p.* 282. On the Upper Arkansas.

Sesleria dactyloides, *Nutt. Gen.* 1, *p.* 65; *Kunth, Enum.* 1, *p.* 323; *Torr. in Emory's Report, p.* 323, *t.* 10. With the last. The flowers are all male in the specimens of this collection. There are thrown out from the root, besides the upright flowering culms, long prostrate runners which produce short verticillate branches and tufts of leaves at the joints, where they also frequently strike root.

Andropogon Torreyanum, *Steud. Syn. Gram. p.* 302.

A. Jamesii, *Torr. in Marcy's Report, p.* 302. A. glaucum, *Torr. in Ann. Lyc. N. York* 1, *p.* 153; *not of Muhl.* Sources of the Arkansas.

Spartina cynosuroides, *Willd. Enum.* 1, *p.* 80; *Torr. Fl. N. York* 2, *p.* 448, *t.* 153. Lowlands of the headwaters of the Arkansas.

Tripsacum dactyloides, *Linn.; Kunth, Enum.* 1, *p.* 469; *Steud. Gram. p.* 362. Plains of the Arkansas.

Elymus Canadensis, *Linn.; Kunth, Enum.* 1. 451; *Torr. l. c.* 476. Between Westport and Bent's Fort.

Panicum capillare, *Linn.; Kunth, Enum.* 1, *p.* 114; *Torr. l. c. p.* 426. With the preceding.

Panicum Crus-galli, *Linn.; Torr. Fl. N. York*, 2, *p.* 424. Damp places. Upper Arkansas. The flowers are hispid and mostly awnless.

EXPLANATION OF THE PLATES.

Plate I. Viola Beckwithii.

Fig. 1, the petals; 2, vertical section of a flower; 3, 4, 5, stamens; 6, pistil; 7, capsule and calyx. All magnified.

Plate II. Sidalcea candida.

Fig. 1, vertical section of the column, ovary, &c.; 2, upper part of the stamineal column, entire; 3, fruit, of the natural size; 4, fruit and calyx; 5, a mature carpel; 6, a seed. All but 3 magnified.

Plate III. Astrgalus Beckwithii.

Fig. 1, vexillum; 2, a wing; 3, keel; 4, calyx and pistil; 4, stamens; 6, pistil, the ovary vertically divided. All enlarged.

Plate IV. Œnothera tanacetifolia.

Fig. 1, vertical section of a flower; 2, stamens; 3, pollen; 4, ovules. All variously enlarged.

Plate V. Tetradymia glabrata.

Fig. 1, a capitulum; 2, receptacle; 3, a flower; 4, corolla and stamens; 5, corolla and stamens laid open; 6, a stamen; 7, transverse section of the ovary; 8, pistil, with the ovary vertically divided; 9, stigmas; 10, a bristle of the pappus. The details variously enlarged.

Plate VI. Pentstemon heterandum.

Fig. 1, a flower; 2, diagram of the æstivation, &c.; 3. 4, normal form for the genus of æstivation of the corolla; 5, vertical section of a flower; 6, corolla laid open, with normal stamens; 7, 8, anterior and posterior view of a perfect stamen; 9, 10, 11, the fifth stamen more or less antheriferous; 12, the fifth stamen reduced to the usual sterile filament; 13, pistil. The details variously enlarged.

Plate VII. Phacelia humilis.

Fig. 1, a flower; 2, corolla laid open, with the stamens; 3, 4, stamens; 5, pistil and calyx; 6, the same in fruit; 7, capsule, &c., vertically divided; 8, a seed; 9, vertical section of the same. The details more or less magnified.

Plate VIII. Phlox canescens.

Fig. 1, a flower; 2, the same laid open; 3, 4, stamens; 5, pistil; 6, ovary horizontally divided; 7, vertical section of the ovary. The details variously enlarged.

Plate IX. Gilia Gunnisoni.

Fig. 1, a flower; 2, calyx laid open; 3, corolla laid open; 4, pistil—pistil with the ovary vertically divided; 6, ovary transversely divided; 7, calyx and capsule. Details variously enlarged.

Plate X. Abronia fragans.

Fig. 1, a flower; 2, the same laid open; 3, anther; 4, stigma; 5, immature fruit.

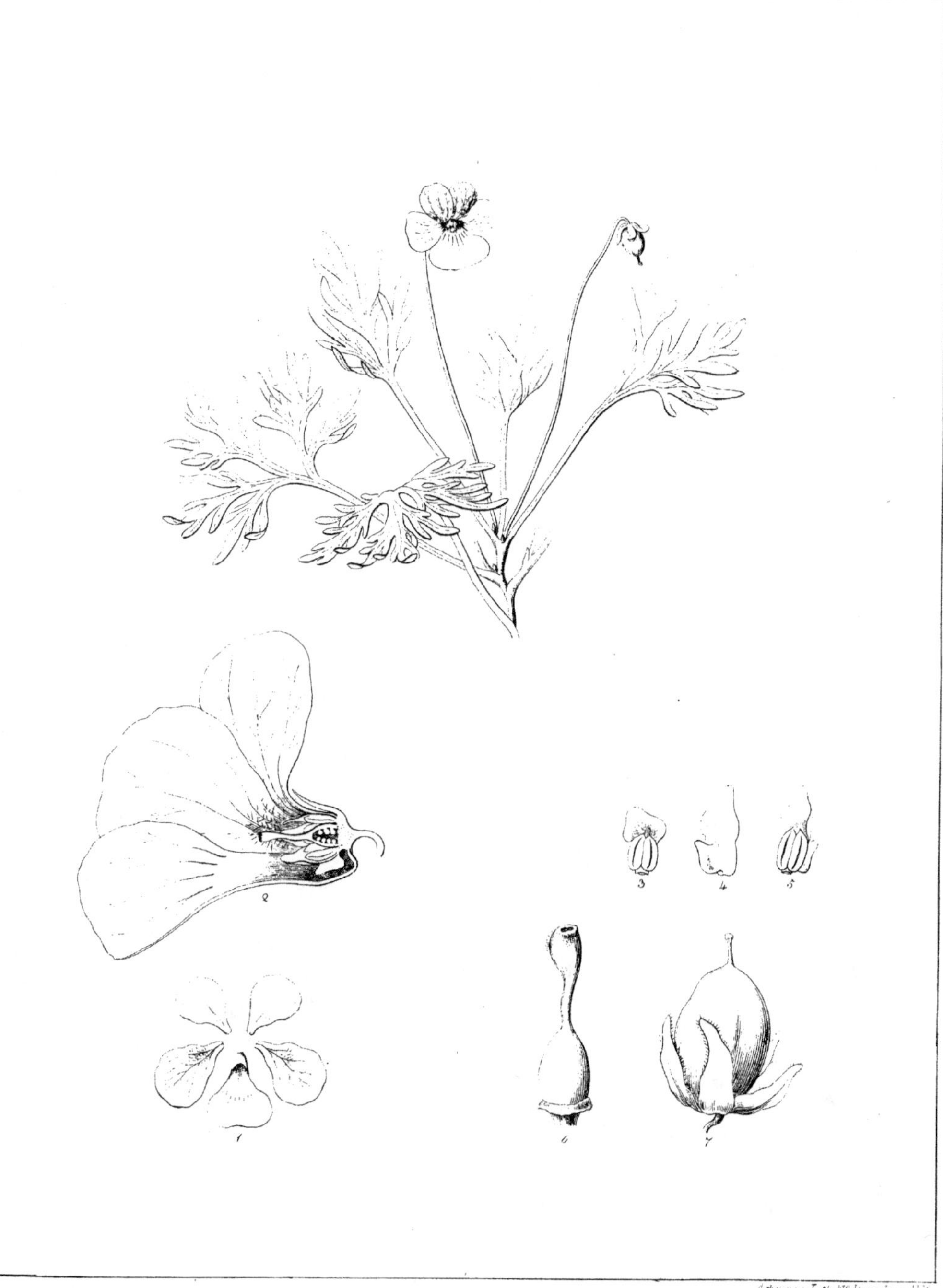

Ackerman Lith. 119 Broadway N.Y.

VIOLA BECKWITHII.

SIDALCEA CANDIDA.

Ackerman Lith. 379 Broadway N.Y.

ASTRAGALUS BECKWITHII.

Ackerman Lith. 379 Broadway N.Y.

ŒNOTHERA TANACETIFOLIA.

Ackerman Lith 379 Broadway N.Y.

TETRADYMIA GLABRATA.

Ackerman Lith 379 Broadway N.Y.

PHLOX CANESCENS.

3 4 5 9 8 1 2 7 6

Ackerman Lith. 379 Broadway N.Y.

PHACELIA HUMILIS.

Ackerman Lith. 379 Broadway N.Y.

PENTSTEMON HETERANDRUM.

Ackerman Lith. 379 Broadway N.Y.

GILIA GUNNISONII.

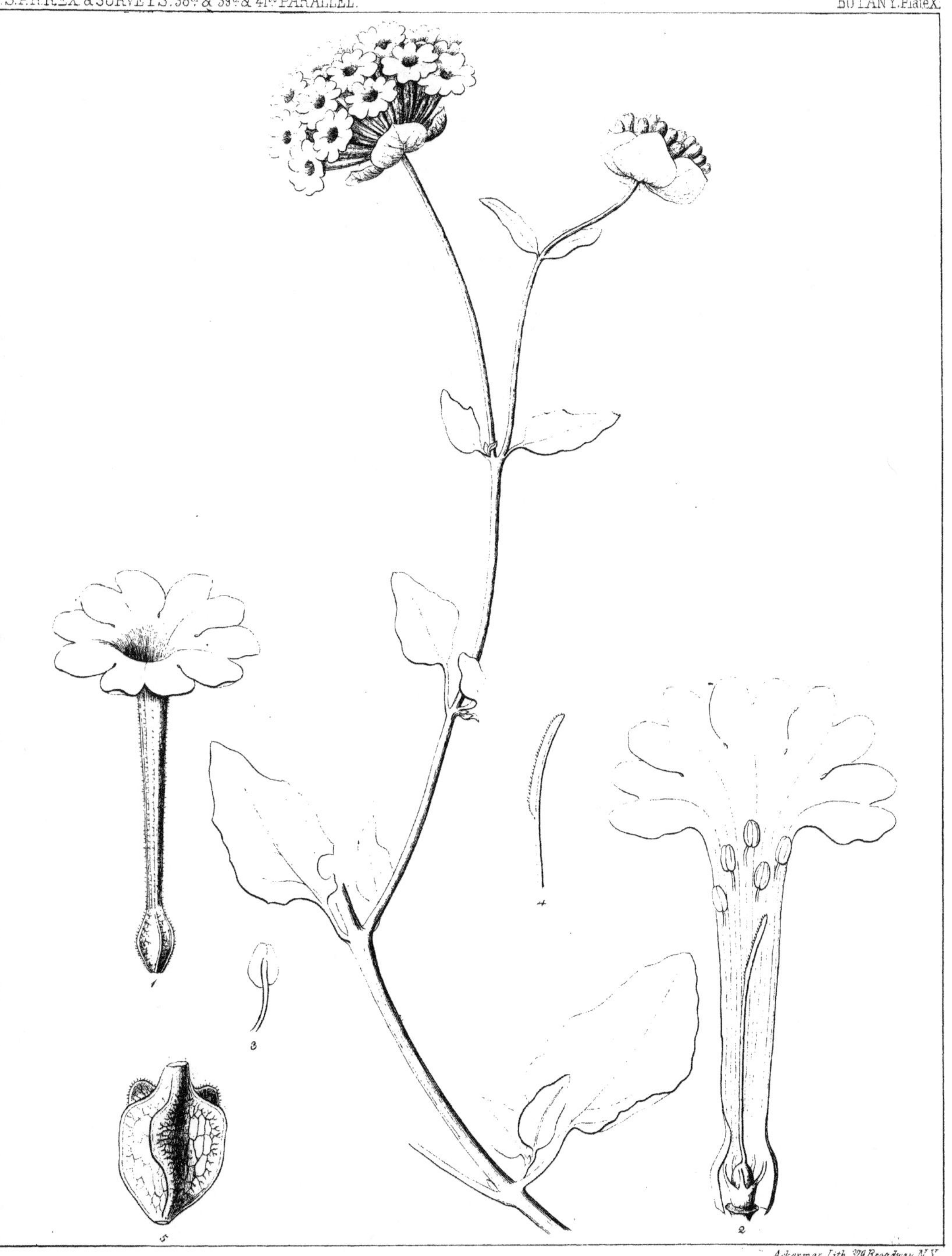

Ackerman Lith. 379 Broadway N.Y.

ABRONIA FRAGRANS.

EXPLORATIONS AND SURVEYS FOR A RAILROAD ROUTE FROM THE MISSISSIPPI RIVER TO THE PACIFIC OCEAN.

WAR DEPARTMENT.

REPORT

ON THE

BOTANY OF THE EXPEDITION:

BY

JOHN TORREY AND ASA GRAY.

ROUTE NEAR THE THIRTY-SECOND PARALLEL OF NORTH LATITUDE, UNDER THE COMMAND OF BREVET CAPTAIN JOHN POPE, CORPS OF TOPOGRAPHICAL ENGINEERS.

BOTANICAL REPORT.

Catalogue of Plants collected on the Expedition. By John Torrey *and* Asa Gray.

RANUNCULACEÆ.

Clematis Drummondii, *Torr. and Gray, Fl.* 1, *p.* 9. On the upper Colorado, Texas; April.

Anemone Caroliniana, *Walt.*; *Torr. and Gray, Fl.* 1, *p.* 12; *Torr. in Marcy's Rep. t.* 1. Delaware creek to the Sacramento, the Pecos, and the Colorado; March, April.

Myosurus minimus, *Linn.* Head of the Colorado; April.

Delphinium azureum, *Michx. Fl.* 1, *p.* 314. Western Texas; April. Broad-leaved varieties.

BERBERIDACEÆ.

Berberis trifoliolata, *Moricand; Gray, Pl. Lindh.* 2, *p.* 142. Base of the Guadalupe mountains, New Mexico; March.

PAPAVERACEÆ & FUMARIACEÆ.

Argemone Mexicana, *Linn.* Western Texas; April.

Corydalis aurea, *Willd.* Delaware creek to the Sacramento and Pecos; March.

CRUCIFERÆ.

Streptanthus petiolaris, *Gray, Pl. Fendl. p.* 7. On the upper Colorado, Texas.

Streptanthus carinatus, *Wright in Gray, Pl. Wright,* 2, *p.* 11. Rocky hills on the Pecos, New Mexico; March. Smaller specimens than Wright's, and, like those, in flower only.

Greggia camporum, *Gray, Pl. Wright,* 1, *p.* 9, *t.* 1. On the Pecos, &c.; March. In flower only.

Sisymbrium canescens, *Nutt.* Delaware creek to the Colorado; March, April.

Erysimum asperum, *DC.; Torr. and Gray, Fl.* 1, *p.* 95. On the Pecos, Llano Estacado, and upper Colorado; March, April.

Dithyræa Wislizeni, *Engelm. in Wisl. N. Mex. p.* 11; *Torr. in Marcy's Rep. t.* 2. On the Pecos, Llano Estacado, &c.

Vesicaria gracilis, *Hook. Bot. Mag. t.* 3533; *Gray, Pl. Lindh.* 2, *p.* 148. On the Pecos, Llano Estacado, and upper Colorado; March, April. Except by its non-stipitate silicles, V. angustifolia, *Nutt.*, is apparently undistinguishable from V. gracilis; and there is some reason to fear that this difference is not constant.

Vesicaria Gordoni, *Gray, l. c., p.* 149. Llano Estacado; April. There is reason to fear that this also passes into the foregoing.

Vesicaria argyræa, *Gray, Pl. Lindh.* 2, *p.* 146. Between Delaware creek and the Pecos; March. Not yet in flower.

Vesicaria Fendleri, *Gray, Pl. Fendl. p.* 9; V. stenophylla, *Gray, Pl. Lindh.* 2, *p.* 149. Everywhere on Delaware creek, the Pecos, Llano Estacado, &c.; March, April. To this, it is now evident, belongs the V. stenophylla; and the species exhibits great diversities in its mode of growth and foliage, as also in the size and even the shape of its pods. The name V. Fendleri is the older one; that of V. stenophylla is applicable only to some of the forms which the species assumes.

Vesicaria Ludoviciana, *DC. Syst.* 2, *p.* 297. On the Pecos; March. Not in flower.

Draba cuneifolia, *Nutt. in Torr. and Gray, Fl.* 1, *p.* 108. Delaware creek to the Colorado.

Selenia dissecta, (n. sp., Plate I.) Leaves bipinnately divided, the segments linear; style not longer than the ovary; valves of the pod imperfectly one-nerved; seeds on short and thick funiculi.—In sandy or gravelly soil, from Delaware springs to the Llano Estacado; March and April. In flower, and with some mature fruit. This second species of Nuttall's genus Selenia is perhaps the most interesting plant of the present collection. It is a sort of biennial, (like so many of this region,) the plant having grown from the seed the preceding autumn, and begun to flower early in the following spring. The earliest flowers, borne on slender peduncles, spring directly from the crown, among the tufted radical leaves. Later, an ascending and sparsely leafy stem rises to the height of from three to six inches, and bears a raceme of leafy-bracted flowers, in the manner of L. aurea. The blossoms appear to be considerably larger than in that species, at least the earlier ones, the petals being fully half an inch long; but their form, and apparently their color, is the same. The leaves are all pinnately divided, with their primary divisions pinnately 3–9-parted. The anthers are linear, rather than oblong. The style, although slender, is hardly as long as the ovary: stigma rather large, depressed. The silicle is elliptical, slightly inclined to obovate, very flat, seven to eight lines long, scarcely stipitate, rounded at the summit, and abruptly tipped with the comparatively short style; valves minutely reticulate-veiny; a mid-nerve is usually evident from the base to the middle, or sometimes even to the summit. Septum complete in the specimens examined, obscurely two-nerved in the middle; the areolæ large, and nearly as in L. aurea. The seeds resemble those of that species, but are borne on short and thick funiculi, the base of which is somewhat adnate to the margin of the septum; and the cœcal pouch at the hilum is small, or indistinct. Cotyledons orbicular, accumbent against the ascending radicle, which is on the side remote from the placenta. As already shown, (*in Gen. Ill.* 1, *p.* 158,) the genus belongs to the Alyssineæ.

Lepidum Alyssoides, *Gray, Pl. Fendl. p.* 10. Llano Estacado; April.

Lepidum Wrightii, *Gray, Pl. Wright.* 2, *p.* 15. On the Pecos, Colorado, &c.

Lepidum intermedium, *Gray, l. c.* Near Fort Washita; April.

CISTACEÆ.

Lechea minor, *Lam.; Torr. and Gray, Fl.* 1, *p.* 153. On the Llano Estacado; March. Without flowers or fruit.

CARYOPHYLLACEÆ.

Silene Antirrhina, *Linn.* On the upper Colorado, Texas; April.

Paronychia Jamesii, *Torr. and Gray, Fl.* 1, *p.* 170. Guadalupe mountains, New Mexico. Without flowers.

MALVACEÆ.

Callirrhöe digitata, *Nutt.; Gray, Pl. Fendl. p.* 17. On the upper Colorado, Texas; April.

Callirrhöe involucrata, *Gray, l. c.* A small variety. On the upper Colorado; April.

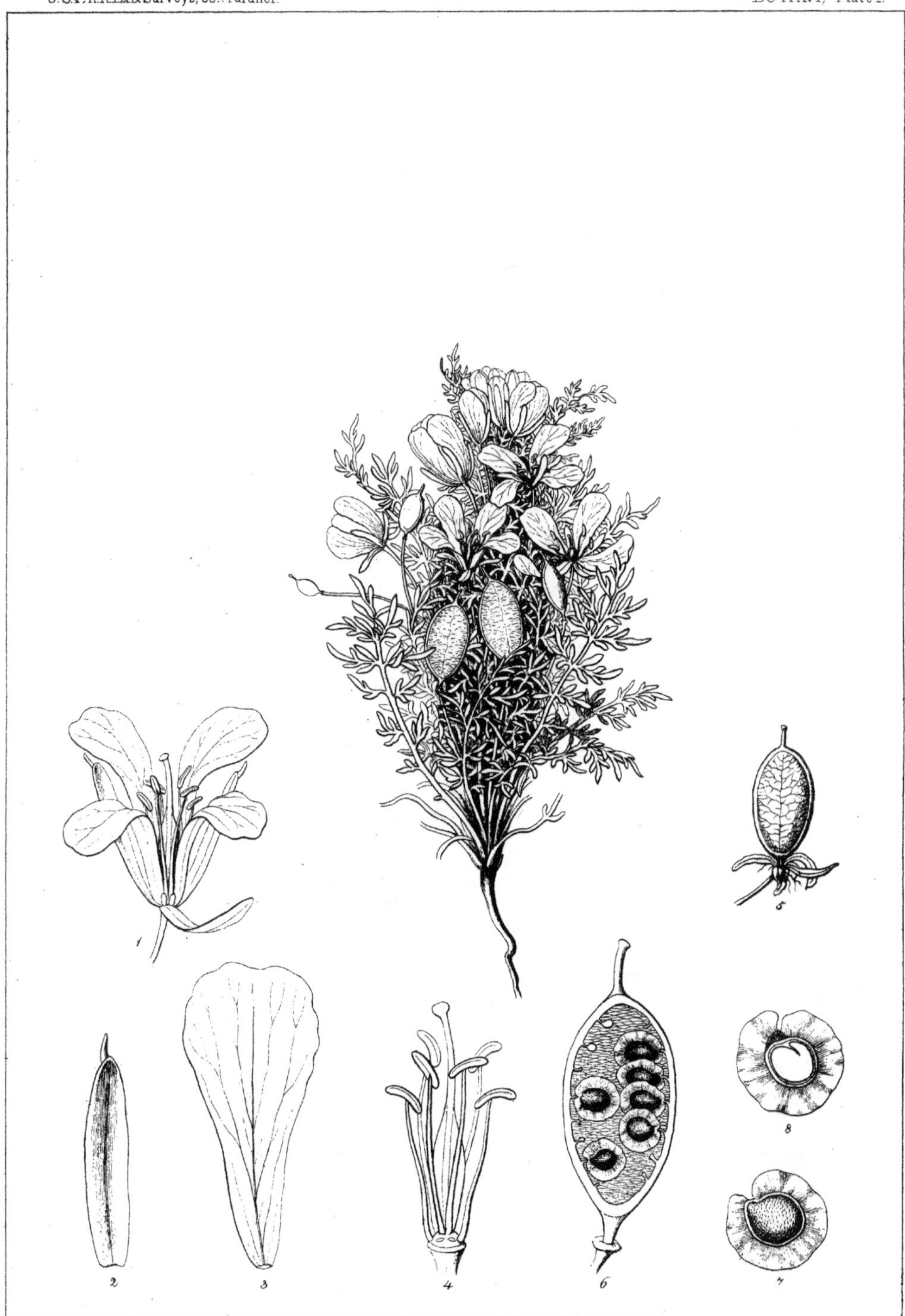

SELENIA DISSECTA.

Sprague del.   P. S. Duval & Co. Lith. Philada.   Prestele sc.

MALVALTRUM COCCINEUM, *Gray, Pl. Fendl. p.* 21. Everywhere between the Rio Grande and the Colorado; March, April.

SPHÆRALCEA HASTULATA, *Gray, Pl. Wright.* 1, *p.* 17. On the Pecos and Colorado.

SPHÆRALCEA ANGUSTIFOLIA, *Spach;* the small flowered variety, S. stellata, *Torr.* Pecos to Llano Estacado; March.

SPHÆRALCEA FENDLERI, *Gray, Pl. Wright.* 1, *p.* 21. Cotton-wood Springs, New Mexico. Fruit only, without foliage.

GERANIACEÆ.

GERANIUM CAROLINIANUM, *Linn.* From Llano Estacado to Colorado, &c.

ERODIUM TEXANUM, *Gray, Pl. Lindh.* 2, *p.* 157; *and Gen. Ill. t.* 151. From the Pecos to the Colorado; March and April.

OXALIDACEÆ.

OXALIS WRIGHTII, *Gray, Pl. Wright.* 1, *p.* 27. On the Pecos; March.

LINACEÆ.

LINUM RIGIDUM, *Pursh, Fl.* 1, *p.* 210. On the Pecos, Llano Estacado, and upper Colorado; March, April.

LINUM MULTICAULE, *Hook. in Torr. and Gray, Fl.* 1, *p.* 678. Llano Estacado; April; Mr. Garrard.

LINUM PERENNE, *Linn.* From New Mexico to the Colorado; March, April.

ZYGOPHYLLACEÆ.

LARREA MEXICANA, *Moricand; Torr. in Emory's Rep. p.* 137, *t.* 3. From the Rio Grande to Llano Estacado, &c. Not yet in flower.

RUTACEÆ.

ZANTHOXYLUM CAROLINIANUM, *Lam.; Torr. and Gray, Fl.* 1, *p.* 214. Western Texas; April. The variety characterized in *Pl. Wright. t. p.* 31.

RUTOSMA TEXANUM, *Gray, Gen. Ill.* 2, *p.* 144, *t.* 155? On the Pecos, &c.; March.

*** Captain Pope collected, on the Organ mountains, specimens, without flowers or fruit, of a remarkable Rutaceous plant, which had been previously gathered there by Mr. Wright, and afterwards by H. B. Gray, Esq. We have also received it from Dr. Edwards, of the United States army, who found it on the Mimbres. Dr. J. M. Bigelow and Mr. Schott were so fortunate as to detect it in fruit, while they were engaged in the Mexican boundary survey, under the command of Major W. H. Emory. The former gentleman collected it, in 1852, on the Florence mountains, which, we believe, are in the southern part of New Mexico, near the Rio Grande; and Mr. Schott obtained it farther down the river. For want of the flowers, a complete description of the plant cannot be given; but there are sufficient materials to show that it is quite a distinct genus, of which a full account will be given in Dr. Torrey's botany of the Mexican boundary survey, under the name of ASTROPHYLLUM DUMOSUM. The plant is a low, much branched shrub, with opposite, palmately 7–10-foliolate, petiolate leaves; the leaflets narrowly linear, coriaceous, marked (as are the petioles and younger branches) with large and prominent glands. These glands on the leaflets are somewhat distant, and form a row along each margin. They are filled with a strong-smelling, acrid, volatile oil. The flowers are hermaphrodite, solitary, on long pedicels, which are lateral and terminal. On one of the specimens was a flower-bud, and on the other specimens were several pedicels supporting unfructified ovaries, besides abundance of ripe fruit. The bud contained ten stamens in two series, with subulate filaments from a broad base, and oblong 2-celled anthers. Opposite the shorter or interior stamens, (and alternating with the exterior ones,) were five ovate scales or petals. The characters of the calyx were not satisfactorily determined. There was no disk perceptible in the bud, and it is very inconspicuous in the flowers that had not matured their fruit. There are five one-celled oblong ovaries, which slightly cohere towards the base, each produced into a short incurved beak or horn. The styles are distinct, and arise from near the middle of the carpels on the inside; but the stigmas are united into an oblong 5-grooved head. Ovules two in each cell, collateral, inserted at the origin of the style. Only two of the carpels ripen. They are sessile, slightly united at the base, broadly ovate, compressed, dotted with small brown glands, and mucronate with the persistent base of the style; but the beak, which in the ovary was at the summit of the cell, has now become a dorsal tooth. At an early period the capsule opens nearly the whole length of the ventral suture, and down the back as far as the tooth. The endocarp also separates almost entirely from the epicarp. The seeds are usually solitary in each cell. They are ovate-globose, black and shining. The embryo is broadly oval, slightly curved, flattish, with a very short radicle; and there is little or no albumen.

ANACARDIACEÆ.

RHUS GLABRA, *Linn.* Near Fort Washita; April.

RHUS TRILOBATA, *Nutt. in Torr. and Gray, Fl.* 1, *p.* 219. On the upper Colorado, Texas; April.

RHUS MICROPHYLLA, *Engelm. in Pl. Wright.* 1, *p.* 31. With the preceding species.

VITACEÆ.

VITIA RUPESTRIS, *Scheele, in Linnæa,* 21, *p.* 591. Western Texas; April 21. In flower.

RHAMNACEÆ.

CEANOTHUS OVATUS, *Desf.* (C. ovalis, *Bigelow.*) Near Fort Chadbourne; also a downy variety on the Colorado, Texas.

ZIZYPHUS LYCIODES, *Gray, Pl. Lindh.* 2, *p.* 168. Western Texas; April.

MICRORHAMNUS ERICOIDES, *Gray, Pl. Wright.* 1, *p.* 34. Near Delaware Springs, &c.; March.

SAPINDACEÆ.

SAPINDUS MARGINATUS, *Willd.; Gay, Gen. Ill.* 2, *t.* 180. Pecos and Llano Estacado. Called *Wild China* in Texas and Arkansas.

UNGNADIA SPECIOSA, *Endl.; Gray, Gen. Ill.* 2, *t.* 178, 179. Big Springs of the Colorado and elsewhere; April.

POLYGALACEÆ.

POLYGALA ALBA, *Nutt. Gen.* 2, *p.* 87. Llano Estacado, Colorado, &c.

POLYGALA MACRADENIA, *Gray, Pl. Wright.* 1, *p.* 38. On the Pecos; March.

KRAMERIA LANCEOLATA, *Torr.; Gray, Gen. Ill. t.* 187, 188. Western Texas; April.

LEGUMINOSÆ.

VICIA LEAVENWORTHII, *Torr. and Gray, Fl.* 1, *p.* 271. On the upper Colorado, Texas; April.

VICIA EXIGUA, *Nutt. in Torr. and Gray, l. c.; Gray, Pl. Wright.* 2, *p.* 32. Llano Estacado; March, April.

TEPHROSIA VIRGINIANA, *Pers. Syn.* 2, *p.* 328. Western Texas; May.

AMORPHA FRUTICOSA, *Linn. var.* On the upper Colorado; April.

Psoralea esculenta, *Pursh, Fl.* 2, *p.* 475, *t.* 22. On the Colorado, Western Texas; April.

Psoralea obtusiloba, *Torr. and Gray, Fl.* 1, *p.* 300. Western Texas; May.

Psoralea floribunda, *Nutt. in Torr. and Gray, Fl. l. c.* Western Texas; May.

Psoralea cuspidata, *Pursh, Fl.* 2, *p.* 741. Western Texas; April.

Psoralea digitata, *Nutt. in Torr. and Gray, l. c.* Western Texas; April.

Dalea formosa, *Torr. in Am. Lyc. N. York,* 2, *p.* 78; *and in Emory's Rep. t.* 1. Everywhere between the Rio Grande and Western Texas.

Petalostemon violaceum, *Michx.* Near Fort Washita.

Petalostemon candidum, *Michx.* Near Fort Washita.

Astragalus mollissimus, *Torr. in Am. Lyc. N. York,* 2, *p.* 178; *Gray, Pl. Wright.* 1, *p.* 53. On the Llano Estacado, in sandy soil; March, April. Plant sometimes considerably caulescent, and a foot high.

Astragalus succumbens, *Dougl. in Hook. Fl. Bor.-Am.* 1, *p.* 151. On the Pecos, Llano Estacado, &c.; March, April. The specimens are only in flower; in which state they very well accord with Douglas' plant. Mr. Gordon also gathered it in flower on the Raton mountains.

Astragalus pauciflorus, *Hook. Fl. Bor.-Am.* 1, *p.* 129. High grounds at the head-waters of the Colorado, Texas; April.

Astragalus Missouriensis, *Nutt. Gen.* 2, *p.* 99. Guadalupe mountains to the Colorado; March, April.

Astragalus cyaneus, *Gray, Pl. Fendl. p.* 34. Between the Pecos and Llano Estacado. Probably too near the preceding species.

Astragalus Nuttallianus, *DC.*, var. trichocarpus and canescens, *Gray, Pl. Wright.* From the Pecos to the Colorado; March, April.

Astragalus Lindheimeri, *Gray, Pl. Wright.* 1, *p.* 52. On the upper Colorado; April.

Astragalus Candensis, *Linn.* Near Fort Washita; April.

Astragalus, *n. sp.?* In flower only. High ground, on the eastern border of the Llano Estacado; April.

Oxytropis Lamberti, *Pursh, Fl.* 2, *p.* 740. Western Texas; May.

Stylosanthes elatior, *Swartz.; DC. Prodr.* 2, *p.* 381. Western Texas; May.

Desmodium canescens, *DC. Prodr.* 2, *p.* 238. Near Fort Washita.

Lespedeza Stuvei, *Nutt. Gen.* 2, *p.* 107. Near Fort Washita.

Sophora sericea, *Nutt. Gen.* 1, *p.* 280. Western Texas; April.

Cercis occidentalis, *Torr. in Pl. Lindh.* 2, *p.* 177. Near Fort Chadbourne; May.

Hoffmanseggia stricta, var. demissa, *Benth. in Pl. Wright.* 1, *p.* 56. Llano Estacado to the Colorado; April. In flower.

Hoffmanseggia drepanocarpa, *Gray, Pl. Wright.* 1, *p.* 58. On the Pecos.

Hoffmanseggia brachycarpa, *Gray, l. c.* On the Pecos.

Hoffmanseggia Jamesii, *Torr. and Gray, Fl.* 1, *p.* 393; *Torr. in Marcy's Rep. t.* 4. Llano Estacado.

Cassia Pumilio, *Gray, Pl. Lindh.* 2, *p.* 180; *and Pl. Wright.* 1, *p.* 59. Llano Estacado, &c.; April.

Cassia Bauhinioides, *Gray, l. c.* Llano Estacado; April.

Cassia Rœmeriana, *Scheele; Gray, Pl. Lindh.* 2, *p.* 179. Western Texas; April.

Strombocarpa pubescens, *Gray, Pl. Wright.* 1, *p.* 60; (Prosopis, *Benth.*) Near Doña Ana. The fruit only; called *Tornio, or Screw-tree;* in some districts *Screw-bean.*

ALGAROBIA GLANDULOSA, *Torr. and Gray, Fl.* 1, *p.* 399. Head-waters of the Colorado, Texas; April. This is the celebrated *Mezquit* of New Mexico.

DESMANTHUS JAMESII, *Torr. and Gray, Fl.* 1, *p.* 402. Llano Estacado, &c. Foliage only.

SCHRANKIA PLATYCARPA, *Gray, Pl. Lindh.* 2, *p.* 183. Western Texas; April.

MIMOSA BOREALIS, *Gray, Pl. Fendl. p.* 39. On the upper Colorado, and near Fort Chadbourne; April, May.

ACACIA HIRTA, *Nutt. in Torr. and Gray, Fl.* 1, *p.* 404. Western Texas; April.

ACACIA TEXENSIS, *Torr. and Gray, l. c.* (Probably the A. cuspidata, *Schlecht.*) Near Fort Washita.

ROSACEÆ.

PRUNUS AMERICANA, *Marsh.; Torr. and Gray, Fl.* 1, *p.* 407. Big Springs of the Colorado; April.

PRUNUS CHICASA, *Michx.; Torr. and Gray, l. c.* On the Colorado; April.

CERCOCARPUS PARVIFOLIUS, *Nutt. in Torr. and Gray, Fl.* 1, *p.* 427. Doña Ana, New Mexico; February. Foliage only.

FALLUGIA PARADOXA, *Torr. in Emory's Rep. t.* 2. Guadalupe mountains, New Mexico. Foliage only.

GEUM VIRGINIANUM, *Linn.* Western Texas; May.

ROSA SETIGERA, *Michx.; Torr. and Gray, Fl.* 1, *p.* 457. Fort Washita; April.

RUBUS TRIVIALIS, *Michx.; Fl.* 1, *p.* 296. Near Fort Washita.

ONAGRACEÆ.

ŒNOTHERA LAVENDULÆFOLIA, *Torr. and Gray, Fl.* 1, *p.* 501. Llano Estacado; April.

ŒNOTHERA HARTWEGI, *Benth. Pl. Hartw. p.* 1; the var. answering to Œ. Fendleri; *Gray, Pl. Fendl.* On the Pecos, Llano Estacado, and Colorado.

ŒNOTHERA TUBICULA, *Gray, Pl. Wright.* 1, *p.* 71. On the Pecos and Llano Estacado.

ŒNOTHERA ALBICAULIS, *Nutt. Gen.* 1, *p.* 245; *Gray, Pl. Wright.* 1, *p.* 59. On the Pecos.

ŒNOTHERA TRILOBA, *Nutt. Gen. l. c.* On the Pecos.

ŒNOTHERA SERRULATA, *Nutt. l. c.* Big Springs of the Colorado to Fort Washita, &c.; April.

ŒNOTHERA SINNATA, *Linn.* Near Fort Washita; April. Western Texas; May.

ŒNOTHERA WRIGHTII, *Gray, Pl. Wright.* 2, *p,* 57. On the Llano Estacado; April. In flower.

ŒNOTHERA MISSOURIENSIS, *Sims, Bot. Mag. t.* 1592. Western Texas; May.

ŒNOTHERA SPECIOSA, *Nutt.; Torr. and Gray, Fl.* 1, *p.* 496. Western Texas; April.

ŒNOTHERA SPACHIANA, *Torr. and Gray, Fl.* 1, *p.* 498. Western Texas; May.

GAURA PARVIFLORA, *Dougl.; Torr. and Gray, Fl.* 1, *p.* 519. Llano Estacado and Western Texas.

GAURA SUFFULTA, *Engelm. in Pl. Lindh.* 2, *p.* 190. Western Texas.

GAURA COCCINEA, *Nutt.; Torr. and Gray, Fl.* 1, *p.* 518. Llano Estacado.

GAURA SINUATA, *Nutt.; Torr. and Gray, l. c.* Western Texas; April.

CUCURBITACEÆ.

SICYDIUM LINDHEIMERI, *Gray, Pl. Lindl.* 2, *p.* 196. On the Pecos, also Western Texas; March, April.

CUCURBITA PERENNIS, *Gray, l. c.* Western Texas; April. Foliage only.

PASSIFLORACEÆ.

Passiflora incarnata, *Linn.; Torr. and Gray, Fl.* 1. *p.* 538. Western Texas; May.

GROSSULACEÆ.

Ribes aureum, *Pursh.* Big Springs of the Colorado, &c.; April.

CACTACEÆ.

Cereus cæspitosus, Echinocactus Texensis, and Opuntia frutescens, *Engelm.*, occur in the collection.

UMBELLIFERÆ.

AMMOSELINUM, n. gen. Margin of the calyx obsolete. Petals ovate, entire, nearly plane. Stylopodium very short, as are the diverging styles. Fruit ovate, laterally compressed. Carpels with five equal, prominent, corky, and scabrous ribs, in the intervals of which there are single oil-tubes, and two in the commisure. Carpophore 2-parted. Seed straight, semiterete, slightly concave on the face.—An annual diffuse herb; the leaves decompound with linear ultimate segments; flowers in compound umbels, white; leaflets of the involucre and involucels simple or compound.

Ammoselinum Popei.—Sandy soil; Llano Estacado, and head-waters of the Colorado; March and April. Mr. Wright found it in Western Texas, but he collected only a few specimens, and it was not distributed with his plants. Some ripe seeds that he collected were cultivated in the Cambridge Botanic Garden, and arrived at perfection. Dr. Parry, while engaged on the Mexican boundary survey, under Major Emory, sent home a single flowering specimen of the plant, found at Eagle Pass in January, 1853. From no other sources have we received any specimens of this apparently new genus. It grows about a span in length, and though usually diffuse, some of Captain Pope's specimens must have grown erect, and only a little branched; but they seem to have been crowded together. The stem and branches are angular, and the angles, as well as the midribs of the leaves, are rough; in other respects the plant is nearly glabrous. The leaves are triternally divided, with narrowly linear segments. Umbels compound, or sometimes decompound. Involucre of several leaves, which in strong-growing specimens are large, and resemble the leaves of the stem, being cut into linear segments: the leaves of the involucels are sometimes cut also, but more commonly they are almost entire. Rays of the umbel seldom more than three or four, unequal: rays of the umbellets 8–10, very unequal. Flowers very small. Fruit about two and a half lines long and two lines broad, compressed laterally, so that the longer diameter is twice as great as the shorter; the ribs scabrous with little points. The lateral ones are less prominent, and are confluent with an accessory, thick, corky margin, which extends through the commissure. We have with reluctance added another genus to the already extensive family of Umbelliferæ, already abounding with ill-defined genera, especially as it is founded on a single species. It is most nearly allied to Chaerophyllum, but differs in the entire petals, ovate fruit with acute ribs, and shallow furrows of the seed, as well as in the involucrum.

Cymopterus montanus, *Nutt. in Torr. and Gray, Fl.* 1, *p.* 624; *Gray, Pl. Fendl. p.* 56, *and Pl. Wright,* 1, *p.* 79. Eastern part of the Llano Estacado and on the upper Colorado; April.

Polytænia Nuttallii, *DC. Prodr.* 4, *p.* 196. On the Colorado, Texas; April. In flower.

Daucus pusillus, *Michx. Fl.* 1, *p.* 164. On the Colorado, Texas; April.

RUBIACEÆ.

Oldenlandia (Houstonia) humifusa, *Gray, Pl. Wright.* 2, *p.* 68. On the Llano Estacado and Pecos; March. A vernal state.

Oldenlandia angustifolia, *Gray, l. c.* Fort Washita and Western Texas; April, May.

Galium Aparine, *Linn.* On the Colorado; April. Not in flower.

VALERIANACEÆ.

Fedia amarella, *Lindh. in Gray, Pl. Lindh.* 2, *p.* 217. On the Colorado, &c., Texas; April, May.

COMPOSITÆ.

Machæranthera tanacetifolia, *Nees; Gray, Pl. Wright.* 1, *p.* 90. On the Llano Estacado and Western Texas; March to May.

Erigeron strigosum, *Muhl.; Torr. and Gray, Fl.* 2, *p.* 176. Near Fort Washita; April.

Erigeron divergens, *Torr. and Gray, l. c.; Gray, Pl. Wright.* 1, *p.* 91. From the Pecos to the Colorado, Texas. Various forms.

Diplopappus ericoides, *Torr. and Gray, Fl.* 2, *p.* 182. New Mexico to the Colorado; March, April. Various forms.

Townsendia sericea, *Hook, Fl. Bor.-Am.* 2, *p.* 16, *t.* 119. Guadalupe mountains, New Mexico; March.

Chætopappa asteroides, *DC. Prodr.* 5, *p.* 301. Western Texas; April, May.

Aphanostephus ramosissimus, *DC. Prodr.* 5, *p.* 310; *Gray, Pl. Wright.* 1, *p.* 93; *Torr. in Marcy's Rep. t.* 9. Big Springs of the Colorado; April.

Aphanostephus Arkansanus, *Gray, l. c.* Western Texas; May.

Bellis integrifolia, *Michx. Fl.* 1, *p.* 131. Western Texas; May.

Aplopappus spinulosus, *DC. Prodr.* 5, *p.* 348. From the Pecos to the Colorado, Texas.

Xanthisma Texanum, *DC. Prodr.* 5, *p.* 94; *Gray, Pl. Wright.* 1, *p.* 98; *Torr. in Marcy's Rep. t.* 10. Western Texas, May.

Solidago Canadensis, *Linn.* Near Fort Washita; April. Not in flower.

Calymmandra candida, *Torr. and Gray, Fl.* 2, *p.* 262. (Plate II.) Western Texas, on the upper Colorado; April. This has scarcely been collected since it was gathered by Drummond.

Filaginopsis multicaulis, *Torr. and Gray, Fl.* 2, *p.* 263. (Plate III.) On the Pecos and Llano Estacado; March. Western Texas; April. Sterile corollas, naked at the summit, but bearing a few long wooly hairs near the base.

Parthenium Hysterophorus, *Linn.* Pecos and Llano Estacado.

Melampodium cinereum, *DC. Prodr.* 5, *p.* 518. Banks of the Pecos to the Colorado; March to May.

Berlandiera lyrata, *Benth.; Gray, Pl. Fendl. p.* 78. Llano Estacado, March.

Engelmannia pinnatifida, *Torr. and Gray, in Trans. Amer. Phil. Soc. and Fl.* 2, *p.* 283; *Torr. in Marcy's Rep. t.* 11. Western Texas to the head of the Colorado; April, May.

Lindheimeria Texana, *Gray and Engelm. Pl. Lindh.* 2 *p.* 225. Western Texas; April.

Zinnia multiflora, *Linn.* Near Fort Chadbourne, Texas.

Echinacea angustifolia, *DC. Prodr.* 5, *p.* 554. Var. Western Texas; April.

Simsia (Barrattia) calva, *Gray, Pl. Lindh.* 2, *p.* 228. On the upper Colorado; April.

Dracopis amplexicaulis, *Cass.; DC. Prodr.* 5, *p.* 558. Near Fort Washita; April.

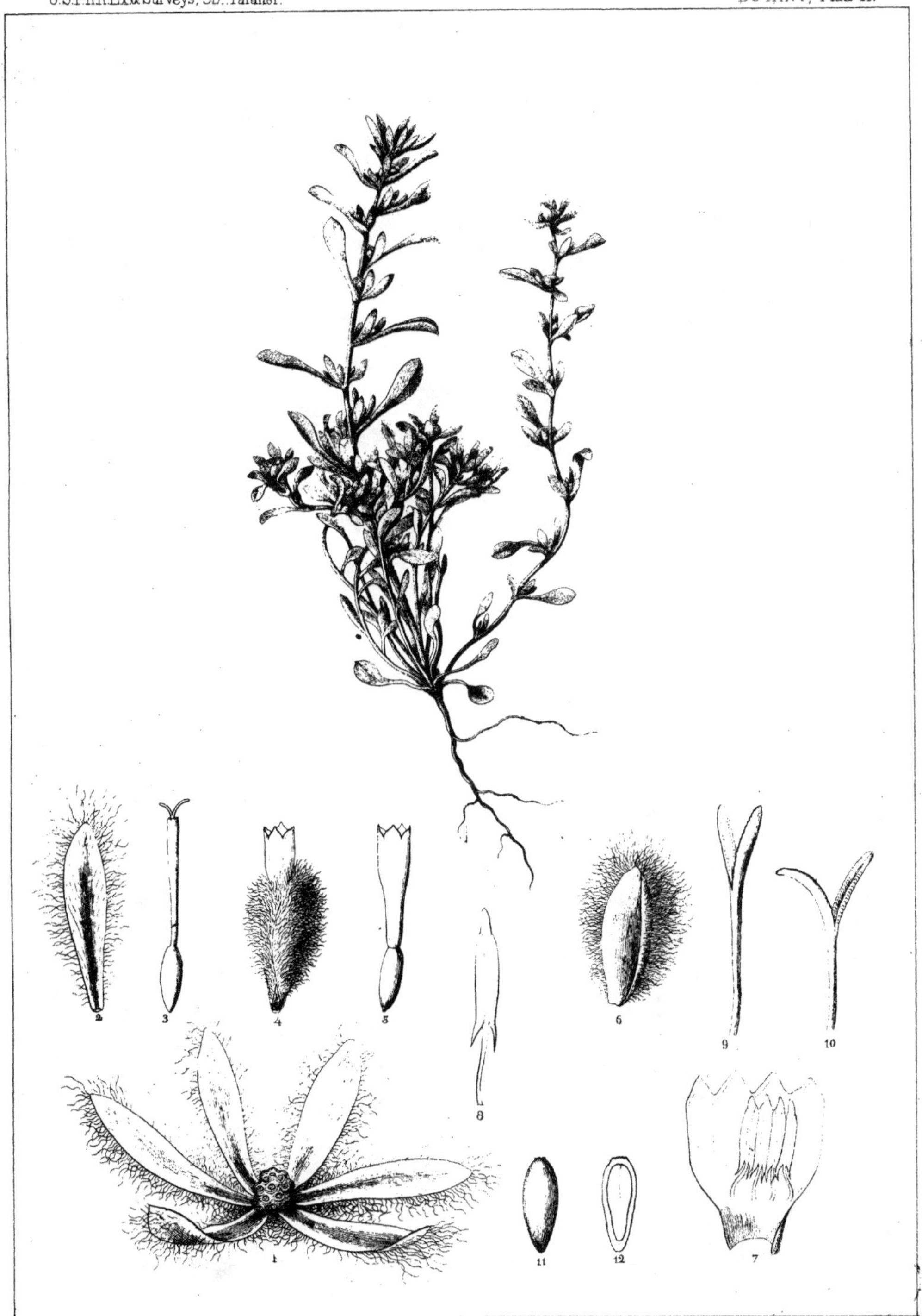

CALYMMANDRA CANDIDA.

Sprague del. P.S.Duval & Co. Lith Phil^a Prestele sc.

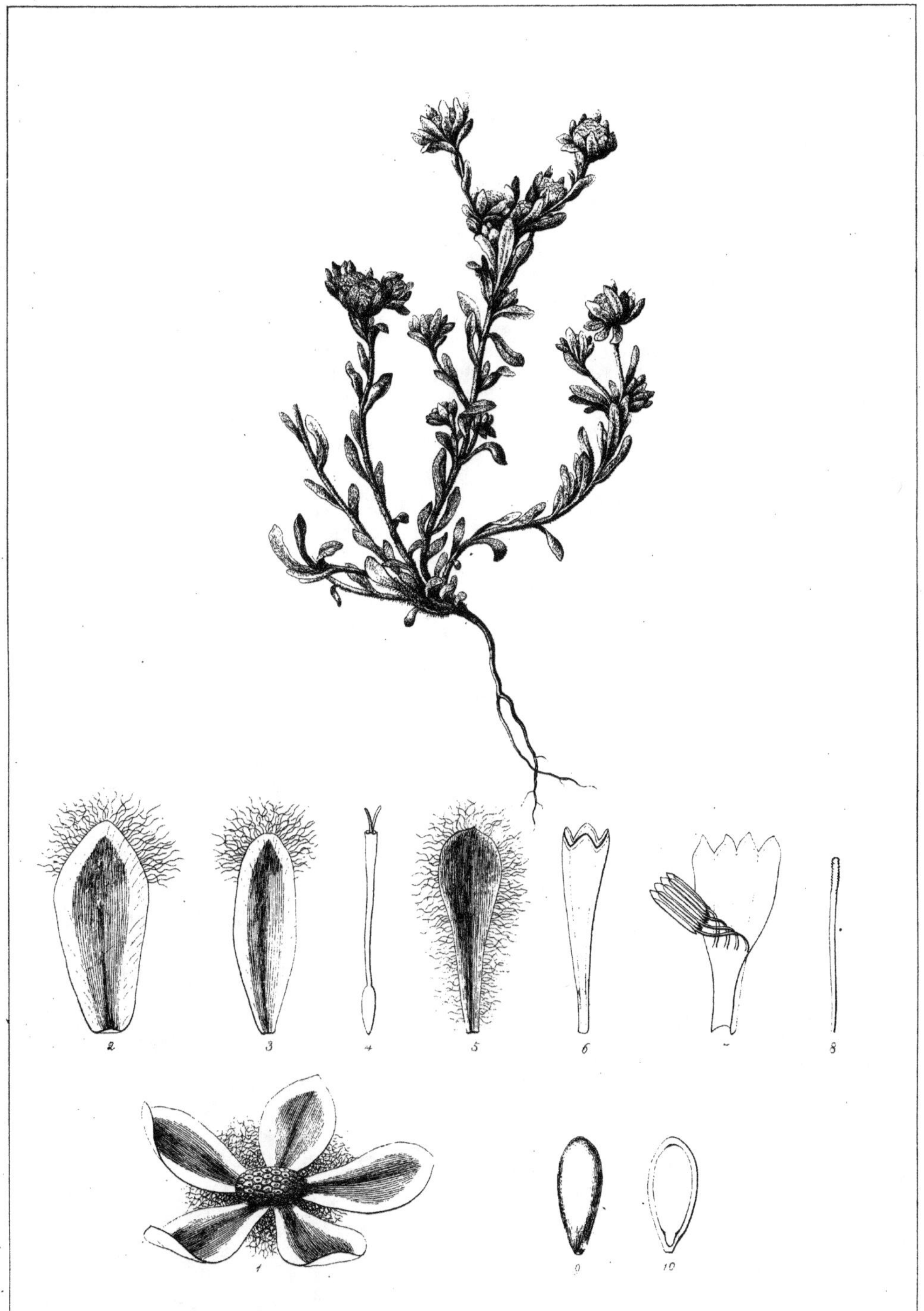

FILAGINOPSIS MULTICAULIS.

Sprague del. P. S. Duval & Co. Lith. Philada. Prestele sc.

ACTINOMERIS HELIANTHOIDES, *Nutt. Gen.* 2, *p.* 181. Near Fort Washita; April.

THELESPERMA FILIFOLIA, *Gray, in Hook. Kew. Jour. Bot.* 1, *p.* 252, *and Pl. Wright.* 1, *p.* 109. Head-waters of the Colorado; April. Also probably T. GRACILIS; but not yet in flower.

COREOPSIS GRANDIFLORA, *Nutt.; Torr. and Gray, Fl.* 2, *p.* 345. On the Colorado; April.

COREOPSIS TINCTORIA, *Nutt.* Near Fort Washita; April.

CHRYSACTINIA MEXICANA, *Gray, Pl. Fendl. p.* 93. Near Independence Spring; March. Without flowers.

HYMENATHERUM (ACIPHYLLÆA) ACEROSUM, *Gray, Pl. Wright.* 1, *p.* 115. On the Pecos and Llano Estacado; March, April.

HYMENATHERUM PENTACHÆTUM, *DC. Prodr.* 5, *p.* 642. On the Pecos; March.

AGASSIZIA SUAVIS, *Gray and Engelm. Pl. Lindh.* 2, *p.* 220. Western Texas; April.

GAILLARDIA AMBLYODON, *Gray; Torr. and Gray, Fl.* 2, *p.* 267; *Gray, Chl. Bor.-Am. t.* 4. Western Texas; April.

GAILLARDIA PINNATIFIDA, *Torr. in Ann. Lyc. New York,* 2, *p.* 214; *Torr. and Gray, Fl.* 2, *p.* 366. Llano Estacado to the Colorado; March, April.

GAILLARDIA PULCHELLA, *Fougeroux; Torr. and Gray, l. c.* Western Texas; April.

HYMENOPAPPUS CORYMBOSUS, *Torr. and Gray, Fl.* 2, *p.* 272. On the Colorado, &c.; April.

BAHIA ABSINTHIFOLIA, *Benth.* var. DEALBATA, *Gray, Pl. Wright.* 1, *p.* 121. On the Pecos; March.

RIDDELLIA TAGETINA, *Nutt.; Torr. and Gray, Fl.* 2, *p.* 262; *Torr. in Emory's Rep. t.* 5. Llano Estacado; March.

AMBLYOLEPIS SETIGERA, *DC. Prodr.* 5, *p.* 568; *Gray, Pl. Wright.* 1, *p.* 121. From the Llano Estacado to the lower Colorado; March, April.

ACTINELLA SCAPOSA, *Nutt. in Torr. and Gray, Fl.* 2, *p.* 382. On the Pecos and Llano Estacado; March.

ACTINELLA LINEARIFOLIA, *Nutt.; Torr. and Gray, l. c.* On the Pecos.

ACTINELLA RICHARDSONII, *Nutt.* Picradenia Richardsonii, *Hook.* Near the Pecos; March.

HELENIUM TENUIFOLIUM, *Nutt.; Torr. and Gray, Fl.* 2, *p.* 385. Western Texas; April.

MARSHALLIA CÆSPITOSA, *Nutt. in DC. Prodr.* 5. *p.* 680. On the upper Colorado; April.

ACHILLEA MILLEFOLIUM, *Linn.* Near Fort Washita and on the Colorado.

ARTEMISIA DRACUNCULOIDES, *Pursh; Torr. and Gray, Fl.* 2, *p.* 216. Sacramento river to the Llano Estacado; March.

ARTEMISIA LEWISII, *Torr. and Gray, Fl.* 2, *p.* 217. Pecos to the Llano Estacado; March.

ARTEMISIA LUDOVICIANA, *Nutt.; Torr. and Gray, Fl.* 2, *p.* 420. Cotton-wood Springs, New Mexico, &c.; March.

GNAPHALIUM LUTEO-ALBUM, *Linn.* New Mexico and Western Texas.

SENECIO FILIFOLIUS, *Nutt.* var. JAMESII, *Torr. and Gray, Fl.* 2, *p.* 444. On the Pecos and upper Colorado.

SENECIO LOBATUS, *Pers.; Torr. and Gray, l. c.* Western Texas; April.

CIRSIUM VIRGINIANUM, *Michx. Fl.* 2, *p.* 90. Western Texas; April.

CIRSIUM UNDULATUM, *Spreng.; DC. Prodr.* 6, *p.* 651. Llano Estacado, &c.

CENTAUREA AMERICANA, *Nutt.* Near Fort Washita; April.

PEREZIA NANA, *Gray, Pl. Fendl. p.* 111. On the Pecos; March. The foliage only.

APOGON HUMILIS, *Ell. Sk.* 2, *p.* 267. Western Texas; May.

KRIGIA OCCIDENTALIS, *Nutt.; Torr. and Gray, Fl.* 2, *p.* 467. Western Texas; May.

Pinaropappus roseus, *Less.; DC. Prodr.* 7, *p.* 99. Western Texas; April.

Lygodesmia aphylla, *DC.* var. Texana, *Torr. and Gray, Fl.* 2, *p.* 484. Western Texas; April.

Pyrrhopappus grandiflorus, *Nutt.; Torr. and Gray, Fl.* 2, *p.* 495. Big Springs of the Colorado, &c.; April.

CAMPANULACEÆ.

Dysmicodon ovatum, *Nutt. in Trans. Amer. Phil. Soc.* (*n. ser.*) 8, *p.* 256. Speculariæ sp. *Torr. Mss.* Western Texas; April to May.

Dysmicodon perfoliatum, *Nutt. l. c.* Campanula perfoliata, *Linn.* Specularia perfoliata, *Alph. DC. Prodr.* 7, *pars* 2, *p.* 490, (in part.) With the preceding.

PLANTAGINACEÆ.

Plantago Virginica, *Linn.* Llano Estacado, and on the Colorado; March, April.

Plantago gnaphalioides, *Nutt. Gen.* 1, *p.* 100. On the Pecos; March.

PRIMULACEÆ.

Dodecatheon Meadia, *Linn.* Western Texas; May.

ACANTHACEÆ.

Stenandrium barbatum, (n. sp.; Plate IV): dwarf, multicipital, bearded all over with long and shaggy white hairs; scape at first shorter than the oblanceolate, or narrowly spatulate, entire, and scarcely petioled radical leaves; bracts oblong-lanceolate, acute, entire, nearly equalling the corolla; anthers bearded on the back and tip; stigma funnel-form, its oblong margin not ciliate; capsule oblong, 4-seeded. On the Pecos; March. First collected by Mr. Wright on a lower part of the same river. It is No. 1423 of his distributed collection.

Dipteracanthus strepens, *Nees in DC. Prodr.* 11, *p.* 121. Western Texas; April, May.

Calophanes oblongifolius, *Don; Nees in DC. Prodr.* 11, *p.* 107, and var. Texensis, *Nees.* Western Texas; April, May.

SCROPHULARIACEÆ.

Linaria Canadensis, *Don.* On the Pecos, Llano Estacado, and Western Texas; March, May.

Veronica peregrina, *Linn.* Llano Estacado, &c.; March.

Pentstemon Cobæa, *Nutt.; Benth. in DC. Prodr.* 10, *p.* 326. Western Texas; April, May.

Pentstemon grandiflorus, *Nutt. in Fras. Cat.; Benth. in DC. l. c.* Near Fort Chadbourne; May.

Pentstemon albidus, *Nutt. Gen.* 2, *p.* 53. Upper Colorado, Texas; April.

Pentstemon Fendleri, (n. sp.; Plate V): erect, glabrous throughout, glaucous; leaves coriaceous, entire, the radical ones ovate or obovate, and tapering into a short petiole, the cauline ovate or oblong, and closely sessile; flowers cymulose, or sometimes subsolitary in the axils of the upper leaves and obovate bracts, forming a strict interrupted panicle or series of apparent verticils; segments of the calyx ovate, with scarious margins; corolla (blue or purple) funnel-form, scarcely bilabiate, sparsely bearded or smooth in the throat; sterile filament dilated and densely (yellow) bearded at the summit. On the Pecos and Llano Estacado; March, April. A species which occurs in all the collections made in this region, and is considerably variable in size, foliage, the number of the flowers, (which are handsome, and eight or ten lines long,) the size of the bracts, &c. It is most nearly related to P. acuminatus and P. nitidus, especially to the latter.

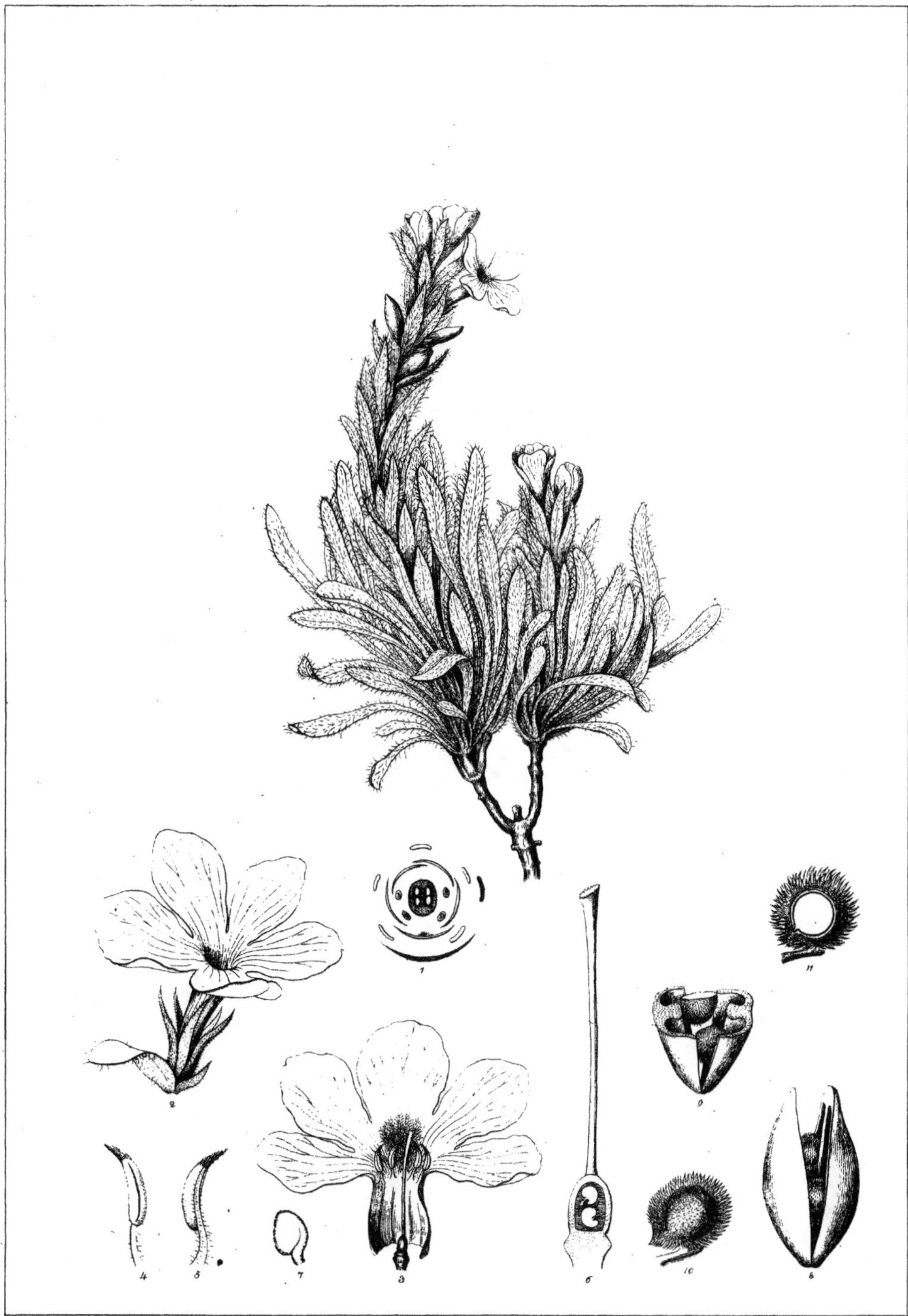

STENANDRIUM BARBATUM.

Sprague del. P. S. Duval & Co. Lith. Phil.a Restele sc.

PENTSTEMON FENDLERI

Sprague del. P. S. Duval & Co. Lith. Philada. Prestele sc.

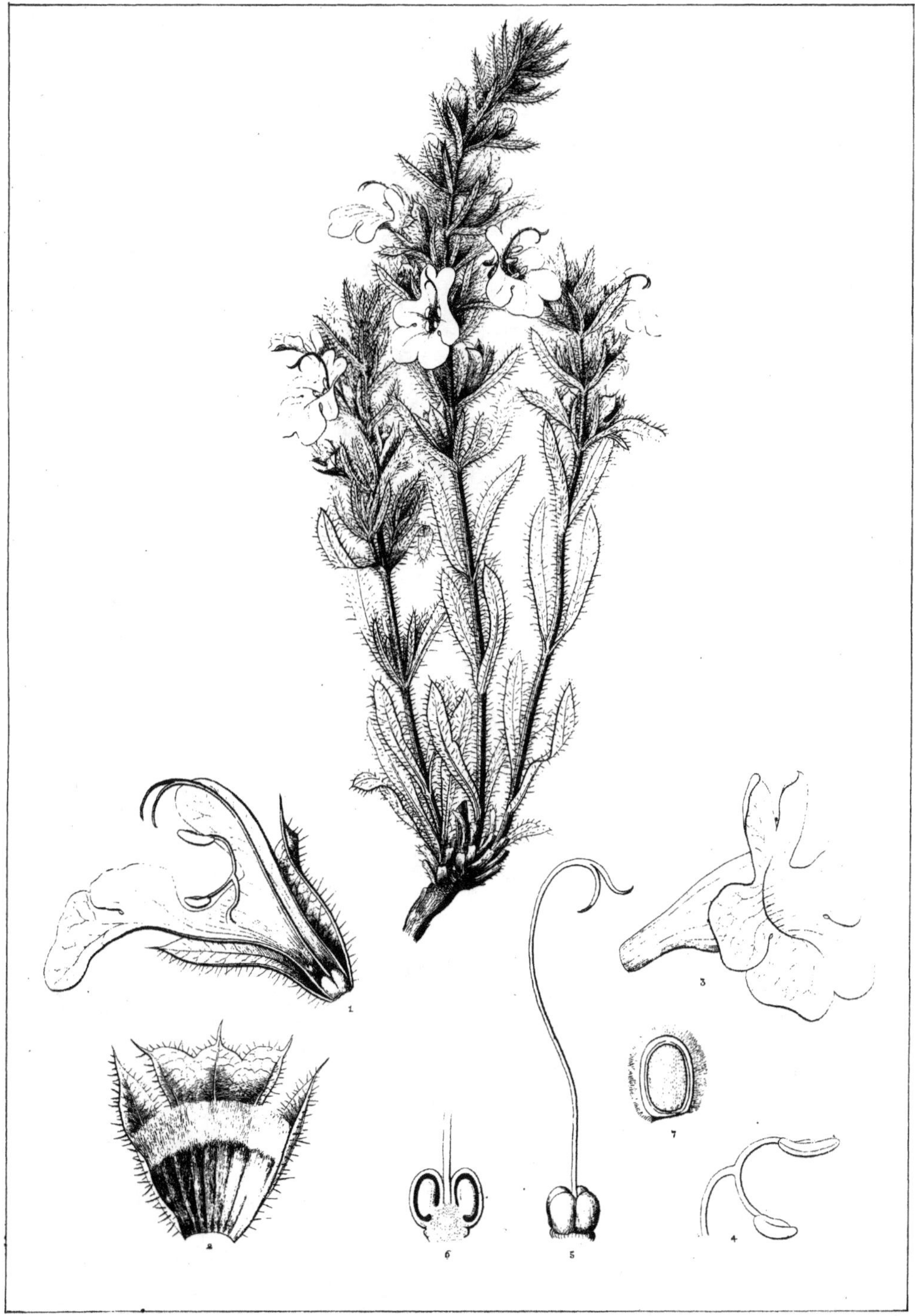

SALVIASTRUM TEXANUM.

Sprague del. P. S. Duval & Co. Lith. Philad.a Prestele sc.

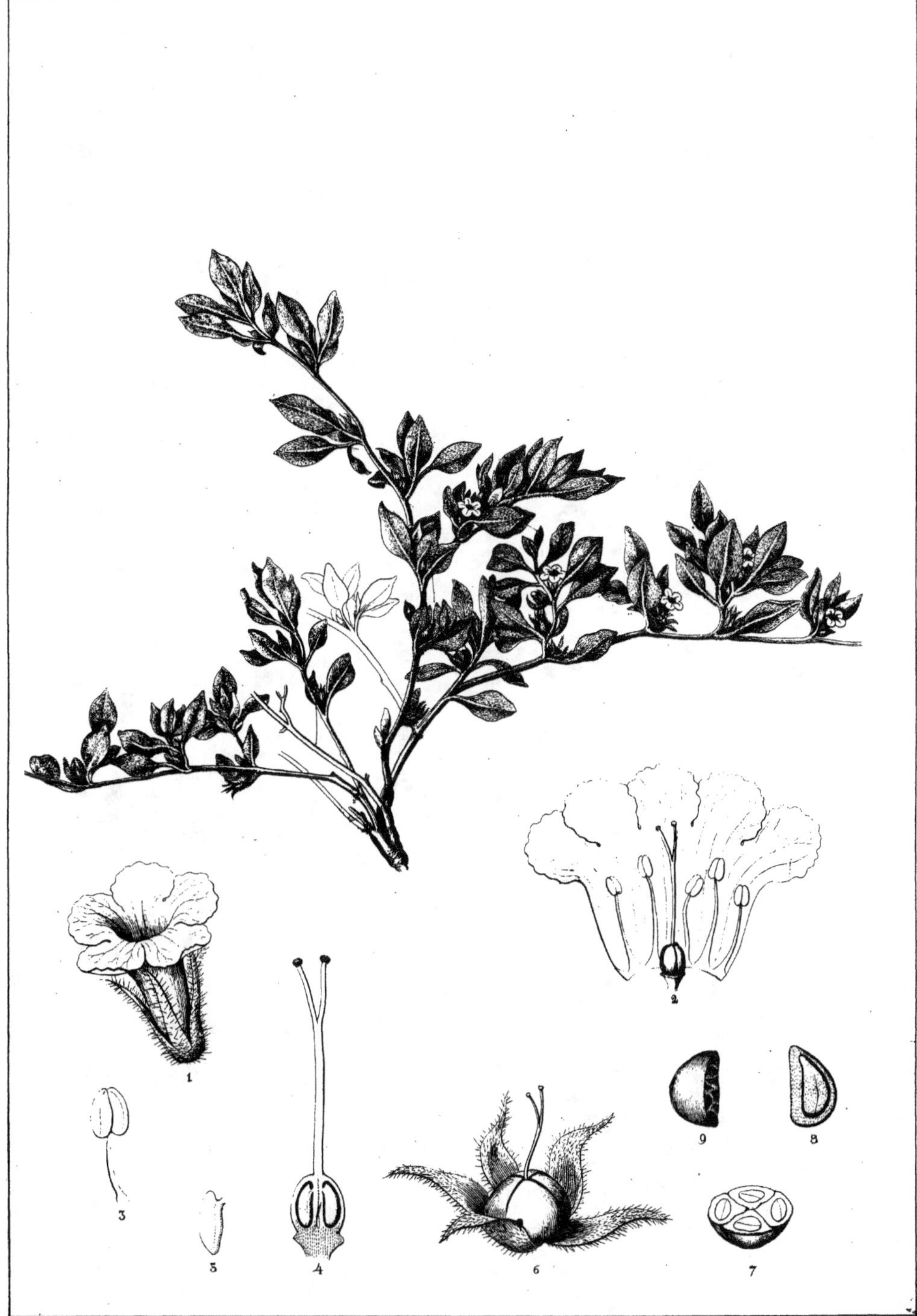

STEGNOCARPUS CANESCENS.

Sprague del. P.S.Duval & Co.Lith.Phil^a. Restele sc.

PENTSTEMON PUBESCENS, *Soland.; DC. Prodr.* 10, *p.* 327. Western Texas; May.

CASTILLEJA PURPUREA, *Don; DC. Prodr.* 10, *p.* 531. Llano Estacado and Western Texas; March, April.

VERBENACEÆ.

VERBENA BIPINNATIFIDA, *Engelm. and Gray, Pl. Lindh.* 1, *p.* 49; *Schauer, in DC. Prodr.* 11, *p.* 553. Glandularia bipinnatifida, *Nutt.* Delaware creek to the Colorado; March, April.

VERBENA AUBLETIA, *Linn.* Upper Texas, &c.; April.

VERBENA BRACTEOSA, *Michx. Fl.* 2, *p.* 14. On the Pecos and Llano Estacado; March.

VERBENA OFFICINALIS, *Linn.* V. spuria, *Linn.*, etc. Western Texas; April, May.

LABIATÆ.

SALVIA FARINOSA, *Benth. Lab. p.* 274. On the Colorado; April. Probably not distinct from S. Pitcheri, *Torr.*

SALVIASTRUM TEXANUM, *Scheele, in Linnæa.* 22, *p.* 584. (Plate VI.) Gravelly soils, Llano Estacado; April. A common plant in Texas and New Mexico.

SCUTELLARIA RESINOSA, *Torr. in Ann. Lyc. New York,* 2, *p.* 232. On the Pecos and the headwaters of the Colorado; April.

TEUCRIUM CANADENSE, *Linn.; Benth. in DC. Prodr.* 12, *p.* 581. Near Fort Washita.

TEUCRIUM CUBENSE, *Linn.; Benth. l. c.; Torr. in Marcy's Rep. p.* 293. On the Pecos, &c.; April.

MONARDA ARISTATA, *Nutt. in Trans. Amer. Phil. Soc.* (*n. ser.*) 5, *p.* 186. In clayey soil; Western Texas. Annual.

MONARDO MOLLIS, *Nutt. l. c.* Near Fort Washita. Seems to be distinct from M. fistulosa.

BORAGINACEÆ.

STEGNOCARPUS, *DC.* (a section of COLDENIA). Calyx deeply 5-cleft; the lobes lanceolate-subovate. Corolla funnel-salverform; the throat naked; border 5-lobed, flat. Stamens five, inserted into the tube of the corolla. Style filiform, terminal, 2-parted: stigmas capitate. Ovary ovate, slightly 4-lobed. Fruit globose-quadrangular, depressed, consisting of four closely joined nutlets which are even, glabrous, (except a slight hairiness at the summit when young,) and at length separate.—A prostrate, much-branched, small under-shrub, canescent with appressed hairs. Leaves numerous, small, ovate, and petiolate. Flowers axillary, solitary or somewhat clustered, sessile, white.

S. CANESCENS, *Torr. in Emory's Rep. of Mex. Bound. Commiss.* (*ined.*) Coldenia (sect. Stegnocarpus) canescens, *DC. Prodr.* 9, *p.* 559. (Plate VII.) In decomposing gypseous gravel, on the Pecos. It is common in the valley of the Rio Grande, from El Paso to Monterey. Dr. Edwards found it near the latter place. It is the same as No. 1554–1556 of Wright's New Mexican collection. De Candolle founded the species and subgenus on specimens collected in Mexico by Berlandier, and numbered 2256* in his collection. He states that the stamens are inserted at the summit of the tube of the corolla, and that the nutlets are silky-pubescent; whereas we found the stamens inserted near the base of the tube, and the nutlets glabrous. We therefore at first supposed our plant to be a distinct species, and called it S. leiocarpa. Having, however, recently obtained original specimens of Berlandier's No. 2256, we found that only the young fruit is a little pubescent near the summit. As to the insertion of the filaments, no great reliance is to be placed on that character in this family, owing to the tendency to a kind of dioicality that occurs in a number of the genera, such as has long been

* No. 2389 of Berlandier's Collection is the same plant.

known to exist in certain Labiatæ and Rubiaceæ. De Candolle (l. c.) asks whether his section Stegnocarpus of Coldenia ought not to constitute a proper genus. If he had had as complete a series of specimens as we possess, no doubt he would have made the separation. It belongs to the tribe Ehretieæ, but has a fruit like that of some Eritrichia. The Stegnocarpus has a decidedly woody base, and seems to be usually prostrate. The leaves are 5–8 lines long (including the petiole) and 1–3 lines broad, ovate or oblong, rather acute at each end, and thickly clothed with appressed whitish hairs. The flowers are often solitary, but sometimes two or three together. Calyx 5-parted below the middle; the lobes subulate from a rather broad base. Corolla about four lines long; the tube ample, and a little longer than the calyx; the lobes crenulate. Stamens five, rather unequal: filaments subulate, usually inserted near the base of the corolla: anthers oblong. Ovary scarcely lobed: style compressed, about as long as the stamens, cleft to the middle; the segments filiform, erect, strongly capitate. Fruit consisting of four closely fitting nutlets, which separate at maturity. When young, there is often more or less pubescence towards the summit; but it finally disappears, and the fruit becomes smooth and shining on the back. The sides (where they come in contact) are somewhat wavy. The pericarp is coriaceous, and there is little or no albumen.

PTILOCALYX, (n. gen.) Calyx 5-parted nearly to the base; the segments subulate-filiform, plumose with spreading hairs. Corolla campanulate-salverform; the throat naked. Stamens five, inserted near the base of the tube. Ovary somewhat 4-lobed, 4-celled, with an obscure glandular ring at the base. Style filiform, terminal, 2-parted: stigmas minute, simple. Fruit coriaceo-chartaceous, one-celled (by abortion), with vestiges of three other cells. Seed solitary, terete; the embryo with little or no albumen. A low, much branching shrub, with small, ovate, entire, and somewhat fascicled leaves, and white flowers in short capitate terminal spikes. The name alludes to the feathery segments of the calyx.

PTILOCALYX GREGGII. (Plate VIII.) Western Texas; April. Common in New Mexico; *Mr. Wright and Dr. Parry.* (It is No. 492 of Mr. Wright's distributed collection.) Near Buena Vista, &c., Mexico; *Dr. Gregg.* A shrub of an ashy gray color, sometimes attaining the height of three feet, the bark separating in loose shreds. Leaves 3–5 lines long, thickish, on short petioles, revolute when dry. Heads of flowers half an inch in diameter. Calyx longer than the corolla; the segments villous-plumose with spreading hairs. Corolla white; the border obtusely 5-lobed. Stamens equal, included; filaments subulate, glabrous; anthers ovate, 2-celled. Ovary globose-ovate, glabrous, 4-celled, with an ovule suspended from the summit of each cell. Style 2-cleft about one third of its length. Fruit brown and shining, retrorsely hispid near the summit, crowned with the persistent style; only one of the cells fertile, the others very indistinct and collapsed; their place being indicated externally by a broad stripe on one side. This plant, which seems to have been hitherto undescribed, agrees in many respects with Ehretia; but differs in the remarkable fruit, which is unlike that of any other Boraginea.

EDDYA, (n. gen.) Calyx deeply 5-parted. Corolla salver-form, with the throat naked. Stamens inserted towards the summit of the tube of the corolla. Style terminal, elongated, 2-cleft: stigmas capitate. Ovary 4-lobed. Nutlets 4, globose-ovate, cohering by the inner angle, but finally separating, muriculate-scabrous. Cotyledons ovate, entire: radicle very short: albumen none, or very thin.—A small, prostrate, much branched, and very hispid undershrub, with crowded linear entire revolute leaves, and small axillary and solitary white flowers. Named in memory of Caspar Wistar Eddy, M. D., formerly of New York, a zealous and promising botanist, who died young, soon after publishing a catalogue of the plants growing around Plandome, Long Island.

EDDYA HISPIDISSIMA. (Plate IX.) Ehretia? hispida, of the 1st edition of this report. Common on the Rio Grande about El Paso. It is the same as No. 845 of Mr. Wright's Texan collection, (1849) and No. 1557 of his New Mexican collection. The plant is much branched from the base, which is decidedly woody. Leaves 3-5 lines long, acute, and very hispid with

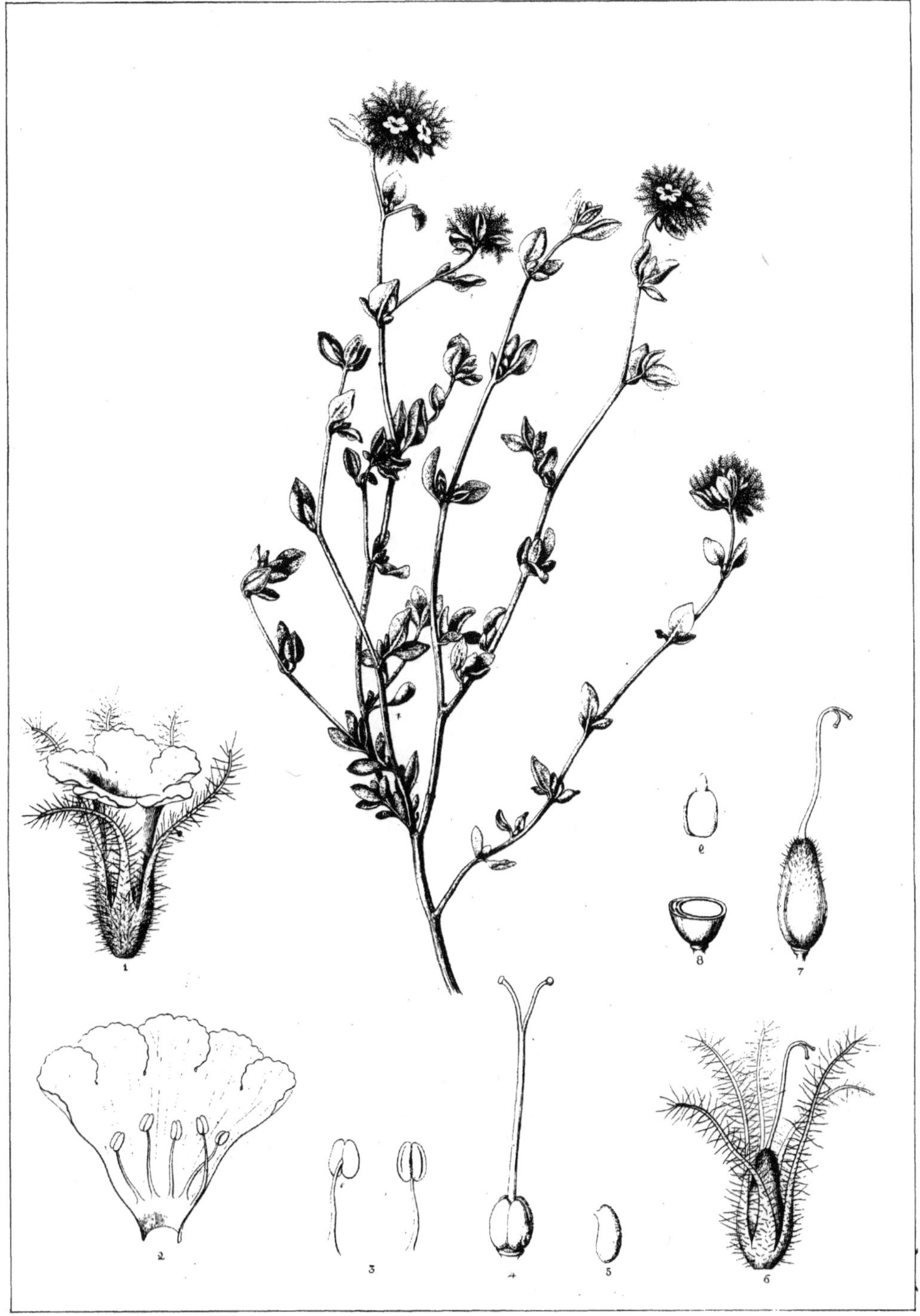

PTILOCALYX GREGGII

Sprague del. P. S. Duval & Co. Lith Philada. Restele sc.

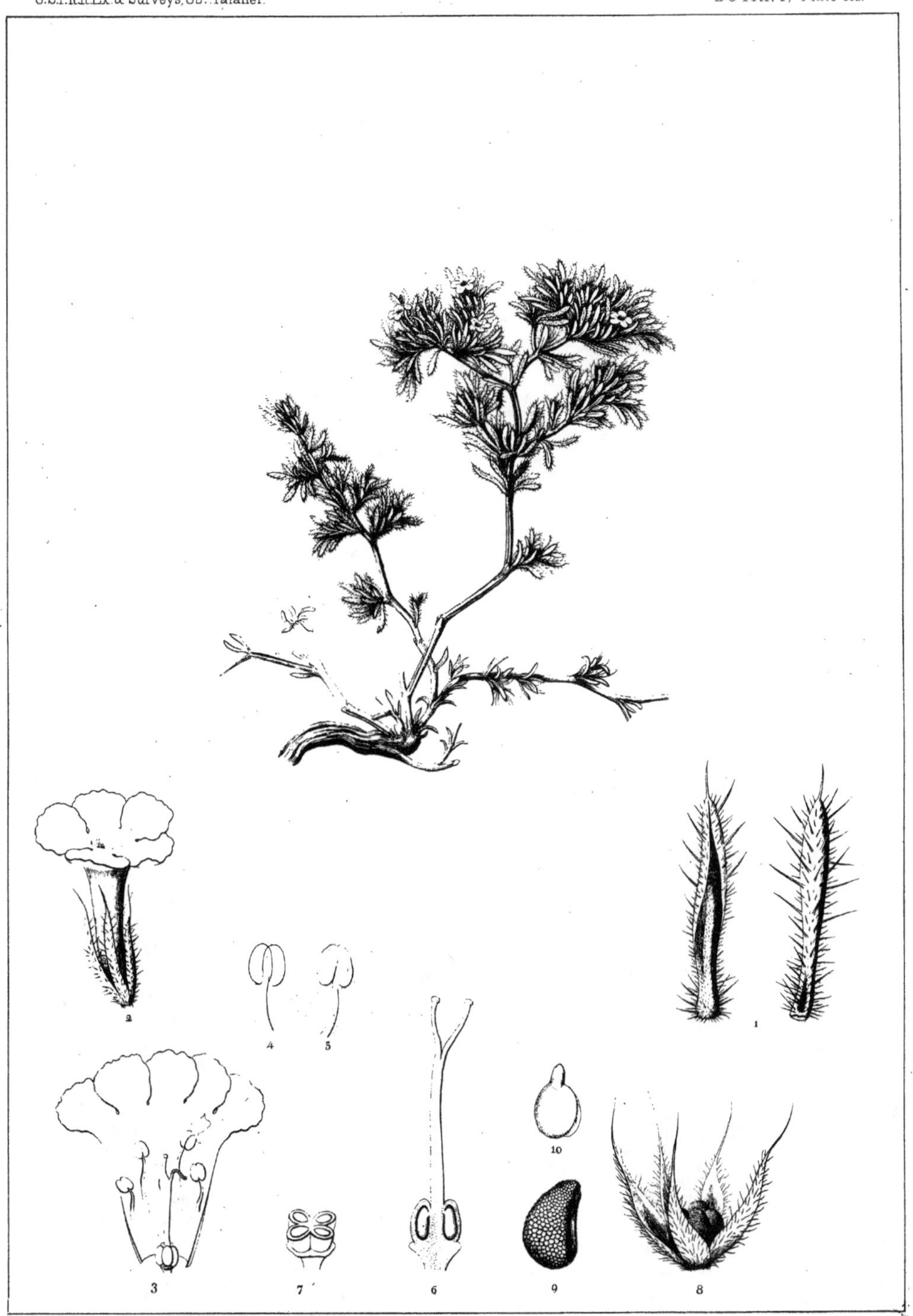

EDDYA HISPIDISSIMA.

Sprague del. P.S.Duval & Co.Lith.Phila. Prestele sc.

rigid whitish hairs: towards the summit of the numerous short branches they are much crowded, so as to appear fasciculate. Flowers sessile, 2-3 lines long. Calyx hispid, like the leaves; the tube somewhat indurated in fruit. Stamens unequal, included. Style cleft about one third of the way down, about as long as the stamens. Nutlets scarcely one third of a line in diameter, two or three of them usually abortive, of a dull gray color, roughened with very minute papilllæ; the endocarp crustaceous and brittle.—Nearly allied to Tiquilia of Persoon, a genus very distinct from Coldenia, to which it was referred as a subgenus, with a mark of doubt, by De Candolle. Both genera seem to be more allied to the tribe Borageæ than to Ehretieæ.

Heliotropium Curassavicum, *Linn.; DC. Prodr.* 9, *p.* 538. Pecos to Llano Estacado; March to April.

Onosmodium Bejariense, *DC. Prodr.* 10, *p.* 70. Western Texas; May.

Pentalophus longiflorus, *Alph. DC. Prodr.* 10, *p.* 86. Batschia longiflora, *Nutt. Gen.* 1, *p.* 114. Gravelly soil; Llano Estacado, &c.; March to April.

Lithospermum breviflorum, *Engelm. and Gray, Pl. Lindheim, part* 2, *no.* 278. Gravelly soil, on the Pecos; April.

Eritrichium Jamesii, *Torr. in Marcy's Rep. p.* 294. Myosotis suffruticosa, *Torr. in Ann. Lyc., New York,* 2, *p.* 225. Sandy soil, Llano Estacado; March.

Eritrichium multicaule, *Torr. in Marcy's Rep. l. c.* On the Pecos; March.

Eritrichium crassisepalum, (n. sp.): annual, very hispid with spreading hairs; stem branching from the base; the branches ascending; leaves obovate-lanceolate, rather obtuse; racemes bracteate (except the upper portion); flowers on short pedicles; fructiferous calyx ventricose at the base, closed and contracted above the middle, the segments thickened and indurated on the back; nutlets heteromorphous, ovate, acute, convex on the back, three of them muriculate-granulate, the fourth larger and nearly or quite glabrous. On the Pecos, Llano Estacado, &c.; in sandy soil; March. A common species in Western Texas and New Mexico. It was found by Frémont on the Upper Platte. It is the same as No. 640 of Fendler's New Mexican collection. The flowers are white and variable in size, being in some specimens minute, and not much longer than the calyx, and in others quite conspicuous, as in the section Cryptantha of Alph. DC. This species, however, belongs to the section Rutidocaryum, as does the following.

Eritrichium pusillum, (n. sp.): annual, dwarfish, hispidly pilose; stem branching from the base; leaves spatulate-linear; racemes many-flowered, ebracteate; flowers sessile, approximate; calyx deeply 5-parted, the segments lanceolate and very hispid; corolla about as long as the tube of the calyx; nutlets ovate-subtriangular, acute, verrucose-granulate on the back. Rio Pecos to Llano Estacado; March. It is the same as No. 1571 of Mr. Wright's New Mexican collection. A very small species, being not more than two or three inches high even in fruit. It either branches from the base, or throws up numerous simple stems, which are somewhat spreading. The flowers are minute and white. The nutlets are light brown, scarcely one third of a line long, and roughened with somewhat distant granules or papillæ.

Echinospermum patulum, *Lehm.; DC. Prodr.* 10, *p.* 137. Common in Western Texas.

Echinospermum strictum, *Nees, in Maximill. Trav. App.* Cynoglossum pilosum, *Nutt. Gen.* 1, *p.* 114? Llano Estacado; March to April. The nutlets are armed with 6-8 strong and short prickles on each side of an obtuse border surrounding a deep open cavity in front of each. Sometimes one of the nutlets is of a different form from the others. De Candolle refers Nuttall's Cynoglossum pilosum to Pectocarya pencillata, not from having seen the plant, but because it was said to resemble so strongly the figure of that species in the Flora Peruviana; but Mr. Nuttall (in Plant Gamb.) says it is "a true Myosotis," or rather an Eritrichium; so that it is wholly unlike Pectocarya.

HYDROPHYLLACEÆ.

Phacelia integrifolia, *Torr. in Ann. Lyc. New York*, 2, *p.* 222, *t.* 3. Delaware creek to the Pecos; March. Barely commencing to flower.

Phacelia Popei, (n. sp.; Plate X): vicosely pubescent, hispidulous with spreading hairs; leaves bipinnately parted, or pinnately cut, the circumscription linear-oblong; segments oblong, pinnatifid; the lobes 5–9, short and obtuse; spikes corymbose, densely flowered; segments of the calyx spatulate, about half the length of the campanulate corolla, and a little longer than the globose capsule; stamens somewhat exserted. On the Llano Estacado and Pecos, in gravelly soil; March and April. Stem four inches to a foot high from a biennial root, hispid, as are the branches, &c., with rather small and weak bristly hairs. Leaves 2–4 inches long; the primary divisions 3–10 lines long, or the lower ones more reduced in size, on the radical leaves barely a line or so in length, clothed with a minute and almost viscid pubescence, with stronger hairs intermixed; the lobes oval or oblong, very obtuse, entire or 2–3-toothed. Spikes an inch or more in length, not much elongated in fruit, dense; the flowers sessile, or nearly so. Calyx viscid-pubescent and hirsute rather than hispid; the segments spatulate, obtuse, a line and a half long, little increased in fruit. Corolla apparently white, about five lines in diameter when expanded; the rounded lobes entire or obsoletely crenulate; the ten appendages at the insertion of the filaments reduced to very short and rounded teeth. Filaments naked, at first slightly, at length considerably exserted. Style nearly naked. Ovary hirsute-pubescent. Capsule a line or a line and a half in diameter. Seeds four, oval, with the inner face strongly bilunate; the central keel very prominent. Albumen conformed to the testa. Fruiting specimens of this very distinct Phacelia are in Wright's collection, (No. 1578.) An abundance of flowering specimens were gathered by Dr. Garrard, as well as by Captain Pope, whose name we desire the species to bear.

POLEMONIACEÆ.

Gilia longiflora, *Don; Torr. in Sitgreaves' Exped. t.* 7. On the Pecos and Llano Estacado; March.

Gilia rigidula, *Benth. in DC. Prodr.* 9, *p.* 312. Llano Estacado and upper Colorado.

Gilia coronopifolia, *Pers.; Benth. in DC. l. c.* Llano Estacado and near Fort Washita; March, April.

Phlox Drummondii, *Hook. Bot. Mag. t.* 3441; *Benth. l. c.* Western Texas; May.

Phlox pilosa, *Linn.; Benth. l. c.* Western Texas; May.

CONVOLVULACEÆ.

Evolvulus argenteus, *Pursh, Fl.* 1, *p.* 187. On the upper Colorado, Texas; April.

Convolvulus lobatus, *Engelm. and Gray, Pl. Lindh.* 1, *p.* 44. On the Colorado, Texas; April.

SOLANACEÆ.

Solanum elæagnifolium, *Cavan. Ic. t.* 243; *Dunal in DC. Prodr.* 13, *p.* 290. S. Texense, *Engelm. and Gray, Pl. Lindh.* 1, *p.* 19. S. Rœmerianum, *Scheele in Linnæa.* 21, *p.* 767. S. flavidum, *Torr. in Ann. Lyc. New York*, 1, *p.* 227. Western Texas; April, May.

Solanum ———, the S. mammosum, *Engelm. and Gray, Pl. Lindh. l. c.*, and the S. platyphyllum, *Torr. in Ann. Lyc.?* Western Texas; April. Not yet identified with any in De Candolle's Prodromus.

Solanum rostratum, *Dunal, Solan. t.* 24; *and in DC. Prodr.* 13, *p.* 329. S. heterandrum, *Pursh, Fl.* 2. *p.* 731, *t.* 7. Western Texas; May.

PHACELIA POPEI.

Sprague del. P.S. Duval & Co. Lith. Phil.a Restele sc.

Physalis lobata, *Torr. in Ann. Lyc. New York*, 1, *p.* 226. On the Pecos and Llano Estacado; March, April. Several forms, including, perhaps, more than one species. They are not true species of Physalis. We know not what Dunal has done with them; but he must have seen specimens in Berlandier's and other collections. There is also a genuine Physalis from Upper Texas, but not in a condition to name.

Nicotiana rustica, *Linn.?* Upper Colorado, Texas; April.

GENTIANACEÆ.

Sabbatia campestris, *Nutt. in Trans. Amer. Phil. Soc.; DC. Prodr.* 9. *p.* 50. Near Fort Washita; April.

JASMINACEÆ.

Menodora heterophylla, *Moricand, in DC. Prodr.* 8, *p.* 316; *Gray, in Sill. Jour.* 14, 1852. Western Texas; April. This is, doubtless, the Boliviara Grisebachii, *Scheele in Linnœa.* 25, *p.* 254.

APOCYNACEÆ.

Amsonia ciliata, *Walt. Fl. Car. p.* 98. On the upper Colorado; April.

Amsonia salicifolia, *Pursh, Fl.* 1, *p.* 184. On the Pecos. Only the broad-leaved form was in the collection.

ASCLEPIADACEÆ.

Asclepias tuberosa, *Linn.; Michx. Fl.* 1, *p.* 117; var. angustifolia. Western Texas; May 10.

Acerates paniculata, *Decaisne, in DC. Prodr.* 8, *p.* 521. Anantherix paniculatus, *Nutt.* Sandy soil, head-waters of the Colorado; April. This is the snake-weed of the Camanche Indians.

Acerates viridiflora, *Ell. Sk.* 1, *p.* 317. Var. 1. Leaves broadly ovate, mucronate, somewhat fleshy, smoothish. Var. 2. Leaves narrowly ovate, acute, somewhat hoary-pubescent. Llano Estacado.

Acerates longifolia, *Ell. l. c.; Decaisne, l. c.* Big Springs of the Colorado and Llano Estacado, in gravelly soil; April.

Gonolobus biflorus, *Nutt. in herb. DC.* Chthamalia biflora, *DC. l. c. p.* 605. With the preceding.

CHENOPODIACEÆ.

Obione canescens, *Moq. Chenop. p.* 74. Atriplex canescens, *Nutt. Gen.* 1, *p.* 197. Mesilla valley, and from Delaware creek to Sacramento river; March.

Obione confertiflora, *Torr. and Frem. in Frem. 2d Report, p.* 318. Gravelly soil, head-waters of the Colorado.

Obione argentea, *Moq. Chenop. p.* 76. Atriplex argentea, *Nutt. Gen.* 1, *p.* 198. Llano Estacado.

Anthrocnemum fruticosum, *Moq. Chenop. p.* 111, *and in DC. Prodr.* 13, *p.* 181?; *Torr. in Stansb. Rep. p.* 394. In a saline, decomposed, gypseous soil, also on the borders of a salt lake on the Guadaloupe mountains.

Chenopodina maritima, *Moq. in DC. Prodr.* 13, (*pars.* 2,) *p.* 164. Sueda maritima, *Dumort.* Chenopodium maritimum, *Linn.* Saline soils between the Pecos and Llano Estacado. Not in flower.

PHYTOLACCACEÆ.

Phytolacca decandra, *Linn.* Near Fort Washita; April.

POLYGONACEÆ.

Polygonum lapathifolum, *Linn.? Willd. Sp. pl.* 2, *p.* 442. Near Fort Washita. Perhaps not distinct from P. Persicaria.

Eriogonum longifolium, *Nutt. in Trans. Amer. Phil. Soc.* (*n. ser.*) 5, *p.* 164. E. Texanum, *Scheele.* Gravelly soil, on the Pecos; April.

Eriogonium cernuum, *Nutt. in Pl. Gambel.?* Llano Estacado, sandy soil. It differs in the pubescence of the leaves being rougher and more persistent.

Rumex venosus, *Pursh, Fl. supp.* 2, *p.* 733. Delaware creek, and along the Pecos; March.

Rumex Acetosella, *Linn.; Pursh, Fl.* 1, *p.* 249. Western Texas. Probably introduced.

Rumex Britannica, *Linn.; Torr. Fl. New York*, 2, *p.* 155. Western Texas.

NYCTAGINACEÆ.

Abronia cycloptera, *Gray, in Sill. Jour.* (*n. ser.*) 15; *Torr. in Marcy's Rep. t.* 18. Llano Estacado to Fort Chadbourne; April, May. In flower only.

Oxybaphus angustifolius, *Torr. in Amer. Lyc. New York*, 2, *p.* 237. On the upper Colorado; April.

Oxybaphus hirsutus, *Sweet; Hook. Fl. Bor.-Am.* 2, *p.* 124. On the Colorado; April.

Acleisanthes Berlandieri, *Gray, in Sill. Jour. l. c.* On the Pecos; March, Foliage only.

EUPHORBIACEÆ.

Tragia ramosa, *Torr. in Ann. Lyc. New York*, 2, *p.* 245. Gravelly soils; March.

Cnidoscolus stimulosus, *Engelm. and Gray, Pl. Lindl., part* 1, *p.* 26. Sand-hills of Llano Estacado and Western Texas; March to May. Flowers larger than in the eastern plant.

Stillingia lanceolata, *Nutt. in Trans. Phil. Soc.*, (*n. ser.*) 5, *p.* 176. Sandy soil, Western Texas; April to May.

Hendecandra crotonoides, *Hook. and Arn. Bot. Beech, p.* 388. This is the same as No. 1800, Pl. Wright. It was found also by Frémont on the Gila. It is quite a distinct species from H. procumbens. The Mexicans call it *Yerba del Gato,* and use it as a purgative.

Euphorbia Arkansana, *Engelm. and Gray, l. c. no.* 303. Intermediate between E. platyphylla and E. Helioscopia. Sandy soil. Collected in a journey to Fort Chadbourne, and on the head-waters of the Colorado.

Euphorbia Geyeri, *Engelm. and Gray, Pl. Lindh.* 1, *p.* 52. Western Texas; May.

Euphorbia Wrightii, (n. sp.): stem herbaceous from a somewhat ligneous base, erect, much branched; leaves opposite, sessile, narrowly lanceolate-linear, entire; involucres solitary, pedunculate, mostly terminal or in the uppermost forks of the stem, pubescent; glands transversely oblong, entire, with a large petaloid broadly obovate denticulate appendage; capsule very minutely papillose-pubescent; seeds glabrous. Head-waters of the Colorado; April. This is the same as No. 1827 of Mr. Wright's New Mexican collection, (1851–52). It is about a foot high, branching from the base; the branches green and angular. Leaves an inch or more in length, and 2–3 lines wide. Peduncles variable in length, occasionally 2–3 times longer than the hemispherical involucre, but usually shorter. Petaloid appendages conspicuous. Styles very short, spreading, 2-cleft about half-way down. Capsule coriaceous. Seeds subglobose.

Euphorbia albomarginata, (n. sp.): perennial, slender, much branched, smooth; leaves stipulate, opposite, suborbicular, subcordate, entire, distinctly petiolate; involucre solitary, shorter than the peduncles; glands transversely oval, with an entire or slightly crenate petaloid border, which is twice as broad as the gland itself; seeds obovate, somewhat rugose transversely, dull, gelatinous when moistened. In red sand and clay: with the preceding. Resembles the following, but more slender and of a more diffuse habit. It is readily distinguished by the broad petaloid appendages of the involucral glands.

EUPHORBIA DILATATA, (n. sp.): whole plant clothed with a soft pubescense; stem much branching from a somewhat woody base, diffuse; leaves without stipules, opposite, ovate, sessile, dilated and somewhat unequal at the base, rather obtuse, entire, (often purplish underneath) thickish; involucres mostly solitary, axillary and terminal, nearly sessile, ovate; glands transversely linear-oblong, with a narrow petaloid crenate margin; capsule somewhat hairy; seeds oblong, even, gelatinous when moistened. Western Texas. Not uncommon in New Mexico. Resembles No. 1840 of Mr. Wright's New Mexican collection, (1851–52); but that is hairy, the leaves are lanceolate, tapering to a mucronate tip, and the petaloid appendages of the involucral glands are much broader.

EUPHORBIA FENDLERI, (n. sp.): branching and diffuse from a somewhat woody candex, smooth; leaves stipulate, opposite, broadly ovate or orbicular-ovate, on very short petioles, subcordate and oblique at the base; involucres solitary, on short peduncles; gland transversely oval, with a narrow entire somewhat 2-lobed border; capsule smooth; seeds obovate, a little rugose transversely, gelatinous when moistened. Big Springs of the Colorado; April. This species is No. 800 of Fendler's New Mexican collection. It is a small plant, throwing off many branches that spread on the ground, forming a little patch from three to six inches in diameter. The leaves are 3–4 lines long, and are often of a purplish tinge, especially underneath.

SANTALACEÆ.

COMANDRA UMBELLATA, *Nutt. Gen.* 1, *p.* 157. Gravelly soil. Big Springs of the Colorado, &c., Texas; April.

SALICACEÆ.

SALIX. Two undetermined species were found in the sand-hills of Llano Estacado.

CUPULIFERÆ.

QUERCUS UNDULATA, *Torr. in Ann. Lyc. New York*, 2, *p.* 248, *t.* 4. Head-waters of the Colorado and Llano Estacado; in sandy soil. In flower April 12.

QUERCUS PALUSTRIS, *Du Roi.* Near Fort Chadbourne, Texas.

URTICACEÆ.

PARIETARIA PENNSYLVANICA, *Willd?* Delaware creek to the Pecos; March.

CELTIS RETICULATA, *Torr. in Ann. Lyc. New York,* 2, *p.* 247. Upper Colorado, Texas; April.

PLANERA RICHARDI, *Michx. Fl.* 2, *p.* 248. Western Texas; April.

MORUS RUBRA, *Linn.?* Near Fort Washita; April.

CONIFERÆ.

EPHEDRA ANTISIPHILITICA, *Berland.; Endl. Conif. p.* 263. High rocky and sandy places; Llano Estacado and on the Pecos. The fertile aments are 1–2-flowered; but usually perfect only one seed, which in that case is triangular. When two seeds ripen they are less angular, and the opposite faces are flat. The scales of the ament become fleshy at maturity.

JUNIPERUS VIRGINIANA, *Linn.; Michx. f. Sylv.* 2, *p.* 253, *t.* 155. Head-waters of the Colorado, and in various parts of Western Texas.

SMILACEÆ.

Smilax hastata, *Willd. Sp. p.* 782; *Ell. Sk.* 2, *p.* 696. High plains, Llano Estacado.

COMMELYNACEÆ.

Tradescantia Virginiana, *Linn.; Kunth, Enum.* 4, *p.* 81. Head-waters of the Colorado and on the Pecos; March and April. Very variable as to size, pubescence, and breadth of the leaves.

Commelyna angustifolia, *Michx. Fl.* 1, *p.* 24. Near Fort Washita.

IRIDACEÆ.

Sisyrinchium Bermudiana, *Linn.;* var. anceps. S. anceps, *Cav.* Dry soils, Llano Estacado.

LILIACEÆ.

Camassia Fraseri, *Torr. in Whipple's Report, ined.* Scilla esculenta, *Gawl. in Bot. Mag., t.* 1574; (excl. syn. *Pursh.*) β. angusta. S. angusta, *Engelm. and Gray, Pl. Lindheim., part* 1, *No.* 198. Western Texas.

Allium mutabile, *Michx. Fl.* 1, *p.* 195. On the Pecos and the head-waters of the Colorado; March to April. Flowers varying from deep rose red to nearly white.

Pseudoscordum striatum, *Herb.* Nothoscordum striatum, *Kunth, Enum.* 4, *p.* 458. Allium striatum, *Jacq.* With the preceding.

Yucca angustifolia, *Pursh, Fl.* 1, *p.* 227. On the Pecos; April. Flowers in a long, narrow raceme, as large as in *Y. filamentosa*, greenish yellow mixed with purple.

JUNACEÆ.

Juncus tenius, *Willd.; Torr. Fl. New York,* 2, *p.* 329. Low grounds. Hueco Tanks.

NARIADACEÆ.

Potamogeton prælongus, *Wulf.; Gray, Bot. North. States, p.* 456. Western Texas.

CYPERACEÆ.

Scirpus lacustris, *Linn.; Torr. Cyp., p.* 321. In water; Llano Estacado; March.

Eleocharis obtusa, *Schultes; Torr. l. c., p.* 302. With the preceding.

GRAMINEÆ.

Ceratochloa unioloides, *Beauv. Agrost. p.* 75, *t.* 15, *f.* 7. Bromus Willdenovii, *Kunth, Enum.* 1, *p.* 416. Head-waters of the Colorado; April.

Tripsacum dactyloides, *Linn. fil. Decad.* 17, *t.* 9; *Steud. Pl. Glum. p.* 362. Llano Estacado. A tall rank grass, affording good fodder.

Chloris verticillata, *Nutt. in Trans. Amer. Phil. Soc.* (n. ser.) 5, *p.* 143. Sandy plains northeast of the Pecos; April. β.? aristulata; spikes much shorter; awns scarcely half the length of the paleæ; lower glume obovate, rather obtuse. With the preceding. Not uncommon at the lower Rio Grande, where it was collected by Dr. Gregg, who says it is good fodder. The spikes are usually purplish, but sometimes yellowish.

Panicum pauciflorum, *Ell. sk.* 1, *p.* 120? On the Pecos; April.

Phalaris angusta, *Nees; Trin. Gram. t.* 78. Head-waters of the Colorado.

Poa aranifera, *Torr. in Marcy's Rep. p.* 301. Head-waters of the Colorado; April 13. Also the var. β. With the preceding, and Big Springs of the Colorado.

FESTUCA TENELLA, *Willd. Enum.* 1, *p.* 116. High sandy plains northeast of the Pecos, and head-waters of the Colorado; March to April.

FESTUCA MACROSTACHYA, (n. sp.) On the Pecos. This is one of numerous Grama-grasses of Texas and New Mexico.

HORDEUM PUSILLUM, *Nutt. Gen.* 1, *p.* 87; *Kunth, Enum.* 1, *p.* 457. Sandy soil; Llano Estacado; March.

ELYMUS CANADENSIS, *Linn.; Kunth, Enum.* 1, *p.* 457. Near Fort Washita.

FILICES.

ADIANTUM CAPILLUS-VENERIS, *Linn.* Big Springs of the Colorado. We follow Hooker in uniting this and several other allied forms of Adiantum.

NOTHOCHLÆNA SINUATA, *Kaulf.* Between the Rio Grande and Llano Estacado.

GYMNOGRAMMA TARTAREA, *Desv.* With the preceding.

CHEILANTHES LINDHEIMERI, *Hook. Spec. Fil.* 2, *p.* 101, *t.* 107. Llano Estacado. This is the same as No. 2126 of Wright's New Mexican collection.

PTERIS (PLATYLOMA) ANDROMEDÆFOLIA, *Kaulf, Enum. Fil. p.* 188. Hueco Swamps, Texas. This is a common fern in California.

EXPLANATION OF THE PLATES.

Plate I. SELENIA DISSECTA. Page 160.

Fig. 1, a flower, moderately magnified; fig. 2, a sepal; fig. 3, a petal; fig. 4, the stamens; fig. 5, the young pod; fig. 6, the mature pod—all more magnified than fig. 1; fig. 7, seed, still more magnified; fig. 8, section of the same, equally magnified.

Plate II. CALYMMANDRA CANDIDA. Page 166.

Fig. 1, involucre and receptacle; fig. 2, chaff of the pistillate flowers; fig. 3, a pistillate flower; fig. 4, a perfect flower, partly enclosed in its woolly chaff; fig. 5, the same, without the chaff; fig. 6, chaff of the perfect flower; fig. 7, corolla of the perfect flower laid open—all moderately enlarged; fig. 8, a stamen, more magnified; fig. 9, upper portion of the style from a perfect flower, equally magnified; fig. 10, the same from a pistillate flower; fig. 11, achenium, pretty highly magnified; fig. 12, longitudinal section of the same.

Plate III. FILAGINOPSIS MULTICAULIS. Page 166.

Fig. 1, involucre and receptacle; figs. 2 and 3, paleæ of a pistillate flower; fig. 4, a pistillate flower; fig. 5, palea of a staminate flower; fig. 6, staminate flower; fig. 7, corolla of the same, laid open and showing the stamens; fig. 8, its abortive style; fig. 9, achenium; fig. 10, vertical section of the same—all the figures variously magnified.

Plate IV. STENANDRIUM BARBATUM. Page. 168.

Fig. 1, plan of the flower; fig. 2, a flower; fig. 3, the corolla laid open, showing the stamens and pistil; figs. 4 and 5, stamens, shown in two positions—all moderately enlarged; fig. 6, pistil, more magnified, the ovary laid open vertically, showing the ovules; fig. 8, a capsule, moderately magnified; fig. 9, cross-section of the same; fig. 10, a seed, more highly magnified; fig. 11, longitudinal section of the same.

Plate V. Pentstemon Fendleri. Page 168.

Fig. 1, corolla laid open, and moderately enlarged; fig. 2, longitudinal section of a flower, more magnified; fig. 3, a perfect stamen, still more magnified; fig. 4, upper portion of the imperfect stamen; fig. 5, pistil, its ovary laid open vertically.

Plate VI. Salviastrum Texanum. Page 169.

Fig. 1, vertical section of a flower; fig. 2, the calyx laid open; fig. 3, corolla; fig. 4, a stamen; fig. 5, pistil; fig. 6, vertical section of the ovary; fig. 8, vertical section of a seed—all the figures variously magnified.

Plate VII. Stegnocarpus canescens. Page 169.

Fig. 1, a flower, enlarged; fig. 2, the corolla laid open, showing the stamens and pistil, equally magnified; fig. 3, a stamen, more magnified; fig. 4, pistil, with the ovary cut longitudinally; fig. 5, an ovule, highly magnified; fig. 6, the fructiferous calyx, moderately enlarged; fig. 7, cross-section of the fruit; fig. 8, a nutlet, more magnified; fig. 9, vertical section of the same.

Plate VIII. Ptilocalyx Greggii. Page 170.

Fig. 1, a flower, magnified; fig. 2, the corolla laid open vertically; fig. 3, a stamen, more magnified; fig. 4, the pistil, equally magnified; fig. 5, an ovule, highly magnified; fig. 6, fructiferous calyx; fig. 7, the fruit and persistent style; fig. 8, transverse section of the fruit, showing one perfect cell containing a seed, and three abortive, collapsed cells; fig. 9, embryo—the last five figures moderately magnified.

Plate IX. Eddya hispidissima. Page 170.

Fig. 1, leaves, showing the upper and lower surface, magnified; fig. 2, a flower, equally magnified; fig. 3, the corolla laid open vertically; figs. 4 and 5, stamens, front and back views; fig. 6, pistil, with the ovary cut vertically; fi . 7, cross-section of the ovary; fig. 8, fructiferous calyx; fig. 9, a nutlet; fig. 10, embryo.

Plate X. Phacel.a Popei. Page 172.

Fig. 1, flower enlarged; fig. 2, corolla laid open, showing the stamens and pistil; fig. 3, stamens, more magnified; fig. 4, calyx and pistil; fig. 5, pistil, with the ovary vertically divided; fig. 6, transverse section of the ovary; fig. 7, ovule, more magnified; fig. 8, fruit scarcely matured, with the persistent calyx; fig. 9, seed, more magnified; fig. 10, vertical view of a seed transversely divided; fig. 11, embryo, still more magnified.

INDEX.

D.

E.

K.

L.

M.

N.

O.

P.

EXPLANATORY NOTE TO GEOLOGICAL REPORT.

WASHINGTON, *February* 18, 1857.

The mineralogical collections made by me were placed in the hands of M. Jules Marcou for examination, and carried by him to France. They were subsequently returned in a confused condition, and with many of the labels displaced. This fact will account for many errors in the report, map, and section prepared by Mr. Blake.

JOHN POPE,
Captain Topographical Engineers.

33d Congress, 2d Session. | SENATE. | Ex. Doc. No. 78.

REPORTS

OF

EXPLORATIONS AND SURVEYS,

TO

ASCERTAIN THE MOST PRACTICABLE AND ECONOMICAL ROUTE FOR A RAILROAD

FROM THE

MISSISSIPPI RIVER TO THE PACIFIC OCEAN.

MADE UNDER THE DIRECTION OF THE SECRETARY OF WAR, IN

1853-4,

ACCORDING TO ACTS OF CONGRESS OF MARCH 3, 1853, MAY 31, 1854, AND AUGUST 5, 1854.

VOLUME IV.

WASHINGTON:
BEVERLEY TUCKER, PRINTER.
1856.

IN SENATE—February 24, 1855.

Resolved, That there be printed, for the use of the Senate, ten thousand copies of the several reports of surveys for a railroad to the Pacific, made under the direction of the Secretary of War; and also of the report of F. W. Lander, civil engineer, of a survey of a railroad route from Puget's Sound, by Fort Hall and the Great Salt lake, to the Mississippi river; and the report of John C. Frémont, of a route for a railroad from the head-waters of the Arkansas river into the State of California; together with the maps and plates accompanying said reports, necessary to illustrate the same; and that five hundred copies be printed for the use of the Secretary of War, and fifty copies for each of the commanding officers engaged in said service.

Attest: ASBURY DICKINS, *Secretary*.

THIRTY-SECOND CONGRESS, SECOND SESSION—Chapter 98.

Sect. 10. *And be it further enacted*, That the Secretary of War be, and he is hereby authorized, under the direction of the President of the United States, to employ such portion of the Corps of Topographical Engineers, and such other persons as he may deem necessary, to make such explorations and surveys as he may deem advisable, to ascertain the most practicable and economical route for a railroad from the Mississippi river to the Pacific ocean, and that the sum of one hundred and fifty thousand dollars, or so much thereof as may be necessary, be, and the same is hereby, appropriated out of any money in the treasury not otherwise appropriated, to defray the expense of such explorations and surveys.

Approved March 3, 1853.

THIRTY-THIRD CONGRESS, FIRST SESSION—Chapter 60.

Appropriation: For deficiencies for the railroad surveys between the Mississippi river and the Pacific ocean, forty thousand dollars.

Approved May 31, 1854.

THIRTY-THIRD CONGRESS, FIRST SESSION—Chapter 267.

Appropriation: For continuing the explorations and surveys to ascertain the best route for a railway to the Pacific, and for completing the reports of surveys already made, the sum of one hundred and fifty thousand dollars.

Approved August 5, 1854.

CONTENTS OF VOLUME IV.

PART V, VI, AND APPENDICES OF THE REPORT OF LIEUTENANT A. W. WHIPPLE, CORPS OF TOPOGRAPHICAL ENGINEERS, UPON THE ROUTE NEAR THE THIRTY-FIFTH PARALLEL.

PART V.

EXPLORATIONS AND SURVEYS FOR A RAILROAD ROUTE FROM THE MISSISSIPPI RIVER TO THE PACIFIC OCEAN.

WAR DEPARTMENT.

ROUTE NEAR THE THIRTY-FIFTH PARALLEL, EXPLORED BY LIEUTENANT A. W. WHIPPLE, TOPOGRAPHICAL ENGINEERS, IN 1853 AND 1854.

REPORT

ON

THE BOTANY OF THE EXPEDITION.

WASHINGTON, D. C.
1856.

CONTENTS.

No. 1.

GENERAL DESCRIPTION OF THE BOTANICAL CHARACTER OF THE COUNTRY.

BY J. M. BIGELOW, M. D.

GENERAL DESCRIPTION OF THE SOIL AND PRODUCTIONS ALONG THE ROUTE TRAVERSED.

No. 2.

DESCRIPTION OF FOREST TREES.

BY J. M. BIGELOW, M. D.

FOREST TREES ALONG THE ROUTE TRAVERSED.

DESCRIPTIONS OF VALUABLE OR REMARKABLE CALIFORNIA FOREST TREES.

No. 3.

DESCRIPTION OF THE CACTACEÆ.

BY GEORGE ENGELMANN, M. D., OF ST. LOUIS, AND J. M. BIGELOW, M. D.

EXPLANATIONS OF THE PLATES OF THE CACTACEÆ.

No. 4.

DESCRIPTIONS OF THE GENERAL BOTANICAL COLLECTIONS.

BY JOHN TORREY.

No. 5.

DESCRIPTION OF THE MOSSES AND LIVERWORTS.

BY W. S. SULLIVANT, Esq.

No. 1.

GENERAL DESCRIPTION

OF

THE BOTANICAL CHARACTER OF THE COUNTRY.

BY J. M. BIGELOW, M. D.

GENERAL DESCRIPTION OF THE SOIL AND PRODUCTIONS ALONG THE ROUTE TRAVERSED.

WASHINGTON, D. C., *August*, 1854.

SIR: In compliance with your instructions, I have the honor to submit to you a report on the forest trees, the productions of the soil, and its capacity for sustaining a civilized population, upon the railroad route near the 35th parallel, over which you had command.

Very respectfully,

JOHN M. BIGELOW.

Lieut. A. W. WHIPPLE, *Topographical Engineer, U. S. A.,*
in charge of exploration for railroad route near the 35*th parallel.*

SECTION I. *Napoleon, on the Mississippi, to Fort Smith, Arkansas.*—From Napoleon to Fort Smith, our way being on steamboat, I could, of course, give but a limited account, either of its forests or of its soil. The banks of the river were densely lined with timber-trees of great variety. Among the kinds observed we particularly noticed the black walnut, sweet-gum, (liquid ambar styraciflua,) pecan, white ash, three kinds of elms, five or six species of oaks, Osage orange, and sassafras, with their dark green foliage; all most luxuriant and beautiful. At Little Rock, among some of those just mentioned, we saw the American holly, (Ilex opaca,) spice-wood, and June berry, (Amelanchier canadensis.) Near Piney Point, at the Sugar-loaf mountain, as well as on our route in the Indian Territory, was found what was considered to be *Pinus mitis*, the common yellow pine of the southern States, quite different from the one in New Mexico, known there by the same common name. We also observed, in passing, witch-hazel, hop-horn beam, birch, Kentucky coffee-bean, honey-locust, black locust, sour-gum, red-bud, box-elder, mulberry, dogwood, blackberry, &c., &c., all indicating a soil of the utmost fertility. It is unnecessary to extend the list beyond the few seen from the boat, as the botany of this country has been described and is well known, having been visited by Nuttall, and other eminent naturalists and botanists.

SECTION II. *Fort Smith to Valley river.*—The range of country embraced between these two points is about four hundred and sixty miles. The western limit of this section is some distance west of the line between Texas and the Indian reservation. Consequently, it embraces the entire limits of the Indian Territory, from east to west. It constitutes a most natural division, being in nearly its whole breadth a beautiful and fertile country, of vast agricultural capacity, and of sufficient dimensions for forming two or three large and magnificent States. The eastern portion is densely covered with timber, of the same varieties and qualities as those enumerated between Napoleon and Fort Smith. The western portion has by no means so great a variety, being mostly grassy plains, with intersections of timber along the streams, arroyos, and ravines. The celebrated "Cross Timbers" is situated along and crosses our line of survey, extending some distance north, and, according to Captain Marcy, about two hundred miles south of it.

The streams are Sans Bois creek, Gaines' creek, Topofki creek, Deer creek, False Washita, Walnut creek, Dry creek, Valley creek, &c., with their various tributaries, as also others of the Canadian and Washita rivers. Near old Fort Arbuckle, and in the vicinity of the "Cross Timbers," the scenery is most beautiful and picturesque. Belts of timber crossing the more elevated plateaux in various directions many times, at right-angles with each other, give them the appearance of vast cultivated fields, formed on a scale of great magnificence, stretching away in every direction as far as the eye can reach. The same beautiful views were noticed in the vicinity of Delaware Mount, near the centre of the Indian territory.

The first appearance of the celebrated "grama-grass" was here noticed, opposite Little river, a small branch from the north side of the Canadian, in about longitude 96° west. This important grass is found, in greater or less abundance, from this point across the continent, or as far as to the mountains of the Sierra Nevada, which, where we crossed it with our line of survey, was not far from the Pacific shore. The great importance of these western prairie grasses, of which we have several species besides this and the buffalo grass, consists in their retaining their nutritive qualities the whole year round, sustaining the life and condition of the beast of the traveller, thereby enabling them to pursue their journey at leisure at all seasons of the year. Were it otherwise, much hazard would be encountered, as it is impossible to transport forage in sufficient quantities to supply a long train over a country of such vast extension. When the tops of these grasses become dry, the stems near their roots retain their vitality and nutritive juices until the plains are again renovated with a new crop. Many of our farmers express a wish to introduce the culture of these grasses at home; but it is to be presumed, from the peculiarities of their situation, that they are only well adapted to the arid climates, where they are found in their native state.

The trees in the western portion of this region consist of several species of oak, black walnut, cotton-wood, buck-eye, elm, mulberry, and a few cedars. Helianthi, Convolvulaceæ, Euphorbiaceæ, Vernoniæ, Eupatoriæ, with shrubby and herbaceous Mimosæ, are common in this region. The Wild China, (Sapindus Marginatus,) common all over Texas, was found here. Mirabilis, (Marvel of Peru,) Evening primrose, Ambrosia, Silphium, (rosin plant,) Golden rods, &c., are abundant on the plains. American and Chickasaw plums are quite common on the banks of the Canadian and other streams, but on the plains is found a small shrub, bearing in abundance what is called prairie plums, which is probably undescribed.

A considerable number of cactaceæ, which always indicate a dry climate, begin here to make their appearance, especially when we come into what appropriately may be termed the grama-grass region. Among them I recognised Opuntia Macrorhiza, (?) having tuberous roots, which appears to be quite extensively diffused in this region. One very similar, if not the same, was detected as far east as Fort Smith. A plant nearly allied to O. Engelmanni was collected at Delaware Mount. The little *Cereus cæspitosus,* so common in lower Texas, was also found here in great abundance. We were sorry not to find a flower or fruit of this pretty little plant, which would have enabled us to solve some obscure points in the natural history of the unique and interesting tribe of plants to which it belongs. The cactaceæ have not heretofore been well studied in the United States, Dr. Engelmann, of St. Louis, being almost the only botanist who has paid any special attention to them.

The whole of this region from Fort Smith to Valley river is eminently calculated to sustain a large population. Although the soil itself, probably, is not as rich as that of Arkansas, yet the ease of raising stock, for which few other countries are better adapted, and the exemption from sickness, will greatly counterbalance this difference. Water, in most places, will be found abundant for all agricultural purposes. In some places, however, especially on the head-waters of the Washita and Red rivers, it is quite brackish, being impregnated with the salts of lime and magnesia, but not sufficiently so to prevent it from being used for domestic purposes. Should a purer kind be required for railroad uses, I presume it can be obtained from the Canadian, which appears to be much more free from mineral impregnation.

SECTION III. *Llano Estacado.*—It would seem proper to include in this region the space on our route between Valley river and Fossil creek, near Tucumcari hills. This is a dry, and generally timberless tract of country, extending over a distance of about one hundred and ninety miles. Over this region, and the western portions of the last, immense herds of buffaloes range at certain seasons of the year, but they evidently make no prolonged stay here; passing from the waters of the Arkansas and Canadian rivers, south, to those of Red river and its tributaries, and thence back again. If not in these days, they formerly ranged south as far as the waters of the Brazos, Colorado, and other Texan rivers, where there are vast hunting grounds for the great Comanche and Kioway tribes of Indians. The noble wild animal upon which these red men of the plains mainly subsist is already becoming greatly diminished in numbers, by the restraints of the settlements, and by the military occupancy of their grounds. Certainly the *manifest destiny* of the Indian is to disappear from the face of the earth, and become extinct, unless he conform to the usages and habits of civilized life, which at present seems quite improbable.

Along the banks of arroyos, or dry creeks, may be found a few alamos; and under the northern and eastern bluffs of the Llano Estacado, and detached surrounding hills, may be found Piñon pine, (Pinus edulis,) and two kinds of cedars. They are, probably, too much stunted and shattered by the prevailing winds to form very useful timbers. It is to be remarked, that the wind blows with tremendous force over these immense denuded plains, and this, we have reason to believe, is one great cause of the destitution of timber in this region. In confirmation of this opinion is the fact, that wherever the least shelter by a bluff or rock is afforded, the modest cedar will rear its head, thankful, as it were, for this partial protection. The stature of the tree appears to be limited to the height and amount of shelter it thus receives. The timber that may be needed for railroad purposes here, will have to be supplied from other districts each way, probably from the Indian territory on the east, and the mountains of the Pecos and Rio Grande on the west, where timber of excellent quality abounds, and from whence it can be easily procured.

Although grass is abundant, yet the scarcity of water will greatly lessen its value as an agricultural district. Very little of this indispensable element is to be found, except along the course of the larger rivers. However, during the more moist seasons of the year, sheep can be grazed, without doubt, over large tracts of this district; as in New Mexico they are driven, herded, and grazed, hundreds of miles from their usual places of abode. Sheep can be grazed a much greater distance from water than cattle or horses. So that when the country between the Eastern States and New Mexico comes to be settled, the difficulties from the depredation of Indians obviated, and security established, this country may prove highly valuable for grazing purposes.

This is more emphatically the region of cacti than the one just left on the east. The singular and rather pretty, but formidable *Opuntia arborescens*, described by Dr. Engelmann, is first found here. It extends west as far as Zuñi, and in southern Texas as low as Presidio del Norte. In this region were found several new and undescribed species, which will be described in another and more appropriate form. The piñon, or *nut pine of New Mexico*, here first makes its appearance, and is presumed to be its eastern limit, extending west as far as the Sierra

Nevada mountains of California. The real grass-leaved dasylirion was first seen here, on the bluffs of the Llano Estacado. It is identical with the one found on the San Pedro, or Devil's river, in Texas. There is another species, with the leaves and habit somewhat of a Yucca, named *D. graminifolia*, I suppose because it does *not* resemble a grass. A rosaceous shrub (*Cerco carpus*) and a shrubby oak (*Q. Emoryi?*) are also common under the bluffs. We have not now the means at hand to determine whether they are the same as occur in lower Texas and New Mexico. Eriogoneæ, another characteristic tribe of plants peculiar to dry climates, begin here to make their appearance in considerable numbers. Mentzelias and asteroid composites are also quite abundant. An Ephedra, much used as a diuretic, especially for horses, was first seen here. The genus is also common in lower Texas, where I know two or three distinct species of it.

SECTION IV. *Tucumcari and Pecos Valleys.*—Although the waters of these two valleys flow into the Gulf of Mexico, by widely-separated channels, yet they may well be considered in one district—being included in the space of about one hundred and seventy miles, from Fossil creek to the dividing highlands between the Rio Pecos and Rio Grande del Norte.

At Tucumcari we have a broad, beautiful, and fertile valley, abounding in most luxuriant grasses, and extending north to the Canadian, but its exact limits we had not time to explore. Although the timber is somewhat scarce, yet, ascending the hills on either side, cedars and piñon become much more abundant, and both attain a higher stature than on the Llano Estacado. Along the banks of the streams there are a few cotton-woods and box-elders of very pretty size. The Gallinos, whose outlet is south into the Pecos by narrow defiles near our line, is a beautiful, bold, clear, running stream, affording water at all seasons of the year, while the Tucumcari and Pajarito creeks, in the immediate vicinity of the Tucumcari hills, flowing north into the Canadian, will afford water doubtless nearly all the year. At any rate, when we passed, (21st September,) there was plenty, flowing in a rapid, turbid stream. The water of Laguna Colorado, which is near, or forms, the sources of these streams, is somewhat brackish.

We collected here, for the first time, specimens of another shrubby cactus, (Opuntia frutescens,) which is so abundant all over southern New Mexico and Texas, as far south as Eagle Pass and San Antonio. It is a very ornamental species, especially when loaded with its scarlet berries. On the hills in this region were found, and collected, several new mamillaria; beautiful flowering and fruiting specimens of which are now growing in the Congressional gardens, in Washington. *Opuntia Engelmanni*, which is probably the most widely spread of the whole tribe of American cactaceæ, was first detected in the rocky cañons of the Gallinos. *Fallugui paradoxa* and *Fendlera rupicola*, two beautiful shrubs, are common here; both of them common to Texas also. There are, likewise, several other Texan plants in this region, among them a *Parthenum*, *Thymophylla greggi*, and a great variety of leguminous and asteroid plants. Several species of eriogoniæ also make their first appearance here. As their geographical limits extend westwardly some distance, most of the eriogoniæ which were collected here will most probably prove to be those which are figured, and well characterized, by my excellent friend *Dr. Torrey*, in Captain Sitgreaves' report of the Zuñi expedition. As we proceed a little further west, we come to the Pecos valley, where, in addition to the piñon and cedars met with before, and already mentioned, we find pine-trees of a majestic size, (Pinus brachyptera, *Engl.*,) that are as valuable for timber as almost any in the world.

The Pecos river is here clear and rapid, its waters pure and sweet, forming quite a contrast to those at the several crossings from San Antonio to El Paso, where they are always turbid, brackish, and disagreeable. Indeed, by some travellers on its lower borders, and on some maps, this river, from these circumstances, has acquired the name of Puerco, the Spanish appellation for muddy waters. There, its valley, for hundreds of miles, is a blank and dreary waste, with scarcely a shrub to relieve the eye of the traveller; here, its fertile banks are dotted with innumerable small plantations, and towns, so characteristic of New Mexico.

This river, with the Gallinos, will form a never-failing supply of water for the erection of all kinds of mills and machinery, when the time for such wants has arrived. These considerations, in connexion with the fact of its forming a middle and connecting link between the Atlantic and Pacific shores, give it a high degree of interest at the present time. The region is large enough for a State of the first magnitude, and contains all the natural elements of self-sustenance, excepting, probably, commerce. The difficulties which alone now prevent this district, and that of the valley of the Rio Grande, from rising to its proper scale of importance, will in a great measure be obviated as soon as any Pacific railroad is established and finished. Should any other route than this be adopted, the road, either north or south, can be easily tapped, so as to diffuse its beneficial influences to this whole country. The quality of the soil, though not equal to that of the Indian territory west of Arkansas, is superior to that of the Rio Grande valley, either in New Mexico or Texas. It is probably as well adapted to sheep grazing as any other country in the world. There can be no doubt, when properly settled, and easy communications can be safely had with the great Eastern States and with California, that it will prove equal, also, to any other country, as a resort for consumptive invalids.

SECTION V. *Rio Grande Valley.*—What there is to be remarked of this valley will be brief, because it is an old and well known region, having been settled by the Spaniards about three hundred years ago. Gregg's Commerce of the Prairies gives a vivid, and generally truthful, view of this country, and its capabilities for agricultural productions. There is not time now, nor indeed is it in place, to enter into a comparative view of the adaptation of this country to consumptive invalids, with those of foreign countries, or with other places in the United States; but little is hazarded in asserting, that in no long time this, and the upper Pecos valley, will become one of the most important and eligible places in the whole world for such purposes. As soon as communications with the Eastern States and California become speedy, cheap, and regular, as well as free from the danger with which they are at present attended, and when the ordinary means and comforts of living are easily and cheaply procured, so as to come within the reach of the yeomanry of the land, a trip and sojourn to this country will form as pleasant an excursion as to any part of our country can, and many an invalid will then avail himself of the recuperative influences of this climate. The summer heat is greatly modified by the peculiar aridness of the atmosphere, which, by rapidly carrying off the perspiration before it has time to accumulate to any sensible degree, cools the surface of the body, and makes the summer truly delightful, especially to an invalid. The winter is mild, being screened from the penetrating winds of the north by intervening mountains. The terrible *norther*, so well known and dreaded by the inhabitants and travellers in lower Texas, is not known here. Many invalids who at present resort to San Antonio for their health, experience various bad effects from the sudden changes of the weather, resulting mainly from those "northers."

The width of the Rio Grande valley, at the point where we crossed it (which was at Albuquerque) from the dividing ridge between it and the Pecos, and the highlands or mountains between its waters and those flowing westward into the Gulf of California, is about one hundred and seventy miles. Its length in the Territory of New Mexico is embraced between about the thirty-second and thirty-eighth degrees of north latitude; which, with its tortuous course, would give it a length of about four hundred and thirty miles. This of course embraces a great variety of climate, independently of the effect produced by the highly elevated ranges of mountains which partly environ it on the east and west.

The soil is well adapted to the cultivation of all the finer fruits and vegetables, as well as the cereals; but it requires irrigation. Grapes, apricots, pears, and melons, are produced in the utmost perfection and abundance. The grapes, especially, are far superior to any that can be cultivated at home, in the open air. Beets, sweet potatoes, and pumpkins do equally well, if not better than in the Eastern States. But the Irish potato does not succeed, excepting in the mountainous regions. On account of the cost of irrigation, wheat and corn cannot be raised as cheaply as in the Western Atlantic States; nevertheless, by irrigation they do very well, and large quantities of both are produced.

SECTION VI. *Valley of Zuñi.*—In this region, we would embrace the scope of country between the summit of the Sierra Madre, or mountains bordering the Rio Grande valley on the west, and Mount San Francisco; the principal and pervading stream of which is the Colorado Chiquito, a tributary of the Colorado Grande, or, as it is more aptly termed, the great Colorado of the West. The general course of this valley is northwest and southeast; the extent of which (in our rapid exploration) we were unable to determine. Its width, travelled, is about two hundred and fifty miles.

At Zuñi, the Indians of the Pueblo tribes raise corn, and many other vegetables, without resorting to irrigation; but from the appearance of the soil on the bottoms of the Colorado Chiquito, it was considered by most of our party that irrigation might be necessary. In the immediate vicinity of the mountains there is evidence of an amount of moisture in the soil, which is wanting in the centre of the valley, more remote from their influence. The water of the Colorado Chiquito is sufficient to irrigate a portion of the central part of the valley, but probably not enough to make all the tillable lands available for agricultural purposes. There are many beautiful streams of water of limited extent, on both ranges of the mountains, which look into this valley from the east and the west. These streams would be sufficient for small settlements in their immediate neighborhood; but on descending into an almost unlimited arid plain, they are lost by the absorptive power of the soil, and the rapid evaporation caused by the dry atmosphere. The Rio Mimbres, in the valley of which is situated Fort Webster, southeast of the Mogoyon, (which has been made well known by the operations of the Mexican Boundary Commission) is a good example of these facts. Such is the case, also, with nearly all the mountain streams in these arid regions.

Grass throughout this whole country is very abundant, and of a most excellent quality, especially around the mountain bases, and on the more elevated plateaus. Large herds of cattle and sheep might be reared and sustained here, were it not for the depredations of the Indians. We were told by Mr. Leroux, that the wild Indians of this country, in their blind eargerness to obtain the flesh of mules, have been known to shoot one down with their arrows while a traveller was yet seated on his back, for which, in a case that he mentioned, the poor savage paid the penalty of his life.

Unfortunately, we passed this region between the 18th of November (when we crossed the crest of the Sierra Madre) and the 25th of December. At the latter date, we encamped at the base of the San Francisco mountain. This was the most unpropitious season of the whole year for the collection of herbaceous plants, and must account for the meagreness of my collections in this part of our journey.

The entire eastern, southern, and part of the western, angles of this region, are well timbered with Douglas's spruce, New Mexican yellow pine, piñon, and balsam fir. The Rocky mountain white pine (Pinus flexilis) grows on the San Francisco mountain, and no doubt on the higher peaks and ranges of the Sierra Madre and Mogoyon. Oaks and black walnut also grow here. The banks of all the streams that are crossed produced cotton-wood and mezquite—in some places in great abundance. Three kinds of cedar abound at the base of the mountains, frequently extending (in more limited quantities) down to the banks of the Colorado Chiquito, wherever the evenness of the surface appears to be broken by dry arroyos or broken banks.

On the slopes east and south of San Francisco mountain, looking into this valley, and also westwardly, are vast forests of piñon, intermingled with cedars, perfectly black in the distance, by their density. From elevated points near the southern base of Bill Williams' mountain we had extensive and beautiful views of these forests, which extended southwestwardly, apparently some fifteen or twenty miles. This one we denominated the "Black Forest." With the aid of the telescope, we could detect (*January 3d, side reconnoissance*) the camp-fires of the Tonto Indians, in several places, in the forest. We were informed by our guide, Mr. Antonio Leroux, who has had much experience, and even desperate forays, with the Indians of this neighborhood, that, at the proper season of the year, large parties of the Yampai, Tonto, Coyotero,

Garretero, and other sub-tribes of the great Apacherian race, resort here for the purpose of collecting the fruit of this pine. It probably forms one of the most important articles of their subsistence. In an economical view of this country, it should not be forgotten or overlooked.

Immediately on our entrance into this valley, (November 19th,) we found and collected a new species of Opuntia, with prostrate, nearly terete joints, entirely devoid of woody fibre; and at Zuñi, soon after, another, with a woody stem, low and prostrate, clearly distinct from O. arborescens, to which it somewhat approaches in its reticulated woody axis. Its fruit, seeds, spines, and general habit, however, separate it from that well-known and widely disseminated species. Very pretty specimens in fruit were obtained, but none in flower, which is much to be regretted. As this tribe of interesting plants was almost the only one we could find and study, at this late season of the year, our party rivalled each other in daily bringing some of them into camp that had not been before seen or collected. Sometimes one would come in ahead of the others, but more frequently several would arrive at the same time with new specimens, and then a great shout would ensue, in deciding upon the claims of priority. Lieutenant Whipple discovered the first specimen of our new *Cactodendron*, as we were pleased to call it, to distinguish it from the O. arborescens. We saw this same species afterwards growing six to eight feet high, retaining all its peculiar characteristics, with the exception of not being prostrate. While on the banks of the Colorado Chiquito, and only in that vicinity, we found a new Echinocactus, the first of this genus met with on our route, but it was neither in flower nor fruit. It is quite limited in its range, having been found only along the bottom lands of the Rio Colorado Chiquito. In the rocky ravines, soon after leaving the river bottoms, we discovered a densely aggregated Cereus, growing in large oval masses, which contained hundreds of low, ovate, fleshy stems, from one root. Our highly esteemed friend, Dr. Engelmann, has made several species of such forms of cerei, which are difficult to identify in the absence of flowers or fruit, on account of the great variety in the number, size, and color of spines in the same species. The spines in the plant just mentioned are angular, like those of Dr. Engelmann's Cer. enneacanthus; but they also very much resemble those of his Cer. polyacanthus. The cactaceæ can only be well characterized by their inflorescence, fruit, and general habit. Opuntia fragilis is very common in this valley, offering many varieties of shape, size, and color of the spines. Nearly all cactaceæ assume a red, shrivelled, drooping appearance at this season of the year, very different from what they exhibit when in vigorous growth. Cereus Fendleri, which is very common about the Pecos and Rio Grande, has nearly its western limit here, soon to be replaced by *Cer. Chloranthus*, an unpublished species of Dr. Engelmann. Among the shrubs peculiar to this part of the country is the beautiful and very aromatic Cowania Stansburiana. In Capt. Sitgreaves' reports, Dr. Woodhouse mentions having seen an *aromatic* Fallugia paradoxa in this region, which must be a mistake. It was this plant; for, although the fallugia and cowania somewhat resemble each other, the former is never aromatic and balsamic, like the latter. The cowania grows on much more elevated positions than the fallugia, and is considered by the Mexicans as a most valuable medicine; often selling at the rate of half a dollar an ounce, under the name of *alouseme*. It is highly esteemed as a styptic, and astringent in hæmorrhagic discharges. A beautiful blue-berried barberry (Berberis pinnata) is very common here, called by the Mexicans *leña amorilla*. This shrub is very different from the one at the Copper Mines, (*Santa Rita del Cobre*,) collected when I was on the Mexican boundary commission. The berries are very pleasant to the taste, being saccharine with a slight acidity. Fallugia, cercocarpus, and another thornless rosaceous shrub, probably a cratægus, is common along the arroyos and rough low places. The Obione canescens, and other species of the same genus, though not peculiar to this region, are met with here in great abundance. The former is called by Mexicans *chamizo*, and by our people *greasewood*. It belongs to the tribe of chenopods, and we noticed that our sheep were very fond of browsing upon it, choosing it in preference to grass. It is an unsightly weed, with a sub-shrubby stem, but withal very useful when we could get no better material for fuel.

SECTION VII. *San Francisco Valley.*[1]—It is doubtful whether the name used to characterize this region is strictly proper. A part of the waters which flow southwardly into the San Francisco river, (Rio Verde,) a tributary of the Gila, and another part flowing in a westwardly direction into the Rio Colorado, are embraced in what we call the San Francisco valley. Between Leroux's springs, situated at the southwestern base of the San Francisco mountain and Cactus Pass, the western limit of this division is a space of about one hundred and sixty miles, so interesting that a volume could easily be made of the materials which are collected in it, without exhausting the subject. In general terms, we could say it was well timbered, although there were large plains situated between the hills and mountains, nearly destitute of trees.

Mounts San Francisco, Bill Williams, and Sitgreaves constitute the highest peaks of this region. They stand upon an elevated, somewhat broken plain, which is about 8,000 feet above the level of the sea. They are environed on the east and west by a large number of beatifully rounded volcanic hills, which, with the intervening forests and glades, give it the most inviting and romantic appearance we had probably seen on our route. Between this elevated plateau, extending some seventy-five miles west of Mount San Francisco, and a low range which we named the Aztec mountains, there is a wide valley, (about eighteen miles by the diagonal path in which we crossed it,) averaging some ten or fifteen miles in width. It is so densely covered with the best grama grass, that we named it "Val de China." This valley we were unable to explore except to a limited degree, for it extends northwest probably to the Colorado, and southeast to the Gila.

Partridge and Pueblo creeks, uniting in this valley from different directions, form what we suppose must be an affluent of the Rio San Francisco, constituting one of its heads and draining the valley to the south. We explored it north about forty miles, where it retained its characteristic appearance, with the exception that there seemed to be less indications of water-courses in that direction. So our attention was turned further south as the only hope of getting an easy way to the Colorado. The hills bordering this valley, especially on the west, are densely covered with cedars, pines, spruces, oaks, &c., which are sufficiently abundant to serve all the purposes of agriculture, domestic economy, and railroads. Much of the timber is of the most valuable kind, consisting of the yellow pine of this country, (Pinus brachyptera,) and the Oregon pine or Douglas spruce, (P. Douglasii,) the value of which will be more fully treated of hereafter. Besides Partridge creek, which enters this valley from the east, there is a beautiful little stream from the mountains west, entering from the opposite direction, a little further south. We named it Pueblo creek. The remains of broken pottery and the ruins of stone buildings and ancient fortifications that occur here give evidence that the country has once been inhabited by an intelligent, enterprising and warlike race of men. These remains exhibit marks of extreme antiquity.

One of the highest peaks in this range, which we named Mount Hope, is situated fifteen or twenty miles south of our explorations. It appears to be the source of the moisture of this region, and no doubt waters many such little valleys as that of the Pueblo, although we had not time to explore in that direction as far as desired.

The importance of this point is still further enhanced by the fact that from this place railroad timber, when needed, will have to be supplied westward as far as the Colorado Grande, which is distant, in a direct line, about one hundred miles; but by the route we travelled, through the valley of the Santa Maria or Bill Williams' fork, it is about one hundred and seventy miles.

My opportunities for making botanical collections in this region were about as unfavorable as on the preceding part of our journey. We passed through it from the 8th to the 31st of January. In the valley west of Aztec Pass, and between it and Cactus Pass, (25th January,) was found the first spring plant in bloom. It is one of the umbilliferous tribe, with a spindle-

[1] The name of the mountain at the head of this valley is San Francisco. The stream is usually called Rio Verde.

shaped, parsnip-like root, but much softer, sweeter, and more tender than that wholesome esculent. It is much sought after by the Mexicans, who name it *gamote*, a name that is also applied by them to the sweet potato. Mr. Leroux informed us that Indian females in this region, especially the Utahs and Pai-utes, spend much time in the early months of the year, when the root is soft and tender, in collecting it in large quantities. It is prepared by slicing, drying, and grinding on matats, and, after which, stored away for future use. They make a soup of the meal. The root becomes hard and cortical as it advances in age, and unfit to be eaten.

Besides the *grama grass*, which has been mentioned while describing the Val de China as so fine and abundant, we had a grass, peculiar to this region, called by our woodsmen "bunch grass." It was quite green, and our animals were immoderately fond of it. We were unable to secure specimens of it in flower or fruit, and therefore could not determine its name. Mr. Leroux says it is well known and prized in the great Salt Lake valley, fattening animals faster than the *grama*, but it does not afford them the same amount of strength and muscle.

A narrow filamentose-leaved Yucca was found near Picacho, and specimens of the young plants were brought home. It was not in fruit. It is quite different from the two species found east of the Rio Grande; but whether different from the one of a similar habit in Texas, can only be determined by an examination and comparison of the flower and fruit. In the waters of Partridge creek we found *Polygonum amphibium*, which, although it grows on land as well as in water, is nevertheless a sure index of the permanency of the water in its neighborhood.

In this valley we saw and collected, growing upon the piñon, a mistletoe, (*Arceuthobium*,) never before seen, and quite distinct from the one found on the other pine, (*P. brachyptera*.)

At the foot of Bill Williams' mountain, we first met the celebrated INDIAN MAGUEY, (Agave sp. undetermined.) This to the wild Indian tribes is probably one of the most important plants of the whole interior of the continent south of the 35th parallel of north latitude. It is a matter of curious interest to know how much further north it grows. We presume, however, that it will be found very little further north than our line. It flourishes on the roughest, most rocky, and apparently most inhospitable spots that can be found; and, generally, it occurs only in such places. An allied species (*Agave Americana*) is common in Mexico, and in our gardens under the title of century plant, so named from the popular notion that it blooms every hundred years. Our plant is a long time (not nearly a hundred years, however) in coming to maturity. It then blooms, bears fruit and dies, leaving many offsets which come to maturity yearly. These likewise perform their great function of fructification, and die, to give place in turn to their successors. The great value of the plant to the Indian is, that it forms a never-failing source of subsistence at all seasons of the year. At the proper season, which is about the 1st July, the stalk that bears the flower shoots up and grows with amazing rapidity. It is then very juicy, tender, and sweet, much resembling the pith of the sugar-cane; and the Indians now devote their time to preparing their *mezcal*, which will keep preserved for several months. When the time for preparing food from the flower-stock is passed, they resort to the heart or central part of the older plants that have not yet come to maturity; the most tender portions being at the base of the inner leaves. The heart can be found in different stages of development at all seasons of the year. They roast it in temporary ovens, made of earth and stones, about two days being required to cook it sufficiently. We used the juice of the plant successfully as an anti-scorbutic while on the Mexican boundary commission, my attention being first called to it by a circular from General Lawson, Surgeon General of the United States army, recommending it on the authority of Dr. Perrin, of the United States army.

Besides the trees already mentioned, we have here two or three species of cedars; one with a large, sweet, edible berry. In times of great scarcity of food, I believe this fruit is resorted to by nearly every animal in this region. Pinus edulis (piñon) grows in great abundance nearly the whole length of this district. The highlands which form spurs to the San Francisco, Bill Williams', and Sitgreaves mountains are covered with these trees; their deep green foliage giving the forests a peculiarly dark and sombre aspect, forming a strong contrast with the surrounding grassy plains. Two very distinct species of oak occur here, one of which I have marked on the profile as *Quercus Gambellii,* of Nuttall; the other is probably new. In the deep ravines or cañons of this district we found an ash, (Fraxinus velutinus,) common also to the copper mine region, and associated with it also a cherry, which may be a new species. Willow-leaved poplar is occasionally found along the arroyos, where water has lately been standing. Among the shrubs abounding in this region are found the blue-berried barberry, a species of currant, (Ribes,) and a species of very thorny Solanaceæ, of unknown genus. A new shrub, interesting on account of its botanical affinities, was found here, belonging to the small order of Garryaceæ, natives only of western North America and the West Indies. A second species of the genus Garrya is very common about the copper mines of New Mexico, which was also detected here, but not in fruit. Which of the two, if either, is the plant of Douglas, upon which the genus was founded, we are unable at present to determine. We find great difficulty in procuring publications of American plants, in the arrangement of orders subsequent to compositæ, up to which point we have been supplied, by the indefatigable zeal and learning of those excellent co-laborers in the field of botany, Drs. Torrey and Gray, in their Flora of North America. Since the acquisition of Texas, New Mexico, and California, with their consequent explorations and discoveries, the new genera and species, in orders previously passed over, are so many and important, that a new edition is now imperatively called for, before their great work is finished.

A walnut was found in this region, collected heretofore in the region of the copper mines of New Mexico, very nearly related to the black walnut of the Eastern States. From Devil's river, in Texas, while on the boundary commission, were sent specimens and a figure of what was thought to be a new species, to Dr. Torrey, a description of which was read by him before the meeting of the American Association of the Sciences, in August, 1851, under the title of *Juglans Whippleana;* which was not published. Dr. Engelmann had previously obtained, and named it *J. rupestris.* Dr. Torrey has published figures of both of them, in Captain Sitgreaves' report; our present plant, provisionally, a variety of that species. The differences between them, however, are greater, in my opinion, than those between the present variety and Juglans nigra; so that they may all ultimately come to be forms of one species, when still other and more closely connecting varieties are found.

A Ptelea, closely allied if not identical with the shrubby treefoil of the States, is found here. A Condalia also, which is a Rhamnaceous shrub, bearing small dark-colored berries, several species of which are eaten by Mexicans and Indians. A beautiful shrubby spiraea, or a species of some nearly allied genus, was found here.

Along the banks of Turkey creek, Pueblo creek, and the streams which we first passed after crossing Aztec Pass, we observed large quantities of willows, which is rather an unusual occurrence in this country. On the hills surrounding the Aztec mountains, for the first time, we met with the beautiful shrubby arbutus, (*Arctostaphylos,*) called by the Mexicans *manzanita;* the bark of the plant is handsomely polished, of a dark mahogany color. From this place to the Pacific, and in California, there are several species of this genus, most of them bearing an edible berry, similar to the whortleberry. In California, a most valuable timber-tree of this genus grows all along the Coast range of mountains. It bears a larger edible berry, which is much sought after by Mexicans and Indians, who know it by the name of *Madrona.* It is a beautiful tree. The wood is very hard, taking a polish equal to, and much resembling *lignum-vitæ.*

Near Bill Williams' mountain we found in considerable quantities the aggregated Cereus, noticed before; but the species cannot well be determined, on account of the want of blossom and fruit. It is very nearly allied to Dr. Engelmann's *Cereus polyacanthus,* which yields an edible fruit, called by Mexicans *pitahaya.* It is sometimes in large oval masses, densely set with formidable spines. The arborescent Opuntia, first found near Zuñi, which, to distinguish from the true O. arborescens, we called Cacto-dendron, finds its western limits near the termination of this region. We also find here a mamillaria, very common, and the only one we saw between this point and the Rio Grande.

At the southern base of Bill Williams' mountain we found an Opuntia never before seen on our route, and from its peculiar appearance, it will doubtless prove to be a new species. It is an upright flat-jointed species, thickly beset with yellow spines, of a much lighter green color than most other species, or, indeed, any other that I have seen. Lieutenant Tidball, of our escort, kindly sketched it for me, and provisionally named it after him, to distinguish from other allied species. *Opuntia fragilis*, and *Cer. Fendleri*, also occur here. There is an Opuntia in this region, very near, if not identical with the one on the Rio Grande, with long brown spines. It is published in Plantae Fendlerianæ, by Dr. Engelmann, as *Op. phœacantha.* As we proceed westward into the neighborhood of Picacho and Val de China, the *O. Tidballii* becomes much more frequent, and we observed that it was never found on the northern and western exposures of the hills and rocky arroyos, but mostly on the southern, (as where we first found it,) and more seldom on the eastern exposures. In Cañon creek, the head-waters of Bill Williams' fork near the western extremity of this region, it grows seven or eight feet high, spreading so as to form an immense head, with upwards of one hundred joints, all branching from a single stalk. At Aztec Pass an Opuntia was found, which in the size of the joints, and appearance of the spines, was very similar to *Opuntia Engelmanni*, but, unlike this well known species, it is spreading and prostrate. Unfortunately, we could obtain no fruit of it.

SECTION VIII. *Santa Maria Valley.*—The space embraced within this section lies between Cactus Pass and the Colorado Grande, following the course of Bill Williams' fork, from near its sources, to the great river of the west. Cactus Pass is the last of the highlands that we cross before reaching the Rio Colorado. The distance from this point, in a direct line, to the Colorado, is only about sixty miles; but by the road we travelled, through the valley of Bill Williams' fork, it is about one hundred and thirty miles.

The timber of this valley is composed almost exclusively of cotton-wood, or *alamo*, mezquite, "green-barked acacia," of Major Emory's report, curly mezquite, (*Strombocarpa pubescens*,) two other leguminous trees, and some willows. One of the leguminous trees is the *Olneya Tesota* of Dr. Gray, in *Plant. Nov. Thurberianae*, pages 313 and 328.—1854. It was collected by Mr. Thurber on the Gila. It has very much the habit of a Robinia. The foliage of the tree is very dense and heavy, and although dark green, the leaves were sometimes crisped as though they had been bitten by frost; yet there were no evidences of frost on other tender vegetables in its vicinity. Our Mexicans were not acquainted with it, nor with the name *Tesota.* The alamos grow to a good large size, and are quite abundant. The two mezquites are rather small in this valley, seldom attaining more than fifteen or twenty feet in height. The *Tesota*, "green-barked acacia," and the other leguminous tree, grow fully as large as the mezquites, and in an economical respect, it is presumed, will prove equally useful for domestic purposes. Although willows in many places grow quite large and abundantly, yet, for anything but browsing animals in times of great scarcity of grass, and for fire-wood, they appear to be nearly useless.

Grass in the upper portions of this valley is quite good, and sufficient to support considerable numbers of mules and stock in passing through. But in the lower portions, as we approach the Rio Colorado, grass of all kinds becomes quite scarce; mules then resort to the twigs of the willow, and the twigs and bark of the alamo, upon which they have been known to subsist the whole winter.

The water of Bill Williams' fork, in many places, flows in a bold current; but, like the Mimbres, and other streams in this country, it sinks again in the sand, sometimes within a very short distance of its head. It rises and sinks this way, alternately, until it reaches the Rio Colorado. This valley, which is generally narrow, cannot be worth much for agricultural purposes; yet there are several places where it widens, so as to form very pretty sites for settlements. We passed through this valley from the 1st to the 20th February, when the weather was warm and genial, as in the month of May in the Atlantic States.

The seasons appear to be two or three weeks earlier here than at the Mojave village in the Colorado valley. We were unable to determine from observation whether the soil here can be cultivated without irrigation, because we had not time to make any experiments on this subject in our rapid reconnoissance. From the fact that the Mojave Indians, but a short distance further west in the Colorado valley, cultivate corn, wheat, beans, pumpkins, melons, and probably other culinary vegetables, without irrigation, one can have little doubt but that the same may be done also in this valley. Should this prove to be true, there are several places, especially in the vicinity of White Cliff creek, which will be of great importance on this account. The valley here spreads out to quite a wide space, and is, moreover, convenient to good timber near Aztec Pass, besides the cotton-wood and mezquite in its own immediate valley.

This may emphatically be called the region of Cacti of our route. One of the first of them that we found after entering this valley was the *Echinocactus Wislizeni* of Dr. Engelmann, called by the Mexicans "visnada," the juice of which is said to serve as a substitute for water when it cannot otherwise be procured. Instances have been known among the white trappers of this wild region, where the lives of men have been saved by this plant. On the morning of February 3, we found one of them left by the Yampai Indians, who had been on the ground the previous night. The spines were burned, and two-thirds of the inside were scooped out so as to form a sort of kettle. Mr. Leroux informed us that they scoop a space of its centre, introduce other vegetables, and with the introduction of heated stones cook the whole together. These vegetable boilers are not transported from one camp to the other, but, on account of their abundance, new ones are formed at every camping ground where they are required. A Cereus was recognised to-day, very nearly akin, if not the same, as one that is very common around El Paso, (*Cer. chloranthus Engl. ined.*,) and heretofore only known in that region. We were unable to get its flower or fruit to compare with the El Paso plant, which was much to be regretted, as the spines of these plants vary so much as to form by themselves but poor distinctive characteristics of the species. There also was found a globose mamillaria, with from one to three or four central-hooked spines. It differs from the one collected on the Pecos, by its red clavate fruit. We noticed also a new arborescent opuntia, very nearly allied to *O. arborescens*, the last of which we saw at the ruins near the Pueblo de Zuñi. This plant differs from that in having spiney fruit and a larger seed, but in other respects it resembles it very much. The beautiful scarlet-berried *Op. frutescens* was found in this region. It was collected also at Laguna Colorado, sixty miles east of the Rio Pecos, showing it to have a wider geographical range than the *O. arborescens*, which is supposed by Dr. Engelmann to be the widest diffused of all North American cacti. In addition to those already mentioned, we gathered a beautiful Opuntia, common in this region and quite different from any we had heretofore seen. It is a flat-jointed, spineless variety, growing in a handsome rosette manner, and covered with a beautiful velvety bloom or pubescence. The minute barbed bristles of the pulvilli are very annoying when handled. It is even said to be destructive to the eye if permitted to touch that delicate organ.

By far the most interesting cactus of this region, and probably of the whole world, is the *Cereus giganteus*. We saw it for the first time, in this valley, on the 4th of February, growing about forty-five feet high; but along the valley of the Gila, it is said to reach sixty feet in height. It frequently occurs from twenty-five to thirty feet high without a single branch. Among the skeletons of wood, after the fleshy parts of the plant had decayed and fallen away, we observed in the old trees a perfect net-work of the bundles of woody fibres, reticulated on a large scale, exactly after the manner of the woody fibres of the *Opuntia arborescens*. Our observations do not accord fully with the account given by Drs. Engelmann and Parry,[1] who had

[1] Silliman's Amer. Jour. of Science and Arts, Vol. XIV, Nov., 1852.

probably taken their description from younger plants, before the interlacing or anastomosing process had been carried to any considerable extent. We have seen the skeletons of young plants which exactly corresponded with their description. The fruits of many Cerei are edible, with something of the flavor and shape of a large gooseberry. They are thickly covered with sharp spines; but as soon as the fruit ripens, these can be brushed off with ease. By peeling the rind, there is left a large, sweet, delicate pulp, that will rival any gooseberry. The top of this giant Cactus, however, yields a *pitahaya*, far sweeter and more delicious than those which grow on more humble stems. The Indians collect large quantities of it by tying a fork to the little end of a long willow pole, which enables them to reach and bring down the fruit without injuring it. They make a syrup, or conserve, from the juice, which serves them for luxury, as well as for sustenance, and which can be preserved a long time. The Mexicans call the tree "suwarrow;" the Indian, "harsee;" and the syrup manufactured from the juice, "sistor." The juice of the flesh of the tree is quite bitter.

We find (February 7) a new species of Opuntia, with a reticulated woody stem, very fragile at the joints before hardening into wood, and armed with spines worse than those of a porcupine. It is called by the Mexicans, "chug." The plant is the horror of man and beast. Our mules are as fearful of it as ourselves. The barbed spines stick so fast in the flesh that the joint of the plant is separated from the main stem before the spines can be withdrawn. We found this species sometimes ten and twelve feet high, branching very fantastically, in consequence of the fragility and decay of the younger stems and joints. In a landscape by Mr. Stanley, (plate 16 of Major Emory's report,) in the foreground is the figure of a cactus, of which, in the text, no account is given. It has a faint resemblance to our plant; but Lieutenant Whipple, who has travelled and explored much in that region, is pretty confident that it represents a different species, which he has also seen. The figure is too regular in its outlines and curves to represent the peculiarly angled and irregular appearance of our plant. It is, without doubt, an undescribed species. We find here what is supposed to be *Opuntia ramossissima* of Dr. Engelmann, collected on the desert between the Colorado and San Diego by Dr. Parry. In places favorable for its growth, it is found six feet high, as robust and tree-like as the *O. arborescens* itself.

The fact that on the 7th February we collected a Drabá, a Thelopodium, and a Vesicaria in full bloom, is a proof of the forwardness of the season in this valley. February 11th we collected, along the banks of Bill Williams' fork, fine specimens of a Lepidium and a Hosackia.

SECTION IX. *Valley of the Colorado.*—From the mouth of Bill Williams' fork to the point above where we crossed the Rio Colorado, is about sixty miles; and from thence to Soda lake, on the Mojave creek, where, at ordinary seasons of the year, water is first found, is about one hundred miles further west. Along the valley of this river, alamo, mezquite, and willow form the principal, and almost entire, kinds of trees. The Mojave Indians make use of willow twigs in the formation of their granaries, where they store away the fruit of the *Tornillo*, (curly mezquite,) and various other vegetable products, for winter consumption, or for times of scarcity. Their depositories are built in a circular form, four or five feet high, and about the same, or a little less, in diameter. After being filled with their stores, they are covered with willow bushes or reeds, over which is laid another cover of earth. The climate is so dry, they find no difficulty in thus preserving their winter grain. We passed their villages the last days of February, and found them in the possession of plenty of corn, wheat, beans, pumpkins, &c., which they gladly traded for our old worn-out clothes. They brought us one watermelon that had been preserved from last year. We travelled about sixty miles through their territory without seeing any appearance of irrigation, from which we may safely infer that they cultivate their crops without having recourse to this process. There can be no doubt, however, but that it would add very materially to the amount of agricultural productions, if irrigation were employed.

Very little grass is to be seen in this valley. Our sheep ate readily of the *Obione canescens*, (grease-wood,) which grows abundantly throughout this whole region. Our mules were very fond of an aromatic shrub, of quite a low stature, which grows in considerable quantities on the gravelly ridges of both sides of the Colorado. It had shed its seed, but, accidentally, a few poor specimens were found—enough to determine it to belong to ambrosiæ, a sub-division of compositæ. Of this tribe there are in the Eastern States several species, of which cattle and horses are very fond.

The value of the Colorado valley, in affording subsistence to a civilized population, was considered nearly equal to that of the Rio Grande valley, which, in some respects, it a good deal resembles. The soil is better adapted to the cultivation of cereals than that of the Rio Grande, where it can only be done by the assistance of irrigation, which, in this country, is a costly process.

On leaving the valley of the Colorado, we ascended very rapidly about four thousand feet above the level of the sea, where the change of climate is very strongly marked. At the Colorado it is very warm and summer-like, while at our camp (6th March) on the northern slopes of the hills and in deep ravines there was snow. Here we met with cedar (Juniperus occidentalis) and pine, (Pinus edulis,) which, however, only greet the eye but a short distance. It may be possible that the New Mexican yellow pine (*Pinus brachyptera*) will be found in still higher points of this range in this neighborhood, but, on account of our necessarily rapid movements, we had not time to determine. In addition to the trees already mentioned, we noticed here vast quantities of the tree Yucca, called by the Mexicans *Palma*. It was seen before on Bill Williams' fork, but it is found here from twenty-five to thirty-five feet in height, and eighteen inches or two feet in diameter, with a bark on the lower part of the trunk very much resembling that of white oak. Although not good for fuel, we were sometimes under the necessity of resorting to it for camping purposes. Besides these, we saw here a variety of shrubs, the principal of which are two species of Rhus, (one of which I had never before seen,) blue-berried Berberis, Cowania Stansburiana, Fallugia paradoxa, Shrubby artemisia, Obione, and a shrubby Amygdalus or Cerasus, which very much resembles one common on Devil's river, in lower Texas. A species of Chilopsis, a bignoniaceous shrub, or small tree, with beautiful large flowers, much resembling those of a Catalpa, is frequently found in the dry ravines here, as also all over the western wilds. An undetermined species of Lycium, a solanaceous shrub, with an edible berry, was also collected here.

Besides some new cactaceæ, which will be mentioned soon, we found here several species, supposed to be peculiar to the Rio Grande valley; among them are Opuntia clavata and O. fragilis. A flat-jointed Opuntia, with long brown spines, collected before as far back as the Llano Estacado, which was considered very near *Op. phœacantha* of the Rio Grande valley, was also found on this part of our route. Also an aggregate Cereus, which cannot be distinguished, in the absence of flower and fruit, from allied species on the Rio Grande. Besides the *Echinocactus Wislizeni*, which is quite common here, we found a new species of the same genus, aggregated in large globose or ovate heads.

The fruit is crowned with the dry flower, and is thickly covered with a whitish wool; the scales are lanceolate-subulate; and the seeds pyriform, black, and rugose. The aggregated form of this plant is peculiar, and an exception to the general habit of the genus. It had already passed flowering, (March 2d,) and matured its fruit.

After crossing the dividing ridge between the Rio Colorado and Mojave creek, we saw the celebrated, but totally useless, *Larrea Mexicana*, or creosote plant, giving the surrounding scenery a most beautiful and verdant appearance. This plant is one of the most repulsive that can well be imagined. It is the surest indication of a sterile, worthless soil that can be found in the vegetable kingdom; for wherever it flourishes, little else can be found.

Section X. *Mojave Valley.*—This region extends from Soda lake to Cajon Pass, a distance of about one hundred and thirty miles. With the exception of the last twenty-five miles, it is entirely along the Mojave creek. There are beautiful grassy plains in this valley, within reach of clear, sweet, running water, where, we were told, it was a great grazing resort for those mules, horses, and cattle, preparatory to crossing the desert of a part of the Salt Lake valley; before the California gold excitement, animals were sent from the valley of Los Angeles, and its vicinity, to Santa Fé, with profitable returns. Large herds were annually brought out to this place and grazed for that purpose. Since the revolution, stock of all kinds is in great demand, at very high rates, in California; and New Mexico, in her turn, now sends out large flocks of sheep, to supply, in part, those demands. Sometimes they are sent by the way of Salt Lake valley, and from thence, up this valley, to California. After crossing the desert of Salt Lake valley, they are generally permitted to stop here, and at the Cajon to recruit, so as to render them saleable on arriving at the settlements of California. At other times they are sent by the way of the valley of the Gila, and thence across the desert to San Diego. Our route is much more direct than either of the others, and better, too, if we may judge from our own explorations and the accounts of travellers. The enterprising Captain Aubrey would have taken his sheep over this route the present season, but for the hostility of the Mojave and other tribes of Indians who infest this region.

The stream of the Mojave is not continuous, but sinks and rises every few miles, after the manner of Bill Williams' fork, and the Rio Mimbres, in New Mexico. In some places the stream is large and bold, running with a swift current, like the Mimbres. The soil in the widened valleys is rich, and appears to be capable of cultivation without irrigation. In such case it will make a valuable territory, well suited to settlements and military posts.

The timber of the valley is much like that of the Colorado, consisting of cotton-wood, (*Populus monilifera,*) mezquite, (*Algarobia glandulosa,*) curly mezquite, (*Strombocarpa pubescens,*) and willow, (*Salix,*) of several species. On arriving at the Cajon Pass, two kinds of cedars occur; pines, three or four kinds—Oregon pine, (*Pinus Douglassii,*) piñon, or nut pine, (*P. monophylla, Torr.;*) and on the neighboring mountains, the sugar pine, (*P. Lambertiana,*) and one other species, somewhat resembling, but different from, the New Mexican yellow pine. All of these occur in great abundance, and of the best quality. Immediately on passing the crest of the Cajon, the vegetation changes like magic. Many of the shrubs being such as we had never before seen, the mountains and hills were covered and green with their perennial foliage. Among the most beautiful we found several species of Ceonothus, (represented at home chiefly by the New Jersey tea,) ornamented with bright, cerulean blue flowers, in charming contrast with the leafless waste that we had just left. We collected at this place specimens of the new remarkable genus *Fremontia*, which is described and figured in *Plantæ Fremontianæ*, (*p.* 6, *pl.* 2: 1850,) by Dr. Torrey. The whole tree has very much the habit of Hibiscus syriacus, or common Althea shrub; but, according to Dr. Torrey, it belongs to the family of Bombaceæ, and is very closely allied to the celebrated hand-tree of Mexico, (*Cheirostemon of Humboldt.*) A species of Yucca, different from the five or six other Texan and New Mexican species that we had seen before, was collected at this place. A beautiful evergreen oak, with very large cups and acorns, was first found at this pass. Not having proper books of reference at hand, it is impossible at this time to determine the species. But the acorn is the one on which the *Digger Indians*, of California, are known to subsist for a great portion of the year. When standing in an open space, it forms one of the most beautiful and graceful trees of the forest.

The Cactus tribe in this valley is not so plentiful in species or numbers as in some of the regions just described; yet we found an Echinocactus here that had not been seen before. It may be the *E. viridescens, Nutt. Var? cylindraceus,* collected by Dr. Parry "near San Felipe, on the eastern slope of the California mountains;" but in the absence of the fruit, or flower, or even a good description of the original plant itself, it is impossible to decide with certainty. Dr. Engelmann's *Mamillaria tetrancistra,* collected by Dr. Parry on the desert between San Diego and the junction of the Gila with the Colorado, was collected here, as also on Bill Williams' fork; but the long, hooked central spines vary from one to four in number.

Section XI. *Los Angeles Valley.*—From Cajon Pass to the sea, at San Pedro, is a distance of about eighty miles through a beautiful valley, requiring very little description, in consequence of its having been long known. It was first settled by the Spaniards soon after the discovery of this part of the continent. It is well wooded and watered. We had not time to examine the timber of the mountains in this vicinity on account of our hasty march. In the preceding portion of our route we mentioned the trees seen at Cajon Pass; and as we passed down Cajon creek we saw the California sycamore, (*Platanus Mexicanus*,) alder, (*Alnus*,) of quite a respectable size, and cotton-wood; and as we proceeded on to the plains there were collected two other species of oaks which grew in great abundance; neither of them in fruit, however, at the time we passed. The base of the mountains to our right was covered with this timber.

Grass and wild oats are abundant in the valley from one end to the other. Nature has peculiarly favored this region, and adapted it to grazing, by furnishing it with a succession of plants, which come on in regular succession; so that no trouble or expense is experienced in raising cattle and horses, except for salting and keeping them tame. The first crop is called "pin-grass," (*Erodium cicutarium*,) belonging to the family of *Geraniaceæ;* the next is a crop of leguminous plants, such as Medicago, and several species of clover, (*Trifolium*,) which spring up one after another; then follow wild oats (*Avena*) and other species of grass in great abundance.

At the Cajon valley there are several species of cactaceæ, both flat-jointed and cylindrical, with a woody axis, which are somewhat different from those passed in the Colorado valley.

At Cocomungo, in this valley, we found vast and dense patches of an Opuntia, nearly akin to *O. Engelmanni*, which had the appearance of having been introduced; but whether it really is so, cannot be determined. The Spanish *Tuna*, (*Opuntia Tuna*,) which is cultivated for its fruit, forms hedges fifteen or twenty feet high. The Indians and Mexicans are very fond of the fruit, which serves them for food during its season.

At the mission of San Gabriel we saw large orchards of orange trees laden with its golden fruit, which ripens perfectly in the open air, (22d May.) We could say nothing more favorable of the climate of this delightful region. There are many other exotic plants that would succeed with very little trouble; the tea plant especially we think would do well, and deserves a thorough trial. The grapes cultivated here are said to be equal to any in the world.

No. 2.

DESCRIPTION OF FOREST TREES.

BY J. M. BIGELOW, M. D.

PINUS (Abies) DOUGLASII.—*Douglas Spruce*, or called simply *Spruce* in some regions; *Oregon Pine* about *San Francisco;* and *Hemlock* in other places.

The first place on the route where it is found is on the Sandia mountains, east of the Rio Grande, and between it and the Rio Pecos. It grows there abundantly. It next occurs on what is called the Sierra Madre, about ninety miles west of the Rio Grande, and is there also quite abundant. We again observed it, but rather sparingly, in the mountains around Zuñi.

After crossing the Rio Colorado Chiquito we come to a range of mountains, of which the most elevated and prominent peaks, near where we passed, were San Francisco, Bill Williams, and Mount Sitgreaves. Here was a belt of forty-five miles or more in width, stretching in a southeasterly direction to the Mogoyon or Sierra Blanca, probably as far as the headwaters of the Gila. At the Copper Mines, near the Gila, I found it in abundance in 1851, as well as at the Organ mountains, near Doña Ana, while connected with the Mexican boundary survey. At Aztec Pass, one hundred miles west of San Francisco, it is found again, but not so abundantly as at the latter mountain. As soon as we reached the Sierra Nevada, and along the whole Coast range as far as Los Angeles, it showed itself in the greatest abundance. It grows also in almost every mountainous region of California, from the coast to the highest range of the Sierra Nevada. On the mountains of the Sierra Madre, east and west of the Rio Grande, at San Francisco and its vicinity near the two Colorados, at the Organ mountains and those of the Mimbres near the Copper Mines, this tree grows from ninety to one hundred and twenty feet in height, and from three to six feet in diameter. In California it is found of a much larger size, frequently attaining the height of two hundred feet or more, and from six to nine feet in diameter. The wood is coarse-grained, tough, and hard—so much so as to preclude its being used as pine lumber; but it forms most excellent building timber. At San Francisco, Sacramento, and other cities of California, this timber is used almost exclusively for making plank-roads, side-walks, and piling. Probably one-fourth of the city of San Francisco is thus built on piles, driven from ten to fifteen feet into the ground. The wharves at the latter place are built exclusively of this timber.

From its abundance and widely-extended range, it will be seen that this tree will form one of the most valuable timber products of the proposed line; and, from what I have seen of its applicability to purposes of this kind, I have no hesitation in affirming that it will make railroad ties, equal, if not superior, to those of any other wood in the West. This tree has been well characterized, and a good figure of the fruit, cone, and branch given in Hooker's Flor. Boreali Americana.

PINUS (Abies) BALSAMEA.—Common name *Balsam*, or *Balsam Fir*.

It is identical with the one growing in the eastern States in such abundance. We found it only on the more elevated points of the Sandia, San Francisco, and Sierra Nevada mountains. It was not seen by us at the Cajon Pass of the Sierra Nevada, but I have no doubt it exists on the more elevated peaks of that region. Near Sonora and Downieville, in California, it grows to a great height, equalling that of the sugar and yellow pines. It forms a beautiful tree; but, from the perishable nature of the wood, it can scarcely be used for railroad purposes, except in places where it is protected from the disorganizing influences of the weather. The process of kyanization would probably have the effect to render it more valuable. It is an old and well-known species. In places where it abounds it is used for various building purposes, where not exposed to the weather, for which it is admirably adapted by its straight axis and beautiful taper. The balsam, which is an exudation from the bark, is medicinal, and held in high esteem as a remedy for burns and various other diseases.

PINUS BRACHYPTERA.—Called *Yellow Pine* in some regions, and *Pitch Pine* in others.

This is quite a different tree from either of the pines so called in the Eastern States. It is very common all over New Mexico and California. This tree is most generally associated with Douglas spruce, first making its appearance on the mountains between the Pecos and the Rio Grande. It grows abundantly about Santa Fé, in New Mexico, and was described first by Dr. Engelmann, from specimens collected by Dr. Wislizenus. Dr. Torrey (Report of Sitgreaves' Expedition, p. 173) mentions that Dr. Engelmann's *P. Macrophylla* was found at the Zuñi mountains. He says, however, it does not agree well with Engelmann's description. We found only this one so common in all that region, and suspect it is the one to which he has reference. It occurs at the Sandia and Organ mountains, east of the Rio Grande, at the Mimbres mountains, Sierra Mogoyon, San Francisco, Aztec Pass, and on the Sierra Nevada, near Mount San Bernardino. In every region of California, also, where the Douglas spruce is known to exist, this tree grows. I think, however, that it is found more abundantly in the interior of California, along the spurs and heights of the Sierra Nevada, than along the Coast range, where the Douglas spruce is the most abundant. In all these places it forms a beautiful timber tree. East of the Sierra Nevada it rises to the height of one hundred feet, with a diameter of five or six feet. On the western slopes of the Sierra Nevada, like the spruce and other pines, it grows much larger and taller. In favorable situations, it equals in height the other pines of those regions.

The wood of this tree is soft and easily worked, and varieties of it are equal in beauty and utility to the wood of any other pine. About Santa Fé, Albuquerque, Anton Chico, San Miguel, and all the towns on the upper Rio Grande, and Pecos, it forms their principal lumber. It exists so abundantly on the Mimbres, the Organ mountains, and on the mountains further east, bordering the Pecos, as to supply San Elizario, El Paso, Doña Ana, and all the lower towns of the Rio Grande, with lumber. It is also used in every part of California for building and other domestic purposes. On account of the softness of the wood, it is thought it would not answer as well for railroad ties as the Douglas spruce. The accompanying profile, on which I have attempted to illustrate the relative ranges of these trees above the level of the sea, approximates pretty nearly the truth. Although the range of this pine is very intimately associated with the Douglas spruce, yet, on reference to the profile, we shall see that it is found at a greater altitude, although the two species frequently overlap each other on the sides of mountain slopes. The Douglas spruce occupies the lower, and this species the upper portions of the mountain chains.

I am not aware that a good figure of this tree has ever been made. It was first brought to the notice of botanists and the public by Dr. Engelmann, in Wislizenus' Report, in 1848.

PINUS EDULIS.—Called *Piñon* by the Mexicans; *Nut Pine of New Mexico,* by Americans. The fruit of it is called by Mexicans *Piñones.*

In every place, from the bluffs of the Llano Estacado, about one hundred and sixty miles east of the Rio Pecos, to the Cajon Pass of the Sierra Nevada, this tree is found to be closely associated with cedars. It seldom grows large. A little west of the San Francisco mountain, and at the Cajon, it is found from forty to fifty feet high, but further east it seldom attains more than twenty-four. Its usual height, however, is about thirty feet. The timber is seldom used for domestic purposes, and I am, therefore, unable to express an opinion of its fitness for railroad lumber. The wood is tough and elastic, but with regard to its durability when exposed to the vicissitudes of the weather, I am unable to give an opinion.

From its extensive diffusion along the route, it would be of great value should it prove durable, for in other respects it would be well adapted to railroad purposes. On the other hand, should it be subject to early decay, I have no doubt but that subjecting it to the process of kyanization, as resorted to in the English railroad system, would obviate the difficulty, and prove with us, as with them, more economical in the end, although rather expensive at first. This might be the case even with our more durable species.

Its range of elevation above the sea-level is wider, and it is more extensively diffused than the species before mentioned. I have not seen it, however, on the western slopes of the Sierra Nevada above Los Angeles, nor in the upper portions of California.

The nut is sweet and edible, about the size of a hazel-nut. It is used as an article of trade by the New Mexicans of the upper Rio Grande with those below, and about El Paso. The fruit has a slightly terebinthine taste; but the New Mexicans are very fond of it. When it is considered how expensive it is to cultivate corn in those arid regions, where irrigation is necessary, one would naturally infer that an oil-nut as easily and abundantly produced as the piñon, would be an article of the first importance; and I have no doubt such will be the case when the country comes to be occupied by an enterprising and intelligent race. In the fattening of swine, this tree would receive a share of public attention. Bears and other animals, in large numbers, are known to subsist upon the fruit in those regions.

Dr. Engelmann (Bot. Sketch, Wislizenus' Report, p. 4, 1848) gave a description of this tree under the name used above, and Dr. Torrey (Sitgreaves' Report, Pl. 20) has given an excellent figure of the same. Three years previously, Dr. Torrey (Report Fremont's Exploring Expedition, p. 319, 1845) described and figured a species of pine under the name of P. MONOPHYLLUS, or the *Nut Pine of California,* which, according to Fremont, is "extensively diffused over the mountains of northern California, from longitude 111° to 120°, and through a considerable range of latitude." Dr. Engelmann, in the work previously referred to, describes another closely allied species under the title of *P. osteosperma,* the *Nut Pine of northeastern Mexico,* collected by Dr. Gregg on the battle-field of Buena Vista, with the remark, that the "cone and seeds are similar to both others," *i. e., P. edulis* and *P. monophyllus.* A comparison of the two figures of Dr. Torrey, in Fremont's and Sitgreaves' Reports, will hardly fail to convince the most skeptical that they are varieties of one species;[1] and consequently, Dr. Torrey's name having the priority, will have to be retained and adopted. The principal characteristics of the three species being in the number of leaves in the sheaths, varying from one to three, they fail to be distinctive marks. In Dr. Engelmann's two species, the leaves are exactly alike in both; the only difference being in the hard and soft shell, which is scarcely sufficient for a specific separation. Indeed, the California specimens I found at the Cajon had a testa as hard as that of Dr. Engelmann's Mexican species; a fact also observed by Mr. Leroux with regard to the nut pine north of our line, on the Sierra Nevada mountains, about Walker's and Fremont's Passes. The extent of the eastern and western range of Fremont's plant is 9°

[1] See Dr. Torrey's remarks on *P. edulis,* in the Botanical Report of the Expedition.

of longitude. Mine extends from the Llano, 103°, to the Cajon, 118°, a range of 15°. I have also seen it south as far as the mountains of the Limpia, in about latitude 31° ; and Dr. Parry has collected it still further south, in the cañons of the Rio Grande, below Presidio del Norte.

Pinus flexilis.—*Rocky Mountain White Pine.*

We found this tree at the Sandia mountains of New Mexico, at an elevation of about 12,000 feet above the level of the sea. Dr. Engelmann observes, that it was collected about Santa Fé by Mr. Fendler. In its cones and habit it is closely allied to *Pinus strobus,* which is the white or Weymouth pine of the North and East. On the authority of Dr. James, who first discovered this species, it is asserted that the seeds are large and edible. The piñones in use about Santa Fé, however, Dr. Engelmann remarks, are the produce of the *P. edulis.*

At an elevation of the San Francisco mountain nearly equal that of the Sandia mountain, it was found again forming a large and beautiful tree one hundred to one hundred and thirty feet in height. These are the only two localities on our route where this pine was detected. I was not high enough on any of the points of the Sierra Nevada to know whether it grows there ; but at the proper elevation, there can be little doubt that it may be found there also.

With the quality of its wood, either for lumber or for railroad ties, I am entirely unacquainted ; but from its close affinity (as before intimated) with the Weymouth pine, which is a most valuable species, I have no doubt this tree will yet prove to be one of the most important on our route.

Juniperus virginiana.—*Red Cedar.*

In places along the Canadian river, near Sans Bois creek, and even as far west as Old Fort Arbuckle, this tree grows quite large, and in abundance. Large specimens of it, however, were not seen further west. Although it would be as durable as almost any other timber that could be procured, yet it is said to be too brittle for railroad ties.

On the bluffs of the Llano Estacado, and from that point west as far as the Cajon Pass, occur in many places, and sometimes in great abundance, two or three other species of cedar. Of a collection made by Dr. Woodhouse, Dr. Torrey, in the "Report of an Expedition down the Zuñi and Colorado rivers, by Captain Sitgreaves," observes "that one may be *Juniperus occidentalis,* (*Hook,*) the second *J. tetragona,* (*Schlect.,*) while the third is probably new." Mine are probably all included in his list ; and if so excellent a botanist as Dr. Torrey is in doubt in reference to the species and varieties of these plants, it would be folly in me to attempt to reduce or determine them.

The trunks of the western varieties are too short to render them of much value for timber. The berries of most of them (especially those of *J. occidentalis,* which has a large, slightly tuberculate fruit) are sweet and nutritious, affording sustenance to bears, wolves, and a variety of other animals, if not the Indian himself.

Algarobia glandulosa.—*Mezquit.*

Trees of this species are found considerably east of the Pecos and Rio Grande valleys, but mostly in a shrubby state. In the valleys of the Colorado Chiquito, San Maria, Colorado Grande, and Mojave, this tree grows to a considerable size. In Southwestern Texas and in the eastern regions of Mexico it is considered invaluable from its extreme durability. Fences made of this timber in that part of Texas have been known to stand in a perfect state of preservation more than fifty years. From its hardness and durability, there can be no doubt but that it would make ties equal to the lignumvitæ of tropical climates ; to which it is, indeed, closely allied botanically, belonging to the section Mimoseæ of leguminous plants.

Besides the Strombocarpa Pubescens, (Mexican *tornillo,*) a genus closely allied to Algarobia, there are other trees of this order abounding along the valley of Bill Williams' fork, attaining the size of the mezquit; but I have not had an opportunity of determining their names. One of them is described by Major Emory, in his report, as the "Green-bark Acacia." An interesting fact respecting this tree is, that it forms a shelter for the propagation of the *Cereus giganteus* of that region. Every young cereus is protected and fostered by this tree until the cactus attains the size and hardihood that enables it to withstand the war of elements waged against it, when it ungraciously spurns its protector, ultimately destroying it, as we saw in numerous instances on our journey.

POPULUS MONILIFERA—in Spanish, *Alamo.—Cotton-wood.—Poplar.*

This tree is somewhat different from the cotton-wood of the Mississippi, which I believe is *P. angulata.* It is found east as far as the Canadian, and west until we cross the Sierra Nevada. In the Rio Grande valley it is used by the Mexicans for building. It is also employed for farming utensils, the most unique of which is their cart, or *caretta,* the wheels being made of a section of the tree. They are six or eight inches thick, and manufactured in the rudest manner. The timber is tough and hard; and although probably not as durable when exposed to the weather as some other kinds, yet I have no doubt it would answer very well for railroad ties, until a road could be formed to regions where more desirable timbers abound. It does not grow here near as tall as on the Mississippi river, but occasionally it is quite large and spreading.

QUERCUS.

Of the valuable genus of *Oaks,* we find about Fort Smith, and west as far as the Cross Timbers, all the varieties that are common to the more eastern States, all of which are well known. Besides the several species mentioned by Dr. Torrey, in Captain Sitgreaves' Report, most of which are doubtless in my collection, we found, at the Cajon Pass of the Sierra Nevada, a live-oak with a cupule an inch or an inch and a half in diameter. It is a beautiful and valuable timber tree, and doubtless it is a well-known Californian oak. It grows in various parts of California; but how widely it is diffused, I am unable to determine. It attains the height of eighty to one hundred feet, and is from two to four feet in diameter. The timber, from the character of the tree, must be valuable.

DESCRIPTIONS OF VALUABLE OR REMARKABLE CALIFORNIA FOREST TREES.

PINUS LAMBERTIANA, OR SUGAR-PINE.

This is one of the most magnificent pines of the Sierra Nevada. We first noticed its appearance at San Bernardino, not far from San Diego; and it probably follows the course of the Sierra Nevada to Oregon. At Sonora, Mokelumne Hill, Nevada City, Downieville, and every place where I visited those mountains, at an elevation of 4,000 or 5,000 feet above the level of the sea, this noble tree is found in perfection. It ordinarily attains the height of two hundred feet, and is six to ten feet in diameter. It is very symmetrical and beautiful in shape, with a slender but graceful foliage, in which characters it probably exceeds every other pine tree of California. It forms a timber equal to that of any other in the world. Its grain is so straight and even, that thousands of houses in California are weather-boarded with shingles, which are merely split, without any other expense or work. There are many mills in the vicinity of Downieville, Nevada City, Grass Valley, and Sonora, where lumber is manufactured and planed, by means of machinery, in quantities sufficient to supply vast regions in that country. Were it not that transportation is so expensive in California, the rapidly-increasing cities of San Francisco, Sacramento, and all the coast region could be supplied with lumber of a quality far superior to that brought from Oregon, with which their markets are now mainly furnished.

Professor Lindley (Vegetable Kingdom, page 228) observes of this tree and *Abies Douglasii*, that "they are probably the most valuable fir timbers of the whole family." And it will be remembered, the pine tribe stands at the head of the list of timber trees.

Wellingtonia gigantea.

This tree is popularly known, in the district where it grows, as the "*Mammoth Washington Tree.*" At this time it probably possesses more interest than any other American tree. Our backwoodsmen have known of its existence ever since the beginning of the California gold excitement, for it grows very near a rich auriferous region, about equidistant from Sonora and Mokelumne Hill, both of which districts are much resorted to by emigrants and gold-seekers. The so-called Mammoth Grove is north of those places, near the head-waters of Calaveras and Mokelumne rivers. Dr. Randall, the worthy president of the California Academy of Natural Sciences, had his attention called to the tree several years ago, and was persuaded it possessed characters generically distinct from the redwood, (*Sequoia sempervirens,*) and sent, more than eighteen months ago, large and beautiful specimens of this tree, besides many other rare and new botanical specimens, to Drs. Torrey and Gray. Most unfortunately, the specimens were lost in the transit of the isthmus. Doubly unfortunate has it happened to us as *Americans*, because we have been anticipated, and prevented from giving it a proud American name, the Washingtonia. Dr. Randall and his friends, being convinced of its being the type of a new genus, proposed to call it after our revered Washington, but not having books of reference at hand, he sent specimens (which, as before stated, were lost) to Drs. Torrey and Gray, for the purpose of having the tree described and published. In the mean time, Mr. Lobb, a seed collector for some society in Scotland, sent home enough to characterize the plant, which was done by Professor Lindley, in the London Gardeners' Chronicle. However, we must now be contented with the possession of the tree, as England must be with the empty name. From recent researches of Dr. Torry, I believe he is pretty well satisfied that this tree is not generically distinct from the redwood, and has bestowed on it the name of Sequoia gigantea. A good generic character of this family is contained in the staminate flowers and stamens; and when these are procured and examined, this question can be satisfactorily settled.

As considerable discussion has already been had with regard to the age of this tree, I may state, that when I visited it in May last, at a section of it eighteen feet from the stump, it was fourteen and a half feet in diameter. As the diminution of the size of the annual rings of growth, from the heart or centre, to the circumference or sapwood, appeared to be pretty regular, I placed my hand midway, roughly measuring six inches, and carefully counted the rings on that space, which numbered one hundred and thirty, making the tree 1,885 years old. Since I came home, Dr. Torrey tells me he has actually counted every ring of a section of the tree, and found the number a little over 1,100. This makes a great discrepancy with Professor Lindley's account in the Gardeners' Chronicle, where it is estimated at more than 3,000 years. I believe it is asserted in the Chronicle that it must have germinated when Moses was a little boy!

A verbal or written description of the size of this tree, however accurate, cannot give one an adequate idea of its dimensions. It required thirty-one of my paces (of three feet each) to measure thus rudely its circumference at the stump. The only way it could be felled was by boring repeatedly with pump augers. It required five men twenty-two days to perform the operation. After they had succeeded in severing it at the stump, the shoulders were so broad, and the tree so perfectly equipoised, that it took the same five men two days in driving wedges with a battering-ram on one side of the cut, to throw it out of its equilibrium sufficiently to make it fall. The mere felling of the tree, at California prices for wages, cost the sum of $550.

A short distance from this tree was another of larger dimensions, which, apparently, had been overthrown by accident some forty or fifty years ago. It was hollow for some distance, and when I was there, quite a rivulet was running through its cavity. The trunk was three hundred feet in length; the top broken off, and by some agency (probably fire) was destroyed.

At the distance of three hundred feet from the butt the trunk was forty feet in circumference, or more than twelve feet in diameter. Fragments of the same kind of tree, which had apparently been exposed to the vicissitudes of climate and weather the same length of time, and supposed to be from the individual tree that lies prostrate, are to be found projected in a line with the main body, one hundred and fifty feet from the top; proving to a degree of moral certainty that the tree, when standing alive, must have attained the height of four hundred and fifty or five hundred feet!! At the butt it is one hundred and ten feet in circumference, or about thirty-six feet in diameter. On the bark, quite a soil had accumulated, on which considerable-sized shrubs were growing. Of these I collected specimens of currants and gooseberries on its body, from bushes elevated twenty-two feet from the ground.

The mammoth trees are situated in a dense forest of sugar and yellow pines, balsam fir, white cedar, (*Libocedrus decurrens*, which, in its foliage, much resembles the American arbor vitæ,) and a little yew, supposed to be *Taxus canadensis*. Although it does not greatly exceed some of these in height, yet its stately and majestic bearing strikes the beholder with awe and wonder, and one almost involuntarily bows to it as the king of the forest. The bark is of a dull brown color, varying much in thickness, sometimes being fifteen inches or more. The whole number of these trees in existence, young and old, does not exceed five hundred, and all are comprised within an area of about fifty acres. Only eighty or ninety of them are of a gigantic size. Their extremely limited locality and number forcibly impressed me with the belief that the species is soon to become extinct, as is further evinced by its slow reproduction. Indeed these giants of the forest are so marked in their rusty habit from their present associates, that we can hardly view them in their present relations, except as links connecting us with ages so long past, that they seem but reminiscences of an eternal bygone. They seem to require but the process of petrifaction to establish a complete palæontological era. If Professor Lindley's estimate of its age be correct, one tree only is propagated in six years; or, if Dr. Torrey be correct, one only in two years. A remarkable peculiarity I observed with regard to their fruit cones, namely, they were in every state of development, from the germ to the ripe fruit. I was near them about the middle of May, when the ground was literally covered with their cones and seed.

The leaves are triangular and scale-like, as in the cedars, but never dimorphous or expanded into flat lamina, like many others of the same tribe of Cupressinæ, as Dr. Gray supposed might be the case. The wood is deep red, much resembling that of the celebrated redwood of the Coast mountains, so that the two trees were confounded for a long time. The value of the wood for timber is a matter of speculation merely, as it is too limited in quantity and locality to excite much interest, except, indeed, to wrest it from its apparent doom by cultivating it in plantations. Such an experiment with so noble a tree would surely be worthy an assiduous and laborious trial.

SEQUOIA SEMPERVIRENS.—*Redwood.*

This, which was long known as the *Taxodium sempervirens* of Don, is a noble and splendid tree. It is found along the Coast mountains of California, from near the region of Monterey to Russian river, above the bay of Bodega; but, whether those are its extreme limits, I am unable to learn. It does not reach into the interior of the State, and is never found at any considerable distance from the Coast range of mountains. In the neighborhood of San Francisco, amid the deep mountain gorges, I have measured fallen trees eleven feet in diameter, and paced their length two hundred feet; and I have seen others standing which appeared very much taller, but I had not the time, nor the means at hand, to measure them. I have been told, however, by men of credibility, that they grow from one hundred and eighty to three hundred feet high. It has been but lately separated from the genus *Taxodium*. The gifted, but unfortunate Douglas, was among the first to notice the peculiar gigantic forms of these trees of California, and from this fact many English botanists ascribe to him the credit of discovering the still more gigantic Washingtonia. Another reason assigned for this opinion is, that he penetrated as far north as 38° 45′ north latitude, and saw gigantic trees, whence it is inferred he must have seen them both. But I have been assured by Dr. Randall, who was well acquainted with Douglas' botanizing localities, that he never penetrated inland while in California, much less that he visited the mountains of the Sierra Nevada; and, consequently, he could not have encountered the mammoth Washington tree.

Little has been written of the valuable qualities of the redwood for timber, it having come into general use but for a comparatively short time—that is, since the settlement of California by Americans. The wood resembles the cedar a good deal in lightness and susceptibility of polish, but it is of a slightly darker shade of red. In the rural districts, along the coast, farmers use it for making fencing rails; and it is almost certain to excite incredulity, to state the number of rails that can be made from a single tree. They are counted by thousands, as we count them by hundreds in the eastern States. For building purposes and cabinet work, it probably excels every other tree in California. In the cities and towns, where its transportation can be afforded, it takes the place of every other wood. Oregon lumber is frequently brought into the San Francisco market at a cheaper rate than it can be brought from the surrounding hills, only a few miles distant. The foliage of this tree is dimorphous, as in most of the cypress tribe; the younger and more thrifty branches having a two-ranked dilated lamina, as in the spruce, while the older ones assume the scale-like foliage of the cedar. I collected the old cones of last year's growth, but fear I failed to procure the seeds, all having already been shed.

LIBOCEDRUS DECURRENS.—*White Cedar.*

This tree, in California, is called "white cedar," but it is quite different from the tree of the same name in the eastern States. I presume it is so called from its having somewhat of a resemblance, in foliage and habit, to the American arbor vitæ. The fruit-cone, and the arrangement of the leaves, however, are quite different, and justify the botanist in separating it from the genus *Thuya*, to which it is closely allied. The excellent representation given by Dr. Torrey, in Plantæ Fremontianæ, (*Smithsonian Contributions to Knowledge*,) Plate 3, pp. 7 and 8, is correct, excepting that the fruit-cones are represented as being erect, whereas they are pendulous. This error probably resulted from the drawing having been made from dried specimens, rather than from nature. The tree is only to be found at an elevation of some four or five thousand feet above the level of the sea, in the Sierra Nevada mountains of California. I found it fifteen or twenty miles southeast of Sonora, on the head-waters of the Stanislaus and Tuolumne rivers, (both of which are considerable affluents of the San Joaquin,) south of 38° north latitude; and also on the head-waters of the Calaveras and Mokelumne rivers, in juxtaposition with the Washingtonia. Dr. Torrey remarks, that it ranges as high as 41° on the head-waters of the Sacramento river. In company with the Washingtonia, it appeared nearly as tall as that tree. It certainly attains a height of over two hundred feet. The timber is much sought for by farmers in that region for making rails and fencing-timber, as it is considered superior in durability to the other species of pine in the neighborhood. The wood is very light, of a dirty yellowish hue, and is thought to be more durable than redwood.

TORREYA CALIFORNICA.—*Nutmeg tree* of California.[1]

I found this interesting tree not very far from the coast, near Tomales bay, in a deep ravine, called "the Redwoods." I am told that it grows also on the American fork of the Sacramento river. I was anxious to obtain the one from the latter locality, in order to determine whether it might not be a different species from that which grows near the coast, as the plants of the coast and Sierra Nevada mountain seldom intermingle. It has a foliage very similar to the spruce, but the fruit is very characteristic and different in appearance from any of the family in

[1] See a description of this tree by Dr. Torrey, in the New York Journal of Pharmacy, Vol. 2. It has since been described by Sir William Hooker, in the Botanical Magazine, under the name of Torreya Myristica.

America. It very much resembles the nutmeg—so much so, indeed, as at one time to deceive some pretty well informed persons, and make them believe it was not a "*wooden nutmeg,*" but a nutmeg in *fact*—in quality as well as in appearance. It is a great pity that dame Nature should amuse herself by playing such pranks, and endanger the monopoly of our good Yankee friends in the manufacture of this aromatic luxury!

This tree grows from forty to fifty feet high, with very slender, drooping branches, and a thin, light foliage. The bark is smooth, somewhat resembling that of the common black mulberry, and the wood hard and firm. Very little is known with regard to its durability or fitness for timber for railroad or domestic purposes. It is closely related to the Podocarpus of tropical regions, and yews, which are common to the temperate regions of Europe and America. According to Professor Lindley, these, and kindred genera, yield "timber which is unsurpassed for durability and elasticity;" from which we may safely infer that the timber of this tree, when it comes to be known and tried, will prove to be truly valuable.

Unfortunately, we were not in California at the season for collecting the nuts, all of these having been long before destroyed by squirrels, rats, and other vermin, which are said to be exceedingly fond of them. According to the statement of Dr. Randall, the nut is too bitter and terebinthinate to be of any use in domestic economy; but no doubt it would make an excellent remedial agent in many diseases.

The true nutmeg is a native of the tropics of India and America, and widely separated from this tree in its botanical relationship.

TAXUS CANADENSIS.—*Yew.*

I much regretted being unable to obtain the fruit of this plant. It grows in the forest, with the giant Washingtonia, and also at Downieville, about a degree and a half further north. Mr. Lobb, while there, pronounced it (without seeing the fruit, however) the *Taxus baccatus*, which is the European species. The tree is small, but the wood is very tough and elastic, being much prized by the Indians for making their bows. On examination of its fruit and seeds, it may turn out to be quite a distinct species from its Eastern congener.

PINUS SABINIANA.—*Sabine's pine.*

This tree is so called by Dr. Randall and other California botanists, who have paid special attention to this department of botany. From not having proper books at hand for reference, we are unable to determine by whom it was first noticed or described. It is found on the lower western slopes of the Sierra Nevada, about Sonora, Mokelumne Hill, Grass valley, and Nevada city. On ascending the mountains its place is taken by Douglas' spruce, sugar-pine, balsam-fir, white cedar, and the yellow pine, of that region. It bears a very large ovate cone, the scales of which are armed with large upturned, hooked spurs. The nut is said to be large and edible. This tree has not the erect and rigid appearance of most other pines, but is flexuous and crooked, like many deciduous-leaved trees. The foliage is also thin, of a very light green, giving it a very peculiar aspect, different from that of all other species of pine in California. The wood is tough and elastic; but with regard to its durability, when exposed to the weather, no means of determination were had, from the fact that it is seldom or never used in the districts where it grows. This results from the sugar and yellow pines being abundant, and much superior to it for lumber.

PINUS INSIGNIS.—*Seal pine.*

This pine, which I have named on the authority of Dr. Randall, is found along the Coast mountains, in the neighborhood of the city of San Francisco. It is found also on the Yuba river, in the vicinity of Nevada city. As it is not a very large tree, and neither used nor sought for in the neighborhood where it grows, the presumption is that it cannot be very valuable. This, however, is only a negative testimony against it, for it is surrounded and associated with other trees which are much superior to it in size and beauty.

PINUS.—*An undetermined species.*

High up in the mountains east of Sonora, (almost in the snowy regions,) and also at Cajon Pass, a pine was discovered very nearly related to the yellow pine of this country, (*P. brachyptera*,) but the cone is larger and more cylindric; the scales armed with a strong recurved spine; the leaves longer, regularly in threes, and with a longer sheath. A very good figure was made of this pine by our artist, Möllhausen. It is a large tree, with a lighter-colored bark than the *P. brachyptera*, and fully as valuable for its timber. I am not certain that it is a new species.

5. E. Emoryi, Engelm. in Emory's Report, 1848: globosus, costis 13 tuberculatis, tuberculis prominentibus obtusis distantibus; areolis ovatis; aculeis subæqualibus robustis annulatis subcompressis recurvatis s. rectiusculis fuscis versus apicem corneis, radialibus 7 (lateralibus 6, singulo inferiore breviore) s. addito summo rarius 8; centrali singulo teretiore paulo longiore robustioreque, porrecto s. demum deflexo curvato s. subuncinato. (Plate III, fig. 3.)

Collected west of the Colorado, in the valley of the Mojave, mixed with *E. Polycephalus*, and therefore not further noted. The only specimen preserved is 9 inches in diameter, sub-globose, below contracted, pear-shaped, or almost stiped.

On the lower part of the plant the areolæ are elevated on distinct ovate or sub-cylindric tubercles, which higher up become connected in 8 and on the upper part of the plant in 13 ribs; tubercles on this part of plant ½–¾ inch in height and diameter; areolæ 1½ inch distant, ½ inch long, a little less wide; the floral areolæ smaller, closely connected with the former, separated from it by 1–3 sub-globose glandular bodies, half or mostly hidden in the tomentum. Radial spines 1½–2 inches long; the four upper lateral ones longer and stouter, the two lower ones more slender; the lowest spine the shortest, (1–1½ inch long,) secured like the others, or rarely hooked, similar to the shape of that spine in *E. Viridescens*.

An eighth upper radial spine, similar to the others, is sometimes observed. The stouter central spine is about 2 inches long, at the point strongly recurved, or often almost hooked. Spines of a reddish-brown color, lighter horn-colored, and somewhat transparent at tip.

This is probably the plant collected and figured by Major William H. Emory, in General Kearny's expedition to California in the fall of 1846, and then named after him. We collected only one young specimen, probably on the Lower Colorado, from which this description is taken. Mr. Schott has found the plant abundantly south of the Gila river, and it is known to extend to the Gulf of California. We procured a large specimen in San Francisco, (said to have been brought from Guaymas,) which is now flourishing in the public garden at Washington. This species has, when full grown, a height of 3 and a diameter of 2 feet, and 18–21 ribs. The large flowers are deep red, similar in form to those of *E. Wislizeni*.

6. E. polycephalus (sp. nov.): globosus, demum ovatus cylindricusque multiceps, (e basi ramosus,) vertice dense tomentoso, costis 13–21 acutis; areolis ovate-orbiculatis junioribus tomentosissimis; aculeis 8–12 robustissimis compressis annulatis plus minus recurvatis junioribus puberulis cinereo rubellis apice nudatis rubicundis; aculeis radialibus 4–8 infimo deficiente, superioribus si extant gracilioribus; centralibus 4 robustissimis 4-angulatis compressis, superiore latiore suberecto s. sursum curvato, inferiore longiore decurvo; floribus in vertice congestis; ovario lana nivea ex axillis sepalorum 90–100 linearium demum spinescentium orta densissime vestito, sepalis tubi infundibuliformis 100–120 lineari-lanceolats aculeato-aristatis purpurascenbus, interioribus margine petaloideis, petalis laciniato-fimbriatis herbacea-aristatis sub-30 flavis, stigmatibus 8–11 linearibus acutis; bacca globosa sicca flore coronata, lana densa involuta; seminibus magnis irregulariter angulatis minutim (sub lente) verrucosis, opacis. (Pl. III, fig. 4–6.)

Stoney and gravelly hills and dry beds of torrents from 20 miles west of the Rio Colorado to about 150 miles westward up the Mojave; found in fruit in the beginning of March. This distinguished species is simple only when quite young; even the small globose plants show several heads from one base, and older cylindric stems have as many as 20 or 30 heads, all pretty nearly of the same size; the globose ones are 6–9 inches in diameter; the ovate heads are 12–15 inches high by 8–10 in diameter, and the largest cylindric stems seen were 2–2½ high by less than a foot in diameter. The number of ribs varies, in old specimens it is generally 21. Areolae about half an inch in diameter, and ¼–½ inch distant from one another; floral areolae smaller, without the ligneous glandular organs noticed in others. The spines in a young 5-ribbed living specimen before us are 7 radial and 1 central one; very soon, however, the 4 upper larger spines become central and 4 lower spines are arranged radially; even in old and full grown specimens sometimes not more than these 8 spines are found, the 4 upper ones (which are in this case perhaps rather improperly designated as central) stouter and cruciate, and the 4 lower ones arranged around the lower half of the areola. Generally, however, 2 upper radial spines, weaker and less curved than the 4 lower ones, make their appearance; and in a few specimens before us we find 3–4 upper radial spines, the uppermost ones being quite slender.

In the field we noted as many as 15 spines occasionally, when no doubt 7 occupy the place of upper radial ones. The central spines are always very stout but very different in size; in some specimens we find them 1¼ to 1¾, while in others they are 2 to 3½ inches long; they are nearly straight or very much curved; the upper one is often 1½ to 2 lines wide, the lower one the longest.

The yellow flowers seem to make their appearance in February as the fruit ripens in March; the ovary and the fruit are enveloped in dense pure white cottony wool, which originates from the axis of the lower sepals and through which only the dark reddish-brown spinulose points of the sepals are visible. The incomplete description of the flowers was made from withered specimens adhering to the fruit. Tube of flower funnel-shaped, short and rapidly widening towards the upper end, naked (without free stamina) at the lower part. Petals about 1 inch long and 2 lines wide. Style 1–1½ inch long, stigmata 4 lines long. Fruit dry 8–10 lines in diameter, together with the remnants of the flower about 2 inches long, open at base when falling off; like the fruit of many if not most of our *Echinocacti*, seeds 2 lines long, 1½ line broad, irregularly shrivelled, appearing rugose and angular, much like those of the nearly allied *E. laticostatus*, (*horizonthalonius Lem.*); hilum transversely oval; embryo curved, the cotyledons buried in the large albumen, accumbent, sometimes oblique.

This species is very nearly allied to *E. Parryi*, Englm. Synops. Cact. of the neighborhood of El Paso, but this latter species is depressed globose, much smaller, simple, with only 13 ribs, whiter, less flattened spines; fruit and seed are said to be the same, but unfortunately have been lost and cannot be compared; no doubt satisfactory diagnostic characters will be dicovered in the seeds; the fruit of *E. horizonthalonius* and *E. Texensis* are also similar, the latter, however, though woolly, is not dry.

Very different in flower and fruit but very similar in shape, in the many heads, numerous ribs, and stout curved annulated spines, is *E. cylindraceus*, discovered by Dr. Parry a few degrees further south on the eastern slope of the Sierra. We shall repeatedly have occasion, especially among the *Opuntiæ*, to indicate the remarkable analogies in the external form or in the more essential character of *Cactaceæ* in different geographical divisions of the southwest.

CEREUS, Haw.

Subgen. Echinocereus.

1. Cereus viridiflorus, Englm. in Wisl. Rep. Subnom. *Echinocereus*.

On the plains east of New Mexico, near the 100th degree of longitude, to the mountains of the Rio Grande, September 12, 1853.

2. C. cæspitosus, Englm. in Plant. Lindh. l. c. The most eastern of all our *Cerei!* and only found in the plains. It was first seen about 170 miles west of Fort Smith, near the 96th degree, about the same longitute where Mr. Lindheimer first discovered it on the Brazos, four degrees further south. Its western limit seems to be near the 100th degree, where the range of *C. viridiflorus* commences.

It may not be uninteresting to observe that this is the first time that this interesting genus has been recognized within the boundaries of the United States under the acquisition of Louisiana.

3. C. Fendleri, Englm. in Pl. Fendl.: Seen first on the high plains 50 miles east of the Pecos, about the 105th degree, and extending from there over the mountains of New Mexico westward to the Aztec mountains, near the 113th degree. Southward it has been seen as far as El Paso.

The ovate or mostly elongated cylindric heads are simple or few together, and of a dark green color; they are characterized by the dark central spine, which is very bulbous and curved upwards, and by the lower radial spines being by far the stoutest, the lowest being 4–angular. Flower and fruit have been described elsewhere.

Var. β. pauperculus, with only about 6 spines, the central one assuming the place of an upper radial spine, was also found near the Pecos. It hardly deserves the designation of a distinct variety, as occasionally complete bunches of spines occur on the same plants with the depauperate ones.

4. C. Mojavensis (sp. nov.): ovatus, dense cæspitosus, 10–11–costatus, glaucescens; areolis orbiculatis junioribus dense albo-tomentosis distantibus; aculeis basi bulbosis teretiusculis s. subangulatis robustis elongatis curvatis, radialibus 7–8, infimo superioribusque debilioribus, lateralibus longioribus, centrali singulo angulato sursum incurvato. (Plate IV, fig. 8.)

Var. β? zuniensis: dense cæspitosis 10-costatus, areolis paulo minoribus, aculeis tenuioribus basi bulbosis quadrangulatis rectis s. paulo curvatis flexuosisve, radialibus 8 infimo graciliore, summo robustiore longioreque, centrali singulo robustiore longiore recto s. sursum incurvo. (Pl. IV, fig. 9.)

Found between the Rio Colorado and Mojave creek, with *Echinocactus polycephalus* and *Opuntia erinacea*, etc., a region rich in rare *Cactaceæ*. The oval heads, 2–3 inches high, and 1½–2 inches in diameter, form dense cespitose masses much like *C. phœniceus*. The areolæ are 3 lines in diameter, 6 lines or more distant from one another. The long and very bulbous spines are curved and interlocked so as almost to hide the body of the plant. Upper and lower radial spines 9–15 lines, the uppermost one wanting or weaker than the rest; lateral spines 15-25 lines long, ashy-red when young; central spine more angled 1½–2½ inches long, dusky; all spines ashy-gray when old.

C. Zuniensis seems to form an intermediate link between this and the next species, but resembles most the former, to which for the present—not knowing flower and fruit—we doubtfully draw it as a variety. It was found near Cañon Diablo, on the Colorado Chiquito, about 120 miles west of Zuñi. Its manner of growth and whole appearance is very much like that of the Mojave species, the spines are weaker, straighter, and more angular; the principal difference consists in the stout upper radial spine, which is similar to the central spine. Young areolæ nearly 3 lines in diameter, 4–6 lines distant; lowest radial spine 6–9 lines, lateral ones 9–15, and upper one 12–18 lines long; central spine 1½–2 inches long, very bulbous at base. Young spines straw colored, old ones ashy.

C. Mojavensis seems to be nearly allied to *C. Fendleri*, (in both the spines are very bulbous at base, the central one single, angular, and curved upwards,) but the cespitose growth, glaucous color, longer radial spines, the lowest one of which is weakest, seem to distinguish it. The examination of numerous specimens *in loco*, and the flower and fruit only can decide here whether they are distinct, or forms of a single species, and this indeed is the case with all those *Cactaceæ* the flower and fruit of which are unknown to us. *C. Zuniensis* was collected December 18, 1852, and the Mojave plant March 4, 1854.

5. C. gonacanthus (sp. nov.): ovatus simplex s. e basi parce ramosus costis 7 interruptis, areolis magnis orbiculatis distantibus, aculeis robustis angulatis rectis s. varie curvatis flexuosisve, radialibus 8, inferioribus lateralibusque quadrangulatis flavidis basi et sæpe apice obscuris,

infimo breviore, summo elongato robusto multangulo obscuro erecto aculeum centralem similem multangulatem erecto-patentem subæquante, rarius excedente. (Plate V, fig. 2–3.)

On high sand-bluffs, covered with scattering cedars, near the natural well, about 40 miles west of Zuñi, near the 109th degree. Only seen in that locality. This species resembles, in its growth and the character of its species, *C. triglochidiatus;* it is simple or has 2 or 3 heads, 3–5 inches high; the young areolæ are very tomentose, 3–4 lines in diameter, and 6–10 lines distant from one another; the lower radial spine is 8–12, the others 10–15 lines long, pale or dirty yellow when young; the upper radial spine is much stouter and longer than the others, and resembles the central spine in shape, size, and color; in the few specimens at our disposal, we find it from 1¼ to 2½ inches long; sometimes it assumes a more central place in the areolæ, the the two upper lateral spines almost closing above it, very rarely a small tenth spine appears above it. The central spine is 1½–2½ inches long, 1 line in diameter, deeply furrowed, and 6 or 7 angled; it is longer, equal to or rarely shorter, than the upper radial spine. Both those spines are almost black or mottled yellowish and black when young, and become, with all the others, gray when old. Collected November 29, 1853.

6. C. TRIGLOCHIDIATUS, Englm. in Wisl. Report, Sub-Echinocereo: In rocky cañons at the Rio Gallinas, east of the Pecos, and from there to the Sierra Madre, near Mount Taylor; not noticed farther west; always with few branches, or nearly simple. Major Brooks, the commandant of the fort at Santa Fé, informed me that the fruit of this species is edible, like many other allied species. Collected September 28, 1853.

7. C. HEXAËDRUS, (sp. nov.): ovatus, simplex seu e basi parce ramosus; costis 6 obtusiusculis subinterruptis, sulcis latis superficialibus, areolis orbiculatis distantibus; aculeis tenuioribus rectis rigidis subangulatis basi bulbosis, radialibus 5–7 e flavido rubellis, inferiore breviore, summo sæpe robustiore, centrali robustiore longiore acute-angulato juniore fuscato, sæpe deficiente. (Plate V, fig. 1.)

On sandy hills, under cedars, about fifteen miles west of Zuñi. Few heads 4–6 inches high, 2–2½ in diameter, with six obtusish ribs, separated by wide and shallow grooves. Areolæ tomentose when young, only 1½ line in diameter, 6 or 8 lines distant. Spines slender, but stiff; quite bulbous at base; lower ones 5–10, upper ones 8–15 lines long; mostly 6 radial spines, without a central one, the uppermost being the stoutest, longest, and darkest one, but smaller where a central spine is present. In a single instance, we found 7 radials, and in another one 2 compressed central spines; central spine usually 12–15 lines long. From the nearly allied, more southern *Cereus paucispinus*, Engl. ined., this northwestern form is principally distinguished by the slender and angular spines. But as of neither of them we know the flower and fruit, we cannot form definite conclusions as to their specific distinction. These forms and *C. triglochidiatus* have a smaller number of ribs than any other species of this section. Collected November 28, 1853.

8. C. PHOENICEUS, Englm. in Synop. Cact., *E. coccineus;* Englm. in Wisl. Rep. non De C. nec. Salm. (Pl. IV, fig. 1.) Found from the Upper Pecos to Albuquerque and Santa Fé, also five degrees further west, on the San Francisco mountains. The specimens perfectly agree with the description given in Wislizenus's report. The numerous heads, 2–3 inches high, about 2 inches in diameter, form dense cespitose masses, often one foot or more across. Areolæ 3–4 lines distant, large; spines slender, almost setaceous, with very slightly bulbous base, 8–12 radial ones, 3–6, 1–3 central ones 5–10 lines long; upper radial spines much shorter than lower ones.

The following form seems very distinct, especially in its manner of growth; but we have seen intermediate forms which seem to indicate the necessity of uniting both. Such questions, however, can only be solved satisfactorily by careful examination of flower and fruit, which are as yet unknown, and by extensive observation of these plants in their native wilds.

9. SUB-SPECIES C. CONOIDEUS: ovatus versus apicem conoideo-acutatus parce e basi ramosus, costis 9–11 tuberculatis, areolis orbiculatis s. subovatis junioribus albo-tomentosis, aculeis basi bulbosis, radialibus 10–12 tenuibus rigidis rectiusculis, summis brevibus, lateralibus inferioribusque longioribus, centralibus 4, (rare 3–5,) superioribus radiales vix superantibus infimo multo longoire 4–angulato sæpe complanato porrecto s. deflexo. (Plate 4, fig. 4–5.)

On rocky and mountainous localities on the Pecos, *Cer. Roemeri*, Muhlenpf., not Englm., from the San Saba, in Texas, seems to agree well with our plant, but the description is not full enough to decide about their identity.

Heads 3 4 inches high, single or few, of unequal height together; remarkable on account of their conical or acutish shape uniformly observed. Areolæ 4-6 lines distant; spines white or straw colored, larger central one often dusky when young; radial spines slightly bulbous at base; upper ones 2–5 lines, lateral ones 6–15 lines long, and lower ones hardly a little shorter; central spines very bulbous; upper ones not much longer than the lower radial ones; lower central spine sharply quadrangular, mostly compressed, often deflexed and curved, 1–3 inches long.

On the San Francisco mountains, a specimen was collected with 11 ribs, 8–9 radial spines, (4–12 lines long,) the uppermost shortest, and 3–4 reddish-gray central spines, very bulbous at base, the lowest longest (12–20 lines long) and angular. In superficial appearance, this plant resembles *C. Mojavensis*, but it must be referred here, and seems to indicate a range of this form through seven degrees of longitude.

A specimen from Anton Chico, on the Pecos, seems to unite *C. conoideus* with *C. phœniceus*. Areolæ more distant than the latter; spines longer; 3 central spines, lower one somewhat curved and angular. Collected September 28 and December 18, 1853.

10. C. ENGELMANNI, Parry, var. and VARIEGATUS: ovato-cylindricus simplex s. parce e basi ramosus 12-costatus, areolis orbiculatis approximatis, aculeis exterioribus sub-13 gracilibus rigidis albis apice sphacelatis adpressis lateralibus longioribus, summis deficientibus; aculeis centralibus 4 cruciatis (raro 5) plus minus curvatis infimo elongato angulato albo decurvato, ceteris brevioribus teretiusculis nigris corneisque variegatis; floribus ex axillis areolarum vetustiorum inferiorum; bacca ovata sicca pulvillis numerosis setas tenues albidas plurimas gerentibus stipata; seminibus obovato-subglobosis compressis rugoso-tuberculatis opacis. (Plate V, fig. 4–7.)

Var. *β?* CHRYSOCENTRUS, cylindricus parce e basi ramosus 10–12-costatus, areolis magnis; aculeis radialibus 12–14 albis superioribus setaceis brevibus, inferioribus longioribus robustioribus angulatis compressis rectis s. paulo incurvis, centralibus 4, superioribus rigidis robustis basi bulbosis angulatis rectiusculis elongatis, erectis vitellinis, inferiore angulato compresso albo recto paulo breviore deflexo; floribus ex inferiore plantæ parte; bacca ovata pulvillis paucis aculeos setosos longiores albos gerentibus stipata. (Plate V, fig. 8–10.)

On the Cactus mountains and at the head of Williams river, degrees 113½ longitude. Heads 4–9 inches high, single or few, not more than 4–6 together; areolæ 2–4 lines distant; radial spines 3–5 lines long, upper central spines 3 or sometimes 4, black on the upper, and horn-colored on the lower side and towards the point, 1–1½ inches long, lower central white, 1½–2 inches long. Position of fruit on lower half of plant much like that of *C. chloranthus*, *E. ined*, only 6–8 lines long, crowned with the remains of the (red?) flower. Seed 0.6–0.7 line long compressed, tubercles sometimes irregularly confluent and leaving pits between the ridges, lower part of the back with a smooth carina, hilum oval.

Var. *β* CHRYSOCENTRUS, named after its deep golden-yellow spines, is, probably, not specifically distinct, though the straighter, stouter, and less divergent spines give it a very peculiar appearance. It was found where *C. variegatus* disappears on the lower part of Williams' river, and was seen from there to the Mojave creek, and up that stream to the Sierra Nevada. Stems 5–10 inches high, areolæ 6–7 lines distant, young ones 2½–3 lines in diameter. Upper radial spines 3–5, lateral 5–7, and lower ones 7–12 lines long; the latter flattened and often curved up.

Upper central spines 3 or sometimes 4, 2–3 inches long, bulbous and angular at base, terete above; lower central spine 1½–2½ inches long, flattened. Spines on fruit 3–8 lines long, fewer and stouter than in the other form.

Cereus Engelmanni, Parry, has been found abundantly by Mr. A. Schott on the lower Gila; a specimen brought home evidently seems to unite them, and consequently *C. variegatus* and *C. chrysocentrus* are to be considered forms of it.

I am acquainted with the *habitus* of about 15 or 16 species of the subgenus Echinocereus. All of them are of low growth, (I write of those only with which I am acquainted,) never more than 12, seldom more than 8, and often less than 5 inches in height. All, also, are more or less cespitose, or branching from the root; some of them slightly, others very much so. *Cereus viridiflorus, chloranthus, dasyacanthus, ctenoides, cæspitosus, longisetus, Fendleri, gonacanthus, hexædrus, paucispinus*, and *Engelmanni*, grow in small irregular tufts, or masses, some of the joints or stems being much taller than others. Some of them, such as *C. viridiflorus, dasyacanthus, ctenoides, cæspitosus*, and *Fendleri*, are often nearly simple, or having but few branches; while others, such as *C. chloranthus, longisetus, gonacanthus, hexædrus, paucispinus*, and *Engelmanni*, have usually 8–20 joints. *C. polyacanthus, phœniceus*, and *enneacanthus* are much branched, and grow in somewhat flattened masses, sometimes with a circular outline, but not always, all the joints being of nearly an equal height. *C. stramineus* always forms a dense hemispherical mass, of a perfectly regular contour—the central joints being the oldest and longest—9–12 inches high, gradually subsiding towards the circumference of the mass until the extreme outer stems are not more than 2 inches high. *C. Mojavensis* often grows similarly, but I have also seen it in much broader masses, containing 500–800 heads or joints; in such cases it is always flattened on the top. Where this state occurs, the central joints are as high as in the hemispherical masses, but the hemispheric contour is destroyed by the longitudinal extension of the joints, forming masses sometimes 4 or 5 feet in diameter. *C. phœniceus* and *C. conoideus*, two forms which Dr. Engelmann has united into sub-species, are quite different in their manner of growth. *C. pheniceus*, as stated above, grows in irregular flattened masses, while *C. conoideus* has the more elevated and somewhat hemispherical shape of *C. stramineus.* On account of the unfavorable season of the year (October—March) during our journey through regions of these cacti, we were unable to procure the flower or fruit of any of these plants. In our friendly correspondence with Dr. Engelmann, I insist that *C. phœniceus* and *C. conoideus* are distinct species, and (from analogy only) I assume that when the flower of *C. conoideus* is obtained, it will be found to be a *purple*, while that of *C. phœniceus* is *crimson.* Time and observation, however, are the only decisive arbiters of such controversies.

Subgen. Eucereus.

Of *Cereus* proper only one species was seen, viz:

11. Cereus giganteus, Englm.: Williams' river to the Colorado of the west, February 4 to February 22, 1854. This is the most northern true *Cereus* that we have, being found as high as latitude 34°, while *Cer Greggii* and *Emoryi* are found only a little above latitude 32°. This plant has a considerable range, extending south, from this place to near latitude 28° in the vicinity of Guaymas Sonora. The fruit under the Mexican name of *Pitajaya*, pronounced Pit-a-zi-ah or Pit-ai-yah, is a great source of sustenance to the Mexicans and Indians of the regions where it grows. Conserves and molasses, or syrup, are made from them which are preserved during the winter season for future use. They are very pleasant to the taste in a fresh state. As the fruit grows near the top of the tree at an altitude of 25 to 50 feet and being very large and pulpy, if permitted to ripen and drop to the ground, they burst and are almost rendered unfit for use. The Indian mode of collecting them is to take a long light pole, make a fork at the top by tying a short piece to it, by which they contrive to bring them within reach. Birds and every kind of animal and insect that can reach them are so fond of them that man

of them are thus destroyed. My friend, Mr. Schott, of the Mexican boundary, who has lately returned from that desolate but rather interesting region, informs me that still further south this interesting plant is replaced by another not so large—but still a great cactus. This is very probably the one collected by Mr. Thurber, described and named by Dr. Engelmann, in Silliman's Journal, *Cer. Thurberi.* The pitajaya of this species, according to Mr. Schott, is the principal support of the Papige Indians. It is much larger, sweeter, more juicy than that of the *Cer. giganteus.* The color of the pulp is also of a much brighter red.

In consequence of the remote and unhospitable region of this curious and interesting cactus, our acquaintance with it became very gradual. Dr. Englemann thinks that Baron Von Humboldt, in his work on New Spain, must have had reference to this plant, but this is quite uncertain because no characteristics are given of his cacti (organos del Lunal) except size and edible fruit, and many other large species of both cerei and opuntiæ are long and well known to yield them. In 1846, Major Emory first collected seeds and made figures of it which, on being presented to Dr. Engelmann, he was unable to pronounce it a true *Cereus* and at that time very appropriately named it. Subsequently, (winter and spring of 1852,) Dr. Parry, under Major Emory, visited that region, collecting spines, wood, &c., and making copious notes on the ground, enabled Dr. Engelmann to give a good diagnosis of it. Still Dr. Parry was unable to procure the flower or fruit on account of the lateness of the season. It was reserved for Mr. Thurber, who repassed this region in the summer of 1852, to collect complete specimens, and Dr. Engelmann, in a subsequent number of Silliman's Journal, has given a complete description of it. (Vide Amer. Jour., Vol. XVII, 2d series, March, 1854.) To the several excellent accounts given of this tree by Dr. Engelmann, little of interest can be added. As noticed by Drs. Parry and Engelmann, the number of ribs at the base is about 12, and they "increase upward, by bifurcation and addition," to the largest circumference of the tree, which is about 15–18 feet from the ground, and where also usually the few branches are given off. Here the ribs sometimes number 30, and from this point upward they decrease in number to 18–20. The wood at the base of old specimens becomes a perfect hollow cylinder, and from thence upward to the first branches, instead of being solid it becomes a reticulated net-work of bundles of wood continuing the hollow cylinder as is seen on a smaller scale in the wood of *Opuntia arborescens.* These trees in abundance give the landscape a very peculiar appearance, and from their novelty and entire dissimilarity to any others, at first is not only curious but pleasing, but as the eye becomes accustomed to it, a gradual transition takes place in ones feelings and from being pleasing they at last become monotonous and repulsive. This feeling, however, may be somewhat accounted for by the surrounding sterility of the land. As far as the eye can reach in the vallies or on the mountains, little else but rocky boulders and the stately yet awfully sombre aspect of the cereus giganteus can be seen.

OPUNTIA, Tourn.

Subgenus 1. PLATOPUNTIA, Englm.

1. OPUNTIA ENGELMANNI, Salm. At Delaware, about 170 miles west of Fort Smith, a specimen of this plant was observed about four feet high. This seems to be the northern limit of a species which is widely spread from lower Mexico to the mouth of the Rio Grande, and on both sides of that river, northward and southward. In the southern regions it grows much taller than in the north.

2. OP. ENGELMANNI, β? CYCLODES: erecta articulis orbiculatis, pulvillis remotis tomento griseo setisque stramineis rigidis inæqualibus instructis; aculeis subsingulis rectis validis compressis stramineis basi fuscis deflexis, adjectis sæpe 1–2 inferioribus brevioribus pallidioribus; bacca globosa late umbilicata, seminibus late undulato-marginatis. (Plate VIII, fig. 1.)

About the mouth of the Gallinas into the Pecos, near Anton Chico, New Mexico; collected in fruit in September. Plant 4 feet high; joints orbicular, or even transversely oval, about 7 inches in diameter; pulvilli 1 inch apart, large, with a semi-circle of large, coarse bristles, 3–4 lines long at the upper edge, and a single stout spine, 1¼–1¾ inch long, on the upper pulvilli, often with 1 or 2 additional ones, 4–9 lines length. Flower not seen. Fruit globose, 1–1¼ inch in diameter, of a purple color. Seed 2.0–2.3 lines in diameter, with a broad and thick acutish undulate rim. The circular joints with fewer spines, and the small globose fruit with large seeds, distinguish this form from *O. Engelmanni*, as it usually appears further south.

3. Op. occidentalis, (sp. nov.): erecta patulo—ramosissima, caule demum lignose terete corticato, articulis grandibus obovatis rhomboideisve, pulvillis remotis griseo-tomentosis, setis flavis s. flavo-fuscis gracilibus confertis, aculeis 1–3 validis compressis angulatis rectis deflexis divergentibusve, uno alterove ad articuli marginem superiorem erecto, albidis corneisve subannulatis basi flavo-fuscis cum adventitiis 1–2 gracilioribus pallidioribus deflexis; flore flavo intus aurantiaco, ovario obovoto pulvillis fusco-villosis vix fulvo-setosis sub-25 notato subinde parce aculeolato, sepalis (extus rubellis) 10–12 dilatato-obovatis cuspidatis, patalis (8?) obovatis obtusis subintegris; bacca obovata late umbilicata succosa, seminibus majoribus irregularibus undulato-marginatis, crenulatis. (Plate VII, fig. 1–2.)

On the western slope of the California mountains, from QuiqualGungo, east of Los Angeles, to San Pasquale and San Isabel, northeast of San Diego, (A. Schott,) at an elevation of 1,000 to 2,000 feet, in immense patches, often as large as half an acre. Flowers in June. Stout ligneous stems, with innumerable branches, sometimes over one hundred joints, spreading far, and then often bent to the ground; joints 9–12 inches long, 6–8 inches wide; pulvilli 1½–2 inches distant, with slender and closely set (much more so than in *O. Engelmanni*) bristles, only 2–3 lines long on the upper part of the pulvillis; spines 1–1¼, smaller ones ½–¾ inch long. Flower yellowish and orange, deeper colored inside at the base, 3–3½ inches in diameter; ovary I½ inch long, not one inch in diameter; pulvilli pretty equally distributed over it, (not as much congregated toward the top as in *O. Engelmanni*;) sepals short and unusually broad; petals only 9 or 10 lines wide by 15 lines in length, rounded, and not emarginate in my specimen, nor mucronate. Fruit 2 inches long, 1¼–1½ inches in diameter, "very juicy, but of a sour and disagreeable taste." Seeds 2½–2¾ lines in diameter. The young plants, raised from the seeds which we brought home, fail to exhibit the very hairy pulvilli which all the young of *O. Engelmanni* show; they bear only the numerous bristly spines seen in most young *Opuntiœ*, at least of this section.

To Mr. A. Schott, who has considerably enriched our knowledge of the vegetation of the countries along the boundary line and in the Gadsden purchase, is due the credit of having discovered the flower of this plant, heretofore unknown, and of many valuable notes about its general habits.

The plant mentioned in Silliman's Journal, November, 1852, (Dr. Parry's collections,) as being common "on the hill-sides and plains near San Diego," and which Mr. Schott seems to have also found "on the sea-beach near San Diego," may be a form of *O. Engelmanni*, as suggested in the above publication; or it may be a naturalized wild state of *O. Tuna*, which is cultivated about the missions there. Enough material has not been obtained to decide about it. At all events, it seems to be distinct from the plant of the western mountain slopes.

4. Op. chlorotica, (sp. nov.): erecta grandis, caule demun-lignoso terete, cortice cinereo-fulvo aculeis flavis numerosissimis fasciculatis armato; articulis orbiculato-obovatis magnis pallide flavo-virescentibus s. subglaucis; pulvillis subremotis griseo-tomentosis, setis stramineis difformibus exterioribus brevioribus tenuioribus subæqualibus confertis, interioribus uniseriatis robustioribus longioribus; aculeis in pulvillis inferioribus 1–3, in superioribus 3–6 inæqualibus stramineis plus minus compressis (nec acute angulatis) plerisque deflexis, interiore breviore

subinde erecto; flore flavo, ovario tubercula pulvilli-gera conferta sub-50 gerente; sepalis tubi sub-20 oblanceolatis cuspidatis, petalis sub-10 obovato spathulatis, obtusis mucronatis, stigmatibus 8 patulis; bacca obovata tuberculosa profunde umbilicata. (Plate VI, figs. 1–3.)

On both sides of the Colorado, from the San Francisco mountains to the headwaters Williams' river, sometimes called "Bill Williams' fork," and to the Mojave creek. The only erect, flat-jointed *Opuntia* in this section of country, 4–5 and sometimes even 7 feet high, forming large bushes, on one of which upwards of one hundred joints were counted. The large trunks have a scaly, grayish, or light-red brown bark; the pulvilli are not obliterated on it, as they are on *O. Engelmanni*, but are largely developed, 4–6 lines in diameter, pulvinate, densely covered with a thick brown tomentum, surrounded by numberless straw-colored bristles, 4 lines in length, and bearing 20–30 or more yellow, compressed spines, often 1–2 inches in length, stellately radiating in every direction, and covering and shielding the whole surface of the stem. The only *Opuntia* which I find described as having a similarly armed stem is *O. Karwinskiana*, Salm., which is said to have 18–20 gray spines on the oldest pulvilli.

Joints 8–10 inches long by 6–8 wide, always of a very pale glaucous, or rather more yellowish green color, which is strikingly characteristic, even at a distance, and which has procured our name for the plant; pulvilli about 1 inch apart, strongly pulvinate; bristles two-fold and distinct, the upper and outer, and by far the most numerous ones are shorter and thinner, and cover the upper semi-lunar area of the areola; inside of them is a semi-circular row of stouter and longer bristles, 4–6 lines long, which unite with the outer and shorter spines of the outer and lower margin of the areola. This arrangement is most distinct on the upper and more fully developed pulvilli; among our *Opuntiæ* it is only seen again, as far as known, in the obscure *O. dulcis* from Presidio del Norte. Spines proper 1–1½ inches long, pale straw color, with faint transverse markings, hardly darker at base; shorter spines 4–9 lines long.

The description of the flower was drawn from an old withered specimen gathered in winter; it seems pale yellow, between 2 and 3 inches in diameter; sepals and petals remarkably narrow, the latter about 1 inch long, and not half as wide. The ovary and fruit (all the specimens found were sterile) are quite tuberculous; pulvilii crowded, bearing brown wool and short, yellow bristles. Specimens of sterile fruit seen 1¼–1½ inches long.

5. Op. procumbens, (sp. nov.): prostrata, articulis orbiculato-obovatis grandibus pallide viridibus, pulvillis remotissimus griseo-tomentosis, setis flavis robustis valde inæqualibus, aculeis validis 2–4 subinde (in articulis vetustioribus?) 7–9 compressis angulatis inæqualibus, stramineis s. pallidioribus versus basin obscurioribus, sæpe rufis fuscisve, deflexis. (Plate VII, figs. 4–5.)

From the San Francisco mountains to the Cactus Pass, at the head of Williams' river, in rocky localities. Joints 9–13 inches long, 7–9 broad, prostrate, always on edge; pulvilli 1½–2 inches apart; bristles 2–4 lines long, comparatively stout; spines 1–2 inches long; no flower or fruit seen. Very similar to *O. Engelmanni;* but prostrate, with even more distinct pulvilli, and stouter and often more numerous spines.

6. Op. angustata, E. & B.: prostrata s. adscendens, articulis elongato-obovatis versus basin sensim angustatis suberectis; pulvillis remotis griseo-tomentosis, setis fulvis gracilibus; aculeis paucis (2–3) validis compressis albidis s. stramineis, versus basin rufis s. fulvis, adjectis sæpe infra 1–2 debilioribus omnibus deflexis; bacca obovata, tuberculata rubella, late profundeque umbilicata pulvillis 24 stipata seminibus magnis subregularibus late marginatis. (Plate VII, figs. 3–4.)

From the foot of the Inscription rock, near Zuñi, to Williams' river, and westward as far as the Cajon Pass of the California mountains. Prostrate in the first and last-mentioned localities, but sub-erect in the bottoms of Williams' river. Joints 6–10 inches long, and at the upper third 3–4 inches wide, gradually narrowed downwards, rounded above; puluilli over 1 inch apart, oblong, quite strongty pulvinate, 3 lines long, bearing slender brown bristles; spines in the specimens collected east of the Colorado sharply angular, pale straw colored or whitish, brownish only at the very base, 1—1½ inch long; sterile fruit obovate-subglose, 1–1¼ inch long, with large pulvilli crowded toward the upper end of the fruit, covered with grayish-brown wool and bright brown bristles. The specimen from Cajon Pass has brighter colored spines, with the lower half red brown, not so angular; some erect spines, at the upper end of the joint, almost terete. On this specimen a ripe fruit was collected, from which the above description has been taken; it is 1½ inch long, nearly one inch in diameter, with the wide and flat umbilicus immersed about half an inch; pulvilli on tubercular elevations about 14 on the upper part of the fruit, and 10 along the rim; seeds 3 lines or more in diameter, much compressed, with the broad rim almost curled. Some of the seeds have germinated, and the young plants grow vigorously.

This plant cannot be confounded with any others of one species; some southern *Opuntiæ* have similar, or even more elongated joints, but are erect and almost unarmed, such as *O. structa, O. tuberculatus, O. lanceolata, etc.* *O. polyantha* from South America, seems to be similar, but has smaller and more spiny joints, etc.

7. Op. phæacantha, var. major E. in Pl. Fendl. Mem. of American Acad. IV, page 52.

Near Zuñi.—As both Mr. Fendler and ourselves failed to collect the fruits of this form, it remains doubtful whether it has been justly referred here, or whether it is more closely allied to *O. Camanchica.*

Op. Mojavensis, E. & B. : prostrata, articulis grandibus suborbiculatus, pulvillis remotis, setis grandibus fulvis, aculeis 2–6 validis compressis acute angulatis elongatis plus minus curvatis, fuscis versus apicem pallidioribus annulatis, adjectis infra 1–3 minoribus tenuioribus pallidis; bacca pulvillis 20–25 fusco-setosis stipata. (Plate IX, fig. 6–8.)

On Mojave creek; at the time it was considered identical with the following species, and no further notice taken of it; only a few fragments were brought home, together with a sterile fruit. Spines 1-2½ inches long, stout, bright-brown; fruit 1¾ inch long, oblong; pulvilli crowded towards the upper end. It is possibly a distinct species, but the material too incomplete to permit us more than merely to indicate it.

8. Op. Camanchica (sp. nov.): articulis adscendentibus majusculis obovato-orbiculatis pulvillis remotis orbiculato-ovatis tomentum griseum setasque paucas stramineas fulvasve (in pulvillis terminalibus demum elongatis rigidiores) gerentibus plerisque armatis; aculeis 1–3 s. ad marginem pluribus compressis fuscis s. atro-fuscis versus apicem pallidioribus superioribus elongatis suberectis ceteris deflexis gracilioribus flore? Bacca ovata late umbilicata atro-rubente succosa pulvillis remotis obsoletis seminibus majusculis irregularibus angulatis late marginatis (Plate IX, fig. 1–5.)

On the Llano Estacado, at the base of the hills, in rather fertile soil, from the easten slope of that elevated plain to the Tucumcari hills, near the upper course of the Canadian river. A large plant, spreading extensively, with large rounded joints 6–7 inches long by 5½–7 wide; pulvilli about 1¼ inch remote; bristles dirty-yellowish, greenish or brown, inconspicuous, except at the upper edge, where they often become elongated and stouter; only the lowest pulvilli are spineless, the others bear 2–3 and the marginal ones 3–6 spines; larger ones 1½–2 and in some specimens almost 3 inches long. Flower unknown; fruit very characteristic, distinguishing this species from the nearly allied *O. phœacantha.* It is oval, not narrowed or constricted at base; 1½–2 inches long, 1–1¼ inch in diameter, with a large flat umbilicus ¾–1 inch in diameter, considerably resembling the fruit of *O. Engelmanni*; of a deep-red color and a very sweet juicy pulp. Seeds 2¼–3 lines in diameter, very irregular, angular and often twisted, with sides impressed, mostly with a broad and thick acute or obtuse rim deeply notched at the hilum.

9. Op. tortispina (sp. nov.): prostrata articulis majusculis adscendentibus obovato-orbiculatis pulvillis subremotis stramineo s. fulvo-setosis; aculeis 3–5 majoribus compressis angulatis subinde canaliculatis sæpe spiraliter tortis, albis basi apiceque sæpe corneis, adjectis infra aculeolis 2–3 gracilibus albis; flore ——; bacca ovata areolis sub-20 parvulis notata, late umbilicata, seminibus mujusculis regularibus crassis. (Plate V, fig 2–3.)

On the Camanche plains, near the Canadian river, east of the plateau of the Llaño Estacado. Similar in growth to the more western *O. Camanchica.* Joints rounded, 6–8 inches long; pulvilli 1–1½ inches apart; bristles short, except on the edges, where they are 2–3 lines long, but rather slender; spines more numerous than in any other of our species, with juicy fruit, often 6–8, lower smaller ones ⅓–1 inch, larger ones 1½–2½ inches long, entirely white or yellowish horn-colored at base and tip; on the upper areolæ one erect spine, the others spreading in different directions, lower ones deflexed. Fruit similar to that of last species, large, oval, not contracted at base, perhaps less juicy and with a somewhat smaller and deeper umbilicus, 1¾–2 inches long, 1–1¼ in diameter. Seeds 2–3 lines across, thick and quite regular, with a very slight indentation at the hilum.

I had observed that sometimes 2 plants are produced from the same seed; this I found to be the case occasionally with *Opuntia occidentalis, Engelmanni* and *dulcis,* one of the young plants always much larger and more vigorous than the other. In examining different seeds of this speceis, I succeeded in finding one with two embryos (see figure), one spirally coiled around the other, both together appearing like one large one.

10. Op. Rafinesquii, Engelm.: diffusa radice fibrosa, articulis mediis s. majusculis obovatis s. suborbiculatis per-viridibus; foliis subulatis elongatis patulis pulvillis sub-remotis albido-s. griseo-villosis setas graciles rufas demum elongatas gerentibus plerisque inermibus; aculeis paucis plerumque solum marginalibus validis teretibus rectis albidis sæpe basi apiceque rufescentibus erectis s. patulis, singulis s. uno alterove graciliore deflexo adjecto; floris alabastro conico acuto, ovario clavato pulvillis 20–25 griseo-villosis rufo-setosis instructo; sepalis tubi sub-13 oblanceolatis acuminatis, interioribus late petaloideo-marginatis cuspidatis; petalis 10–13 late obovatis eroso-denticulatis sub-marginatis sulphureis basi intus miniatis, stigmatibus 7–8 erectis adpressis fluvo-albidis; bacca ovata basi angustata clavata subnuda pulposa purpurascente, umbilicoinfundi buliformi immerso; seminibus subregularibus compressis, margine plerumque lato compresso sub-acuto. Var. *microsperma* subinermis seminibus minoribus regularibus angustius marginatis. (Plate XI, fig. 1–3.)

In sterile, sandy, or rocky (consisting as well of sandstone as of limestone) localities in the Mississippi valley, Illinois, Missouri, Arkansas, and north to Wisconsin, east to Kentucky, and south, probably, to Louisiana and Texas; westward it has not been found west of the western boundary of Missouri and Arkansas. Flowers in May and June; fruit ripens in the same season, but remains on the plant till the following spring. Joints rather large, orbicular 3–4 inches in diameter, or obovate, 4–5 inches long by 3 in width; a small variety with orbicular joinsts only 2 inches in diameter occurs on sandstone rock in southern Missouri. The color of the plant is dark or fresh-green. Leaves 2½–4 lines long, diameter about one-fourth of the length; pulvilli 9–12 lines apart with short whitish or grayish wool, and bright red-brown bristles conspicuous even in the youngest joints. Spines rarely none, generally few in var. *microsperma,* sometimes disappearing entirely in fertile soil in gardens, etc.; mostly only on the upper part or the edge of the joint, single or rarely 2–3, 9–12 lines long, rather stout, white with a darker tip and sometimes also darker base. Flowers 2½–3½ inches in diameter, sulphur-yellow, mostly with a red centre. Fruit 1½–2 inches long, less than half that in diameter, narrowed at base, the seminiferous cavity not extending to the base; umbilicus funnel-shaped, but with shallow bottom, much wrinkled and scarred; naked by the disappearance of the bristles of the pulvilli, and edible, somewhat acid or sweetish. Seeds 2½ lines in diameter, hardly more than one line in thickness; rim rather narrow, thick, but acutish. Var. *Microsperma* has seeds only 0.8 or 0.9 line in diameter, more compressed, with quite a narrow rim.

This species has, by western botanists, generally been considered identical with the eastern *O. vulgaris*. Riddell mentions it as occurring in Kentucky and Illinois, Torrey & Gray in their Flora do not give any locality in the Mississippi valley; but Rafinesque had already observed it in Kentucky, and, in his usual carelèss manner, had indicated 3 species: *Cactus humufusus*, (which growing, "from New York to Kentucky and Missouri," probably comprised both *O. vulgaris* and our species,) *O. cæspitosa*, from Kentucky and Tennesse, and *O. Mesacantha*, from Kentucky to Louisiana. As it seems impossible from his incomplete descriptions to make out what he meant by three different names, and as we know only one species in those States of the Mississippi valley, I take the liberty of discarding those names and of substituting the name of the author for the western species. It is not improper to state here that Rafinesque's vague and partly erroneous descriptions have found their way into Seringe's Bulletin, 1831, page 216, into the Linnæa, vol VIII, into Pfeiffer's Enumeratio Cactearum, page 146, and into other works, but with the substitution of Nuttalls for Rafinesque's name as authority; the "rounded joints" have, in these works, been taken for "globose" or "cylindric" joints, and our plant has been classed with the *Opu tiæ glomeratæ* from Chili and Mendoza.

A large form of *O. Rafinesquii* was coll cted near Fort Smith, on the western border of Arkansas; further west, where no true *O. Rafinesquii* has been found, several forms were met with, which, though they exhibit some distinctive characteristics, are, perhaps, not sufficiently different to constitute distinct species. The flowers of most of them are unknown as well as the leaves, but fruit and seed were carefully preserved, which not only furnish important characters, but also the means to propagate, cultivate, and further to study them. We append them as sub-species.

1. RADICE FIBROSA.

a. O. CYMOCHILA: diffusa articulis orbiculatis pulvillis subremotis griseo-tomentosis stramineo s. fulvo-setosis, plerisque armatis; aculeis 1–3 robustioribus elongatis teretibus s. subcompressis tortisque albidis basi saepe rufescentibus, patulis deflexisve, additis saepe 2–3 gracilioribus radiatim deflexis; flore? stigmatibus 8; bacca obovata umbilico plano s. parum depresso pulvillis 20–24 griseo-tomentosis parce setulosis, demum nudatis; seminibus irregularibns angulosis margine undulato acuto. (Plate XII, fig. 1–3.)

On the Camanche plains east of the Llaño Estacado, near the 100th degree of longitude, and from there to Tucumcari hill, 80 miles east of the Pecos. Joints 2½–3 inches in diameter, orbicular or very slightly obovate; pulvillis 6–8 lines apart; the very light yellowish-brown bristles numerous, and conspicuous only on the older joints; only the lowest pulvilli of a joint unarmed, upper ones with 2–5 spines, 2 or 3 larger ones, often reddish-brown at lower half, 1–2 inches long, lower, smaller, paler ones 3–9 lines long. Fruit oval, 1–1¼ inches long, about 10 lines in diameter, purplish, pulpy, sweet, and edible, less contracted at base than *O. Rafinesquii;* seed remarkably irregular and twisted, 2½ lines in diameter, with a wavy or twisted very sharp rim, whence the name which indicates the undulated border.

The orbicular joints, the numerous spines, the oval not clavate fruit, and curiously twisted seed, seem to distinguish this form sufficiently from *O. Rafinesquii*, but these characters may not be sufficiently constant or important to constitute specific difference. The characters of *Opuntiæ* are not yet sufficently studied to permit us to form satisfactory conclusions about their diagnostic importance; so we find a form collected on the Sandia mountains, near Albuquerque, which, in habit and appearance, does not differ from the common form of *O. Rafinesquii*, but which has the seeds of *O. cymochila.*

O. CYMOCHILA, *β.* MONTANA: articulis orbiculatis majoribus inermibus s. margine superiore solum aculeatis; pulvillis remotis stramineo-setosis; aculeis singulis binisve validis albidis infra fuscis; bacca obovata subclavata seminibus irregularibus acute undulateque marginatis. Joints 3–4½ inches in diameter, pulvilli 9–12 lines apart, spines 12–18, smaller ones 4–6 lines long, on some plants entirely wanting. Fruit 1½ inches long, much contracted at base, with a much depressed, almost funnel-shaped, umbilicus. Seeds cannot be distinguished from those of the plant of the plains.

b. O. STENOCHILA: prostrata articulis obovatis, pulvillis remotis stramineo-setosis superioribus solum armatis; aculeis singulis albidis patulis, 1–2 minoribus deflexis sæpe adjectis; bacca obovata clavata pulposa, umbilico lato parum immerso, seminibus regularibus crassis anguste obtuseque marginatis. (Plate XII, fig. 4–6.)

At the cañon of Zuñi. Joints 4 inches long and 3 wide, flaccid or often lying flat on the ground, (in November;) pulvilli 12 lines apart, small, with yellowish or greenish bristles; larger spines 1–1¼ inches long, smaller ones less than half as long; fruit green or pale red, very juicy; 1½ inches long, but sometimes much enlarged, even more juicy, and 2–2½ inches long and 1 inch in diameter above, long clavate towards the base. Seeds quite characteristic, about 2½ lines in diameter, 1½ line thick, regular, with a very narrow and somewhat obtuse rim, whence the name.

In the same neighborhood another plant was found with similar seed, but smaller, more rounded, and somewhat more spinous joints, fruit less clavate, smaller, seeds similar, but a little smaller.

2. RADICE TUBEROSA.

c. O. FUSIFORMIS: diffusa s. adscendens, radicibus fusiformibus elongatis, irregulariter incrassatis; articulis suborbiculatis majusculis, foliis elongatis subulatis patulis pulvillis subremotis griseo villosis, setas elongatas virescente-fuscas gerentibus, plerisque s. solum superioribus armatis; aculeis 2–3 gracilibus inæqualibus deflexis s. patulis, albidis; floris minoris flavi (basi rubelli?) ovario pulvillis 25 stipato, stigmatibus 8, bacca ovata basi vix clavata demum nudata, pulposa rubella, umbilico immerso subinfundibuliformi; seminibus subregularibus crassis majusculis acute marginatis. (Plate XII, fig. 7–8.)

Cross-timbers longitude 97°–99°; west of the region inhabited by *O. Rafinesquii*, and east of that of *O. cymochila;* also collected by Dr. Wislizenus in the same longitude, but farther north on Cow creek and the Little Arkansas, (on the road from Independence to Santa Fé,) and by Dr. Hayden, of the United States army, on the Missouri, below the Big Bend. Fl. in May. Roots form elongated tubers, attenuated at one or both ends ½–1 inch in diameter; joints 4 or even 5 inches in length; leaves 2½–3½ lines long, pulvilli 9–12 lines apart, with numerous stout yellowish-brown bristles, often 2 lines long, spines 1 or 2, 1–1¼ inches long, with a smaller one of half the length, more slender than in most other allied forms. Flowers 2–2½ inches in diameter, yellow apparently with red base, smaller and with fewer sepals than *O. Rafinesquii*, but the same mumber of stigmata. Fruit 1½ inches long, umbilicus ½ inch wide; seed rather larger and thicker than in *O. Rafinesquii*, 2¾ lines in diameter and 1½ thick. The description of the flower is from the specimens collected by Dr. Wislizenus.

O. MACRORHIZA, Engl., of Texas, also belongs here as another tuberous rooted form in the wide circle of *O. Rafinesquii.*

11. O. BASILARIS (sp. nov.): humilis, articulis obovatis s. subtriangularibus glaucescentibus pubescentibus adscendentibus e basi proliferis, fere rosulatis; foliis subulatis minutis erectis rubellis tomentum axillare vix superantibus; pulvillis subconfertis fulvo-tomentosis setas gracillimas demum numerosissimas breves fulvidas et subinde aculeolos setiformes caducos gerentibus; floris purpureis ovario obovato pubescente pulvillis plurimis (40–60) confertis fulvo-tomentosis instructo, sepalis 20-25 exterioribus oblanceolatis acuminatis, interioribus late obovatis cuspidatis, petalis sub-10 obovato-orbiculatis retusis s. obcordatis sæpe tenuiter mucronatis,

stigmatibus 8 brevibus in capitulum conicum congestis; bacca (sicca?) breviter obovata late umbilicata, seminibus magnis crassis subregularibus. (Plate XIII, fig. 1–5.)

On hills and in ravines from the Cactus Pass down the valley of Williams river to the Colorado, and to Mojave creek; Mr. Schott met with it on the lower Gila; and both he and Mr. Albert H. Campbell obtained the beautiful purple flowers of this plant in April and May, 1855. The habit of this plant is very different from any other of our *Opuntiæ*, as the stout obovate or often fan-shaped or sometimes almost obcordate joints originate from a common base form a kind of rosette, resembiing somewhat an open cabbage head. Among thousands of specimens observed, none deviated from this peculiar manner of growth, none was proliferous in the shape of the other elliptic *Opuntiæ*. Joints 5–8 inches long, ½ inch in thickness, minutely pubescent; leaves only 1 line in length, slenderly subulate, smaller than any other of our species; next in size are the leaves of *O. Missouriensis*, *O. fragilis*, and *O. filipendula;* the largest leaves are produced by the cylindric *Opuntiæ*, some of which have them 10 lines long.

Pulvilli somewhat immersed, 4–6 lines apart. Flower of a beautiful and rich purple color, about 2½ inches in diameter, ovary nearly 1 inch long, crowded with 40–60 elevated areolæ, with light brown wool and brighter brown bristles; filaments not very numerous, leaving the inner base of the tube naked; stigmata about 2 lines long, or less, apparently green. Fruit seems to be perfectly dry, short and thick; seeds 3 lines in diameter, nearly 2 lines thick, with a rather narrow but very thick rim, regular or sometimes quite irregular.

12. O. HYSTRICINA, (sp. nov.): diffusa, articulis obovato-orbiculatis, compressis, pulvillis subconfertis magnis griseo-tomentosis setas pallidas rutilasve gerentibus, omnibus armatis aculeis 5–7 inferioribus gracilioribus brevioribus albidis deorsum radiantibus, superioribus 5–8 elongatis validioribus angulatis sæpe tortis flexuosisve 3–4 deflexis albidis, uno alterove longissimo, ceteris 2–4 superioribus patulis suberectisve sæpe basi s. ad medium fuscatis; flore ——, bacca obovata subclavata, umbilico parum immerso planiusculo, pulvillis 25–30, inferioribus inermibus, superioribus confertis aculeolos paucos gerentibus; seminibus maximus irregularibus late crasseque marginatis. (Plate XV, fig. 5–7.)

This beautiful species was found abundant from the Rio Grande westward to the San Francisco mountains, mixed with *O. Missouriensis*, to which it is nearly allied. The specimens before us were obtained at the Colorado Chiquito and on the San Francisco mountains. Joints 3–4 inches long and nearly as broad. Pulvilli 5-6 lines apart, unusually large; lower radiating spines 4–9 lines, the others 1½–3 and even 4 inches long, irregularly arranged as we generally find it in this species. We notice many specimens where 3 or 4 larger spines are placed above the lower short radiating ones, the uppermost one of them is usually the longest; somewhat above these are 2–4 other spines, the lower one of which is the darkest and often not much shorter than the one just mentioned, the others are shorter and whitish or dark only at the base. The bristles are yellowish in some and brown in other specimens; sometimes we find short pale and longer darker bristles together. The fruit is 1 inch long and half as thick, with a very shallow umbilicus; only the upper larger pulvilli bear 4–6 spines (2–5 lines long,) the lower ones on the contracted part of the fruit are very small, distant, and unarmed. Seed among the largest in this genus 3½ lines in diameter, the thick and broad rim acutish. The name indicates the porcupine-like armature of this species.

13. *O. Missouriensis*, D. C.: prostrata radice fibrosa, articulis obovatis suborbiculatisve tuberculatis compressis laete viridibus adscendentibus, foliis subulatis minutis patulis, pulvillis subconfertis albo s. griseo-tomentosis stramineo—setosis omnibus armatis; aculeis in pulvillis inferioribus gracilioribus paucioribus, in superioribus 5–10 exterioribus minoribus radiantibus albidis, 1–5 interioribus robustis teretiusculis longioribus patulis, rarius suberectis, albidis s. rufescentibus; floribus sulphureis basi intus sæpe aurantiacis, ovario obovato subgloboso, pulvillis 25–35 albo tomentosis aculeolatis instructo; sepalis tubi sub-13 exterioribus oblanceolatis,

interioribus obovatis cuspidatis petaloide-marginatis, petalis sub-13 obovato-orbiculatis emarginatis s. obcordatis crenulatis sæpe mucronulatis; stigmatibus sub-8 viridibus in capitulum globosum s. conicum confertis; bacca ovata s. subglobosa, umbilico parum depresso, pulvillis 25–35 albo tomentosis setos albidas stramineas s. rufescentes aculeolos que numerosos breves s. elongatos gerentibus; seminibus magnis plerumque irregularibus late subacuteque marginatis. (Plates XIV and XV, flig. 1–10 and 1–4.)

This variable species extends from the country north of the Upper Missouri river to the regions south of the Canadian and of Santa Fé, latitude 48° 35′; and from longitude 99° east of Fort Pierre, on the Missouri, to 112° on the San Francisco mountains. It has not been found south of Albuquerque, along the Rio Grande, nor in the Salt Lake valley, Utah, as far as at present known. Flowering in May, fr. same fall. Nuttall discovered this common western species on the Upper Missouri in 1811, and described it under the name of *Cactus ferox;* he noticed "8–10 greenish stigmata" and the "dry spring fruit." The deep purple fruit, as large as a hen's egg," attributed to our species on the authority of Dr. James, by Torrey and Gray, in their Flora, perhaps belongs to our *O. Camanchica*; it certainly cannot belong to *O. Missouriensis.*

It forms large spreading masses, much dreaded by travellers and their animals. Joints mostly suborbicular, 2–4 inches long, and 2–3½ wide, light green, somewhat tuberculated from hemispherical elevations which bear the leaves and pulvilli, 4–6 lines apart; leaves 1½–2 lines long, hardly more than ½ line in diameter at the base, nearly twice as long as the wool in their axills; numerous small white spines radiating downwards and laterally, sometimes a few rather longer ones obliquely upwards, mostly 3–6 lines long, rarely more elongaged; central spines in the Missouri specimens mostly 1, rarely 2; in the southern ones, often 2–4, 1–1½, or even 2 inches long, terete or somewhat angular, white, or mostly with a reddish base when young, entirely brown red, with lighter tips. On the lower pulvilli the stouter spines are mostly wanting; in some Missouri specimens, I find few and weak spines on the upper, and none at all on the lower part of the joints; in other plants, from the same region, all the pulvilli are nearly equally armed with 5 weaker (2–3 lines long) lower deflexed, and 5 inner stouter (4–6 lines long) spreading spines. Flowers 2–3 inches in diameter, ovary, with subulate sepals, similar to the leaves, spines already present, but not as long and stiff as in the fruit. Petals yellow towards the base, or sometimes almost entirely rose-colored, orange, or brick-colored, sometimes only the margin remaining yellow. Exterior filaments much the longest, deep red; interior ones paler, shorter; pistil pale yellowish, thickened below the middle, as in almost all the species of this genus; stigmata united into a small subconic head.

Fruit ovate, or sometimes globose, umbilicus shallow, spines on the pulvilli numerous, 6–12, usually short, 1–4, sometimes 6 lines long. Seeds about 3 lines in diameter, sometimes larger, in one form much smaller, mostly irregular, twisted, angular, much compressed, with a broad and thick but rather acutish rim. Embryo of different shapes, conform to the shape of a seed, always with a small albumen.

The following forms, we think, must be included under this species, though the whole history of most of them is not known; some of them may not even be constant varieties.

α. RUFISPINA: articulis orbiculatis s. transversis setis parcis rufescentibus, aculeis radialibus 6–8 albidis rufo-variegatis, interioribus validis fuscis apice pallidioribus, 2–4 deflexis, singulo patulo s. suberecto robustissimo; bacca ovata.—(Plate XIV, fig. 1–3.)

This is the shortest form of our species, and greatly deserves Nuttall's original name ferox; It was collected on rocky places on the Pecos; Dr. Hayden has also sent it from the Yellowstone, and it no doubt is met with in all the intervening territory. Joints 2–3 inches in diameter, pulvilli 4–5 lines apart; bristles fewer, but longer and darker than in other forms; central spines 1¼–2 inches long; fruit 1 inch long, half as thick, with shallow umbilicus, about 30 pulvilli, spines on the upper ones 4–6 lines long. Seeds 2½–3 lines in diameter.

β. PLATYCARPA: articulis obovato-orbiculatis, setis parcis stramineis, aculeis exterioribus

5–10, inferioribus albidis, superioribus robustioribus rufescentibus centrali subsingulo robusto fusco patulo s. deflexo; bacca depresso-globosa, umbilico lato plano, pulvillis sub-25 aculeolos 5–10 breves gerentibus.—(Plate XIV, fig. 4.)

Sent from the Yellowstone by Dr. Hayden. A stout form; joints 3 inches long, 2½–2¾ wide; pulvilli 4–6 lines apart, the dirty yellowish bristles visible only on the older joints. Central spine single, or only on vigorous specimens on the upper pulvilli 2, mostly brownish, deeper colored on the margin. Fruit 8–9 lines long, umbilicus, of the same diameter, spines only 1–3 lines long, deflexed. Seed 3 lines in diameter, rim rather narrower than in the first-mentioned form.

γ MICROSPERMA: articulis ut in præcedente; stigmatibus 5; bacca ovata, umbilico parum depresso, pulvillis, 20–30 setosis et breviter aculeolatis, seminibus anguste acuteque marginatis. (Plate XIV, figs. 5–7.)

On the Missouri, about Fort Pierre; brought down 10 years ago by the fur traders. Very similar to the last form in the general appearance; also with only 1, or at most 2, central dark spines; flowers only with 5 stigmata, otherwise same as the one described above; fruit short, oval, with 10–20 very short spines on the numerous pulvilli; seed only 2 lines in diameter, more regular, thicker in proportion, with a narrow and acute rim. It might be supposed that these characters were important and constant enough for a specific difference, if we did not know the great variability in this genus, and if we did not find among Dr. Hayden's plants seeds of intermediate shape and size.

δ SUBINERMIS: articulis elongato-obovatis, pulvillis subremotis, inferioribus, inermibus, superioribus aculeos paucos breves gerentibus.

Brought from the Upper Missouri by Dr. Hayden; remains constant in three years cultivation. Joints 3½–5 inches long, half as wide, gradually narrowed down at base; leaves entirely similar to those of the common form; pulvilli 6–9 lines apart; spines entirely wanting, or on the upper pulvilli 2 or 3 short and slender ones, rarely one or the others more robust, ¼–½ inch long; flowers not seen.

ε ALBISPINA: articulis late obovatis, setis stramineis, aculeis omnibus albis gracilioribus, exterioribus 6–10 setaceis, interioribus in pulvillis superioribus 1–3 robustioribus elongatis deflexis s. patulis; bacca ovata, seminibus magnis. (Plate XIV, figs. 8–10.)

Sandy bottoms and dry beds of streamlets on the Upper Canadian, 250 miles east of the Pecos; on the Sandia mountains, near Albuquerque; also, on the Upper Missouri. This was the first form of this species met with in travelling up the Canadian; the stouter and more compact forms were found further west, in higher elevations. Joints 3–4 inches long, 2½–3 wide; pulvilli 4–6 lines apart; spines all ivory white, rarely with a yellowish tinge, larger ones 1–¼ inch long; fruit with very shallow umbilicus, and very slender and short spines; seed 3–3½ lines in diameter, irregular, rim broad acutish. A form from the Sandia mountains with pulvilli more remote; spines longer, more slender, some of them flexuous; seems to unite this with the next variety.

ζ TRICHOPHORA: articulis ovatis, pulvillis confertis parce albo-tomentosis setas stramineis demum albidas breves gerentibus, omnibus armatis; aculeis 10–18 setiformibus albis, exterioribus 8-12 brevioribus radiantibus, interioribus longioribus deflexis, rarius singulo suberecto; pulvillis in articulis vetustioribus lignosis confertissimis setas numerosas aculeosque 15–25 capillaceos elongatos flexuosos gerentibus; bacca ovata, umbilico parum immerso pulvillis 35–40 albo-tomentosis stramineo-setosis fasciculum aculeolorum 12–18 plerumque deflexorum gerentibus; seminibus maximis valde compressis irregularibus latissime acuteque marginatis. (Plate XV, figs. 1–4.)

Only on the volcanic rocks about Santa Fé, and on the Sandia mountains. The hoary appearance of the older joints is very characteristic, and reminds one strongly of *Pilocereus senilis*. These hairs are from a few lines to 2 or 2½ inches in length, and of the appearance and about as fine as an old man's beard. The older joints become thick and of a solid ligneous substance; younger joints 4½ inches long, 2½ inches wide, or larger; pulvilli 4–5 lines apart; exterior spines 3–6 lines, interior ones 9–18 lines long. Fruit ovate, 10 lines long, 7 in diameter; very slender and numerous spines, 3–6 lines long. Seeds, with those of *O. hystricina*, the largest known to us, 3½ lines in diameter, sometimes larger; rim large, almost of the tickness of the seed itself. This is, perhaps, a distinct species, and must be further studied.

14. O. SPHÆROCARPA, (sp. nov.): diffusa articulis orbiculatis transversisve tuberculatis; pulvillis confertis albo-tomentosis, setas stramineas breves gerentibus, plerisque inermibus, summis solum et marginalibus aculeos 1–2 reflexos s. patulos, adjectis subinde 1–3 brevioribus gerentibus; bacca globosa, umbilico minore plano, pulvillis sub-25 tomentosis setosis vix aculeolatis, seminibus mediis acute marginatis. (Plate XIII, figs. 6–7.)

On tho eastern declivity of the Sandia mountains, near Albuquerque. Joints in the specimen before us 3 inches wide, less in length, strongly tuberculated; pulvilli 4–5 lines apart; spines on the upper lateral pulvilli mostly single, deflexed, ½ inch long; on the middle or lower ones none; on the uppermost and marginal ones mostly 2, rarely 3 lines long, reddish brown, with darker tip; 1–3 smaller additional spines, 2–4 lines long also reddish. Fruit perfectly globose, 9 lines in diameter; umbilicus 5–6 lines wide; pulvilli bristly, but only the upper ones with one or a few small spines. Seeds 2½ lines in diameter, very irregular, with a rather narrow, but sharp rim.

The arrangement of the spines is so different from any form of *O. Missouriensis,* which always shows the numerous slender radiating spines, and always has spiney fruits, that we feel obliged to separate this plant as a distinct species. The seeds brought home by the expedition have germinated, and are growing vigorously.

15. O. ERINACEA, (sp. nov.): diffusa adscendens; articulis tumidis ovatis s. teretiusculis, pulvillis confertissimis ovato-orbiculatis albo-tomentosis demum stramineo-setosis omnibus armatis; aculeis 3–5 gracilibus elongatis e cinereo-rubellis 1–3 superioribus brevioribus sursum porrectis, centrali longior patulo vel declinato, ceteris deflexis, additis 2–4 minoribus inferioribus; bacca ovata umbilico infundibuliformi pulvillis 30–40 setal stramineas et aculeolos 12–20 gerentibu·; seminibus magnis subregularibus late acuteque marginatis. (Plate XIII, fig. 8–11.)

West of the great Colorado near the Mojave creek; joints 2–2½ inches long, 1–1½ inches wide, and about ½–¾ inch thick, sometimes elongated, almost cylindric, densely covered with the large white pulvilli, which are only 2–3 lines apart, and numerous reddish-gray spines with red points bristling hedgehog-like (whence the specific name) in every direction. Spines 6–14 or in old joints even 20 lines long, with smaller ones very slender, flexible, but stiff. Young plants cylindric, covered with bunches of 15 or 20, or more, white hair-like spines. Bristles dirty-yellow even in young joints present, in old ones densely crowded, and 2–3 lines long; in a dead flower a 6-parted stigma was noticed. Fruit 1–1¼ inches long, about ½ an inch in diameter, with a deep funnel-shaped umbilicus; pulvilli crowded, prominent, white-tomentose with yellowish bristles and numerous, mostly deflexed, spines, 3–6 lines long. Seed nearly 3 lines in diameter, much compressed, more regular than in the three foregoing species.

15. O. BRACHYARTHRA, (sp. nov.): prostrata s. adscendens, articulis ovatis s. orbiculatis tumidis saepe subglobosis, tuberculatis; pulvillis confertis magnis albo-tomentosis parce setulosis plerisque armatis; aculeis 3–5 albidis s. fuscatis patulis; 1–2 validioribus sursum versis, caeteris minoribus minimisqe subdeflexis; floris parvi; ovario subgloboso, pulvillos 12–15 tomentosos setosos superiores aculeolatos gerante, sepalis tubi exterioribus obovatis cuspidatis stigmatibus 5. (Plate XII, fig. 9.)

At the foot of the inscription rock near Zuñi under pine trees, only seen in that single locality. A singular looking plant with short tumid joints (10–15 lines long, 10–12 wide and nearly the same in thickness) one growing on the top of the other so as to resemble, somewhat, a jointed finger. In the absence of ripe fruit we are unable, with certainty, to class this species; the shape of the joints and the somewhat spinulose fruit seem to bring it very near to *O. fragilis*, and it may possibly be a small and compact form of this species, though the appearance is very different; on the other hand the subglobose joints seem to refer it to the section *Glomeratæ*, Salm.

Pulvilli 2–4 lines apart, large, white or when old grayish tomentose with very few short yellowish bristles, even in the old joints; spines 9–12 lines long, rather stout, terete, often with 1 or 2 short ones not more than 1–2 lines long. No ripe fruit was found (Novr.) which is also often the case with *O. fragilis*, but many remains of flowers with globose-ovate fleshy sterile red ovaries, 3–4 lines long, some of them becoming larger and probably proliferous, generally only some of the upper pulvilli bear a few short spines. The flower seems to have been about 1 inch in diameter, with about 5 sepals, 8 or 9 petals, and style with 5 stigmata.

O. FRAGILIS, Haw., the seed of which we give a figure of, (pl. XXIV, fig. 5,) grows on the upper Missouri and Yellowstone and probably down to Santa Fé. The joints are small, ovate, compressed or turned, or even terete, 4 larger spines on the upper fully developed pulvilli cruciate, the upper one suberect, stouter and longer than the others, mostly yellowish-brown; on the lower margin 4–6 small white radiating spines; bristles few. Fruit apparently somewhat fleshy, getting dry much later with 20–28 pulvilli, almost naked, only the upper ones with a few short spines; seeds few, large, regular.

Subgen. 2. CYLINDROPUNTIA, Engelm.

§ 1. *Clavatæ.*

17. O. CLAVATA, E. in Wisl. Rep. (Plate XXII, fig. 1–3.) Found from Santa Fé to Albuquerque, where Wislizenus and Fendler had already collected it, and no where else. A remarkable and well characterized species, the type of this section. We add to the characters previously published, (Wislizenus' Report note 12, and Plantæ Fendlerianæ in Mem. Amt Acad. vol. IV, page 49,) that the leaves are long and subulate, 2–2½ lines long; the broades. spines were 1½ lines wide; fruit 1½–1¾ inch long, lemon-yellow, almost covered with 30–50 hemispherical pulvilli, which bear innumerable white slender bristles, spreading ray-like in every direction. Seeds large for this section, and, as in all the allied species, transverse or broader than high; 2¼–3 lines in the longest diameters, rostrate, somewhat angular; commissure (which in the cylindric and clavate opuntiæ replaces the rim of the flat-jointed ones), impressed, linear or a little wider; cotyledons in several seeds examined by me oblique.

18. O. PARRYI, E. in Sillim. Journ., Nov., 1852: Articulis ovatis basi clavatis, tuberculis oblongo-elongatis, pulvillis albo-tomentosis setas paucas rigidas gerentibus; aculeis angulatis scabris rubello-cinereis, interioribus validioribus sub-4 triangulato-compressis, exterioribus 5–8 angulatis supra infraque divergentibus, extimis 6–10 gracilibus rigidis radiantibus; bacca ovato basi clavata pulvillis sub-40 setosissimis stipata; seminibus regularibus latius commissuratis. (Plate XXII, fig. 4–7.)

On the gravelly plains 30 miles west of the Colorado, near the Mojave river; southward to the eastern slope of the California mountains near San Felipe, Dr. Parry. Joints 2½–3 or 4 inches long, 1¼ inch in diameter, attenuated not only below but also somewhat above in the specimen before us. Tubercles about 9 lines long, pulvilli small, bristles few, coarse and long. Spines very numerous in 3 series; the 4 inner ones 12–16 lines long, ½–¾ lines broad, the lower one somewhat flattened, the others triangular; the next series consists usually of 2–3 upper ones and 3–5 lower ones, angular, more slender and shorter than the first, 4–8 lines long; the third or external circle consists of 6–10 bristly slender spines, 3–4 lines long, some above, but most of them lateral or inferior. Young spines reddish-grey with paler margins, older ones ashy. Fruit 1½ inch long; seed rather regular, 2–2½ lines in the transverse diameter, less than 2 lines high, not beaked, commissure broader and more distinct than in any other of this section examined by us. Cotyledons in all the seeds examined oblique.

This discription refers to the plant brought by the expedition from the Mojave river. Several years before Dr. Parry had described a plant discovered by him "on the hills and plains about San Felipe on the eastern slope of the California mountains," which had been named after the discoverer. We presume that both plants were identical, but have to remark that Dr. Parry's plant is much larger, having joints of 4–8 inches in length, with tubercles 6–12 lines long, spines whitish, half an inch long; he describes the flowers as 1½ inch in diameter, greenish-yellow with green stigmata. Fruit not mentioned. Further investigation will be necessary to clear up those doubts.

From *O. clavata* (which grows 8 or 9 degrees east and on much greater elevation) the Mojave species is distinguished by the shape of the joints, the color, much narrower, more numerous spines and the smaller more regular seeds, with the broad commissure.

§ 2. *Cylindricæ.*

19. Opuntia Davisii, (sp. nov.): caule dense lignoso ramosissimo divaricato adscendente, articulis junioribus erectis elongatis, basi attenuatis; tuberculis oblongo-linearibus prominulis, setis stramineis tenerrimis; aculeis interioribus 4–7 subtriangularibus rufis apice pallidioribus, vagina straminea laxa fulgida indusiatis divergentibus s. deflexis, aculeis gracilioribus inferioribus 5–6; bacca ovata pulvillis sub-25 setas stramineas aculeolosque paucos gerentibus; umbilico lato. (Plate XVI, fig 1–4.)

Common on the upper Canadian, eastward and westward of Tucumcari hills, near the Llano Estacado. A very much branched shrubby, somewhat procumbent, plant, with erect joints, about 18 inches high; wood dense and hard; joints 4–6 inches in length, and half an inch or more in thickness; tubercles not very prominent, 7–8 lines long; very slender bristles, forming a thick brush at upper end of pulvillus; interior spines 1–1¼ inches long, covered with a very loose glistening membranaceous sheath, which makes the plant an object of remark for a long distance; lower spines 3–6 lines long. All the fruits seen on the route were sterile, and most of them elongated, 1–1¼ inch long; on many pulvilli 1–4 sheathed spines were observed, which possibly are peculiar only to the sterile and proliferous fruits.

We have named this well-marked and pretty species after our enlightened Secretary of War, Colonel Jefferson Davis, under whose auspices the expeditions for the exploration of a proper route for the Pacific railroad were organized, and were enabled to accomplish so much, not only for this specific object, but also for the elucidation of the natural history of this hitherto almost unknown country.

20. O. echinocarpa, (sp. nov.): caule reticulato-lignoso, erectiusculo, ramis numerosis patentissimis subinde pene decumbentibus, articulis ovatis basi clavatis, tuberculis ovatis prominentibus confertis, setis paucis stramineis; aculeis albidis stramineo s. albido-vaginatis, majoribus sub-4 cruciatis, ceteri, minoribus 8–16 undique radiantibus; floris flavi (?) ovario pulvillis 30–40 villosis subaculeolatisque confertis stipato, sepalis sub-13, exterioribus ovatis acutis; interioribus obovatis mucronatis, petalis sub-8 obovatis obtusis s. subemarginatis denticulatis, stigmatibus 6; bacca globoso-depressa s. hemispherica, late profundeque umbilicata pulvillis sub-40 aculeolos vaginatos elongatos 8–12 gerentibus dense stipata floris, rudimento subpersistente coronata; seminibus subregularibus s. angulatis, crassis, late commissuratis, cotyledonibus parallelis.

In the Colorado valley, near the mouth of Williams' river. Mr. Schott found a stouter form further south. The more northern plant forms a low shrub 6–18 inches high, spreading, and often partially prostrate; the cylindric tubular wood is reticulated with short meshes. Joints 1–2½ inches long, less than 1 inch thick, tubercles not more than 4 or 5 lines long; bristles few and rather coarse; spines 12–20; the 4 larger ones are somewhat central, 9–12 lines long; the others radiating from 4–9 lines long; the smaller ones, as in all these *Opuntiæ*, hardly vaginate. Flower described from a withered specimen found attached to a fruit, to which it somewhat adhered, but perhaps held more by the long intricate spines than by an organic attachment. Flower 1½–1¾ inches in diameter, apparently yellow, which is uncommon among the *Cylindric Opuntiæ;* petals about 9 lines long and three broad, stigmata about 2 lines long. The fruit is very peculiar, and with the seed, characterizes this species well. The wide umbilicus on the shallow fruit gives it the appearance of a saucer, and the seeds find their place more around the edge of the umbilicus than in the body of the fruit. Spines on fruit from 4–10 lines long. Seed 2 lines or more in diameter, with a broader commissure than any of the allied species, cotyledons always, all the specimens examined regularly accumbent or parallel; the only species, so far, where this regularly is the case, albumen unusually large.

O. Serpentina, from San Diego, is very nearly allied to our species, but seems sufficiently distinct by its elongated cylindric joints and different growth.

21. O. Bigelovii, *Englm.:* caule arborescente erecto crasso reticulato-lignoso, ramis erectis adscendentibusve numerosis congestis, inferioribus demum refractis, articulis ovatis s. ovato-cylindricis tumidis læte s. pallide viridibus fragilibus; tuberculis subhemisphericis depressis confertis; pulvillis immersis ovatis setas pallidas penicillatas et aculeos 6–10 robustiores pallidos stramineo-vaginatos, 3 deflexos, ceteros divergentes et 6–10 graciliores inferiores radiantes gerentibus; ovario tuberculis plurimis stipato parce aculeolato; bacca ovata profunde umbilicata tuberculata pulvillos immersos 60–70 setigeros inermes s. aculeolos sub-3 vaginatos gerente; seminibus parvis.—(Plate XIX, fig. 1–7.)

On Williams' river, a branch of the Colorado; 10-12 feet high, stem ¾ inch in diameter; skeleton forming a large hollow tube, much reticulated with numerous small roundish or somewhat rhombic meshes in 13 or 21 spiral rows. Branches forming a dense head; younger joints erect, adpressed very fragile, often shaken off by the wind and covering the soil around, taking root everywhere, or sticking to the clothes of the passers-by like burrs. The joints on the older part of the stem are often persistent and reflexed, becoming withered and brown. Joints 2–6 inches long, 1–2 inches in diameter, light flesh green, covered with the small almost hemisherical, and not very prominent, tubercles, which are 3–4 lines long, and arranged mostly in 13 spirals; the areola is immersed at the apex of the tubercle, and surrounded by an elevated paler or almost whitish ridge, having the appearance of 2 lateral glands. Larger spines about 1 inch long. Flower or complete fruit not seen; an ovary or young fruit before me is clavate, 1 inch long, and has a few spines on the pulvilli; some empty (sterile?) fruits brought home are oval 1½–1¾ inches long, 1 inch in diameter, strongly tuberculated, and spineless; others again are even larger, with more numerous tubercles, and the pulvilli beset with 3–6 sheathed spines 4–7 lines long. These are evidently undergoing a change into joints; proliferous seeds, said to be small, but most unfortunately the specimens were lost, so that we were unable to compare them with those allied species found further south, (*O. fulgida,*) and on the Pacific coast, (*O. prolifera.*) Our plant is distinguished from these forms by its short tubercles, immersed pulvilli, and large tuberculated and somewhat spiny fruit.

[I have thought proper to consecrate this remarkable species, so conspicuous in its desert wilds, to my colaborer Dr. J. M. Bigelow, through whose intelligent exertions and indefatigable assiduity so many new Cactaceæ, described in this report, have been discovered and brought home.—G. E.]

22. O. Whipplei, (sp. nov.): caule erecto s. rarius patulo s. subprocumbente, reticulato-lignoso, divaricato ramoso, articulis cylindricis; tuberculis ovatis confertis, pulvillis pulvinatis

parce tomentosis vix setosis; aculeis brevibus cinereo s. stramineo vaginatis, 1—4 majoribus divaricatis, inferiore longiore deflexo, minoribus 2–8 solum ad inferiorem pulvilli marginem deflexis s. undique radiantibus; flore rubro, ovario ovato tuberculato pulvillis 20–30 tomentosis setas stramineas et aculeolos paucos mox deciduous gerentibus stipato sepalis tubi sub-8 orbiculatis cuspidatis, petalis 8–10 spathulatis cuspidatis; bacca subglobosa leviter tuberculata subcarnosa flava inermi; umbilico infundibuliformi seminum subregularium commissura lineari.

α. LÆVIOR humilior, aculeis brevioribus paucioribus seminibus minoribus.

β. SPINOSIOR elatior aculeis plurimis longioribus seminibus majoribus. (Plate XVII, fig. 1–4.)

From the elevated country about Zuñi to the head of Williams's river, at first seen only 8–15 inches high, subprostrate, afterwards 20–30 inches, and sometimes even 5–6 feet high. Var. *β.* was found by Mr. A. Schott south of the Gila river, and he also discovered the flower of this plant, which, like the flowers of all the other new species, remained unknown to us, unless winter remains were picked up here and there. Ligneous skeleton tubular, with small meshes, dense at base of stem; joints elongated, 2–4 inches to a foot long, ½ or ¾ of an inch in diameter; tubercles ovate or sometimes almost rhombic, about 5 lines long; spines very variable in number, sometimes only with 1 larger and 2 or 3 smaller ones; in other instances, especially in Var. *β.*, with 12 or 14; spines 3–9 lines long, bristles few, generally only on older joints; flowers 1¼–1½ inches in diameter; ovary 6–9 lines long with 20 or 25 pulvilli; fruit about 1 inch long, a little less in diameter, somewhat fleshy and sweet, with 25–35 not very prominent tubercles; seeds with linear or almost linear commissure, 1½–1¾ lines in diameter; cotyledons regularly incumbent or sometimes oblique. The seeds of *β.* are 2 lines in diameter.

This is easily distinguished from all the allied species of the slender elongated branches, the short, crowded tubercles, and the short spines. We have dedicated this *Opuntia*, characteristic of the desert mountains under the 35th degree, between the Rio Grande and the Colorado, to Captain A. W. Whipple, the commander of the expedition who, by his zealous and liberal cooperation, afforded every facility in his power in the various collections of natural history- (Plate XVII, fig. 5–6, and Plate XVIII, fig. 4.)

23. O. ARBORESCENS, *Englm.*: found first 200 miles east of the Pecos, and from there abundantly as far west as Zuñi, where other cylindric *Opuntiæ* take its place. In this region it does not grow higher than 5–8 feet, and can scarcely be called arborescent; it is always well characterized by the verticillate often somewhat pendulous branches, the cristate-tuberculate spineless fruit, and the smooth seeds with a distinct and broadly linear commissure. Seeds of specimens collected at Zuñi smaller than others, ouly 1½ line in diameter.

24. O. ACANTHOCARPA, (sp. nov.): caule arborescente erecto reticulato-lignoso, ramis adscendentibus divaricatis articulis cylindricis tuberculatis pallide virescentibus, tuberculis oblongolinearibus pulvillis ovato-orbiculatis breviter tomentosis vix setosis, aculeis numerosis s. plurimis (8–25) stramineo-vaginatis undique porrectis, stellatis; bacca subglobosa late umbilicata tuberculata; pulvillis 12–15 tomentosis parce setosis aculeolis validis 8–10 munitis; seminibus magnis muetangulis late commissuratis. (Plate XVIII, fig. 1–3.)

On the mountains of Cactus Pass, about 500 miles west of Santa Fé. Stout, stem 5–6 feet high, wood forming a hollow reticulated tube, solid at base; branches few, never verticillate, separating at acute angles; joints 4–6 inches long, 1 inch in diameter, tubercles 9–10 lines long; pulvilli in some with one central and 6 or 8 exterior spines, in others with 3–7 interior and 10–20 exterior stellately radiating spines. Central spines 1–1¼ inch, exterior 4–10 lines long, with a yellowish or brownish sheath. Fruit 1 inch long with a large but not deep umbilicus, and 12–15 rather shallow tubercles; spines of fruit stout, 3–6 lines long, stouter and more crowded toward the top of the fruit. Seeds unlike any other of our *Opuntiæ*, 2½–3 lines in diameter, with rather broad commissure, often spongy on the margin, and on the sides with many even or concave faces separated by sharp ridges.

This peculiar species cannot be confounded with any other, but comes, in the arrangement of spines, nearest to *O. arborescens*, from which it is easily distinguished by its manner of growth, its elongated tubercles, and especially the much less tuberculated and spiny fruit, and the peculiar seed.

25. G. TESSELATA, Englm.: caule frutescente erecto s. diffuso, dense lignoso, ramosissimo, ramis divaricatis, articulis gracilibus teretibus, plano-tuberculatis cæsiis, tuberculis 5–6 angulatis confertissimis depressis, planiusculis; pulvillo lineari tomentoso vix setis paucis deciduis instructo, inermi s. medio s. versus basin aculeo elongato porrecto s. subdeflexo albido flavido s. fulvo vagina laxi basi constricta flava s. e flavo fulva indusiato, singulo s. rarissime binis; aculeis paucis brevibus setaceis infra sæpe adjectis; floris purpurei ovario obovato s. clavato pulvillis 30–50 villoso-tomentosis inermibus s. parce aculeolatis dense stipato; sepalis tubi sub-8 obovato-orbiculatis cuspidatis petalis 5 late obovato-orbiculatis emarginatis; filamentis exterioribus latioribus persistentibus, stigmatibus 5 brevibus ovatis adpressis; bacca ovata basi apiceque contracta sicca pulvillis villosis aculeo-latissimus confertissimis stipata, floris rudimentis coronata; seminibus subregularibus margine spongioso crasso parum prominente cinctis. *O. ramosissima*, E. in Sill. Journ., November, 1852. (Plate XXI, figs. 1–7.)

Valley of the Lower Colorado, and from thence to the California mountains; first discovered by Dr. Parry in the Colorado desert, afterwards found by Dr. Bigelow from the valley of Williams' river to 70 miles east of Cajon Pass, in the California mountains. The flower was first noticed by Mr. A. Schott, in western Sonora, towards the Lower Colorado. Fl. May to September. Stems 2–6 feet high, mostly branching from the base below, 1–3 inches in diameter, covered with a dark-gray scaly bark; wood of young branches reticulate, very soon becoming solid, but even then the reticulated structure remains visible in the different layers of wood. Annual layers not as distinct as the medullary rays, but more so than in *O. frutescens;* in a stem of near 2 inches diameter we counted 35 annual layers, 8 or 9 of which belong to the alburnum; branches numerous and slender, of an ashy or grayish green color, younger ones 3 or 3½ lines in diameter, well characterized by the remarkable flattened tubercles, which, by closely crowding together, become 5 or 6 angular, diamond-shaped; the areola is linear, extending down to the middle of the tubercle; its short tomentum usually extends upwards between the next adjoining tubercles. Tubercles 2½–3 lines long, and a little less in diameter. Spines 1½–2 inches long, usually from the middle or at least above the base of the pulvillus, generally only on the upper tubercles of each year's growth, which gives the whole plant a singular appearance, showing the fasciculate spines at some, and having no spines at all on other parts of the apparently homogeneous branches. Sheath contracted at base, and firmly adhering to the spine, loose and saccate above. Small bristly spines at the base of the pulvillus, 2–3, sometimes even 5 in number, 1–4 lines long. Flower purple, about 6 lines in diameter, lowest part of the tube naked. Fruit 9–10 lines long, resembling much the fruit of the *Clavate Opuntiæ* in shape, being contracted above, with a narrow and deep umbilicus, and retaining the dead remains of the flower, of which the broad, scale-like exterior filaments are most conspicuous; pulvilli large and woolly, almost entirely covering the fruit, and beset with 30 to 50 reddish-brown, bristly, flexuous spines, 2–3 lines long. Seeds few, regular, nearly or quite 2 lines in diameter.

O. VAGINATA, Englm.: caule frutescente erecto dense lignoso, ramis virgatis demum teretibus junioribus tubercula oblongo-elongata subprominentia gerentibus læte viridibus; foliis subulatis pulvillis orbiculatis magnis breviter albo-tomentosis, setarum stramineurum penicilla paro brevi, aculeis ex imo pulvillo singulis elongatis corneis s. fuscis laxe stramineo s. aurantiaco-vaginatis, adjectis subinde supra aculeis minoribus 1–2; bacca ovata tuberculata pulposa flava pulvillos 15–20 majusculos albo-tomentosos setosos gerentibus, umbilico angusto immerso, seminibus subregularibus marginatis. (Plate XX, fig. 1.)

About Albuquerque, where Dr. Wislizenus had already collected it in 1846; apparently extending into Mexico, as Dr. Gregg collected what seems to be the same species about San Luis Potosi. Shrub 3–5 feet high; lower part of stem 1–1½ inch thick, covered with scaly, light-yellowish-brown bark; older branches smooth terete, younger ones 3–4 lines in diameter, strongly tuberculated; tubercles 6–9 lines long; leaves slender, about 3 lines long, and apparently somewhat persistent, as they are sometimes found adhering, though withered, even to fruit-bearing branches, which, of course, are over a year old. The same, though to a less extent, is sometimes seen in *O. frutescens*. Pulvilli unusually large; bristles in the young ones forming a small but distinct bunch at the upper edge of the areola, but disappearing on the older joints, contrary to the usual occurrence, when the bristles become stouter and more numerous in older joints. Spines 1–2½ inches long, dark, with very loose and glistening sheaths; second or smaller spine sometimes lateral, but usually above the principal one, not below it, as in most others. Flower unknown. Fruit ovate, 8 or 9 lines long, the pulvilli often bear 2–5 obtuse bodies, almost hidden in the tomentum, apparently glandular, but of a fibrous structure. Seeds, 12–15 in each fruit, about 2 lines or a little more in diameter, commissure broad, prominent, forming a distinct, somewhat spongy, rim. (See plate XX, fig. 1, and plate XXIV, figs. 13–15.) In Dr. Wislizenus' report, the long-spined form of *O. frutescens* was confounded with this species. It is possible, however, that *O. vaginata*, as described here, may be a stouter, tuberculated form of *O. frutescens*, with lighter colored, tuberculated fruit, and larger seed.

27. O. FRUTESCENS, Engelm. This well known species was observed from Laguna Colorado, 60 miles east of the Pecos, to Williams' river, a branch of the great Colorado, always with the same characters. The bark is scaly, almost papery, with a silvery reflection; the wood shows the medullary rays very distinctly, especially 5 of them; much less the annual layers. Fruit deep scarlet, smooth, small, sometimes almost obliterated pulvilli, 5–9 lines long; seeds 5–10, about 1½ lines in diameter, with a narrow and often acute margin. The forms collected on the expedition belong to var. *α. longispina;* the var. *β. brevispina* has been observed only in Texas and northeastern Mexico. (See Plate XX, fig. 2–5, and Plate XXIV, fig. 16–19.)

EXPLANATIONS OF THE PLATES OF CACTACEÆ.

Pl. I. Echinocactus Whipplei, E. & B.: fig. 1, whole plant; fig. 2, bunch of spines of the usual size; fig. 3, same, uncommonly large and broad; fig. 4, same, lateral view; fig. 5, same, very young; fig. 6, seed—*a* natural size, *b* magnified 8 diameters, *c* part of the surface still more magnified to exhibit the tuberculated appearance.

Pl. II, Fig. 1–2. Echinocactus polyancistrus, E. & B.: 1, upper part of a rib with older and younger bunches of spines, the youngest one with a flower bud in the axil; 2, one of the largest and most fully developed bunches of spines.

Fig. 3–5. Echinocactus Le Contei, E.: 3, part of a rib, with 2 bunches of spines; 4, a single bunch of spines from another specimen; 5, seed—*a* natural size, *b* magnified 8 diameters, *c* part of the surface still more magnified to exhibit the oval pits.

Pl. III, Fig. 1–2. Echinocactus Wislizeni, E.: 1, side view of a bunch of spines; 2, seed—*a* natural size, *b* magnified 8 diameters, *c* part of the surface still more magnified to exhibit the reticulation. This species, collected by Captain Whipple on the Gila, and common about El Paso, on the Rio Grande, has been introduced here to show those characteristics which distinguish it from the nearly allied *E. Le Contei*, on the foregoing plate.

Fig. 3. Echinocactus Emoryi, E.: two bunches of spines on part of a rib.

Fig. 4–6. Echinocactus polycephalus, E. & B.: 4, part of a rib, with 3 bunches of short, stout, and straightish spines; 5, a young bunch of spines of unusual dimensions and much curved, with a woolly fruit in the axil; 6, seed—*a* natural size, *b* magnified 8 diameters, *c* part of the surface more magnified to show the warty appearance, *d* seed after the removal of the outer integument, embryo, together with a considerable quantity of albumen in the endopleura, *e* embryo curved with accumbent cotyledons.

Pl. IV, Fig. 1–3. Cereus phœniceus, E.: 1, upper part of a head bearing a flower; 2, a bunch of spines of the usual size; 3, part of a rib, with 3 bunches of spines from an uncommonly large form.

Fig. 4–5. Cereus phœniceus, sub. sp. conoideus, E. & B.: 4, upper part of a head; 5, part of a rib, with 2 bunches of spines.

Fig. 6–7. Cereus triglochidiatus, E.: 6, upper part of a large head, with a flower; 7, part of a rib of another specimen, with smaller curved spines.

Fig. 8. Cereus Mojavensis, E. & B.: part of a rib, with 3 bunches of spines.

Fig. 9. Cereus Mojavensis, E. & B., var. zuniensis: part of a rib, with 2 bunches of spines.

Pl. V, Fig. 1. Cereus hexædrus, E. & B.: upper part of a head.

Fig. 2–3. Cereus gonacanthus, E. & B.: 2, part of a rib, with two bunches of spines; 3, another fascicle of spines; the 3 bunches of spines show all a different proportion of the central and the upper radial spines.

Fig. 4–7. Cereus Engelmanni, var. variegatus, E. & B.: 4 and 5, two bunches of spines, showing a different arrangement of central spines; 6, fruit; 7, seed—*a* natural size, *b* magnified 8 diameters, *c* part of the surface still more magnified to show the irregular tuberculation.

Fig. 8–10. Cereus Engelmanni, var. chrysocentrus, E. & B.: 8, part of two ribs, with numerous spines; 9, a single bunch of spines; 10, fruit, sterile and perhaps not fully developed.

Pl. VI, Fig. 1–3. Opuntia chlorotica, E. & B.: 1, joint with a flower. The flower to be reconstructed from a withered specimen collected in January; 2, sterile and probably undeveloped fruit; 3, fragment of the bark of the lower part of the plant, with several large bunches of spines.

FIG. 4–5. OPUNTIA PROCUMBENS, E. & B.: 4, part of a joint; 5, larger bunch of spines from another specimen.

PL. VII, Fig. 1–2. OPUNTIA OCCIDENTALIS, E. & B.: 1, joint of the usual shape and size; 2, fruit.

FIG. 3–4. OPUNTIA ANGUSTATA, E. & B.: 3, a large and less spinous joint with a sterile degenerate spinous fruit; 4, a smaller, more spinous joint with a full grown ripe fruit.

PL. VIII, Fig. 1. OPUNTIA ENGELMANNI, var. CYCLODES, E. & B.: with ripe fruit.

FIG. 2–3. OPUNTIA TORTISPINA, E. & B.: 2, fragment of a joint with fewer spines and ripe fruit; 3, part of a more spiny joint.

PL. IX, Fig. 1–5. OPUNTIA CAMANCHICA, E. & B.: 1, a joint with shorter and lighter colored spines; 2, a joint with larger and darker spines; 3, fragment of a joint with more numerous an, docwded spines; 4 and 5, ripe fruit of the smaller and largest size.

FIG. 6–8, OPUNTIA MOJAVENSIS, E. & B.: 6, a younger bunch of spines · 7, another from the oldest part of the plant; 8, a sterile and degenerate fruit.

PL. X. Fig. 1–2. OPUNTIA VULGARIS, Mill.: 1, a young joint with leaves, the older one has a single spine and bears, a flower bud; 2, a single leaf magnified 4 diameters. The figures of this species have been introduced to exhibit the diagnostic characters and its difference from the next species.

FIG. 3–5. OPUNTIA RAFINESQUII, E.; 3, an older joint with a flower and a bud, and a younger half-grown joint with leaves. This represents the spinous form common in Illinois, Missouri, and Arkansas. 4, an older joint of the variety with few spines, bearing numerous fruits of different shapes, as they often occur in the same plant; 5, two leaves of different sizes magnified 4 diameters.

PL. XI, Fig. 1, OPUNTIA RAFINESQUII, var. MINOR, E.: the larger joint spineless, the upper one spiny on the margin.

FIG. 2–3. OPINTIA RAFINESQUII, var. GRANDIFLORA, E.: 2, a joint with flower; 3, fruit.

FIG. 4. OPUNTIA FUSCOATRA, E.: a joint with a young fruit just after flowering, fragment of an older, very bristly, joint visible.

PL. XII. Fig. 1–3. OPUNTIA CYMOCHILAS, E. & B.: 1, a joint; 2, a single bunch of spines; 3, ripe fruit.

FIG. 4–6. OPUNTIA STENOCHILA, E. & B.: 4, a joint; 5 and 6, a smaller and large fruit.

FIG. 7–8. OPUNTIA FUSIFORMIS, E. & B.: 7, a joint; 8, a fruit.

FIG. 9. OPUNTIA BRACAYARTHRA, E. & B.: a whole plant with two withered flowers.

PL. XIII. Fig. 1–5. OPUNTIA BASILARIS, E. & B.: 1, a joint somewhat shrivelled as it appears in winter; a late young joint near its base appears more plump and fresh; 2, flower; 3, style; 4, undeveloped sterile fruit; 5, a whole plant reduced in size to show the singular manner of growth.

FIG. 6–7. OPUNTIA SPHÆROCARPA, E. & B.: joint and fruit.

FIG. 8–11. OPUNTIA ERINACEA, E. & B.: 8, joint of the usual shape, (only partly finished;) 9 and 10, bunches of spines; 11, fruit.

PL. XIV. Fig. 1–3. OPUNTIA MISSOURIENSIS, var. RUFISPINIS, E. & B.: 1, a joint, (only partly completed;) 2, a very full bunch of spines; 3, fruit.

FIG. 4. OPUNTIA MISSOURIENSIS, var. PLATYCARPA, E.: fruit.

FIG. 5–7. OPUNTIA MISSOURIENSIS, var. MICROSPERMA, E.: 5, joint (unfinished) with flower; 6, bunch of spines; 7, fruit.

FIG. 8–10. OPUNTIA MISSOURIENSIS, var. ALBISPINA, E. & B.: 8, joint (unfinished); 9, bunch of spines; 10, fruit.

PL. XV, Fig. 1–4. OPUNTIA MISSOURIENSIS, var. TRICHOPHORA, E. & B.: 1, part of an old stem showing the thickness and hairy spines, upper younger joints (unfinished); 2, bunch of spines from a younger joint; 3, same from an older part of the plant; 4, fruit.

Fig. 5–7. Opuntia hystricina, E. & B.: 5, a joint (unfinished); 6, a large bunch of spines; 7, fruit.

Pl. XVI. Opuntia Davisii, E. & B.: 1, a branch showing the structure of the older parts, an older and young joints with two fruits; 2, a tubercle with its bunch of spines, the membranaceous sheaths partly torn, showing the spine itself; 3, a degenerate sterile spiny fruit in its transition to a branch, as it is often seen in this species and others, especially cylindric opuntia; 4, the whole plant reduced.

Pl. XVII, Fig. 1–4. Opuntia Whipplei, E. & B.: 1, a branch of the more common form of the plant covered with ripe fruit. At (*a*) the fruit is undeveloped, probably not different from the ovary of the flower, only more shrivelled; 2, branch of a larger specimen, spines more numerous, fruit larger; 3, a single bunch of spines of this specimen; 4, whole plant reduced.

Fig. 5–6. Opuntia arborescens, E.: 5, a stout branch with numerous spines and large fruit; 6, a bunch of spines of same.

Pl. XVIII, Fig. 1–3. Opuntia acanthocarpa, E. & B.: 1, an older branch with fruit; 2, a young branch; 3, whole plant reduced.

Fig. 4. Opuntia arborescens, E.: whole plant reduced.

Fig. 5–10. Opuntia echinocarpa, E. & B.: 5, a branch of the plant densely covered with the sheathed spines; 6, 7, and 8, bunches of spines; 9, fruit, side view; 10, same, top view.

Pl. XIX. Opuntia Bigelovii, E.: 1, a single joint; 2 and 3, tubercles, with bunches of spines; 4, young undeveloped fruit; 5, an apparently full-grown fruit, sterile, and perhaps degenerating into a branch; 6, part of the ligneous skeleton, forming a wide tube, and showing in the reticulated structure the traces of the tubercles and branches; 7, an entire plant reduced; on the left of the main stem is a younger shoot, with vigorous erect joints.

Pl. XX, Opuntia vaginata, E.: 1, an older joint bearing two fruits, and a young vigorous shoot.

Fig. 2–3. Opuntia frutescens, E., var. longispina: from Williams' river of the Colorado; 2, a branch with fruit; 3, lower part of the trunk, with some roots; the sections show the structure of the dense wood.

Fig. 4–5. Opuntia frutescens, E., var. brevispina: 4, a branch with fruits, most of them sterile, one producing young branches from its upper areola; 5, a flower.

Pl. XXI. Opuntia tesselata, E.: 1, a branch with fruit *a*, *a*, and a withered flower *b*; 2 and 3, flowers as they probably are reconstructed from withered specimens; 4, a small joint magnified so as to show distinctly the appearance of the tubercles and areolæ; 5, part of the stem with a section of the wood above and a fracture below, so as plainly to show the ligneous structure; the bark of the younger branches exhibits the tesselated surface, while in the older trunk it is lost in the irregular scales; 6, ligneous skeleton of a young branch; 7, a whole plant reduced.

Pl. XXII, Fig. 1–3. Opuntia clavata, E: 1, joint with a ripe fruit; 2, one of the upper bunches of spines; 3, part of the central spine magnified 4 diameters.

Fig. 4–7. Opuntia Parryi, E: 4, joint with ripe fruit; 5, bunch of spines, side view; 6, another one, front view; 7, part of the central spine magnified 4 diameters.

The remaining figures of this and all the two following plates represent seeds and their details of almost all the *Opuntiæ* described in this report. Fig. *a* represents a side view of the seed, natural size; *b*, same, four times magnified, as are all the following figures; *c*, posterior view; *d*, anterior view; *e*, vertical section of seed, exhibiting the position and proportion of the embryo and the albumen; *f*, embryo and albumen coated by the endopleura, after the removal of the testa; *g*, lateral view of embryo. The other letters *h*, *i*, *k*, etc., will be explained wherever they occur.

Fig. 8–9. Seeds of Op. Engelmanni, var. cyclodes.

Fig. 10. Seed of Op. occidentalis: One of the embryos, *g*, shows the cotyledons in an oblique almost incumbent position.

Fig. 11. Seed of Op. angustata.

Fig. 12–15. Seeds of Op. Camanchica, of different sizes and shapes.

Pl. XXIII, Fig. 1–5. Seeds of Op. tortispina: 1–3, seeds of different sizes and shapes; 4, two embryos in one seed; *g–h*, different views of both embryos together as they lay in the seed; *i*, interior layer, and *k*, exterior smaller embryo; 5, germination of a double embryo; two young plants from one seed, the larger one still bearing the shell of the seed.

Fig. 6. Seed of Op. fusiformis.

Fig. 7–12. Seeds of Op. Rafinesquii, and some of its varieties and sub-species; 7, usual form from Missouri, (see pl. X, fig. 3;) *h*, *i*, *k*, germination in different stages of development; *l*, seedling with three cotyledons.

Fig. 8. Small seed from the fruit, (represented on pl. X, fig. 4.)

Fig. 9. Op. stenochila.

Fig. 10–12. Op. cymochila: 10 and 11, different forms of the usual variety; 12, seed of the variety *montana*.

Fig. 13. Seed of Op. vulgaris.

Fig. 14. Seeds of Op. basilaris: An irregular and a very regular one from the same fruit.

Fig. 15. Seed of Op. hystricina.

Fig. 16–19. Seeds of different forms of Op. Missouriensis: 16, var. rufispina 17, var. platycarpa; *h*, seedling of same; 18, var. albispina; 19, var. tricophora.

Pl. XXIV, Fig. 1–2. Op. Missouriensis: 1, var. with smaller fruit and seeds from the Upper Missouri; 2, var. microsperma. (See pl. XIV, Fig. 5–7.)

Fig. 3. Seed of Op. sphærocarpa.

Fig. 4. Seed of Op. erinacea: The embryo, *g*, shows considerable obliquity of the cotyledons.

Fig. 5. Seed of Op. fragilis: From the Yellowstone river.

Fig. 6. Seed of Op. clavata: The embryo, *g*, oblique.

Fig. 7. Seed of Op. Parryi: Embryo, *g*, nearly accumbent.

Fig. 8. Seed of Op. echinocarpa: One of the seeds quite regular, the other irregular; embryo, *g*, *g*, always regularly accumbent; *h*, and *i*, seedlings with the very narrow and thick cotyledons crossing each other, one of them bearing the shell of the seed.

Fig. 9–10. Seeds of Op. Whipplei: 9, seed of the plant represented Pl. XVII, fig. 2, seed larger, commissure perfectly linear, cotyledons oblique; 10, seeds of the other specimen, Pl. XXII, fig. 1, seeds smaller, of different shapes, commissure a little wider, cotyledons oblique, in *i* somewhat separated; in *k* three cotyledons, of which *l* is a transverse section, *h*, seedling with very narrow and long cotyledons.

Fig. 11. Seeds of Op. acanthocarpa, of different shapes all from one fruit.

Fig. 12. Seeds of Op. arborescens, of different shapes belonging to the plant, figured Pl. XVII, fig. 5, smaller than those sent by other collectors, embryo *g*, regularly incumbent.

Fig. 13–15. Seeds of Op. vaginata: 13–14, seeds of different sizes from the plant, Pl. XX, fig. 1., the smaller one is empty and perhaps not fully formed; 15, seed of the same species collected in Mexico by Dr. Gregg. Cotyledons regularly incumbent.

Fig. 16–19. Seeds of Op. frutescens: 16, var. longispina from the Llano Estacado (Pl. XX, fig. 2); 17, same from Mexico Dr. Gregg; 18, same from Williams River branch of the great Colorado; 19, var. brevispina, from Texas, Lindheimer. In all these the cotyledons of the embryo are regularly incumbent.

Fig. 20. Seeds of Op. tesselata: embryo oblique or almost accumbent.

All the figures are of natural size unless the contrary is expressly stated. They were drawn with the greatest accuracy, partly from living and in part from dried specimens, by Mr. Paulus

Roetter of St. Louis, under the personal superintendence of Dr. Engelmann. The drawings made on the spot by Mr. H. B. Möllhausen, the artist of the expedition, greatly aided the work and were made use of, and even partly copied, especially in the plates exhibiting the Cylindric Opuntiæ.

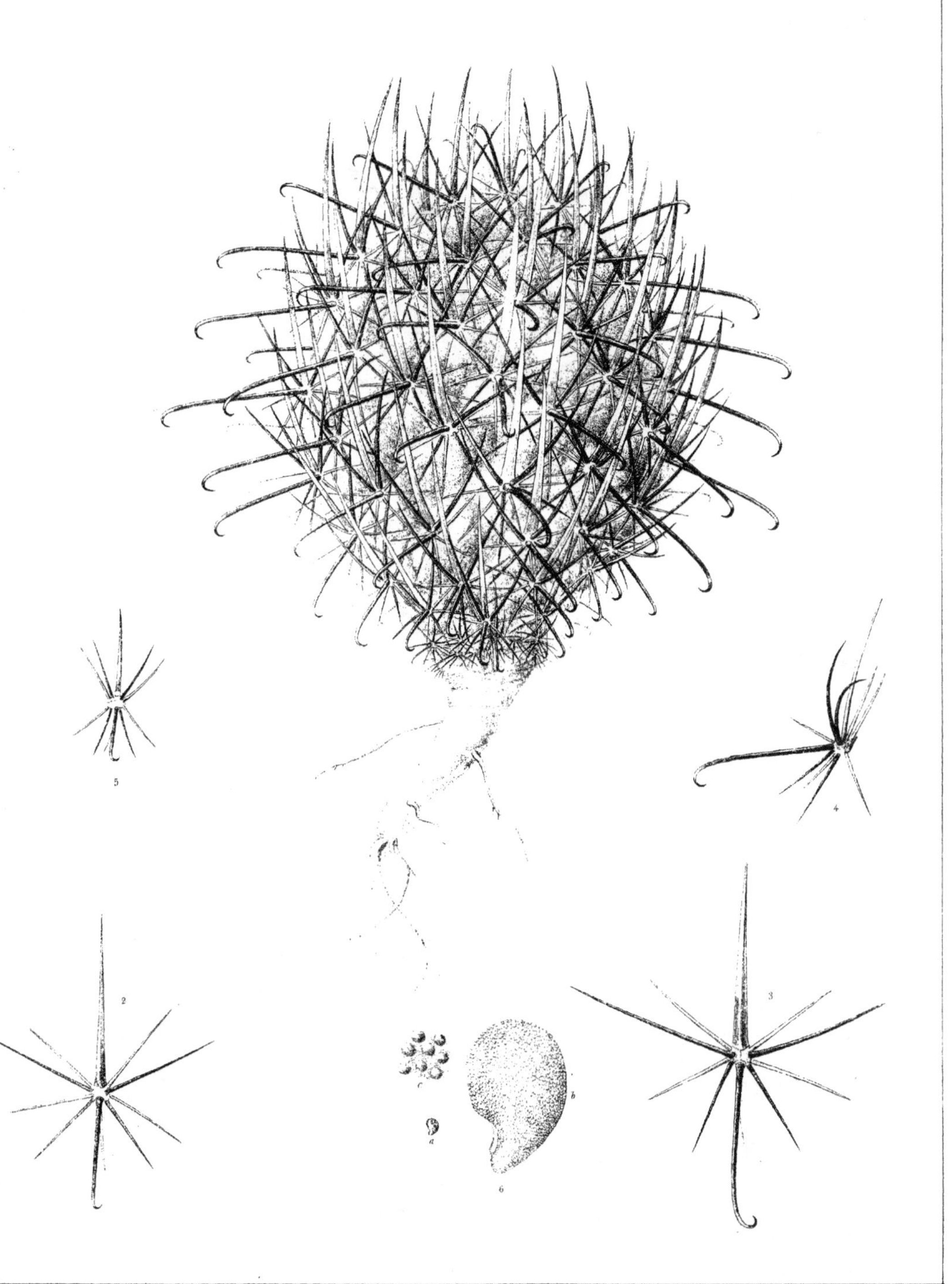

Ackerman Lith. 379 Broadway N.Y.

ECHINOCACTUS WHIPPLEI. E. & B.

1-2. ECHINOCACTUS POLYANCISTRUS, E.&B. 3-5. ECHINOCACTUS LECONTEI. E.

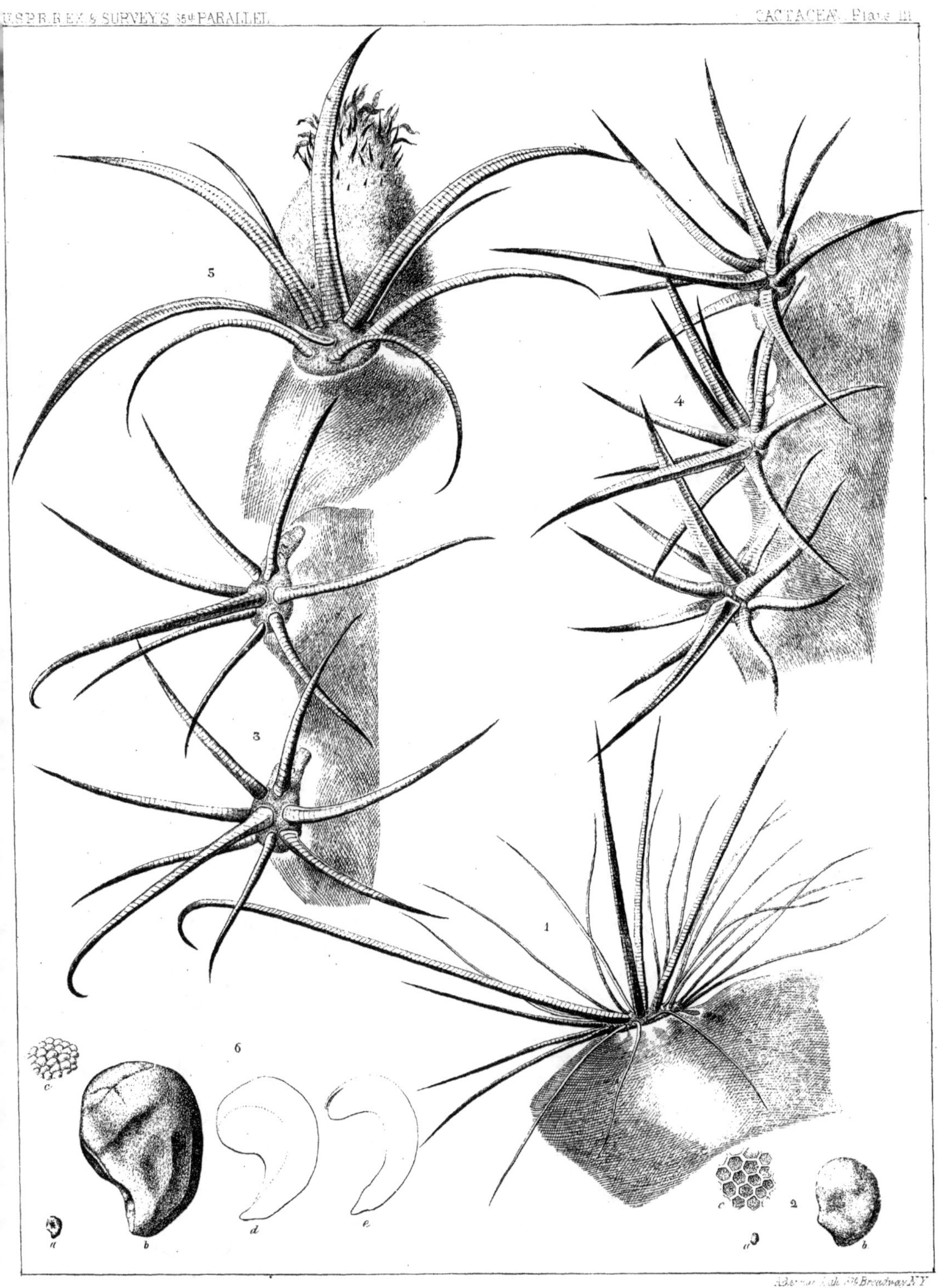

Ackerman Lith. 379 Broadway N.Y.

1-2 ECHINOCACTUS WISLIZENI, E. 3. E. EMORYI, E. 4-6 E. POLYCEPHALUS, E & B.

Ackerman Lith. 379 Broadway N.Y.

1–3. CEREUS PHŒNICEUS, E. 4–5. CEREUS CONOIDEUS E. & B. 6–7 CEREUS TRIGLOCHIDIATUS, E.
8. C. BIGELOVII. 9. C. BIGELOVII β. ZUNIENSIS.

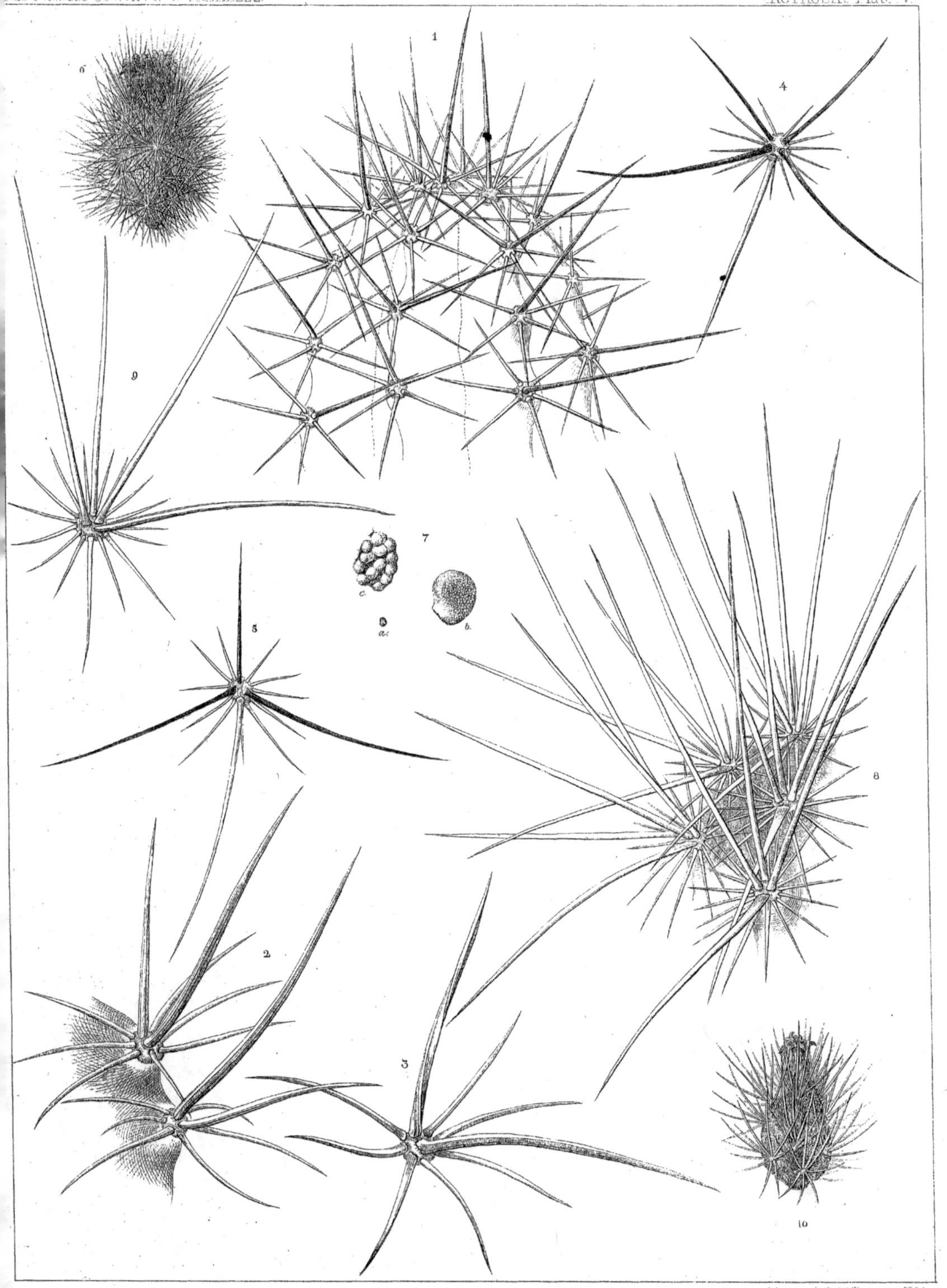

Ackerman Lith 379 Broadway N.Y.

1. CEREUS HEXAEDRUS. E&B., 2–3. C. GONACANTHUS. E&B. 4–7. C. ENGELMANNI, var VARIEGATUS.
8–10: var CHRYSOCENTRUS.

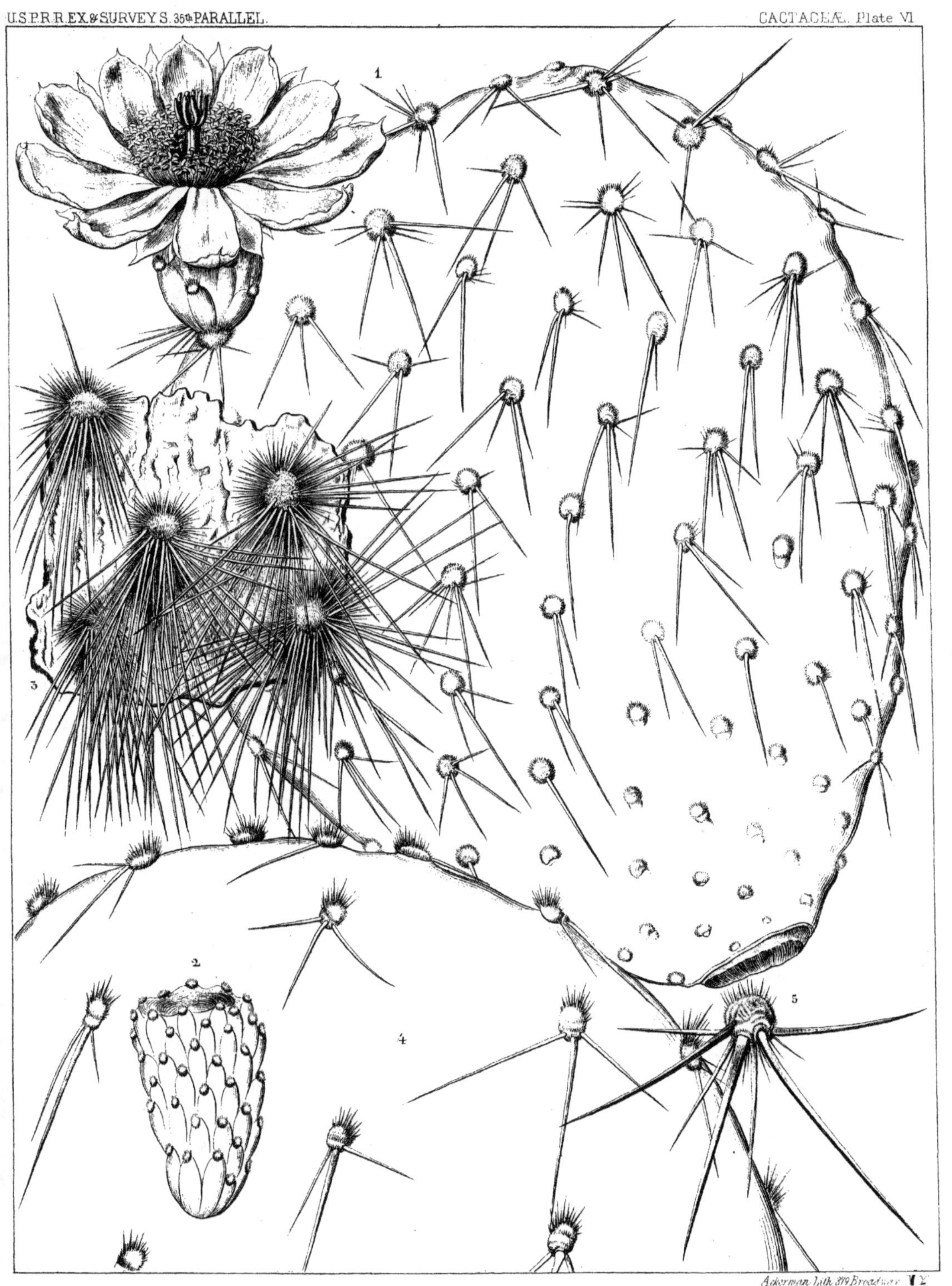

1–3 OPUNTIA CHLOROTICA, E & B. 4–5 O. PROCUMBENS, E & B.

Ackerman Lith. 379 Broadway N.Y.

1–2. OPUNTIA OCCIDENTALIS, E. & B. 3–4. O. ANGUSTATA, E. & B.

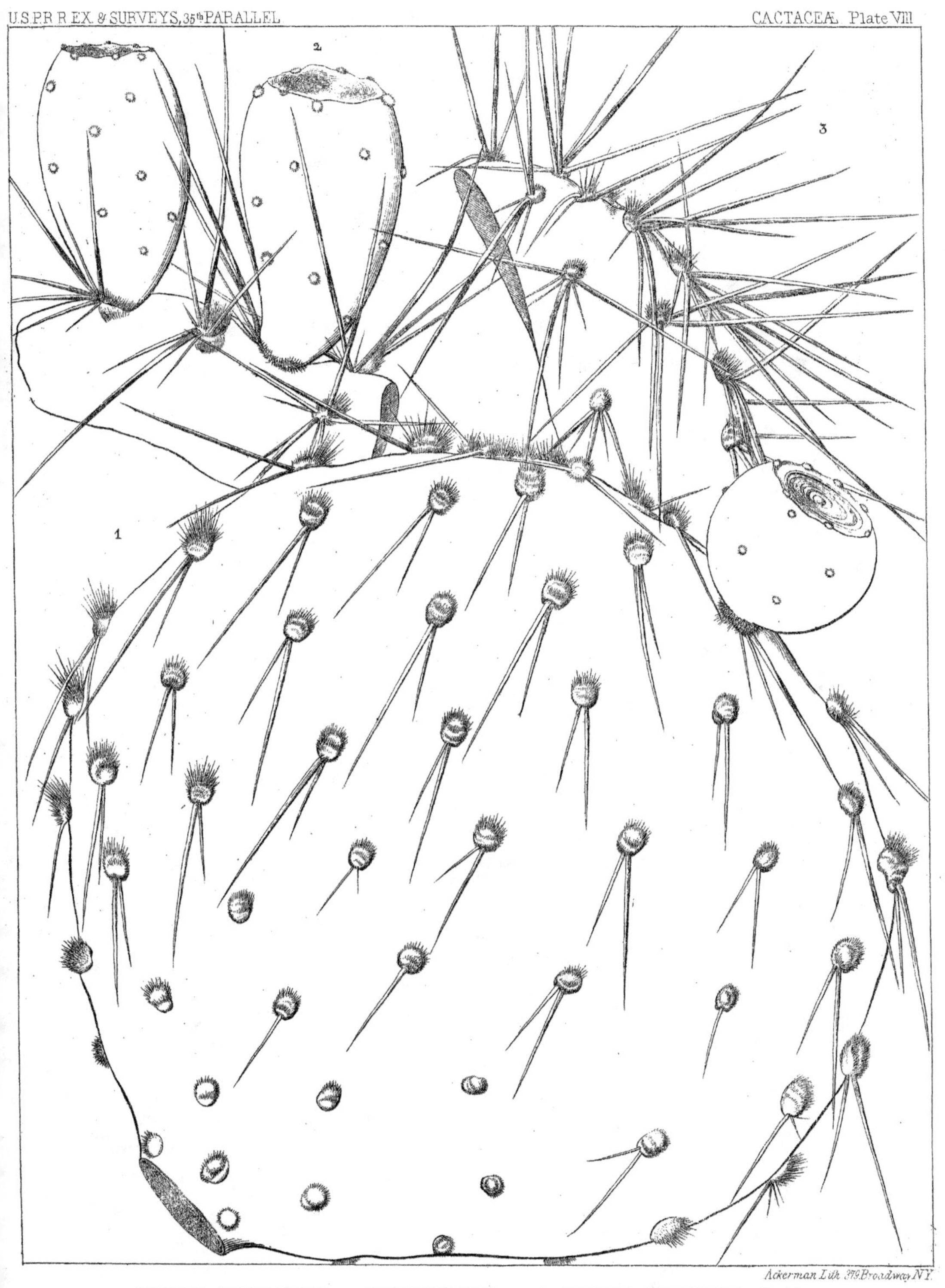

1. OPUNTIA ENGELMANNI *var.* CYCLODES. E.&B. 2–3. OPUNTIA TORTISPINA. E.&B.

Ackerman Lith. 379 Broadway NY

1–5, OPUNTIA CAMANCHICA, E & B. 6–8, OPUNTIA MOHAVENSIS, E & B.

Ackerman Lith. 379 Broadway N.Y.

1-2. OPUNTIA VULGARIS., *Mill.* 3-5. OP. RAFINESQUII, E.

1, OPUNTIA RAFINESQUII, *minor*, E. 2-3. OP. RAFINESQUII, *grandiflora*. E.
4, OPUNTIA FUSCO-ATRA. E.

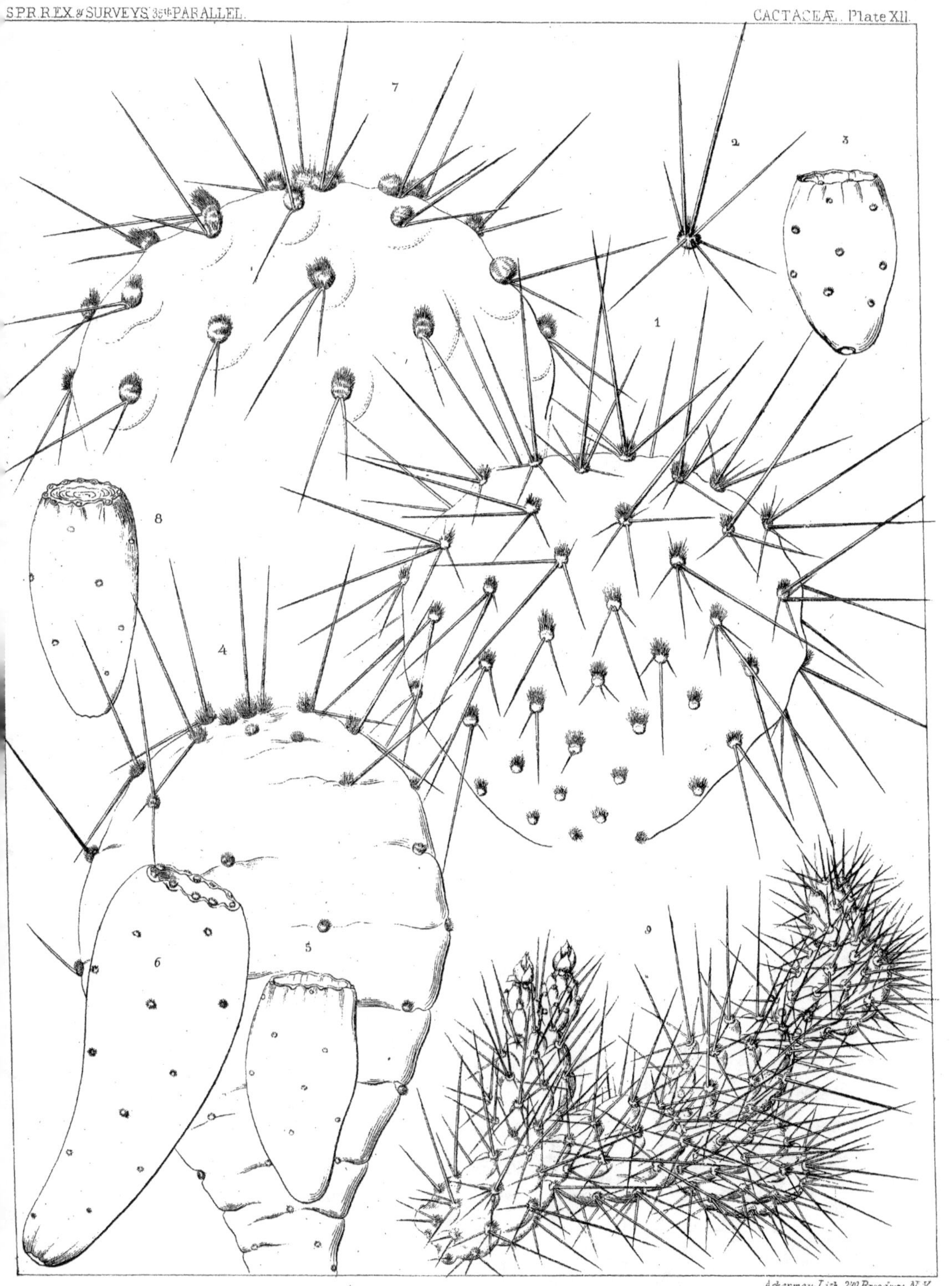

1-3, OPUNTIA CYMOCHILA, E & B. 4-6. OPUNTIA STENOCHILA, E & B. 7-8, OPUNTIA FUSIFORMIS, E & B.
9, OPUNTIA BRACHYARTHRA, E & B.

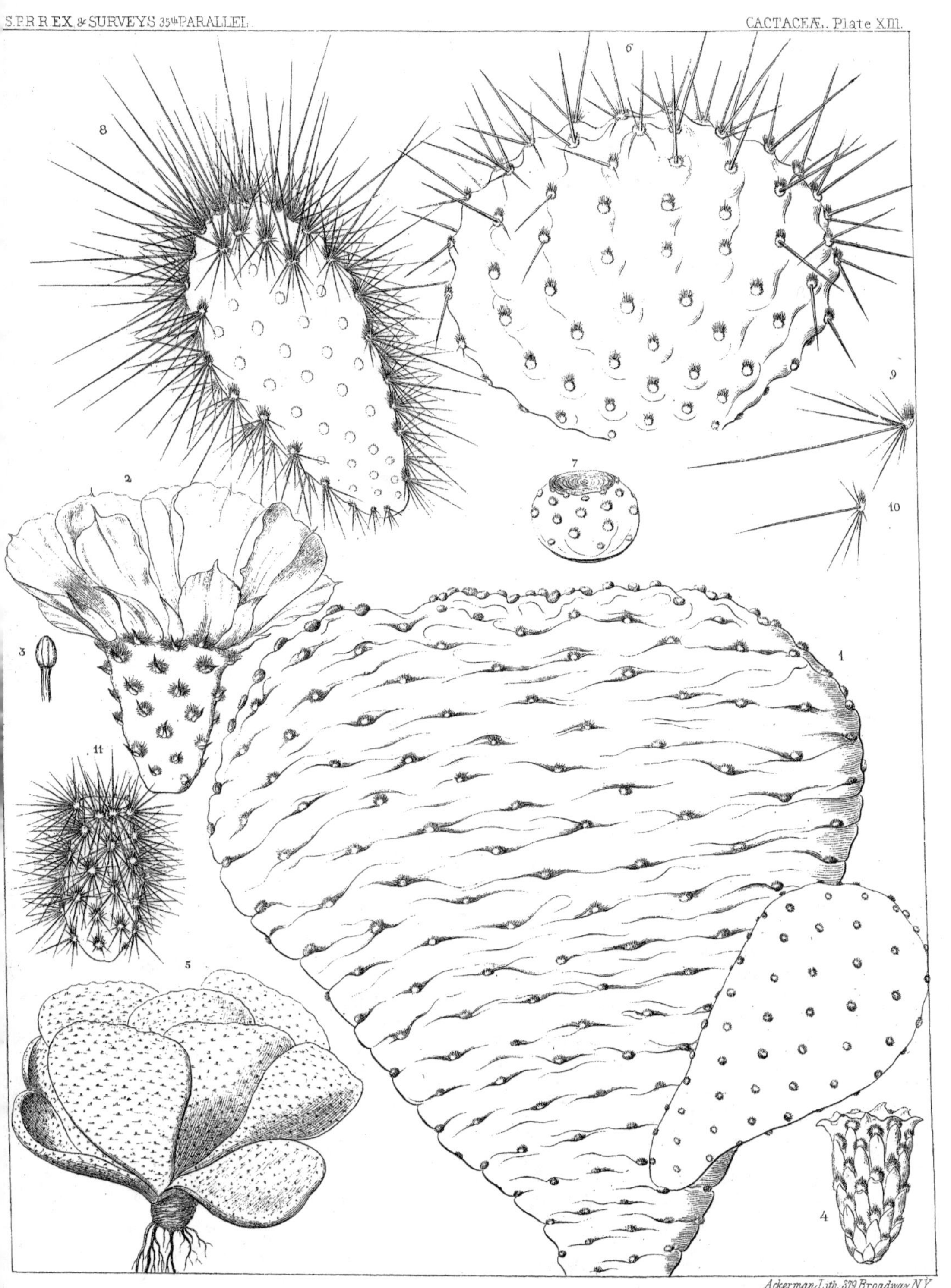

Ackerman Lith 379 Broadway N.Y.

1–5 OPUNTIA BASILARIS, E & B. 6–7. OPUNTIA SPHÆROCARPA, E & B
8–11 OPUNTIA ERINACEA, E & B.

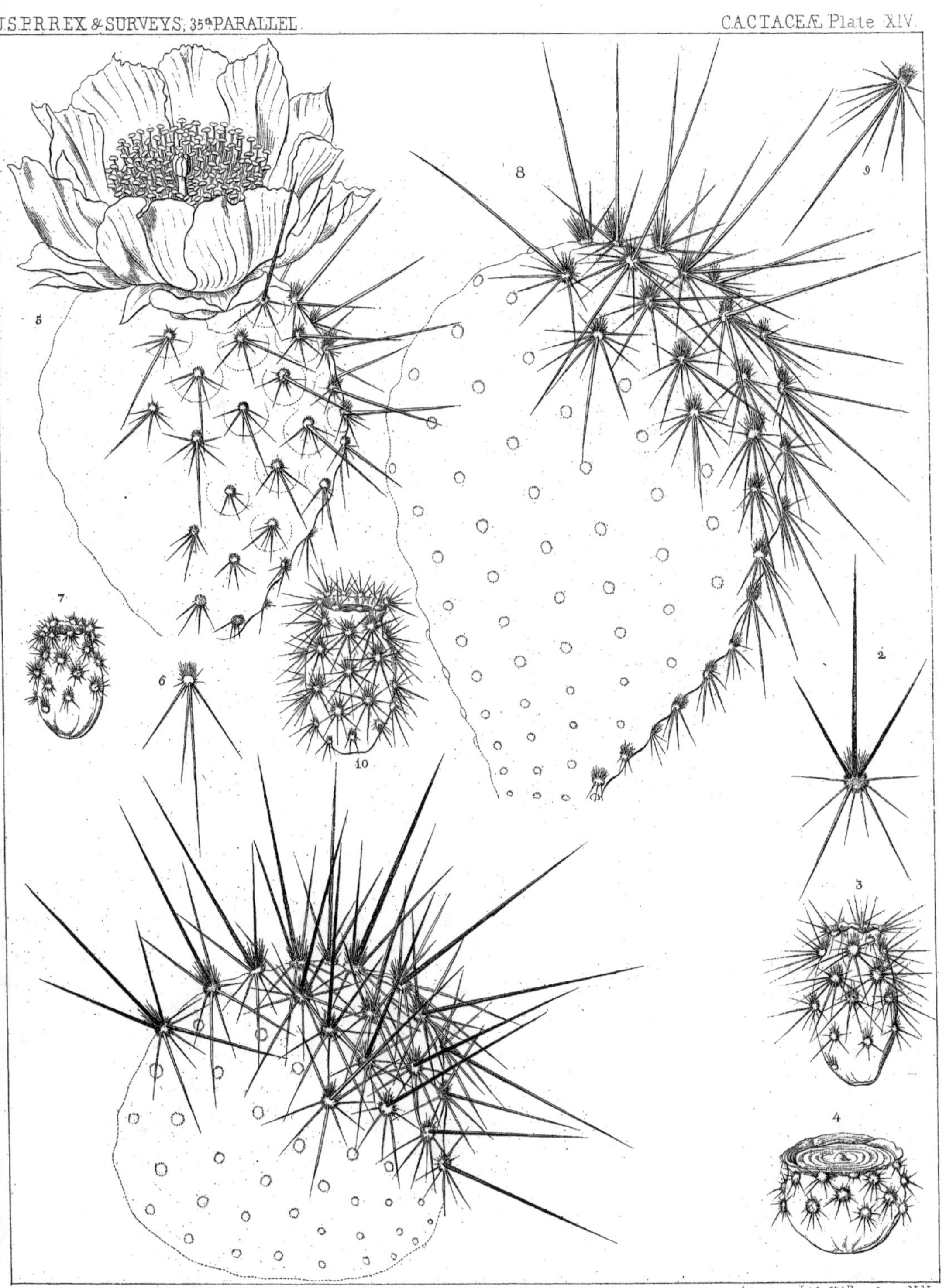

Ackerman Lith. 379 Broadway N.Y.

OPUNTIA MISSOURIENSIS, D.C.

1-3, *var.* RUFISPINA. 4, *var.* PLATYCARPA. 5-7, *var.* MICROSPERMA. 8-10. *var.* ALBISPINA.

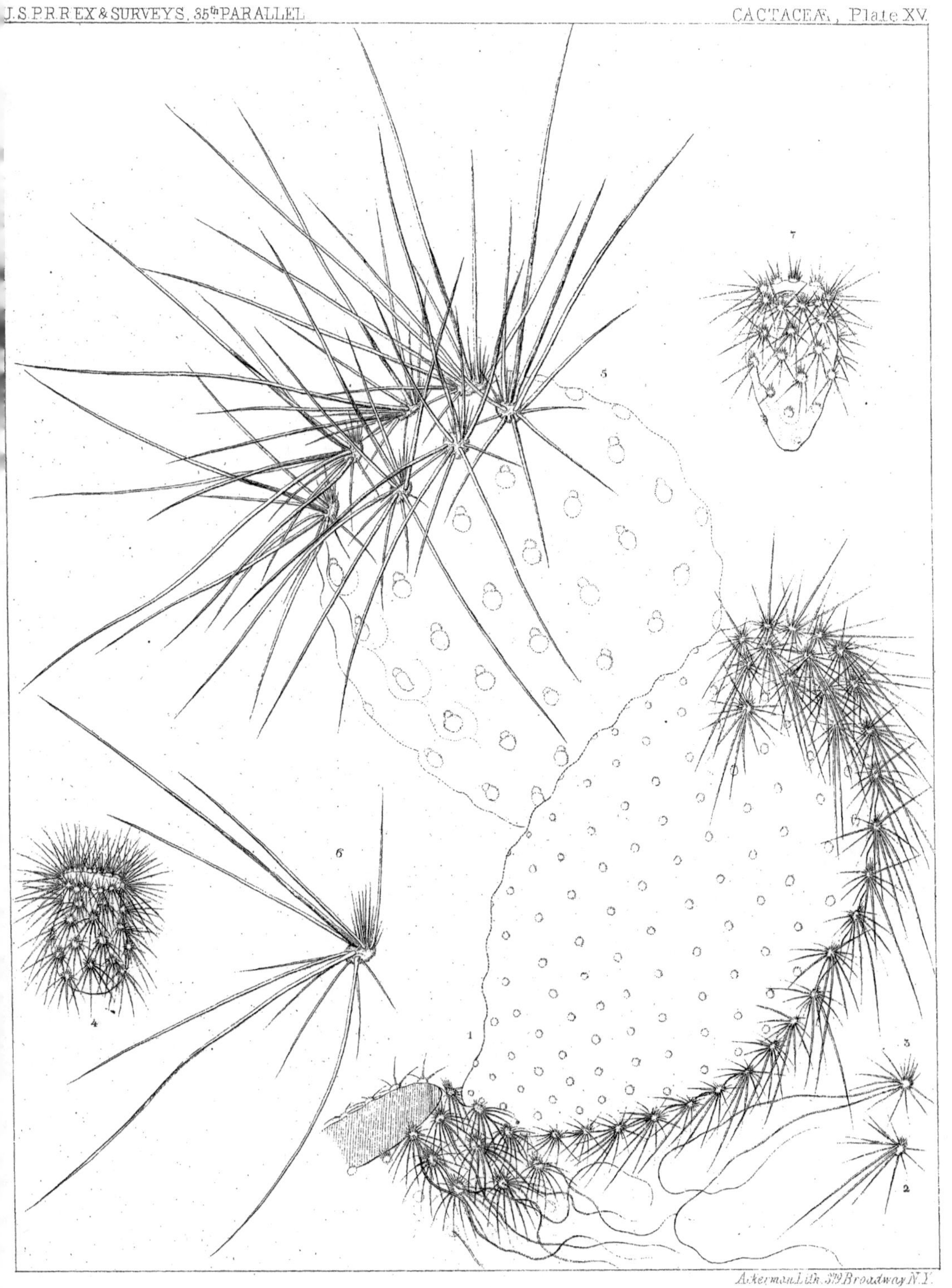

1-4. OPUNTIA MISSOURIENSIS. DC. var TRICHOPHORA. E & B.
5-6 OPUNTIA HYSTRICINA, E & B.

OPUNTIA DAVISII E. & B.

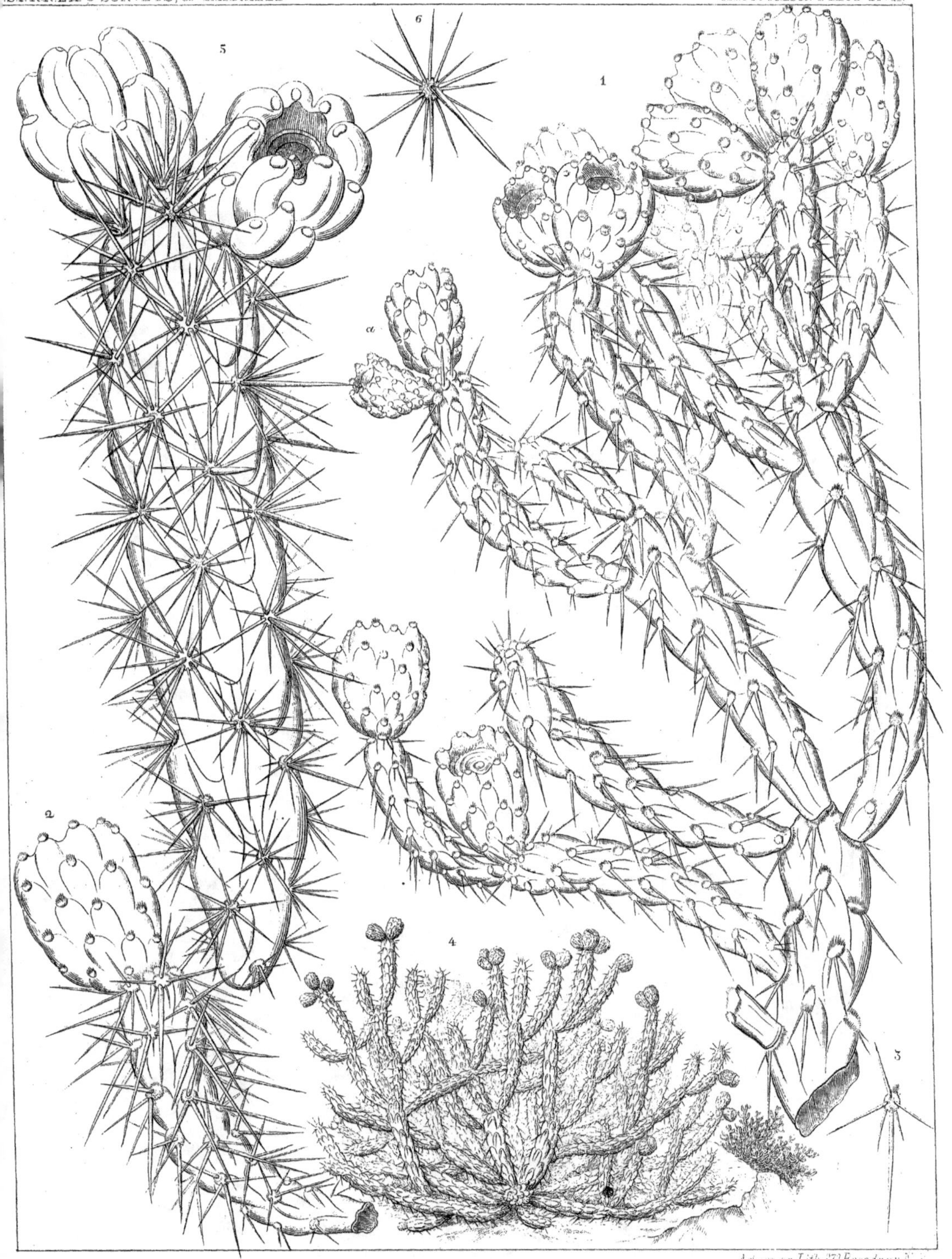

Ackerman Lith 379 Broadway N.Y.

1-4 OPUNTIA WHIPPLEI, E&B. 5-6 OP. ARBORESCENS, E.

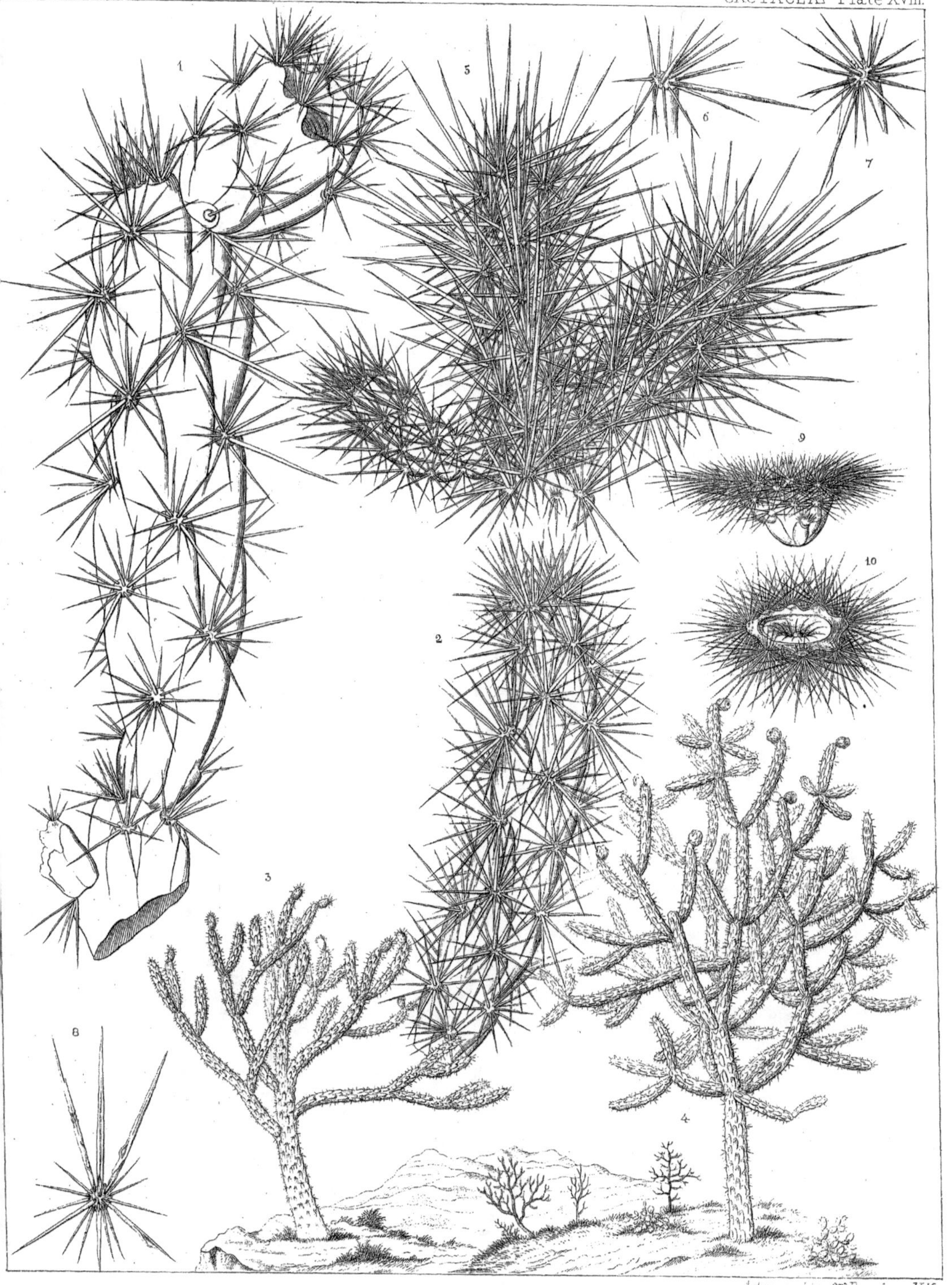

Ackerman Lith. 379 Broadway N.Y.

1-3. OPUNTIA ACANTHOCARPA, E. & B. 4, OP. ARBORESCENS, E. 5-10. OP. ECHINOCARPA, E. & B.

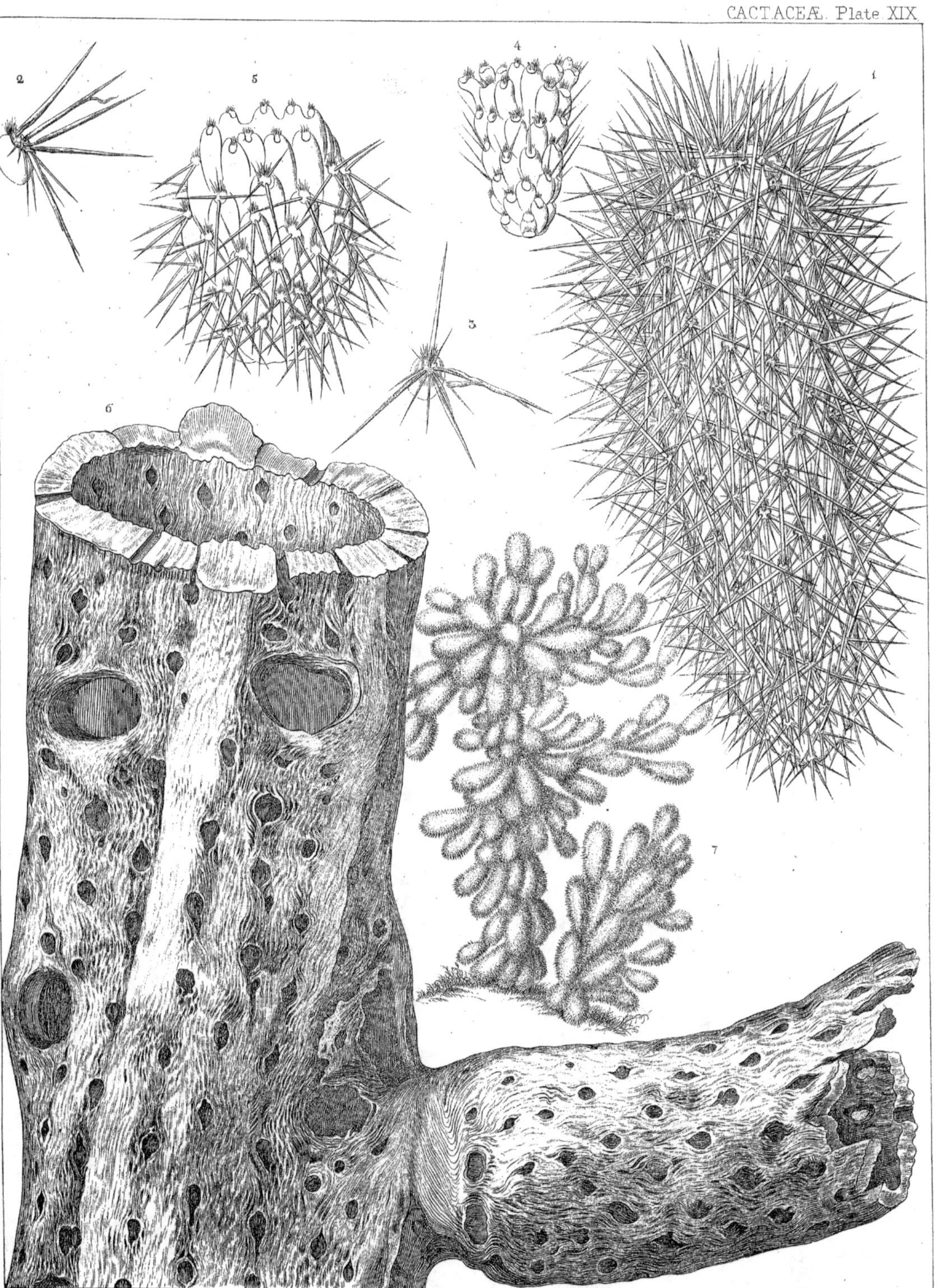

Ackerman Lith. 379 Broadway N.Y.

OPUNTIA BIGELOVII, E.

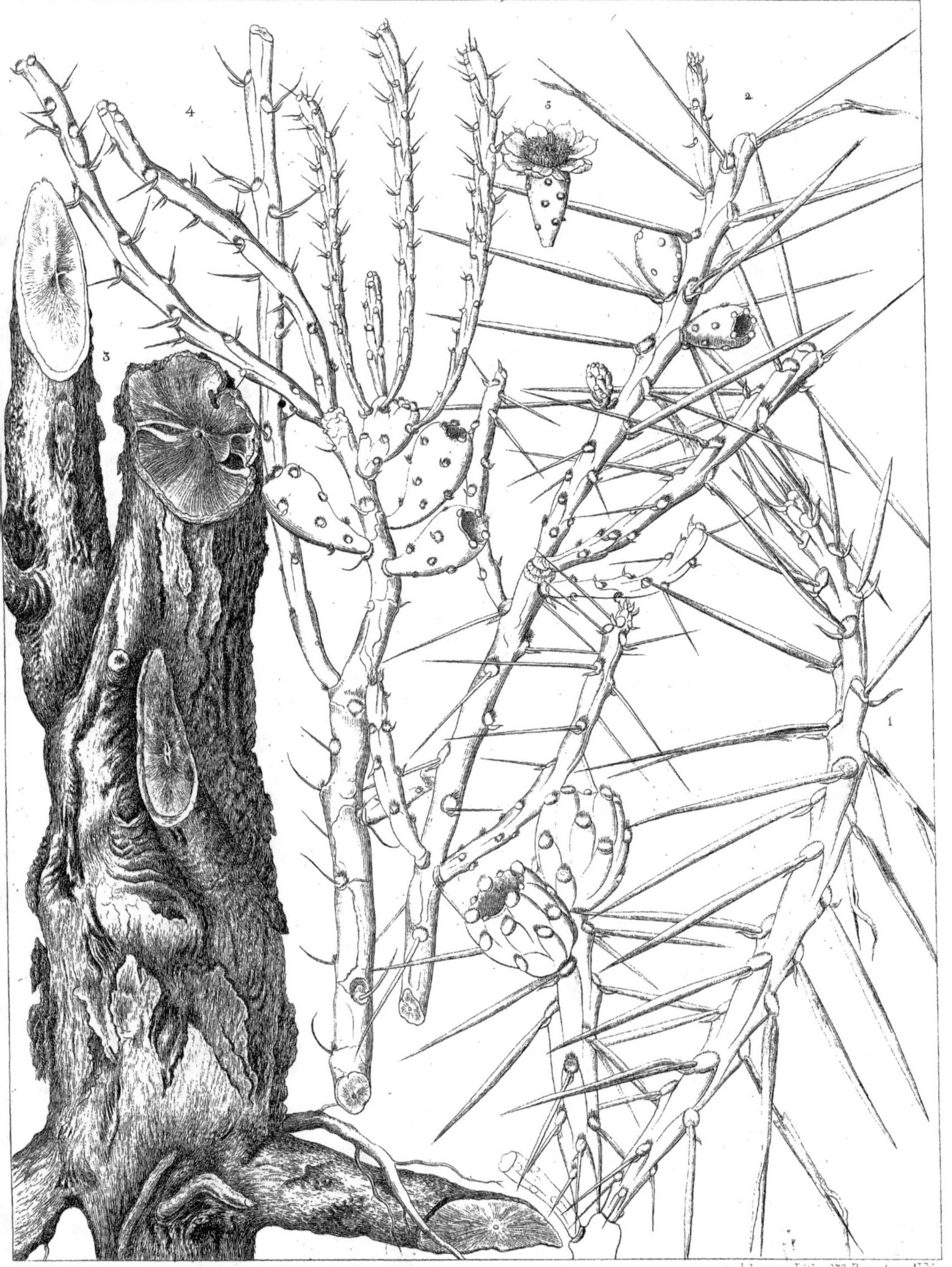

1. OPUNTIA VAGINATA, E. 2-5 OPUNTIA FRUTESCENS, E.
2-3. *var.* LONGISPINA. 4-5 *var.* BREVISPINA.

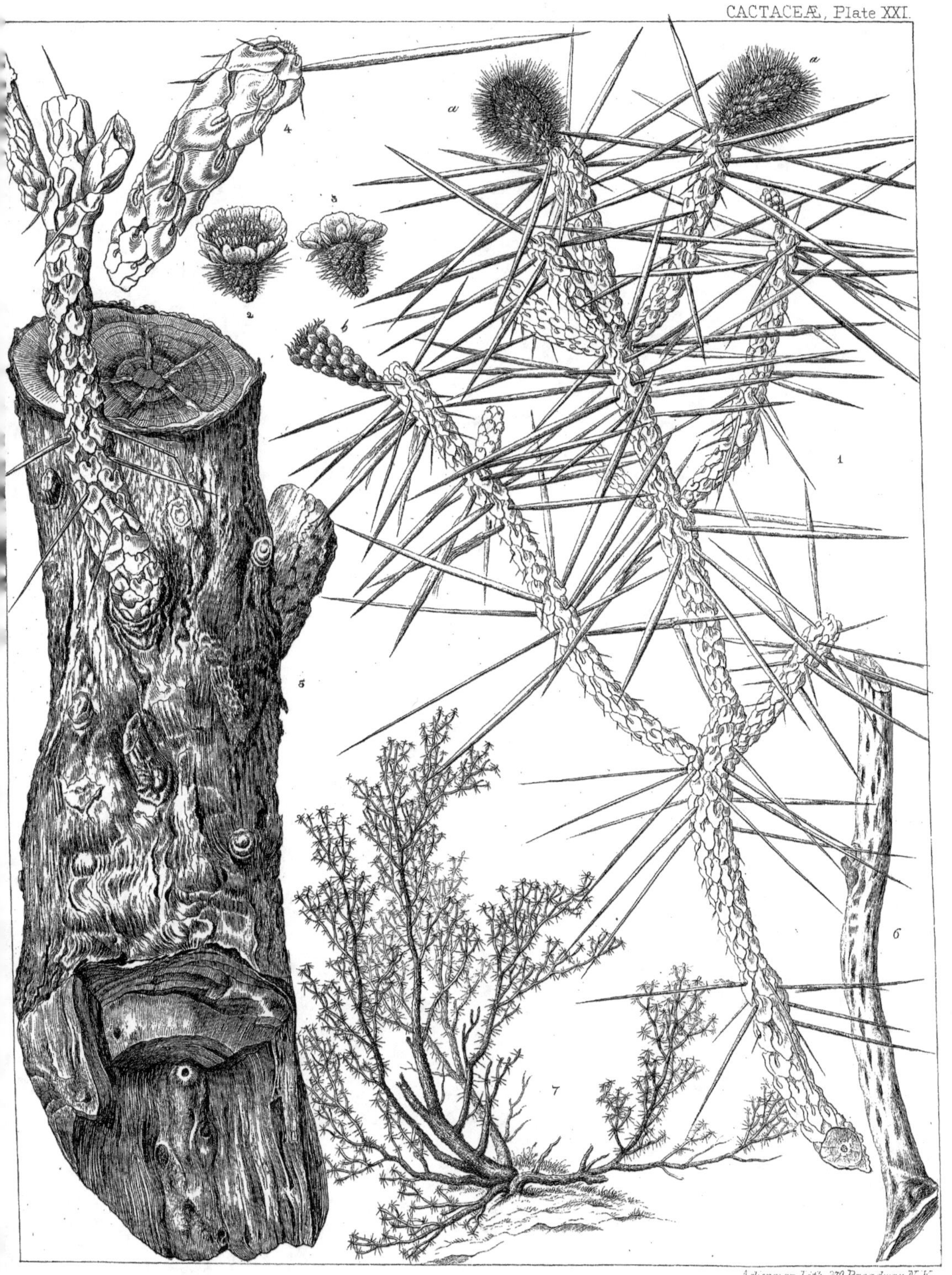

Ackerman Lith. 379 Broadway N.Y.

OPUNTIA TESSELLATA, E.

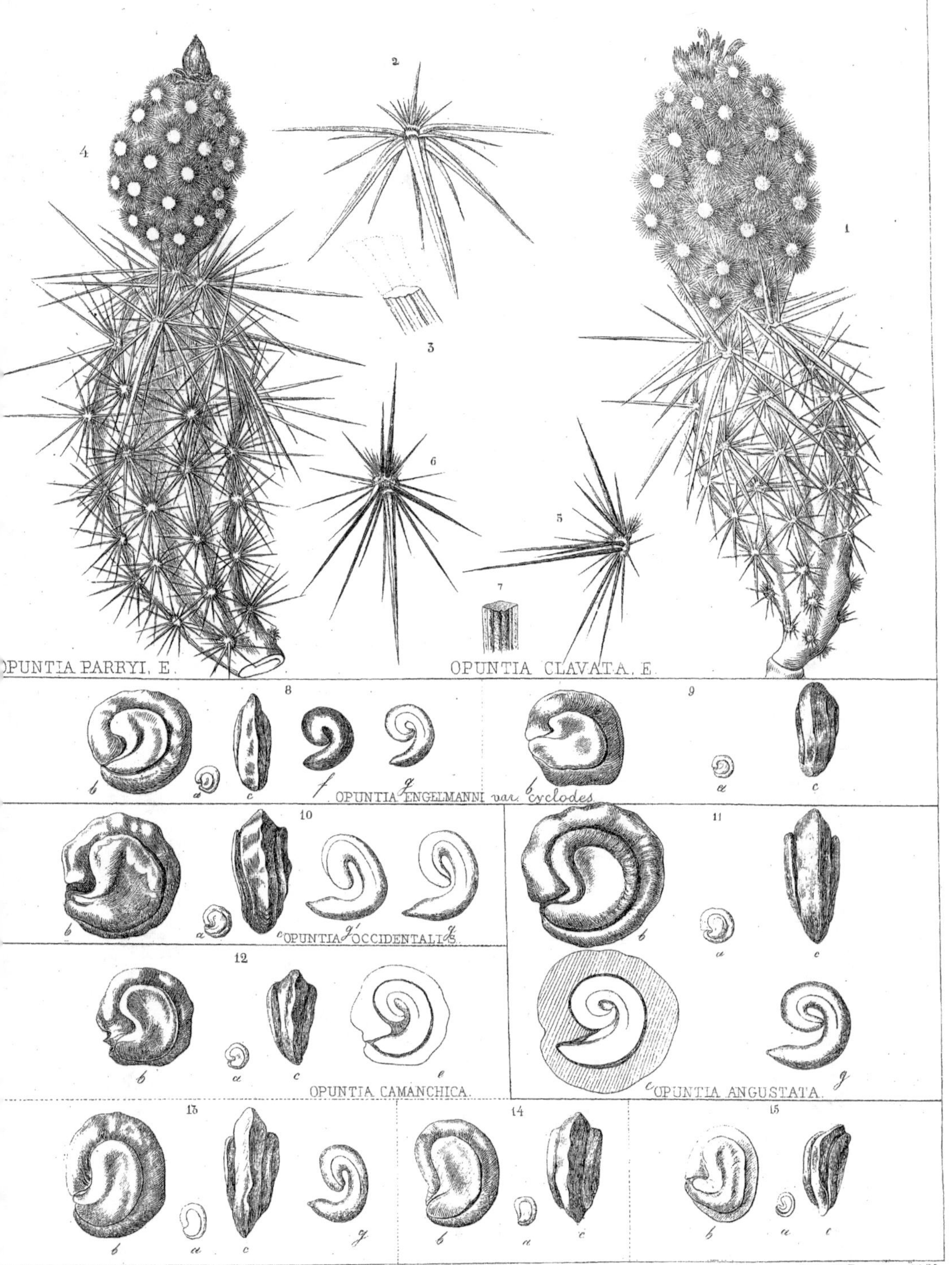

Ackerman Lith. 379 Broadway N.Y.

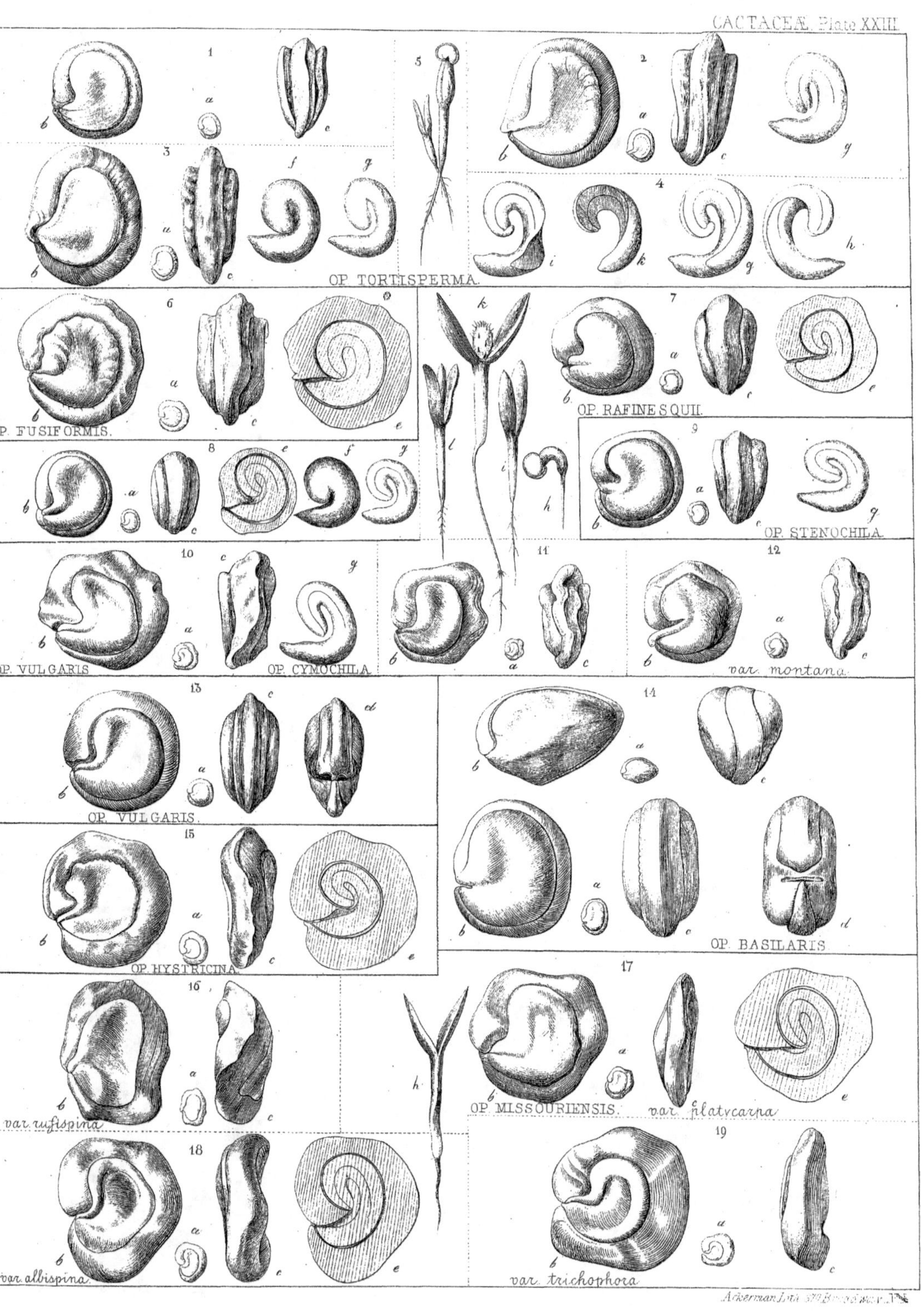
OP. TORTISPERMA.
OP. FUSIFORMIS.
OP. RAFINESQUII.
OP. STENOCHILA.
OP. VULGARIS.
OP. CYMOCHILA.
var. montana.
OP. VULGARIS.
OP. BASILARIS.
OP. HYSTRICINA.
var. rufispina.
OP. MISSOURIENSIS.
var. platycarpa.
var. albispina.
var. trichophora.
Ackerman Lith. 379 Broadway N.Y.

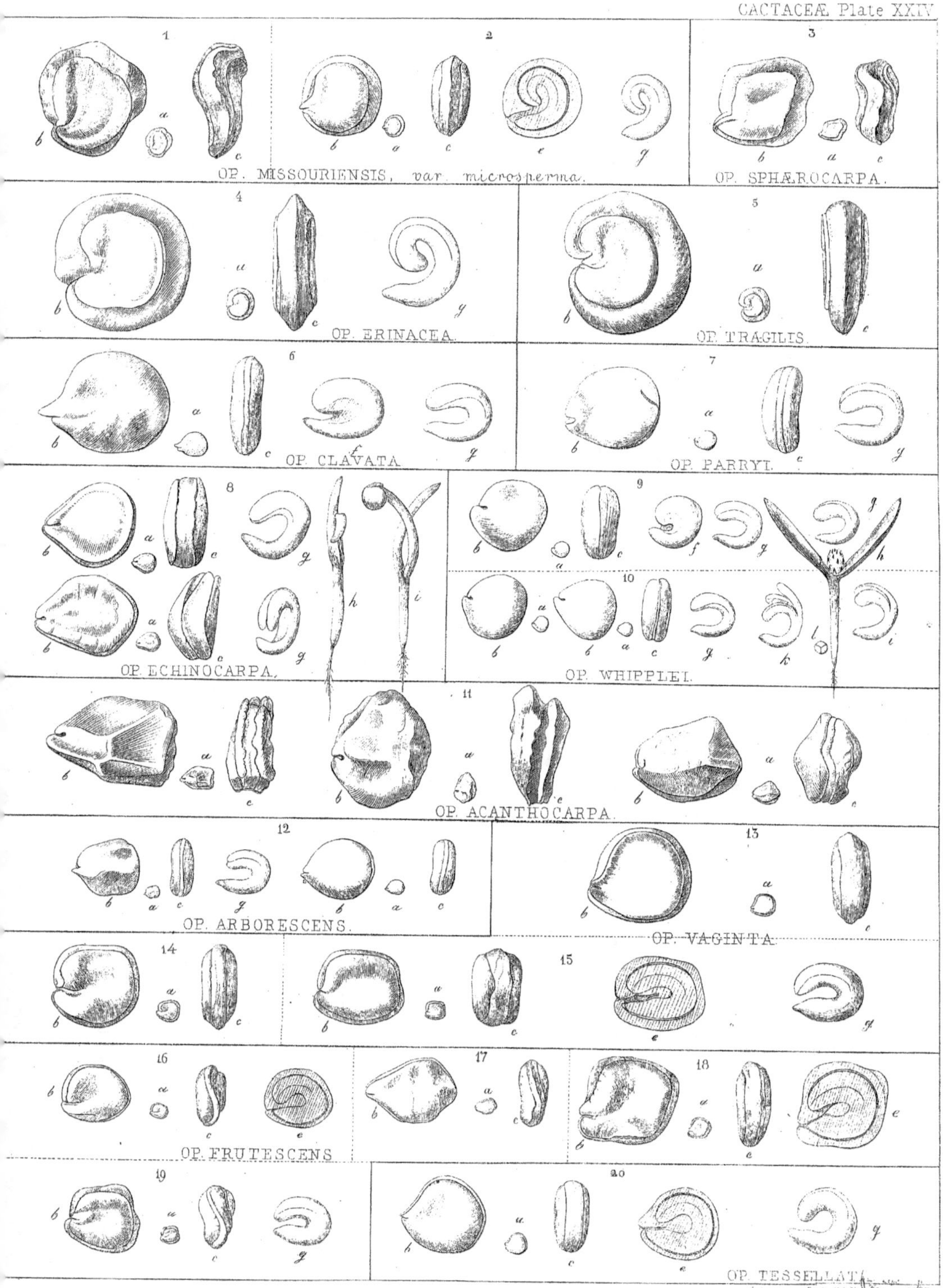

1, 2. OP. MISSOURIENSIS, *var. microsperma.*

3. OP. SPHÆROCARPA.

4. OP. ERINACEA.

5. OP. FRAGILIS.

6. OP. CLAVATA.

7. OP. PARRYI.

8. OP. ECHINOCARPA.

9, 10. OP. WHIPPLEI.

11. OP. ACANTHOCARPA.

12. OP. ARBORESCENS.

13. OP. VAGINTA.

14, 15, 16, 17, 18. OP. FRUTESCENS.

19, 20. OP. TESSELLATA.

Ackerman Lith. 379 Broadway N.Y.

INTRODUCTION.

The greater part of the botanical collections made by Dr. J. M. Bigelow, in the Pacific Railroad Survey, under the charge of Captain Whipple, were submitted to me for examination, in accordance with the instructions of the War Department. The plants that were collected before reaching Fort Smith, on the western borders of Arkansas, are of comparatively little interest, and are not included in the following list. The surveying party, in proceeding from Fort Smith to Albuquerque, travelled near the Canadian river, through the Indian territory and northern Texas ; thence through northeastern New Mexico to the Rio Grande. This river was crossed on the 10th of November, at which time the flowering season of most plants had passed ; and the explorations continued through western New Mexico, chiefly between the parallels of 35° and 36°, to the Great Colorado, which was reached on the 28th of February. The most interesting region of this part of the route is the valley of Williams' river, (commonly called Bill Williams' Fork,) a tributary of the Colorado. Some of the most remarkable plants of the collection were found here, and it is a matter of regret that a country so rich and peculiar in its Flora (and I am informed by Professor Baird that its Fauna is equally remarkable) was not visited at a more favorable season. From the Colorado the route was across the California desert to the Cajon Pass, in the southern part of the Sierra Nevada ; thence through Coco Mungo and Los Angeles to San Pedro, on the Pacific coast. Here the surveys of Captain Whipple terminated ; but Dr. Bigelow remained in California until near the first of June, and improved the time in exploring considerable portions of the valleys of the Sacramento and San Joaquin, as well as numerous tributaries of those rivers. His ample collections were brought home in perfect order, and the following report affords abundant proof of the zeal and success with which he labored. A number of new genera, and more than sixty new species, have been discovered by Dr. Bigelow, and he has added much valuable information upon many heretofore imperfectly known plants.

The observations of Dr. Bigelow upon the geographical botany of the regions explored are interesting, and are embodied by him in a separate memoir, as also are his notes upon the more interesting forest trees of the country.

The Cactaceæ collected in the Expedition have been elaborated conjointly by Dr. Engelmann and Dr. Bigelow, and are described by them in a separate portion of Captain Whipple's report. The Compositæ and Scrophulariaceæ were described by my friend Dr. Gray, to whom I am indebted also for much valuable aid in drawing up this catalogue, as will be seen by the frequent quotation of his manuscript names in the following pages. The drawings were, with few exceptions, executed by Sprague and Riocreux, two of the most skilful botanical artists now living. All the engraving has been done upon stone by Prestele, who excels in this branch of the art.

JOHN TORREY.

NEW YORK, *January* 12, 1857.

No. 4.

DESCRIPTION OF THE GENERAL BOTANICAL COLLECTIONS.

BY JOHN TORREY.

RANUNCULACEÆ.

Clematis ligusticifolia, *Nutt. in Torr. & Gray, Fl.* 1, *p.* 9. Near San Antonita, New Mexico; October. In fruit.

Clematis Bigelovii, (sp. nov.): humilis? herbacea? glabella; foliis pinnatis vel subbipinnatis; foliolis 7–9 trilobis tripartitisve longiuscule petiolulatis, lobis subovatis integerrimis nunc incisis; pedunculis solitariis unifloris; calyce subcampanulato, sepalis anguste oblongis haud crassis apice obtuso patentibus; caudis carpellorum dense plumosus. On the Sandia mountains, New Mexico; October. Of this apparently new Clematis there is only a single flowering specimen and a few mature carpels in the collection. The stem appears to be low and nearly herbaceous, but it probably elongates and climbs by the petioles. The leaflets are only from half an inch to an inch in length, membranaceous and inconspicuously veined; those of the lower pinnæ more divided. Peduncle an inch or two in length, nodding in flower. Sepals scarcely over half an inch in length, pale, membranaceous in the dried state, probably a little thickened in the living plant, but not leathery as in C. Viorna, C. Pitcheri, etc., almost glabrous, except the densely *tomentose margin, not appendaged, but the obtuse tip spreading. Carpels silky* pubescent, becoming glabrate; the tails over an inch long, plumose as in C. Viorna. The flowers are smaller than in any other North American species of this division.

Clematis lasiantha. *Nutt. in Torr. & Gray, Fl.* 1, *p.* 9. Hill sides, Napa valley, April 27. Only the male plant of this showy species was collected by Dr. Bigelow. The female was not known when the Flora of North America was published; but it has since been found by Colonel Frémont. The carpels have tails of about an inch and a half in length.

Thalictrum Fendleri, *Engelm. in Gray, Pl. Fendl. p.* 5; var.? polycarpum: glaberrimum; carpellis numerosioribus eglandulosis. Mountain ravines, New Mexico. In fruit October, &c. Sides of rivulets, Napa valley, California, April 25, (with immature fruit). It occurs in Coulter's California collection, in flower only. Leaves mostly petiolate, ternately decompound: leaflets obovate and cuneate, incisely 3-lobed; the lobes cut or entire. Panicle contracted, few-flowered. Sepals ovate, rather acute. Carpels 15–25, ovate, compressed, with two prominent ribs on each side. Stigma linear, elongated. T. Fendleri has a more compound and spreading panicle than our plant, and the carpels are more or less glandular.

Thalictrum dioicum, *Linn.; Torr. & Gray, Fl.* 1, *p.* 38. Mountains near San Gabriel; March 23. Only the male flowers are in the collection; and it is possible the plant may be distinct from T. dioicum. That species occurs in Oregon.

Anemone nemorosa, *Linn.;* var. caule gracili elongato; foliis utrinque pubescentibus. San

Geronimo Ranch; April 12. Differs from the ordinary form of A. nemorosa, in its tall stem (which is a foot or more below the involucre), the elongated petioles, and the pretty strong pubescence of the leaves. The leaflets are rhombic-ovate, incised and rather coarsely toothed, but the lateral ones are not two-parted in any of the specimens. Such leaflets, however, occur now and then in the eastern A. nemorosa. Rev. Mr. Spalding found the same plant on the Kooskooskee, in Oregon, and it exists in Geyer's collection.

RANUNCULUS AQUATILIS, *Linn. sp. p.* 556. Corte Madera; in water; April 10–13. This seems not to be the form or species which almost universally represents the section Batrachium in North America, but what is called R. aquatilis by those European authors, who do not subdivide the Linnæan species extremely. It is a state destitute of emersed leaves.

RANUNCULUS HEDERACEUS, *Linn.* var. With the preceding. Nearly the R. tripartitus, *D.C.*, as to the leaves, etc.; but the receptacle of the fruit is glabrous. The petals are oblong-obovate and twice the length of the calyx. This is the first Batrachium, bearing emersed leaves, which we have received from any part of North America.

RANUNCULUS TRACHYSPERMUS, var.? LINDHEIMERI, *Engelm. in Pl. Lindh.* 1, *p.* 3. Napa valley, in wet places; April 26. The granulate roughened carpels principally distinguish this from R. pusillus (to which R. oblongifolius, *Ell.*, with large bright yellow petals, numerous stamens, and apiculate achenia, does not properly belong). The heads of carpels incline to become oblong.

RANUNCULUS DIVARICATUS, *Schrank; Gray, Pl. Wright.* 2, *p.* 8. In the bed of the Pecos; October.

RANUNCULUS AFFINIS, *R. Br.; Var. β. Hook. Fl. Bor.-Am.* 1, *p.* 13, *t.* 6. Near San Antonita; October. In fruit.

RANUNCULUS CALIFORNICUS, *Benth. Pl. Hartw. p.* 295. R. dissectus, *Hook. & Arn. Bot. Beech. p.* 316. R. delphinifolius, *Torr. & Gray, Fl. Suppl. p.* 659, *non H. B. & K.* Los Angeles; March 21. This is R. acris *β. Torr. & Gray* = R. Deppii, *Nutt. Mss.* It agrees exactly with Nuttall's specimens. Two forms of the plant were collected by Dr. Bigelow. 1. About a span high, manifestly pubescent, and the leaves with narrowly linear segments. 2. Tall and stout; less pubescent; leaves with oblong-cuneate segments. Fremont gathered the latter in 1846, near San José.

RANUNCULUS REPENS, *Linn.; Torr. & Gray, Fl. l. c.* San Francisco; April 5. Resembles the European. In the long styles it agrees with some of the forms of this polymorphous species, though not with the ordinary state of it, that we find in the northern States.

RANUNCULUS CANUS, *Benth. Pl. Hartw. p.* 295. Hill sides, Duffield's Ranch, Sierra Nevada; May 11. A less white-hairy form; some of the radical leaves only 3–5-parted. The plant is probably only a state of R. repens.

RANUNCULUS HEBECARPUS, *Hook. & Arn. Bot. Beechey, p.* 369. R. parviflorus, *Torr. & Gray, Fl.* 1, *p.* 25. Along rivulets, Sonora, May 9th; and hill-sides, Knight's Ferry, Stanislaus; May 8. Not an uncommon species in the southern part of California. It is regarded by most of our botanists as a variety of R. parviflorus, which, indeed, it very much resembles. This species differs, however, it being much less hairy; the lobes of the leaves are broader and less acute; the fruit is decidedly tuberculate, while in R. hebecarpus it is merely a little roughened, and the pubescence longer. In the latter the beak of the fruit is decidedly shorter than in the former.

AQUILEGIA CANADENSIS, *Linn.; Torr. & Gray, Fl.* 1, *p.* 29; var. sepalis limbo petalorum duplo-longiorius, calcare subæqualibus. A formosa, *Fisch. in DC. Prodr.* 1, *p.* 20*; Torr. & Gray, l. c.* Plains near Oakland, California; April 5.

DELPHINIUM NUDICAULE, *Torr. & Gray, Fl.* 1, *p.* 33, *&* 661. D. sarcophyllum, *Hook. & Arn. Bot. Beechey, p.* 317. Hill sides, Napa valley, April 27, and near San Geronimo Ranch, California, April 12. A beautiful species with large scarlet flowers. It would be a great acquisition to our gardens.

A splendid scarlet-flowered Delphinium was discovered by Dr. Parry, in 1850, on the mountains east of San Diego. It is D. coccinium, *Torr.* (Bot. Mexican Boundary Survey, with a figure). It differs from D. nudicaule in the leaves, the lobes of which are deeply 3-cleft, with linear-lanceolate acute segments.

DELPHINIUM AZUREUM, *Michx. Fl.* 1, *p.* 314: var. floribus cœruleo-albidis, *Benth. Pl. Hartw. p.* 296. Plains, etc., Knight's Ferry, Stanislaus; May 7.

DELPHINIUM PATENS, *Benth. Pl. Hartw., p.* 296. Hills, Napa; and on mountains near Oakland; April 4–25.

DELPHINIUM SIMPLEX, *Dougl. in Hook. Fl. Bor.-Amer.* 1, *p.* 25; *Hook. & Arn. Bot. Beechey, p.* 317. Napa valley; April 26.

DELPHINIUM VARIEGATUM, *Torr. & Gray, Fl.* 1, *p.* 32; D. decorum, *Benth. Pl. Hartw. p.* 295. Napa valley; April 26. Flowers sometimes almost white.

DELPHINIUM DECORUM, *Fisch. & Mey. Index sem.* (3) *Petrop., p.* 33. Plains near Punta de los Reyes; April 17. Perhaps D. variegatum is not distinct from this.

DELPHINIUM SCOPULORUM, *Gray, Pl. Wright.* 2, *p.* 9. In the Sandia mountains, New Mexico; October. In fruit.

ACTÆA SPICATA, *Linn.* var. ARGUTA, *Nutt. in Torr. & Gray, Fl.* 1, *p.* 35. Redwoods, Corte Madera, and Oakland; April 4–10. Not found before south of Oregon. We are of opinion that A. rubra and A. alba are likewise only varieties of A. spicata.

PÆONIA BROWNII, *Dougl. in Hook. Fl. Bor.-Amer.* 1, *p.* 27; *Bot. Reg.* 25, *t.* 30. Cocomungo, March 17; and Duffield's ranch, Sierra Nevada, May 10. P. Californica, *Nutt.*, is not a distinct species.

CROSSOSOMA CALIFORNICA, (Tab. I,) *Nutt. Pl. Gamb. in Journ. Acad. Philad.* (*ser.* 2) 1, *p.* 150. Cañons on Williams' River, a branch of the Colorado, western New Mexico; February 8. In the memoir above quoted, Mr. Nuttall does not express any opinion as to the affinities of this genus, owing to the embryo being unknown, the seeds in all his specimens being imperfect; but he says that it "may well form a Suborder Crossosomeæ." On the ticket of a fragment of this plant, which he sent us, he has written: Nat. Order Pæoniaceæ. Unfortunately, our specimens are only in flower, and the ripe seeds are still wanting. Although the stamens are decidedly perigynous, and the seeds are furnished with an ample fimbrillate arillus, the plant may nevertheless belong to the tribe or Suborder Pæoniaceæ. We were once inclined to refer it to tribe Spirææ of Rosaceæ, to which it has some resemblance in the flowers; but it is destitute of stipules, and arillate seeds are not found in that order. We should place this remarkable plant in Dilleniaceæ, were it not for the perigynous stamens. These are inserted in several series into the upper part of a thin disk which, lining the tube of the calyx, projects in a somewhat tumid border around the base of the pistils, as in Pæonia.

BERBERIDACEÆ.

VANCOUVERIA HEXANDRA, *Morr. & Dec. in Ann. Sc. Nat.* (2 *ser.*) 2, *p.* 351; *Torr. & Gray, Fl.* 1, *p.* 52. Epimedium hexandrum, *Hook. Fl. Bor.-Am.* 1, *p.* 31, *t.* 13. Deep ravines and shady woods, Napa valley; April 27.

BERBERIS AQUIFOLIUM, *Pursh, Fl.* 1, *p.* 219, *t.* 4, (*excl. fig.* 4.) Hill-sides Downieville, Yuba; May 22. In the specimens from this locality, the leaflets are mostly reduced to a single pair, and are sometimes even solitary. The Var. REPENS was found in the Sandia mountains of New Mexico.

BERBERIS PINNATA, *Lag. Elench.* 1803, *p.* 6; *Benth. Pl. Hartw., p.* 296. Mahonia fascicularis, *DC. Syst.* 2, *p.* 19, *and in Deless. Ic.* 2, *t.* 3. Mountains near Oakland; April 4. This agrees pretty well with Delessert's figure, but we are not confident that it is distinct from B. aquifolium. The short petioles are pretty constant, but we can find no other reliable characters. This plant occurs also near San Francisco.

BERBERIS TRIFOLIATA, *Moricand, Pl. Amer. t.* 69? In arroyas and cañons; Lithodendron creek western New Mexico; December 4, (in fruit.) This species grows 15 feet high. The leaves have frequently two pairs of leaflets, which are furnished with 2–4 (sometimes more) very strong angular teeth. The fructiferous racemes are loose, and the pedicles of the dark-blue berries are half an inch long. The same plant grows between the Rio Grande and the Gila, where it was collected by Major Emory, and it is the B. pinnata of Sitgreave's report. Colonel Frémont found it on the tributaries of the Virgin river. Dr. Gregg collected, near the battle-field of Buena Vista, what seems to be the same species, except that he says the berries are reddish; but they may be so only when they are unripe.

Berberis Fendleri, *Gray, Fl. Fendl., p.* 5. Mountain arroyas and bluffs on the Pecos, New Mexico; October. In fruit. The lower cauline leaves are spinulose-toothed, and the racemes appear not to have been many-flowered; otherwise the specimens accord with those of Fendler.

PAPAVERACEÆ.

Eschscholtzia Californica, *Cham.; Torr. & Gray, Fl.* 1, *p.* 664. Sandy plains, Cocomungo; March 19. Common in most parts of California.

Eschscholtzia Douglasii, *Hook. & Arn. Bot. Beech., p.* 320; *Torr. & Gray, l. c.*—Hill-sides Knight's ferry, Stanislaus; May 8. We find the acumination of the calyx nearly as long as in the preceding species. The flowers, too, are smaller than in the Oregon plant.

Eschscholtzia Douglasii, Var. *tenuifolia.* E. tenuifolia, *Benth. in Trans. Hort. Soc.* (*ser.* 2) 1, *p.* 408. With E. Douglasii, from which it differs only in its usually very short stem, long sub-radical peduncles, and very narrow segments of the leaves; characters which are by no means constant. What appears to be a diminutive form of this variety, was collected on Williams' River of the Great Colorado, early in February.

Dendromecon rigidum, *Benth. in Hort. Trans.* (*ser.* 2) 1, *p.* 407; *Hook. Ic. t.* 37. Gravelly hills near Oakland, California; April 5.

Meconella Californica, *Torr. & Frêm. in Frêm.* 2*d Rep.* Mokelumne hill, California; May 17. Also found on the American river by Mr. Rich, and near San Francisco by Mr. Thurber. We have also specimens collected in California by Mr. Gibbes. It differs from M. Oregana in having 11 or 12 stamens, and in its much larger flowers.

Platystigma lineare, *Benth. in Hort. Trans.* (2 *ser.*) 1, *p*, 407; *Hook. Ic. t.* 38; *Torr. & Gray, Fl.* 1, *p.* 65. Low places near San Francisco; April 8. A much rarer plant than the next.

Platystemon Californicum, *Benth. l. c.; Lindl. Bot. Reg. t.* 1679; *Torr. & Gray, Fl. l. c.* Cocomungo, March 17; plains near San Gabriel, March 23. β leiocarpum, *Torr. & Gray, l. c.* Hills and plains, Benicia, April 24; Knight's ferry, Stanislaus, May 8.

Meconopsis heterophylla, *Benth. l. c.; Torr. & Gray, Fl.* 1, *p.* 61; *Hook. Ic.* 8, *t.* 732. Hill-sides, Martinez, California; April 23.

Argemone Mexicana, *Linn.* Plains of Deer creek, Arkansas; August.

FUMARIACEÆ.

Dicentra formosa, *DC. Syst.* 2, *p.* 109; *Torr. & Gray, Fl.* 1, *p.* 603, (not 67.) Fumaria formosa, *Dryand. Bot. Mag. t.* 1335. Mountains near Oakland, April 5; hillsides and ravines, Duffield's ranch, Sierra Nevada, May 12.

CRUCIFERÆ.

Cheiranthus capitatus, *Dougl. in Hook, Fl. Bor.-Amer.* 1, *p.* 38; *Torr. & Gray, Fl.* 1, *p.* 71. C. asper, *Cham. & Schlecht. in Linnæa* 1, *p.* 14, (excl. syn.) Erysimum grandiflorum, *Nutt. in Torr. & Gray, Fl.* 1, *p.* 96. Sand Hills, near the sea-shore, Punta de los Reyes, April 17. A true Cheiranthus.

Nasturtium palustre, DC.: the usual short-fruited form. On the Pecos, and St. Domingo; October.

NASTURTIUM OBTUSUM, *Nutt. in Torr. & Gray, Fl.* 1, *p.* 74. River banks, Middle Yuba, May 2. The North American species of this genus need a careful revision. Thei are probably too many of them described in our books.

NASTURTIUM CURVISILIQUA, *Nutt. l. c.* Gravelly hills near the Colorado; Feb uary. Without full-grown fruit.

BARBAREA VULGARIS, *R. Br.*; var. pedicellis angulo recto patulis, etc. *Benth. Fl. Hartw., p.* 297. Near San Francisco and Punta de los Reyes, April.

STREPTANTHUS FLAVESCENS, *Hook. Ic.* 1, *t.* 34; *Torr. & Gray, Fl.* 1, *p.* 77. River banks, Benicia, April 24. Sepals hairy. Pods about an inch and a half long, nearly terete, sparsely hirsute, with a long tapering point, strictly erect. Pedicles almost hispid, with spreading or reflexed hairs.

STREPANTHUS LINEARIFOLIUS, *Gray, Pl. Fendl., p.* 7. Gravelly and rocky places, on Hurrah creek; September. The radical and some of the lower cauline leaves are spatulate or obovate, and short.

STREPANTHUS CORDATUS, *Nutt. in Torr. & Gray, Fl.* 1, *p.* 77. River banks, Middle Yuba, May 21. Stem 2–3 feet high, paniculately branched above; whole plant very smooth and somewhat glaucous. Lower leaves and sometimes the cauline ones repandly or sharply denticulate; the latter about an inch long, mostly obtuse, strongly clasping. Pedicles usually almost as long as the flower, spreading and curved upward. Flower buds acute. Calyx very obtuse at the base. Sepals with a long narrow acuminate point, the exterior ones carinate, petals spatulate, shorter than the calyx. Torus or receptacle dilated. Pods not seen. We have specimens of the plant collected in California by Colonel Frémont and Mr. Gibbes.

STREPANTHUS LONGIFOLIUS, *Benth. Pl. Hartw., p.* 10, *No.* 52. *Gray, Pl. Fendl., p.* 6, var. glaber; pedicellis brevioribus. Sandy hills near the Colorado of the West. New Mexico, February 22. Root annual. Stem about a foot high, slender. Lower leaves acutely repand-dentate; upper ones linear-oblong, entire. Pedicles shorter than the closed calyx, recurved after flowering. Petals linear-spatulate, pale purple, a little exserted. Pods (immature) an inch long, with a tapering summit.

TURRITIS GLABRA, *Linn.; Torr. & Gray, Fl.* 1, *p.* 78. T. macrocarpa, *Nutt. in Torr. & Gray, Fl. l. c.* Near San Francisco, April 3. A dwarf state of this species was found on Cajon creek, March 17. We reduce Nuttall's T. macrocarpa to T. glabra, as there are often intermediate forms between the two.

TURRITIS PATULA, *Graham, in Edinb. Phil. Jour.*, (1829,) *p.* 7; *Torr. & Gray, Fl.* 1, *p.* 79 *Gray, Pl. Wright.* 2, *p.* 10. Yuba river, May 22. In all Dr. Bigelow's specimens of this plant the stem-leaves are nearly as hairy as the radical leaves.

TURRITIS PATULA, *Graham; Hook. Fl. Bor.,–Am.* 1, *p.* 40: var. magis hispidula. Hill sides, Downieville; May 22.

ARABIS HIRSUTA, *Scop.; Torr. & Gray, Fl.* 1, *p.* 80. *β.* GLABRATA, *Torr. & Gray, l. c.* Wet ravines, Duffield's ranch, Sierra Nevada, May 11, (in flower.)

CARDAMINE ANGULATA, *Hook. Bot. Misc.* 1, *p.* 343, *t.* 69; *Torr. & Gray, Fl.* 1, *p.* 84. C. paucisecta, *Benth. Fl. Hartw., p.* 297. Hill-sides, Duffield's ranch, Sierra Nevada, May 10; mountains near Oakland, April 4; and plains near San Gabriel, March 23. Radical leaves sometimes entire; but more commonly 3-parted, with the segments petiolulate, roundish, entire, or obscurely repand-toothed; stem-leaves 3–5-parted; the segments varying in form from broadly ovate and cordate to lanceolate, and narrowed at the base, entire, toothed. Flowers as large as in Cardamine rhomboidea. Pods erect, an inch and a half long, on a stalk of about the same length, 1½ line wide, tapering to a long point. Seeds narrowly margined, distant. Root tuberiferous.

CARDAMINE OLIGOSPERMA, *Nutt. in Torr. & Gray, Pl.* 1, *p.* 85; *Benth. Fl. Hartw.* Near San Francisco; April 3. Very near C. hirsuta, but differs in the broader pods and less numerous seeds.

SISYMBRIUM OFFICINALE, *Scop.; Torr. & Gray, Fl.* 1, *p.* 91. Near Benicia, April 24. Doubtless introduced.

SISYMBRIUM CANESCENS, *Nutt. Gen.* 2, *p.* 68; *Torr. & Gray, Fl.* 1, *p.* 92. Var. CALIFORNICUM, *Torr. & Gray, l. c.* Williams' River of the Colorado, New Mexico. February 6–18.

SISYMBRIUM DEFLEXUM, (*Harvey, Mss. in herb. Gray*:) annuum, pilis patentibus hispidulum; caule stricto, folioso simplici, foliis oblongis inferioribus pinnatifidis seu pinnatipartitis, segmentis lineari-lanceolatis distantibus laciniato-dentatis integrisve, sinubus obtusis; foliis supremis linearibus integris; pedicellis brevibus cum siliquiis angustissimis rectis elongatis teretiusculis arcte deflexis. Turritis? lasiophylla, *Hook. & Arn. Bot. Beechey, p.* 321? Hill-sides, Napa valley, April 26. About three feet high, slender, the lower half almost hispid, with short spreading hairs. Lower leaves petiolate, 2–3 inches long, more hispid than the stem; middle leaves sharply toothed; the highest 2–3 lines wide, and usually entire. Flowers about as large as in Cardamine hirsuta, and apparently white. Petals oblong-spatulate. Pods 2–3 inches long, and scarcely half a line wide. Pedicles 2 lines long. Cotyledons incumbent. This plant resembles a Sisymbrium from Coulter's Californian collection, sent to us by Dr. Harvey under the name of S. deflexum *Harv.*, of which we believe no description has yet appeared. A smoother and more humble form of it (some of the specimens only 2 or 3 inches high) was collected near San Francisco, April 3.

SISYMBRIUM INCISUM, *Engelm. in Pl. Fendl., p.* 8. Mountain arroyas, near San Antonita, New Mexico; October.

ERYSIMUM ASPERUM, *DC.* Laguna Blanca to the Sandia mountains.

THELYPODIUM WRIGHTII, *Gray, Pl. Wright.* 1, *p.* 7. Rocky places on the Pecos; September. Many of the flowers are in an enlarged and abnormal state, probably from the stinging of insects.

TROPIDOCARPUM GRACILE, *Hook. Ic.* 1, *t.* 43; *Torr. & Gray, Fl.* 1, *p.* 94. T. scabriusculum, *Hook. l. c.; Torr. & Gray, l. c.* Plains near San Gabriel, March 23. We find the two species of Hooker to pass into each other.

ERYSIMUM ASPERUM, *DC. Syst.* 2, *p.* 506; *Torr. & Gray, Fl.* 1, *p.* 94 Near San Francisco, April 3, and mouth of Santa Rosa creek, May 1, (with flowers and immature fruit.) Flowers cream-color or pale yellow, becoming deeper in drying. A variety (or possibly distinct species) with much larger and orange-yellow flowers, was found at Cocomungo, March 17, without fruit; also found by Mr. Wallace. We are unable to find characters that will clearly distinguish E. Arkansanum and E. elatum from this species. The leaves and degree of pubescence are very variable, and the pods seem to be the same in all of them.

VESICARIA ARGYREA, *Gray, Pl. Lindheim.* 2, *p.* 147. Arroyas and cañons, Williams' River of the Colorado, New Mexico, February 7–26.

VESICARIA FENDLERI, *Gray, Pl. Fendl., p.* 9. Bluffs and rocky places, New Mexico; October. To this very polymorphus species must be referred V. stenophylla, *Gray, Pl. Lindh.* 2, *p.* 149.

DRABA AUREA, *Vahl; Hook. Bot. Mag. t.* 2934. San Antonita, New Mexico, and in the Sandia mountains, in rocky places; October. Mostly in fruit. From these specimens the plant appears to have a biennial root, while those of Fendler would seem to be perennial. The silicles are mostly twisted.

DRABA CUNEIFOLIA, *Nutt. in Torr. & Gray, Fl.* 1, *p.* 108. Williams' River of the Colorado; February 11.

DITHYREA WISLIZENI, *Engelm. in Wisl. Mem. New Mex., p.* 11; *Torr. in Marcy, Expl. Red River, t.* 11. On prairies and sandy bottoms of the Canadian, near Antelope Hills; September. It is from this region doubtless that the plant was first collected by Dr. James.

DITHYREA CALIFORNICA, *Harv. in Hook. Lond. Jour. Bot.* 4, *p.* 77, *t.* 5; *Engelm. in Wisliz. Mex. p.* 95. Sandy hills on the Colorado of the West. February 22. The radical leaves are deeply lyrate-pinnatifid. The calyx is 4 or 5 lines long; much longer, narrower, and more closed than that of D. Wislizeni. The petals appear to have been purple.

LEPIDIUM NITIDUM, *Nutt. in Torr. & Gray, Fl.* 1, *p.* 116. Sandy plains, Cocomungo; March

17. A humble annual; seldom more than a span high. The flowers are tetrapetalous in all of Dr. Bigelow's specimens.

LEPIDIUM ALYSSOIDES, *Gray, Pl. Fendl. p.* 10. San Antonita and Galisteo, New Mexico; October.

LEPIDIUM WRIGHTII, *Gray, Pl. Wright.* 2, *p.* 15. On Williams' River of the Colorado, New Mexico; February 11. There are 4 minute petals in all the specimens.

LEPIDIUM FLAVUM (sp. nov.): annuum, pusillum, acaule, demum prolifero-ramosum, depressum glabrum; foliis crassiusculis oblongo-spathulatis pinnatifidis, lobis rotundatis brevibus; floribus capitato-congestis flavis; petalis obovatis unguiculatis; siliculis ovatis, sinu lato emarginato truncatis breviter bidentatis stylo bis longioribus. Sandy places near the Mohave creek; March 13. These are early specimens of a minute depressed plant, in flower only. But a single specimen was gathered by Fremont, in the same region, in his second expedition, from which the fruit is here characterized. The leaves are half an inch or more in length, and mostly rosulate around the sessile capitate or umbellate cluster of small *yellow* flowers: and the axis of the inflorescence apparently does not elongate in fruit. Stamens tetradynamous. Silicle a line long. Valves minutely reticulated. Cotyledons incumbent.

THYSANOCARPUS ELEGANS, *Fisch. & Mey. Ind. Sem. St. Petersb., Dec.* 1835; *Torr. & Gray, Fl.* 1. *p.* 118. Hill sides, Napa; April. The pods are perforated only when they are quite mature and dry. They vary in shape from nearly orbicular to orbicular-obovate. The stem is usually simple or with very few branches. T. pulchellus, *Fish. & Mey.*, and T. radians, *Benth.*, seem to be only forms of this species.

THYSANOCARPUS CRENATUS, *Nutt. in Torr. & Gray, Fl. l. c.* Hill sides, Sonora, California; May 9. Chiefly distinguished from T. elegans by its smaller pods and paniculately branching stem.

THYSANOCARPUS LACINIATUS, *Nutt. in Torr. & Gray, Fl. l. c.* Plains near San Gabriel, March 23, and sandy places, Cajon creek. Radical leaves pinnatifid; the segments very narrow and entire.

THYSANOCARPUS OBLONGIFOLIUS, *Nutt. in Torr. & Gray, Fl. l, c.* Sides of hills, Napa; April 26.

THYSANOCARPUS PUSILLUS, *Hook. Ic.* 1, *t.* 43; *Torr. & Gray, Fl. l. c.* Low wet places near San Francisco, April 8, and Murphy's, May 14.

CAPPARIDACEÆ.

CLEOME (PERITOMA) INTEGRIFOLIA, *Torr. &. Gray, Fl.* 1, *p.* 122; *Gray, Gen. Ill. t.* 76, *Pl. Fendl. p.* 11. Comanche plains, on the banks of rivulets; September. The form with lanceolate leaflets, and very densely crowded, large flowers. Galisteo, and on the Rio Grande near Santa Domingo, in low places; October: a form with oblong or obovate leaflets, and smaller as well as fewer flowers, mostly on short axillary branchlets, appearing considerably different, but doubtless of the same species. Fendler's No. 49 is intermediate. The leaflets are entire in all the specimens I have seen. Probably, however, C. serrulata, *Pursh* is not distinct.

CRISTATELLA JAMESII, *Torr. & Gray, Fl.* 1, *p.* 124; *Gray, Gen. Ill. t.* 77. Gravelly hills, on the Canadian; September.

POLANISIA UNIGLANDULOSA, *DC. Prod.* 1. *p.* 242; *Gray, Pl. Wright.* 1, *p.* 10. P. trachysperma *Torr. & Gray, Fl.* 1, *p.* 669. On the Canadian, and at Anton Chico; August, September.

VIOLACEÆ.

VIOLA SHELTONII, (sp. nov.): glabra, caulibus adscendentibus brevibus; foliis circumscriptione reniformi-cordatis trisectis, segmentis subsessilibus, irregulariter palmatim 5–8-fidis lobatisve, lobis lineari-cuneatis obtusis; stipulis parvulis ovatis apice ciliatis, sepalis lineari-lanceolatis; petalis luteis, calcare brevi sacciforme, (TAB. II.) Hill sides, Yuba, near Downieville; May 8. A neat little species resembling V. Beckwithii, *Torr. & Gray in Beckwith's Report;* but that has the divisions of the leaves conspicuously petiolulate, and the two upper petals purple.

VIOLA LOBATA, *Benth. Pl. Hartw. p.* 298. Moist and shady places, Napa valley, April 27; Grass valley, May 21. Rhizoma short, throwing down a tuft of long thick fibres. Stem sometimes a foot high, naked below. Leaves variable in the lobing. Flowers large, the petals yellow, often tinged with purple, especially on the outside; the lateral ones bearded near the base.

VIOLA CHRYSANTHA, *Hook. Ic.* 1, *t.* 49; *Torr. & Gray, Fl.* 1, *p.* 143. Hill sides and plains, Knight's ferry, Stanislaus, and Murphy's, California; May 8–14.

VIOLA PEDUNCULATA, *Torr. & Gray, Fl.* 1, *p.* 141. Sandy plains, Cocomungo, March 17; Benicia, April 24; Duffield's Ranch, Sierra Nevada, May 10. A pubescent form was collected near Santa Rosa creek, May 1. This species, V. præmorsa, *Dougl.*, V. linguæfolia, *Nutt.*, and V. Nuttalli, *Ph.*, are nearly allied, and should, perhaps, be united.

VIOLA SARMENTOSA, *Dougl. in Hook. Fl. Bor.-Am.* 1, *p.* 80; *Torr. & Gray, l. c.* Mountains near Oakland, April 4; Red woods, April 12.

VIOLA OCELLATA, *Torr. & Gray, Fl.* 1, *p.* 142. Deep ravines, Napa valley. Mr. Thurber found this species near the quicksilver mines of New Almaden.

VIOLA ADUNCA, *Smith in Rees Cyclop.* V. longipes, *Nutt. in Torr. & Gray, Fl.* 1, *p.* 140. Santa Rosa creek; May 1. The specimens are tall and slender, with the peduncles much elongated; but a short cespitose form of the plant (which is the same as Hartweg's No. 1660,) with the peduncles scarcely longer than the leaves, was collected at Duffield's Ranch, Sierra Nevada. There can be scarcely a doubt that the little known V. adunca of Smith is identical with Nuttall's V. longipes. The description of Smith agrees with our plant, but we have seen no authentic specimen for comparison.

VIOLA CUCULLATA, *Ait.; Torr. & Gray, Fl.* 1, *p.* 139. Pecan creek, Arkansas, and on the Pecos. August–October; Cocomungo, California; March 18. The style is more slender and the stigma less rostrate in the Californian than in the eastern plant; but in other respects we find no difference.

VIOLA CANADENSIS, *Linn.* In the Sandia mountains, New Mexico; October. In flower and fruit.

HYPERICACEÆ.

HYPERICUM ANAGALLOIDES, *Cham. & Schlecht. in Linnæa* 3, *p.* 127; *Torr. & Gray. Fl.* 1, *p*, 160. Wet places, Laguna Santa Rosa, May 1, and Punta de los Reyes, April 18. Leaves varying from oblong to broadly ovate, sparsely pellucid-punctate. Not very distinct from H. mutilum*.

* A remarkable shrub, bearing ripe pods only, was found by Dr. Bigelow in western New Mexico, on the hills bordering Williams' river, from near its source to its confluence with the Great Colorado. The Mexicans call it *Canotia.* It usually grows from 9 to 10 feet high, but was sometimes found attaining the height of nearly 20 feet. The branches are very numerous, alternate, rigid, terete, of a greenish color, and terminate in very long thorns. The epidermis is smooth and finely striate. Between the elevated striae there are 2 or 3 rows of impressed perforations. There were no leaves on the plant when Dr Bigelow saw it, and he thinks that it never bears any; but there are distant alternate brown scars, where minute leaves or scales appear to have been. The pedicles are somewhat racemose towards the summit of the branches. They are about half an inch long, somewhat spreading, then curved upward, and are articulated below the middle. Calyx persistent, 5-cleft, small, free from the ovary. The corolla, if any, is deciduous. Stamens 5, hypogynous; filaments slender and distinct. The fruit is nearly an inch long, oblong, acute at each end, and pointed with a short persistent subulate style, covered with a thin red flesh; the endocarp ligneous; 5-celled, septicidally dehiscent about two-thirds of the way down, and loculicidally at the summit, which thus presents 10 subulate points in pairs. Seed solitary in each cell, suspended from near the summit at the inner angle, oblong, compressed with a broad somewhat falcate wing at the inferior extremity. Testa coreaceo-chartaceous, dull, minutely granulated. Albumen very thin. Embryo nearly the length of the seed; cotyledons thin and flat. Radical inferior, terete, short, straight.

We can scarcely form a conjecture as to the affinities of this plant, but may note that the fruit is not unlike that of Eucryphia, which Lindley, following Choisy, refers to Hypericaceæ, nothwithstanding its superior radicle. The fruit has the same thin fleshy covering that occurs in our plant, and the large seeds (of which there are only three or four in each carpel) are also furnished with a conspicuous wing on the lower side; but the radicle is certainly superior. It is yet uncertain whether the New Mexican plant ever bears leaves. Dr. Bigelow saw it early in the spring, when other shrubby plants of the region were beginning to assume their foliage, but it was entirely naked. We must wait for other observations on this strange shrub, and especially for its flowers, before assigning it a place in the system. As, however, there can be but little doubt of its constituting an undescribed genus, we may bestow upon it the provisional name of *anotia holacantha.*

CARYOPHYLLACEÆ.

SILENE CALIFORNICA, *Durand, Pl. Pratt. in Jour. Acad. Philad.*, (*n. ser.*) 2, *p.* 83. S. pulchra, *Torr. & Gray, Fl.* 1, *p.* 675; *excl. syn. Cham. & Schlecht.*; S. Virginica, *Benth. Pl. Hartw. No.* 1653. Sides of hills, Mammoth Grove, and Duffield's Ranch, Sierra Nevada, May; Mormon island, *Mr. Rich. var?* viscido-pubescens; foliis ovatis sessilibus, cymis subtrifloris; petalis profunde bipartitis, lobis bifidis, segmentis bidentatis v. integris. Valley of the Sacramento, Mr. Shelton. This variety has leaves sometimes as broad as those of S. latifolia. At the base of the limb of the petals there is remote linear lobe or tooth. In the specimens from Mormon island the middle lobes of the petals are somewhat toothed on the margin, especially near the summit. Lychnis pulchra, *Cham. & Schlecht.*, which was founded on a Mexican plant, seems clearly to be Silene laciiata, *Cav.* We are not sure that it grows in California, unless, which is possible, S. Californica passes into it.

SILENE QUINQUEVULNERA, *Linn.*; *Torr. & Gray, Fl.* 1, *p.* 191. Hills near Sonoma; May 3. Doubtless introduced from Europe.

SILENE DRUMMONDII, *Hook. Fl. Bor.-Am.* 1, *p.* 89; *Torr. & Gray, Fl.* 1, *p.* 91 *and* 675. Near San Francisco; April 8. On the Sandia mountains, New Mexico; October. In fruit.

SILENE ANTIRRHINA, *Linn.*; *Torr. & Gray, Fl.* 1, *p.* 191. Hill sides, Napa valley; April 16.

SAGINA DECUMBENS, *Torr. & Gray, Fl.* 1, *p.* 177. Spergula saginoides, *Linn.*; *Michx. Fl.* 1, *p.* 276. Damp places near San Francisco. Sepals and petals 4–5, equal in length. Stamens 10.

ALSINE DOUGLASII, *Fenzl.*; *Torr. & Gray, Fl.* 1, *p.* 674. Napa valley; April 26. Seeds orbicular-reniform, compressed, not margined.

ALSINE MICHAUXII, *Fenzl.* Arenaria stricta, *Michx. Fl.* 1. *p.* 274. Walnut creek; August: on rocks. In fruit.

ARENARIA MACROPHYLLA, *Hook. Fl. Bor.-Amer.* 1, *p.* 102, *t*, 37; *Torr. & Gray, Fl.* 1, *p.* 182. Mœhringia umbrosa, *Fenzl.?*; *Gray, Pl. Fendl. p.* 13. We are uncertain of the station of this plant, as the ticket belonging to it was lost; but it is probably the valley of the Sacramento. Dr. Bigelow's specimens are rather smaller than Nuttall's from Oregon, and the leaves are narrower. They accord pretty well with *Mœhringia umbrosa* from Songaria, in our herbarium, except that the leaves are narrower. Our California plant is not sufficiently mature to show the character of the seeds.

ARENARIA DIFFUSA, *Ell. Sk.* 1, *p.* 519; *Gray, Pl. Wright.* 2, *p.* 18. San Antonita, New Mexico; October.

ARENARIA FENDLERI, *Gray, Pl. Fendl. p.* 13. Laguna Blanca, in pine woods; September. The specimens bear mature fruit. The capsule is slightly longer than the calyx, and six-valved. Seeds obliquely obovate, with a minute uncinate micropyle, papillose-scabrous. Embryo unequally hyppocrepiforme.

STELLARIA JAMESII, *Torr. in Ann. Lyc. New York*, 2. *p.* 169. In the Sandia mountains; October. This striking species has not been collected, since its discovery by Dr. James, until now. The weak stems (a foot in length) and the older leaves are glabrous; the branches, etc., viscid-pubescent. The larger leaves are 3 or 4 inches long, and two-thirds of an inch in width.

STELLARIA NITENS. *Nutt. in Torr. & Gray, Fl.* 1. *p.* 184. Near San Gabriel, March 23. In our specimens the leaves are fringed with weak hairs, the lowest ones are oblong-ovate, on long petioles, the middle ones lanceolate-spatulate, and the uppermost linear. Sepals subulate-lanceolate, acuminate, 3-nerved. Petals oblong, deeply two-parted with linear segments. A similar form occurs in Oregon. We have also an apetalous triandrous state of the plant from hills near Murphy's; May 14.

STELLARIA LITTORALIS, (sp. nov.): undique pubescens; caule adscendente? superne cymoso-ramoso; foliis ovatis acuminatis basi rotundatis arcte sessilibus; pedicellis foliis vix longioribus; petalis profunde bipartitis, laciniis linearibus, sepala lanceolata excedentibus. Seashore, Punta de los Reyes; April 17. Stems about a foot long, clothed, like the leaves, with a short woolly (and somewhat viscid?) pubescence. Leaves nearly an inch long and half an inch wide; the upper ones almost amplexicaul. Flowers few in leafy cymes, about as large as in Cerastium vulgatum. Sepals lanceolate, acute, obscurely 3-nerved. Petals about one-fourth longer than the sepals. Stamens 10. Styles rarely 4. Ovary and young fruit globose-ovate. This species resembles S. pubera, but that has less pubescence on the stem in two lines; the leaves are much larger, narrow at the base, and nearly smooth, except on the margin, and the sepals are broader as well as more obtuse. The present plant has much the aspect of a Cerastium, but the styles are almost invariably only three, and never five.

Cerastium oblongifolium, *Torr. in Sill. Jour.* 4, *p.* 63; *Torr & Gray, Fl.* 1, *p.* 188. Near Punta de los Reyes, California; April 17. Except in the larger flowers, we see nothing in which this differs from the eastern plant.

Paronychia ramosissima, *DC. Mém. Paronych. p.* 12, *t.* 4; *Torr. & Gray, Fl.* 1, *p.* 72. San Francisco; April 8.

Paronychia sessiliflora, *Nutt. Gen.* 1, *p.* 150; *Hook. Fl. Bor.-Amer.* 1, *p.* 226, *t.* 79. Gravelly natural mounds on the Canadian; September.

Paronychia dichotoma, *Nutt. l. c.* On the Canadian, in rocky prairies; August.

Drymaria glandulosa, *Bartl.; Gray, Pl. Wright.* 2, *p.* 18. La Cuesta, New Mexico, on mountains, under pine trees; September. A small state.

Spergularia rubra, *Pers. Syn.* 1, *p.* 504, (*Sect.* Arenariæ); *Gray Gen. Ill.* 2, *p.* 25, *t.* 107. Arenaria rubra, *Linn.* Spergula rubra, *Torr. & Gray, Fl.* 1, *p.* 174, *and Torr. & Gray, Fl.* 1, *p.* 157. Arenaria media, *Linn.* A. marginata, *DC. prodr.* 1, *p.* 401. Low places where the tide flows, Martinez, Corte Madera, &c.; April 10–23. All the specimens have the seed broadly margined.

PORTULACACEÆ.

Portulaca pilosa, *Linn.* Pecan creek, in dry, rocky places; August.

Portulaca retusa, *Engelm. in Pl. Lindh.* 2, *p*, 154. On the upper Canadian; September.

Calandrinia Menziesii, *Hook. Fl. Bor.-Amer.* 1, *p.* 223, *t.* 10; *Torr. & Gray, Fl.* 1, *p.* 197. Cocomungo, March 18, Corte Madera, April 20. C. speciosa, *Lindl.*, seems to be scarcely distinct from this species. Dr. Bigelow collected at Cahon Pass, March 16, a Calandrinia scarcely an inch high, but with conspicuous bright purple flowers. It is, probably, C. Menziesii in a very early state.

Claytonia Caroliniana, *Michx. Fl.* 1, *p.* 160; var. sessilifolia: minor, racemo foliis ovato-oblongis sessilibus vix longiore; petalis obovatis integris. C. lanceolata, *Hook. Fl. Bor.-Am.* 1, *p.* 234. On hills near Downieville, May 22. Whole plant only 2 or 3 inches high. Tuber globose, about half an inch in diameter. There were no radical leaves on any of the numerous specimens. Stem leaves from half an inch to three-fourths of an inch or more in length. Raceme 6–10-flowered, a little overtopping the leaves, even when the lower capsules were nearly mature. Flowers about half as large as in the eastern plant. (They are quite as large in specimens of C. lanceolata, *Hook.*, collected in the Rocky mountains by Burke). Calyx one-third the length of the petals. Corolla apparently pale rose-color. This is the only perennial (corm-bearing) Claytonia that we have received from California. Pursh's C. lanceolata (as intimated in the Flora of North America), is a spurious species, made up of C. Caroliniana and C. alsinoides. The leaves, in all the species of this genus that we have examined, are furnished with a fine intra-marginal vein, in which all the veinlets terminate.

Claytonia alsinoides, *Sims, Bot. Mag. t.* 1309; *Torr. & Gray, Fl.* 1. *p.* 199. Marshes, Punta de los Reyes, April 17; deep woods, Bolinas bay, April 19.

Claytonia perfoliata, *Don, Hort. Cant. ed.* 4, *p.* 50; *Bot. Mag. t.* 1335; *Torr. & Gray, l. c.* Corte Madera, April 12; Cocomungo, March 18; Cajon creek, March 18. In the specimens from the two latter stations, some of the radical leaves are rhomboidal, others are linear-spatulate, showing a tendency to pass into C. parviflora.

C. PERFOLIATA, var. PARVIFLORA: foliis radicalibus lineari-spathulatis, caulinis in unum ovale perfoliatum coalitis. C. parviflora, *Dougl. in Hook. Fl. Bor.-Amer.* 1, *p.* 225, *t.* 73; *Torr. & Gray, l. c.*; C. gypsophiloides, *Fisch. & Mey. Index. Sem. St. Petersb.* (1835), *p.* 33. Hills, Middle Yuba (fine specimens, nearly a foot high). A dwarf form was collected near San Francisco, April 3.

C. PERFOLIATA, var. EXIGUA: nana; radicalibus anguste linearibus; caulinis lanceolatis vel linearibus, subconnatis. C. exigua, *Torr. & Gray, Fl. l. c.* San Francisco; April

A careful examination of our numerous specimens of annual Claytoniæ has led us to reduce several species to C. perfoliata, and we would add to the list of varieties C. spathulata. Intermediate forms connect all these. Hereafter it may be found necesasry to include C. tenuifolia.

CLAYTONIA LINEARIS, *Dougl. in Hook. Fl. Bor.-Am.* 1, *p.* 224, *t.* 71; *Torr. & Gray, l. c.* Wet places, Napa valley; April 26. The specimens are considerably larger than those of Douglas. The seeds are larger than in any other species of this genus; they are lenticular, acute on the margin, and highly polished. A very distinct species.

MONTIA FONTANA, *Linn.; DC. Prodr.* 3, *p.* 361; *Torr. & Gray, Fl.* 1, *p.* 202. In water; Duffield's ranch, Sierra Nevada, May 11; San Francisco, April 8; Corte Madera, April 20. On the western side of America, the range of this plant extends from Sitcha to Quito, but on the eastern side it has not been found south of Newfoundland. Chamisso (in Linnæa 6, p. 565) considers the Quito plant as a distinct species, which he calls M. lamprosperma, and states that it occurs also in the island of Unalaschka, and at the Bay of Eschscholtz. In plate 7, figs. 1–2, of the volume quoted, he has given figures of the seeds of that species, and of M. fontana. Our Californian plant has exactly the seeds of M. fontana, and Mr. Nuttall's Oregon specimens have the same; but M. fontana β. from Sitcha, is M. lamprosperma of Chamisso. We find the seeds to vary in size and color, and Dr. J. D. Hooker, in *Fl. Antarct.*, *p.* 13, has shown that the two species are almost certainly not distinct.

LEWISIA REDIVIVA, *Pursh, Fl.* 1, *p.* 368; *Hook. Bot. Misc.* 1, *p.* 344, *t.* 70; *Torr. & Gray, Fl.* 1, *p.* 677. Rocky places, Napa valley; April 25. This interesting plant extends as far south as the American fork of the Sacramento.

STERCULIACEÆ.

FRÉMONTIA CALIFORNICA, *Torr. in Smithson. Contrib.* 6, *p.* 5, *t.* 2. Cajon Pass of the Sierra Nevada. The plants found by Dr. Bigelow were about 15 feet high, which is much taller than the specimens seen by Col. Frémont and Rev. Mr. Fitch. They were bearing ripe fruit on the 16th of March, which must have been formed the previous season. The capsules are in perfect condition, and show that no part of the calyx is deciduous. The seeds are about as large as in Hibiscus Syriacus, ovate, black, smooth, and somewhat shining. Testa thick and crustaceous. Embryo straight, lying in fleshy and oily albumen; cotyledons ovate, foliaceous, nearly flat. In all of Dr. Bigelow's specimens of the Frémontia, the leaves were small, few of them being more than an inch in diameter.

MALVACEÆ.

CALLIRRHÖE INVOLUCRATA, *Gray, Pl. Fendl.*, *p.* 15, *and Gen. Ill. t.* 117. On the Canadian; September.

MALVASTRUM COCCINEUM, *Gray, l. c.* Upper Canadian, and near Galisteo, New Mexico.

MALVA BOREALIS, *Wallm.; Gray, Pl. Fendl.*, *p.* 15. M. obtusa, *Torr. & Gray, Fl.* 1. *p.* 225, A common weed in California.

SIDALCEA DIPLOSCYPHA, *Gray, Gen. Ill.* 2, *t.* 222; *Plant. Fendl.*, *p.* 19. Sida diploscypha. *Torr. & Gray, Fl.* 1, *p.* 234. Plains, Ione valley, California; May 18.

STELLARIA HIRSUTA, *Gray, Pl. Wright.* 1, *p.* 16. S. delphinifolia, *Gray, Pl. Fendl., p.* 19, *and Gen. Ill.* 2, *t.* 12, *f.* 10–12, *and in Benth. Pl. Hartw. p.* 300, *excl. syn. Nutt.* In low places, on the sides of rivulets; Knight's ferry, Stanislaus river, California; May 7.

STELLARIA HARTWEGI, *Gray, Pl. Fendl., p.* 209, *and in Benth. Pl. Hartw., p.* 300. Plains and hill-sides, Napa valley; May 5. Fine specimens of this rare plant are in the collection; some of them are sparingly branched above, and the racemes are somewhat compound. The fruit is still unknown.

STELLARIA MALVÆFLORA, *Gray, Pl. Wright.* 1, *p.* 16. Sida malvæflora, *Moç. & Sesse.; DC. Prodr.* 1, *p.* 194. Sidalcea Neo-Mexicana, *Gray, Pl. Fendl. p.* 23. S. Oregana, *Gray, l. c.* Mokelumne hill, May 17; plains of Napa valley, May 5.

STELLARIA HUMILIS and var. *β. Gray Pl. Fendl. p.* 20. Hills near Oakland, April 5; Punta de los Reyes, April 18; *β.* Napa valley. Perhaps not distinct from S. malvæflora.

SIDA LEPIDOTA, var. SAGITTÆFOLIA, *Gray, Pl. Wright.* 1, *p.* 18. Plains, Laguna Colorado; September.

SIDA SPINOSA, *Linn.* Shawneetown, Indian Territory; August.

ABUTILON PARVULUM, *Gray, Pl. Wright.* 1, *p.* 21. Rocky hills near Anton Chico; September.

SPHÆRALCEA ANGUSTIFOLIA, var. (S. stellata, Torr. & Gray.) Plains of the Upper Canadian, etc.; September.

STELLARIA INCANA? Var. OBLONGIFOLIA, *Gray, Pl. Wright.* 2, *p.* 21. Galisteo, in low places; October.

HIBISCUS MOSCHEUTOS, Linn. Sandy bottoms of the Canadian; September.

LINACEÆ.

LINUM PERENNE, *Linn.* Gravelly hills and plains near Galisteo, New Mexico; October. In fruit.

LINUM RIGIDUM, *Pursh, Fl.* 1, *p.* 210; *Gray, Pl. Wright.* 2, *p.* 25. Prairie hills, on the Canadian; September.

LINUM CALIFORNICUM, *Benth. Plant. Hartw. p.* 298. Plains of Feather river, near Marysville; May 25. Petals rose color in the bud; white when expanded. In all the flowers that we examined, there were but 3 styles, and the ovary was tricarpellary. Some of our specimens are more than a foot high.

GERANIACEÆ.

GERANIUM CAROLINIANUM, *Linn.; Torr. & Gray, Fl.* 1, *p.* 207. Corte Madera, April 12; hill-sides, Murphy's, May 14. One of the most widely diffused plants of North America.

GERANIUM RICHARDSONII, *Fisch. & Meyer; Engelm. in Pl. Fendl. p.* 26. G. albiflorum, *Hook.* In the Sandia mountains, New Mexico; October.

GERANIUM CÆSPITOSUM, *James, in Long's Exped.; Gray, Pl. Fendl. p.* 25. Mountain arroyas, near San Antonita; October. A low and diffuse state, mostly in fruit, and an erect form, near Wright's No. 910, but with long peduncles.

ERODIUM MACROPHYLLUM, *Hook. & Arn. Bot. Beech., p.* 227; *Torr. & Gray, Fl.* 1, *p.* 679. Hill-sides, Murphy's, May 14. All the specimens are small leaved.

ERODIUM CICUTARIUM, *L'Herit.; DC. Prodr.* 1, *p.* 646; *Torr. & Gray, Fl.* 1, *p.* 208. In various parts of New Mexico; also plains near Los Angeles, and on Williams' river, near the Colorado, February and March. In the specimens from the latter station the leaves are more cut than usual.

OXALIDACEÆ.

OXALIS OREGANA, *Nutt. in Torr. & Gray, Fl.* 1, *p.* 211. O. Acetosella, *Hook. Fl. Bor.-Am.* 1, *p.* 118, (ex parte.) Tamul Pass, April 11. Perhaps not distinct from O. Acetosella; the chief difference being the greater proportionate breadth of the leafless. The rhizoma is sometimes a foot or more in length. It is only the portion near the leaf-bearing extremity that has the scales imbricated; on the other parts they are distant and alternate.

OXALIS STRICTA, *Linn.; Torr. Fl., New York*, 1, *p*. 123. Plains near San Gabriel, March 23.

LIMNANTHACEÆ.

LIMNANTHES ROSEA, *Benth. Pl. Hartw., p*. 302; "*Jour. Hort. Soc.* 4, *t*. 78." Low wet places, Corte Madera; Stanislaus; Los Angeles, etc. March—May. Scarcely distinct from L. Douglasii; the divisions of the leaves being, in some of Douglas' original specimens, quite as narrow as those of L. rosea. In cultivated specimens of the latter the ultimate segments of the leaves are broader than in the wild plant.

LIMNANTHES ALBA, *Benth. l. c.* Hill-sides, Duffield's ranch, Sierra Nevada, May 12. This seems to be a very distinct species, and is obviously distinguished by its hairiness.

RUTACEÆ.

THAMNOSMA MONTANUM, (Torr. & Frém.:) fruticosum, ramosissimum; ramis spinescentibus; foliis crassiusculis lineari-spathulatis obscure punctatis; antheris sagittatis promisse mucronatis; disco parvo stipite fructifero (sesquilineari) columnari multum breviore; capsula didyma basi retusa; seminibus cochleatis lævibus. (Tab. III.)—*Torr. & Frém. in Frém. 2d. Rep., p*. 313. Dry ravines of the Mohave, near the Colorado, March 3–9. The description in the work here quoted was drawn from imperfect materials, and the plant was incorrectly referred to Zanthoxylaceæ, instead of Rutaceæ proper. The æstivation of the corolla is imbricated, not valvate. The stamens and filiform style are more or less exserted. Stigma small and capitate. Albumen thin. Rutosma of Gray must be included in this genus.

PTELEA TRIFOLIATA, *Linn.* B. MOLLIS, *Torr. & Gray, Fl.* 1, *p*. 680; *Gray, Pl. Wright.* 1, *p*. 31. Rocky hills of the Upper Canadian; September. In fruit.

ANACARDIACEÆ.

RHUS TRILOBATA, *Nutt. in Torr. & Gray, Fl.* 1, *p*. 219. Hilly prairies on the Canadian; September. In fruit.

RHUS DIVERSILOBA, *Torr. & Gray, Fl.* 1, *p*. 218. R. lobata, *Hook. Fl. Bor. Am.* 1, *p*. 127, *t*. 46, *non Poir.* Plains and mountains near San Gabriel, March 23; Martinez, April 23. The specimens are all male.

STYPHONIA INTEGRIFOLIA, *Nutt. in Torr. & Gray, Fl.* 1, *p*. 220; *Nutt. Sylv.* 3, *p*. 4, *t*. 82. Ravines, Cojon Pass; March 17. The leaves are three inches long, and nearly two inches wide, ovate, with a short acumination. Dr. Parry collected similar specimens near Santa Barbara. S. serrata is probably not a distinct species.

LITHRÆA LAURINA, *Walp. Repert.* 1, *p*. 551. Rhus laurina, *Nutt. in Torr. & Gray, Fl.* 1, *p*. 219. Near San Gabriel, March 23, (in fruit; doubtless of the preceding season.) The thin pulp of the dry fruit consists chiefly of a white waxy material, which is soluble in very strong alcohol, and seems to be almost entirely cerine.

VITACEÆ.

VITUS INCISA, *Nutt. in Torr. & Gray, Fl.* 1, *p*. 241. Gypsum rocks, Elm creek; August.

VITUS RUPESTRIS, *Scheele in Linnœa* 21, *p*. 291, On the Canadian, Pecos, etc. August—September. In fruit.

ACERACEÆ.

NEGUNDO ACEROIDES, *Mœnch.* In a cañon on the Pecos; September. In fruit.

ACER TRIPARTITUM, *Nutt. in Torr. & Gray, Fl.* 1, p. 247; Gray, Pl. Fendl., p. 28. Arroyas in the Sandia mountains; October. In fruit. While some of the leaves are trifoliate, others on the same branch are only three-lobed, and so much resemble those of A. glabrum that the species probably cannot be kept distinct.—*Gray, Mss.*

ACER MACROPHYLLUM, *Pursh, Fl.* 1, *p.* 267; *Hook. Fl. Bor.-Am.* 1, *p.* 112, *t.* 38; *Nutt. Sylv.* 2, *p.* 76, *t.* 67.

NEGUNDO ACEROIDES, *Mœnch. Meth., p.* 334; *Torr. & Gray, Fl.* 1, *p.* 260; N. Californicum, *Torr. & Gray, l. c.; Nutt. Sylv.* 2, *p.* 90, *t.* 72. Acer Negundo, *Linn.* Corte Madera, April 10, (in flower.)

SAPINDACEÆ.

ÆSCULUS CALIFORNICA, *Nutt. in Torr. & Gray, Fl.* 1, *p.* 251; *and Sylv.* 2, *p.* 69, *t.* 64. Hill-sides, Sonoma, May 3, in flower; mountains near Oakland, (leaves only.)

ÆSCULUS FLAVA, *Art.; Pursh, Fl.* 1, *p.* 255. On the Canadian, near the Shawnee villages, and Deer creek; August. In fruit.

SAPINDUS MARGINATUS, *Willd.; Gray, Gen. Ill.* 2, *t.* 180. Creek bottoms, on the Upper Canadian; September. In fruit.

CARDIOSPERMUM HALICACABUM, *Linn.* Deer creek; August.

CELASTRACEÆ.

PACHYSTIMA MYRSINITES, *Raf. in Amer. Month. Mag.*, 1818; *Gray, Pl. Fendl., p.* 29. Ilex? Myrsinites, *Pursh, Fl.* 1, *p.* 119. Oreophila myrtifolia, *Nutt. in Torr. & Gray, Fl.* 1, *p.* 259.—Sandia mountains, New Mexico; October; in fruit. Hill-sides. South Yuba, California; May 26. The leaves are larger than in the Oregon plant, and sharply serrate. The woody stem is of extremely slow growth, several annual circles being included with one-tenth of an inch.

EUONYMUS OCCIDENTALIS, *Nutt. Mss.* E. atropurpureus *β? Torr. & Gray, Fl.* 1, *p.* 258. Head of Tomales bay; April 17. Leaves ovate, mostly obtuse, at the base quite smooth. Peduncles 3-flowered. Flower pentamerous, larger than in E. atropurpureus. The fruit is unknown.

CELASTRUS SCANDENS, *Linm.* Pecan creek; August. In fruit.

GLOSSOPETALON SPINESCENS, *Gray, Pl. Wright.* 2, *p.* 29, *t.* 12. Cañons in the Llano Estacado; September. Without flowers or fruit.

RHAMNACEÆ.

RHAMNUS CROCEUS, *Nutt. in Torr. & Gray, Fl.* 1, *p.* 261. Hills near Sonora, May 9; Rocky hills, 80 miles west of the Colorado. Leaves often green underneath.

FRANGULA CALIFORNICA, *Gray, Gen. Ill.* 2, *p.* 178; *and Pl. Wright.* 2, *p.* 28. Rhamnus Californicus, *Esch.; Torr. & Gray, Fl.* 1, *p.* 263. R. oleifolius, *Hook. Fl. Bor.—Am.* 1, *p.* 123, *t.* 44. R. laurifolius, *Nutt. in Torr. & Gray, Fl. l. c.* Hill-sides, Robinson's ferry, Stanislaus, May 14; a variety, with larger leaves, softly pubescent on both sides; Napa valley, May 5, (leaves nearly glabrous both sides, and with obtuse serratures;) mountains near San Gabriel, March 23, (glabrous leaves, with acute serratures): var. TOMENTELLA, *Gray, Pl. Wright. l. c.* Rhamnus tomentellus, *Benth. Pl. Hartw. p.* 303. Butte mountains, near Marysville, May 25. A plant of very diverse appearance; but its extreme forms pass insensibly into each other. In favorable situations it attains the height of 18 feet.

CEANOTHUS THYRSIFLORUS, *Esch.; Torr. & Gray, Fl.* 1, *p.* 266; *Bot. Reg.* 30, *t.* 38; *Nutt. Sylv.* 2, *p.* 43, *t.* 57. Punta de los Reyes, April 18; San Francisco, April 3; hill-sides, Napa valley, April 27. A beautiful shrub, known in its native country under the name of California lilac.

CEANOTHUS SOREDIACUS, *Hook. & Arn. Bot. Beech. p.* 328; *Torr. & Gray, Fl. l. p.* 686. Hill-sides, Grass valley; May 9–19. A neat little shrub, 4–5 feet high, (sometimes prostrate,) with numerous clusters of bright-blue flowers, and resembling C. thyrsiflorus, only much smaller. A trailing form, with more pubescent branches and leaves, and short-peduncled panicles, was found at Duffield's ranch, Sierra Nevada, (May 12,) and at the Washington Mammoth grove, (May 15.)

Ceanothus divaricatus, *Nutt. in Torr. & Gray, Fl. l. c.* Var.? grosse-serratus: foliis majoribus, grosse-serratus, acutiusculis. Station not recorded. Branches thorny at the extremity; serratures of the leaves acute; flowers blue.

Ceanothus incanus, *Torr. & Gray, Fl.* 1, *p.* 265. A single specimen, of a slender form, of this species exists in the collection. It is without a ticket, but was probably found in the valley of the Sacramento.

Ceanothus crassifolius, (*Torr. in Emory's Mex. Bound. Rep., cum tab. ined.*:) fruticosus, ramulis pubescentibus; foliis ovatis, integerrimis, vel remote spinuloso-denticulatis coriaceis crassis penninerviis, supra demum glabratis, subtus albo-tomentosis, thyrsis subsessilibus umbelliformibus (floribus albis.) Hills and sandy plains, Cajon Pass, March 16; Teyung, California, *Mr. Wallace*, 1854. Dr. Parry discovered this well-marked species in the mountains south of Los Angeles, while acting as botanist, under Major Emory, in the Mexican boundary survey.

Ceanothus integerrimus, *Hook. & Arn. Bot. Beechey, p.* 329; *Torr. & Gray, Fl. l. c.; Benth. Pl. Hartw. p.* 302, *No.* 1684. Grass valley, May 20; Los Angeles, May 14; hill-sides, Nevada, May 20.

Ceanothus divaricatus, *Nutt. l. c. var.* eglandulosus: foliis integerrimis (margine nec denticulatis glanduliferis) obtusissimis. On mountains near San Gabriel; March 22. Also with vestiges of last year's fruit. Cohon Pass, March 16. (Collected by Dr. Parry on the mountains east of San Diego; in fruit and in flower by Mr. Wallace, at Boca de Teyunga, April.) This has the flowers, the divaricate spinescent branches with whitish bark, and also the foliage of C. divaricatus, except that none of the specimens show a trace of the glandular denticulations so manifest in the specimens of Douglas and of Coulter; nor is the pubescence on their ribs quite so evident. Some of the leaves are slightly cordate.—*Gray, Mss.*

Ceanothus cuneatus, *Nutt. in Torr. & Gray, Fl.* 1, *p.* 267. C. macrocarpus, *Nutt. l. c.*, (non *Cavan.*) Cocomungo, March 17; San Giovana, April 12; Napa valley, April 27; Knight's ferry, Stanislaus, May 7, (fruit.) A very variable species in the size and form of the leaves. It should, perhaps, include *C. verrucosus* of Nuttall.

Ceanothus dentatus, *Torr. & Gray, Fl.* 1, *p.* 268; *Lindl. & Paxt. Fl. Gard.* 1, *p.* 17, *t.* 4. Santa Rosa Laguna; May 1. This pretty species has much the appearance of C. sorediacus, but the leaves are hardly 3-nerved.

Ceanothus rigidus, *Nutt. in Torr. & Gray, Fl. l. c.; Lindl. & Paxt. Fl. Gard.* 1, *p.* 74, *t.* 51; *Bot. Mag.* 78, *t.* 4664. Var. grandifolius. Punta de los Reyes; April 18. The leaves are three times larger than in the ordinary form of this species, and strongly spinose-toothed on the sides, as well as at the extremity. This variety seems to show almost a transition to C. prostratus, through the broad-leaved form of that plant noticed below; but we are not willing to unite the two species, without seeing a more extensive suite of specimens for comparison.

Ceanothus prostratus, *Benth. Pl. Hartw. p.* 302. Grass valley, May 20; with immature fruit. The leaves vary from oblanceolate and entire to cuneate and tricuspidate. The fruit is crowned with 3 strong protuberances. A variety, with much larger obovate-cuneate leaves, coarsely spinose-toothed down to the middle, or at the apex only, was found at the Washington Mammoth grove. Colonel Frémont collected the same on the Upper Sacramento in 1846.

Ceanothus Fendleri, *Gray, Pl. Fendl. p.* 20. Sandia mountains; October. In fruit.

MESEMBRYANTHEMACEÆ.

Mesembryanthemum dimidiatum, *Harv.?* Sea-shore, Punta de los Reyes, April 18. The plant is abundant in several other places on the coast of California, and was probably introduced.

FRANKENIACEÆ.

Frankenia grandifolia, *Cham. & Schlect. in Linnæa* 1, *p.* 35; *Torr. & Gray, Fl.* 1, *p.* 168. Corte Madera; April 10.

POLYGALACEÆ.

Polygala cucullata, *Benth. Pl. Hartw. p.* 229. Hill-sides, Napa valley; April 27. We have seen no other Polygala from California, nor from any other part of the Pacific coast, and we strongly suspect that *P. Nutkana, Moç. Sesse.* (if really from the northwest coast) and *P. Californica, Nutt.*, are not distinct. The leaves are variable in breadth. In some of Frémont's specimens, collected on the Sacramento, they are acute at the base, and the apex is scarcely blunt. The little appendage which takes the place of this crest at the summit of the keel is sometimes rostrate, and either straight or curved. Although there are no flowers or radical sarments in Dr. Bigelow's specimens, there are vestiges of them, and it is probable that in the early state of the plant it usually produces such flowers.

Polygala Lindheimeri, *Gray, Pl. Lindh.* 2, *p.* 150. On the Llano Estacado; September. A form with mostly linear leaves.

KRAMERIACEÆ.

Krameria lanceolata, *Torr. in Am. Lyc., New York*, 2, *p.* 168. Sandy prairies on the Canadian; August.

LEGUMINOSÆ.

Vicia exigua, *Nutt. in Torr. & Gray, Fl.* 1, *p.* 272; *var.?* Californica. River banks, Benicia, April 24. We have not seen the Californian variety of the plant noticed by Mr. Nuttall. The specimens collected by Dr. Bigelow seem to be quite as near V. exigua, and perhaps the two species are not distinct. The former has been found in Alabama by Mr. Buckley, and in Florida by Dr. Chapman. All the specimens of Dr. Bigelow have single-flowered peduncles, which are of not half the length of the leaves. They are usually 6 leaflets, which are about an inch long and two lines wide, glabrous and emarginate, with a mucro, or acute and entire. The stipules are minute, and narrowly semi-sagittate. The pod is fully an inch long, sabre-shaped, and 5–7-seeded.

Vicia gigantea, *Hook. Fl. Bor.-Amer.* 1, *p.* 157; *Torr. & Gray, Fl.* 1, *p.* 270. Mountains near Oakland; April 4; Punta de los Reyes, April 18. This agrees well with our Oregon specimens from Dr. Scouler and Mr. Nuttall, except that the lower teeth of the calyx are not so long. It also occurs in Coulter's Californian collection.

Vicia Oregana, *Nutt. in Torr. & Gray, Fl. l. c.* V. truncata, *Nutt. l. c.* Mountains, near Oakland, April 4; hill-sides, Benicia, April 24. We find Nuttall's two species to run into each other.

Lathyrus vestitus, *Nutt. in Torr. & Gray, Fl.* 1, *p.* 276. Var.? multiflorus: foliolis ovato-oblongis, pedunculis folio multo longioribus 20–25-floris, dentibus inferioribus calycis superioribus triplo-longioribus. Hills, Tomales bay, April 19; Corte Madera, April 10. About one foot high, clothed with a short soft pubescence. Leaflets 6 pairs, nearly three-fourths of an inch long, cuspidate. Peduncles 2–3 times longer than the leaves. Flowers nearly as large as in L. palustris. Lower teeth of the calyx linear-lanceolate, three times longer than the upper triangular ones. Stipules lanceolate, semi-sagittate, entire.

Lathyrus venosus, *Muhl. in Willd. Sp.* 3, *p.* 1092? *Torr. & Gray, Fl.* 1, *p.* 274, (the var. γ.;) *Benth. Pl. Hartw., No.* 1705. L. decaphyllus, *Hook. Fl. Bor.-Amer.* 1, *p.* 159; non Pursh. Grass valley, May 19. A stout plant, with a winged stem. Leaflets 6 pairs, an inch and a half long, ovate-elliptical, minutely pubescent on both sides. Peduncles 4–6 inches long, (exclusive of the 10–14-flowered raceme.) Upper teeth of the calyx very short, and broadly triangular, with a minute point; all the teeth shorter than the tube. The stipules are larger than in the eastern plant, but much smaller than the leaves. We have not seen the pods.

LATHYRUS VENOSUS, var. GRANDIFLORUS: caule nudo; foliolis (subdecum) minoribus supra glabris; pedunculis folio subduplo longioribus; floribus maximis, dentibus calycis tubo subæqualibus. Cocomungo, March 17. The flowers are twice as large as in the ordinary form of this species.

LATHYRUS VENOSUS, var. δ. *Torr. & Gray, l. c.* L. pubescens, *Nutt. Mss.* Hill-sides, Benicia; April 24. This agrees with our Oregon specimens from Nuttall. It is between L. venosus and vestitus, and seems almost to unite the two species.

LATHYRUS VENOSUS: var. OBOVATUS: caule nudo; foliolis sub-4-jugis plerumque obovatis obtusis puberulis; racemo 3–4-floro; calcycis dentibus subæqualibus. Near the Mammoth Grove and at Duffield's Ranch, Sierra Nevada, May 15. A mountain form, with larger flowers than usual.

LATHYRUS OCHROLEUCUS, *Hook. Fl. Bor.-Am.* 1, *p.* 159? Var. pedunculis 12–20-floris, folio subæquantibus. Hill-sides, Murphy's, May 12. Leaflets of a firm texture, and more approximated than in the eastern plant.

We are by no means satisfied with the results of our examination of the Lathyri in Dr. Bigelow's collection. The species of this genus are extremely variable, especially those of Oregon and California. It is possible that the true L. venosus does not grow on the northwest coast; but we have not been able to discover characters sufficient for distinguishing from that species any of the varieties enumerated above.

LATHYRUS POLYMORPHUS, *Nutt. Gen.* 2, *p.* 97; *Gray, Pl. Fendl., p.* 30. Laguna Colorado, New Mexico, September; and Santa Domingo, October; in low and wet places.

OROBUS LITTORALIS, *Gray, in Stevens' Rep. ined.* Astrophia littoralis, *Nutt. in Torr. & Gray, Fl.* 1, *p.* 278. Specimens of this plant were given to Dr. Bigelow by Dr. Andrews. They were probably collected on the coast, near San Francisco.

PHASEOLUS DIVERSIFOLIUS, *Pers.; Torr. & Gray, Fl.* 1, *p.* 279. Sand banks of the Canadian River, near the Shawnee villages, etc. August.

PHASEOLUS PAUCIFLORUS, *Benth.; Gray, Pl. Wright.* 1, *p.* 44. With the preceding.

AMPHICARPÆA MONOICA, *Torr. & Gray, Fl.* 1, *p.* 292. Ravines of Pecan creek; August.

PSORALEA PHYSODES, *Dougl. in Hook. Fl. Bor.-Amer.* 1, *p.* 304; *Torr. & Gray, Fl.* 1. *p.* 304 *and* 689. Near Mark West's Creek, California. April 30. The stem is wholly free from glands.

PSORALEA CUSPIDATA, *Pursh, Fl.* 2, *p.* 741. Rocky hills of the upper Canadian; September. In fruit.

PSORALEA DIGITATA, *Nutt. in Torr. & Gray, Fl.* 1. *p.* 301. Sand-banks of the Canadian, near the Shawnee villages; August. In fruit.

PSORALEA LINEARIFOLIA, *Torr. & Gray, l. c.* Gypsum hills, Comanche plains; September.

PSORALEA MICRANTHA (sp. nov.): cinereo-puberula, minute glanduloso-punctata; caulibus e radice seu rhizomate longissimo repente assurgentibus paniculato-ramosissimis; stipulis subulatis minimis; foliis palmatim trifoliolatis; foliolis lineari-filiformibus incisve anguste linearibus mucronato-acutis; pedunculis folio paullo brevioribus; spica brevi densiflora; bracteis minimis caducis; calycis dentibus brevibus obtusissimis; fructu glabro.—Sand hills, near the last camp on the upper Canadian; September. Plant a foot high, from a horizontal root or slender rootstock of several feet in length. Branches slender, leafy. Leaflets an inch or less in length, canaliculate and nearly filiform, or the lowest flat and about a line wide, punctate with fine brown dots. Peduncles half an inch long, about the length of the subtending petioles, bearing a short and oval or oblong spike of 10–20 small flowers, which are usually closely approximate or crowded. Calyx short, scarcely a line long, rather longer than the pedicel, campanulate, dotted with coarse brown glands; the short teeth broad and very obtuse, equal. Corolla barely a line and a half long beyond the calyx, narrow, white, except the tip of the keel, which is blue.

Anthers uniform. Fruit globular, flattened, glabrous or nearly so. This should be compared with P. laxiflora, *Nutt.*, which we have never seen, and which is compared with P. lanceolata, a species having much affinity with the present one. Nuttall's plant, however, is characterized as having the leaflets longer than P. lanceolata, and linear or oblong, the peduncles longer than the leaves, the flowers somewhat distant, etc.—*Gray, Mss.*

AMORPHA CANESCENS, *Nutt. Gen.* 2, *p.* 92. Prairies Indian Territory; August.

PETALOSTEMON VIOLACEUM, *Michx. Fl.* 2, *p.* 50, *t.* 37. Sand banks of the Canadian river, near the Shawnee villages ; August.

PETALOSTEMON MULTIFLORUM, *Nutt. ; Torr. & Gray, Fl.* 1, *p.* 309. Prairies on the Canadian, near Delaware mountain ; August.

PETALOSTEMON VILLOSUM, *Nutt. Gen.* 2, *p.* 85 *; Torr. & Gray, l. c.* Sand banks of the Canadian, near the Shawnee villages ; August.

DALEA SPINOSA, *Gray, Plant. Thurb. p.* 315. Arroyos near Williams' River of the Colorado, New Mexico ; February 16. In fruit.

DALEA FORMOSA, *Torr. in Anner. Lyc. New York*, 2, *p.* 178, *& in Emory's, Rep. t.* 1. Rocks and cañons on the upper Canadian ; September.

DALEA LAXIFLORA, *Pursh, Fl.* 2, *p.* 741. Prairies of the upper Canadian ; August.

DALEA ALOPECUROIDES, *Willd.* Santo Domingo, New Mexico, on the banks of streams ; October.

DALEA LANATA, *Spreng. Syst.* 3, *p.* 327. Sand banks of the Canadian, near the Shawnee villages ; August.

DALEA NANA, *Torr. in Pl. Fendl. p.* 31. Plains of the upper Canadian and New Mexico ; September—October.

DALEA AUREA, *Nutt. Gen.* 2, *p.* 101. Prairies of the upper Canadian ; September.

DALEA JAMESII, *Torr. & Gray, Fl.* 1, *p.* 308. Plains of the upper Canadian; September.

TRIFOLIUM INVOLUCRATUM, *Willd. ; Benth. Pl. Hartw. n.* 54 *; Gray, Pl. Fendl. p.* 33. Banks of streams near Santo Domingo, New Mexico ; October.

TRIFOLIUM MACRÆI, *Hook. & Arn. in Hook. Bot. Misc.* 3, *p.* 179, *& Bot. Beech. p.* 330. T. albopurpureum, *Torr. & Gray, Fl.* 1, *p.* 313. Corte Madera, April 10 ; in fields, Benicia, April 23 ; Napa valley, April 26. Variable in height, size of heads, and form of the leaves.

TRIFOLIUM DICHOTOMUM, *Hook. & Arn. Bot. Beech. p.* 330 *; Torr. & Gray, Fl.* 1. *p.* 691. The station of this plant is uncertain, as no ticket accompanied the specimen, but it was probably collected near San Francisco. We are not certain that it is a distinct species from the preceding, although so much larger in all its parts.

TRIFOLIUM CILIOLATUM, *Benth. Pl. Hartw. p.* 304. Corte Madera, April 12 ; Benicia, California; April 23. We have specimens of this plant from the valley of the Sacramento, collected by Dr. Stillman and Mr. Shelton.

TRIFOLIUM GRACILENTUM, *Torr. & Gray, Fl.* 1, *p.* 316. Corte Madera, April 10 ; Napa valley, April 26 ; Hill sides, Sonoma, California; May 3.

TRIFOLIUM MICROCEPHALUM, *Pursh, Fl.* 2, *p.* 478*; Torr. & Gray, Fl.* 1, *p.* 317. Tamul Pass, California ; April 11.

TRIFOLIUM HETERODON, *Torr. & Gray, Fl.* 1, *p.* 318. Low wet places, near San Francisco ; April 3–8. Legume 4–5-seeded. A good species.

TRIFOLIUM TRIDENTATUM, *Lindl. Bot. Reg. sub. t.* 1070. T. involucratum, *Torr. & Gray, l. c., non Willd.* Corte Madera, April 12.

TRIFOLIUM MICRODON, *Hook. & Arn. Bot. Misc.* 3, *p.* 180; *& Bot. Beechey, p.* 330, *t.* 79. Hill-sides, Sonoma, California ; May 3.

TRIFOLIUM FUCATUM, *Lindl. Bot. Reg. t.* 1883 ; *Torr. & Gray, Fl.* 1, *p.* 619. Los Angeles, March 21 ; Benicia and Martinez, April 23–24.

TRIFOLIUM AMPLECTENS, *Torr. & Gray, Fl.* 1, *p.* 319. Corte Madera, April 10 ; and San Francisco, April 3 ; hill-sides, Benicia, April 24.

TRIFOLIUM BARBIGERUM, (sp. nov.): nanum, molliter pubescens; caulibus e radice annua vel bienni adscendentibus, (1–3 poll. longis,) junioribus stipulis scariosis apice truncato setaceo-laciniatis imbricatum vestitis; foliolis obovatis cuneatisve obtusissimis denticulatis; involucro cyathiformi laciniato aristato-dentato flores subæquante; calycis dentibus tubo fere triplo longioribus aristiformi-subulatis plumoso-barbatis, infimo simplici præsertim supremo bi-trifidis; leguminibus dispermis. Near San Francisco, April. The Rev. A. Fitch collected this plant in the same place, four or five years ago.

MELILOTUS PARVIFLORA, *Desf. Fl. Atl.* 2, *p.* 192; *Torr. & Gray, Fl.* 1, *p.* 321. Common in New Mexico and California, on banks of streams; probably introduced.

MEDICAGO DENTICULATA, *Willd. Sp.* 3, *p.* 1414; *Torr. & Gray, Fl.* 1, *p.* 332. Cocomungo, California; March 18. Introduced.

HOSACKIA BICOLOR, *Dougl. et Benth. in Bot. Reg. t.* 1257; *Hook. Fl. Bor.-Am.* 1, *p.* 134; *Torr. & Gray. Fl.* 1, *p.* 323. Hills near Punta de los Reyes; April 17; and wet ravines, Grass Valley, California; May 19. A showy perennial species. The stipules are not always "very obtuse," but are sometimes rather acute.

HOSACKIA STOLONIFERA, *Lindl. Bot. Reg. t.* 1977; *Torr. & Gray, Fl.* 1, *p.* 323. River banks, Mokelumne Hill, and Mammoth grove, California; May 15–17. Var. PUBESCENS. Corte Madera, April 16. In this variety the peduncles are sometimes naked, and sometimes (even on the same specimen) furnished with a sessile, unifoliolate, or pinnately 2–7-foliolate bract. The whole plant is conspicuously pubescent.

HOSACKIA GRANDIFLORA, *Benth. in Bot. Reg. sub. t.* 1257; *Torr. & Gray, Fl.* 1, *p.* 323. Hillsides, mouth of the Yuba, California; May 21. The bract is occasionally trifoliolate, and not unfrequently it is wanting altogether, or only rudimentary.

HOSACKIA PUBERULA, *Benth. Pl. Hartw., p.* 305; *Gray, Pl. Wright.* 1, *p.* 50. On Williams' River of the Colorado, western Mew Mexico, February 11.

HOSACKIA (EUHOSACKIA) INCANA (sp. nov.): perennis, undique et mollissime cano-villosa; caule erecto simplici; foliolis 11–13 ovatis acutiusculis; stipulis ovatis folioformibus; pedunculis folio multo brevioribus; umbellis 6–9-floris; bractea 5-foliolata; floribus pedicellatis; calycis dentibus subulato-lanceolatis tubo duplo brevioribus. (Tab. IV.) Dry hills, near South Yuba, California; May 23. Plant 6–10 inches high, densely clothed with soft greyish-white villous pubescence. Stem rather stout, leafy. Leaflets nearly half an inch long, mostly opposite, varying from broadly to narrowly ovate. Stipules about two-thirds the size of the leaflets, and resembling them in form. Peduncles (floriferous) half an inch or more in length. Flowers as large as in H. bicolor, apparently purple, mixed with yellow; the pedicels about one-third the length of the calyx. Pods not seen. Allied to H. stipularis, but abundantly distinct.

HOSACKIA PARVIFLORA, *Benth. in Bot. Reg. sub t.* 1257; *Torr. & Gray, Fl.* 1, *p.* 326. Napa Valley, April 25. Hills near Punta de los Reyes, and Tomales bay, April 17–19. H. microphylla and H. nudiflora of Nuttall seem to be only reduced forms of this species.

HOSACKIA STRIGOSA, *Nutt. in Torr. & Gray, Pl.* 1, *p.* 326. Cocomungo, March 26. We think that H. rubella, *Nutt.*, should be united to this species.

HOSACKIA SUBPINNATA, *Torr. & Gray, l. c.* Lotus subpinnatus, *Lagas. Gen. and Sp. p.* 33; *Hook. & Arn. Bot. Beech., p.* 17, *t.* 8. Corte Madera, April 10; hill-sides, Martinez, California; April 23.

HOSACKIA PURSHIANA, *Benth. l. c.; Torr. & Gray, l. c.* Lotus sericeus, *Pursh, Fl.* 2, *p.* 489. Low ravines, Grass valley, May 19. The four remaining species of the section Psycopsis of Nuttall (*in Torr. & Gray, Fl. l. c.*) are probably only forms of H. Purshiana.

HOSACKIA CYTISOIDES, *Benth. l. c.; Torr. & Gray, l. c.* Near San Francisco. Bracts mostly unifoliolate.

ROBINIA NEO-MEXICANA, *Gray, Pl. Thurb., p.* 314. Mountain arroyos, near San Antonita, New Mexico; October. In fruit.

GLYCYRRHIZA LEPIDOTA, *Nutt. Gen.* 2, *p.* 106. Sand banks of the Canadian, near the Shawnee villages; August. With ripe fruit.

INDIGOFERA LEPTOSEPALA, *Nutt. in Torr. & Gray, Fl.* 1, *p.* 298. With the preceding, and at Upper Crosstimbers, Indian Territory; August.

PHACA DENSIFOLIA, *Smith in Rees Cycl.; Torr. & Gray, Fl.* 1. *p.* 344 & 693; *Hook. Ic. t.* 283. P. Nuttallii, *T. & Gr. l. c.* Cocomungo, California; March 18. Legumes an inch and a half long, and more than three-fourths of an inch broad. Seeds numerous, not half the size of a pepper-corn. Our plant differs somewhat from Douglas's, as figured by Hooker in his Icones, especially in being smoother and the flowers larger, as well as in the larger calyx-teeth; but it is undoubtedly the same.

ASTRAGALUS DIDYMOCARPUS, *Hook. & Arn. Bot. Beech., p.* 334, *t.* 81; *Torr. & Gray, Fl.* 1, *p.* 693. Fields near Benicia, and Corte Madera; April 10–23. The specimens are much smaller than those collected by Douglas, Mr. Rich, and Dr. Parry. The legumes are scarcely three lines long, and of about the same breadth. When young they are villous, but nearly glabrous (though strongly rugose) when old. The leaves vary in breadth from half a line to two lines or more. We have little doubt that A. nigrescens and A. Catalinensis, *Nutt.* (*Pl. Gamb.*,) are varieties of this species.

ASTRAGALUS MISSOURIENSIS, *Nutt. Gen.* 2, *p.* 99; *Torr. & Gray, Fl.* 1, *p.* 331, *excl. syn. Pursh.* Gravelly hills, New Mexico, and on Williams' fork of the Colorado, February 6.

ASTRAGALUS FRÉMONTII (sp. nov.): molliter strigoso-cinerea; radice perenni; caulibus adscendentibus (10 poll. longis) crassiusculis; foliolis 9–21 ovalibus vel rotundatis retusis; stipulis triangulatis basi tantum petioli adnatis; pedunculis folium æquantibus, floribus laxiuscule spicatis patentibus subsessilibus; calycis dentibus subulatis tubo campanulato brevioribus; "corolla purpurea;" leguminibus immaturis membranaceis inflatis ovatis acuminatis bilocellatis polyspermis estipitatis. Banks of the Rio Virgin; May 3, 1844, Frémont. Var. caule breviori (2–3-pollicari); floribus majoribus; calyce magis cylindraceo et nigro-hirsuto. On the Mohave creek; March 3. An early state, only in flower, apparently of the same species as that gathered in the same region by Colonel Frémont. Leaflets 3–6 lines long. Flowers half an inch long; the calyx 3 lines long; the corolla apparently white, or whitish; all the petals tipped with deep violet purple. The half-grown pods of Frémont's specimens are over half an inch in length, nearly glabrous, very thin, and completely bilocellate.—*Gray, Mss.*

ASTRAGALUS HUMISTRATUS, *Gray, Pl. Wright.* 5, *p.* 45. Arroyos, near San Antonita, New Mexico; October. In fruit.

ASTRAGALUS MOLLISSIMUS, *Torr. in Ann. Lyc., New York,* 2, *p.* 178; *Gray, Pl. Wright.* 1, *p.* 53. Rocky ridges of the False Washita, August; and plains of the Upper Canadian, September. In flower.

ASTRAGALUS DIPHYSUS, *Gray, Pl. Fendl., p.* 34. Sandy places, near Albuquerque; October. In fruit.

ASTRAGALUS (PHACA) LONCHOCARPUS. Phaca macrocarpa, *Gray, Pl. Fendl., p.* 36. Bluffs and rocky places, on the Llano Estacado; September. The few specimens of this interesting plant bear only old and dehiscent pods, which are shorter than in Fendler specimens, and are follicular, opening as they do only by the ventral suture, and at length spreading out into a perfectly plane lamina. The leaflets are nearly all wanting, and the filiform naked petioles are rather persistent. The root is perennial. The name has to be changed, on account of the Astragalus macrocarpus of De Candolle.

OXYTROPIS URALENSIS, *DC. Prod.* 2, *p.* 276; *Hook. Fl. Bor.-Am.* 1, *p.* 145. Sandia mountains, New Mexico; October. In flower and fruit.

OXYTROPIS LAMBERTI, *Pursh Fl.* 2, *p.* 740. Rocky hills, of the Upper Canadian; September. Narrow-leaved and loosely-flowered forms. Pods slender and very minutely silky-puberulent; in one specimen of which the flowers are unknown, shorter and thicker, and strigose-hirsute.

OXYTROPIS SERICEA, *Nutt. in Torr. & Gray, Fl.* 1, *p.* 339. Bluffs and rocky places, on the Llano Estacado; September. There is scarce a doubt that this passes into O. Lamberti.

KENTROPHYTA MONTANA, *Nutt. in Torr. & Gray, Fl.* 1, *p.* 353. Inscription Rock, New Mexico;

November 18, (in fruit.) K. viridis is hardly a distinct species, and the genus itself might be reduced to a section of Astragalus.

LUPINUS SPARSIFLORUS, *Benth. Pl. Hartw., p.* 303. Gravelly hills, on the Colorado, western New Mexico, February 26. A form with less hirsute leaves. Also a larger form, February 17.

LUPINUS NANUS, *Dougl.; Benth. in Hort. Trans., p.* 459, *t.* 14, *f.* 2. Corte Madera, California; April 12–15. Some of the specimens are a foot or more in height. Those with broader eaflets accord with "L. nanus var. latifolius," *Benth.* in Herb. Coulter. The flowers are sometimes white.

LUPINUS DENSIFLORUS, *Benth. in Hort. Trans. n. ser.* 1, *p.* 409. L. Menziesii, *Agardh, Syn. Lup., p.* 2. Woods and shady places, Knight's Ferry, on the Stanislaus river; May 7. Mr. Bentham (in *Pl. Hartweg p.* 303) points out that Agardh has founded his L. Menziesii upon the Douglasian plant, which he had described as L. densiflorus. All confusion about the synonymy may be avoided, however, for the two species, L. densiflorus and L. Menziesii, *Ag.*, cannot be kept distinct. Both have white flowers, (Agardh wrongly attributes yellow corollas to his L. Menziesii, but his guess from the appearance in dried specimens is not correct in this, nor in some other instances;) and the longer bracts and very villous calyxes of Agardh's L. densiflorus are evidently not available for a specific distinction. Dr. Bigelow's specimens, however, corresponds in this respect with L. Menziesii.

LUPINUS BICOLOR, *Lindl. Bot. Reg. t.* 1109; *Agardh, l. c. p.* 14. L. micranthus, *Dougl. in Bot. Reg. t.* 1251; *Torr. & Gray, l. c.* Wet places, near San Francisco, April 8. Plains, near San Gabriel; March 23.

LUPINUS LEPTOPHYLLUS, *Benth. in Hort. Trans. l. c. t.* 14, *f.* 2; *Torr. & Gray, l. c.* Hills and rocky places, Knight's Ferry, Stanislaus river; May 7.

LUPINUS LATIFOLIUS, *Agardh, l. c.* L. cytisoides, *Agardh, l. c.; Torr. & Gray, l. c.* Corte Madera, April 12; and hill-sides, Martinez, California; April 23. L. cytisoides was supposed by Agardh to have yellow flowers, but he saw only dried specimens, and was very probably mistaken.

LUPINUS RIVULARIS, *Lindl. Bot. Reg. t.* 1595; *Torr. & Gray, Fl.* 1, *p.* 377. Plains, near San Gabriel, March 23. Rather more silky than the ordinary state of the plant. Except in the entire calyx, it scarcely differs from L. Douglasii.

LUPINUS LAXIFLORUS, *Dougl. in Bot. Reg. t.* 1140; *Torr. & Gray, l. c.* Hill-sides, Stanislaus river, near Carson's, May 14. We are doubtful about our determination of this plant, as the calyx is not very decidedly gibbous.

LUPINUS DECUMBENS, *Torr.* var. ARGOPHYLLUS, *Gray, Pl. Fendl. p.* 37. Gravelly hills, near San Antonita, New Mexico; October. L. laxiflorus, Dougl., probably passes into this species.

LUPINUS ALBIFRONS, *Benth. in Hort. Trans.* 1, *c. p.* 410; *Lindl. Bot. Reg. t.* 1642; *Torr. & Gray, l. c.* Sand hills, on the sea-shore; Punta de los Reyes; and near San Francisco. April 3–17. A fine shrubby species.

LUPINUS ORNATUS, *Dougl. in Bot. Reg. t.* 1216; *Agardh, l. c. p.* 28; *Torr. & Gray, Fl.* 1, *p.* 378. Butte mountains, California; May 25.

LUPINUS MACORCARPUS, *Hook. & Arn. Bot. Beech., p.* 138. On sand hills, near the sea; Punta de los Reyes, California; April 17. This species was discovered many years ago by Menzies, and seems not to have been found again till Dr. Bigelow collected it in Whipple's expedition. It resembles L. arboreus (which Dr. Parry obtained near San Diego) in its shrubby stem and large yellow flowers, but that species is minutely pubescent; this is very hirsute, and the leaves are silky underneath. The petioles of both are shorter than the leaflets, and in our specimens of L. macrocarpus the flowers are decidedly verticillate. We have not seen the pods.

THERMOPSIS MACROPHYLLA, *Hook. & Arn. Bot. Beech., p.* 329; *Torr. & Gray, Fl.* 1, *p.* 388. L. montana, *Nutt. in Torr. & Gray, Fl. l. c.* Corte Madera, April 15. Leaflets often broadly obovate. Nuttall's T. montana can hardly be considered as more than a smoother form of this plant, with usually narrower leaves. We have specimens that are intermediate between the two.

Sophora speciosa, *Benth. in Gray, Pl. Lindh.* 3, *p.* 178. Dermatophyllum speciosum, *Scheele in Linnæa,* 21, *p.* 459. Cactus Pass and White Cliff creek, New Mexico, January 29.

Hedysarum boreale, *Nutt. Gen.* 2, *p.* 110. With the preceding; in flower and fruit.

Desmodium pauciflorum, *DC. Prod.* 2, *p.* 230. Creeks, on the Canadian river; August.

Desmodium cuspidatum, *Torr. & Gray, Fl.* 1, *p.* 360. Near Shawnee town; August.

Desmodium Canadense, *DC.; Torr. & Gray, l. c.* Wet places, on the Canadian; September. In fruit.

Desmodium paniculatum, *DC.; Torr. & Gray, l. c.* Sandy soil, on the Canadian; September.

Lespedeza violacea, *Pers.* On the Canadian; August.

Lespedeza capitata, *Michx.* Near Beavertown; August.

Cercis occidentalis, *Torr. in Gray, Pl. Lindh.* 2, *p.* 177. C. Siliquastrum, var. *Benth. Pl. Hartw., p.* 307. Hill-sides, Robinson's Ferry, Stanislaus river; May 14; with immature fruit. This species has a very extensive range, being found from the upper Sacramento, northern California, to the high lands near Saltillo, Mexico.

Olneya Tesota, *Gray, Pl. Thurb., p.* 328. Arroyos, near Williams' river of the Colorado, western New Mexico; February 6. The specimens are in fruit only. Some of them are destitute of prickles.

Parkinsonia microphylla, *Torr. Bot. of Mex. Boundary Survey, ined.* Banks of the Colorado, and on Williams' river; February 12–22; in fruit. A very distinct species with minute roundish leaflets.

Cercidium floridum, *Benth. in Gray, Pl. Wright.* 1, *p.* 58. In arroyos, near the Colorado. February 11; in fruit. This is the *Green Acacia* of Major Emory's report. It is a common tree on the Gila; attaining the height of 25 or 30 feet.

Cassia Rœmeriana, *Scheele in Linnæa,* 21, *p.* 458. Hurrah creek, New Mexico; September. In fruit.

Hoffmanseggia Jamesii, *Torr. & Gray, Fl.* 1, *p.* 393; *Torr. in Marcy's Rep. t.* 4. Prairies of the Canadian; September.

Hoffmanseggia stricta, *Benth. Var.* demissa, *Gray, Pl. Wright.* 1, *p.* 56. Dogtown praries, on the Llano Estacado; September.

Hoffmanseggia drepanocarpa, *Gray, Pl. Wright.* 1, *p.* 58. Plains, near Hurrah creek, New Mexico; September. In fruit.

Strombocarpa pubescens, *Gray, Pl. Wright.* 1, *p.* 60. Prŏsopis (Strombocarpa) pubescens, *Benth. in Hook. Lond. Jour. Bot.* 5, *p.* 82. P. (Strombocarpa) Emoryi, *Torr. in Emory's Rep., p.* 139. Low sandy shore of the Colorado. Western New Mexico, (in fruit.) Prosopis odorata, *Torr. in Frém. Rep., p.* 313, *t.* 1, is a var. of P. glandulosa, (in flower only,) with the pods of Strombocarpa pubescens. The error arose from the mixing of specimens in Frémont's collections.

Algarobia glandulosa, *Torr. & Gray, Fl.* 1, *p.* 399. Plains, on the Canadian; September.

Schrankia uncinata, *Willd.; Torr. & Gray, Fl.* 1, *p.* 400. Prairies, near Deer creek, Indian Territory; August.

Desmanthus brachylobus, *Benth. in Hook Journ. Bot.* Sand banks of the Canadian; August.

Calliandra humilis, *Benth. in Lond. Journ. Bot.* 5, *p.* 103; *Gray, Pl. Wright.* 2, *p.* 53. C. herbacea, *Englm.* Gravelly hills, near Santa Antonita, New Mexico; October. In fruit.

ROSACEÆ.

Prunus subcordata, *Benth. Pl. Hartw., p.* 308. Hills, Sonora, May 9; near Duffield's Ranch, Sierra Nevada, May 11, and hill-sides, near Middle Yuba, California; May 23. A shrub 2–6 feet high. Fruit small, with a thin pulp. The leaves are sometimes pubescent underneath.

Prunus Americana, *Marsh. Ait.; Torr. & Gray, Fl.* 1, *p.* 407. Banks of Bogg creek, near Shawneetown, Indian Territory; August. In fruit.

Prunus Chicasa, *Michx. Fl.* 1, *p.* 284. Banks of the Canadian, near Shawneetown; August. With ripe fruit.

PRUNUS GRACILIS, *Engelm. & Gray, Pl. Lindh.* 1, *p.* 35. Prairies, Gains' creek, Indian Territory; August. In fruit. Cultivated under the name of Prairie Cherry. This appears to belong to the *Microcerasus* group.

CERASUS VIRGINIANA, DC. Banks of the Pecos, and in cañons of the Llano Estacado; September. Sandia mountains; October. In fruit.

CERASUS DEMISSA, *Nutt. in Torr. & Gray, Fl.* 1, *p.* 411. Deep ravines, Sonora, California, May 9; and Duffield's Ranch, Sierra Nevada; May 12.

CERASUS EMARGINATA, *Dougl. in Hook. Fl. Bor.-Amer.* 1, *p.* 169; *Torr. & Gray, Fl.* 1, *p.* 410. Hill-sides, near Downieville, California; May 21. A small shrub, with numerous slender branches. Flowers in short corymbose racemes. Leaves ¾ of an inch to an inch and a half long, entire at the summit. Teeth of the calyx obtuse and reflexed.

CERASUS MINUTIFLORA, *Engelm. in Gray, Plant. Lindh.* 2, *p.* 185, *sub Pruno; Gray, Pl. Wright.* 2, *p.* 68. Williams' fork of the Colorado, Western New Mexico. Fruit only.

CERASUS ILICIFOLIA, *Nutt. in Torr. & Gray, Fl.* 1, *p.* 411; *& Sylv.* 2, *p.* 16, *t.* 47; *Hook. & Arn. Bot. Beechey, p.* 340, *t.* 83. Topographical Hill, near Williams' fork of the Colorado. With leaves only.

NUTTALLIA CERASIFORMIS, *Torr. & Gray, in Hook. & Arn. Bot. Beechey, p.* 336, *t.* 82; *& Fl.* 1, *p.* 413. Mountains, near Oakland; April 5, (in flower and young fruit,) and hill-sides, Napa valley, California; April 27, (with mature fruit.)

SPIRÆA OPULIFOLIA, *Linn. Sp.* 1, *p.* 489; *Torr. & Gray, Fl.* 1, *p.* 413. Arroyos, in the Sandia mountains, New Mexico, October. Banks of streams and hill-sides, Napa valley, etc., California; April 27.

SPIRÆA ARIÆFOLIA, *Smith in Rees, Cycl.; Torr. & Gray, Fl.* 1, *p.* 416. Banks of streams, Sonoma, California; May 3.

SPIRÆA CÆSPITOSA, *Nutt. in Torr. & Gray, Fl.* 1, *p.* 418; *Gray, Pl. Fendl., p.* 40. Rocky places, Pass of Mt. Hope, Western New Mexico; January 23. The wood of the stem has no annual rings, even when several years old, and the medullary rays are as wide as the woody wedges.

SPIRÆA MILLEFOLIUM (sp. nov.): lanoso-tomentosa; foliis circumscriptione oblongo-lanceolatis pinnatis multijugis, pinnis pinnatisectis partitisve oblongo-linearibus cum foliolis minutissimis oblongis confertissimis; floribus racemoso-paniculatis. (Tab. V.) Low hills and valleys, near Williams' mountain; January 5. A shrub, apparently 1–2 feet high. Leaves crowded on short branches or spurs, scarcely an inch long; pinnæ oblong-linear, in 20 or more pairs; the upper ones sometimes confluent; leaflets very numerous, about one-fourth of a line long, densely tomentose, and of a somewhat fleshy texture. Stipules linear, minute, deciduous. Racemes in a long and rather loose terminal panicle. Calyx turbinate; the teeth acute, erect, rather longer than the tube. Petals orbicular-obovate, longer than the calyx. Stamens about 70; the filaments distinct at the base, inserted into the margin of a disk, which is wholly adnate to the tube of the calyx. Ovaries 5, distinct, at first woolly; styles filiform; stigmas somewhat capitate. Ovules 8–10, pendulous from the upper part of the ovary, narrowly oblong. Mature carpels nearly glabrous, erect, 2-valved to the base. All the mature seeds had fallen, but the immature ones were somewhat attenuated at each end. Although so very remarkable, this appears to be a genuine Spiræa, and to resemble more the Euspiræa than any other of the admitted sections of the genus. The leaflets are almost as small and crowded as in Chamæbatia. The specimens collected by Dr. Bigelow seem to have the persistent inflorescence and fruit of the preceding autumn, and the young leaves of the new year. Many of the flowers exhibited the withered petals, and there were a few imperfect undeveloped buds.

CERCOCARPUS PARVIFOLIUS, *Nutt. in Torr. & Gray, Fl.* 1, *p.* 427; *Gray, Pl. Fendl., p.* 41; *Hook. Ic. Pl. t.* 323. Hills on the Llano Estacado; also sandy hills, Cañon Pass and Cocomungo, April 16–17; hills and ravines, Sonora, California; May 9. A shrub about 10 feet high. C. betulaefolius seems to pass into this species.

CHAMÆBATIA FOLIOLOSA, *Benth. Pl. Hartw. p.* 308; *Torr. Pl. Frémont., p.* 11, *t.* 6. Hill-sides and ravines, Sonora; May 9.

COWANIA MEXICANA, *Don in Linn. Trans.* 14, *p.* 574, *t.* 22; *Gray, Pl. Wright.* 2, *p.* 55. Mountains near the Zuni river. In leaf only.

COWANIA STANSBURIANA, *Torr. in Stansb. Rep., p.* 386, *t.* 3. Ojo Piscado; November 19. San Francisco mountain, and Lithodendron creek, New Mexico; December. Although very near C. Mexicana it seems to retain its characters.

ACÆNA TRIFIDA, *Ruiz & Pav. Fl. Peruv.* 1, *p.* 67, *t.* 104. A pinnatifida, *Hook. & Arn. Bot. Beechey, p.* 339; *Torr. & Gray, Fl.* 1, *p.* 430, non *Ruiz & Pav.* San Geronimo Ranch; April 12.

ADENOSTOMA FASCICULATA, *Hook. & Arn. Bot. Beechey, p.* 139 *&* 338, *t.* 30; *Torr. & Gray, Fl.* 1, *p.* 430. Sandy hills near Cajon Pass, March 16, (with the fruit of the preceding year.) Hill-sides, near Ion valley; May 18.

ALCHEMILLA ARVENSIS, *Scop. Fl. Carn.* 1, *p.* 115; *Torr. & Gray, Fl.* 1, *p.* 432. A. occidentalis and A. cuneifolia, *Nutt. in Torr. & Gray, Fl. l. c.* Hill-sides, Benicia, April 24. Low places near San Francisco, April 8. We find the characters of this species to be quite variable, so as to include the two species of Nuttall.

FALLUGIA PARADOXA, *Torr. in Emory's Rep.* 2. Cañons of the Pecos, New Mexico; September.

HORKELIA CAPITATA, *Lindl. Bot. Reg. sub fol.* 1997; *Torr. & Gray, Fl.* 1, *p.* 434. San Gabriel, California; March 21. In Dr. Bigelow's specimens, as also in those collected at Los Angeles by Mr. Wallace, the petals are quite as long as the calyx. Agrees pretty well with our Douglasian specimen, except that the cymes are not capitate; but in most of the species of this genus the inflorescence is at first dense, and unfolds with age.

HORKELIA FUSCA, *Lindl. Bot. Reg. t.* 1997. Var. TENUILOBA: canescenti-villoso; foliolis 25–30, latissime-cuneatis profunde-palmitifidis; laciniis anguste-linearibus; cymis laxiusculis; bracteolis calycis dentibus subæqualibus; petalis cuneatis, apice bilobis. Laguna of Santa Rosa creek, California; May 1. Radical leaves 4–6 inches long, mostly villous with greyish hairs; leaflets less than half an inch long, palmately 5–7-cleft; the segments scarcely half a line wide; cauline leaves with a much smaller number of leaflets, with 3–4 segments. Stem about a foot high. Cyme somewhat open when the inflorescence is fully developed. Flowers about as large as in H. parviflora. Proper segments of the calyx triangular-lanceolate; the bracteoles narrowly lanceolate. Petals white, narrowly cuneiform, deeply notched at the summit.

HORKELIA TRIDENTATA (sp. nov.): subsericeo-villosa; caulibus patenti-diffusis; foliolis 7–11 oblongo vel obovato-cuneatis apice plerumque tridentatis; stipulis profunde laciniatis; cymis densifloris; bracteolis calycis segmentis brevioribus et angustioribus; petalis obovato-spathulatis. (Tab. VI.) Wet ravines, Duffield's Ranch, Sierra Nevada; May 10; and hill-sides, Mammoth Grove, California; May 15. A span or more in height. Leaflets of the radical leaves 9–11, about half an inch long, almost uniformly 3-toothed at the apex, the intermediate tooth often smaller, otherwise entire; those of the cauline leaves (5–7) narrower. Petals at first narrowly spatulate, but broader when fully expanded. Somewhat resembling H. parviflora; the flowers being quite as small as in that species.

POTENTILLA PENNSYLVANICA, var. HIPPIANA, *Torr. & Gray, Fl.* 1, *p.* 438. Sandia mountains, New Mexico; October; in fruit. Some of the specimens nearly accord with P. diffusa, *Gray, Pl. Fendl. p.* 41, which Prof. Lehmann, the learned monographer of the genus, has no doubt correctly arranged as a variety of his P. Hippiana, viewed by him as distinct from P. Pennsylvanica.

POTENTILLA ANSERINA, *Linn. Sp.* 1, *p.* 495; *Torr. & Gray, Fl.* 1, *p.* 444. Wet places, San Domingo, New Mexico; October. Near San Francisco, California; April 3.

POTENTILLA RIVALIS, *Nutt. in Torr. & Gray, Fl. l. c.* Wet places near San Francisco, April 8.

POTENTILLA GLANDULOSA, *Lindl. Bot. Reg. t.* 1583; *Torr. & Gray, Fl.* 1, *p.* 446. Mountains near Oakland, California; April 4.

FRAGARIA VESCA, *Linn.; Torr. & Gray, Fl.* 1, *p.* 448. San Antonita, New Mexico, October. Ravines on the Yuba, near Downieville, May 22, and mountains near Oakland, California; April 5.

FRAGARIA CHILENSIS, *Ehrh.; Torr. & Gray, l. c.* Near San Francisco; April 3.

RUBUS NUTKANUS, *Moçino; Lindl. Bot. Reg. t.* 1368; *Torr. & Gray, Fl.* 1, *p.* 450. Corte Madera, California, April 10.

RUBUS VITIFOLIUS, *Cham. & Schlecht. in Linnæa,* 2, *p.* 10? Near San Francisco; April 3. Stems long and apparently prostrate. Leaves (of flowering specimens) about an inch and a half in length and breadth, strongly 3-lobed, a little pubescent on both surfaces when young. Flowers smaller than the species is described to have. Sepals ovate-lanceolate, with a long subulate (not foliaceous) point. Petals white, a little longer than the calyx.

RUBUS LEUCODERMIS, *Dougl.*; *Torr. & Gray, Fl.* 1, *p.* 454? Leroux's spring, foot of San Francisco mountain, New Mexico; December. Prickles numerous, slender, short and somewhat recurved. Leaves mostly pinnately 5-foliolate, very white underneath, much smaller than usual. Peduncles 5–6-flowered. The specimens are imperfect, the plant having been gathered late in the season.

RUBUS URSINUS, *Cham. & Schlecht. in Linnæa,* 2, *p.* 11; *Torr. & Gray, l. c.* R. Menziesii, *Hook. Fl. Bor.-Am.* 1 *p.* 141; *Hook. & Arn. Bot. Beech. p.* 140. Ravines and low grounds near Punta de los Reyes; April 17. A showy species, with large red flowers. The obovate petals are 7 or 8 lines long, much larger than they are said to be by Chamisso and Schlecthendal, who do not mention the color, and whose description of the species applies better to what we take for a state of R. macropetalus than to this plant.

RUBUS MACROPETALUS, *Dougl. in Hook. Fl. Bor.-Amer.* 1, *p.* 178, *t.* 59; *Torr. & Gray, l. c.* Cocomungo, California; March 18. The main stems are often prostrate, throwing up short erect branches. The leaves are mostly trifoliolate, except the uppermost ones, which are sometimes simple and 3-lobed. All the specimens seem to have perfect flowers.

RUBUS TRIVIALIS, *Michx. Fl.* 1, *p.* 296. Low places near Mark West's creek, California; April 30. Petals elliptical-lanceolate, nearly twice the length of the sepals. Leaves all trifoliolate; leaflets rhombic-oblong. Perhaps only a state of R. macropetalus.

ROSA FOLIOLOSA, *Nutt. in Torr. & Gray, Fl.* 1, *p.* 460. Upper Canadian river, and in the Sandia mountains; September—October. In fruit.

ROSA GYMNOCARPA, *Nutt. in Torr. & Gray, Fl.* 1, *p.* 461. Near Bolinas, April 19; wet ravines, Grass valley, May 20, (in flower); also mountains near Oakland; April 5, (with the fruit of the preceding season). A very neat slender species. The leaflets vary from less than half an inch to three-fourths of an inch long. The flowers are scarcely an inch in diameter.

ROSA BLANDA, *Ait. Kew.* (*ed.* 1,) *p.* 202; *Torr. & Gray, Fl.* 1, *p.* 459. R. fraxinifolia, *Bork.; Torr. & Gray, l. c.* R. Californica, *Cham. & Schlecht. in Linnæa,* 2, *p.* 35. R. Woodsii, *Lindl.; Torr. & Gray, l. c.* Knight's ferry, Stanislaus river, May 7; Grass valley, May 19; low places, Mark West's creek, California; April 30 (with fruit of the preceding season.) This is a variable species, including, as we think, all those quoted above.

PYRUS RIVULARIS, *Dougl. in Hook. Fl. Bor.-Amer.* 1. *p.* 203, *t.* 68; *Torr. & Gray, Fl.* 1, *p.* 71; *Nutt. Sylv.* 2. *p.* 22. *t.* 49. Santa Rosa creek, California; May 1.

PHOTINIA ARBUTIFOLIA, *Lindl. in Linn. Trans.* 13. *p.* 103, *& Bot. Reg. t.* 491; *Torr. & Gray, Fl.* 1, *p.* 473; Cajon Pass, March 16, (with unexpanded flowers.) Martinez, April 23, (young fruit;) Mark West's creek, California; and April 30 (mature fruit).

AMELANCHIER CANADENSIS, var. ALNIFOLIA, *Torr. & Gray, Fl.* 1, *p.* 473. Near Punta de los Reys, April 17. Hill sides, Nevada, May 20. Hills near Williams' fork of the Great Colorado. Another form of this species was found on the middle Yuba. It has ovate or obovate leaves, which are often nearly entire, or with only a few serratures at the summit. The racemes are 6–8-flowered, and the peduncles as well as the segments of the calyx are woolly.

CRATÆGUS COCCINEA, *Linn.* Var. VIRIDIS, *Torr. & Gray, l. c.* In the Sandia mountains, New Mexico; October. With ripe fruit.

CRATÆGUS SUBVILLOSA, *Schrad. Hort. Gœtt.* C. coccinea, *var.* mollis, *Torr. & Gray, l. c.* Shawnee villages on the Canadian River; August. In the great size of the fruit, no less than in the foliage, this differs from C. coccinea.

CALYCANTHACEÆ.

CALYCANTHUS OCCIDENTALIS, *Hook. & Arn. Bot. Beechey, p.* 340, *t.* 84; *Torr. & Gray, Fl.* 1, *p.* 476; *Bot. Mag. t.* 4808. Deep ravines, Napa Valley, California; (with old fruit).

LYTHRACEÆ.

AMMANNIA LATIFOLIA, *Linn.; Torr. & Gray, Fl.* 1, *p.* 480. Near Beavertown, on the Canadian River, in low places; August.

ONAGRACEÆ.

EPILOBIUM COLORATUM, *Muhl.* Wet places, near San Domingo, New Mexico; October.

EPILOBIUM PALUSTRE, *Linn.* In a spring, on the Upper Canadian; September.

EPILOBIUM TETRAGONUM, *Linn.; Hook. Fl. Bor.—Am.* 1, *p.* 206. Corte Madera, California; April 20. Near San Francisco Dr. Bigelow also gathered, early in April, specimens of an Epilobium, with purple flowers as large as those of E. montanum or E. parviflorum, but too young for satisfactory determination.

EPILOBIUM MINUTUM, *Lindl. in Hook. l. c.; Torr. & Gray, Fl.* 1, *p.* 490. Hill sides, Napa valley; April 24. Knight's Ferry on the Stanislaus river; May.

ŒNOTHERA JAMESII, *Torr. & Gray, Fl.* 1, *p.* 493. Comanche Plains, etc., New Mexico; September.

ŒNOTHERA CORONOPIFOLIA, *Torr. & Gray, l. c.* Laguna Blanca, New Mexico; September. The corolla is sulphur color in the dried specimens: it was probably white in the living plant.

ŒNOTHERA ALBICAULIS, *Nutt.; Gray, Pl. Wright.* 1, *p.* 69. One of the cinereous varieties, with leaves toothed at the base. Sandy bottoms of the Upper Canadian; September.

ŒNOTHERA SPECIOSA, *Nutt.; Torr. & Gray, l. c.* Near Shawneetown and Beaverstown, on the Canadian river; August.

ŒNOTHERA MISSOURIENSIS, *Sims.* Naked prairies of the Upper Canadian. The smooth and broader-leaved form. Var. INCANA. False Washita and Comanche Plains; September.

ŒNOTHERA SERRULATA, *Nutt. Gen.* 1, *p.* 246. Walnut Creek, etc.; August.

ŒNOTHERA LEPIDA, *Lindl. Bot. Reg. t.* 1849. Plains near Stockton and Knight's Ferry, California; May 7.

ŒNOTHERA VIMINEA, *Dougl. in Bot. Mag. t.* 2873. Hill-sides and plains, Knight's Ferry; May 8. Var.? PARVIFLORA, *Hook. & Arn.* Napa valley, May 5.

ŒNOTHERA TENELLA, var. TENUIFOLIA, *Lindl.; Hook. & Arn. Bot. Beech. p.* 342. Hill-sides, Knight's Ferry, California; May 7.*

ŒNOTHERA DENSIFLORA, *Lindl. Bot. Reg. t.* 1593. Knight's Ferry, Stanislaus river; in dry ravines and on plains; May 8.

ŒNOTHERA CLAVÆFORMIS, *Torr. in Frêm. 2d Rep. p.* 314. Mohave Creek; March 2. Rocky arroyos of the Colorado; Feb. 22. The petals barely equal the stamens, (2 or 3 lines long,) and the style is soon much exserted. The corolla would seem to be whitish; but specimens gathered at the foot of the Sierra Nevada, by Lieut. Beckwith, (Beckwith's Report, p. 115,) are plainly yellow-flowered. The following is a third and very striking species of the same group, (Chylismia of Nuttall,) connecting it with Sphærostigma.

* Œbiloba, *Durand, Pl. Pratten. Calif. in Jour. Acad. Philad.* 1855, (the same as Hartweg's, No. 1,728,) appears to be a well-marked species. The petals vary, however, in the degree in which they are obcordate or two-lobed. In specimens raised by Dr. Short, from seeds collected in California by Dr. Dayton, the petals ("delicate rose-color, changing to violet") are nearly two-cleft.—*Gray, Mss.*

ŒNOTHERA (CHYLISMIA) BREVIPES (sp. nov.): villoso-hirsuta vel glabra; caule simplici (3–9 pollicari) inferne foliato; foliis lyrato-pinnatisectis, segmentis denticulatis, lateralibus parvis irregularibus nunc obsoletis, terminali maximo ovato vel subcordato; petalis calyce staminibusque duplo longioribus, capsula longe lineari tubum calycis et pedicellum multoties excedente. Gravelly hills on and near the Colorado; February 17 and 20. We have seen an imperfect specimen of this plant in a small collection made on the Gila, etc., by A. B. Gray, Esq., surveyor, in the possession of Mr. George Thurber. The stem is pretty stout, much thicker than that of O. scapoidea and the nearly related O. clavæformis; and the flowers are very much larger, the light yellow petals being from half an inch to an inch in length; they are rounded, obovate, and entire. The pedicels are about as long as the bracts, varying from 1 to 5 lines in length, while the ovary is usually an inch long. The latter, like the limb of the calyx, is very villous in some specimens, and sparingly so or entirely glabrous in others. Ripe pods arcuate ascending, about an inch and a half long. Veins of the leaves often purplish beneath, as in O. clavæformis. The raceme is nodding at the undeveloped summit, and scorpioid, as in the related species.—*Gray, Mss.*

ŒNOTHERA OVATA, *Nutt. in Torr. & Gray, Fl.* 1, *p.* 507. San Francisco, and on mountains near Oakland; April 3 and 4.

ŒNOTHERA GRACILIFLORA, *Hook. & Arn. Bot. Beech., p.* 341; *Hook. Ic. t.* 338. San Gabriel, California; March 23.

ŒNOTHERA DENTATA, *Cav.?; Torr. & Gray, Fl.* 1, *p.* 510. Gravelly hills near the Great Colorado; February 17. Knight's ferry, on the Stanislaus; May; a much branched and larger flowered variety.

ŒNOTHERA STRIGULOSA, *Torr. & Gray, l. c.* Cocomungo; March 8, and San Francisco; April 8.

ŒNOTHERA CHEIRANTHIFOLIA, *Hornem.; Torr. & Gray, l. c.* San Francisco; April 8.

ŒNOTHERA VIRIDESCENS, *Hook. Fl. Bor.-Am.* 1, *p.* 214. Seashore at Punta de los Reyes, California; April 17.

GAYOPHYTUM NUTTALLII, *Torr. & Gray, Fl.* 1, *p.* 514. Hillsides on the Yuba, near Downieville; May 22.

EUCHARIDIUM CONCINNUM, *Fischer & Meyer; Lindl. Bot. Reg., t.* 1962. Bolinas bay, California; April 19. Also, a specimen collected by Dr. Andrews; the habitat not recorded. This plant rarely occurs in Californian collections.

CLARKIA ELEGANS, *Lindl. Bot. Reg., t.* 1575. Also, C. unguiculata, *Lindl.?* Hillsides, Knight's ferry; May 7–8.

LUDWIGIA NATANS, *Ell. Sk.* 1, *p.* 581. Beavertown on the Canadian in wet places; August.

STENOSIPHON VIRGATUS, *Spach. Monogr. Onagr., p.* 64. Rocky prairies on the Canadian; August.

GAURA PARVIFLORA, *Dougl. in Hook. Fl. Bor—.Am.* 1, *p.* 208. Sand banks of the Canadian; August.

GAURA BIENNIS, *Linn. β.* PITCHERI, *Torr. & Gray, Fl.* 1, *p.* 517. Near Beaverstown, Indian Territory; August. San Domingo; October.

GAURA VILLOSA, *Torr. in Ann. Lyc. New York,* 2, *p.* 200. Prairies and hills on the Upper Canadian; September.

GAURA COCCINEA, *Nutt. Gen.* 1, *p.* 249. Prairie hills on the Canadian; September.

GAURA HETERANDRA (sp. nov.): glabella, annua; caule ramoso; foliis membranaceis ovato-lanceolatis summis anguste lanceolatis acuminatis petiolatis; spicis paniculatis laxis; floribus tetrameris parvis, inferioribus folioso-bracteatis; tubo calycis infundibuliformi lobis dimidio brevioribus; petalis obovato-spathulatis conformibus; staminibus 8, alternis brevioribus fere anantheris, 4 longioribus antheris cordato-rotundis; stigmate integro; fructu brevissime pedicellato obovato gibboso 3-4-loculari. River banks, Mokelumne Hill, California; May 17. Stem a foot or more in height, erect, paniculately branched above; the branches, etc., slightly puberulent. Cauline leaves two inches in length, and with a slender petiole of half or two-thirds of an inch in length, those of the branches smaller and narrower ; all thin, entire, or obscurely repand, loosely feather-veined. Flowers apparently purple, small, the lobes of the calyx and the petals about two lines long. Stamens apparently not declined ; the four longer ones equaling the petals, and with very short basi-fixed anthers; the alternate ones (opposite the petals) much shorter, and with the anthers abortive. Style long; stigma hemispherical, entire, or nearly so. Fruit globular-obovate, gibbous, obscurely ribbed, a line and a half long, indehiscent. This is the only Gaura yet known from California, and a very peculiar one, but apparently of this genus, notwithstanding the abortive shorter stamens and the short anthers of the others.

HIPPURIS VULGARIS, *Linn. Spec.* 1, *p.* 4. Ponds near Tomales bay, California ; April 19.

GROSSULACEÆ.

RIBES CALIFORNICUM, *Hook. & Arn.*, R. Californicum, occidentale, and subvestitum, *Hook. & Arn. Bot. Beech., p.* 346 ; *Torr. & Gray, Fl.* 1, *p.* 545, 548. Dr. Bigelow's specimens, with others, collated with those of Douglas, plainly show that the three above-mentioned nominal species must be reduced to one, which should stand next to R. Menziesii, (the anthers of which are slightly mucromate,) and for which the name of R. Californicum is to be preferred. The subaxillary spines are sometimes solitary, geminate and ternate on the same branch; the branches are setose or naked on otherwise similar plants ; the foliage is either glabrous, glandular-pubescent beneath, or simply pubescent, and either moderately or deeply lobed and incised ; the flowers in all are reddish or purple; the ovary, etc., more or less strongly glandular and setose, and with or without a soft or hirsute pubescence. R. Californicum was founded on a small-leaved and smaller-flowered state of the species. R. subvestitum on a larger-leaved and large-flowered form. Dr. Bigelow's collection comprises the following: 1. From rocky ravines, Cajon Pass ; March 16 : the R. subvestitum, *Hook. & Arn.*, except that the branchlets are not setose, and the pubescence of the leaves scarcely glandular.—2. Mammoth Grove, on the prostrate trunk of a huge Sequoia gigantea ; May 11 : similar to the preceding, but the leaves more cleft, and the calyx-tube more pubescent.—3. Mountains near San Gabriel; March 28: like No. 1, but more glabrous leaves, glandular-dotted beneath.—4. Duffield's ranch, Sierra Nevada, with young fruit, which is large, hairy, and prickly.—5. Grass valley ; May 20, with young fruit : the same, with glabrous leaves.—6. Duffield's Ranch, on hillsides, and near San Francisco : forms with the foliage and calyx, etc., perfectly glabrous ; the fruit glandular and prickly. This answers to R. occidentale, but the subaxillary spines are often in pairs, threes, or fives. It is the same as Hartweg's No. 1736.—*Gray, Mss.*

RIBES DIVARICATUM, *Dougl. in Hort. Trans.* 7., *p.* 515*; Torr. & Gray, l. c.* ; San Francisco ; April 3. This accords entirely with the Californian plant of Douglas's collection, except that the racemes are 4–5-flowered. Nuttall's R. villosum is merely a pubescent form of it.

RIBES GLUTINOSUM, *Benth. in Hort. Trans. n. ser.* 1, *p.* 476; San Francisco ; April 3. Duffield's Ranch ; May 12. Also, at Mammoth Grove, on the prostrate trunk of a huge Sequoia, at the height of twenty feet from the ground.

RIBES MALVACEUM, *Smith ; DC. Prod.* 3, *p.* 383 ; *Torr. & Gray, l. c.* Cajon Pass ; March 16. San Francisco ; April 28.

RIBES AUREUM, *Pursh, Fl.* 1, *p.* 164, Var. R. tenuiflorum, *Lindl. Bot. Reg., t.* 1,274. Rocky hills on the upper Canadian river. Plains near San Gabriel, California; March 23, in flower.

RIBES LEPTANTHUM, *Gray, Pl. Fendl., p.* 53. Laguna Blanca, New Mexico, in rocky places at the foot of mountains ; September.

RIBES OXYACANTHOIDES, *Linn. ?* Rocky hills near San Domingo, New Mexico; October, without flowers or fruit.

CUCURBITACEÆ.

MELOTHRIA PENDULA, *Linn.* On the Canadian River and Deer creek ; August.

Cyclanthera dissecta, *Arn. in Hook., Jour. Bot.* 3, *p.* 280. Banks of the False Washita; August.

Cucurbita perennis, *Gray, Pl. Lindh.* 2, *p.* 193. Cucumis perennis, *James.* Camanche plains, on the banks of streams; September.

LOASACEÆ.

Eucnide lobata, *Gray, Pl. Lindh.* 2, *p.* 192. Rocky ravines of the Colorado, near the confluence of Williams' River, in western New Mexico. The specimens were winter vestiges, with good fruit of the preceding season.

Mentzelia albicaulis, *Torr. & Gray, Fl.* 1, *p.* 534. Bartonia albicaulis, *Hook. Fl. Bor.-Amer.* 1, *p.* 222. Mohave creek, California; March 2.

Mentzelia Lindleyi, *Torr. & Gray, l. c.* Gravelly hills along the Great Colorado; February 20.

Mentzelia oligosperma, *Nutt. in Bot. Mag. t.* 1760. Rocky hills on the False Washita, etc.; August.

Mentzelia (Bartonia) nuda, *Nutt.; Torr. & Gray, Fl.* 1, *p.* 534. On Elm creek and the False Washita; August. Denuded plains of the Upper Canadian; September.

Mentzelia (Bartonia) multiflora, *Nutt. Pl. Gamb. p.* 180; *Gray, Pl. Wright. p.* 74. Rocky cañons, from the Llano Estacado to Galisteo, New Mexico; October.

CRASSULACEÆ.

Sedum Wrightii, *Gray, Pl. Wright.* 1, *p.* 76. Sandia mountains, New Mexico; October. A dwarf and condensed state.

Sedum spathulifolium, *Hook. Fl. Bor.-Amer.* 1, p. 227; *Torr. & Gray, Fl.* 1, *p.* 559. Hill-sides and rocky places, Napa valley, California; May 5. Stems ascending, simple, or sparingly branched, throwing off from the base prostrate sterile runners or offsets, which bear a rosulate tuft of leaves at the extremity, and strike root.

Echeveria lanceolata, *Nutt. in Torr. & Gray, Fl.* 1, *p* 561. Rocks and hill-sides, Sonoma, and Knight's Ferry, Stanislaus river, California; May 3–9. The leaves vary in form, from lanceolate to obovate. The pedicels are from one-third to more than half the length of the flower.

SAXIFRAGACEÆ.

Saxifraga Virginiensis, *Michx. Fl.* 1, *p.* 269; *Torr. & Gray, Fl.* 1, *p.* 571; *Benth. Pl. Hartw. p.* 311. Mountains near Oakland, California. The leaves are less toothed, and the petals broader than in the eastern plant, but in other respects there is little difference. Dr. Bigelow collected in Napa valley (May 5) an unusual state of this species, with large, thin, nearly entire glabrous leaves, and a very loose sparsely-flowered panicle; characters which may be owing to the plant having grown in a moist shady place.

Saxifraga integrifolia, *Hook. Fl. Bor.-Amer.* 1, *p.* 249, *t.* 86: var. foliis oblongo-lanceolatis, basi angustatis; cymis in paniculam elongatam sub-contractam dispositis; floribus brevi-pedicellatis; calycis segmentis oblongis recurvis; petalis lineari—lanceolatis, obtusis. Swamps near Santa Rosa, California; May 3. Plant 24–30 inches high; leaves 2–3 inches long; corolla apparently white. This variety has a strong resemblance to S. Pennsylvanica. The panicle remains contracted even in fruit.

Heuchera micrantha, *Dougl. in Bot. Reg. t.* 1302; *Torr. & Gray, Fl.* 1, *p.* 579. Rocky ravines, Yuba, near Downieville, May 22; and shady hill-sides, Napa valley, California; May 5. The solitary specimen from the latter locality is leafy to the summit, and more hairy than is usual in this species. This accords with Hartweg's No. 1742, but it can hardly be H. pilosissima of Fischer and Meyer.

LITHOPHRAGMA HETEROPHYLLA, *Hook. & Arn. Bot. Beech. p.* 346; *Torr. & Gray, Fl.* 1, *p.* 585. Hill-sides, near Napa, California; April 26. A smaller form occurs on the mountains near Oakland.

TELLIMA GRANDIFLORA, *Dougl.; Lindl. Bot. Reg. t.* 1178; *Torr. & Gray, Fl.* 1, *p.* 583. Head of Tomales bay, and Redwoods, California; April 12—17. In the dried specimens from Tomales bay the petals are bright crimson. We have not received this plant before, except from Oregon.

PHILADELPHUS CALIFORNICUS, *Benth. Pl. Hartw., p.* 309. Ravines, Mokelumne Hill, May 17, (flowers unexpanded.) Frémont collected fine specimens of this plant on the rocky banks of the American river; June 14, 1846. It grows from 8 to 12 feet high. We fear it is scarcely distinct from P. Lewisii.

PHILADELPHUS LEWISII, *Pursh, Fl.* 1, *p.* 329. Var. PARVIFOLIUS: foliis ovato-oblongis utrinque acutis remote denticulatis margine ciliolatis cæteris glabriusculis; thyrso pedunculato, multifloro. Hill-sides, Duffield's Ranch, Sierra Nevada; May 12. The specimens are without flowers, but bear the fruit of the last season. It is therefore uncertain whether the inflorescence was naked, as the leaves of the preceding year had fallen. The leaves are scarcely an inch long, and the thyrsus is 6–12-flowered.

JAMESIA AMERICANA, *Torr. & Gray, Fl.* 1, *p.* 593; *Gray, Pl. Fendl. p.* 55. Arroyos in the Sandia Mountains, New Mexico; October. In fruit.

FENDLERA RUPICOLA, *Engelm. & Gray, Pl. Wright.* 1, *p.* 77, *t.* 5. Cañons of the Pecos, New Mexico; September.

WHIPPLEA, Nov. Gen.

Flores hermaphroditi. Calyx 5–6- fidus, tubo brevissimo turbinato cum ovarii basi connato, segmentis oblongo-lanceolatis æstivatione valvatis? Petala 5–6, perigyna, rhomboideo-ovata, basi angusta subunguiculata, æstivatione imbricata? marginibus involutis, decidua. Stamina 10 vel 12, cum petalis inserta, iisdem opposita et alterna, ea sepalis anteposita breviora: filamenta subulata: antheræ didymæ, subintrorsæ, longitudinaliter dehiscentes. Ovarium quadriloculare, quadriovulatum: styli discreti, ovario subæquilongo, subulato-lineares, intus plani longitrorsum stigmatosi. Ovulum in quoque loculo solitarium, suspensum, anatropum. Capsula[1] 4–5-cocca, parva, basi calysis tubo accreta, coccis coriaceis; intus dehiscentibus. Semen pendulum. Embryo minutus, in apice albuminis, rectus; radicula supera. Suffrutex—Californicus, sarmentosus; foliis oppositis membranaceis deciduis ovatis trinervatis paucidentatis; stipulis nullis; pedunculis gracilibus terminalibus racemum parvum confertum gerentibus; floribus parvis albis.

WHIPPLEA MODESTA. (Tab. VII.) Red-woods, California; April 12. A slender, nearly simple or moderately branching under-shrub, about a foot long, sparsely clothed with strigose scabrous hairs. Leaves on very short petioles, about an inch long, membranaceous, obtuse, 2–3-toothed on each margin, green on both sides, 3-nerved from the base, softly strigose-pubescent; the hairs of the upper surface arising from a slightly tuberculate base. Peduncles terminal, 1–2 inches long: raceme 6–12-flowered, the flowers mostly opposite; pedicels about 2 lines long, spreading. Calyx whitish, the tube pubescent; segments lanceolate, rather acute, one-nerved, erect. Petals exceeding the sepals, about a line and a half long, slightly imbricated, the margin involute in the bud. Stamens twice as many as the petals, (very rarely 4,) in a double series: filaments subulate, flat, inserted with the petals at the base of the free portion of the calyx: anthers didymous, the cells roundish, opening on the margin from the summit to the base; pollen extremely minute, globose. Ovary ovate-globose, the base adherent to the tube of the calyx; styles (rarely 3) linear, flat, slightly united at the base, the upper half stigmatose on the inside. Ovules large for the size of the ovary, suspended from the inner angle of the cell at the summit,

[1] From Dr. T. L. Andrews, lately of California, we have received, just in time for this publication, the Whipplea with nearly ripe fruit.

furnished with a small caruncle at the micropyle. Fruit subglobose, about a line and a half in diameter. There can be little doubt of the affinities of this interesting plant. Notwithstanding some of its anomalies, it must be referred to the suborder Hydrangeæ of Saxifragaceæ. In Eremosyne of Saxifrageæ proper the cells of the ovary are one-ovuled; also in Aphanopetalum, and in the new genus Spiræanthemum[1] of the suborder Cunoniaceæ. The hairs, especially those of the leaves, exhibit the same muricate-scabrous appearance that occurs in those of Deutzia, Philadelphus, Fendlera, and other genera of Hydrangeæ. It is somewhat difficult to determine the æstivation of the petals of this genus, as the flower is open while the bud is yet very young; but in one or two instances they were slightly overlapping. We dedicate this new genus to the accomplished commander of the expedition.

UMBELLIFERÆ.

Eryngium diffusum, *Torr. in Ann. Lyc. New York*, 2, *p.* 207, *& in Marcy's Report, t.* 6. Prairies on the False Washita; August. The root appears to be annual.

Sanicula bipinnata, *Hook. & Arn. Bot. Beechey, p,* 347; *Torr. & Gray, Fl.* 1, *p.* 603. Hill-sides, Martinez, California, April 23, (with mature fruit.) The heads or umbellets are about 3 lines in diameter, on long slender rays. Pedicels of the sterile flowers shorter than the fruit. Root fusiform.

Sanicula bipinnatifida, *Dougl. in Hook. Fl. Bor.–Amer.* 1, *p.* 258, *t.* 92; *Torr. & Gray, Fl. l. c.* Cocomungo, San Francisco and Benicia; March and April. This is rather a common plant in California and Oregon.

Sanicula tuberosa (sp. nov.): caule gracili e tubero globoso; foliis pinnatisectis, segmentis angustis pinnatifidis inciso serratis vel dentatis; foliolis involucralibus profunde trifidis, laciniis plerumque dentatis; floribus sterilibus longe pedicellatis; calycis tubo tuberculato. Hill-sides, Duffield's Ranch, Sierra Nevada; April—May. Tuber half an inch in diameter, fleshy and farinaceous. Stem (fructiferous) 12–14 inches high, moderately branching. The primary divisions of the leaves are rather ternate than pinnate. The secondary ones are pinnately and deeply cut, with pinnatifid or sometimes finely dissected segments. Umbels compound, or sometimes decompound; the rays seldom more than two, unequal. Heads nearly half an inch in diameter. Sterile flowers 15–20, on pedicels 3–4 lines long. Fertile flowers 1–5, sessile. Calyx-tube in fruit covered with conical obtuse tubercles, which are not at all hooked at the point. Teeth of the calyx lanceolate. Styles elongated, recurved. This remarkable species was first collected by Colonel Frémont in 1844 on the American river, and afterwards on the upper waters of the Sacramento, but without fruit. The specimens of Dr. Bigelow have the fruit not quite mature, but fully formed, and yet without any appearance of prickles; instead of which there are rather soft tubercles. In all the other North American species of Sanicula the calyx-tube, in its youngest state, shows the uncinate prickles distinctly. Our plant most resembles S. bipinnata, but is distinguised by its long-stalked sterile flowers and unarmed fruit.

Sanicula Menziesii, *Hook. & Arn. Bot. Beech., p.* 142 *&* 347; *Hook. Fl. Bor.-Amer.* 1, *p.* 258, *t.* 90; *Torr. & Gray, Fl. l. c.* Hill-sides, San Francisco and Martinez, April; in flower and fruit.

Sanicula laciniata, *Hook. & Arn. l. c.; Torr. & Gray, l. c.* β. nudicaulis, *Hook. & Arn. l. c.; Torr. & Gray, l. c.* Hill-sides, Napa valley, California; April 27, with flower and young fruit. S. nudicaulis can hardly be regarded as more than a variety of S. laciniata; the chief difference being the less finely cut leaves of the latter.

Sanicula arctopoides, *Hook. & Arn. l. c.; Hook. Fl. Bor.–Amer.* 1, *p.* 258. *t.* 91; *Torr. & Gray, l. c.* San Francisco, April 3.

Apium graveolens, *Linn.; DC. Prodr.* 4, *p.* 101; *Hook. & Arn. Bot. Beechey, p.* 142. The

[1] Gray, Botany of the United States Exploring Expedition, 1, p. 666.

label of this plant got misplaced, but we suppose the specimens were collected near the coast. They agree with others found near San Luis Rey, California, by Dr. Parry.

BERULA ANGUSTIFOLIA, *Koch; Gray, Pl. Fendl. p.* 55, *and Pl. Wright.* 2, *p.* 65. In water, near San Domingo, New Mexico; October. In fruit.

CYMOPTERUS MONTANUS, *Nutt. in Torr. & Gray, Fl.* 1, *p.* 624; *Gray, Pl. Fendl., p.* 56. William's river, New Mexico; January 26, (scarcely in full flower.) Called by the Mexicans *Gamote* or *Camote*. The root is about as thick as a man's thumb, and seems to be farinaceous.

PEUCEDANUM LEIOCARPUM, *Nutt. in Torr. & Gray, Fl.* 1, *p.* 626. Seseli leiocarpum, *Hook. Fl. Bor.-Amer.* 1, *p.* 262, *t.* 93. Hill-sides, Napa, California, April 25; in flower. The segments of the leaves are broader than in the Oregon plant; so that we suspect P. latifolium may be only a variety of this species.

PEUCEDANUM NUDICAULE, *Nutt. in Torr. & Gray, Fl. l. c.* Ferula Nuttallii, *DC. Prodr.* 4, *p.* 173. *β?* ellipticum, *Torr. & Gray, in Beckwith's Rep.* Hill-sides, Sonoma, May 3; (with flowers and immature fruit), and Feather river, near Marysville, California; with mature fruit. The fruit is so much longer and narrower in proportion than in the normal form of P. nudicuale that we would have described this plant as a distinct species, were there other marks of difference; which, however, we have not been able to find. Besides, in other species of this genus there is considerable variation in the form and size of the fruit.

PEUCEDANUM TOMENTOSUM, *Benth. Pl. Hartw., p.* 312. Knight's Ferry, Stanislaus river, May 7; with immature fruit; and Corte Madera, California, on hills. We have a strong suspicion that this species, P. dasycarpon, macrocarpon, and fœniculaceum (at least the western plant) are not distinct. We have many intermediate forms that appear to connect them; but are unwilling, at present, to unite them.

PEUCEDANUM DASYCARPUM, *Torr. & Gray, Fl.* 1, *p.* 628. Knight's Ferry, Stanislaus river, May 7; with immature fruit. Peduncles 15 inches long. Ultimate segments of the leaves narrowly linear. Fruit (not mature) elliptical-obovate, very woolly. Segments of the involucels lanceolate. Perhaps not sufficiently distinct from P. fœniculaceum. The number of North American species of this genus will doubtless be reduced when they are carefully studied with more ample materials than we now possess.

PEUCEDANUM CARUIFOLIUM, *Torr. & Gray, Fl. l. c.* Ferula caruifolia, *Hook. & Arn. Bot. Beech. p.* 348. Mark West's creek, Napa valley, and on hill-sides, near Sonoma, California, April—May. The specimens are much larger than the original ones of Douglas and Nuttall, being about a foot and a half high. This is pretty certainly P. marginatum, *Benth. Pl. Hartw. p.* 312, *No.* 1752; and we suspect that it is also P. abrotantifolium, *Nutt. Pl. Gambel.*

PEUCEDANUM UTRICULATUM, *Nutt. in Torr. & Gray, l. c.* Hill-sides, Martinez; mountains near Oakland; Mark West's creek, and Cocomungo, California; March—April.

LEPTOTÆNIA? CALIFORNICA, *Nutt. in Torr. & Gray, Fl.* 1, *p.* 630. Hills, near Tokeloma creek, April 17, (with flowers and young fruit;) Napa valley, April 26, (with nearly ripe fruit.) This plant, which Nuttall referred with doubt to Leptotænia, and thought (as he had not seen the fruit) might perhaps be a species of Polytænia, does not accord entirely with either genus. From the former it differs in having emarginate petals with a long inflexed point, and 6 vittæ on the commissure, with numerous true vittæ on the back, and nearly obsolete ribs; the involucels also are wanting. From the latter it disagrees in the toothless calyx, as well as in wanting the involucels. The fruit is oval or elliptical, about 5 lines long, and the border is rather thin. Many of the flowers are abortive, and in some of the umbels all are so. The primary rays are about 3 inches long.

HERACLEUM LANATUM, *DC. Prodr.* 4. *p.* 192. *Torr. & Gray, Fl.* 1, *p.* 632. H. Douglasii, *DC. l. c.* Corte Madera, California, April 10; in flower. Scarcely more pubescent than the eastern plant.

DAUCUS PUSILLUS, *Michx. Fl.* 1, *p.* 164; *Torr. & Gray, Fl.* 1, *p.* 636. Hill-sides, Napa, April 25. This plant has some reputation among the Mexicans as a remedy for the bite of venemous serpents; but its efficacy is very doubtful.

DAUCUS BRACHIATUS, *Sieb.; DC. Prodr.* 4, *p.* 514; *Gray, Bot. U. S. Expl. Exped.* 1, *p.* 711. Scandix glochidiata, *Labill. Pl. N. Holl.* 1, *p.* 75, *t.* 102. Caucalis microcarpa, *Hook. & Arn. Bot. Beech. p.* 348; *Torr. & Gray, Fl.* 1, *p.* 636. Hill-sides, Knight's ferry, Stanislaus, May 1, (in fruit.) A widely diffused plant, being found in Australia, New Zealand, Peru, Chili, many parts of Mexico, and California. It may have been brought to California by cattle. An original specimen of Labillardiere differs from our plant only in the rather denser prickles of the fruit. It is more nearly related to Caucalis than to Daucus, but does not accord wholly with either genus.

CHÆROPHYLLUM? CALIFORNICUM (sp. nov.): perenne, erectum, elatum, glaberrimum; foliis triternatisectis, lobis linearibus integris vel paucidentatis; involucro polyphyllo; calycis margine 5-dentato; fructibus oblongis utrinque obtusis, costis vix elevatis. Wet ravines, Knight's ferry, Stanislaus, May 8; in flower and fruit. Stem 3–4 feet high, nearly simple. Leaves (including the petioles) a foot in length; the primary divisions biternately or bipinnately divided; the segments either all (except the elongated terminal one) coarsely 2–3-toothed, or nearly entire and linear; uppermost leaves simply 3-parted with entire divisions. Umbels on very long peduncles, the primary one wholly female, 9–12-rayed. Involucre 9–12-leaved, scarcely one-fifth the length of the rays. Lateral umbels wholly male. Umbellets many-flowered, about an inch long. Involucels of numerous entire lanceolate leaves. Petals white, broadly oval, emarginate, with a small inflexed point. Calyx with 5 distinct acute teeth. Stylopodium broadly conical. Styles half the length of the ovary, recurved. Fruit about five lines long, often a little curved, or gibbous, laterally compressed: mericarps obscurely ribbed, with large single vittæ in the intervals and 4 in the commissure. Seed deeply furrowed on the face, but not involute, with an elevated central ridge; carpophore 2-cleft at the summit. We are by no means satisfied with our disposition of this plant. It rather falls into this genus than into any other known to us; yet it differs much in habit and in several characters from Chærophyllum.

OSMORHIZA BRACHYPODA, *Torr. in Durand's Plantæ Pratt.* (*Jour. Acad. Phil. n. ser.* 2, *p.* 79). Hill-sides, Yuba, Downieville, California; May 22. It was also found with mature fruit by Dr. Parry near Monterey, and by Mr. Pratten on Deer creek. The flowering specimens collected by Dr. Bigelow are only a foot high. Easily distinguished from O. brevistylis and O. longistylis by the very short pedicels of the fertile flowers and fruit, the minute stylopodium, and shorter trapezoidal segments of the leaves. In the short styles it is nearest O. brevistylis, but it is quite glabrous, and the fruit is much more hispid on the angles than in that species.

OSMORHIZA NUDA (n. sp.): stylis brevissimis; fructibus obtusis; involucris et involucellis nullis; pedicellis fructu longioribus. Shady woods, Napa valley, April 27. Plant about two feet high. Leaves on long petioles, which, as well as the lower part of the stem, are strigosely pubescent; segments broadly ovate, often deeply 3-lobed, coarsely dentate-serrate. Peduncles enlongated. Umbel about 4-rayed; umbellets 4–6-flowered. Flowers like those of O. brevistylis. Fruit (immature) very hispid, especially towards the base, crowned with a short conical stylopodium. This species is intermediate between Osmorhiza and Glycosma. In its bristly fruit it is like the former, and in the short stylopodium and styles, as well as in the entire absence of the involucres, it resembles the latter. The two genera should, perhaps, be united.

CYNAPIUM APIIFOLIUM, *Nutt. in Torr. & Gray, Fl.* 1, *p.* 640. Tamul Pass, April 11; in flower. This plant had not been found before in California.

SUBGENUS? MICROTÆNIA. Calycis margo obsoletus. Petala ovata, cum lacinula elongata inflexa. Stylopodium minutum, depressum. Styli elongati, recurvi. Fructus ovalis, a latere contractus. Mericarpia jugis obtusissimis; valleculis 3–5-vittatis. Commissura 6–8-vittata, crassa, spongiosa. Herba Californica, glabra. Folia decomposita. Involucrum oligophyllum. Involucella 6–8-phylla.

CYNAPIUM? (MICROTÆNIA) BIGELOVII. Hill sides, near Murphy's, California; May 16. Stem 3 feet or more in height. Lower leaves a foot long, ternately decompound; segments pinnately incised, with linear-lanceolate lobes. Umbels on long naked peduncles. Rays about 12, 2 or 3 inches in length. Involucre of 5–6 linear leaves. Involucels somewhat lateral, the leaflets lanceolate and reflexed, longer than the flowers. Umbellets monœcious, many-flowered; the male flowers mostly central. Petals apparently white. Fruit (immature) about 3 lines long; the ribs very indistinct. Vittæ extremely minute, forming an almost uninterrupted circle around each mericarp. Differs from Cynapium in its much more compressed fruit, nearly obsolete ribs, and in having an involucrum. Very likely the mature fruit would show other differences.

THASPIUM MONTANUM, *Gray, Pl. Fendl. p.* 57, *and Pl. Wright.* 2, *p.* 65. Sandia mountains, New Mexico; October.

CONIOSELINUM CANADENSE, *Torr. & Gray, Fl.* 1, *p.* 69. Near Santa Antonita, in mountain marshes; October. In fruit.

DEWEYA? ACAULIS (sp. nov.): humilis; foliis 5–9-foliolatis e rhizomate repente crasso scapum nudum simplicem subæquantibus; foliolis cuneatis sessilibus acute trifidis quandoque 3–5-fidis lobis patentibus acutis integerrimis; umbella solitaria; fructu subtereti, valleculis univittatis In crevices of rocks near Santa Antonita, New Mexico; October. Of this there are only one or two specimens in the collection, with some mature fruit, but no flowers. The genus is altogether doubtful; but it may, perhaps, be referred to Deweya until it is better known; although the fruit is but slightly campylospermous, so that the plant should, perhaps, be referred to the Seselineæ. The seeds and the root-stock have a pleasant aromatic odor, much as in Ligusticum; from which genus, as well as from Deweya, our plant differs in the single large vittæ which fill the narrow intervals between the thick and corky, almost winged, rather obtuse ribs.

DEWEYA ARGUTA, *Torr. & Gray, Fl.* 1, *p.* 641. Near San Gabriel; March 22; in flower. *β.* foliis triternati-sectis; involucellis elongatis. D.? (n. sp.) *Benth. Pl. Hartw., p.* 312; *Durand, Pl. Pratt. p.* 89. Mountains near Oakland; April 5; in flower only. The Oakland plant must be only a form of D. arguta, with the leaves more divided than usual.

APIASTRUM ANGUSTIFOLIUM, *Nutt. in Torr. & Gray, Fl.* 1, *p.* 644. Hill sides, Napa valley; April 26; plains near San Gabriel; March 23. We doubt whether A. latifolium is a distinct species from this.

ARALIACEÆ.

ARALIA RACEMOSA, *Linn. Spec.* 1, *p.* 273? Bolinas bay, California; April 19; scarcely in flower. The inflorescence is less compound, and the serratures of the leaves are much coarser than in the eastern plant. Very likely this will prove to be a distinct species.

CORNACEÆ.

CORNUS NUTTALLII, *Audubon, Birds of Amer. t.* 367; *Torr. & Gray, Fl.* 1, *p.* 655; *Nutt. Sylv.* 3, *p.* 51, *t.* 97. C. florida, *Hook. Fl. Bor.-Am.* 1, *p.* 277, (ex parte.) Hill sides and ravines, Duffield's Ranch, Sierra Nevada; May 12; in full flower. This beautiful tree attains its highest perfection in lower Oregon, where Mr. Nuttall found it growing seventy feet high. The involucral leaves vary in form. They are sometimes nearly as broad as in C. florida.

CORNUS SESSILIS, *Torr.* (*in Durand, Pl. Pratt. p.* 89): floribus paullo ante folia late ovata subtus pubescentia nascentibus; involucri foliis acutis; petalis acuminatis. (TAB. VIII.) Wet ravines near Grass valley, California; May 20; with young fruit. A small tree, (10–15 feet high,) with smooth, slender, flexile branches. Leaves 2½ inches long and 1½ inch wide, dull, closely approximated towards the extremity of the flowering branches. Umbel 15–20-flowered, appearing rather before the leaves, usually becoming lateral from the development of only one of the buds near the extremity of the flowering branch: pedicels 4–6 lines long, villous. Involucre nearly as long as the pedicels, very deciduous; the leaflets ovate, acute, yellowish, or tinged with purple. Teeth of the calyx minute, crowning the ovary. Petals lanceolate, or ovate-lanceolate, acuminate. Style filiform; stigma slightly dilated. Immature fruit twice as long as broad, somewhat hairy. This species, remarkable as the only one of the section Tanycrania found in America, is closely allied to C. mas of Europe and C. officinalis of Japan, differing only, so far as our imperfect materials show, in the slight characters given above. Dr. Bigelow's specimens have the foliage and the young fruit. A branchlet gathered by Mr. Pratten exhibits the flowers just developing.

CORNUS PUBESCENS, *Nutt. in Torr. & Gray, Fl.* 1, *p.* 652, (sub var. C. sericea,) *& Sylv.* 3, *p.* 54. C. circinata, *Cham. & Schlecht. in Linnæa* 3, *p.* 139. C. sericea, *β?* occidentalis, *Torr. & Gray, l. c.* River banks and ravines. Grass valley and Middle Yuba; May 20. Also, hill-sides, Duffield's Ranch, Sierra Nevada; May 12; with unexpanded flowers. We incline to the opinion that this species is more nearly allied to C. alba (stolonifera) than to C. sericea. It varies in the degree of pubescence and in the breadth of the leaves.

CAPRIFOLIACEÆ.

LONICERA INVOLUCRATA, *Banks; DC. Prodr.* 4, *p.* 336. Near San Francisco, California.

LONICERA CALIFORNICA, *Torr. & Gray, Fl.* 2, *p.* 7. Knight's ferry on the Stanislaus. A small-leaved form: L. hispidula is a more or less hairy state, apparently of the same species.

SYMPHORICARPUS ROTUNDIFOLIUS, *Gray, Pl. Wright.* 2, *p.* 66. In the Sandia mountains near Santa Antonita, New Mexico; October. In fruit.

SAMBUCUS MEXICANA, *Pres. in DC. Prodr.* 4, *p.* 323; *Gray, Pl. Wright.* 2, *p.* 66. S. glauca, *Benth. Pl. Hartw. p.* 313, (non *Nutt.*) S. velutina, *Durand & Hilg. Pl. Heerm. in Journ. Acad. Sc. Phil.* (*n. ser.*) 3, *p.* 39, (a more pubescent form.) Knight's ferry, Stanislaus river, May 7, (in flower;) also on Mark West's creek, California. Our specimens agree very well with the plant collected in New Mexico by Mr. Wright.

SAMBUCUS PUBENS, *Michx. Fl.* 1, *p.* 181; *Torr. & Gray, l. c., p.* 13. Hills near Oakland, California.

RUBIACEÆ.

OLDENLANDIA (HOUSTONIA) RUBRA, *Gray, Pl. Wright.* 2, *p.* 68. Hills and plains near Galisteo, New Mexico; October.

GALIUM APARINE, *Linn. Sp.* 1, *p.* 108. San Francisco and Napa valley; May. A small-fruited form, apparently of this species, occurring in various collections from California, New Mexico, and western Texas.

VALERIANACEÆ.

PLECTRITIS CONGESTA, *Lindl.; DC. Prodr.* 4, *p.* 631. Mountains near Oakland; April—May.

PLECTRITIS MACROCERA, *Torr. & Gray, Fl.* 2, *p.* 50. P. brachystemon, *Fisch. & Mey.* Napa valley; April.

COMPOSITÆ. (By A. GRAY.)

ELEPHANTOPUS CAROLINIANUS, *Willd.* On the Canadian River; August.

VERNONIA JAMESII, *Torr. & Gray, Fl.* 2, *p.* 58. On the Canadian; and Llano Estacado; August—September.

PECTIS (PECTIDOPSIS) ANGUSTIFOLIA, *Torr. in Ann. Lyc. New York* 2, *p.* 214; *Gray, Pl. Fendl. p.* 61. Head waters of the Canadian. September.

Hofmeisteria pluriseta (sp. nov.): fruticulosa, puberula; foliis oppositis et alternis parvis plerumque hastato-trifidis inciso-dentatis; involucri squamis floribusque 20–25; pappi paleis 10–12 lineari-lanceolatis (aut muticis aut partim acuminato-aristatis,) cum setis totidem tenuibus denticulatis. (Tab. IX.) In a cañon at Bill Williams' fork, now called Williams' river; February This is evidently a congener of Helogyne fasciculata, *Benth.*, of southern California, and apparently of Phania? urenifolia, *Hook. & Arn.* also, although the number of scales and awns of the pappus (2–3 in the former and 4–5 in the latter) is thrice or twice greater. On account of the earlier Helogyne of Nuttall, (founded on an obscure Eupatoriaceous plant from Peru, but apparently with good characters,) the late Dr. Walpers has changed the name of Bentham's genus to Hofmeisteria, in honor of one of the best phytotomists of the age. This genus, strengthened by a third species, is well marked in habit as well as character. All have palmately-lobed or divided leaves on very long petioles. In H. pluriseta the petioles are an inch or an inch and a half long, while the blade is only 4 to 6 lines long. The latter is ovate or deltoid in outline, and irregularly cut into 3–6 coarse teeth or lobes, the two basal ones usually largest and divergent. Involucre as in Brickellia; the scales acuminate. Corolla ochroleucous; the slightly dilated summit 5-toothed. Style, &c., as in H. fasciculata. Achenia oblong, nearly terete, 5-ribbed, minutely hirsute. Paleæ of the pappus 10 or 12, hyaline, with somewhat erose margins, entire at the summit, which is either obtuse, retuse, or several of them more commonly produced into an acuminate point, or into a short awn, the latter above half the length of the achenium. Bristles of the pappus as many as the paleæ, and alternate with them, forming an inner series as long as the corolla, nearly capillary, minutely denticulate.

Liatris punctata, *Hook. Fl. Bor.-Am.* 1, *p.* 306, *t.* 55. Rocky prairies, from the Canadian river, August 26, to the Llano Estacado; August–September.

Liatris squarrosa, *Willd.* Prairies; August 26.

Liatris elegans, *Willd.; Torr. & Gray, Fl.* 2, *p.* 48. Shawnee villages, Canadian; August.

Carphochæte Bigelovii, *Gray, Pl. Wright.* 1, *p.* 89; *&* 2, *p.* 71. On the mountains near the Mimbres; April; *Dr. Henry.*

Kuhnia eupatorioides, *Linn.*, Var. corymbosa, *Torr. & Gray, Fl.* 2, *p.* 78. Deer creek, of the Canadian; August.

Kuhnia eupatorioides, Var. gracillima, *Gray, Pl. Lindh.* 2, *p.* 218. Anton Chico; September; and on the San Domingo, New Mexico; October.

Brickellia brachyphylla, *Gray, Pl. Wright.* 2, *p.* 84. Clavigera brachyphylla, *Gray, Pl. Fendl. p.* 63. On bluffs and rocky plains of the Llano Estacado; September. Root thick and long. Pappus nearly plumose.

Brickellia Wrightii, *Gray, Pl. Wright.* 2, *p.* 72. Arroyos and washed places, near the Llano Estacado; September.

Brickellia Californica, var. *Gray, Pl. Fendl. p.* 64. Rocky hills and plains on the San Domingo, New Mexico, &c. This is the same as Fendler's plant; but its bushy habit, cordate leaves, and smaller heads indicate it as probably distinct from B. Californica; and it is very likely to pass into B. Wrightii.

Brickellia grandiflora, *Nutt.; Gray, Pl. Fendl. p.* 63. La Cuesta, New Mexico; September.

Eupatorium ageratoides, *Linn. f.* Shawneetown, on the Canadian; August.

Eupatorium ageratifolium, var.? herbaceum, *Gray, Pl. Wright.* 2, *p.* 74. Anton Chico, New Mexico; in rocky arroyos, &c. A small-leaved form.

Eupatorium serotinum, *Michx. Fl.* 2, *p.* 100. Grande Prairie, on the Canadian; August 22.

Eupatorium altissimum, *Linn.* On the Canadian, &c.; August.

Conoclinium cœlestinum, *DC.* Shawnee villages; August.

Nardosmia palmata, *Hook. Fl. Bor.-Am.* 1, *p.* 308. Tussilago palmata, *Ait. Hort. Kew. ed.* 1, 3, *t.* 2. Wet places along mountain streams, Oakland, California; April 5. A plant of wide range, yet of very rare occurrence.

Machæranthera tanacetifolia, *Nees. Ast., p.* 224; *Gray, Pl. Wright.* 1, *p.* 90. On the Canadian, &c.; September.

Machæranthera canescens, *Gray, Pl. Wright.* 1, *p.* 89. Banks of the Pecos, &c., northwestern Texas, (smooth varieties); gravelly hills near the Colorado of the west; February.

Aster Bigelovii (sp. nov.): ramis viscido-hirsutis ad apicem usque foliosis; ramulis corymbosis monocephalis; foliis membranaceis oblongo-lanceolatis semiamplexicaulibus grosse serratis tenuiter triplinerviis hirto-puberulis glabratis; capitulis magnis globosis; involucri pluriserialis squamis attenuato-subulatis basi appressis superne longe caudato-appendiculatis squarroso-recurvis glanduloso-viscidis; acheniis glaberrimis. Arroyos in the Sandia mountains; October. A wholly new and most remarkable Aster, of the Grandiflori group; but the apparently showy heads larger than those of A. grandiflorus, being an inch in diameter, and the numerous (blue and violet) rays an inch long. It is probably a tall plant; but the base of the stem was not collected. Cauline leaves two or three inches long, coarsely dentate-serrate throughout; the uppermost, and those of the short branchlets, smaller and less toothed. Scales of the imbricated involucre half an inch long when extended, very slender; the long and almost filiform appendicular portion recurved, spreading and very glandular. Receptacle flat, alveolate; the alveolæ short and entire. Achenia perfectly glabrous, linear, compressed, three lines long. Pappus not abundant, nearly in a single series.

Aster Novi-Belgii, *Linn.; Gray, Pl. Wright.* 2, *p.* 76. Sandia mountains, New Mexico.

Aster lævis, *Linn.; Torr. & Gray, Fl.* 2, *p.* 116. San Antonio, New Mexico; October; in mountain ravines.

Aster patens, *Ait.; Torr. & Gray, l. c.* On the Canadian, &c.; August–September.

Aster multiflorus, *Ait.* Rocky dell, Eastern New Mexico; September 17.

Aster Nuttallii, *Torr. & Gray, Fl.* 2, *p.* 126; var. Fendleri; foliis rigidioribus hispido-ciliatis; involucri squamis granuloso-glandulosis. A. Fendleri, *Gray, Pl. Fendl. p.* 66. Rocky ravines and cañons, Llano Estacado; September. Exactly Fendler's plant; but it appears to differ from A. Nuttallii only in its greater rigidity, and the more manifest hispid bristles on the branches and the margin of the leaves.

Aster (Oxytripolium) pauciflorus, *Nutt.; Gray, Pl. Wright.* 2, *p.* 76. San Domingo, New Mexico; October.

Aster (Oxytripolium) divaricatus, *Nutt.; Torr. & Gray, Fl.* 2, *p.* 162. Sand-banks of the Canadian; August.

Aster (Oxytripolium) angustus, *Torr. & Gray, l. c.; Gray, Pl. Wight.* 2, *p.* 76. In wet springs, Eastern New Mexico.

Diplopappus ericoides, *Torr. & Gray, l. c.* Laguna Colorado, New Mexico, September.

Erigeron (Cænotus) divaricatum, *Michx., Fl.* 2, *p.* 534. Dogtown prairies; September.

Erigeron (Cænotus) subdecurrens. Conyza subdecurrens, *Gray, Pl. Fendl. p.* 78. Plains and prairies, Eastern New Mexico; September 21.

Erigeron macranthum, *Nutt.; Gray, Pl. Fendl. p.* 67. Mountain arroyos, near San Antonio, New Mexico.

Erigeron Bellidiastrum, *Nutt.; Torr. & Gray, Fl.* 2, *p.* 170. Sand-hills on the Upper Canadian; September.

Erigeron Philadelphicum, *Linn.; Torr. & Gray, Fl.* 2, *p.* 171. Near Santa Rosa, Benicia, and Cocomungo, California; March–May.

Erigeron divergens, *Torr. & Gray, Fl.* 2, *p.* 175; *Gray, Pl. Wright.* 2, *p.* 77, (nearly the var. cinereum.) Hills in the Butte mountains near Marysville, California; May 25. The lower leaves are mostly lobed or almost divided, and the stems become lignescent at the base.

Erigeron Douglasii, *Torr. & Gray, l. c.* Hill-sides on the Stanislaus river at Robinson's Ferry, California. Mr. Thurber and others have gathered a very narrow-leaved state of this near San Diego.

Erigeron modestum, *Gray, Pl. Fendl. p.* 68, & *Pl. Lindl.* 2, *p.* 220; excl. syn. DC. Rocky ravines on the Llano Estacado; September.

ERIGERON STENOPHYLLUM (sp. nov.): humile, cæspitosum, pube appressa tenuiter cinereum; caulibus floriferis simplicibus e caudice perenni inferne foliosissimis apice nudo monocephalis; foliis angustissime linearibus integerrimis; capitulo magno; ligulis (semipollicaribus et ultra) circiter 40 albis uniseriatis involucro pubescente multo longioribus; acheniis hirsutissimis; pappo simplici. On hill-sides and steep banks of the Pecos; October. Stems six to ten inches high, growing in dense tufts. Leaves one to three inches long, about a line wide, many of them almost filiform; the lower ones tapering to the base, which is not ciliate nor hirsute; all merely cinereous with a very fine and close strigose pubescence. Scales of the involucre all nearly equal and similar, scarcely biserial, linear-lanceolate, acuminate, three or four lines long, somewhat tomentose-pubescent. Rays linear, broad for the genus, apparently pure white or slightly tinged with purple, certainly not ochroleucous. Achenia flat, two-nerved, densely hirsute with long and white hairs. Pappus similar in the ray and disk, composed of a single series of scabrous capillary bristles of about the length of the disk-corolla, not fragile nor caducous, of equal length, and not accompanied by short setæ or squamellæ. This most resembles E. ochroleucum, *Nutt.*; but the leaves are hoary with a finer pubescence, and are not hirsute towards the base; the heads are longer and more showy, the rays not ochroleucous, the achenia remarkably villous-hirsute, and the exterior pappus wanting.

EREMIASTRUM BELLIOIDES, *Gray, Pl. Nov. Thurb., p.* 320. Gravelly hills near the Colorado, interior of California; February. Precocious specimens, less than an inch high, just beginning to flower. Mature fruit of this plant is a desideratum.

TOWNSENDIA GRANDIFLORA, *Nutt. in Trans. Amer. Phil. Soc.* 7, *p.* 305; *Torr. & Gray, Fl.* 2, *p.* 186. Erigeron? florifer, *Hook. Fl. Bor.-Am.* 2, *p.* 20. Sand-hills and rocky ridges of the Antelope hills on the Canadian; September.

TOWNSENDIA EXIMIA, *Gray, Pl. Fendl. p.* 70. Laguna Blanca, in pine woods, and Santa Antonita, New Mexico, in mountain ravines; October. The root of this striking and well-marked species is perhaps perennial. The branching stems sometimes attain the height of a foot and a half.

APHANOSTEPHUS ARKANSANUS, *Gray, Pl. Wright.* 1, *p.* 93. Valley of the Canadian, at Shawneetown; August.

AMPHIACHYRIS DRACUNCULOIDES, *DC.; Torr. & Gray, Fl.* 2, *p.* 122. Ravines on Walnut creek, of the Canadian; August.

GUTIERREZIA EUTHAMIÆ, *Torr. & Gray, Fl.* 2, *p.* 123. Antelope hills of the Canadian; September.

GUTIERREZIA SPHÆROCEPHALA, *Gray, Fl. Fendl. p.* 73. Prairies and plains near the Pecos, New Mexico, September 21.

SOLIDAGO RIGIDA, *Linn.* At Beavertown, on the Canadian; August.

SOLIDAGO PUMILA, *Torr. & Gray, Fl.* 2, *p.* 210. On the Pecos, New Mexico; October.

SOLIDAGO TENUIFOLIA, *Pursh.*. Sand-hills and Antelope hills on the Canadian; September.

SOLIDAGO RADULA, *Nutt. in Jour. Acad. Philad.* 7, *p.* 102. With the foregoing, and on the Llano Estacado; September.

SOLIDAGO CANADENSIS, *Linn.* Deer creek, of the Canadian; August.

LINOSYRIS WRIGHTII, *Gray, Pl. Wright.* 1, *p.* 95. Between the Canadian and the Pecos, September 15.

LINOSYRIS (CHRYSOTHAMNUS) GRAVEOLENS, *Torr. & Gray, Fl.* 2, *p.* 234. Wet places and banks of creeks between the Canadian and the Pecos rivers.

LINOSYRIS (CHRYSOTHAMNUS) BIGELOVII (sp. nov.): fruticosa, ramosissima, cinerea; ramis flexuosis fastigiato-polycephalis; foliis filiformibus supra canaliculatis; capitulis 5-floris; involucro elongato floribus tertia parte breviore, squamis 5-floris 4–5-seriatis pallidis carinatis arachnoideo-ciliatis subacutis appressis, extimis oblongis, intimis lineari-lanceolatis; acheniis acute 5-angulatis glaberrimis; pappo copioso, setis tenuibus inæqualibus. (Tab. XII.) Hills and arroyos, Cienegella, above Albuquerque, New Mexico. A dense and fastigiate shrub, apparently of two or more feet in height; the branchlets whitish or yellowish, but with scarcely a perceptible pubescence. Leaves more hoary, about an inch long, involute-filiform, slender. Heads fasciculate, 9 or 10 lines long, about a line and a half in diameter, therefore more slender than those of L. pulchella; the scales of the involucre almost as strikingly five-ranked as in that species, but thinner, not so sharply carinate, not green on the back, and not so much pointed, the somewhat scarious margins, especially of the outer ones ciliate with arachnoid and apparently viscid hairs. Corolla, style, and the slender achenia nearly as in L. pulchella; but the bristles of the pappus rather less copious, evidently finer and softer, and unequal in length, therefore intermediate between that of the latter species and of L. graveolens. This species is a peculiarly interesting discovery, on account of the transition it establishes between L. pulchella, a strikingly aberrant form, and the rest of the group to which I had referred to that plant.

LINOSYRIS (CHRYSOTHAMNUS) PULCHELLA, *Gray, Pl. Wright.* 1, *p.* 96, *&* 2, *p.* 80; *Torr. in Sitgreaves' Rep. t.* 4. Gravelly hills on the upper Canadian, September. The margins of the leaves are denticulate-ciliolate, which was not observed in Mr. Wright's specimens. Dr. Schultz (Bipont,) informs me, in a letter, that he has indicated this as a new genus, "Tetragonospermum pulchellum, *C. H. Schultz, Mss.*" I think that the preceding species forbids its separation from Nuttall's Chrysothamnus, whatever view we take of that group.

APLOPAPPUS (BLEPHARODON) SPINULOSUS, *DC.* and var. GLABER, *Gray, Pl. Fendl. p.* 75. On the Canadian, and Deer creek; August, September.

APLOPAPPUS (BLEPHARODON) RUBIGINOSUS, *Torr. & Gray, Fl.* 2, *p.* 240. Sandy bottoms of the Canadian; September.

APLOPAPPUS (PRIONOPSIS) CILIATUS, *DC. Prodr.* 5, *p.* 346; *Gray, Pl. Wright.* 1, *p.* 98. Prairies on the Canadian; September.

APLOPAPPUS (ISOPAPPUS) DIVARICATUS. Isopappus divaricatus, *Torr. & Gray, Fl.* 2, *p.* 239. Sand-banks of the Canadian, near the Shawnee villages; August. A state with rather larger heads, approaching Isopappus Hookerianus, which most probably is not distinct.

APLOPAPPUS (ERICAMERIA) LARICIFOLIUS, *Gray, Pl. Wright.* 2, *p.* 80. White Cliff creek, New Mexico; on hills and rocks. Cañon creek, Western New Mexico. The flowers have all fallen; but there is little doubt about the species, which Dr. Bigelow formerly gathered in the Organ Mountains, near El Paso.

AMMODIA OREGANA, *Nutt. in Trans. Amer. Phil. Soc.* 7, *p.* 321; *Torr. & Gray, Fl.* 2, *p.* 235, California, on the Stanislaus; May 8. This was also gathered in northern California by the United States South Sea Exploring Expedition, and by Mr. Allen on the Yuba river.

STENOTUS LINEARIFOLIUS, *Torr. & Gray, Fl.* 2, *p.* 238. Cañon Pass, New Mexico; March 16, 1854; California.

CHRYSOPSIS HISPIDA, *Hook.; Nutt. in Trans. Amer. Phil. Soc. n. ser.* 7, *p.* 316. Sandstone rocks and hills, on the Canadian; August—September.

CHRYSOPSIS FOLIOSA, *Nutt. l. c.* Hilly prairies on the Canadian; September. Intermediate between C. villosa and C. canescens.

HETEROTHECA GRANDIFLORA, *Nutt. in Trans. Amer. Phil. Soc. n. ser.* 7, *p.* 315. Cocomungo, California.

GRINDELIA HIRSUTULA, *Hook. & Arn. Bot. Beech. p.* 147 & 351. Hill-sides, at Knight's ferry, on the Stanislaus, California; May 7. A narrow-leaved state.

PENTACHÆTA AUREA, *Nutt. l. c.; Torr. & Gray, Fl.* 2, *p.* 249. Corte Madera, California; April. Very like Nuttall's original specimens, except that the leaves are broader.

APHANTOCHÆT, A Nov. Gen.

Capitulum heterogamum, 8–10-florum; floribus radii 3–5 fœmineis, tubulo corollæ stylo breviore truncato eligulato; disci 4–5 hermaphroditis, corolla tubuloso-infundibuliformi apice 5-dentata. Involucrum circiter 10-phyllum, biseriale; squamis æqualibus oblongis membranaceis margine lato hyalinis dorso subcarinatis obtusis mucronatis. Receptaculum parvum, alveolato-dentatum. Antheræ ecaudatæ. Styli rami fl. fœm. lineari-filiformes prorsus stigmatosi; fl. herm. plani appendice longa subulato-filiformi hispida superati. Achenia conformia, vel disci substerilia, hirsuta, oblonga, compresso-pentagona, 5-nervia. Pappus e setulis 5 brevissimis ad nervos respondentibus, vix manifestus. Herba annua, tenerrima; caulibus filiformibus 2–4-pollicaribus erectis parce arachnoideo-villosis ramisque paucis superne nudis monocephalis; foliis alternis filiformibus integerrimis; floribus ut videtur luteis mox purpurascentibus.

APHANTOCHÆTA EXILIS. (Tab. XI.) Hill-sides in the Napa Valley, California; April 25. A delicate, almost capillary little plant, becoming glabrous; the stems or branches naked above for an inch or so, and terminated by a head of 3 lines in length, below rather leafy, the leaves half an inch or more in length. Scales of the involucre greenish, except the margins, shining, nearly equaling the flowers. Corolla of the ray reduced to a tube, sheathing the style and about half its length, the apex somewhat obliquely truncate, with no vestige of a ligule. Disk-corollas with rather slender tubes; the throat dilated, the border equally 5-toothed. Appendages of the style twice the length of the stigmatic portion. Mature achenia not seen. The five rudimentary setulæ of the pappus do not exceed the hairs of the achenium in length. This curious little Composita exhibits that modification of the Asteroid style which is seen in Pentachæta, Bradburia, Xanthisma, &c. From the technical characters, the genus would fall into De Candolles div. Solenogyneæ. But the genus to which I imagine it is most related has true rays, namely, the California genus Pentachæta, *Nutt.;* from which it differs mainly in the fewer-flowered heads, the entire suppression of the ligule, the longer proper tube of the corolla in the disk, and the reduction of the five bristles f the pappus to minute rudiments. The latter character furnishes the generic name.

PERICOME CAUDATA, *Gray, Pl. Wright.* 2, *p.* 81. On rocky hills at San Domingo, New Mexico; October. Also gathered by Dr. Henry on the Mimbres.

PERITYLE NUDA, *Torr. in Bot. Emory's Mex. Bound. ined.*: herbacea, ramosissima; foliis plerisque alternis subcordato-rotundis 5–7-lobis crebre laciniato-dentatis incisisve cum ramulis junioribus subpubescentibus glanduloso-viscosis; involucri sqamis oblongis; ligulis oblongis discum haud superantibus; appendicibus styli fl. hermaph. brevibus obtusis; acheniis oblongo-linearibus marginibus villosissimo-ciliatis; pappo e squamellis hyalinis coroniformi-concretis pilis achenii brevioribus; aristis omnino nullis. (On the Rio Gila, near the Pimo village. Dr. Parry.) Arroyos and cañons at Williams' River, and on hills near the Colorado of the West; February 7. Plant a span to a foot or more high, probably annual. Leaves half an inch or more in diameter, moderately lobed, much laciniated and toothed. Heads three or four lines in diameter. Scales of the involucre very thin, hispid-ciliate towards the summit. Disk deep yellow; the small rays nearly white in the specimen. Receptacle convex, scrobiculate Disk-corollas 4-toothed. Achenia a line and a half long, the margin densely villous-hispid. This species, which has no awns to the pappus, together with P. aglossa, *Gray, Pl. Wright.* 2, *p.* 107, which wants the rays, nearly effects a transition to Pericome, *Gray, l. c., p.* 81. The subjoined species, having (so far as the imperfect and scanty specimens show) no pappus at all, and no strong fringe on the margins of the achenium, carries the variations of this genus to an extreme.

PERITYLE FITCHII (*Torr. ined.*): herbacea, humilis, viscosissimo-pubescens; foliis oppositis et alternis cordato-rotundis inciso-crenatis dentibus crenulatis; involucri squamis oblongis; ligulis oblongis discum superantibus; appendicibus styli fl. hermph. subulatis; acheniis lineari-oblongis 3–4-nervatis ad nervos hirsutulis; pappo plane nullo. California; *Rev. Mr. Fitch.* Stems or branches three inches long, probably from a depauperate plant, clothed (as are the leaves in a lesser degree) with a glandular and very viscous villous pubescence. Leaves half an inch or less in diameter, subcordate, on slender petioles. Heads five to six lines in diameter. Scales of the involucre oblong, or oblong-lanceolate, villous, bearded at the tip. Receptacle convex. Flowers yellow; the rays moderately exserted. Disk-corollas 4-toothed, the teeth sparingly bearded on the back. Branches of the style tipped with slender and acute, but rather short, appendages. Achenia compressed, usually with two approximate nerves at each margin, which are barely hirsute, terminated by a small, disk-shaped, rather prominent areola, which is entirely naked, there being no trace of a pappus.

BACCHARIS DOUGLASII, *DC. Prodr.* 5, *p.* 400; *Torr. & Gray, Fl.* 2, *p.* 259; excl. syn. P. Pingræa, &c. Along streams; Napa Valley, (male,) and Cocomungo, (female); California, March and April. The leaves often denticulate.

BACCHARIS SERGILOIDES, (sp. nov.): suffruticosa, glabra, confertim ramosissima; ramis ramulisque angulatis rigidis articulatis sæpissime aphyllis; foliis dum adsunt parvis spathulatis uninerviis, ramulorum ad bracteas minimas reductis, capitulis parvis in ramulos confertis subsessilibus, masculis magis glomeratis; involucro obovato, squamis multiseriatis appressis glabris oblongis, seu interioribus lanceolatis, fœm. acutis, masc. omnibus obtusis; receptaculo conico subpaleaceo; acheniis glabris; pappo brevi. Dry arroyos, fifty miles west of the Colorado, western New Mexico. A very bushy, broom-like plant, with small heads, apparently abundant on the Gila, where Colonel Emory and others have gathered specimens.

BACCHARIS TEXANA, *Gray, Pl Fendl. p.* 75. Prairies, &c. Comanche plains, Northwestern Texas; September.

BACCHARIS SALICINA, *Torr. & Gray, Fl.* 2, *p.* 258. Sand-banks of the Canadian, near the Shawnee villages; August.

PLUCHEA FŒTIDA, *DC. Prodr.* 5, *p.* 452. On the Canadian; August.

TESSARIA (PHALACROCLINE) BOREALIS, *Gray, Pl. Fendl. p.* 75, *& Pl. Wright* 1, *p.* 102. Williams's river; February.

STYLOCLINE GNAPHALIOIDES, *Nutt. in Trans. Amer. Phil. Soc., l. c.; Torr. & Gray, Fl.* 2, *p.* 267; var. BIGELOVII: foliis spatulato-oblongis vel sublinearibus; paleis receptaculi fructiferis dorso multo magis lanatis. (TAB. XIII.) California; along rivulets near Knight's ferry, on the Stanislaus river; May. Plant a span high, rather stouter, and with larger and broader leaves, and larger heads than in our specimens of Nuttall's plant; which, however, are poor, and perhaps depauperate. The heads are not larger in Dr. Bigelow's plant than those of S. gnaphalioides are described to be; but the paleæ are more woolly on the back, which perhaps is more deeply saccate, especially in the upper ones. In both, however, the saccate portion enclosing the fruit is larger than the hyaline wing in the uppermost fructiferous paleæ. The male flowers are subtended by one or two small and linear glabrous paleæ; their scanty pappus is sometimes barely denticulate, sometimes barbellate-toothed.

EVAX (HESPEREVAX) CAULESCENS. Psilocarphus caulescens, *Benth. Pl. Hartw. No.* 1812, *p.* 319. (TAB. XI.) Napa Valley, California; April 25. This plant is no Psilocarphus, but essentially an Evax. The achenia are obcompressed, and the paleæ barely concave (not complicate): the latter are of a firm, chartaceous texture, and persistent on the villous cylindrical receptacle, or the uppermost (which form an involucrate verticil around the 6–8 sterile flowers) herbaceous, all pointless, or nearly so. Achenia smooth.

PSILOCARPHUS TENELLUS, *Nutt. l. c.* Near San Francisco and Mark West's creek, California; April. Quite distinct from P. globiferus, to which Nuttall's P. brevissimus and P. Oreganus are likely to belong.

MICROPUS CALIFORNICUS, *Fisch. & Meyer; DC. Prodr.* 7, *p.* 283. Napa valley and Corte Madera, California; April.

ECLIPTA ERECTA, *Linn.* River banks, Shawneetown, Arkansas; August.

BLENNOSPERMA CALIFORNICUM, *Torr. & Gray, Fl.* 2, *p.* 272. Rancho of San Geronimo, California; April.

POLYMNIA UVEDALIA, *Linn.* Woods, on the Lower Canadian; August.

MELAMPODIUM CINEREUM, *DC. Prodr.* 5, *p.* 518. Prairies, on the Canadian; September.

BERLANDIERA TEXANA, *DC. Prodr.* 5, *p.* 517. Bottom lands and prairies, on the Canadian and Walnut creek; August.

Berlandiera lyrata, *Benth. Pl. Hartw.; Gray, Pl. Fendl. p.* 78. Plains of the Canadian; September.

Engelmannia pinnatifida, *Torr. & Gray.* Prairies, on the Canadian; September.

Parthenium incanum, *H. B. K. Nov. Gen. & Spec.* 4, *p.* 260, *t* 391. Rocky hills, between the Canadian and the Pecos; September.

Euphrosyne xanthiifolia, *Gray, Pl. Wright.* 2, *p.* 85. Cyclachæna xanthiifolia, *Fresenius.* Bottom of creeks, Comanche plains, Northwestern Texas, September.

Iva ciliata, *Willd.; Torr. & Gray, Fl.* 2, *p.* 287. On Deer creek; August.

Ambrosia aptera, *DC. Prodr.* 5, *p.* 527; *Gray, Pl. Lindh.* 2, *p.* 226. On the Canadian; August.

Ambrosia coronopifolia, *Torr. & Gray, Fl.* 2, *p.* 291. With the preceding.

Franseria ambrosioides, *Cav. Ic.* 2, *t.* 200. Mountain cañons, near Bill Williams' fork; February, (in fruit.)

Franseria dumosa, *Gray, in Frém. Report* 2, *p.* 316? On the Mohave river, March. Branches, destitute of inflorescence.

Franseria tenuifolia, var. tripinnatifida, *Gray, Pl. Lindh.* 2, *p.* 227. Plains, between the Canadian and the Pecos; September.

Franseria Hookeriana, *Nutt.; Torr. & Gray, Fl.* 2, *p.* 294. Low places, Pecos to Galisteo; September—October.

Franseria tomentosa, *Gray, Pl. Fendl. p.* 80. Bottoms of the Canadian; September. The specimens resemble those of Fendler, and bear mature fruit.

Xanthium echinatum, *Murray; Torr. & Gray, Fl.* 2, *p.* 295. On the Canadian river.

Zinnia (Diplothrix) grandiflora, *Nutt.; Gray, Pl. Fendl. p.* 81, *& Pl. Wright.* 1, *p.* 105. Dogtown prairies, Northwestern Texas; September.

Wyethia helenioides, *Nutt.; Gray, Pl. Fendl. p.* 82. Alarçonia helenioides, *DC. Prodr.* 5, p. 537. Hill-sides, Oakland, California; April.

Wyethia augustifolia, *Nutt. in Trans. Amer. Phil. Soc. l. c.; Torr. & Gray, Fl.* 2, *p.* 300. Hills, near Punta de los Reyes, California; April.

Wyethia scabra, *Hook. in Lond. Jour. Bot.* 6, *p.* 247: foliis linearibus seu lineari-lanceolatis acutatis (inferioribus sæpe oppositis) integerrimis sessilibus venoso-trinervibus utrinque cum caule stricto gracili ultrapedali hispidulo-scaberrimis; capitulo solitario nudo; involucro hemisphærico disco breviore, squamis pluriseriatim imbricatis appressis coriaceis oblongis, exterioribus appendice foliosa lineari patente auctis, interioribus pungenti-mucronatis; acheniis glaberrimis compresso-quadrangulatis pappo brevissimo calyculiformi irregulariter dentato coronatis. Sand bluffs, near Inscription Rock, on the Puerco of the West, New Mexico. A remarkable species, of which only fruiting specimens were gathered. The stems are over a foot long, and do not show the base; possibly they are only branches, but they are perfectly simple. These, like the leaves, (which are 4 to 6 inches long, and 3 to 7 lines wide,) are very rough with short and close papillose bristles, much as in Helianthus Maximiliani. The short and sparing veins are confluent into a false nerve within the margin on each side, making the leaf appear three-nerved. Head short-peduncled, an inch in diameter. Rays not seen. Disk-corollas slender, glabrous. Achenia about 4 lines long, the angles very acute. This species completes the parallel between Wyethia and Balsamorhiza, having the involucre imbricated as in Balsamorhiza Hookeri, &c., while several species of the latter genus are now known with the entirely foliaceous involucres of Wyethia helenioides, augustifolia, &c. Without doubt, the plant described above is the same as that of Geyer.

Balsamorhiza macrophylla, *Nutt. l. c.*; var. pube minuta molli canescens; foliis plerisque elongatis (radicalibus subpedalibus) circumscriptione lanceolatis 1–2-pinnatipartitis, segmentis sæpe dentatis incisisve; involucri squamis exterioribus magnis foliaceis elongato-oblongis seu spathulatis quandoque dentatis. Hill-sides, near Sonoma, California; May. All the species cf this group are extremely variable in foliage. I possess only a leaf of Nuttall's B. macrophylla, and that shows no hoary pubescence; but a specimen from Frémont's collection (which is remarkable for the foliaceous scales of the involucre being as long as the rays, even two inches in length) connects Nuttall's plant with our own. The foliage is more like that of B. Hookeri, (to which B. hirsuta must belong,) but the involucre is very different.

BALSAMORHIZA DELTOIDEA, Nutt. l. c.; var. GLABRESCENS. B. glabrescens, *Benth. Pl. Hartw.*, No. 1785, p. 317; but with the leaves for the most part coarsely toothed, and some of them not cordate at the base. Hill-sides, Sonora, California; May. This was also collected by Frémont in his second journey, and is mentioned in the account of some new Compositæ of that collection (in Bost. Jour. Nat. Hist.) as a new Balsamorhiza, if not a form of B. deltoidea. There is scarce a doubt that they are all forms of one species.

HELIANTHELLA CALIFORNICA (sp. nov.): hirsutula; caule ramoso; ramis apice longe nudis monocephalis; foliis omnibus longius petiolatis lanceolatis seu spathulato-lanceolatis e medio triplinerivis nitidulis; involucri squamis lineari-subulatis hirsutis ligulas subæquantibus; acheniis (immaturis) leviter obcordatis glaberrimis ala integerrima apice pappum brevissimum squamellato-setulosum gerentibus; aristis atque squamellis intermediis nullis. Napa valley, California, on hill-sides; April. The western species of this genus were founded on very incomplete materials, and greatly need revision. But this appears to be different from any before known, on account of the perfectly glabrous, awnless, neither ciliate nor lacerate achenia, with the pappus reduced to a tuft of very minute setæ or squamellæ at the summit of each smooth and entire wing; and the scales of the involucre are uniformly attenuate-subulate, not at all foliaceous. The naked peduncles are from 5 to 15 inches long. Leaves slightly scabrous, most of them opposite, 3 to 7 inches long, half an inch or an inch wide, or some of the larger occasionally rhomboid-dilated upwards, and these 2 inches wide; the cauline all on petioles of one or two inches in length.

ENCELIA CALIFORNICA, *Nutt. l. c.; Torr. & Gray, Fl.* 2, *p.* 317. Los Angeles, California; March.

ENCELIA FARINOSA, *Gray, in Emory's Rep. p.* 143. A species of which no character has been published, but which is likely to prove not distinct from the E. nivea, *Benth. Bot. Voy. Sulph. p.* 27. Gravelly hills on the Colorado of the west; February.

HELIOMERIS MULTIFLORA, *Nutt. in Jour. Acad. Philad.* (*n. ser.*) 1, *p.* 171; *Gray, Pl. Fendl. p.* 171, *& Pl. Wright.* 2, *p.* 87. Banks of streams, San Domingo and New Mexico; October.

LEPACHYS COLUMNARIS, *Torr. & Gray, Fl.* 2, *p.* 315. Shawneetown; August. Var. PULCHERRIMA, *Torr. & Gray, l. c.* Upper Canadian to New Mexico; September, October.

LEPACHYS TAGETES. L. columnaris, var. Tagetes, *Gray, Pl. Wright.* 1, *p.* 106. Rudbeckia Tagetes, *James, in Long's Exped.* 2, p. 68. Prairies on the Canadian; September. This appears to hold its characters, and to claim a place as a distinct species.

VIGUIERA LAXA, DC. and V. CORDIFOLIA, *Gray, Pl. Wright.* 1, *p.* 107, & 2, *p.* 88, were collected on the Mimbres, by *Dr. Henry*.

HELIANTHUS LENTICULARIS, *Dougl. in Bot. Reg. t.* 1265. On the Canadian; August.

HELIANTHUS PETIOLARIS, *Nutt. in Jour. Acad. Philad.* 2, *p.* 115. Pecan creek, a tributary of the Canadian; August.

HELIANTHUS CILIARIS, *DC.* Prairies of the upper Canadian; September. A dwarf state of this well-marked species.

HELIANTHUS RIGIDUS, *Desf.; Torr & Gray, Fl.* 2, *p.* 322. Prairies near Walnut creek, of the Canadian; August.

HELIANTHUS LÆTIFLORUS? *Pers.; Torr. & Gray, l. c.* Pecan creek, of the Canadian; August.

HELIANTHUS MAXIMILIANI, *Schrader; Torr. & Gray, l. c.* Prairies and ravines on the Canadian; August.

HELIANTHUS GROSSE-SERRATUS, *Martens; Torr. & Gray, l. c. p.* 326. Bottoms, Deer creek, Arkansas; August.

HELIANTHUS DORONICOIDES, *Lam.; Torr. & Gray, l. c., p.* 327. On the Canadian, in low places; August.

ACTINOMERIS SQUARROSA, *Nutt. Gen.* 2, *p.* 131. Near Shawneetown, on the Canadian river; August.

THELESPERMA GRACILIS, *Gray in Kew Jour. Bot.* 1, *p.* 252, *& Pl. Wright* 1, *p.* 109. Denuded prairies on the False Washita; August.

COSMOS BIPINNATUS, var. PARVIFLORUS, *Gray, Pl. Wright.* 2, *p.* 90. Plains and pine woods in the mountains near Laguna Blanca; September; (in fruit.)

BIDENS CHRYSANTHEMOIDES, *Michx.* San Domingo, New Mexico, in wet places; October.

BIDENS TENUISECTA, *Gray, Pl. Fendl. p.* 86. Banks of the Pecos; October.

BIDENS BIPINNATA, *Linn.* Hurrah creek, in rocky places; September.

LEPTOSYNE DOUGLASII, *DC. Prodr.* 5, *p.* 531. San Gabriel and Cocomungo, California; March.

PUGIOPAPPUS, Nov. Gen.

Capitulum, etc., fere Coreopsides; sed flores radii fœminei fertiles; tubus corollæ disci (fauce infundibulari-campanulata haud longior) apice annulatus. Ovaria plano-obcompressa, ovalia, glabra; radii ala angusta cincta, calva; disci marginata, pappo gerentia e squamellis 2 pugioniformibus triquetris, angulis anguste alatis denticulatis, corolla vix dimidio brevioribus, constante. Herba monocarpica, pumila, glabra, subcaulescens, facie Leptosynis; caulibus scapisve sub-1–2-foliatis monocephalis; foliis alternis pinnatisectis, segmentis cum rhachi anguste linearibus; corollis radii et disci flavis.

PUGIOPAPPUS BIGELOVII. On the Mohave creek, in the desert east of the Colorado; March. The accessions which may be expected are not unlikely to efface the distinctions between several admitted genera, mostly founded on single plants, resembling Coreopsis or Bidens except in having fertile rays. The present plant, which we possess only in an early flowering state, approaches the incompletely-known Narvalina, *Cass.* (a West Indian opposite-leaved shrub) in floral characters, but it could hardly be joined to that genus with our present knowledge. It is to Leptosyne much what Agarista is to some sections of Coreopsis; but it is distinguished by the short tube of the disk-corolla, marked at the summit by a beardless ring, as well as by the pappus; yet, from the analogous case of Coreopsis, one should not be surprised if future discoveries were to connect them.

HETEROSPERMUM TAGETINUM, *Gray, Pl. Fendl. p.* 87. With the preceding.

SANVITALIA ABERTI, *Gray, Pl. Fendl. p.* 87, *& Pl. Wright.* 1, *p.* 111. La Cuesta; September.

XIMENESIA ENCELIOIDES, *Cav.* Plains from the Canadian to New Mexico; September.

VERBESINA VIRGINICA, *Linn.; Torr. & Gray, Fl.* 2, *p.* 359. Prairies on the Canadian; August.

FLAVERIA ANGUSTIFOLIA, *Pers.; DC. Prodr.* 5, *p.* 635. Sandy bottoms of the upper Canadian; September. In all probability not distinct from F. Contrayerba.

DYSODIA CHRYSANTHEMOIDES, *Lagasca; DC. Prodr.* 5, *p.* 640. Plains from the Canadian to the Galisteo, New Mexico; August—October.

HYMENATHERUM (ACIPHYLLÆA) ACEROSUM, *Gray, Pl. Wright.* 1, *p.* 115. Bluffs of the Llano Estacado; September.

HYMENATHERUM TENUIFOLIUM, *Cass.; Gray, Pl. Wright.* 1, *p.* 118. Bill Williams' fork, West New Mexico; February.

LOWELLIA AUREA, *Gray, Pl. Fendl. p.* 91, *& Pl. Wright.* 1, *p.* 118. Dogtown prairies, on the Llano Estacado, &c.; September.

GAILLARDIA PINNATIFIDA, *Torr. in Ann. Lyc. New York* 2, *p.* 214; *Torr. & Gray Fl.* 2, *p.* 366. Prairies of the Llano Estacado; September.

GAILLARDIA PULCHELLA, *Foug.; Torr. & Gray, l. c.* Prairies on the Canadian; September.

PALAFOXIA HOOKERIANA, *Torr. & Gray, Fl.* 2, *p.* 368. Sand-hills on the Canadian, from Shawneetown; August–September.

PALAFOXIA TEXANA, *DC. Prodr.* 5, *p.* 125. Shawneetown; with the foregoing species.

CHÆNACTIS GLABRIUSCULA, DC. var. MEGACEPHALA. Hill-sides and near rivulets, at Knight's ferry, on the Stanislaus, and Ione valley, California; May. Heads from 6 to 9 lines in length. Flowers yellow; the ray-corollas conspicuously ampliate. Pappus mostly of 4 silvery paleæ;

which in the outermost flowers are often oblong, obtuse, and barely half the length of the corolla, but in the others lanceolate, mostly acutish, and almost as long as the corolla. Although the heads are larger than in Douglas' plant, described by De Candolle, and notwithstanding differences in the characters, yet I think that both these specimens and what I called Chænactis filifolia, in *Pl Fendl. p.* 98, belong to C. glabriuscula, *DC.* For, although De Candolle in the generic character assigns 5 or 6 paleæ to the pappus, I find only four in Hooker's, and his own specimens of C. glabriuscula, and these are in many flowers almost as long as the corolla, although in others (probably from the exterior part of the head) they are only half that length, as De Candolle described them. In this and the allied genera, little reliance is to be placed upon the particular size and shape of these paleæ.

HYMENOPAPPUS FLAVESCENS, *Gray, Pl. Fendl., p.* 97, *& Pl. Wright.* 2, *p.* 94. Dogtown prairies on the Pecos; September. Also, the fine-leaved variety, La Cuesta, New Mexico; September 29.

HYMENOPAPPUS TENUIFOLIUS, *Pursh, Fl.* 2, *p.* 742; *Torr. & Gray, Fl.* 2, *p.* 372. Plains and dry arroyos from Hurrah creek to the Galisteo; September–October. The characters of all the species need revision. The length of the tube of the corolla and rise of the pappus varies considerably. This species probably includes H. corymbosus, Var. Nuttallii, *Torr. & Gray, l. c.*

HYMENOPAPPUS LUTEUS, *Nutt.; Torr. & Gray, l. c.; Gray, Pl. Wright.* 2, *p.* 94. Sandy, denuded plains, on the Upper Canadian; September.

RIDDELLIA TAGETINA, *Nutt.; Torr. in Emory's Rep. t.* 5; *Gray, Pl. Fendl. p.* 93. Plains, &c., from the False Washita to the Llano Estacado; August–September.

BAHIA OPPOSITIFOLIA, *DC. Prodr.* 5, *p.* 656; *Gray, Pl. Fendl. p.* 99; *Torr. in Sitgreaves' Rep. t.* 3. Prairies, &c., near Hurrah creek, N. W. Texas; September.

BAHIA (ERIOPHYLLUM) CONFERTIFLORA, *DC. Prodr.* 5, *p.* 657. Hill sides, Sonora, California.

BAHIA (ERIOPHYLLUM) LANATA, *Nutt.; DC. l. c.* California; banks of the Mokelumne river, and near Marysville; May: also, Napa Valley; April: a form with the heads no larger than in B. tenuifolia, DC., but much branched to the top and leafy; the lobes of the leaves rather broad and short, much laciniate and toothed. Knight's ferry, on the Stanislaus; May: the very large form, with the involucre almost half an inch in diameter; the same with Hartweg's No. 1787.

BAHIA (ERIOPHYLLUM) ARACHNOIDEA, *Fisch. & Lallem. Ind. Hort. Petrop.*, 1842; *Gray, Pl. Fendl. p.* 100. B. latifolia, *Benth. Bot. Voy. Sulph. p.* 30. Bolinas Bay, California; April. Pappus reduced to a crown of minute paleæ, shorter than the diameter of the achenium. In a small collection made by Mr. Wm. A. Wallace, in the vicinity of Los Angeles, there is an interesting dwarf Bahia, which, with B. rubella, (an unpublished species found by Dr. Parry in the interior of California,) is intermediate in character between true Bahia and Eriophyllum, and both species are remarkable for having a conical receptacle. The characters are subjoined.

BAHIA WALLACEI (sp. nov.): annua, humilis, e basi diffusa ramosissima, albo-lanosissima; pedunculis solitariis monocephalis; foliis alternis obovatis vel spathulatis integerrimis; involucro hemisphærico 8-phyllo lanuginoso, squamis subpatentibus margine scariosis discum subæquantibus; ligulis 8 rotundis subintegerrimis aureis; styli fl. disci ramis cono acuto superatis; receptaculo conico; acheniis glabellis; pappi paleis 10 brevissimis enerviis obtusissimis. Teyunga, near Los Angeles, California; May; *Mr. Wm. A. Wallace.* Plant 2 or 3 inches high, but doubtless acquiring a greater size later in the season, white, with a dense covering of long and loose floccose wool, the branches terminated by peduncles of about an inch in length. Leaves numerous, 3 to 6 lines long, tapering into a slight petiole. Involucre 2½ lines long and broad; the scales obovate-oblong, acute, membranaceous, with a hyaline margin. Ligules 1½ to 2 lines in length and breadth, either retuse or obsoletely emarginate, three-toothed at the truncate-summit, abruptly contracted at the base into a very short tube. Disk-flowers, 20 or more, like those of true Bahia. Branches of the style much as in Bahia ambrosioides, but with a proportionately larger, triangular, more flattened, acute, and hispid cone or appendage.

Paleæ of the pappus oblong, or the alternate ones oval, about one-sixth of the length of the corolla, scarcely longer than the breadth of the achenium. Receptacle proportionately large, ovoid-conical.

I append the characters of what must be regarded as a new genus, allied to Bahia, Burrielia, and Actinolepis, and remarkable for its multisetose rather than paleaceous pappus.

SYNTRICHOPAPPUS, Nov. Gen.

CAPITULUM multiflorum, heterogamum; floribus radii 5 ligulatis fœmineis; disci tubulosis hermaphroditis. Involucrum obovatum, e squamis 5 erectis membranaceis discum æquantibus. Receptaculum convexum, nudum. Corollæ glabræ; disci infundibuliformes, limbo quinquelobo, lobis lineari-oblongis; ligulæ breves, late ovales, apice trilobæ. Antheræ lineares, in appendicem lanceolatam longe productæ. Styli rami fl. disci appendice triangulata complanata hispidula conspicua superati. Ovaria oblongo-linearia, hirsuta. Pappus (radii et disci conformis) e setis plurimis (35–40) uniserialibus filiformibus hispidulis æqualibus basi inter se pl. m. coalitis constans, corolla disci paullo brevioribus. Herba monocarpica, e basi ramosa, depressa, floccoso-lanata, deinde glabrescens; foliis alternis cuneato-spathulatis apice trilobatis; capitulis breviter pedunculatis; floribus flavis.

SYNTRICHOPAPPUS FREMONTII. (TAB. XV.) Gathered by Colonel Fremont (a single specimen) in his journey across the continent in 1853–4, probably in the spring of 1854, and somewhere between the Rocky Mountains and the Sierra Nevada. A small herb, intermediate in habit between Actinolepis, DC., and Bahia § Trichophyllum. Leaves 6 to 10 lines in length, tapering from the summit into a long, narrowed base. Heads somewhat glomerate on the branches, 3 lines long. Scales of the involucre concave, with narrow scarious margins. Pappus white, composed of 30 to 40 uniform and equal slender bristles, which are all usually connate at the very base into a ring, so as to fall away together; and also for the most part further united in twos, threes, &c.; the combined base somewhat paleaceous.

AMBLYOPAPPUS NEO-MEXICANUS. Schkuhria (Amblyopappus vel Achyropappus ligulus nullis) Neo-Mexicana, *Gray, Pl. Fendl. p.* 96. Hills and rocky places near La Cuesta, &c., between the Pecos and the Rio Grande; September. The same as Fendler's No. 458. Except in the want of rays, this is an Achyropappus; the species of which (along with an unpublished one, gathered by Dr. Bigelow on the Limpio, in 1852, Bahia (Achyropappus) Bigelovii) I am unable to keep generically separate from true Bahia. Its characters accordingly associate it with Amblyopappus, *Hook. & Arn.* (Aromia, *Nutt.*; Infantea, *Remy*,) which may perhaps be kept distinct for the sake of convenience, unless, as is likely, radiate and rayless heads should occur in the same plant.

VILLANOVA CHRYSANTHEMOIDES, *Gray, Pl. Wright* 2, *p.* 96. Rocky places near Hurrah creek; September. In a few heads some traces of a chaffy pappus were detected, showing that this is really only an epappose Bahia.

MONOLOPIA MAJOR, *DC. Prodr.* 6, *p.* 74. A small form, Napa valley, Feather river, &c., California; May.

MONOLOPIA LANCEOLATA, *Nutt. Pl. Gamb. in Jour. Acad., Philad., n. ser.* 1, *p.* 175. Los Angeles, California; March. This comes from the same district as Nuttall's M. lanceolata, and was likewise gathered by Coulter, (No. 323.) The leaves are lanceolate, nearly all toothed, and less woolly than those of M. major; but the lowest are opposite, and the scales of the involucre are united to about the middle.

LASTHENIA (HOLOGYMNE) GLABRATA, *Lindl.*; *DC. Prodr.* 5, *p.* 665. Near Tamul-Pass Mountain, California; April 11.

BURRIELIA (BAERIA) CHRYSOSTOMA, *Torr. & Gray, Fl.* 2, *p.* 379; and var. MACRANTHA. San Francisco; the variety on hills near Punta de los Reyes, California; April. The stems, foliage, &c., of the variety accord with the larger states of Burrielia chrysostoma; but the head is of extraordinary magnitude, the involucral scales being half an inch, and the rays an inch in length.

Burrielia tenerrima, *DC. Prodr.* 5, *p.* 663. Cocomungo, California; March. In the same head some of the flowers present a pappus of a single large palea, (awned from a broad base;) others have a minute rudiment of a palea, the greater number none at all; thus destroying all claims of Baeria to rank as a genus. Perhaps the epappose state of more than one Burrielia may have been referred to B. chrysostoma.

Burrielia (Dichæta) lanosa (sp. nov.): pygmæa, arachnoideo-lanata, foliosa; foliis linearibus plerumque integerrimis; capitulo sessili; involucri squamis oblongis ligulisque ovalibus (albis?) 8; antheris appendice setiformi auctis; pappo ex aristis 4 subulatis scabris corolla paullo brevioribus et squamis totidem oblongis obtusis denticulatis alternantibus. Gravelly hills near the Colorado of the West; February. The specimens are barely an inch high from a slender annual root, leafy to the head, and clothed throughout with a loose white wool. They are evidently early seedling plants, flowering at the first approach of spring, but probably branching and increasing considerably in height as the season advances. They were found growing along with equally pigmy specimens of Eremiastrum bellidioides. Perhaps the wool is deciduous with age. Leaves half an inch long, tapering downwards, one of them is two-lobed at the apex. Involucre campanulate, two and a half or three lines long, resembling that of a Bahia Eriophyllum. Ligules two lines long, broadly oval, truncate and emarginate or three-toothed at the summit. Disk-flowers yellow. Anthers tipped with a setiform appendage almost of their own length. The intermediate paleæ of the pappus almost half the length of the aristiform ones, which are about two-thirds the length of the disk-corolla. Ovaries linear, minutely hairy.

Helenium autumnale, *Linn.* Springs and wet places on the upper Canadian; September. A roughish and rigid-leaved state.

Helenium Mexicanum, *H. B. K. Nov. Gen. & Spec.* 4, *p.* 299; *DC. Prodr.* 5, *p.* 666. Bolinas Bay, California; April. The same as No. 357 of Coulter's California collection. The pappus is from a third to half the length of the disk-corolla, as it is in Humboldt's plant.

Helenium Bigelovii (sp. nov.): subglabrum; caule bipedali simplici apice longe nudo monocephalo vel superne parce ramoso; ramis monocephalis; foliis lineari-lanceolatis integerrimis parallele triplinerviis basi plerumque in caulem decurrentibus; ligulis palmatifidis involucri squamis subulatis et disco hemisphærico paullo longioribus; pappi paleis 5–7 ovato-lanceolatis aristatis corolla 5-dentata tertia parte breviore. Swamps near Santa Rosa Creek, California; May. Plant, when single-stemmed and simple, with much the aspect of a Leptopoda and of Hecubæa; the striate stem moderately leafy below, its naked summit or peduncle 10 or 12 inches long, thickened under the head. One specimen, however, is considerably branched above. Leaves from 3 to 6 inches long, 3 to 5 lines wide, erect, tapering to each end; the lower ones again dilated at the insertion, and mostly decurrent on the stem into a slight or manifest wing; the radical leaves similar, or rather shorter and broader. Rays numerous and crowded, bright yellow. Disk two-thirds of an inch in diameter, between hemispherical and depressed-globose, as is the receptacle, considerably larger than in any form of H. autumnale, but the rays not so long in proportion. This handsome and well-marked species is dedicated to the discoverer.

Actinella Richardsonii, *Nutt. in Trans. Amer. Phil. Soc. l. c.; Gray, Pl. Fendl. p.* 101. Pine and Cedar woods near Galisteo, New Mexico; October.

Actinella leptoclada, (sp. nov.): caulibus e caudice perenni crasso multicipiti gracilibus ramosis foliosis; ramis apice longe nudis monocephalis; foliis lineari-spathulatis, radicalibus in petiolum attenuatis subtrinerviis subtus vel utrinque sericeo-canescentibus, superioribus viridulis; involucri squamis biserialibus oblongis cano-villosis; receptaculo acute conico; pappi paleis 5 obovato-rotundis integerrimis subito longiuscule aristatis. In mountains and rocky places near Santa Antonita, New Mexico; October. Caudices 1 or 2 inches long, cespitose, clothed with the scaly bases of former leaves mixed with villous hairs, as in other species; the slender and loosely-branched flowering stems 8 or 9 inches high, 4–6-leaved. Leaves 1 or 2 inches long, 1½ to 3 lines wide, the radical often spatulate and silky-canescent, at least beneath, nearly as in A.

acaulis, but the cauline or upper ones green and merely silky-pubescent, strongly punctate. Peduncles or naked branches 3 to 4 inches long, almost filiform. Head small, the involucre barely 3 lines in diameter. Rays 5 to 8, glandular-puberulent underneath. Pappus similar in the disk and ray; the thin silvery scales very obtuse, marked with an indistinct mid-nerve, which is abruptly produced into a slender awn rather shorter than they, and a little shorter than the disk-corolla. Achenia silky-villous. The perennial root, thick caudices, and broader leaves, the lower at least appressed-silky and canescent, distinguish this from any form of A. linearifolia; the much smaller heads, the less silvery foliage, the acute receptacle, and the rounder paleæ of the pappus forbid its being viewed as an attenuated form of A. argentea.

ACTINELLA ACAULIS, *Nutt. l. c.; Torr. & Gray, Fl.* 2, *p.* 389. On the crest of the Sandia mountains, New Mexico; October 10. The scape, 2 or 3 inches long, and seldom exceeding the linear silvery radical leaves, occasionally bears one or two similar leaves.

ACTINELLA SCAPOSA, var. A glabra, *Nutt. l. c.; Torr. & Gray, l. c.* Rocky ridges of the Antelope hills, on the Canadian; September. This is the same as the A. scaposa var. mutica, *Gray, Pl. Fendl. p.* 101; and the pappus is sometimes awnless, sometimes short-awned. It is without doubt the A. glabra of Nuttall, (whose specimen probably came from the same district, not from the Missouri,) but only a narrow-leaved and glabrate form of A. scaposa.

ACHYRACHÆNA MOLLIS, *Schauer; DC. Prodr.* 7, *p.* 492. On plains, Benicia and Ione valley, California; April–May.

LAYIA CALLIGLOSSA, *Gray, Pl. Fendl. p.* 103. Calliglossa Douglasii, *Hook. & Arn. Bot. Beech. p.* 356. Fields at Benicia, California; April.

LAYIA (CALICHROA) PLATYGLOSSA, *Gray, l. c.* San Francisco and Los Angeles, California; March–April.

LAYIA (CALLICHROA) PENTACHÆTA, (sp. nov.): villoso-hispida; foliis linearibus, inferioribus parce pinnatifidis, superioribus integerrimis; pappo ex aristis 5 tenui-setiformibus lævibus ter se æqualibus achenio pubescente et fere corolla æquilongis. (Tab. XVI.) Hillsides at Knight's ferry, on the Stanislaus, California; May. This adds another to the already numerous species of this genus, which so closely resemble one another that they can scarcely, if at all, be distinguished, except by the pappus, or sometimes by the chaff of the receptacle. The present species falls naturally into the section Callichroa, and is only to be distinguished from the more slender forms of L. platyglossa, perhaps, by the rather smaller heads and less hairy achenia, but principally and surely by its pappus of only five longer and smooth awns. These are slender and bristle-like, naked, and only obscurely denticulate under a strong lens. Receptacle chaffy only at the very margin. Rays cuneate, yellow throughout.

LAYIA (MADAROGLOSSA) GAILLARDIOIDES, *Hook. & Arn. Bot. Beech. p.* 148 *& p.* 357. Napa Valley and Tamul Pass, California; April. This is undoubtedly Hooker and Arnott's species, on which the genus was originally founded. But there is seldom any chaff on the receptacle within the exterior disk flowers, so that it wholly falls into the section Madaroglossa. Its large rays trifid at the apex distinguish it from L. hieracioides. The fuscous pappus is villous with rather scanty wool only next the base.

LAYIA (MADAROGLOSSA) CARNOSA, *Nutt. in Trans. Amer. Phil. Soc.* 7, *p.* 393, *& in Torr. & Gray, l. c.* Sandy beach, Punta de los Reyes, California; April.

LAYIA (MADAROGLOSSA) HETEROTRICHA, *Hook. & Arn., l. c.; Hook. Ic. Pl. t.* 326. Plains at Knight's Ferry, on the Stanislaus, California; May.

LAGOPHYLLA DICHOTOMA, *Benth. Pl. Hartw. p.* 317. Plains of Feather river, near Marysville, California; May. The rays are bright yellow. The genus is distinguished from Hemizonia by the obcompressed fertile achenia, completely enclosed by the subtending involucral scale, and by the cuneiform, deeply trifid rays. The habit also is peculiar. Yet the genus may perhaps pass into Hemizonia, although it is more distinct from it than Calycadenia is.

HEMIZONIA LUZULŒFOLIA, *DC. Prodr.* 5, *p.* 692. Hillsides near Benicia, California; April.

Hemizonia Fitchii (sp. nov.): annua, pilis longissimis patentibus arachnoideo-villosa; caule rigido erecto superne demum ramoso; foliis caulinis elongatis pinnatifidis vel pinnatipartitis, (imis nunc fere bipinnatipartitis,) summis et ramealibus subulato-linearibus integerrimis seu rariter dentatis rigidis pungenti-cuspidatis, floralibus capitulum sessile arcte involucrantibus et bis superantibus; involucri squamis 7–9 subulatis glandulis nonnullis parvis claviformibus obsitis ligulis oblongis apice bidentatis flavis paullo brevioribus; floribus disci (plusquam 30) omnibus paleis receptaculi oblongis scariosis muticis ad apicem herbaceum longe crinitis fulcratis; pappo (fl. disc. ster.) corollam subæquantibus e paleis 8–12 auguste linearibus rigidis basi in tubum vel in phalanges sæpius pl. m. coalitis superne fimbriato-barbatis; ovariis radii apice valde gibbosis. Plains of the Sacramento, California; May; where it was previously detected by the Rev. Mr. Fitch. A well-marked and peculiar species, which will fall into none of the sections of the genus, as they are limited in the Flora of North America; but in some respects it approaches that section of Calycadenia which is formed of Nuttall's Osmadenia, and of which some additional species are now known. The present plant has a rigid and usually stout stem, from three to twelve inches high, at first simple, and terminated by a single sessile head, (of about an inch in diameter,) at length corymbosely branched, often from within the circle of involucrate leaves, so as to appear proliferous. Cauline leaves of linear outline, two to three inches long; the rigid and springy-pointed rameal ones an inch or less in length, often fascicled. Ligules three lines long, including the tube. Lobes of the disk-corolla short, ovate. Receptacle chaffy throughout; the paleæ distinct, partly wrapped around the disk-flowers. The very immature fertile achenia are obovate-trigonal, with a short inflexed stipe, a large dorsal hump, and a short inflexed apical beak.

Hemizonia congesta, *DC. Prodr.* 5, *p.* 692. California. Besides these specimens, I have seen no indigenous ones except those of Douglas, who seems to have collected it sparingly. I have, however, a specimen taken from a plant raised in the Cambridge Botanic Garden, in 1850, from seeds received the previous year from the London Horticultural Society, under the name of "Madaria corymbosa." Indeed, it is distinguishable from Madaria by the shape of the fertile achenia alone. The foliage and young parts are more cinereous and soft-downy than in Madaria, and many of the leaves are serrulate-toothed.[1]

Madaria elegans, *DC. Prodr.* 5, *p.* 692. Hill-sides, Knight's Ferry, on the Stanislaus River; May.

Madia sativa, *Molina; DC., l. c.* With the preceding, and in Napa Valley.

Madia racemosa, *Nutt. in Trans. Amer. Phil. Soc.; Torr. & Gray, Fl. N. Amer.* 2, *p.* 405. Hill-sides, with the preceding.

Harpæcarpus madarioides, *Nutt., l. c.; Torr. & Gray, Fl. N. Amer.* 2, *p.* 406. Hill-sides, Napa Valley; April: a small form; and Knight's Ferry; May: a larger state.

Calycadenia cephalotes, *DC. Prodr.* 5, *p.* 695; also, C. multiglandulosa, *DC. l. c.*, which is a more elongated and glandular state. Hill-sides and plains, Knight's Ferry, on the Stanislaus; May.

Maruta Cotula, *DC. Prodr.* 6, *p.* 13. Knight's Ferry, on the Stanislaus, California; May. Doubtless introduced.

Achillea Millefolium, *Linn.* Stony mountain streams, New Mexico; October: Benicia, California; April.

Baileya pleniradiata, *Harv. & Gray, in Pl. Fendl. p.* 106. Gravelly hills and arroyos, New Mexico; October–November.

Baileya multiradiata, *Harv. & Gray, l. c.; Torr. in Emory, Rep. p.* 144, *t.* 6. Williams' River; February.

Matricaria discoidea, *DC. Prodr.* 6, *p.* 52. Corte Madera, California; April.

[1] Hemizonia filipes, Hook. & Arn., is doubtless a third Lagophylla, L. filipes. Hartmannia ciliata, *DC.*, is surely Oxyura chrysanthemoides. There is no specimen in the Candollean herbarium; whence I suppose that De Candolle had discovered the fact and united the specimens, but omitted to erase the species under Hartmannia from his manuscript.

Cotula coronopifolia, *Linn.; DC. l. c. p.* 78. Swampy places, Beniçia, California; April. Laguna, near San Francisco, *Mr. H. G. Bloomer*. Dr. Bigelow does not seem to have thought this an introduced plant; but it was probably brought to California from the Old World.

Artemisia dracunculoides, *Pursh., Fl.* 2, *p.* 742; *Torr. & Gray, Fl.* 2, *p.* 416. Rocky hills along the Canadian River; August.

Artemisia caudata, *Michx. Fl.* 2, *p.* 129. Sandy bottoms of the Canadian; September.

Artemisia filifolia, *Torr. in Ann. Lyc. New York* 2, *p.* 211, *& in Marcy's Rep. t.* 12. Rocky hills on the Canadian; August.

Artemisia Bigelovii (sp. nov.): fruticosa, humilis, incana; foliis utrinque albo-sericeis cuneato-linearibus seu augustissime cuneatis apice tridentatis, floralibus parvis integerrimis; capitulis obovatis parvis glomeratis longe spicato-paniculatis; involucro tomentoso sæpissime trifloro; floribus 2 hermaphroditis, unico fœmineo; corolla glabra. Rocks and cañons on the Upper Canadian and Llano Estacado. A much branched, shrubby species, apparently only a foot high, and of the section Abrotanum; very canescent all over, the crowded leaves and branchlets with a fine and close silvery sericeous pubescence, the heads (which are glomerate, into a strict and virgate, interrupted, spicate panicle, of fully the length of the leafy branches) more tomentose. Leaves 3 to 7 lines long, 1 to 2 lines broad at the truncate and 3-toothed or 3-lobed apex, thence tapering to the base, equally silky-canescent on both sides, the broader ones triplinerved above; the floral ones very small, filiform-linear, entire, scarcely as long as the glomerules they subtend. Heads a line and a half long, usually three-flowered, sometimes only two-flowered, but one of them always slender and pistillate only, apparently all of them fertile. Scales of the involucre oblong, obtuse; the exterior with slight scarious margins, the innermost scarious, villous-ciliate. This might be mistaken for a small and narrow-leaved state of A tridentata, *Nutt.;* but the heads are smaller, more hoary, fewer-flowered, and heterogamous, while in that species (rightly referred to the section Seriphidium) the flowers are all hermaphrodite.

Artemisia Ludoviciana, *Nutt.:* an entire-leaved variety. Hills and plains, with the last species.

Artemisia frigida, *Willd.; DC. Prodr.* 6, *p.* 125. La Cuesta, New Mexico; on mountains and plains; September.

Filago parvula, *Torr. & Gray, Fl.* 2, *p.* 432. Hill-sides, Napa Valley, California; April. Plant a span to nearly a foot high, the fascicles of capituli terminating the corymbose branches. Involucral scales and chaff mostly obtuse, the exterior with a narrowed apex.

Antennaria luzuloides, *Torr. & Gray, Fl.* 2, *p.* 430: var. foliis inferioribus oblongo-spathulatis. A. argentea, *Benth. Pl. Hartw. no.* 1810, *p.* 319. Duffield's Ranch, in the Sierra Nevada, California; May. The male plant only. Stem 12 to 18 inches high. Scales of the involucre either white or tinged with rose-color.

Gnaphalium Californicum, *DC. Prodr.* 6, *p.* 224. San Francisco. Punta de los Reyes; April. San Gabriel; March.

Gnaphalium Sprengelii, *Hook. & Arn.* Between the upper Canadian and the Rio Grande, New Mexico. Cocomungo, California; March.

Gnaphalium palustre, *Nutt.; Torr. & Gray, Fl.* 2, *p.* 427. Knight's Ferry, Stanislaus River, California; May; on the sides of rivulets. Albuquerque, New Mexico; October: the variety with smooth achenia.

Gnaphalium purpureum, *Linn.* San Francisco; April.

Gnaphalium microcephalum, *Nutt.; Gray, Pl. Wright.* 1, *p.* 124. Rocky places. Hurrah Creek, New Mexico; September.

Gnaphalium strictum (sp. nov.): annuum, cano-lanatum; caule simplici stricto; foliis angustissime linearibus elongatis; capitulis in axillis arcte glomeratis; glomerulis subsessilibus folioso-bracteatis foliis multo brevioribus longe interrupto-spicatis; involucro campanulato, squamis exterioribus lanceolatis subfuscis, intimis linearibus apice albidis; acheniis lævibus.

Banks of the Rio Grande, near Albuquerque; October. Stems 3 to 9 inches high, virgate. Leaves uniform from the base to the apex of the stem, an inch or an inch and a half long, rather crowded, almost filiform. Heads rather larger than those of G. uliginosum, densely congested into woolly capitate glomerules, one in each axil, and forming a long and virgate, interrupted, leafy spike. Flowers very numerous. Receptacle broad and flat. Involucre about the length of the disk. To this apparently well-marked species belongs a specimen gathered by Frémont, in his first expedition, on the Sweet-water of the Platte. Its strict and virgate stems and inflorescence, and the very narrow leaves, distinguish it at once from G. uliginosum and any allied species.

Senecio filifolius, *Nutt.* var. Jamesii, *Torr. & Gray, Fl.* 2, *p.* 444; and var. Fremontii, *Torr. & Gray, l. c.* Rocky hills of the Upper Canadian; September.

Senecio longilobus, *Benth. Pl. Hartw.* var. Rocky places, Hurrah Creek, New Mexico; September.

Senecio Fendleri, *Gray, Pl. Fendl. p.* 108. Sandia mountains, New Mexico; October. The specimens exactly accord with those of Fendler's collection.

Senecio eremophilus, *Richards.; Gray, Pl. Fendl. p.* 108. Mountain arroyos, near Santa Antonita, New Mexico; October.

Senecio eurycephalus, *Torr. & Gray, Pl. Fendl. p.* 109, var. major; foliis tantum pinnatifidis, radicalibus superne integris inferne dentatis rariter laciniato-lobatis. On plains, near Murphy's, California; May. The heads and flowers accord with those of Frémont's and Hartweg's specimens of S. eurycephalus; but the plant is larger, apparently 3 or 4 feet high; the cauline leaves are 6 to 9 inches long, lanceolate in outline, obtuse, laciniate-pinnatifid, with irregular and unequal oblong lobes; the radical leaves oblong or ovate-oblong, sparingly and irregularly pinnatifid only at the base. All these species may be expected to be polymorphous in foliage.

Senecio exaltatus, *Nutt.; Torr. & Gray, Fl.* 2, *p.* 439. Hill-sides, near Downieville, California; May.

Senecio exaltatus, Nutt., var. unifloscululus. Hill- ides, Grass Valley, California; May. A slender form, and with a solitary ray, or sometimes perhaps rayless.

Senecio aronicoides, *DC. Prodr.* 6, *p.* 426. Hills, near San Francisco and Punta de los Reyes; April. Also, with slightly-toothed leaves and few heads, Duffield's Ranch, in the Sierra Nevada; May.

Senecio Californicus, *DC. l. c.*, var. foliis caulinis laciniato-pinnatifidis. Cocomungo, California, in sandy plains; March. This appears to differ from S. Californicus, *β. DC.*, only in the laciniate-pinnatifid or toothed leaves. The heads are larger than in Nuttall's S. Coronopus.

Senecio Bigelovii (sp. nov.): glabra; caule simplici e radice perenni apice racemoso-3–15-cephalo; foliis ovato-lanceolatis acuminatis argute calloso-dentatis in petiolum longum marginatum contractis, supremis lanceolatis basi augusta semiamplexicaulibus; capitulis magnis nutantibus homogamis; involucro late campanulato 10–12-phyllo basi bracteolis paucis brevibus setaceis calyculato, squamis acutis æqualibus, exterioribus lanceolatis, interioribus latioribus scarioso-marginatis; ligulis nullis; acheniis glaberrimis. In mountain arroyos, near Camp Douglas, New Mexico; October. Plant entirely glabrous. Stem rather stout, erect, 18 inches to 2 feet or more in height, rather leafy to the top; the uppermost leaves reduced to bracts. Lower leaves 3 to 5 inches long, abruptly contracted at the base into a margined or winged petiole of 2 or 3 inches in length; the upper successively narrower and with shorter petioles, or at length sessile. Heads racemose, nodding on the summit of erect and naked or slightly bracteolate peduncles of 1½ to 3 inches in length, very large for a Senecio, from half to three quarters of an inch in length and breadth, many-flowered. Involucre rather fleshy, a little shorter than the flowers, very minutely bracteolate; the scales 5 or 6 lines long, herbaceous, with abrupt hyaline-scarious margins, which on the alternate and interior scales are broad and conspicuous. Corollas yellow, narrowly infundibuilform-tubular, rather deeply 5-toothed at the summit, externally callous-thickened, and reticulated at the tip. Stamens, style, &c., as in Senecio. Achenia linear, perfectly glabrous, strongly ribbed or angled, fully 3 lines long. Pappus soft and fine, white, minutely scabrous. This striking species may perhaps be taken for a Cacalia; but I see nothing to distinguish it from Senecio. There is no North American species with which I can compare it, except S. Frémontii, *Torr. & Gray*, which has much smaller and radiate heads.

HAPLOESTHES GREGGII, *Gray, Pl. Fendl. p.* 109. Gypsum hills, on the Upper Canadian; September.

CIRSIUM UNDULATUM, *Spreng.; DC.; Torr. & Gray, Fl.* 2, *p.* 456. Plains of the Upper Canadian to Anton Chico, in the mountains; September.

CIRSIUM ALTISSIMUM, *Spreng.; Torr. & Gray, l. c.* Woods, near Shawneetown; August. "Stem 10 feet high."

CIRSIUM CALIFORNICUM (sp. nov.): elatum, ramosum; foliis caulinis lanceolatis basi subdecurrentibus infra medium sinuato-pinnatifidis denticulatis spinulosis supra glabris vel glabratis subtus ramisque arachnoideis; capitulis longe pedunculatis hemisphæricis; involucro ebracteato glabrato, squamis subulato-lanceolatis superne subfoliaceis patulis spinula brevi cuspidatis. Hill-sides, near Knight's Ferry, on the Stanislaus, California; May. Only the upper part of an apparently tall plant was collected. The largest leaves (upper cauline) are 5 or 6 inches long, an inch wide, obtusely sinuate-pinnatifid from the middle to the base, the summit entire; the upper surface green, sparingly arachnoid when very young, soon glabrous and smooth, the lower clothed with a thin and whitish arachnoid wool, not more dense than that of C. lanceolatum. Heads solitary, terminating nearly naked branches or peduncles of 5 to 8 inches long, erect, rather smaller than those of C. lanceolatum. Scales of the involucre occupying only about five series, slightly arachnoid, soon glabrous, smooth; the coriaceous base appressed; the upper half of all except the innermost spreading, and more or less green, narrow, tapering into a small prickle of not more than two lines in length. Flower apparently pale purple or pink. Pappus not very copious, 7 lines long.

ONOPORDON ACANTHIUM, *Linn.?* San Francisco; April. The heads undeveloped.

SILYBRUM MARIANUM, *Gærtn.* Stanislaus River, near Knight's Ferry, California; May. A single specimen occurs in the collection; its ticket has no indication of the plant being otherwise than indigenous; but it was doubtless introduced from the south of Europe.

PEREZIA NANA, *Gray, Pl. Fendl. p.* 111, *& Pl. Wright.* 1, *p.* 125. Plains, near Laguna Colorado, New Mexico; September.

CALAIS MACROCHÆTA, *Gray, Pl. Fendl. p.* 112, *adn.** San Francisco, California; April. The

* The recent accessions to this group of plants render the union of Scorzonella, *Nutt.* and Ptilophora, *Gray, Pl. Fendl. l. c.*, with calais inevitable, as will be seen by the following synoptical view:

CALAIS, *DC. Prodr.* 7, *p.* 85, char. auct.

Capitulum multi-(rarius pauci)-florum. Involucrum cylindraceum vel campanulatum, aut simplex basi calyculatum, aut imbricatum pauciseriale. Receptaculum epaleaceum planum. Achenia teretia, 10–14-costata, aut erostria aut sursum rostrato-attenuata. Pappus simplex, e paleis scariosis aristatis 5–10 vel 14–22, aristis scabris barbellatis vel plumosis. Herbæ Americæ Boreali-Occidentalis, scapis ramisve superne longe nudis monocephalis, floribus flavis.

§ 1. CALOCALAIS, *DC.* Achenia gracilia, apice attenuata vel breviter rostrata. Pappus (sæpissime niveus) e paleis 5 apice bifidis ex sinu aristam nudam proferentibus. Involucri squamæ exteriores breviores. Ligulæ breves vix exsertæ. Monocarpicæ, leptorhizæ, subcaulescentes.

1. C. LINEARIFOLIA, *DC. l. c.*, excl. syn. C. Lindleyi, *DC.*

2. C. MACROCHÆTA, *Gray, Pl. Fendl. p.* 112, excl. syn.

3. C. PARRYI (sp. nov.): scaposa, fere glabra; involucri squamis triseriatis ovatis oblongisve subobtusis, exterioribus graduatim brevioribus; pappi paleis oblongis apice bifidis arista e sinu exserente barbellato-scabra dimidio brevioribus. Near San Diego, California, *Dr. Parry.* (Achenia not seen.)

§ 2. EUCALAIS, *DC.* Achenia breviora, linearia vel oblonga basi attenuata, erostria, apice truncata, extima villosa. Pappus (sordidus vel rufidulus) e paleis 5 integris in aristam barbellato-scabram productis. Involucrum basi calyculatum; squamæ propriæ inter se æquales. Ligulæ breviusculæ, exsertæ. Monocarpicæ, leptorhizæ, scaposæ.

4. C. DOUGLASII, *DC. l. c.*

specimens are barely in flower, and therefore too young for ascertaining the form of the achenia. But the pappus and the lanceolate very taper-pointed involucral scales are just as in C. macrochæta, and the whole plant resembles the Oregon specimens, except that the leaves are mostly pinnatifid with longer linear lobes; a character of no specific value in this and other Cichoraceous genera, and not uniform in these specimens. These plants, like so many others of the same and similar regions, spring from seed apparently in the autumn, and flower in the vernal season; so that one is in doubt whether to call them annuals or biennials, between which there is no marked distinction in such climates.

Calais Douglasii, *DC. Prodr.* 7, *p.* 85. Low or wet places, Mark West's creek, California; April. A depauperate state, with slender and only about 10-flowered heads, none of the exterior achenia hirsute. Still the few specimens gathered (mixed with another species) cannot safely be regarded as specifically distinct from C. Douglasii.

Calais Bigelovii (sp. nov.): scaposa, spithamæa; foliis pinnatipartitis, lobis plerumque crebris linearibus acutis, majoribus sæpe laciniatis; involucro calyculato; acheniis oblongo-turbinatis apice truncatis, (nec rostratis nec sursum angustatis,) externis villosissimis; pappi paleis 5 oblongo-ovatis in aristam barbellulatam iisdem longiorem subito productis. (Tab. XVII.) Corte Madera, California; April. This species is most nearly related to C. Douglasii; but the heads are smaller and shorter; the (ovate-lanceolate) scales of the involucre broader; the achenia barely 2 lines long when apparently full grown, and tapering from the broad truncate summit to the base, the exterior densely villous, the others smooth, or nearly so; the fuscous paleæ of the pappus are of nearly the length of the achenium, their strong midnerve produced abruptly from the apex into an arwn, which is about a third longer than the palea itself.

Calais cyclocarpha (sp. nov.): scarpsra, glaberrima; foliis scapis dimidio brevioribus integris et pinnatifidis, lobis integerrimis; involucro calyculato; acheniis oblongis sub apice truncato levissime contractis, extimis villosissimis; pappi paleis 5 orbiculatis integris achenio dimidio arista barbellulata circiter triplo brevioribus. (Tab. XVIII.) Napa Valley, California, on grassy plains and hill-sides; May. Root annual, slender, as in all the species of true Calais. Leaves 5 to 9, the naked scapes 6 to 18, inches long. Involucre 5 to 6 inches long, campanulate, glabrous, of 10 or 11 ovate-lanceolate equal proper scales, and of 6 or 7 very short

5. C. Bigelovii, sp. nov. Vide supra.

6. C. cyclocarpha, sp. nov. Vide supra.

7. C. platycarpha (sp. nov.): pappi paleis latissime ovalibus integerrimis brevissime aristatis. San Luis Rey, California, *Dr. Parry.*

§ 3. Aphanocalais. Achenia clavato-oblonga, erostria, apice obtuso areola parva terminata! omnia glabra. Pappus Scorzonellæ, sed paleis multum paucioribus (1–5) et deciduis, quandoque nullus! Involucrum fere Eucalaidis, 8–12 florum. Ligulæ exsertæ. Herbula scaposa monocarpica, radice exili.

8. C. tenella, sp. nov. Vide supra, p. 112.

§ 4. Scorzonella. (Scorzonella, *Nutt.*) Achenia brevia, truncata, hand apice vix basi angustata. Pappus e paleis 10 brevissimis lato-ovatis integerrimis, arista capillari scabro-denticulata multoties brevioribus, constans. Involucri squamæ gradatim imbricatæ, acuminatæ. Caules subramosi plures, e radice perenni tuberosa fusiformi.

9. C. laciniata. Hymenonema? laciniatum. *Hook. Fl. Bor.-Am.* 1, *p.* 301. Scorzonella laciniata and S. leptosepala? *Nutt. in Trans. Amer. Phil. Soc. n. ser.* 7, *p.* 426; *Torr. & Gray, Fl.* 2, *p.* 470. Hymenonema? glaucum, *Hook. l. c.*, (Scorzonella glauca, *Nutt. l. c.*,) is either an allied species, or only an entire-leaved state of C. laciniata.

§ 5. Anacalais. Achenia linearia, erostria, omnia glabra. Pappus (sordidus) e paleis 6–9 vel sæpissime 10 lanceolatis integerrimis in aristam longam barbellatam desinentibus. Involucri squamæ subgradatim imbricatæ, acuminatæ. Ligulæ exsertæ, elongatæ. Caulis simplex e radice bienni? gracili vel subfusiformi, basim versus foliosus.

10. C. sylvatica. Vide supra, p. 112. Scorzonella sylvatica, *Benth. Pl. Hartw. p.* 320.

§ 6. Ptilophora. (Ptilophora, *Gray*, non *Kutzing.*) Achenia oblongo-linearia, erostrata. Pappus (albus) e paleis 14–22 brevissimis aristam prælongam molliter plumosam gerentibus. Involucri squamæ inæquales, extimæ breviores. Ligulæ exsertæ. Caules ramosi, e radice perenni fusiformi vel tuberosa.

11. C. nutans. Crepis nutans, *Geyer.* Ptilophora nutans, *Gray, Pl. Fendl. p.* 113.

12. C. major. Ptilophora major, *Gray l. c.*

This last group has greater claims than any of the preceding to rank as distinct from Calais, but too close a transition is found in section 5. The name *Ptilophora* is preoccupied in the Algæ. Still it may serve to designate a subgenus in the present instance; otherwise the latter may be called *Ptilocalais.*

and small calyculate ones. Flowers numerous. Achenia only 3 lines long, terete and strongly 10-ribbed in the manner of the genus, narrowed at the base, very slightly contracted underneath the large and truncate summit, the inner ones scabrous on the ribs. Paleæ of the pappus of a firm scarious texture, overlying each other in a convolute manner, or else imbricated, a line and a half long, and of equal breadth, whitish, appressed-puberulent or scabrous externally (at least the exterior ones) as in Eucalais generally, entire, or erose-denticulate near the summit, where the thick midnerve is abruptly produced into a long and rather stout arwn. This is well distinguished by the pappus, &c., from any one yet described, and is most nearly related to an unpublished species (C. platycarpha) found by Dr. Parry at San Luis Rey, of which better materials are wanted, but which appears to be clearly distinguished by the larger paleæ of the pappus, tipped with very short arwns. Both in the achenia and the pappus C. cyclocarpha makes an approach to Scorzonella.

CALAIS (APHANOCALAIS) TENELLA (sp. nov.): annua, scaposa, fere glabra; foliis linearibus integerrimis et laciniato-pinnatifidis scapo filiformi subæquilongis; capitulo 8–12-floro; involucro calyculato, squamis lanceolatis obtusiusculis; acheniis conformibus glabris oblongo-clavatis erostratis, areola terminali parva; pappo aut nullo aut sæpius e paleis 1–5 brevissimis lato-deltoideis in aristam tenuem nudam iisdem multoties longiorem productis decidius. (Tab. XVII.) Napa Valley, California, in plains and grassy places; May. (On the Sacramento river, *Rev. Mr. Fitch.*) Plant about a span high, slender, glabrous. Head nodding before anthesis. Involucre 3 lines long, of 7 to 10 equal scales, and of 5 or 6 minute calyculate scales. Corolla yellow. Achenia nearly 2 lines long, narrowed at the base, not at all contracted towards the summit, strongly 10-ribbed, the ribs upwardly scabrous, the apex obtuse, but not truncate, the terminal areola being much smaller than the diameter of the achenium. Some of the achenia are destitute of pappus, at least in many specimens; others in the same head bear from one to four, or sometimes five, capillary, barely scabrous arwns, which are abruptly dilated at the base into a very short and broad palea, just as in Scorzonella laciniata. So that this connects Scorzonella, and the following connects Ptilophora, with Calais.

CALAIS (ANACALAIS) SYLVATICA. Scorzonella sylvatica, *Benth. Pl. Hartw. No.* 1815, *p.* 320. Sonora, California; on hills; May. The slender but sometimes fusiform-thickened root is that of a biennial. Pappus sordid, of 6 to 9, or more commonly 10 paleæ; the long arwns strongly barbellate, almost plumose. The leaves in these specimens are scarcely, if at all, pinnatifid. On Mark West's creek, April 30, in low wet places, was gathered a specimen of what may (on account of an intermediate form gathered by Dr. Stillman) be received as a variety of this species, with the involucral scales all lanceolate and taper-pointed, and the arwns of the pappus less strongly barbellate.

RAFINESQUIA NEO-MEXICANA, *Gray, Pl. Wright.* 2, *p.* 103. Gravelly hills of the Rio Colorado; February. In the single specimen the rays of the pappus are only 8, or even sometimes fewer.

STEPHANOMERIA MINOR, *Nutt. in Trans. Amer. Phil. Soc. n. ser.* 7, *p.* 427. Plains, between the Canadian and the Rio Grande, New Mexico; September, This and S. runcinata are doubtless the same.

LYGODESMIA JUNCEA, *Don; Hook. Fl. Bor.-Am.* 1, *p.* 295, *t.* 103. Buffalo plains, Upper Canadian; September.

PYRRHOPAPPUS CAROLINIANUS, *DC. Prodr.* 7, *p.* 144. Beavertown, Arkansas; and on the grassy bottoms of the Rio Grande, New Mexico.

MACRORHYNCHUS RETRORSUS, *Benth. Pl. Hartw. No.* 1817, *p.* 320. Hill-sides, Sonora, California; May. Plant stouter than Hartweg's specimens, and the fully developed head larger, but otherwise the same. Stems a foot high. Head from an inch to an inch and a half, or in fruit two inches long, cylindraceous, or at length cylindrical; the scales of the involucre all acute, somewhat tinged with purple; the exterior short, lanceolate or ovate-lanceolate, obscurely foliaceous above. Achenia all alike, oblong, smooth, and glabrous, wingless, acutely ribbed and angled, somewhat muricate-toothed in a ring at the abrupt origin of the very long and capillary beak, which is more than thrice the length of the achenium. The latter is only 2½ lines long, while the beak is three-fourths of an inch long; the pappus fully half an inch long. The lobes of the leaves are all retrorse and callous-tipped, as described by Mr. Bentham.

MACRORHYNCHUS GRANDIFLORUS, *Torr. & Gray, Fl.* 2, *p.* 492, (Stylopappus grandiflorus, *Nutt.*): var. involucri squamis exterioribus aut ovatis appendice acuminatis aut oblongo-lanceolatis. Hill-sides, Napa Valley, near Sonoma; May. Head in fruit an inch and a half long, broader and proportionally shorter than in M. retrorsus, the external calyculate scales more foliaceous and spreading. Achenia smooth and glabrous, oblong, acutely ribbed and angled, barely 2½ lines long, abruptly tapering into a filiform beak of three-fourths of an inch in length; the pappus only 4½ lines long. This may be a larger state of M. laciniatus, (of which I have only a miserable flowering specimen,) but it plainly passes into M. grandiflorus. The achenia differ from those of M. retrorsus, and the lobes or laciniæ of the leaves are either spreading or ascending.

MACRORHYNCHUS HUMILIS, *Benth. Pl. Hartw. No.* 1816, *p.* 320. Hills, near Punta de los Reyes, California; April. The leaves are larger and more glabrate than in my specimen of Hartweg's plant; the scape 6 to 10 inches high. The fusiform achenia are from 1½ to 2 lines long; the external rather longer than the inner ones; the latter more strongly and sharply ribbed, as Mr. Bentham remarks. The beak, though apparently full grown, is not longer than the achenium. If it varies so as to be "more than twice the length of the achenium," as Bentham characterizes the species, then it must pass, I should think, into M. Lessingii, *Hook. & Arn.;* of which we have no fruiting or certain materials; but it is said to have the beak "nearly thrice the length of the achenium."

MACRORHYNCHUS HETEROPHYLLUS, *Nutt. in Trans. Amer. Phil. Soc. l. c.; Torr. & Gray, Fl.* 2, *p.* 493. M. Chilensis, *Hook. in Lond. Jour. Bot.* 6, *p.* 256. Fields, Benicia and San Geronimo Ranch, California; April. This abounds in California and Oregon, where it is the only annual species known. Hooker pronounces this to the M. Chilensis; and it doubtless must be so considered, if that is held to include all the Chilian species. But the short wing-ribbed achenium (1½ to 2 lines long) and long beak (of 3 to 4½ lines) distinguish it from M. lævigatus, and less decidedly from M. pterocarpus, to one or the other of which Lessing's M. Chilensis is referred, though in neither are the achenia "plano-obcompressed." The ribs or wings of M. heterophyllus vary considerably in strength; they are scarcely, if at all, serruelate. When less salient and acute, they remain straight and even; when more developed, especially in the exterior achenia, these wings become strongly undulate at or before maturity, sometimes very strikingly so, giving the body of the achenium a remarkable corrugated appearance. Some different state of the marginal achenia has probably served as the basis of Nuttall's Cryptopleura Californica; but I have seen nothing that accords with his character of it.

TROXIMON PARVIFLORUM, *Nutt. in Trans. Amer. Phil. Soc. l. c., p.* 434. Macrorhynchus cynthioides, *Hook. Pl. Geyer, in Lond. Jour. Bot.* 4, *p.* 256, ex char. Sandia mountains, New Mexico; October. The specimens, with mature fruit, are taller than Nuttall's; the scapes 9 inches high; the scales of the involucre tinged with purple, and the ligules of a remaining flower appear to have been purple. I suspect that T. roseum, *Nutt.*, is only a variety of this with pinnatifid leaves and purplish or rose-colored flowers. I should confidently refer the present specimens to Macrorhynchus purpureus, *Gray, Pl. Fendl.*, were it not for the short and stouter beak, of less than half the length of the body of the achenium; and the pappus is, perhaps, a little stiffer. Whether the difference holds constant or not, it is evident that the present plant effects a real transition between Troximon and Macrorynchus.

MULGEDIUM PULCHELLUM, *Nutt. l. c.* Banks of the Pecos, New Mexico; October.

SONCHUS OLERACEUS, *Linn.* Near San Gabriel, California; March.

LOBELIACEÆ.

Downingia pulchella. Clintonia pulchella, *Lindl. Bot. Reg. t.* 1909; *Hook. & Arn. Bot. Beechey, p.* 362. C. corymbosa, *DC. Prodr.* 7, *p.* 347. Borders of pools, on the Stanislaus River; May 8: and Santa Rosa creek; May 1. As the Clintonia of Rafinesque was published some years earlier than Douglas', we propose to dedicate this beautiful genus of annuals, now so frequent an ornament of our gardens, to the memory of the late A. J. Downing, Esq., whose name, in every part of the world, is associated with horticulture.*

CAMPANULACEÆ.

Heterocodon rariflorum, *Nutt. in Trans. Amer. Phil. Soc. (n. ser.)* 8, *p.* 255. Grassy plains, Napa Valley, California; May 5. Dr. Parry and Rev. Mr. Fitch also found this plant in California. It is a neat and very delicate annual, with flowers only 2 or 3 lines in diameter.

Dismicodon Californicum, *Nutt. l. c.* Plains and mountains near Marysville, California; May 25. Very near D. ovatum, and perhaps not distinct from that species. The uppermost flowers are nearly as large as in D. perfoliatum, and blue.

Githopsis specularioides, *Nutt. l. c.* Hill-sides and plains along the Stanislaus and Sacramento, also at Martinez; April—May. Most of the specimens belong to the vari. hirsuta, of Nuttall l. c.

ERICACEÆ.

Vaccinium ovatum, *Pursh; Dunal, in DC. Prodromus* 7, *p.* 570. Mountains near Oakland; April 4.

Arbutus Menziesii, *Pursh Fl.* 1, *p.* 282; *DC. l. c., p.* 582. Mountains near Oakland, and in other parts of California. A tree 40 feet high.

Arctostaphylos tomentosa, *Dougl.; DC. Prodr.* 7, *p.* 585. Xerobotrys tomentosus, cordifolius, etc., *Nutt. in Trans. Amer. Phil. Soc.* Los Angeles; March 22. A shrub 4 or 5 feet high.

Arctostaphylos glauca, *Lindl. Bot. Reg. sub t.* 1791? Xerobotrys glaucus, *Nutt. l. c.* Hills near Downieville; May 21.

Arctostaphylos pungens, *H. B. K. Nov. Gen. & Sp.* 3, *p.* 278; *Hook. Bot. Mag. t.* 3027. A. Hookeri, *Don.* Andromeda? venulosa, *DC.* Xerobotrys venulosus, etc., *Nutt.* Daphnidostylis pungens Hookeri, *Klotzsch, in Linnæa* 24, *p.* 81. Hills near Downieville, and San Francisco; May 22: in flower. Napa Valley; April 25: with old fruit.*

Azalea occidentalis, *Torr. & Gray, Fl. ined.* A. calendulacea, *Benth. Pl. Hartw. p.* 321. Rhodedendron calendulaceum, *Hook. & Arn. Bot. Beech. p.* 362. Laguna de Santa Rosa, in low and wet ravines; May 1. Differs from A. calendulacea, among other characters, in its *white* flowers.

Pyrola chlorantha, *Nutt. Gen.* 1, *p.* 273; *Hook. Fl. Bor.-Amer.* 2, *p.* 46. Hills near Downieville, Yuba river; May 22.

Chimaphila Menziesii, *Hook. Fl. Bor.-Amer. p.* 49, *t.* 138. C. dasystemon, *Haw. Supp.* Hill-sides near Downieville, (with unexpanded flower buds.)

Pterospora Andromedea, *Nutt. Gen.* 1, *p.* 269; *Torr. Fl. N. York* 1, *p.* 458. Hill-sides, Duffield's Ranch, Sierra Nevada; May 11, (in fruit.) The only specimen collected is more than two feet high.

*Kunth (Enum. 5, p. 156, adnot.) proposed to change the later name of Lindley to Wittia, in honor of the same distinguished statesman and patron of science (De Witt Clinton) to whom the earlier genus was dedicated. But it would be inadmissible to bestow two genera on the same person.

* "The genera recently severed from Arctostaphylos are not well founded. Different fruits of A. Uva-Ursi, both American and European specimens, exhibit the characters of Daphnidostylis, *Klotzsch*, Xerobotrys, *Nutt.*, and even of Comarosathtphylis, *Zucc.* Indeed, one of Klotzsch's new species of Daphnidostylis (D. Fendleri) is only Arctostaphylo Uva Ursi" *Gray, Mss.*

Sarcodes sanguinea, *Torr. in Smithson. Contrib.* 6, *p.* 19, *t.* 10. Hill-sides, Duffield's Ranch, Sierra Nevada; May 12. Fine specimens, in full flower, of this rare plant were collected by Dr. Bigelow. They differ from Fremont's only in the scales being more strongly ciliate.

PLANTAGINACEÆ. (By A. Gray.)

Plantago maritima, *Linn.* Corte Madera, California, within reach of the tide; April. The sepals, especially the posterior ones, are strongly crested, more so perhaps than in the plant of the Atlantic States, which seems to pass by gradations into the northern crestless form, (P. juncoides, *Lam.*, P. pauciflora, *Pursh,* and P. decipiens, *Barnéoud.*)

Plantago Patagonica, *Jacq.* var. gnaphalioides. P. gnaphalioides, *Nutt. Gen.* 1, *p.* 100. Williams' Fork of the Great Colorado; February: a depauperate form. Cocomungo; March: a still more diminutive and glabrate form. A widely diffused species, extending nearly the whole length of the continent on the western side, and with us exhibiting some remarkable varieties; for to this species we must refer not only the Chilian P. Patagonica, (P. mollis, *Hook. & Arn.*,) but P. Hookeriana, *Fisch, & Meyer*, P. gnaphalioides, *Nutt.*, P. spinulosa, *Decaisne*, P. curta, *Engelm.*, P. Wrightiana, *Decaisne*, P. Xorullensis, *H.B.K.?*, P. aristata, *Michx.*, P. squarrosa, *Nutt.*, and P. filiformis, *Decaisne*. This species is *diœcio-dimorphous*, some individuals having small anthers on short filaments, and mostly included in the throat of the corolla, while others bear large anthers on long exserted filaments as in the genus generally. Both sorts perfect fruit, but the former (as is usual in such cases) is the most fruitful.

Plantago Bigelovii (sp. nov.): pusilla, parce minutim hirsuta vel glabrata, annua; foliis carnulosis lineari-filiformibus obtusis integerrimis; spica brevi-oblongo 3–12-flora densa; staminibus 2; capsula oblongo-ovoidea 3-4-sperma bractea ovata acuta calyceque longiore. Benicia, California; April 23. Leaves 1–2 inches long, half a line wide. Scape 2–3 inches high. Bracts carinate, the margins broadly scarious. Sepals broadly oval, very obtuse, scarious, with a green and thickened centre. Flowers twice as large as those of P. pusilla, in the specimens all perfect and fertile; the two stamens more or less exserted, but not so long as the style. Lobes of the corolla ovate, open or spreading in fruit. Capsule a line and a half long at maturity, when it becomes one-third longer than the calyx. Ovules 2 in each cell. Seeds oblong, nearly as in P. pusilla. By the latter we mean, of course, Nuttall's P. pusilla, not what Decaisne has taken for it, and characterized in DeCandolle's Prodromus. His plant, as also his P. perpusilla, is P. heterophylla, *Nutt. in Trans. Amer. Phil. Soc. n. ser.* 5, *p.* 177, which, although often larger and with sparingly-toothed or incised leaves, is to be distinguished with certainty only by its 10–28-seeded capsule, more oblong or conoidal in form, and exserted to twice the length of the calyx when mature. P. pusilla has only a pair of ovules and seeds in each cell. These three species accord in being *diandrous*, (a fact first noted for P. pusilla by Dr. Torrey in his Flora of New York, where, however, the capsule is inadvertently said to be *two-seeded*, instead of four-seeded;) but P. tenuiflora, *Kit.*, is not so: they are also *subdiœcious* or *diœcio-dimorphous*, more decidedly so than P. Patagonica, and with the corolla inclined to be closed in the more fertile form, but less so than in P. Virginica* and its allies.

* It is remarkable that the diœcio-dimorphous character of the wide-spread and variable P. Virginica (which includes P. occidentalis, rhodosperma, echioides, Cumingiana? and purpurascens, (*Nutt.*, of Decaisne) and some allied species, has not long before this been distinctly made out. Both *subsexes* have been described, indeed; some authors indicating the one, some the other, some mixing up the two incongruously in their descriptions; while others, as Nuttall and Decaisne, have mistaken them for separate species. The *substerile* plant, as we may call it, since it rarely ripens any seeds, exhibits the usual exserted stamens and large anthers of the genus, and its corollas remain open after anthesis; this is Nuttall's P. purpurascens, of which, with other substerile forms of the same and some allied species, Decaisne has made his section *Novorbis*. That these are mostly sterile plants may be inferred from the circumstance that of the fifteen admitted species of the section, only two have the capsule and seed described, although specimens of all of them have been examined by Decaisne himself; yet in such a spicate inflorescence it rarely happens that a dried specimen of a truly fertile plant fails to offer some full-grown fruit and seed. The truly fertile form, which is the most common in herbaria, bears flowers all of which are provided with short or included filaments and

They compose a small section section of the genus, quite otherwise characterized, however, than is Decaisne's Micropsyllium, and not embracing all his species.

PLUMBAGINACEÆ.

ARMERIA VULGARIS, *Willd.*, var. A. Andina var. Californica, *Boiss. in DC. Prodr.* 12, *p.* 682; *Benth. Pl. Hartw. p.* 332. Hills near San Francisco; and Laguna of Santa Rosa creek; April. We are not satisfied with the characters on which the acute Boissier has separated into many species what may, perhaps, better be regarded as variations of A. vulgaris.

STYRACACEÆ.

STYRAX CALIFORNICUM, *Torr. Desc. Darlingt. in Smithson. Contrib.* 6, *p.* 4, *t.* 12. Hill-sides and river banks, Mokelumne Hill, California; May 17: in blossom. Some of the racemes are 5–6-flowered. This is quite an ornamental shrub, and well deserves cultivation.

PRIMULACEÆ.

TRIENTALIS EUROPÆA, *Linn.* var. LATIFOLIA. T. latifolia, *Hook. Fl. Bor.-Am.* 2, *p.* 121. Tokeloma creek; April 16. Mountains, near Oakland, California; April 5.

GLAUX MARITIMA, *Linn.* Martinez, California; April 23.

ANAGALLIS ARVENSIS, *Linn.* There was no label to this plant. It is, however, common in California, and was doubtless introduced from Europe.

DODECATHEON MEADIA, *Linn.* var. D. integrifolium and D. frigidum, (*Cham.*) *Hook. Fl. Bor.-Am.* 2, *p.* 118. Cocomungo; March 17; and mountains, near Oakland, California; April 4. We can recognize but one species of Dodecatheon. The length of the tube of filaments is exceedingly variable.

OROBANCHACEÆ. (By A. GRAY.)

BOSCHNIAKIA STROBILACEA (sp. nov.): squamis orbicularibus vel obovato-rotundis obtusissimis ubique confertim imbricatis, floralibus flores subæquantibus; calyce postice truncato haud obliquo, dentibus 3 lineari-subulatis tubo longioribus; labio corollæ inferiore patente superius adæquante, lobis oblongis; filamentis basi barbatis; placentis 4 æquidistantibus. Dry and rocky hills, South Yuba, California; May. A span high, thick, resembling Conopholis Americana in aspect, the scales larger and broader, about half an inch wide, brown in the dried state. The three slender teeth of the calyx are anterior and lateral, a line and a half long; the two others obsolete or indistinct. Anthers sparsely hairy. The shape of the scales and of the calyx teeth at once distinguishes this from B. tuberosa and B. glabra of Oregon, etc.

PHELIPÆA CALIFORNICA, *Don, Syst.* 4, *p.* 632. Orobanche Californica, *Cham. & Schlecht. in Linnæa*, 3, *p.* 134. Plains, near Marysville, California; May. The specimen renders it probable that P. Californica is not distinct from P. Ludoviciana, which has a wide range. It is nearly allied on the other hand to P. comosa, (the Orobanche comosa of Hooker,) which must find a place in this genus, notwithstanding the bractlets are remote from the calyx.

APHYLLON UNIFLORUM, *Gray, Man. Bot. N. States, ed.* 1, *p.* 290. Napa valley, California; April 27. The range of this species includes all temperate North America, from Newfoundland and Canada, south to Florida and Texas, and west to the Pacific. Had Wallroth's name of Anoplon been generally adopted by succeeding botanists, it might have been unwise to disturb it. But

very small anthers—whether sterile or precocious is uncertain, probably the latter, as the ovary is uniformly fruitful;—and the corolla, as is well known, becomes connivent-closed after anthesis, its broad lobes involutely and imbricately enwrapping each other, so as to form a kind of beak surmounting the fruit. This is the type of Decaisne's section *Cleiosantha.*—*Gray, Mss.*

since Endlicher's name of Anoplanthus has been adopted by Reuter, the monographer of the order in De Candolle's Prodromus, while Nuttall has preferred the prior claim of his unobjectionable name Gymnocaulis, there can be no question of the propriety of restoring the far older name of Aphyllon, under which Mitchell characterized the genus more than a hundred years ago. There is considerable reason for thinking, however, that the genus will be reduced to a mere section of Phelipæa.

SCROPHULARIACEÆ. (By A. GRAY.)

LINARIA CANADENSIS, *Dum.* Near San Francisco, and elsewhere in California; April. A species diffused over all the temperate parts of the American continent.

SCROPHULARIA NODOSA, *Linn.; Benth. in DC. Prodr.* 10, *p.* 309. Corte Madera and Napa Valley; April. A species common to the temperate portion of the whole northern hemisphere.

COLLINSIA BARTSIÆFOLIA, *Benth. in DC. Prodr.* 10, *p.* 318. Bolinas bay and Punta de los Reyes, California; April.

COLLINSIA TINCTORIA, *Hartw.; Benth. Pl. Hartw. p.* 328. Wet ravines, Knight's Ferry, etc., California; May. This and the foregoing are likely to pass into the next.

COLLINSIA BICOLOR, *Benth. in Hort. Trans.* 1, *p.* 480. Hill-sides, Martinez, Mokelumne, etc., California; May.

COLLINSIA PARVIFLORA, *Dougl. in Bot. Reg. t.* 1082. Hill-sides, on the Yuba; May. Var. SPARSIFLORA, *Benth.* (C. sparsiflora, *Fisch & Meyer.*) Corte Madera, Napa Valley, and mountains, near Oakland, California; April. The corolla is not only larger, but longer in proportion to the calyx; still intermediate forms appear to connect it with C. parviflora, as Bentham states.

PENTSTEMON CENTRANTHIFOLIUS, *Benth. Scroph. Ind. p.* 7, *& in DC. Prodr.* 10, *p* 323. Plains, near San Gabriel, California; March.

PENTSTEMON MICROPHYLLUS (sp. nov.): fruticosus, ramosissimus, foliis in axillis crebre fasciculatis (minutis) obovatis ovatisve obtusissimis coriaceis integerrimis subpetiolatis; racemis paniculatis; sepalis fructiferis oblongo-ovatis. On Williams' Fork of the Colorado, New Mexico. The specimens were collected in February, and are without flowers, but they bear the remains of the fruit of the preceding season. The plant is a remarkable one, and may possibly not belong to this genus. The leaves are only one or two lines long, of a thick and firm texture, and arise three or seven together from short spurs or undeveloped branches. The peduncles are opposite and alternate, somewhat spreading, and about as long as the fructiferous calyx. There is nothing peculiar about the capsule; and the aspect of the plant is that of the section Erianthera.

PENTSTEMON LEWISII, *Benth. l. c.?* Rocky ravines, Cajon Pass, California; March 16. The specimen belongs to a shrubb species, and bears only the vestiges of the last year's fruit. The leaves are not so finely and evenly denticulate as those of P. Lewisii; but for the present it may be referred to that species.

PENTSTEMON BREVIFLORUS, *Lind. Bot. Reg. t.* 1946. Knight's Ferry, on the Stanislaus; May. A shrubby species, as already noted by Hartweg.

PENTSTEMON HETEROPHYLLUS, *Lindl. Bot. Reg. t.* 1899. Butte mountains, near Marysville, California; May. The variety with narrower sepals, without manifest scarious margins, (*Hook. & Arn. Bot. Beech.*;) the same as Hartweg's No. 1880, and not to be well separated from P. azureus, *Benth. Pl. Hartw.* No. 1819, which seems, as to the calyx, to connect all the forms.

PENTSTEMON SPECTABILIS (*Thurber in A. B. Gray's Rep. ined.*): undique glaber; caule stricto elato (3–4-pedali) herbaceo; foliis coriaceis serraturis rigidis crebris argute dentatis oblongis seu ovato-lanceolatis sæpius acutis, imis sessilibus, reliquiis connato-amplexicaulibus, superioribus floralibusque orbiculato-disciformibus; panicula ampla elongata virgato-pyramidali; pedunculis 3–9-floris; sepalis orbiculari-ovatis carnosis; corolla e tubo brevi (calyce duplo longiori) angusto subito ventricosa campanulata modice bilabiata, lobis 5 consimilibus rotundatis patentibus; filamento sterili filiformi glabro; antheris (Cepocosmi) glabris. San Francisco Mountain, New Mexico, December 16. Imperfect specimens, with fruit only. But they clearly belong to a species which we first received from Mr. William A. Wallace, from Cocomungo and Los Angeles, California; and soon after from Mr. George Thurber, who gathered it in the same district. Mr. A. B. Gray likewise gathered fragments of the same on the Gila river. It must be one of the showiest species known, and it will appropriately bear the name imposed upon it by Mr. Thurber. The crowded pianicle of purplish blue flowers is often two feet in length, and free from leaves, the lowest bracts not exceeding the peduncles, while the upper are reduced to small and inconspicuous perfoliate disks. Peduncles and spreading pedicels each half an inch to an inch long. Sepals 3 lines long, obtuse or apiculate. Corolla an inch or more in length; the proper tube about twice the length of the calyx, then abruptly expanded into a campanulate throat, glabrous inside; the two lips of equal length, and the lobes very similar. Leaves apparently somewhat glaucous, 3 or 4 inches long; only the radical petioled; all the upper cauline connate into a disk, which is an inch or two in width where it is perforated by the stem.

Diplacus glutinosus, *Nutt.* Hill-sides, Sonoma, Punta de los Reyes, etc., California; May. The species also includes D. leptanthus and D. longiflorus of Nuttall.

Mimulus brevipes, *Benth. Scroph. Ind. p.* 28, *& in DC. l. c.* Hill-sides, on the Stanislaus; May.

Mimulus luteus, *Linn.; Benth. in DC. l. c.* Various forms of this polymorphous plant: Napa Valley, etc., California, and Williams' River; February—May.

Mimulus dentatus, *Nutt. in Herb. Hook.; Benth. l. c.* Hill-sides, at Murphy's, California. Also (a narrow-leaved variety) near Mammoth Grove; May.

Mimulus moschatus, *Dougl. in Bot. Reg. t.* 1118. Wet ravines on the Yuba, near Downieville, California; May.

Mimulus bicolor, *Benth. Pl. Hartw. p.* 328, *No.* 1892. Hill-sides, near Sonora, California; May. A depauperate form.

Mimulus floribundus, *Dougl. in Bot. Reg. t.* 1125. Grass valley, California, in low places; May. A small form.

Mimulus inconspicuus (sp. nov.): annuus, glaber; caule gracili 1–2-pollicari adscendente paucifoliato; foliis ovalibus seu ovatis subintegerrimis obsolete 3–5-nerviis subsessilibus; pedunculis solitariis foliis et flore parvo brevioribus; calyce prismatico, dentibus brevissimis subæqualibus; tubo corollæ paullo exserto. Damp hill-sides, Los Angeles, California, May. Leaves 5 or 6 lines long, the cauline only a single pair in the specimens. Peduncle 2 or 3 lines long. Flower 4–5 lines long; the corolla yellow tinged with rose-color in the dried plant, its lobes very small. Fructiferous calyx not seen.

Eunanus Douglasii, *Benth. in DC. Prodr.* 10, *p.* 374. Gravelly hills, Sonora, and Mokelumne Hill, California; May. The former specimens, like those of Douglas, etc., are very dwarf and simple; the stem, of only 2 or 3 internodes above the cotyledons, barely half an inch long, while the flower it is terminated with is fully an inch long. Those from the latter locality, like Hartweg's No. 1894, are developed into many-flowered branches 4 inches high, the lower part fructiferous. To Bentham's description of the capsule, from Hartweg's specimens, we have only to add that it is often nearly linear, 4 or 5 lines long, not much compressed, of a crustaceous texture, but at length dehiscent; the valves bearing the many-seeded placentæ. The ovoid seeds are apiculate at each end. The calyx, as in the next species, is very oblique at the orifice; in this it is narrow and prismatic, and its teeth are very short and obtuse. The marked difference between this species and E. Frémonti, and perhaps E. Tolmæi, (which we have not seen,) led us to propose its generic separation, as Mr. Bentham has stated; but his judgment in the combination is fully sustained by the characters of the following intermediate species.

Eunanus Coulteri, (*Benth. Pl. Hartw. p.* 320): foliis inferioribus ovatis oblongisve, superioribus spathulato-lanceolatis pollicaribus; calycis infundibuliformis dentibus lanceolatis, supremo tubo vix dimidio breviore; corollae tubo calycem bis terve superante, fauce valde ampliata, labiis subæquilongis; stigma obtuse bilabiato, labiis brevibus latis inæqualibus sed consimilibus; fructu immaturo subgloboso. Low places, Mark West's creek; April, and Knight's ferry, on the Stanislaus; May. (Also communicated by Dr. Andrews, etc.) Flower fully as large as that of E. Douglasii, often an inch and a half or even two inches long, lilac? the throat mottled with deep purple. Immature seeds apiculate at both ends. This is not the E. Coulteri, *Harv. & Gray*, in the herbarium of Trinity College, Dublin, (Coll. Coult., No. 614;) but as no character of that has been published, and as recent specimens lead us to think it not different from E. Fremonti, the name should be retained for the present species, to which Bentham applied it, although we are not sure that it occurs in Coulter's collection.

EUNANUS BIGELOVII (sp. nov.): foliis caulinis oblongo-lanceolatis acutis; calycis subcampanulatis valde plicato-angulatis, ore vix obliquo, dentibus inæqualibus triangulari-subulatis pungentibus dimidium tubi longitudine paullo excedentibus; corollæ tubo calyce subduplo longiore, limbo patentissimo, lobis æquilongis; stigmate integro. Gravelly hills, near the Colorado of California; February 17. On the Mohave creek; March 2. Plant only beginning to blossom, 1–2 inches high, doubtless attaining a greater height as the season advances. Largest leaves an inch long, more or less viscid-pubescent, like the stem. Calyx 4–5 lines long. Corolla 6–8 lines long, of the same shape as in E. Fremonti; the foliage and the calyx quite different.

VERONICA AMERICANA, *Schwein.; Benth. in DC. Prodr.* Santa Rosa creek, California; May.

CASTILLEIA AFFINIS, *Hook. & Arn. Bot. Beech., p.* 154. Cocomungo, California; March. The same as Hartweg's No. 1896.

CASTILLEIA HISPIDA, *Benth. in Hook. Fl. Bor.-Am.* 2, *p.* 105. San Francisco and Punta de los Reys; April.

ORTHOCARPUS PUSILLUS, *Benth. Scroph. Ind., in DC. Prodr.* 10, *p.* 535. Low grounds, San Francisco; April.

ORTHOCARPUS FLORIBUNDUS, *Benth. l. c.* San Francisco, California; April.

ORTHOCARPUS ERIANTHUS, *Benth. l. c.* Benicia, California; April.

ORTHOCARPUS LITHOSPERMOIDES, *Benth. l. c.* Mark West's creek, California; April.

ORTHOCARPUS (TRIPHYSARIA) FAUCIBARBATUS (sp. nov.): foliis linearibus 1–3-nerviis ultra medium pinnatifidis cum caule erecto ramoso lævi glabris, laciniis angusto-linearibus fere filiformibus elongatis; bracteis viridibus scabro-puberulis floribus brevioribus; spicis demum interruptis; calyce tubo corollæ pubescente dimidio breviore, dentibus triangulari-lanceolatis obtusis vix dimidium tubi adæquantibus; corollæ labio inferiore trisaccato, fauce secus plicas 2 palatinas longe barbata, appendiculis brevissimis obtusis; antheris unilocularibus. Corte Madera, California; April 20. Plant rather stout, 9 or 10 inches high, with spreading branches. Cauline leaves 2 inches long; the bracts becoming shorter and broader, the upper ones nearly palmate. Flowers 7–8 lines long. Calyx minutely pubescent. Corolla apparently pale yellow. Allied to O. lacerus and O. lithospermoides of Bentham. The last named has the throat of its corolla somewhat villous-pubescent; that of the others is glabrous. Besides the smoothness and the one-celled anthers, the calyx distinguishes the present species.

ORTHOCARPUS DENSIFLORUS, *Benth. l. c.* Corte Madera and San Gabriel; March and April.

ORTHOCARPUS CASTILLEIOIDES, *Benth. l. c.?* Corte Madera, California; April. Too young for proper determination.

ORTHOCARPUS (ONCORRHYNCHUS) ATTENUATUS (sp. nov.): cinereo-pubescente; caule gracili stricto; foliis anguste linearibus sursum filiformi-attenuatis integerrimis vel summis cum bracteis viridibus trifidis, lobis attenuatis; spica angusta; calyce corolla tertia parte breviore postice fisso, dentibus linearibus obtusis tubo dimidio brevioribus; corollæ labio inferiore vix trisaccato, appendiculis oblongis obtusis ventriculo brevioribus galeam rectam truncatam subæquantibus; antheris bilocularibus. Corte Madera; April 16. A span high. Corolla narrow, 7 lines long, puberulent, white or cream-color, with the slightly ventricose lower lip spotted with purple.

Pedicularis densiflora, *Benth. in Hook. Fl. Bor. Amer.* 2, *p.* 110, *in DC. l. c., p.* 574. Napa Valley, California; April 5. In fruit.

Pedicularis attenuata, *Benth. in DC. l. c.* Mountains near Oakland, California; April 5. In flower.

BIGNONIACEÆ—SESAMEÆ. (By A. Gray.)

MOHAVEA, Nov. Gen.

Calyx alte 5-partitus, laciniis lanceolatis foliaceis fere æqualibus. Corolla hypogyna, profunde bilabiata personata, limbo amplo patenti tubo campanulato multo longiore; labio postico latissimo rotundo emarginato-bilobo, æstivatione exteriore, basi fornice supra antheras arcuata instructo; labio antico consimili subtrilobo, palato prominente medio barbato. Stamina fertilia 2, tubo corollæ inserta: filamenta apice incurva: antheræ approximata rotundo-reniformes, confluentim uniloculares. Filamenta sterilia sæpius 2, exigua. Stylus columnaris: stigma compresso-capitatum, integrum. Ovarium ovoideum, biloculare, placentis axilibus, apice tantum placentis haud coalitis uniloculare, parietibus membranaceis. Ovula multa, pluriseriata, horizontalia vel adscendens, anatropa. Fructus ignotus. Herba humilis, ramosa, diffusa, pilis viscidis et glanduliferis pubescens; radice annua; foliis alternis, imisve oppositis, oblongo seu ovato-lanceolatis, integerrimis vel repando-angulatis, penninerviis, basi angustata parallelinerviis; floribus axillaribus solitariis, pedunculis nudis brevibus; corolla ochroleuca? et purpurascente, fauce cum palato purpureo picta.

Mohavea viscida. Mohave Creek, California; March 2. Leaves 1½ to 2 inches long. Sepals half an inch long, exceeding the short tube of the corolla. Lips of the corolla nearly an inch broad, apparently flat. Filaments and style somewhat hairy towards the base, included within the throat. Ovary 2–celled, except near the summit, with no dorsal introflexion of the walls, the placentæ not bilammelar. Style nearly as long as the stamens. Notwithstanding the ovary, which is strictly 2–celled, except at the top, we suspect this curious plant to belong to the Bignoniaceæ–Sesameæ; but the fruit alone can determine the question. If the seeds prove to be albuminous, we know not where in the order Scrophulariaceæ to place it. In one of our few specimens a singular abnormal body was found growing from the outside of the corolla at its base, resembling a long-clawed petal, with a small, truncate, saccate, and involute limb. It is evidently a monstrosity.

VERBENACEÆ.

Verbena prostrata, *R. Br. in Hort. Kew.* (*ed.* 2) 4, *p.* 41; *Schauer in DC. Prodr.* 11, *p.* 547. Banks of the Mokelumne River, California, May 17.

LABIATÆ.

Pycnanthemum Californicum (*Torr. in Durand, Pl. Pratt. in Jour. Acad. Phil.* 2, *p.* 99): incano-pubescens, foliis ovato-lanceolatis sessilibus parce denticulatis; verticillastris 2–4 densissimis, demum scorpoideo-explanatis multiradiatis; calycis dentibus æqualibus lanceolatis muticis. California, probably from the lower part of the Sacramento Valley. Gathered by Colonel Frémont, (1846), Rev. A. Fitch, & Mr. Shelton.

P. Californicum, var. foliis tenuioribus oblongis glabriusculis viridibus. River banks and ravines, Mokelumne, California, (with the persistent inflorescence of the preceding year).—This plant is a genuine Pycnanthemum, and is most nearly related to P. muticum. No other species is found west of the Rocky Mountains. The inflorescence is at first in the form of compact heads, of which there are usually three on the main axis. Late in the season these unfold into very dense sessile cymes, the branches of which are secund, and nearly an inch in length,

The variety found by Dr. Bigelow was not in flower. It seems to be a tall plant. The leaves are 3–4 inches long and nearly an inch broad.

MONARDELLA CANDICANS, *Benth. Pl. Hartw. p.* 330, (*No.* 1911); *Durand, l. c.* Sides of rivulets, Knight's Ferry, Stanislaus, May 7. The lobes of the corolla in this and some other species have a small hemispherical sac at the tip. The stamens are strongly didynamous. This species is found as far south as San Diego, and north to the Upper Sacramento.

M. CANDICANS, *β.* VENOSA: foliis angustioribus; bracteis mucronatis capitulis longioribus, inter venas validas hyalino-membranaceis. Plains of Feather River, near Marysville, May 25. Also collected in California by Rev. A. Fitch. The bracts of this plant are very remarkable. They are larger than in the ordinary form of M. candicans, and between the strong veins (which are usually of a purplish color) there is no parenchyma, but only the thin transparent epidermis resembling goldbeater's skin. The corolla s much exserted, of a deep rose color, and has the lobes tipped with a little sac, as in the common variety.

POGOGYNE DOUGLASII, *Benth. Lab. p.* 414, *& in DC. Prodr.* 12, *p.* 243. Plains and low places, Stockton, May 7; valley of the Sacramento, May 26. All the species of this genus are annual.

HEDEOMA? SERPYLLOIDES (sp. nov.): annua, e basi ramosa prostrata; foliis obovatis obtusis integris, basi in petiolem attenuatis; verticillastris 2–6-floris sessilibus basi bibracteolatis, bracteolis oblanceolatis flore longioribus; calyce vix bilabiato, profunde quinquefido, segmentis angusto-lanceolatis patulis; corolla calyce paulo breviore, labio superiore plano ovato obtuso labio inferiore trifido, laciniis subæqualibus, intermedio subemarginato. Hill-sides, Martinez, California, April 23. A slender annual, with divaricate puberulent branches. Leaves 5–6 lines long (including the petiole), ciliolate at the base, otherwise nearly glabrous. Early flowers solitary, the later ones in 2–6-flowered cymules. Tube of the calyx very short; the 3 superior segments (upper lip) broader and longer than the others, all of them cuspidate. Stamens 2, the upper pair wanting.

SALVIA CARDUACEA, *Benth. Lab. p.* 302, *& in DC. Prod.* 12, *p.* 349. S. gossypina, *Benth. Pl. Hartw. p.* 330. Plains, Knight's Ferry, Stanislaus, May 7. We have no doubt of S. gossypina being a mere variety (as Mr. Bentham suspected) of S. carduacea.

SALVIA COLUMBARIÆ, *Benth. l. c.* Sides of rivulets, Knight's Ferry, California, May. This is an annual species, and varies greatly in size, as well as in the lobing of the leaves.

AUDIBERTIA HUMILIS, *Benth. Lab. p.* 313, *& in DC. Prodr.* 12, *p.* 359. Hill-sides, near Nevada City, May 20. Leaves most clustered towards the base of the stem; the proper cauline ones being seldom more than a single pair.

SCUTELLARIA TUBEROSA, *Benth. l. c.* Plains, near San Gabriel, March 23. Dr. Parry collected this species near Monterey. It was found also by Mr. Gibbes in Calaveras county; by Dr. Stillman on the Upper Sacramento; by Mr. Thurber and Rev. Mr. Fitch in the lower part of the Sacramento valley. It is variable in its pubescence, being sometimes almost glabrous. The calyx, however, is always villous. The leaves frequently oblong and narrowed at the base. Besides the principal tuber, from which the stem arries, there are often others at the extremity of the fibrous roots, or rather subterranean branches. They are about three-fourths of an inch in length, oblong, pubescent, tapering to the extremity, jointed, and of a fleshy consistence. Sometimes they show a tendency to ramify. They appear to be true tubers, like those of the potato.

SCUTELLARIA ANTIRRHINOIDES, *Benth. in Bot. Reg. fol.* 1493, *& in DC. Prodr.* 12 *p.* 428. Var. foliis dentatis, interdum sessilibus. River banks, Mokelumne Hill, May 17. We have the same variety, collected in California by Frémont (1846) and by Rev. A. Fitch. The leaves are larger than in the Oregon plant, and the upper ones are sometimes closely sessile.

MARRUBIUM VULGARE, *Linn.; Benth. in DC. Prodr.* 12, *p.* 453. River banks, Mokelumne Hill, California, May 17. Introduced from Europe.

STACHYS AJUGOIDES, *Benth. in Linnæa* 6, *p.* 80, *& in DC. Prodr.* 12, *p.* 468. Bolinas bay,

April 19. Bracts shorter than the calyx, ovate. Teeth of the calyx triangular-ovate, spinescent at the tip, somewhat recurved.

STACHYS CHAMISSONIS, *Benth. l. c.* Hill-sides, Napa Valley, California; April 26.

BORAGINACEÆ.

LITHOSPERMUM (BATSCHIA) CANESCENS, *Lehm. Asperif.* 2, *p.* 305? Hill-sides, Grass Valley, California; May 20. Except in being less canescent than the eastern plant, we can find nothing to distinguish this from some of our specimens of L. canescens.

AMSINCKIA SPECTABILIS, *Fisch. & Mey. Index Hort. Petrop.* 1835; *DC. Prodr.* 10, *p.* 118. Los Angeles, March 21. Gravelly hills of the Colorado, February 20. On Mohave creek, March 14. Near San Francisco, April 3. The place of insertion of the stamens is by no means a constant character in this genus. In the same species they sometimes are inserted in the throat, and sometimes towards the base of the corolla. A. intermedia seems to be no more than a variety of A. spectabilis.

ERITRICHIUM FULVUM, *Alph. DC. in Prodr.* 10, *p.* 132. Myosotis fulva, *Hook. & Arn. Bot. Beech. p.* 369. Cocomungo, California; March 17. The fruit is scarcely mature enough for comparison, but our plant is very like specimens of E. fulvum from Chili, and it is certainly Myosotis fulva of Hooker and Arnott.

ERITRICHIUM CALIFORNICUM, *DC. Prodr.* 10, *p.* 130. Myosotis Californica, *Fisch. & Mey. Ind. Sem. Hort. Petrop.* 1835, *p.* 42. Near San Francisco, April 8. E. Scouleri, *DC. l. c.* (Myosotis Scouleri, *Hook. & Arn.*) seems to be a mere variety of this species.

ERITRICHIUM CHORISIANUM, *DC. l. c.* Myosotis Chorisiana, *Cham. in Linnæa*, 1829, *p.* 444. With the preceding, from which it is chiefly distinguished by its much longer pedicels.

ERITRICHIUM PLEBEIUM, *Alph. DC. l. c.* Lithospermum plebeium, *Cham. & Schlecht. in Linnæa*, 1829, *p.* 446. With the preceding. The flowers are much larger than in E. Californicnm.

PECTOCARYA LINEARIS, *DC. Prodr.* 10, *p.* 120. On gravelly hills, near the Colorado of California, February 17. This species differs from all the others of the genus in the nutlets being pectinate with acute teeth, instead of bristles.

PECTOCARYA CHILENSIS, *DC. Prodr.* 10, *p.* 120; var. CALIFORNICA: nuculis obovatis, plano-convexis calyce brevioribus. Hill-sides and wet places, near Los Angeles; May 14. Embryo straight, cotyledons nearly orbicular. We find the radicle inferior (not superior, as stated by Alph. De Candolle) in all the species of this genus that we have examined. P. pencillata was found in California by Frémont in his second expedition, and it is No. 516 of Coulter's Californian collection. In this species the nutlets are somewhat panduriform, and are chiefly pectinate on the upper half. The middle contracted portion is naked, and towards the base the hooked hairs are much smaller than those above.

KRINITZKIA LEIOCARPA, *Fisch. & Mey. Ind. Sem. Hort. Petrop.* 1841, *p.* 52. Myosotis flaccida, *Dougl. in Hook. Fl. Bor.-Amer.* 2, *p.* 82. Hill-sides, Knight's Ferry, Stanislaus river. There are specimens, in a young state, of what seems to be the same plant from gravelly hills along the Colorado of California. We find very often but a single nutlet matured in one flower. Mr. Bentham makes the same remark of Hartweg's specimens.

CYNOGLOSSUM GRANDE, *Dougl. Mss.; Lehm. Pug.* 2, *p.* 25; *Hook. Fl. Bor.-Amer.* 2, *p.* 85. Mountains, near Oakland, California; April 4.

HYDROPHYLLACEÆ.

ERIODYCTION TOMENTOSUM, *Benth. Bot. Sulph. p.* 35. E. crassifolium, *Benth. l. c.* Near San Gabriel, California; March.

ERIODYCTION GLUTINOSUM, *Benth. l. c.* Sonora, Cajon Pass, Mokelumne hill, etc., California; Also, var. ANGUSTIFOLIUM, (E. angustifolium, *Nutt. Plant. Gamb.*,) from hills near Cactus Pass, in the western part of New Mexico; January 30.

NAMA JAMAICENSIS, (*Linn.?*): hispido-hirsuta; caule decumbente; foliis lanceolato-spathulatis in petiolum decurrentibus; floribus subgeminis axillaribus pedicellatis; corolla campanulato-infundibuliformi calyce duplo-longiore; sepalis angusto-linearibus. Gravelly hills near the Great Colorado; February 17. Also found near Fort Yuma by Major G. H. Thomas and Lieutenant Du Barry. It is a common species in the valley of the Rio Grande. We refer it to N. Jamaicensis with much doubt.

ROMANZOFFIA SITCHENSIS, *Cham. in Linnæa.* 2, *p.* 609; *Bong. Veg. Sitch. t.* 4. Redwoods, California; April 12. It is interesting to meet with this species in California, where doubtless it is confined to the mountains. Dr. Bigelow's beautiful specimens accord very well with those we possess from Sitcha, from Mertens' collection. The calyx is glabrous. Choisy, (in *DC. Prodr.* 10, *p.* 185,) who had not seen the plant, has written "calycis *hirsuti*," doubtless by a slip of the pen, in place of *glaberrimi*, the word used by Chamisso.

HYDROPHYLLUM CAPITATUM, *Dougl. in Benth. Hydrophyll.; DC. Prodr.* 9, *p.* 289. Hill-sides, Duffield's Ranch, Sierra Nevada; May. The peduncles are longer than usual, and the leaves are as large as in H. macrophyllum; but the segments are sparingly incised, not coarsely toothed, and the lobes of the corolla have a pubescent line along the back. Perhaps the eastern and western plants may be united.

NEMOPHILA PARVIFLORA, *Benth. l. c.* With the preceding, and near Oakland, California; April.

NEMOPHILA ATOMARIA, *Fisch. & Meyer; DC. l. c.* Borders of fields, Corte Madera; April.

NEMOPHILA MACULATA, *Hartw.; Lindl. in Jour. Hort. Soc.* 3, *p.* 319. Hill-sides, Duffield's Ranch, Sierra Nevada; May. A handsome species, now often seen in cultivation.

NEMOPHILA AURITA, *Lindl. Bot. Reg. t.* 1601. Banks of the Stanislaus, at Robinson's Ferry; May.

NEMOPHILA INSIGNIS, *Benth. l. c.* N. liniflora, *Fisch. & Meyer, Hort. Petrop.* Cajon Pass; March.

PHACELIA TANACETIFOLIA, *Benth. Hydrophyll. l. c.* Los Angeles, San Francisco, etc.; March, April. Various forms.

PHACELIA CIRCINATA, *Jacq. Ecl.* 1. *t.* 91; *Benth. l. c.* Hill-sides at Murphy's, and in many other places in California; May.

PHACELIA CILIATA, *Benth. l. c.* Los Angeles, and on the Great Colorado; February, March.

EUTOCA DIVARICATA, *Benth. l. c.* Near the Redwoods of California; April.

POLEMONIACEÆ.

PHLOX OCCIDENTALIS (Durand, Mss.): glanduloso–puberula; caulibus adscendentibus (subpedalibus); foliis lanceolatis rigidulis mucronatis; pedunculis erectis brevibus; calyce viscido corollæ tubo paullo breviore, dentibus subulatis erectis tubo æquilongis; corollæ (albæ?) lobis late obcordatis contiguis; ovarii loculis uniovulatis. P. divaricata, *Durand, Pl. Pratten in Journ. Acad. Philad. n. ser.* 1855. Hill-sides, near Duffield's Ranch, May. Lower leaves not seen; the upper 12–16 lines long, 2 or 3 wide, usually broadest at the base. Limb of the corolla an inch in diameter, the broad and rounded rather deeply obcordate lobes overlapping each other, not widely separate as in P. divaricata (in which, however, the lobes vary from strongly obcordate-notched to barely retuse). Ovules solitary. Root doubtless perennial. The only species of the first section of the genus known west of the Rocky Mountains.

COLLOMIA GRACILIS, *Benth. in Bot. Reg., & in DC. Prodr.* 8, *p.* 308. Corte Madera and Sonoma; April, May.

COLLOMIA GLUTINOSA, *Benth. l. c.* Sonora, California, along rivulets and ravines; May. A form with the corolla longer than usual; its slender tube half an inch long, and thrice the length of the calyx.

NAVARRETIA HETEROPHYLLA, *Benth. in DC. l. c.* Collomia heterophylla, *Hook.* Mokelumne Hill, and Grass Valley, California; May.

NAVARRETIA PUBESCENS, *Hook. & Arn. Bot. Beech. p.* 368. Ione Valley, in low places; also Knight's Ferry on the Stanislaus, on hill sides; May.

NAVARRETIA COTULÆFOLIA, *Hook. & Arn. l. c.* With the last.

NAVARRETIA LEUCOCEPHALA, *Benth. Pl. Hartw. p.* 324. Low and wet places, Mark West's Creek, California; April 30.

GILIA CAPITATA, *Dougl. in Bot. Mag. t.* 2698. Hill-sides, Sonoma, California; May.

GILIA ACHILLEÆFOLIA, *Benth. in Bot. Reg. & DC. l. c.* Knight's Ferry on the Stanislaus; May.

GILIA TRICOLOR, *Benth, l. c.* Hill-sides, Martinez; April. From Napa Valley are specimens gathered April 16, wholly in fruit, which appear to be either G. tricolor or G. multicaulis, but with the calyx and peduncles glabrous.

GILIA (LINANTHUS) DICHOTOMA, *Benth. in DC. l. c.* Napa Valley, and near San Francisco; April. This and all the sections (formerly genera) of Bentham, with palmatisect usually opposite leaves, we should prefer to regard as one genus, leaving to Gilia the sections Eugilia, Thyrsogilia (of which G. congesta is the type), and Ipomopsis.

GILIA (LINANTHUS) DIANTHOIDES, *Endl. Atakt. t.* 29; Cocomungo, California; in sandy or gravelly places; March.

GILIA (DACTYLOPHYLLUM) PHARNACEOIDES, *Benth. in DC. l. c.* Hill-sides, Napa Valley; April.

GILIA (LEPTOSIPHON) ANDROSACEA, *Steud.; Benth. l. c.* Plains and hill-sides, Napa Valley, etc. April, May.

GILIA (LEPTOSIPHON) CILIATA, *Benth. Pl. Hartw., p.* 324. Hill-sides and grassy plains, Napa Valley, California; May.

GILIA (LEPTOSIPHON) MICRANTHA, *Steud.; Benth. l. c.* Hill-sides, Napa Valley; May: and Benicia, California; April.

GILIA MICRANTHA, var. AUREA, *Benth. Pl. Hartw. l. c.* Hills and plains, Napa Valley; April. The stamens nearly equal in length the lobes of the corolla, which is yellow; otherwise the same as G. micrantha.

GENTIANACEÆ.

FRASERA NITIDA, *Benth. Pl. Hartw. p.* 322. Hill-sides, near Marysville, California; May, Capsule, 4-seeded. Seeds linear-oblong, winged. We have specimens of this species in fruit, collected in California by Mr. Shelton. It is scarcely distinct from F. albescens.

FRASERA PANICULATA (n. sp.): foliis linearibus oppositis; panicula pyramidata nuda laxa; calycis segmentis ovatis acutis corollam duplo brevioribus; foveis oblongo-linearibus binis; corona nulla. Sand-bluffs, Inscription Rock, Zuñi county. Specimens were collected very late in the season, but they are sufficient to show that this is quite a new species. The plant is nearly three feet high, with a long tapering root. Radical leaves in a cluster; stem leaves in three distant pairs. Panicle (fructiferous) about two feet long, loose, compound; pedicels an inch or more in length. Segments of the corolla oblong, obtuse, furnished near the base with two narrow pits, which are nearly half the length of the segment, and are pectinately ciliate around the margin. Filaments somewhat dilated downward, distinct. Capsule about three-fourths of an inch long, very slightly compressed. Seeds 15–20, completely filling the capsule. scabrous, wingless.

As Mr. Bentham remarks, (in Plant. Hartw.) Grisebach's character of the genus Frasera does not agree with the western species, and seems to have been drawn from F. Carolinensis, which is destitute of a corona. This is the more remarkable, as Grisebach elaborated the Gentianaceæ for Hooker's Fl. Bor.-Amer., and described in that work, two species, which are furnished with a conspicuous corona, consisting of fimbriate scales, alternating with the stamens. Our new species agrees with the eastern one in wanting the crown. Dr. Parry found on the mountains east of San Diego another species (F. Parryi, *Torr. Bot. Mex. Bound. Surv., ined.*) still more like F. Carolinensis, and likewise destitute of a crown. It is, perhaps, F. verticillata, *Hook. Fl. Bor.-Am.*, but not of Walter. It has a nearly naked panicle, and lunate solitary glandular pits.

ERYTHRÆA MUHLENBERGII, *Griseb. in DC. Prodr.* 9, *p.* 60, quoad pl. Calif. Fields, Benicia; April.

MENYANTHES TRIFOLIATA, *L.* Near San Francisco; April.

CONVOLVULACEÆ.

CONVOLVULUS CALIFORNICA, *Choisy in DC. Prodr.* 9, *p.* 405. Santa Rosa creek, California; May 1.

IPOMÆA SAGITTATA, Desf.? I. sagittifolia, *Hook. & Arn. Bot. Beech. p.* 151. Hills near Punta de los Reyes, California; April 17. This is probably the plant of Hooker and Arnott, but not Convolvulus sagittifolius, *Michx.* The leaves are broader, and the auricles are deeply emarginate, or even 2-lobed at the summit. The one-flowered peduncles are longer than the leaves, and furnished with two small alternate lanceolate bracts a short distance below the flower. Corolla nearly as large as in Calystegia sepium, whitish, with pale purple stripes.

CONVOLVULUS ARVENSIS, *Linn.; Choisy in DC. Prodr.* 9, *p.* 406; var. VILLOSUS, *Choisy l. c.* Hill sides, Sonora, California; May 9. Stems prostrate, branching from the root. Leaves varying from ovate to narrowly lanceolate, strongly hastate or sagittate. Peduncles longer than the leaves, with a pair of opposite lanceolate mostly sagittate bracts a little below the flower.

CONVOLVULUS (n. sp.?): canescenti-tomentosus; caule prostrato e basi ramoso; foliis latocordatis brevissime acuminatis, auriculis angulari-bilobis; pedunculis unifloris axillaribus- Hill-sides, Downieville, Yuba river, California; May 22. Our specimens have only young flower buds, so that the genus cannot certainly be ascertained. The plant has never come under our observation before.

CUSCUTA CALIFORNICA, *Hook. & Arn. Bot. Beech. p.* 364; *Choisy in DC. Prodr.* 9, *p.* 457. Parasitic on Phacelia circinata and other plants, in various parts of California; February, May.

SOLANACEÆ.

SOLANUM UMBELLIFERUM, *Eschsch. Mem. de St. Petersb.* 10, *p.* 280, *and in Linnæa*, 1828, (*litt.*) *p.* 148; *Dunal in DC. Prodr.* 13, *pars.* 2, *p.* 93. S. Californicum, *Dunal. l. c. p.* 86. Cocomungo, March 17, and San Francisco; April 3. A common species in California. It varies much in the size and form of the leaves, degree of the pubescence, and number of flowers in the raceme or umbel.

NICOTIANA QUADRIVALVIS, *Pursh Fl.* 1, *p.* 141; *Dunal in DC. Prodr.* 13, *pars.* 1, *p.* 571. N. multivalvis, *Lindl. Bot. Reg. t.* 1057? Rocky arroyos, near the Colorado of the West; February 17.

NICOTIANA PLUMBAGINIFOLIA, *Dunal in DC. Prodr.* 13, *pars.* 1, *p.* 569. Var? BIGELOVII: annua; caule glanduloso-pubescente subsimplici; foliis oblongo-lanceolatis acutiusculis glabriusculis, inferioribus in petiolem angustatis, superioribus sessilibus basi angustatis; panicula terminali laxiuscula; calyce glanduloso-pubescente, laciniis lanceolato-linearibus inequalibus, corolla hypocraterimorpha, tubo elongato calyce 2–3-plo longiore, limbi laciniis lato-ovatis obtusiusculis. Knight's Ferry, Stanislaus river; May. We are unwilling to propose this as a new species, since there are so many others in the same genus that are very imperfectly known. Our plant does not agree with any Nicotiana described by Dunal, (l. c.,) but it seems to approach the nearest to N. plumbaginifolia.

LYCIUM, "n. sp. near L. FRAGROSUM," *Miers in lit.* In cañons along Williams' river, February 8. Mr. Miers will describe this new species in a monograph of Lycium that is to appear in the second volume of his Illustrations of South American Plants, shortly to be published.

ASCLEPIADACEÆ.

Asclepias ericoarpa, *Benth. Pl. Hartw. p.* 323, *No.* 1835. Hill-sides, Knight's Ferry, Stanislaus river, California; May 7.

Asclepias (Otaria) n. sp.? Dry arroyos, on the Great Colorado of California. Our specimens are imperfect, having been gathered late in the season, when the leaves had fallen. The plant evidently belongs to the section Otaria of Decaisne, but we can refer it with certainty to none of the species described in the Prodromus. It is tall, (apparently 3–4 feet high,) somewhat branched above, with a minutely pubescent stem. The umbels are numerous, in a terminal panicle or raceme, 15–20-flowered. The flowers are apparently white, about as large as in A. variegata. The petals are reflexed, and the oblong entire cuculli are only about one-third longer than the sessile gynostegium. Horn subulate-falciform, slightly exserted. The pod is about 5 inches in length, even, oblong, tapering to a long point. It seems to be nearly allied to A. subulata of Decaisne, but that is said to have the cuculli twice as long as the gynostegium, and until the leaves are known we cannot be sure that it is a new species.

Acerates cordifolia, *Benth. Pl. Hartw. p.* 323. Knight's Ferry, Stanislaus river, California; May 8. We have this plant also from the Rev. Mr. Fitch. In all our specimens the gynostegium is much shorter than the corolla. The cuculli are about the length of the gynostegium, obliquely truncated downward, and closely appressed to the processes of the anthers.

OLEACEÆ.

Fraxinus pistaciæfolia: glabra seu tomentuloso-velutina; foliolis 2–4-jugis subpetiolulatis ovatis oblongis lanceolatisve serratis vel fere integerrimis pallidis vel supra lucidis venosis; petiolo canaliculato nunc apicem versus marginato; samara ex apice in alam spathulato-oblongam portione seminifera subtereti immarginata vix longiorem producta. F. velutina, *Torr. in Emory's Rep.* (forma tomentosa.) Rocky ravines of Williams' River; January 3: fruit only. A species occurring in almost all the New Mexican collections, excessively variable in its foliage, and so much more generally smooth than pubescent (still less velvety) that we propose to supersede the little-known name under which an extreme form of it was briefly described in Emory's Report some years ago.

Fraxinus Oregona, *Nutt. N. Amer. Sylv.* 3, *p.* 59, *t.* 99. F. pubescens, *var. Hook. Fl. Bor.-Am.* 2, *p.* 51. F. grandifolia, *Benth. Bot. Sulph. p.* 33. Napa Valley, California, in deep ravines and along rivulets; May 5. A small-leaved form.

ARISTOLOCHIACEÆ.

Aristolochia Californica (sp. nov.): caule volubili fruticoso; foliis ovato-cordatis integerrimis membranaceis utrinque pubescentibus; pedunculis solitariis medio unibracteatis; perianthio glabriusculo inflato, limbo trilobo, lobis fere æqualibus subconniventibus. Near Corte Madera, California; April 16, (in flower.) A tall climbing species. Leaves 3–4 inches long, obtuse, velvety-pubescent when young, thinly but softly pubescent when mature. Peduncles an inch and a half or two inches in length, thickened and pubescent under the flower, furnished near the middle with a small ovate bract. Flower dull purple at the base and tip, paler in the middle, about an inch and a half long from the base to the curvature. This rare plant (which we have only received besides from Dr. Hulse, who collected it in the Sacramento valley) resembles A. tomentosa, *Nutt.;* but that has naked peduncles and narrow villous flowers, the lobes of which are widely spreading.

Asarum Hookeri, *Fielding, Sert. Plant. fol. & t.* 32. A. Canadense, *β. Hook. Fl. Bor.-Amer.* 2, *p.* 139. Hill-sides and low places, Downieville, Yuba; Duffield's Ranch, and mountains near Oakland, California; March—April. The specimens from all these stations have the lobes of the flower furnished with a long caudate acumination, and the leaves are much more glabrous than in A. Canadense; but Bentham (*Pl. Hartweg, p.* 335) says that specimens from the mountains of Sacramento are more like the eastern A. Canadénse, of which he thinks the Californian plant may be only a variety.

CHENOPODIACEÆ.

TELOXYS CORNUTA (n. sp.): foliis repando-dentatis pinnatifidisque calycis laciniis acutis dorso brevi-rostellatis, semine compresso margine obtusissimo. Rocky places, Hurrah creek, New Mexico. Near San Francisco mountain, Western New Mexico, *Dr. Woodhouse*, (omitted by accident in the botany of Sitgreaves' report); Wright's Coll., No. 1735. Gregg collected the plant near Saltillo, Mexico, (No. 390.) T. aristata differs in the entire leaves, inappendiculate glabrous calyx with obtuse segments, and acutely margined lenticular seeds. T. cornuta is commonly about a foot or 15 inches high, and is often very much branched. The leaves are deeply pinnatifid, with 2–3 distant lobes on each side. The calyx is beset with minute elevated glands, and on the upper part of the back of each segment is a short acute spine or tooth, so that in fruit the calyx appears somewhat stellate. The seed is exactly orbicular, thick, rounded on the margin, and closely covered with the utricle, which strongly adheres to its surface. In T. aristata the utricle separates spontaneously from the seed.

The genus Teloxys was established by Moquin on Chenopodium aristatum, and has hitherto consisted of that species only. Linnæus, in the second edition of the Species Plantarum, referred to C. aristatum, the Chenopodium Virginicum of his first edition, regarding it as a variety only. Dr. Gray, who saw the original specimens in the Linnæan herbarium, informs me that the plant is nothing more than Suæda maritima; and yet it is difficult to understand how the description of Chenopodium Virginicum, in the Species Plantarum, (ed. 1,) could have been drawn from that plant. The first part of the character ("foliis linearibus obtusis canaliculatis") agrees sufficiently well, but the latter portion ("peduncularibus axillaribus dichotomis") is quite inapplicable. We greatly doubt whether a Teloxys has ever been found in any of the older United States. Moquin (in DC. Prodr.) states that he has seen Mexican specimens of T. aristata in the Vienna herbarium, but it is more than probable that the plant which he refers to is our T. cornuta. Without the leaves, (which fall away late in the season,) the two species are not distinguishable except by the use of a lens.

CYCLOLOMA PLATYPHYLLUM, *Moq. Chenop. p.* 18, *& DC. Prodr.* 13, *pars* 2. *p*, 60. Salsola platyphylla, *Michx.* Sand-hills of the Canadian River; September: flowers and fruit.

CHENOPODIUM ALBUM, *Linn.* Alluvions of the Upper Canadian; September. C. subspicatum, *Nutt.* is hardly distinct.

CHENOPODIUM HYBRIDUM, *Linn.; Moq. in DC. l. c. p.* 68. With the last.

BLITUM CAPITATUM, *Linn.; Moq. l. c. p.* 83. Ravines, Sandia mountains, New Mexico; October. It is difficult to believe that the last three species could have been introduced into a region so far removed from settlements of the whites.

BLITUM BONUS-HENRICUS, *Reich.; Moq. in DC. Prodr.* 13, (*pars* 2,) *p.* 85; *Torr. Fl. N. York* 2, *p.* 136. Plains and banks of the Sacramento, California; April 24.

OBIONE LENTIFORMIS, *Torr. in Sitgreaves' Report, p.* 169, *t.* 14, *β* RHOMBIFOLIA: foliis rhomboideo-ovatis undulatis. On Williams' River of the Colorado of California; February, (with fruit of the preceding autumn.) This species forms impenetrable thickets twelve feet high! The leaves are much larger than in the specimens collected in Captain Sitgreaves' expedition.

OBIONE HYMENELYTRA, *Torr. in Emory's Rep. of Mex. Bound. Surv.* (*ined.*) (Tab. XX.) Hills and gravelly places, on Williams' River. This species was found by Dr. Parry and by Colonel Fremont on the Gila. It is remarkable for its large broad membranaceous fruit-bracts, and roundish-deltoid coarsely and sharply toothed leaves.

OBIONE POLYCARPA, *Torr.* (*in Emory's 1st Report, p.* 149, *sine char.*): suffruticosa, ramosissima; ramulis gracilibus paniculatis; foliis minutis sessilibus obovato-oblongis obtusis integerrimis albido-farinosis; bracteis orbicularibus, supra mediam distinctis argute grosse-dentatis, utrinque cristatis. With the preceding. Leaves 3–5 lines long, crowded. Fruit abundant, aggregated on the long slender branchlets. Fructiferous bracts about 2 lines in diameter.

OBIONE CANESCENS, *Moq. l. c. p.* 212. Llano Estacado; September; fruit. The specimens belong to the form with broadly winged fruit-bracts.

OBIONE ARGENTEA, *Moq. l. c. p.* 115. Atriplex argentea, *Nutt. Gen.* 1, *p.* 198. Upper waters of the Canadian; with ripe fruit, in which state it is seldom collected. The fructiferous bracts are somewhat orbicular, the margin deeply and acutely toothed, and the disk is often more or less cristate with leafy appendages.

EUROTIA LANATA, *Moq. l. c. p.* 121. Diotis lanata, *Pursh, Fl.* 2, *p.* 602. With the last, abundant; September. Hooker refers this to E. ceratoides, but we are inclined to regard it as a distinct species.

CORISPERMUM HYSSOPIFOLIUM, *Linn.; Moq. l. c., p.* 140. C. hyssopifolium, *Nutt. Gen.* 1, *p.* 4. Sandy ravines on the Canadian; also banks of streams, Galisteo, New Mexico; September, October.

SUÆDA MARITIMA, *Dumort.; Torr. Fl. N. York*, 2, *p.* 141. Chenopodina maritima, *Moq. in DC. Prodr.* 13, *pars* 2, *p.* 161. Salsola depressa, *Pursh, Fl.* 1, *p.* 197, *excl. syn.* Wet saline soils along the Canadian River; August, September.

SUÆDA FRUTICOSA, *Forsk.; Moq. l. c. p.* 156. Var.? MULTIFLORA: floribus 6–10 glomeratis, foliis carnosis compressis. Llano Estacado. A shrubby much branched plant, apparently 3–4 feet high. The branches are of a light-brown color, and marked with little knobs, the cicatrices of fallen leaves. Lower leaves not seen; those of the primary branches are nearly half an inch long, and more than half a line wide, compressed, (not semiterete.) The flowers are very numerous, and are crowded on the axils of the leaves. Sepals oblong, a little fleshy, concave and somewhat cucullate at the extremity, the narrow margin scarious. Seeds horizontal and vertical in the same plant, black and shining, with a short rostrum. We fully agree with Fenzl (in Ledeb. Fl. Ross. 3, p. 777) in restoring Chenopodina to Suæda—the only character on which the former genus was founded being inconstant. There are several other species of Suæda, in which both vertical and horizontal seeds are found on the same plant.

SARCOBATUS VERMICULARIS, *Torr. in Emory's Rep. p.* 150, and in *Sitgreaves' Rep. p.* 169. Batis? vermicularis, *Hook.* Alluvions of the Rio Grande, near Albuquerque; October; in fine fruit.

AMARANTHACEÆ.

MONTELIA TAMARISCINA, *Gray. Man. ed.* 2, *p.* 370. Amaranthus tamariscinus, *Nutt. in Trans. Amer. Phil. Soc.* (*2d ser.*) 5, *p.* 165. Wet ravines, Deer creek, Indian Territory; August.

AMARANTUS ALBUS, *Linn.; Moq. in DC. Prodr.* 13, *pars* 2, *p.* 264. Sandy ravines near the Canadian River; September.

AMARANTUS RETROFLEXUS, *Linn.; Moq. l. c., p.* 258. A. græcizans, *Torr. Fl. N. York* 2, *p.* 144. Ravines near Santa Antonito, New Mexico; and prairies (especially around marmot burrows) along the Canadian River; September, October.

GOSSYPIANTHUS TENUIFLORUS, *Hook. Ic. t.* 251; *Moq. l. c., p.* 337. Dry prairies near the Cross Timbers of the Canadian River. Root-stock stout and dark colored, branching into several short heads. Stems numerous prostrate 3–4 inches long. Leaves a little pubescent underneath. Filaments very thin and translucent.

FRŒLICHIA GRACILIS, *Moq. l. c. p.* 420. Dry prairies and rocky places along the Canadian to the Rio Grande. On Hurrah creek a dwarf form (1–4 inches high) was found, in which the inflorescence was reduced to a single terminal cluster or head.

FRŒLICHIA FLORIDANA, *Moq. l. c.* Oplotheca floridana, *Nutt. Gen.* 2, *p.* 79; *Bart. Fl. N. Amer.* 2, *t.* 59; *Hook. Ic. t.* 256. Sand banks of the Canadian; August. F. Drummondii of Moquin seems to be scarcely a variety of this species. The fructiferous calyx has a narrowly winged and irregularly toothed margin. At the base there is usually a central tooth or protuberance on one side, and two protuberances on the other. The same characters occur in F. gracilis.

NYCTAGINEÆ.

OXYBAPHUS GLABRIFOLIUS, *Vahl, Enum.* 2, *p.* 40; *Choisy in DC. Prodr.* 13, (*pars* 2,) *p.* 431. O. lævis, *Benth. Bot. Sulph. p.* 44. Los Angeles; March 21; and mountains near the Colorado, Mexico.

This species is very variable in its pubescence. If O. lævis of Bentham be correctly referred here, it is sometimes wholly glabrous. Our California specimens usually have the branches, peduncles, and margin of the leaves slightly pubescent. Those from near the Colorado have the branches strongly pubescent, and both surfaces of the leaves more or less so. The perianth is rose-colored, and the 5 lobes are emarginate.

QUAMOCLIDION OXYBAPHOIDES, *Gray in Sill. Jour.*, 2*d ser.* 15, *p.* 320. Rocky places, Llano Estacado; September. The involucre is unequally 4–5 cleft. Fruit black when dried before ripening, but mottled when mature.

ABRONIA CYCLOPTERA, *Gray l. c.*, *p.* 319. A. (Tripterocalyx) micrantha, *Torr. in Frem.* 1*st Rep.*, *p.* 96. Banks of the Rio Grande, near Albuquerque, New Mexico; October; with flowers and fruit, the latter more than an inch in length, with very broad membranaceous wings.

ABRONIA MELLIFERA, *Dougl. in Hook. Bot. Mag. t.* 2879; *Moq. in DC. Prodr.* 13, (*pars* 2,) *p.* 435. Sandy hills, Indian Territory; September; with flowers and ripe fruit; and sandy hills near the Colorado, California; February. The figure in the Botanical Magazine (copied by Lindley, *Veg. Kingd.*) erroneously shows the embryo with two cotyledons. We have shown, elsewhere, that in all the species of Abronia, the inner cotyledon is either wholly suppressed, or only rudimentary. Near Galisteo, New Mexico, Dr. Bigelow collected a dwarf variety of A. mellifera, with spatulate leaves tapering at base to a long petiole, and large membranaceous involucres with broadly ovate segments. The fruit resembled that of the ordinary form.

ABRONIA ARENARIA, *Menz. in Hook. Exot. Fl. t.* 193; *Choisy in DC. Prodr.* 13, (*pars* 2,) *p.* 435. Sand-hills near the sea-shore, Punta de los Reyes, California; April 17.

POLYGONACEÆ.

ERIOGONUM POLIFOLIUM, *Benth. in DC. Prodr.* 14, *pars* 1, *p.* 12. Mountain aroyos near Williams' River; February 9. Involucres usually in a capitate cluster, but sometimes on short rays.

ERIOGONUM CORYMBOSUM, *Benth. l. c.* Var. DIVARICATUM, *Torr. & Gray, in Beckwith's Rep.*, *p.* 123. On sandy hills, near Inscription Rock, Western New Mexico; November 18.

ERIOGONUM LONGIFOLIUM, *Nutt. in Trans. Amer. Phil. Soc. n. ser.* 5, *p.* 164. Dry prairies, Upper Cross Timbers of the Canadian River; August.

ERIOGONUM ORTHOCLADON, *Torr. in Sitgreaves' Rep. p.* 167, *t.* 9; *Benth. in DC. Prodr.* 14, *pars.* 1, *p.* 15. Sandy hills, Albuquerque, New Mexico.

ERIOGONUM ALATUM, *Torr. l. c. p.* 168, *t.* 8. Var. GLABRIUSCULUM: caule foliisque vix pube. scentibus; involucris bracteolisque glabris. High prairies, near the Upper Canadian. Plant 4–5 feet high. Differs from the ordinary form of this species in being taller, nearly glabrous in all its parts, (except a slight hairiness on the leaves and lower part of the stem,) and in the slender and more numerous branches. It may be E. alatum β. elatum, *Benth. in DC. Prodr*- 14, *pars.* 1, *p.* 7.

ERIOGONUM LACHNOGYNUM, *Torr. mss.; Benth. l. c. p.* 8. (Tab. XIX.) Hill-sides and rocky dells of the Llano Estacado; September. A remarkable species. At the base of each flower there is an ovate-lanceolate bract, (not represented in the figure,) and inside this a pair of spatulate-linear opposite bracteoles. This appears to be the normal structure in the genus, but we have not detected it in any other species. Usually the bracteoles are solitary, or more rarely, a pair of opposite ones to each flower.

ERIOGONUM WRIGHTII, *Torr. Mss.; Benth. l. c. p.* 15. Gravelly plains, near Albuquerque, New Mexico; October. Stem suffruticose, decumbent, throwing up erect branches which are 6–12 inches high. Flowers very numerous, many of them expanding together, and thus forming heads which are more than half an inch in diameter. Involucre acutely 5-toothed. Segments of the perianth obovate, the exterior a little broader than the others; ovary and achenium with the beak hispid.

ERIOGONUM JAMESII, *Benth. in DC. Prodr.* 14, *pars* 1, *p.* 7. Hills on the upper waters of the Canadian River. September.

ERIOGONUM TENELLUM, *Torr. Ann. Lyc. N. York*, 2, *p.* 241; *Benth. l. c. p.* 19. With the last; in rocky places.

ERIOGONUM ROTUNDIFOLIUM, *Benth. l. c. p.* 21. Sandia mountains, New Mexico; October. Bracteoles 2, spatulate-linear, glandular on the margin, and fringed also with long hairs.

ERIOGONUM EFFUSUM, var. LEPTOPHYLLUM, *Torr. in Sitgreaves' Rep. p.* 168. Hills and ravines, Cienegella, New Mexico; October.

ERIOGONUM EFFUSUM, var.? NUDICAULE: caule brevissimo ramoso basi lignoso; foliis subradicalibus lanceolato-linearibus albolanatis, scapis glabriusculis superne bis bi-trichotomis, involucris turbinato-campanulatis glabris 5-dentatis, dentibus rotundatis brevibus, perigoniis glabris, basi obtusis, laciniis oblongis subæqualibus; ovario glabro. In pine and cedar woods, near Galisteo, New Mexico. Branches of the stem or caudex scarcely an inch long. Leaves 2 inches long, 2–3 lines wide, revolute on the margin (in the dry specimens), tomentose on both sides, but less so above. Scapes 8–12 inches high, naked, mostly twice three-forked with very short bracts at the base of the somewhat spreading branches. Perianth pale purple, segments emarginate, the exterior ones a little broader. Achenium ovate with a long tapering summit, slightly scabrous on the angles above. Embryo incurved-excentric. This resembles some forms of E. effusum, especially the var. rosmarinoides, *Benth.*, but differs in the very short stem, nearly glabrous elongated scapes or peduncles and involucres, looser and more spreading inflorescence. Its habit is that of E. lachnogyuum, but it belongs to a different section, the embryo being strongly curved.

ERIOGONUM POLYCLADON, *Benth. l. c. p.* 16. Gravelly hills, near Albuquerque, New Mexico; October. Annual. Bracteoles filiform, not glandular, with very long fringed hairs on the margin.

CHORIZANTHE MEMBRANACEA, *Benth. in Linn. Trans.* 17, *p.* 419, *t.* 17, *f.* 11. Hill-sides, etc., Knight's Ferry, Stanislaus River; also near Sonora, California; May.

CHORIZANTHE PUNGENS, *Benth. l. c. t.* 19, *f.* 2. With the preceding species, May 8.

PTEROSTEGIA DRYMARIOIDES, *Fisch. & Mey. Ind. Sem. Hort. Petrop.* 1835; *Hook. & Arn. Bot. Beech. p.* 387, *t.* 90. Rocky places, near Marysville; also at Knight's Ferry, Stanislaus River; Napa Valley; and mountains near San Gabriel, March—May. This plant is variable in the size and divisions of the leaves. In the specimens from near San Gabriel the leaves are deeply two-parted, and the divisions two-cleft, with entire or bifid segments. We have little doubt that among its forms must be included P. diphylla and P. microphylla.

ACANTHOGONUM, Nov. Gen.

Involucrum 1–2-florum, tripartitum, basi indurata subtrigonum, segmentis inæqualibus ovatis lanceolatisve apice subulato-pungentibus. Flos hermaphroditus sessilis, ima basi involucri reconditus. Perigonium æqualiter 6-dentatum, fructiferum clausum. Stamina 6, perigoni fauc inserta, dentibus ejusdem opposita: filamenta brevissima. Styli 3, breves; stigmata capitata. Achenium ovato-trigonum, acutum, semen conforme. Embryo in axi albuminis farinacei curvatum; cotyledonibus orbiculatis planis; radicula elongata supera. Herba annua, nana, breviter ramosa, rigida; foliis imis ovatis longe petiolatis tomentosis, reliquiis spinescenti-subulatis confertissimis patentibus exstipulatis; involucris axillaribus sessillibus bracteola trifida spinescente fulcratum.

ACANTHOGONUM RIGIDUM. On Williams' river, a fork of the Colorado, Western New Mexico. Only winter vestiges of this plant were collected by Dr. Bigelow; but the specimens seem to show that it is a new genus of Eriogoneæ. It will stand next to Mucronea, from which it differs in habit, in the short involucral tube, in the 6-toothed closed perianth, and in the insertion of the stamens. The whole plant above ground is not more than 3 or 4 inches high. The lower and radical leaves are about half an inch long, clothed with a white tomentum, and stand on petioles which are nearly an inch in length. The upper leaves are destitute of stipules, rigid, subulate, and spreading. In nearly every axil is a solitary sessile involucre, which is 3-parted; the segments varying from ovate to narrowly lanceolate; all of them mucronate and pungent, carinate, strongly 3-nerved, with transverse connecting veins; the closed base is obtusely triangular, and contains a single sessile flower. Perianth membranaceous, 6-toothed; the teeth ovate, very hairy. Stamens apparently only 6; filaments inserted in the throat opposite the teeth of the perianth; anthers not seen. The achenium is sometimes 3-valved at the summit, or at least easily splits when old. What we have called subulate rigid upper leaves may be only the spine-like persistent midribs.

RUMEX MARITIMUS, *Linn.; Meisn. in DC. Prodr.* 14, *pars* 1, *p.* 59. Low places on the Rio Grande, near Albuquerque. A dwarf form.

RUMEX DOMESTICUS, *Hartm.; Hook. Fl. Bor.-Amer.* 2, *p.* 129? Sandy plains and hills near the Mohave creek, California; March. The fruit too young for determining with certainty the species.

POLYGONUM PARONYCHIA, *Cham. & Schlecht. in Linnœa.* 3, *p.* 51; *Hook. & Arn. Bot. Beech.*, *p.* 158. Near San Francisco; April 3.

POLYGONUM BISTORTA, *Linn.; Meisn. Polyg. p.* 91. P. bistortoides, *Pursh, Fl.* 1, *p.* 371. Laguna of Santa Rosa creek, New Mexico; May 1.

LAURACEÆ.

OREODAPHNE CALIFORNICA, *Nees, Syst. Laur. p.* 463. Tetranthera? Californica, *Hook. & Arn. Bot. Beech. p.* 150. Laurus? regia, *Dougl. in Hook. Comp. Bot. Mag.* Umbellularia Californica, *Nutt. Sylv.* 1, *p.* 87. Drimophyllum pauciflorum, *Nutt. l. c. t.* 22, *excl. syn.* Mountains near San Gabriel, and Oakland, California; March—April, (in flower.) On the Upper Sacramento this fine tree attains a height of 50–70 feet. Douglas estimated the height of some individuals at 120 feet. Towards the south its altitude is much less, being from 15–30 feet. By the slightest friction it emits a strong spicy odor, but is apt to excite sneezing. The fruit is globose, nearly an inch in diameter, and stands on a thick stalk. When immature it is green, but dark-purple when fully ripe. We have no doubt that Nuttall's Drimophyllum is identical with Oreodaphne Californica. His plate agrees very well with a common state of the plant, and also with an authentic specimen of Laurus regia of Douglas. The inhabitants of California call it Mountain Laurel and Spice-tree. It grows throughout the western part of the State, from the borders of Oregon to Santa Barbara.

THYMELACEÆ.

DIRCA PALUSTRIS, *Linn. Spec.* 1, *p.* 358; *Torr. Fl. N. York* 2, *p.* 163. Mountains near Oakland, California; April 4, (with flowers and young fruit.) We have never before received this plant from any part of the United States west of the Mississippi.

SANTALACEÆ.

Comandra umbellata, *Nutt. Gen.* 1, *p.* 157; *Hook. Fl. Bor.-Amer.* 2, *p.* 139, *t.* 179, *fig. A; Torr. Fl. N. York* 2, *p.* 160. Hill-sides, Sonora, California; May 9. This plant has a very extensive range both in latitude and longitude, being found from British America to Georgia and Texas, and from the Atlantic to the Pacific. In the south, and far to the west, it is often suffrutescent, which is not the case in the middle States. Mr. Stauffer, of Mount Joy, Pennsylvania, has clearly established the parasitism of Comandra to be similar to that which M. Mitten had previously ascertained of Thesium.

LORANTHACEÆ.

Phoradendron flavescens, *Nutt. in Jour. Acad. Phil. n. ser.* 1, *p.* 185; *Engelm. in Gray Pl. Fendl. p.* 59. Viscum flavescens, *Pursh, Fl.* 1, *p.* 114. V. Reichenbachianum, *Seem. Bot. Herald. p.* 294 *t.* 62. On Williams' River; February. The anthers are only one-celled, with a transverse terminal slit.

Var. pubescens, *Engelm. in Gray, Pl. Lindh.* 2, *p.* 212. Parasitic on Quercus agrifolia. Napa Valley, Corte Madera, &c., California. Differs from the ordinary form of P. flavescens only in its pubescence, and smaller leaves.

Var. orbiculatum, *Engelm. l. c.* Pass of Mount Hope, and near White Cliff Creek, Western New Mexico; on Quercus Emoryi. Fruit ripe in January. Dr. Bigelow found at Cajon Pass, on what seems to be a dwarf oak, a Phoradendron with ovate nearly sessile and very thick leaves, which are scarcely more than half an inch in length, and clothed (as well as the young branches) with a dense pubescence. There were only a few separate berries accompanying the specimens. It may be P. villosum of Nuttall. Our materials are scarcely sufficient for identifying the species.

Phoradendron pauciflorum (n. sp.): ramis teretibus; foliis spathulatis v. spathulato-linearibus enerviis junioribus pubescentibus demum glabratis crassis; spicis brevipedunculatis simplicibus capitatis oblongisve pauci-(4–8)-floris foliis multo brevioribus; floribus plerumque 3-lobis. On Juniperus occidentalis and Abies Douglasi, Duffield's Ranch, Sierra Nevada. Branches 3–6 inches long, stout. Leaves three-fourths of an inch to an inch long, 2–3 lines wide. Anthers 2-celled, opening by two terminal transverse chinks. There is an abortive ovary with a distinct style in the male flowers. Berries apparently white, about one line in diameter in the dried specimens. This seems to be a widely spread species. Dr. Gregg found it at San Antonio de los Alanzanes, Mexico. It also occurs in Sonora, and Mr. Wright collected it in New Mexico.

Phoradendron Californicum, *Nutt. l. c.; Engelm. l. c.* Williams' River, growing on Parkinsonia microphylla; also near the Colorado, on Cercidium floridum, bearing fruit in February, probably formed in the autumn of the preceding year. Specimens with small flowers were collected near Fort Yuma by Major Thomas. Branches pubescent when young, but at length nearly or quite smooth. Spikes, in the specimens from the Colorado, three-fourths of an inch long and many-flowered, with several approximated whorls; but often only 4–8-flowered. Berries globose, apparently reddish, about two lines in diameter. Perianth 3–4-lobed. Anthers oblong, 2-celled, adnate by the middle to the calyx; the cells opening longitudinally on their face the whole length of the anther. This species differs in the structure of the anthers from the character of Phoradendum as given by Nuttall and Engelmann. When dry, the whole plant is of a grayish-brown color.

Phoradendron juniperinum, *Engelm. l. c.* On Williams' River; also in the Desert, 50 miles west of the Colorado. It grows on different species of Juniperus. Only fruiting specimens were found. This is a common species in New Mexico, but we have never seen the male flowers.

Arceuthobium cryptopodum, *Engelm. in Gray, Pl. Lindh.* 2, *p.* 214. On Pinus brachyptera. Sierra Madre and Leroux's Spring, near San Francisco mountain, Western New Mexico. Our specimens are all female, and mostly in fruit. The plant is of a light-brown when dry. Dr. Engelmann (l. c.) was inclined to refer A. Oxycedri of Hooker's Fl. Bor.-Amer. to this species, but seeing that plant in my herbarium, he thought it was probably A. Americana, *Nutt.*

ARCEUTHOBIUM OXYCEDRI, *M. Bieb.?* A. campylopodum, var. macrathron, *Engelm. l. c.?* On Libocedrus decurrens, Duffield's Ranch, California. The female plant only. A foot long, and of a dark-brown when dry. Stems stout; the branches long and slender, somewhat quadrangular above; the length of the joints 2–3 times more than the diameter. Female flowers mostly 3-cleft. From the Rev. A. Fitch we have specimens of what is undoubtedly Engelmann's plant, collected on a Pinus between Stockton and Stanislaus. It is much smaller than the specimens from Duffield's Ranch, and the color is light-brown.

SAURURACEÆ.

ANEMOPSIS CALIFORNICA, *Nutt. in Tayl. Ann. Nat. Hist.* 1, *p.* 136; *Hook. & Arn. Bot. Beech. p.* 390 *t.* 92. Wet places on the Rio Grande, near Albuquerque; October.

CALLITRICHACEÆ.

CALLITRICHE VERNA, *Linn. Sp.* 1, *p.* 6; *Torr. Fl. N. York*, 2, *p.* 170, var. vulgaris, *DC. Prodr.* 3, *p.* 70. In water, near Tamul Pass, California; April 11. Styles twice as long as the fruit.

CALLITRICHE MARGINATA *n. sp.*: fructibus longepedunculatis; carpellis parallelis dorso alato-membranaceis; foliis lineari-spathulatis trinerviis. Muddy places along Mark West's creek, California; April 30. Upper California; *Rev. A. Fitch*, (locality not recorded.) Stem slender, branching, rooting in the mud. Leaves about one-third of an inch long, distinctly 3-nerved. Styles at first spreading, but finally reflexed over the fruit. Peduncles about two-thirds as long as the leaves, spreading or reflexed. Carpels strongly margined, or with a narrow wing on the back from the base to the summit. A well characterized species, resembling C. Nuttallii; *nob.* (C. pedunculosa, *Nutt. in Trans. Amer. Phil. Soc. n. ser.* 5, *p.* 140; not of Arnott, nor C. pedunculata *DC.*), but differs in the winged fruit. In C. Nuttallii the leaves are very obscurely 3-nerved, not veinless, as they are described.

DATISCACEÆ.

TRICERASTES GLOMERATA, *Presl, Rel. Hænk.* 2, *p.* 88, *t.* 64; *Benth. Pl. Hartw. p.* 335, *No.* 1951. Mokelumne Hill, and sides of rivulets, Sonora, California; May. Our observations on the male flowers of this genus agree with those of Bentham l. c. We have not seen the hermaphrodite flowers which he describes.

EUPHORBIACEÆ.

EUPHORBIA LEPTOCERA, *Engelm. Mss. in herb. Torr.* Prairies of Grass Valley, California; May 20, (fl. and fr.) We regret having mislaid Dr. Engelmann's description of this species. It will, however, be contained in his Monograph of North American Euphorbiæ, which will be published in a few months. The plant has a strong resemblance to E. Peplus, but is more nearly allied to E. commutata, *Engelm.*, (*in Gray's Manal, ed.* 2, *p.* 389,) from which, indeed, it is difficult to distinguish it.

EUPHORBIA MELANADENIA (sp. nov.): caule procumbente ramosissimo herbaceo; foliis breviter petiolatis suborbiculatis inequaliter cordatis crassiusculis integerrimis dense cano-pubescentibus; stipulis minutis; involucris solitariis; glandulis involucri transverse oblongis, appendicibus petaloideis semiorbiculatis; capsulis hirsutis; seminibus lævibus opacis. Low or wet places near San Gabriel, California; March 22. Leaves 2–3 lines in diameter. Glands black in dried specimens, but perhaps very dark purple in the living plant. Capsule without tubercles. This species appears to be annual, and belongs to the group that contains E. herniariodes.

GARRYACEÆ.

Garrya elliptica, *Lindl. Bot. Reg. t.* 1686; *Hook. & Arn. Bot. Beech. p.* 390. Rocky arroyos, near White Cliff Creek, a tributary of Williams' River, New Mexico. The specimens in the collection were gathered in February, and are all female, in fruit. The leaves of the flowering specimens are smaller than the ordinary form of this species, and they are not wavy: those of sterile branches are much larger.

Garrya Wrightii (sp. nov.): foliis elliptico-oblongis utrinque acutis mucronatis crassis planis opacis, margine muriculatis; racemis ramosis; bracteis lanceolatis basi connatis interdum foliaceis et vix connatis; floribus in quisque bractea solitariis masculis pedicellatis, fœmineis sessilibus. On rocks, base of San Francisco Mountain, New Mexico. This species is common at the Copper Mines, New Mexico, and is the same as No. 634 of Mr. Wright's collection of 1849, and No. 1789 of the collection made in 1851–'52. It is nearly allied to G. laurifolia, *Benth. Pl. Hartw. No.* 81 *and* 384; but that has rather obtuse and larger leaves, which are of a thinner texture and without the thickened muriculate margin. Endlicher (*Gen. Suppl. I, No.* 1900) has proposed to separate G. Fadyenii, *Hook. Ic. t.* 333, a native of Jamaica, as a genus, under the name of Fadyenia, on account of the sepals cohering at the tip in the male flower, the absence of a free portion of the perianth in the female, and the short thick recurved styles. In his Suppl. IV, No. 1899, he has added four other species from Mexico to this genus. In G. elliptica, however, (the original species,) the sepals cohere at the tip as much as they do in G. Fadyenii, nor have we detected in the pistillate flower of the former, the two teeth or free portion of the calyx described by Lindley; and the styles are more or less recurved in all the species. The genus Fadyenia is, therefore, without a distinctive character. G. Wrightii is easily distinguished by the roughish, slightly muriculate margin of the leaves. It is a shrub about three feet high. The leaves are 1½–2 inches long, and from three-fourths to nearly an inch wide, with a strongly mucronate tip.

Colonel Frémont found on the Upper Sacramento, "above the Great Cañon," in 1846, a Garrya nearly allied to this species. It may be thus characterized:

Garrya Fremontii: foliis lato-ellipticis utrinque acutis vix mucronatis planis glabris supra nitidis margine integerrimis; racemis (♂) ramosis; bracteis ovatis acuminatis supra medium connatis, inferioribus 3-floris; floribus pedicellatis. A shrub about four feet high. Only the male plant was found. The leaves are broader than in G. Wrightii, and are only slightly hairy in the youngest state. The spikes are 2–4 inches long, and seem to be pendulous. The bracts, by their union, form bidentate cups, which, on the lower part of the spike, and frequently throughout, are 6-flowered, (three flowers on each side.) This seems to be the normal inflorescence of the genus, for in G. elliptica, and often in G. Wrightii, besides the primary flower in each bract, there are two small rudimentary ones.

Another apparently undescribed species of this genus is No. 633 of Wright's Western Texas and New Mexican Collection, (1849.) It is also in the earlier collection of Lindheimer. We have only the male plant. The leaves (including the petioles) are 2½–3 inches in length, oblong and obovate, obtuse, slightly mucronate, nearly glabrous and somewhat shining above, pubescent underneath, smooth and even on the margin; spikes shorter than the leaves, bracts lanceolate or ovate, flowers on short pedicels. Lindheimer and Wright seem to be the only botanists who have collected it. We propose for it the name of G. Lindheimeri.

PLATANACEÆ.

Platanus racemosa, *Nutt. in Audubon's Birds t.* 362, *and North Amer. Sylv.* 1 *p.* 47, *t.* 15. P. Mexicana, *Moric. Pl. Nov. ou rar. d'Amer. t.* 26. P. Californica, *Benth. Bot. Sulph. p.* 54, *and Pl. Hartw. p.* 336. Arroyos and plains, near San Gabriel; March 23, (in flower, with balls of ripe fruit of the preceding year.) This species resembles P. orientalis much more than P. occidentalis.

BETULACEÆ.

ALNUS VIRIDIS, *DC. Fl. Franç.* 3 *p.* 304? Cajon Pass and Creek, California. The specimens are in very young leaf, with old female aments of the past season. The latter are oblong-ovate, and the fruit is narrowly winged. The leaves are glutinous, acute at the base, and doubly serrate. There are needed specimens in a more mature state in order to be certain of the species.

MYRICACEÆ.

MYRICA CALIFORNICA, *Cham. & Schlecht. in Linnœa* 6, *p.* 535; *Hook. Fl. Bor.-Am.* 2, *p.* 260; *Hook. & Arn. Bot. Beech. p.* 390. Near San Francisco; April 3, (only the male plant); near Monterey, *Mr. Rich*, (in fruit.) Hooker and Arnott are inclined to refer the plant to M. Xalapensis, *H.B.K.*

CUPULIFERÆ.

CASTANEA CHRYSOPHYLLA, *Dougl. in Hook. Fl. Bor.-Amer.* 2 *p.* 159; *Hook. Lond. Jour. Bot.* 1843, *t.* 16. Gravelly hills near Oakland, California. The plants found by Dr. Bigelow were only from 2–3 feet high, and yet they bore fruit. In Oregon, where it abounds on the Columbia, it is a large tree, sometimes growing 70 feet high. Dr. Parry and Mr. Rich found it at Monterey. It is a beautiful species, and well deserves cultivation. Nuttall, in his North American Sylva, asks whether this tree and Quercus densifolia, *Hook.*, may not be the same. The Castanea had not been figured when the Sylva of Mr. Nuttall was published, nor had he seen specimens of the plant.

QUERCUS ECHINACEA, *Torr. in Pl. of U. S. Expl. Exped.* (*ined.*): foliis perennantibus lanceolato-oblongis integerrimis vel serrato-dentatis, junioribus subtus cinereo-tomentosis demum glabratis; amentis masculis elongatis densifloris; fructibus sessilibus; cupula hemispherica, squamis filiformibus densis patulis vel reflexis apice plerumque uncinatis; glande brevi ovata. Tokeloma Creek, California; April 17; fruit of the preceding season was collected on the ground. This fine oak was first discovered by Mr. Brackenridge, on the upper waters of the Sacramento Creek, while attached to the United States Exploring Expedition. It was found also by Dr. Parry, botanist of the Mexican Boundary Survey, while under command of Major Emory. We have also received specimens of it from Mr. Burke, and the acorns from Dr. Andrews. It is a near ally of Q. densiflora, *Hook. & Arn.*, which is also a native of California, but is easily distinguished from that species by the remarkable scales of the cup. The leaves are exceedingly variable, for although they are usually more or less lanceolate-oblong, sometimes they are obovate. They are commonly obtuse, but occasionally quite acute, even on the same tree. In the specimens collected by Dr. Bigelow and by Mr. Burke, the leaves are 4–5 inches long, and sharply toothed, as in the chestnut. In those obtained by Mr. Brackenridge they are perfectly entire, except a few of them which are obscurely repand-dentate. The male aments are in clusters, about 4 inches long and about 3 lines in diameter; at their base are a few female flowers. The acorns are 2 or 3 together; the cup is an inch in diameter and thickly covered with rigid subulate or filiform scales, which are at length reflexed or recurved. The acorns are short and thick, about three-fourths of an inch long, obtuse, with a short abrupt point, and of a light-brown color. In the mountains this oak attains the height of 25 or 30 feet, with a trunk six inches in diameter.

QUERCUS CRASSIPOCULA, *Torr. in Williamson's Rep. cum tab.* Cajon Pass, Sierra Nevada. The specimens are not in fruit. According to Dr. Bigelow's notes, this species, in favorable situations, becomes a tree 40 feet high, but in poor soils it is a mere bush. In the former the leaves are toothed; in the dwarf plants they are entire.

Quercus densiflora, *Hook. & Arn. Bot. Beech. p.* 391; *Hook. Ic.* 4. *t.* 380; *Nutt. Sylv.* 1. *p.* 11. *t.* 5. Hill-sides on the Yuba, near Downieville, California. There are no acorns, and only old decayed cups of the preceding season, which show the characters very imperfectly. We are not certain but our specimens may belong to a form of the preceding species.

Quercus Emoryi, *Torr. in Emory's Rep.* 1 *p. t.* 9. San Francisco Mountain, and Aztec Pass, New Mexico. A species of Phoradendron frequently grows on this oak.

Quercus agrifolia, *Née. in Ann. Sc. Nat.* 3, *p.* 271; *Hook. Ic.* 3, *t.* 377; *Nutt. Sylv.* 1 *p.* 5, *t.* 2. Corte Madera, and Laguna of Santa Rosa Creek, California; April, May; with male catkins and old acorns. This is a dwarf species in most situations; often loaded with fruit when only 2 or 3 feet high. Sometimes, however, it becomes a tree 40–50 feet high, with a trunk of a foot or more in diameter. It varies greatly in the size, form, and dentures of the leaves, as well as in the size and shape of the acorns. Q. oxyadenia, *Torr. in Sitgreaves' Rep. t.* 17, is this species with the acorns fully developed.

Quercus tinctoria, *Bartram. Trav. p.* 37; *Michx. f. Sylv.* 1, *t.* 24, var. *Californica:* sinubus folii angustioribus, fructibus majoribus, cupula squamis triangulari-ovatis acutioribus. Hill-sides, Napa Valley. This is a common tree in California. It occurs throughout the valley of the Sacramento, and as far south as San Diego. We have not been able to point out characters sufficient to distinguish it specifically from the Q. tinctoria of the Atlantic States, and yet it is probably a distinct species. The qualities of the bark we had no means of determining. It presents some diversity in the size and lobes of the leaf; but the acorns vary more than in the eastern oak. They are generally larger, and the glands are sometimes more than two-thirds immersed in the cup, with the upper scales elongated; but more commonly the cup is much more shallow and the scales more nearly uniform in size. The largest acorns are an inch and a quarter long.

Quercus Garryana, *Hook. Fl. Bor.-Amer.* 2, *p.* 159; *Hook. & Arn. Bot. Beech. p.* 391; *Nutt. Sylv.* 1, *p.* 1, *t.* 1. Santa Rosa Creek, California. Dr. Bigelow found it growing only about 30 feet high; but in Oregon Mr. Nuttall saw trees of this species 90–100 feet in height, with a diameter of from 3 to 6 feet. It belongs to the section of the genus that includes the White Oak.

Quercus Hindsii, *Benth. Bot. Sulph. p.* 55; *Torr. Bot. of Calif. & Oregon, U. S. Expl. Exped. cum icon.* (ined.) Q. longiglanda, *Torr. in Frémont's Geogr. Mem. of Calif.* Plains near Marysville, Feather River, California. Common in the valley of the Sacramento. Dr. Parry found it as far south as Monterey. It is a tall tree with a trunk 3 feet in diameter, and is remarkable for the usually great length of its acorns. These are sometimes even two inches long, and either tapering to a point, or rather obtuse at the summit. Rarely they are somewhat curved. On some trees they are ovate. The cup is tuberculate with the thickened scales.

SALICACEÆ.

Salix Hindsiana, *Benth. Pl. Hartw. p.* 336, *No.* 1956. Swamps and river banks, Mark West's Creek; April 30, (male;) also valleys and ravines near Butte Mountains, Marysville, California; May 25, (in fruit.) Branches very slender, pale-brown, dull. Leaves about an inch and a half long and 2–3 lines wide, thinly pubescent, at first hoary, but when mature pale-green on both sides, very acute at each end. Aments appearing with the leaves, pedunculate, terminating the short lateral branchlets, about an inch long; the male often 2–3 together. Filaments hairy below the middle. Capsules sessile, pubescent, abruptly narrowed to a long beak; style short, but distinct; stigmas with 2 linear lobes. This species is allied to S. exigua. *Nutt. Sylv. I, p.* 75, but the leaves are narrower, perfectly entire, and not silky; the fertile aments shorter, etc. It also resembles No. 1873, Wright, but that has glabrous fruit, bright reddish-brown branchlets, paler leaves, etc.

Salix lasiandra, *Benth. l. c. No.* 1954. Near Bolinas Bay, California; April, in fruit. The fertile aments only were collected by Dr. Bigelow, while Mr. Bentham describes only the male flowers. There can be little doubt that our plant is the same as his. The fertile aments appear after the leaves are nearly unfolded, and are produced at the extremity of short lateral branches. They are cylindrical, and about two inches long. The capsules are smooth and distinctly pedicellate. Style short, but evident. Stigmas 2-lobed. Leaves 2½ inches long and 6–8 lines wide, distinctly serrulate. There are in Dr. Bigelow's collection more advanced specimens of what appears to be only S. lasiandra. The leaves are fertile, aments are larger, but in other respects there is little difference.

Salix Bigelovii (sp. nov.): foliis obovatis vel cuneato-oblongis obtusissimis integerrimis subtus griseo-pubescentibus supra glabratis nitidulis; amentis (fœmineis) brevi pedunculatis cylindricis elongatis crassis, basi bracteosis; ovariis pedicellatis acutiusculis glabris; stylo elongato; stigmatibus brevibus bilobis; squamis persistentibus villosis. Near San Francisco; April 8, (with immature fruit.) Twigs rather stout, slightly pubescent, dark-brown, and dull. Leaves 1½–2 inches long, and ½ to ¾ of an inch broad, on short petioles of a firm but not coriaceous texture. Female catkins nearly two inches long, and more than one-third of an inch in diameter; the peduncle 3–4 lines long; the small leafy bracts at base deciduous. Ovary ovate, supported on a distinct pedicel. Scale about one-fourth the length of the ovary, dark-brown, but the color is concealed by the strong villous pubescence. We know not what else to do with this well characterized willow but to describe it as a new species. It does not appear to have been noticed by any writer on the plants of California and Oregon. The species to which it seems nearest allied is S. planifolia of Hooker. The male flowers were not found. In the collection of Dr. Bigelow was a Salix with female catkins only, which is perhaps the same species as the one just described, but in a younger state. The leaves are silky-pubescent underneath, and slightly pointed.

Two or three other Salices were collected in California, but we are unwilling to decide on them without a more extensive study of all the allied species than we can give them at present.

URTICACEÆ.

Urtica urens, *Linn. Sp.* 2. *p.* 284; *Torr. Fl. N. York.* 2. *p.* 222. Plains near San Gabriel; March 23. Probably introduced from Europe.

HESPEROCNIDE, Nov. Gen.

Flores monoici. *Masc.* Calyx 4-partitum; foliolis æqualibus concavis patentibus. Stamina 4. Ovarii rudimentum. *Fem.* Perigonium oblongo-ovatum, ventricosum; ore minuto bidentato; Ovarium liberum, ovatum, sessile; stigma sessile, pencillatum. Achenium lato, ovatum lenticulari-compressum, calyce membranaceo immutato tectum. Herba annua Californica; pilis urentibus; foliis oppositis ovatis petiolatis dentatis; floribus laxe glomeratis axillaribus, masculi et fœminei in iisdem glomerulis.

Hesperocnide tenella.—Shady rocks, Napa Valley, California; April 25. Stem slender, 3–8 inches high, simple, armed with scattered conspicuous stinging hairs. Leaves broadly ovate, 5–8 lines in diameter; obtuse, serrate-dentate, beset with a few stinging hairs on both sides, and finely ciliate on the margin; petiole about one-third the length of the lamina. Axillary glomerules 15–20-flowered, on short pedicels, mostly female, there being usually only one or two males in a cluster. *Male.* Calyx deeply 4-parted; the segments concave and somewhat saccate at the summit. Stamens nearly twice as long as the calyx. In the centre of the flower is the rudiment of an ovary. Female flowers articulated to a short stalk. Calyx clothed with short uncinate hairs, acute, the orifice minute, bidentate. Ovary loosely but completely enclosed in the calyx. Stigma terminal, nearly sessile, consisting of a tuft of short-jointed hairs. Achenium enclosed in the thin membranaceous calyx, orbicular-ovate, acute, somewhat coriaceous, brownish. Embryo in thin albumen; cotyledons transversely reniform-orbicular; radicle cylindrical rather shorter than the cotyledons. This little urticaceous plant seems to have been overlooked hitherto. It resembles Bœhmeria, but differs in the inflorescence, pencilliform stigma, and in some other characters. It is still more nearly related to the East Indian genus Pouzolzia, which differs in the "stigma elongatum," and in the fructiferous calyx being "accretum vel 2–4-alatum." The habit is also different: Pouzolzia consisting of perennial shrubs, or under shrubs, with entire leaves.

CONIFERÆ.

EPHEDRA ANTISIPHILITICA, *Berland.; Endl. Syn. Conif. p.* 263. On hills between the Canadian and the Pecos, also along Williams' Fork, (not in flower.)

TAXUS BREVIFOLIA, *Nutt. Sylv.* 3. *p.* 86, *t.* 108. T. baccata, *Hook. Fl. Bor.-Am.* 2, *p.* 167, (ex parte.) T. Lindleyana, *Murray in Edinb. Phil. Mag. April*, 1855. Mammoth Grove, and hill-sides near Downieville; May. A small tree in California, but in Oregon it sometimes occurs 60 feet high, with a trunk 2 or 3 feet in diameter. We follow Mr. Nuttall in separating the Yew of the Northwest coast from the Taxus baccata of Europe. We have not, however, found the differences pointed out by Mr. Nuttall to be constant. The leaves are not always shorter than in the European species, and in T. Canadensis; nor are they flatter than in the other species, and the male aments, when fully grown, are quite as large as in the Canadian Yew. The chief character in which T. brevifolia differs from T. baccata is the cuspidate leaves of the former. From T. Canadensis it is distinguished by its upright stem.

TORREYA CALIFORNICA, *Torr. in New York Jour. Pharm.* 3, *p.* 49. T. Myristica, *Hook. Bot. Mag. t.* 4780. Tokeloma Creek, near Tomales Bay; April 17, (male flower.) This is the famous *California Nutmeg*. It was first made known to North American botanists by the late Mr. Shelton, who travelled extensively in California. For a description of the plant, we refer to the works here quoted, and to Dr. Bigelow's report on the trees collected on the expedition.*

SEQUOIA SEMPERVIRENS, *Endl. Syn. Conif. p.* 198. Taxodium sempervirens, *Lamb. Pin. (ed.* 2,) 2, *t.* 64; *Gray, in Sill. Jour.* (*2d ser.*) 18, *p.* 150. Mountains near Oakland. The popular name of this tree in California is Redwood. Dr. Bigelow has given some interesting details respecting it in his special report.

SEQUOIA GIGANTEA, *Torr. in Sill. Jour. l. c.* Wellingtonia gigantea, *Lindl. Gardner's Chronicle, Dec.* 1853, *p.* 820 *and* 823; *Hook. Bot. Mag. t.* 4777 *and* 4778. A full account of this monarch of the Californian forest will be found in Dr. Bigelow's report, and in the Botanical Magazine, l. c. We have shown that in this tree, as well as in S. sempervirens, the leaves are dimorphous, as they are in many species of Juniperus. We have proved, also, that there is no generic difference between the two trees. The male aments of S. gigantea, which were not known to Lindley and Hooker, prove to be in all respects like those of S. sempervirens. S. gigantea, of Endlicher, (l. c.,) which is founded on Taxodium sempervirens, *Hook. & Arn. Bot. Beech. & Hook. Ic. t.* 379, (not of Humboldt,) has been ascertained by Hooker to be a species of Abies, (A. bracteata, *Bot. Mag. t.* 4640.)

LIBOCEDRUS DECURRENS, *Torr. in Smithson. Contrib.* 6. *p.* 7. *t.* 3. Hills, Duffield's Ranch, Sierra Nevada. Called *White Cedar* in California. It is in Hartweg's California Collection. Dr. Bigelow, in his report, states that the fruit is pendulous, and is incorrectly represented as erect in the plate just quoted; but in most of his own specimens the cones are erect.

PINUS EDULIS, *Engelm. in Wisliz. Rep. p.* 88; *Torr. in Sitgr. Rep. p.* 173, *t.* 20. Rocky places on the Llano Estacado; also near Hurrah Creek, New Mexico; September 20; with ripe seeds. Near Bill Williams' Mountain; January 5. A tree 40–50 feet high, called *Piñon* by the Mexicans, and *Nut Pine* by American travellers. It is found from 150 miles east of the Rio Grande to the Cajon Pass of the Sierra Nevada. How far it occurs to the southward we have

* Dr. Kellogg, of San Francisco, says that it sometimes attains the height of eighty feet, with a trunk 12–15 inches in diameter.

not been able to ascertain. In Mexico its place seems to be taken by Pinus Cembroides, *Zucc.*, which has been found by Dr. Parry on the mountains east of San Diego, in California.

PINUS LAMBERTIANA, *Dougl.; Lamb. Pin. ed.* 2, 1, *p.* 57, *t.* 34; *Endl. Syn. Conif. p.* 150; *Nutt. Sylv.* 3, *p.* 122. *t.* 114. On the eastern slope of the Sierra Nevada. A stately and beautiful tree, not excelled by any in California for its timber. A sweet substance, intermediate between resin and sugar, exudes from it when wounded and partially burned, so that it is generally known in California by the name of *Sugar Pine.*

PINUS ENGELMANNI. P. BRACHYPTERA, *Engelm. in Wisliz. Rep. p.* 89. Hill-sides, Sonora, California. Dr. Bigelow states that this valuable pine makes its first appearance in the mountains between the Pecos and the Rio Grande, and occurs in large quantities on the mountain ranges quite to the Sierra Nevada. See his report. It is called Yellow Pine and Pitch Pine in some parts of New Mexico. We have changed the specific name, because the wing of the seed is not short; Dr. Engelmann himself having ascertained that the specimens from which his description was drawn were not perfect. In our plant the wing is nearly an inch long. The leaves are sometimes nearly six inches in length.

PINUS FLEXILIS, *James, in Long's Exped.* 2, *p.* 27 *&* 35; *Torr. in Ann. Lyc. N. Hist. N. York.* 2, *p.* 249; *Nutt. Sylv.* 3, *p.* 107, *t.* 112. P. Lambertiana, *β. Hook. Fl. Bor.-Amer.* 2, *p.* 162, (ex. Nutt.) Sandia Mountains of New Mexico, "12,000 feet above the level of the sea," and on the San Francisco Mountain, in the western part of the same Territory. It is called *Rocky Mountain White Pine.* The ordinary height of the tree is from 40–50 feet, but Dr. Bigelow saw trunks of it that were more than 100 feet high. The seeds are edible like those of P. Cembra, which this species greatly resembles.

PINUS INSIGNIS, *Dougl. in Loud. Arb.* 4, *p.* 2265, *t.* 2170–2172. Mountains near Oakland; also on the south Yuba and on the Coast mountains, California. The cones, when fully grown, are about six inches long. They are usually gibbous and a little curved; the points of the scales much more developed on the gibbous side. The ordinary height of the tree is from 30–40 feet. This may be the same as the imperfectly described P. Californica, *Lois.*

PINUS SABINIANA, *Dougl. in Lamb. Pin.* (*ed.* 2,) 2, *p.* 146, *t.* 80; *Loud. Arb.* 4, *p.* 2246, *f.* 2138–40, 2142 *&* 2143; *Nutt. Sylv.* 3, *p.* 110, *t.* 103: Duffield's Ranch, etc., at the base of the Sierra Nevada. One of the species called *White Pine* in California. It is remarkable for its very large, heavy cones, the scales of which are produced into a long stout incurved point. See Dr. Bigelow's Report.

PINUS CONTORTA, *Dougl. in Loud. Encl. of Trees, p.* 975, *f.* 9148 *&* 915; *Endl. Syn. Conif. p.* 163. Near Sonora, California. Leaves about 2½ inches long. Cones scarcely 2 inches in length, ovate when closed, but nearly globose when expanded. Its range extends northward to Cape Disappointment.

ABIES DOUGLASII, *Lindl. in Penny Cyclop.* 1, *p.* 32; *Loud. Arb.* 4, *p.* 2319, *f.* 2230; *Nutt. Sylv.* 3, *p.* 129, *t.* 115; *Hook. Fl. Bor.-Amer.* 2, *p.* 162, *t.* 183. From the Sandia Mountains, between the Pecos and Rio Grande, to the coast range of California, on most of the higher mountains. It extends also north to Oregon. Its common name is *Douglas' Spruce.* See Dr. Bigelow's Report.

ABIES BALSAMEA, *Mill.?* Pinus balsamea, *Linn.?* Sandia and San Francisco Mountains; also on the Sierra Nevada. We name this tree on the authority of Dr. Bigelow, who says (in his report) that it is identical with the eastern species; but the leaves are considerably longer. No good cones came with the specimens.

JUNIPERUS TETRAGONA, *Schlecht. in Linnæa,* 13, *p.* 495? *Torr. in Sitgreaves' Rep. p.* 173, var. OSTEOSPERMA, near Bill Williams' Mountain, and on hills fifty miles west of the Colorado of California. This is the smooth-barked Juniperus of Sitgreaves' Report that was supposed might be J. tetragona, *Schlecht.* The short description given of that species by Schlechtendahl leaves us in doubt as to its identity with ours. The berries (not quite ripe) are said to be 3–4 lines in diameter, while in our plant they are nearly half an inch. Neither are the fructiferous branchlets nodding as in that species. Indians are said to use the berries as food. Travellers call this and the following species *Sweet-berried Cedar*. The seeds are as large as a small pea, and the shell is very thick and hard. The branchlets are about a line and a half in diameter. Leaves nearly as broad as long, very closely appressed, (there are no acicular ones in any of our specimens), obtuse, or sometimes rather acute, convex and marked with a depressed gland.

Juniperus pachyphlæa (n. sp.): arborea; foliis omnibus squamiformibus ovatis incrassato-gibbis acutiusculis, dorso glandula elliptica impressa; ramulis obtuse quadrangulatis, fructiferis erectis galbulos globosos minute tuberculatos trispermos brevioribus. Juniperus No. 1, *Torr. in Sitgreaves' Report, p.* 173. On the Zuñi Mountains, Western New Mexico. This is the thick-barked Juniperus of Captain Sitgreaves. It seems to be undescribed, and is distinguished from the preceding species by the character of the bark, and by the berries (which are also very large and sweet) being 3-seeded. From the gland of each leaf a little drop of turpentine exudes. It is possible this may be J. Mexicana, *Schlecht.*, which has berries half an inch in diameter; but in that species the leaves are acuminate, and the berries conspicuously tuberculate, especially at the apex.

Juniperus occidentalis, *Hook. Fl. Bor.-Amer.* 2, *p.* 166. J. Andina, *Nutt. Sylv.* 3, *p.* 95, *t.* 110. Common on the mountains of New Mexico, in various places along the route as far as the Zuñi mountains. The glands are very obscure in the young leaves, but are plainly to be seen in the older ones. The berries are larger and the branchlets much stouter than in J. Virginiana.

Juniperus Virginiana, *Linn. Spec. p.* 1471; *Michx. Sylv.* 2, *p.* 353, *t.* 155. Near Zuñi, Western New Mexico. Resembles the eastern plant, except that the leaves are all scale-like, and the berries are a little larger.

LEMNACEÆ.

Lemna trisulca, *Linn. Spec.* 1, *p.* 1376; *Kunth, Enum.* 3, *p.* 5. Stagnant waters, near San Francisco; mixed with Azolla Caroliniana; also on San Gabriel creek, California. We have never seen North American specimens of this species in flower or fruit.

Lemna minor, *Linn. l. c.; Kunth, l. c.* On the surface of running water; Williams' Fork of the Colorado of California; not in flower.

TYPHACEÆ.

Typha latifolia, *Linn.* Wet places, near Shawneetown, on the Canadian; August; in fruit.

NAIADACEÆ.

Potamogeton hybridus, *Michx. Fl.* 1, *p.* 101. In tributaries of the Canadian River; August; with mature fruit. Easily distinguished by its cristale spiral fruit.

Potamogeton pectinatus, *Linn.; Torr. Fl. N. York*, 2, *p.* 257. With the preceding. Nutlets obovate; the pericarp very thick, with a small lunate cavity.

JUNCAGINEÆ.

Triglochin maritimum, *Linn.; Torr. Fl. N. York*, 2, *p.* 261; *Kunth, Enum.* 3, *p.* 145. Low places in reach of the tide; San Francisco and Corte Madera, April. The fruit, in some of the species, agrees very well with Nuttall's T. elatum, which we fear is not distinct from this species.

ALISMACEÆ.

Damasonium Californicum, *Torr. in Benth. Pl. Hartw. p.* 341:* foliis oblongis seu lanceolatis basi cordatis obtusisve 3–5-nerviis; petals apice incisis; scapis adscententibus; verti-

* We much regret not having received the portion of Bentham's Plantæ Hartwegianæ that contains most of the Endogens.

cillis 6–9-floris; staminibus 6; carpellis 8–10 uniovulatis basi gibbosis abrupte longirostratis. (Tab. XXI. In water, near Ione Valley, California; May, (in flower and fruit.) Tuber subglobose. Leaves all radical, on elongated petioles; the lamina 2–3 inches long, and often nearly an inch wide. On young plants the leaves are much smaller, and sometimes not more than 2–4 lines wide. Scapes 12–18 inches high, usually several from one root; whorls (3–4) distant; the longer pedicels 1–2 inches in length. Flowers nearly twice as large as in A. Plantago, white. Sepals oblong, obtuse. Stamens shorter than the sepals; anthers oblong; filaments subulate from a somewhat dilated base. Ovaries usually 8–9, connected at the base, with a tapering straight style; each with a solitary ascending anatropous ovule arising from near the base of the cell. Carpels 4–5 lines long, much compressed, abruptly narrowed to a long rigid beak, always one-seeded. This species greatly resembles Damasonium stellatum, *Dalech.* of Europe, but that differs in the entire petals, and in the carpels being almost uniformly six, with the beak gradually narrowed from a broad base. It is a little remarkable to find a representative of the genus or subgenus Damasonium in the Western Hemisphere.

Echinodorus rostratus, *Engelm. in Gray, Man. Bot. ed.* 2, *p.* 439. Alisma rostrata; *Nutt. in Trans. Amer. Phil. Soc.* (*n. ser.*) 5, *p.* 159. On Mohave creek, California. The seeds of this plant are collected by the Mohave Indians, and used as food. The species is widely diffused. We have it from Key West, Florida, (*Mr. Blodgett*); Georgia, (*Dr. Leavenworth*); St. Louis, (*Dr. Engelmann*); and Texas, (*Drummond*, Coll. 2, No. 432); the last a form with narrower leaves, which are not cordate at the base.

Sagittaria simplex, *Pursh, Fl.* 2, *p.* 397; *Engelm. in Gray, Man. Bot. ed.* 2, *p.* 439. In water, near the Shawnee villages, on the Canadian River. August. Plant larger than usual; the blade of the leaves being 5–6 inches long, an inch or more in breadth, and the scape a foot high. Flowers not much larger than in Alisma Plantago.

JUNCACEÆ.

Luzula campestris, *DC.* L. campestris, var. *J. E. Meyer, in Linnæa,* 22, *p.* 407. Near San Francisco, April. Stem 1½–2 feet long. Leaves 3–4 lines wide. Flowers in sessile clusters, forming a compact ovate head. L. comosa of E. Meyer, if we may judge from specimens of Scouler and others referred to that species by Hooker and by Meyer himself, is hardly to be distinguished from L. campestris.

Juncus bufonius, *Linn. Sp. p.* 466; *Torr. Fl. N. York,* 2, *p.* 329. Damp places, Los Angeles, etc., California; May. Wholly like the eastern plant.

Juncus xiphioides, *C. A. Mey. in Reliq. Hænk.* 2, *p.* 143, *ex Kunth, Enum.* 3, *p.* 331; *Hook. & Arn. Bot. Beech. p.* 161. Low grounds, Napa Valley, California, April.

IRIDACEÆ.

Sisyrinchium Bermudiana, *Linn. Sp.* 2, *p.* 954; *Torr. Fl. N. York,* 2, *p.* 291, *var.* 1 & 2. Plains, near San Gabriel, California; March 23; mostly the *var.* mucronatum, and with flowers larger than in the eastern plant.

Sisyrinchium lineatum (*Torr. in Emory's Rep. Mex. Bound. ined.*): scapo late alato erecto simplici basi foliato; foliis linearibus gramineis; spatha triflora valde inæquali, folio exteriore flores longe superante; perianthio luteo lato-campanulato, phyllis obtusis, exterioribus 7-nerviis, interioribus 5-nerviis; filamentis brevibus glabris; capsula ovato-pyriforme. Punta de los Reyes, California; April 18. This species was first detected by Dr. Parry, who found it near San Diego. The flowers are one-third larger than in S. Bermudiana. Another yellow-flowered Sisyrinchium occurs in New Mexico.

Iris longipetala, *Herb. in Hook. & Arn. Bot. Beech. p.* 395. Grass Valley, and near San Francisco; May 19. Flowers as large as in I. versicolor.

IRIS DOUGLASIANA, *Herb. l. c.* Hill-sides, Grass Valley, California; May 19. The tube of the perianth is longer than in our original Douglasian specimens of this plant.

Var.? MAJOR: floribus majoribus; pedicellis elongatis (fere unc. longis). Corte Madera, California; April 10.

IRIS MISSOURIENSIS, *Nutt. Jour. Acad. Phil.* 7, *p.* 58? Sandia Mountains, New Mexico; October. In fruit only. Leaves rather rigid, 4–5 lines wide. Scape 1–2-flowered. Capsules 1–1¼ inch long, obtusely triangled, abruptly contracted at the base; statutes slightly prominent. Seeds obovate, somewhat compressed, reddish brown. Rhizoma thick and creeping, clothed with strong brownish lanceolate scales.

IRIS MACROSIPHON (sp. nov.): pumila; subcaulescens; rhizomate gracili; foliis angustis erectis; caule bifloro; perianthii imberbis tubo prælongo exserto; petalis apice denticulatis; ovario attenuato breviter pedunculato. Hill-sides, etc., Corte Madera, California; April 10. Leaves less than one-third of an inch wide. Stem (exclusive of the flower) 2–3 inches high, the bracts somewhat unequal. Flowers as large as in I. versicolor, bright purple. Tube of the perianth 2½ to 3½ inches long, very slender. Exterior sepals broadly obovate; the interior shorter.

MELANTHACEÆ.

PROSARTES HOOKERI: foliis sinu profundo cordatis caulem amplectentibus; umbellis 3–4-floris; perianthio basi obtuso, phyllis lanceolatis obtusiusculis; antheris linearibus glabris; stigmate fere integerrimo. Uvularia lanuginosa β. major, *Hook. Fl. Bor.-Am.* 2, *p.* 174. Mountains, near Oakland, California; April 4. Very near P. lanuginosa of the Atlantic States, but differs in the strongly cordate and clasping leaves, more numerous-flowered umbels, and in the form of the sepals.

PROSARTES TRACHYANDRA (sp. nov.): foliis oblongo-ovatis basi rotundatis seu vix subcordatis arcte sessilibus, inferioribus amplexicaulibus; umbellis 2–3-floris; perianthio basi subacuto, phyllis rhomboideo-lanceolatis; antheris oblongo-linearibus hirtellis; stigmate integerrimo. Hill-sides, Duffield's Ranch, Sierra Nevada; May 10. This species is easily distinguished from the preceding by its scarcely cordate leaves, broader attenuate sepals, and especially by its hispid anthers. The stem is about two feet high, and dichotomously branched. The flowers are as large as in Uvularia perfoliata, and of a greenish white color. At the base of each sepal is a distinct nectariferous pit.

VERATRUM VIRIDE, *Ait. Kew. ed.* 1, 3, *p.* 422; *Torr. Fl. New York*, 1, *p.* 317. Swamps, near the South Yuba, California; May, (with unexpanded flowers); and marshes, near San Gabriel, (leaves only.)

ANTICLEA NUTTALLII, Amianthium Nuttalii, *Gray, Melanth. Revis. in Ann. Lyc. N, York*, 4, *p.* 123. Amiantanthus Nuttallii, *Kunth, Enum.* 4, *p.* 181. River banks, Mokelumne Hill, and Sonora, California; May, (in fruit.) This is the *Poison* or *Death Camass* of the Northwest Indians. The root is a bulb the size of a musket ball, and is covered with a blackish skin, but is white within. We find the sepals to vary in form, from very obtuse and emarginate to acute or acuminate. The gland is a small, roundish, discolored spot, without a very distinct margin.

ANTICLEA FREMONTI: foliis lato-linearibus planis, racemo composito interdum simplici; sepalis ovatis brevi unguiculatis acutiusculis 5–7-nerviis, glandula superne dentata, dentibus cum basis nervos incrassatos confluentibus. Mountains near Oakland, April 4, (in flower.) Also found by Mr. Rich near Monterey; and by Colonel Frémont at Santa Cruz, (flowering in February,) and on the Uinta River, Utah; June, (in fruit.) It is No. 2009 of Hartweg's Californian collection. We have specimens of it collected in California by Mr. Douglas, so that it is probably Zygadenus chloranthus, *Hook. & Arn. Bot. Beech.* (excl. syn.) Bulb tunicated, about as large as a pigeon's egg. The stem is from a few inches to 4 feet high, simple or paniculately branched above, the branches terminating in simple racemes. Flowers hermaphrodite, three-fourths of an inch in diameter, the pedicels 1–2 inches long. Bracts linear-lanceolate, about half the length of the pedicels. Sepals greenish-white, narrowed into a short somewhat callous claw, from which spring 5–7 (rarely more) strong nerves. The gland is obscure, occupying the whole breadth of the base of the sepal, toothed on the upper edge, the teeth running into the thickened bases of the nerves. Stamens shorter than the sepals. Anthers roundish-kidney-form. Capsule about an inch long, almost as broad near the summit as at the base. Seeds broad and shining, compressed, variously indented, and angled. We have thrown this and the preceding species into the genus Anticlea of Kunth, as they are excluded from Amianthium by having a gland on the sepals. The character of Anticlea being drawn from A. Sibirica and A. glauca will require to be slightly modified to receive the species we here refer to it. Zigadenus will retain Z. glaberrimus and other species with a creeping rhizoma. Z. elegans of Pursh is pretty certainly Anticlea glauca.

SCOLIOPUS,* Nov. Gen.

Flores hermaphrodite. Perianthium petaloideum 6-phyllum, patens, deciduum; foliola subæquilonga; 3 exteriora oblongo-lanceolata, multiervia; 3 interiora, angusto-linearia. Stamina 3, perianthii exterioris foliolis opposita; filamenta subulata; antheræ oblongæ, extrorsæ. Ovarium liberum, sessile, triquetrum, uniloculare; placentis 3, parietalibus. Stylus brevis, trigonus, trifidus; lobis lineari-subulatis, apice intus stigmatosis. Ovula plurima, biserialia, adscendentia, anatropa. Capsula (immatura) oblonga, subalato-triquetra, polysperma. Semina compressa, raphe valida percursa. Embryo haud visus. Herba Californica, glabra; caule spithameo e rhizomate brevi erecto vaginato apice diphyllo; foliis ovalibus 7–9-nerviis membranaceis basi vaginantibus umbellam sessilem amplectentibus: pedicellis unifloris prælongis nudis flexuosis, in fructu tortuosis.

Scoliopus Bigelovii. (Tab. XXII.) Tamul Pass, Marin county, not far from San Francisco, on the opposite side of the bay; past flowering early in April. We have specimens in full flower, collected by Mr. Samuels, but in what part of California we have not been informed. The leaves are 6–8 inches long and 2–4 inches broad, varying from acute to rather obtuse. They are marked with from 5 to 7 primary nerves, which are narrowly winged on the under surface, and above they are sprinkled with minute purple dots. The pedicels are from 7 to 12 or more in number, 3–8 inches long, about the size of a packthread, and more or less tortuous. Dr. Bigelow informs us that they spread out and lie upon the ground after flowering. The exterior leaflets of the perianth (or rather sepals) are about 7 lines long, apparently of a dull purplish-color, and widely spreading. The inner leaflets, or petals, are scarcely half a line wide, and about the length of the sepals. Stamens one-third the length of the sepals, and inserted at their base: anthers more than a line long, manifestly extrorse. Ovary tapering upward; style 3-cleft nearly to the base; the segments subulate, recurved. Capsule (immature) about two-thirds of an inch long, acute at the base, apparently loculicidal. Ripe seeds not known. This remarkable new genus is placed at the end of Melanthaceæ chiefly on account of its extrorse anthers, notwithstanding its one-celled fruit and parietal placentation. The somewhat dichlamydeous flowers are suggestive of Trilliaceæ, but the extrorse anthers, as well as other characters, would seem to forbid its being placed in that group. In Melanthaceæ, however, Tofieldia and Pleea have introrse anthers. If it were not for the loculicidal placentation, (so rare a character in Endogens,) we might regard Scoliopus as intermediate between Melanthaceæ and Trilliaceæ.

LILIACEÆ.

Erythronium grandiflorum, *Pursh, Fl.* 1, *p.* 231; *Lindl. in Bot. Reg. t.* 1786; *Kunth, Enum.* 4, *p.* 218. Hills near Forest City, California; May 21. All the specimens from this locality are one-flowered. The stigma is manifestly 3-cleft, with the segments recurved.

* From ϛκολιος and πους, in allusion to the tortuous pedicels.

ERYTHRONIUM GRANDIFLORUM, var. MULTIFLORUM: foliis immaculatis; floribus 1–6 racemosis; sepalis lanceolatis acuminatis a basi fere reflexis; stigmate clavato-capitato. Hill-sides, Downieville, California; May 21. Some of the scapes, which had apparently been stung by an insect, were 10–15 flowered. Sepals bright lilac, yellow at the base on the inside.

FRITILLARIA KAMTSCHATCENSIS, *Fisch. in Hook. Fl. Bor.-Am.* 2, *p.* 181, *t.* 193, *A.* F. biflora, *Lindl. Bot. Reg. fol.* 1663; *Hook. & Arn. Bot. Beech. p.* 397. Laguna of Santa Rosa Creek, California; May, (in fruit.) The specimens are mostly single-flowered; stem about 14 inches high, mostly naked above. Lowest leaves verticillate in threes, the others few and scattered. Capsule subglobose, obtusely 6-angled. A variety? from hill-sides, Sonoma, has the stem 2-flowered, and the (immature) capsule acutely 6-angled.

FRITILLARIA MUTICA, *Lind. l. c.; Hook. & Arn. l. c.* San Francisco, April 30, (in flower;) mountains near Oakland, California, April 4, (also in flower;) hill-sides, Martinez, April 23, (in fruit, but immature.) The capsule of this species is strongly 6-winged, as in F. lanceolata, *Pursh,* from this species is hardly distinct.

FRITILLARIA LILIACEA, *Lindl. l. c.; Hook. & Arn. l. c.* Hill-sides near Nevada; May 21, (flower.)

FRITILLARIA PARVIFLORA (sp. nov.): foliis anguste lanceolato-linearibus, infimis verticillatis, superioribus sparsis; floribus sparsis longe racemosis nutantibus; bracteis pedicellos recurvos multo longioribus; perianthio basi subangusto; stylo usque ad medium fere trifido; capsula hexaptera. Hill-sides near Murphy's, California; May 16, (in flower.) This species is near F. lanceolata, but it has more numerous (5–20) and much smaller flowers, (scarcely three-fourths of an inch long.) Sepals with an obscure nectariferous groove, greenish-purple, with darker striæ, but not spotted.

CYCLOBOTHRA ALBA, *Benth. in Hort. Trans. (n. ser.)* 1, *p.* 413, *t.* 14, *f.* 3; *Lindl. in Bot. Reg. t.* 1661; *Hook. & Arn. Bot. Beech. p.* 399. Grass Valley, May 19, (in fl. & fr.;) hill-sides and ravines, Sonoma; May.

CYCLOBOTHRA PULCHELLA, *Benth. l. c. t.* 14, *f.* 1; *Lindl. in Bot. Reg. t.* 1662; *Hook. & Arn. l. c.* Hill-sides, Napa Valley; April 27.

CYCLOBOTHRA ELEGANS, *Lindl. l. c.; Kunth, Enum.* 4, *p.* 229. Calochortus elegans, *Pursh, Fl.* 1, *p.* 240; *Dougl. in Hort. Trans.* 7, *p.* 278, *t.* 9, *f.* 13. Hills near Punta de los Reys; April 17. The Calochortus Tolmæi, *Hook. & Arn. l. c.* (in a note) is perhaps not distinct from this species. The inflorescence appears racemose from the unequal forking of the stems, each division bearing from two to four flowers. It seems to be the plant described by Pursh, who remarks that the petals are "covered with long down." There are other forms of this species in Dr. Bigelow's collection: one from the mountains of Oakland, (April 4,) in which the petals are sparsely bearded not half way from the base; and another (a dwarf state) from the Sierra Nevada (May 11) with the petals glabrous except an adnate fringed scale at the base.

CALOCHORTUS VENUSTUS, *Benth. l. c. t.* 15, *f.* 3; *Hook. & Arn. l. c.; Lindl. in Bot. Reg. t.* 1669. Hill-sides, Knight's Ferry, Stanislaus River, California; May 7, (fl.)

CALOCHORTUS LUTEUS, *Dougl. Mss.; Lindl. in Bot. Reg. t.* 1567? In the same place as the preceding. This seems to be intermediate between *C. luteus* and *C. uniflorus.* With the former it agrees in its usually 3-flowered stem, and with the latter in its petals. It may perhaps be a variety of C. elegans.

CALOCHORTUS NITIDUS, *Dougl. in Hort. Trans.* 7, *p.* 277, *t.* 9, *f. A.?* Cyclobothra nitida, *Kunth, Enum.* 4, *p.* 230. Grass Valley, May 19; and hill-sides, Sonora, California, May 9. A dwarf plant, scarcely a span high. Stem 2–4-flowered. Pod drooping, ovate, not winged. Petals orange-yellow, copiously bearded.

LILIUM CANADENSE, *Linn.*, var. PUBERULUM: caule pedunculisque minute pubescentibus; foliis lato-lanceolatis margine nervisque puberulis; floribus paucis (2–7) longe pedunculatis; sepalis a medio valde revolutis intus purpureo-maculatis. Grows in all the region between Grass Valley and

Downieville, California. Colonel Frémont found it on Antelope Creek, one of the tributaries of the Upper Sacramento, and it is No. 2004 of Hartweg's California collection. If the character given above prove constant, this fine lily must be considered a distinct species from L. Canadense.

YUCCA ALOIFOLIA, *Linn. Spec. p.* 457; *Kunth, Enum.* 4, *p.* 270? Near a mountain arroyo, Williams' River. "Plant 15 feet high." The specimens are with leaves only. Also found at Cajon Pass, Sierra Nevada, in March, with ripe capsules of the preceding season. The same plant, or one very much resembling it, was found by Mr. Wright in New Mexico, and is his No. 1909. The flowers are very large and white.

YUCCA DRACONIS, *Linn. l. c.; Kunth, l. c.* Var. ARBORESCENS: foliis lineari-lanceolatis rigidis, margine serrulato-scabris. Sandy and gravelly plains west of the Colorado, California. Dr. Bigelow states that this species attains the height of 30 feet, with a diameter of 18 or 24 inches. He found "whole forests" of this tree on the Mohave creek. The leaves are flat, about 3½ inches long, and from ⅓ to ½ an inch wide, thick, convex below, flat or concave above, pointed with a strong spike, the broad flat base about half as long as the upper rigid and narrower portion. For want of more complete specimens we cannot be certain of the species.

YUCCA ANGUSTIFOLIA, *Pursh, Fl.* 1, *p.* 227; *Nutt. Gen.* 1, *p.* 218. Plains of Northern New Mexico. Leaves only: these are 12–15 inches long, and scarcely more than one-fourth of an inch wide, tapering upward, and ending in a strong sharp spine, thick and rigid, filamentous on the margin, along which is a narrow white line.

Dr. Bigelow collected in New Mexico (near Hurrah creek) specimens of a Yucca which seems to be undescribed. The leaves are a foot or more in length, and nearly an inch wide, very thick, entire, abruptly pointed with a short blunt spine, and furnished on the margin (especially towards the base and summit) with coarse tortuous fibres, tapering a little towards the base, and then dilated into a short sheathing base, which is of a brownish-red color. Flowers not seen. Fruit racemose, drooping, oval, as large as a hen's egg, pointed with the thick persistent style. It is of a soft fleshy consistence, and has a sweet taste. Endocarp thin and almost membranaceous, 3-celled, each cell partially divided into two others. Seeds piled horizontally in the cells, somewhat semi-circular, with thick edges, flat, black, wrinkled. Embryo straight, cylindrical, nearly the length of the seed; the albumen fleshy and somewhat indurated, a transverse section (parallel with the flat surfaces) appearing ruminated. The fleshy fruit, on account of the large quantity of grape sugar it contains, can be dried without decomposition, so as to have about the same consistence as a dry fig.

Still another species was found in rocky places near Pecan creek, a tributary of the Canadian. The leaves are a foot long, and three-fourths of an inch wide, flat and rather thin; the margin thin, sparingly furnished with very fine threads. No flowers were obtained. The fruit is in an elongated raceme. The pods are about two inches long, and more than an inch in diameter, erect and pedicellate; the mesocarp thin and somewhat fleshy, when dry a little papillose; cells divided by an accessory septum into 2 locelli. Seeds flat, smooth, and thin, black; the embryo two-thirds the length of the albumen. We need more complete specimens in order to determine whether the species is described.

CAMASSIA ESCULENTA, *Lindl. Bot. Mag. t.* 1486; *Kunth, Enum.* 4, *p.* 347. Phalangium Quamash, *Pursh, Fl.* 1, *p.* 226. Marshes, Punta de los Reyes, California; April 17. The Scilla esculenta, *Gawl. in Bot. Mag. t.* 1574, (Phalangium esculentum, *Nutt.*) is certainly a congener of this plant, and not a Scilla. In our specimens of the C. esculenta, *Lindl.*, we do not find the five upper sepals ascending, and the lowest one deflexed; but it is difficult to decide on such characters in dried specimens. In other respects the Northwest Coast species is so near the eastern one that they can be distinguished only by the considerably larger flowers, usually broader leaves, and more numerous ovules of the former. We find from 16–to 18 ovules in each cell of the ovary of C. esculenta, while in the other, which may be called C. Fraseri, the cells are only 8-ovuled. The genus Scilla has the sepals one-nerved, somewhat campanulate-connivent or urceolate, and the filaments a little adnate to the base of the sepals. In Camassia the sepals are 3–5-nerved, and the filaments are free to the very base of the sepals.

Scilla (Camassia) angusta, *Engelm. & Gray in Bot. Journ. Nat. Hist.* 5, *p.* 29, is only a slender form of C. Fraseri.

CHLOROGALUM POMERIDIANUM, *Kunth, Enum.* 4, *p.* 682. C. divaricatum, *Kunth, l. c.*? Anthericum pomeridianum, *Gawl. Bot. Reg. t.* 561. Phalangium pomeridianum, *D. Don. in Sweet's Flow. Gard.* (*ser.* 2,) *t.* 381. Hill-sides, Stanislaus River, California; May 8. This is the celebrated Amole or Soap Plant of California. It has an extensive range from north to south in that country, being found from the valley of the Upper Sacramento to Monterey. The bulb is ovate-conical, and varies from less than an inch to 4 inches in diameter. It is (especially when old) clothed with the black fibrous vestiges of the outer scales. The inner scales are mucilaginous when bruised, and are used by the Mexicans as a substitute for soap. There is but one Californian species of this genus that has come uuder our observation. The native country of the original species, which has long been cultivated in Europe, is not recorded in the books, but the plant is generally supposed to have been brought from Mexico. It is very doubtful whether C. divaricatum be a distinct species. The characters of the two as given by Gawler and Lindley seem blended in our plant. We suspect that Don was mistaken in describing the cells of the ovary as several-ovuled. In our specimens they have but two ovules, as described by Kunth.

ALLIUM CERNUUM, *Roth; Bot. Mag. t.* 1324; *Kunth, Enum.* 4, *p.* 435. Mountains and rocky places, near Laguna Blanca, New Mexico; September.

ALLIUM ACUMINATUM *Hook. Fl. Bor.-Am.* 2, *p.* 185, *t.* 196; *Hook. & Arn. Bot. Beech. p.* 349. Hill-sides, Sonora, and near Marysville, California; May 3–25. A showy species, with deep rose-colored flowers.

ALLIUM FALCIFOLIUM, *Hook. & Arn. l. c.* Benicia, and on the Yuba River, California; April—May. About a span high. Also a much larger form, with the bracts as long as the flowers. Tamal Pass, April.

ALLIUM TRIBRACTEATUM (sp. nov.): humilis; foliis radicalibus plerumque 2 angusto-linearibus scapum 2–4-pollicarem multo superantibus; umbella multiflora; spatha e bracteis 3 ovatis; perianthio basi acuto, sepalis lanceolatis acutis; filamentis subulatis basi parum dilatatis sepala subæquantibus; capsula late obovato-trigastrica, lobis rotundatis, loculis dispermis. Hill-sides, Duffield's Ranch, Sierra Nevada, May 10. Bulb ovate, three-fourths of an inch long. Leaves mostly 2, about three lines wide, recurved. Scape 3–4 inches long. Umbell 15–20 flowered. Spathe of 3 ovate bracts. Pedicels scarcely longer than the flower. Sepals pale rose-color, with a purple midrib, about 4 lines long, not acuminate. Filaments inserted near the base of the sepals. Style filiform; stigma minute, obscurely 3-lobed. Capsule narrow at the base, but not stipitate; the cells rarely perfecting more than one seed. We cannot refer this Allium to any described species. It is remarkable for its dwarf habit, 3-leaved spatha, and the sepals marked with a strong purple central nerve.

ALLIUM AMPLECTENS (sp. nov.): scapo flexuoso spithamaeo superne bifoliato; foliis filiformibus; umbella pauci-(3–6-) flora; spatha e bracteis 2 orbiculatis concavis subacuminatis flores amplectentibus; sepalis oblongis obtusiusculis; filamentis e basi lata submonadelpha subulatis; capsula trigastrica apice depressa, loculis dispermis. Hill-sides, Sonoma, California; May 3. Bulb large for the size of the plant. Scape 6 inches high, more or less flexous. Leaves scarcely a line wide, overtopping the scape. Easily distinguished by the small few-flowered umbel, which is almost enclosed in the concave purple bracts.

HESPEROSCORDIUM? MARITIMUM (sp. nov.): sepalis a basi fere distinctis; filamentis e basi vix dilatata subulatis Sea shore, Punta de los Reyes, California; April 17. Bulb the size of a small pea. Leaves all radical, narrowly linear. Scape 3–6 inches long, shorter than the leaves. Umbel 10–12-flowered; the lower pedicels an inch in length, the others much shorter.

Bracteal leaves 4–6, subulate-linear, connate at the base. Flowers apparently white. Sepals oblong, rather acute, and minutely sacculate at the lip, slightly united at the base, membranaceous on the margin, the midrib broad and thick. Stamens 6, equal; filaments inserted a little above the base of the sepals, not connected; anthers oblong, 2-celled, inserted near the middle of the back. Ovary ovate, obtuse, 3-celled, with 10 anatropous ovules in each cell, in a double series. Style filiform, erect, slightly clavate upward; stigma minutely 3-cleft. This little plant seems to have been hitherto overlooked. It differs from Hesperoscordium in the sepals being distinct nearly to the base, and in the slender filaments.

Dichelostemma congesta, *Kunth, Enum.* 4, *p.* 470. Brodiæa congesta, *Smith, in Linn. Trans.* 10, *p.* 3, *t.* 1; *Hook. Fl. Bor.-Amer.* 2, *p.* 186. Cocomungo, March 8, and hill-sides, Martinez, California; April 20, (in fruit.) Our numerous specimens of this plant collected in various parts of California have the flowers all hexandrous, (as, indeed, they are shown in the early figure of Salisbury); nor do we find any hypogynous scales, except a slight callosity at the base of each adnate filament.

Brodiæa grandiflora, *Smith, l. c.; Kunth, Enum.* 4, *p.* 471. Var.? brachypoda: umbella multiflora, pedicellis floribus multo brevioribus; staminibus sterilibus lato-lanceolatis integris. Plains of the Sacramento, May 26, (in flower and fruit.) The same plant was collected also by Colonel Frémont on Utah Lake, and by Dr. Stillman on the Sacramento.

Var. macropoda: scapo foliis multo breviore; umbella pauci-(3–6-) flora, pedicellis flores multoties excedentibus; staminibus sterilibus lato-linearibus emarginatis. Swamps, Santa Rosa creek, and Laguna, California; May 1. Tuber the size of a marble. Scape only 2–3 inches high. The longer pedicels 3–4 inches in length. Flowers bright purple, about three-fourths of an inch long.

STROPHOLIRION.* Nov. Gen.

Perianthium corollaceum campanulato-infundibuliforme, 6-fidum; tubo subventricoso 6-sacculato; segmentis æqualibus ovatis obtusis uninerviis suberectis. Stamina fertilia 3, segmentis interioribus perianthii opposita; filamenta tubo adnata, summo apice appendicibus 2 linearibus emarginatis, antheram linearem bilocularem utrinque fissam, adæquantibus, aucta: sterilia linearia, uninervia, emarginata, glanduloso-ciliata fertilibus æquilonga. Ovarium oblongum, basi attenuatum (haud stipitatum), triloculare: ovula in loculis 4, biseriata anatropa, adscendentia: stylus ovario longior, triangularis, superne subfistulosus: stigma 3-lobum, lobis brevibus obtusis fimbriato-papillosis. Capsula ovata, sessilis, trilocularis, loculicida; loculis sæpius abortu monospermis. Semina ovata, nigra, longitudinaliter striata. (Embryo ignotus.) Herba Californica, glabra, foliis lato-linearibus breviusculis et scapo gracili nudo 2–4-pedali volubili e cormo globoso exortis; umbella terminali multiflora densa, bracteis concavis spathaceis coloratis involucrata; pedicellis cum flore articulatis; floribus saturate roseis.

Stropholirion Californicum. (Tab. XXIII.) In rocky places, Knight's Ferry, Stanislaus River, May, (in flower and fruit); also at Sonora, Mokelumne Hill; Valley of the Sacramento, *Colonel Frémont*, *Mr. Rich*, and *Dr. Stillman.* It is No. 1992 of Hartweg's Californian collection. A remarkable plant, of which we have had specimens for many years. It seems to be common in the Valley of the Sacramento. The tall stem, which is not larger than a crow-quill, and often more than 4 feet (Dr. Kellogg, of San Francisco, found it even 12 feet) in length, twines around other plants. In Dr. Bigelow's specimens they were on Calliprora. Not unfrequently several stalks are twined together. The umbel is about 20-flowered, and much resembles that of some species of Allium, so that at first we took the plant for one of that genus. It most resembles Dichelostemma, but differs in having only three perfect stamens, and these furnished with appendages, while the abortive stamens are simple or undivided. There are also other characters, besides the habit, in which it differs from that genus.

* From στρεφξ, to turn or twist, (in allusion to the twining stalk,) and λειριον, lily.

Seubertia laxa, *Kunth, Enum.* 4, *p.* 475. Triteleia laxa, *Benth. in Hort. Trans.* (*n. ser.*) 1, *p.* 413, *t.* 15, *f.* 2; *Hook. & Arn. in Bot. Beech. p.* 401. Plains of Benicia, California, April 14—23. It is No. 1998 of Hartweg's Californian collection. A showy plant, resembling Brodiæa grandiflora, but with larger hexandrous flowers, and the ovary elevated on a very long stipe.

Calliprora lutea, *Lindl. in Bot. Reg. t.* 1590; *Hook. in Bot. Mag. t.* 3588; *Kunth, Enum.* 4, *p.* 476. Hills, near Sonora, and Grass Valley, California; May 19, (in flower and fruit.)

ODONTOSTOMUM,* Nov. Gen.

Perianthium hypocraterimorphum, marcescens; segmentis 6 æqualibus patentissimis, 3 exterioribus 5-nerviis, interioribus 7-nerviis; tubo cylindrico segmentis æquilongo, ima basi ovario accreto, demum paullo supra basim transversim rupto deciduo. Stamina fertilia 6, conformia: filamenta lato-subulata, plana, discreta, fauci calycis inserta, cum appendicibus seu filamentis sterilibus totidem alternantibus: antheræ subrotundæ, biloculares, fissuris 2 transversis apice dehiscentes. Ovarium globosum, 3-loculare, loculis biovulatis: stylus gracilis, filiformis: stigma minutum. Ovula collateralia, e basi loculi adscendentia, anatropa. Capsula globoso-triloba, trilocularis loculicida; loculis dispermis. Herba Californica, bulbifera? caulescens, glabra; caule e basi parce dichotomo; foliis radicalibus lato-linearibus, caulinis angustioribus, summis in bracteas transeuntibus; floribus albidis racemosis vel paniculatis; pedicellis solitariis 1–2-bracteolatis haud articulatis.

Odontostomum Hartwegii. Wet places, Ione Valley, California; May 18. Valley of the Sacramento, *Dr. Stillman.* It is No. 2008 of Hartweg's Californian collection. Plant about two feet high. Radical leaves 3–6 lines wide, flat. Bracts lanceolate-subulate, about as long as the filiform pedicels, which are furnished with a subulate bracteole a little below the flower. Raceme 3–8 inches long. Flowers half an inch in diameter; the segments elliptical-oblong, rather obtuse, as long as the tube, at length reflexed. Seeds all empty shells in our specimens. This genus is allied to Pasithea and Zephyra; but these differ in the want of sterile filaments; the more numerous ovules; in the dehiscence of the anthers, and in several other characters. We received it several years ago from our friend Dr. Stillman, of New York, but it seems to have been first collected by Mr. Hartweg.

Clintonia Andrewsiana (n. sp.): umbellis 2–4 in parte superiori scapi subremotis, terminali multiflora, ceteris paucifloris; floribus erectiusculis; perianthiis subcampanulatis; ovarii loculis 8–10-ovulatis. Hill-sides, Tamul Pass; also along the *Redwood* (Sequoia sempervirens) ravines of Costa County, east of Pablo Bay, California. The only specimens of this interesting plant found by Dr. Bigelow have the flowers scarcely expanded; but we fortunately, while this report was in press, received it in a more advanced state from Dr. Andrews, lately of California, and to this gentleman, who has assiduously examined the botany of that State, we dedicate the species. No ticket accompanied his specimens, but they were probably collected not far from San Francisco. The root consists of numerous thick descending fibres, which proceed from a small fleshy tuber. The leaves grow from the summit of a slender, erect, or curved caudex, which is 5 or 6 inches long, and clothed below with sheathing scales. They are from 7 to 11 inches long, and 3–4 inches broad, narrowed and sheathing at the base, with a short abrupt acumination, glabrous and green on both sides, but the margin sparingly ciliate with slender deciduous hairs. The nerves are very numerous, and run from the base to the apex. The scape is about twice as long as the leaves, terete, and naked, except a lanceolate or linear foliaceous bract at the base of the lower umbel, or at some distance below it. Terminal umbel 10–20-flowered; the lateral ones 2–4-flowered and sessile. Pedicels about the length of the flower, somewhat elongated in fruit. Sepals 6, about 8 lines long, 5–7-nerved, oblong, obtuse, apparently greenish-yellow. Stamens 6; filaments subulate, flat; anthers

* From 'οδους, tooth, and στομα, mouth; in allusion to the tooth-like sterile filaments at the orifice of the flower.

oblong-linear somewhat versatile, the cells opening inward near the margin, the membranous connective produced externally nearly to the base of the cells. Ovary oblong-fusiform, tapering into a cylindrical thickish tubular style; stigma truncate, slightly 2-lipped, and perforate at the extremity. Ovules 8–10 in each cell, in a double series, obliquely ascending. Fruit (immature) subglobose, about one third of an inch in diameter. Seeds 6–8 in each cell, oblong.

This species is remarkable for bearing one or more few-flowered umbels besides the primary or terminal one; otherwise it has a general resemblance to C. umbellata. As in that species, the flowers are erect and numerous, but they are considerably larger and subcampanulate. It differs, too, in the numerous ovules.

SMILACINA RACEMOSA, *Desf. in Ann. du Mus. Paris*, 9, *p.* 51; *Torr. Fl. N. York* 2, *p.* 298, *t.* 130. Near Bolinas Bay; April 19; and mountains near Oakland, California; April 4. It seems to differ in no essential character from the eastern plant.

SMILACINA STELLATA, *Desf. l. c.; Torr. l. c.* Asteranthemum vulgare, *Kunth, Enum.* 5, *p.* 152. Mountains near Oakland, California; April 4.

SMILACINA BIFOLIA, *Desf. l. c.; Torr. l. c.* Maianthemum bifolium, *DC. in Redouté, Lil.* 4, *t.* 216, *f.* 2; *Kunth, Enum.* 5, *p.* 147. Marshes, Punta de los Reys, California; April 17. The plant of Oregon and California differs from the S. bifolia of the Atlantic States in the leaves being more deeply cordate, or almost auriculate, and in the longer petioles. It is much more like the European plant. The leaves are more commonly three than two.

AMARYLLIDACEÆ.

DASYLIRION BIGELOVII (sp. nov.): foliis longissimis (3–4-ped.) lineari-ensiformibus in apicem acutissimum sensim attenuatis integerrimis, margine lævibus; panicula ampla densa; fructibus lato-trialatis trilocularibus sæpissime monospermis, loculis 2 inanibus. Mountain sides, Williams' River. In fruit, February 10, (doubtless from the flowers of the preceding season.) "Scape about 3 feet high." We have not been furnished with Dr. Bigelow's notes on this plant, but it is evidently an undescribed species, of which flowering specimens are desirable. Kunth described the genus as having a one-celled ovary, while in three of his six species it is said to be three-celled!

At Plaza Larga, in Eastern New Mexico, Dr. Bigelow found another Dasylirion, of which the leaves only are in the collection. These are nearly a yard long, and 3–4 lines wide at the base, gradually tapering upward, entire and nearly smooth on the margin, convex on the lower surface and concave above, except towards the apex, where they are somewhat triangular. It is allied to D. Texanum, but seems to be an undescribed species.

SMILACEÆ.

TRILLIUM SESSILE, *Linn. Spec. p.* 484; *Kunth, Enum.* 5, *p.* 123. β. GIGANTEUM, *Hook. & Arn. Bot. Beech. p.* 402. Mountains near Oakland; April 4. The petals are more than three inches long, and of a dark purple color.

γ. ANGUSTIPETALUM, *Torr. in Emory's Rep. Mex. Bound. Comm.* (*ined.*): foliis basi subito contractes; petalis lanceolato-linearibus acutis, sepala purpurea fere duplo superantibus. Wet ravines, Washington Mammoth Grove; May 15.

δ. CHLOROPETALUM: petalis viridulis obovato ellipticis, obtusiusculis, sepala duplo superantibus, Redwoods; April 12.

TRILLIUM OVATUM, *Pursh, Fl.* 1, *p.* 249; *Hook. Fl. Bor.-Am.* 2, *p.* 180; *Kunth, l. c.* Redwoods; April 12.

SMILAX PSEUDO-CHINA, *Linn.?* Banks of rivulets, Shawnee Villages, near the Canadian River; August, in fruit. Leaves orbicular-ovate, with a short abrupt acumination, often somewhat cordate, glabrous on both sides, paler underneath. Peduncles usually twice the length of the petioles. Berries black, mostly one-seeded.

ORCHIDACEÆ.

Spiranthes decipiens, *Hook. Fl. Bor.-Am.* 2, *p.* 203, *t.* 204. Low places, Mammoth Grove, Calaveras County; May, (in fruit of the preceding season.)

Spiranthes cernua, *Rich.; Torr. Fl. N. York*, 2, *p.* 283, *t.* 129. Prairies on the Canadian River, and valley of the Upper Rio Grande; September, October.

Corallorhiza striata, *Lindl. Gen. & Sp. Orchid. p.* 534. Corte Madera, California; April. Scape 12–15 inches high, 20–30-flowered. Flowers larger than in any other North American species. Lip not spotted. C. Macræi, *Gray*, is a nearly allied species. (Tab. XXV.)

Aplectrum hyemale, *Nutt. Gen.* 2, *p.* 197; *Torr. l. c. p.* 270, *t.* 127. Shawnee Villages, on the Canadian; August.

CYPERACEÆ.

Cyperus inflexus, *Muhl.; Torr. Cyp. p.* 273. Low places near Albuquerque, and on the Upper Canadian River. Bentham (*Plant. Hartw.*) refers this plant to C. aristatus of Rottboel, which, indeed, it much resembles, as was remarked long ago in the work just quoted; but we are not yet satisfied that the two species should be united.

Cyperus Michauxianus, *Schultes; Torr. l. c. p.* 259. Wet sandy places, headwaters of the Canadian River. This species is found as far west as the Great Colorado.

Cyperus diandrus, *Torr. Cyp. p.* 264. Wet sandy places near Albuquerque, New Mexico.

Cyperus repens, *Ell. Sk.* 1, *p.* 69; *Torr. l. c.* C. phymatodes, *Muhl.* Grows with the last.

Cyperus lutescens, *Torr. & Hook. in Torr. Cyp. p.* 433. Alluvions of Pecan Creek; August; and prairies near the Upper Canadian. The heads are inclined to be compound, and contain more numerous spikelets than Drummond's specimens, from which the original description of this species was taken. The spikelets, too, become brownish when old, so that the name is not wholly appropriate.

Fuirena squarrosa, var. aristulata, *Torr. Cyp. p.* 291. Borders of running water, Upper Cross Timbers of the Canadian River. Our specimens agree exactly with those collected by Dr. James in Long's Expedition.

Hemicarpha subsquarrosa, *Nees. Cyp. in Endl. & Mart. Fl. Bras. p.* 61, *t.* 4, *f.* 1; *Torr Fl. N. York*, 2, *p.* 362. Isolepis subsquarrosa, *Torr. Cyp. p.* 348. Scirpus subsquarrosus, *Muhl.* Wet sandy places near Albuquerque, New Mexico.

Eleocharis acicularis, *R. Brown; Torr. Cyp. in Ann. Lyc. New York*, 3, *p.* 308. Var.? culmo crasso brevi, spica ovato-lanceolata valde compressa acuta 6–7-flora. Wet places near San Francisco; April 8; not mature. Differs from the ordinary form of the plant in its stout culm, (which is 2–3 inches high,) and much compressed dark chestnut-colored scales. There are 3 stamens and a 3-cleft style, which has a distinct tubercle at its base; but no bristles were found.

Eleocharis pygmæa, *Torr. l. c.* (*excl. syn. Vahl.*) Cocomungo, California; April 18. Although the specimens are rather too young for certain determination, they agree very well with the plant of the Eastern States. Kunth (*Enum.* 2, *p.* 158) retains Scirpus pusillus of Vahl in the genus Scirpus, although he seems to have examined the original specimens of that plant. He also refers to it the S. pusillus of Willdenow's herbarium; but quotes it again under his own Eleocharis reclinata! Vahl's plant was from New England, and seems to be only one of the forms of E. acicularis. Willdenow's is probably not different, as he received most of his North American plants from Muhlenberg, who refers S. pusillus, *Vahl*, to S. trichodes, which is undoubtedly Eleocharis acicularis.

Eleocharis pygmæa, var. anachæta. Moist places near Albuquerque, New Mexico. This variety was noticed in the botany of Nicollet's Report, p. 163. We have it also from the Red River, Louisiana, where it was collected by Dr. Hale.

ELEOCHARIS CAPITATA, *R. Br.; Torr. Cyp. p.* 305. With the last. We have this species from Texas, collected by Drummond, and also by Dr. Leavenworth.

ISOLEPIS CARINATA, *Hook. & Arn. in Torr. Cyp. l. c. p.* 349. Wet places, Laguna of Santa Rosa Creek, California; May 1. This agrees well with the eastern plant, except that the achenium is more minutely roughened, and the spikes are sometimes in pairs.

ISOLEPIS LEPTOCAULIS (sp. nov.): culmo sulcato angulato setaceo elongato basi 1–3-phyllo; spica ovata 10–12-flora; involucro monophyllo spicam superante; squamis ovatis obtusis, infimo bracteiformi acuminato; stylo trifido. Cocomungo, California; March 18. The spike is apparently lateral, and indeed the one-leaved involucre (which is 5–6 times as long as the spike) may be regarded as a continuation of the culm. The species resembles I. carinata, but differs in being much more slender and taller, with smaller heads, and the scales are not acuminate. There were no mature achenia on the specimens.

SCIRPUS TRIQUETER, *Linn.?* Near San Francisco? The specimens are too young for satisfactory determination.

SCIRPUS LACUSTRIS, *Linn.; Torr. Cyp. p.* 321. Overflowed places, Comanche Plains, and near San Domingo, New Mexico.

SCIRPUS MARITIMUS, var. MACROSTACHYOS, *Michx.; Torr. l. c. p.* 323. Sandy alluvions of the Upper Canadian River; probably in saline soils.

SCIRPUS SYLVATICUS, *Linn.; Torr. l. c. p.* 323. Wet ravines, Upper Cross Timbers of the Canadian River.

ERIOPHORUM GRACILE, *Koch; Hook. Fl. Bor.-Amer.* 2, *p.* 232; *Gray, Bot. U. States, p.* 529. E. angustifolium, *Torr. Cyp. p.* 339, not of Roth. Swamps near Sonoma, California; May 3, (with mature achenia.) The peduncles are mostly erect, and much shorter than the spikes.

FIMBRISTYLIS SPADICEA, *Vahl; Torr. Cyp. p.* 346. Borders of streams, Upper Cross Timbers of the Canadian River.

CAREX* SITCHENSIS, *Prescott, in Hook. Fl. Bor.-Am.* 2, *p.* 220, *t.* 221. Marshes at the head of Tomales Bay, and near San Francisco, California; April.

CAREX DECIDUA, *Boott, in Linn. Trans.* 20, *p.* 119. Mountains near Oakland, Los Angeles, Duffield's Ranch, Sierra Nevada, and other parts of California; April, May.

CAREX LACINIATA, *Boott, in Benth. Plant. Hartweg ined.* Swamps on Mark West's Creek, Bolinas Bay, etc., California; April. This is the same as Hartweg's No. 2022, and Coulter's 806. It is likewise (in part) 1241 *Herb. U. S. Expl. Exped.* from the Sacramento. It is very near C. Jamesii, *Torr.*, quæ foliis glaucis, auriculis pallidis discretis elongatis, perigyniis nervosis glabris bracteis brevioribus, squamis non ciliatis differt.

CAREX XALAPENSIS, *Kunth, Enum.* 2, *p.* 380. Low swampy places, Mark West's Creek, and Napa, California; April 25–30.

CAREX DEWEYANA, *Schwein.; Torr. & Schwein. Mon. Car. in Ann. Lyc. N. York,* 1, *p.* 316. Shady hill-sides, Napa Valley, California; May 5. The Oregon specimens and these have 6–8 approximate spiculæ.

CAREX FESTIVA, *Dew. in Sill. Jour.* 29, *p.* 351. Spica oblonga; in uno specimine spicula infima subremota. Punta de los Reyes, California; April 18.

CAREX GEYERI, *Boott, in Linn. Trans.* 20, *p.* 118. Flosculis fœminiis 2–3, squamis inferioribus foliaceis. Hill-sides, Duffield's Ranch, Sierra Nevada, California; May 10–12. This is like Dr. Parry's specimens collected in California. Kunze's figure, t. 47, has a solitary female flower.

CAREX HOODII, *Boott, in Hook. Fl. Bor.-Am.* 2, *p.* 211, *t.* 211. Mark West's Creek, California; May 1.

CAREX LAGOPODIOIDES, *Schk. Car. t. Yyy. f.* 177; *Torr. & Schw. l. c. p.* 313. Mark West's Creek, California; May 1.

* The Carices of this collection were determined by our valued friend Dr. Boott, whose names and remarks are given as they were received from him.

Carex vesicaria, *Linn.; Schk. Car. t. Ss. f.* 106. With the last; April 30. One of the specimens is *var. major, Boott, l. c.*

Carex siccata, *Dewey, in Sill. Journ.* 10, *p.* 278, *t. F. f.* 18; *and* 14, *p.* 353. C. pallida, *Meyer.* With the last species; April 30.

Carex stellulata, *Good. in Linn. Trans.* 2, *p.* 144; *Schk. Car. t.* 3, *f.* 14. Swamps, Santa Rosa, California; May 3.

Carex propinqua, *Nees, et Mey. in Kunth, Enum.* 2, *p.* 396. Swamps, Mark West's Creek, California; April 30. No. 1622 of Coulter's California collection.

Carex Cherokeensis, *Schw.; Torr. & Schw. Car. in Ann. Lyc. N. York,* 1, *p.* 369, *t.* 25, *f.* 1. Swamps, Santa Rosa Creek, California; May 1. We can find no character that will distinguish this from the eastern plant. The specimens are young. The ovate abbreviate spikes and short bracts give it a peculiar aspect. It might be considered a *var. minor.* C. Cherokeensis, like all its allies, is very variable; from solitary to geminate and ternate spikes, (my C. Christiana, *in Bost. Jour. Nat. Hist.*) Bigelow's specimens, if mature, would closely resemble the original figure of C. Cherokeensis, *Torr. & Schwein. Monogr. of N. Amer. Car. in Ann. Lyc. N. York,* 1, *t.* 25, *f.* 1.

GRAMINEÆ.

Alopecurus geniculatus, *Linn. Spec. p.* 89; *Kunth, Enum.* 1, *p.* 24. Low places, Napa Valley, California; April 26. A. borealis, *Trin.*, seems to be only a form of this variable species.

Phalaris arundinacea, *Linn. Spec. p.* 80; *Torr. Fl. N. York,* 2, *p.* 418. P. Californica, *Hook. & Arn. Bot. Beech. p.* 161. Bolinas Bay, April 19, and Napa Valley, California; April 26.

Hierochloa borealis, *Rœm. & Schult. Syst.* 2, *p.* 513; *Hook. Fl. Bor.-Amer.* 2, *p.* 234. Red-woods, California; April 12. Male flowers with a very short awn, or sometimes scarcely mucronate.

Stipa Neesiana, *Trin. & Rupr. Stip. p.* 27; *Steud. Syn. Glum. p.* 124: S. avenacea, *Hook. & Arn. Bot. Beech. p.* 403, *non Linn.* Hill-sides, Sonoma, May 3, and Benicia, California; April 23. It is No. 2028 of Hartweg's collection. It differs from S. avenacea of the eastern States in its much larger flowers, the almost villous lower palea, the hairiness of the awn below the articulation, and in the pubescent leaves.

Agrostis microphylla, *Steud. Syn. Pl. Glum. p.* 164? Mark West's creek, California, May 1. This species was founded on a grass collected by Douglas in "North America;" doubtless in California, though it is not taken up by Hooker and Arnott in the Botany of Beechey's Voyage. It is Agraulus brevifolius, *Nees, Mss.* Our plant differs somewhat from the grass described by Steudel. It is rather stout than "slender," and is nearly two feet high. The leaves are flat, about two lines wide, and, as well as the sheaths, are quite rough to the feel. Panicle about three inches long, contracted; the branches fasciculate and somewhat conglomerate. The flowers are of a purplish tinge. Glumes nearly equal, lanceolate, tapering to a long slender point, the lower one rough on the keel, otherwise glabrous; both of them without lateral nerves. Lower palea less than half the length of the glumes, truncate, with four short teeth at the summit, furnished a little below the middle of the back with a nearly straight slender awn, which is nearly twice the length of the valve. Upper palea wanting, or appearing as a very minute rudiment. Stamens 3. Styles plumose.

Calamagrostis gigantea, *Nutt. in Trans. Amer. Phil. Soc.* (*n. ser.*) 5, *p.* 143. Prairies and ravines, along the Canadian River. Glumes somewhat coriaceous, one-nerved, the superior nearly 2–3 times the length of the paleæ, hairs at the base of the latter more than half the length of the valves. Caryopsis oblong, obtuse at each end, large for the size of the spikelet.

Sporobolus cryptandrus, *Gray, Man. p.* 542. Vilfa cryptandra, *Torr. Fl. N. York,* 2, 440.

Var.? foliis angustioribus; panicula exserta, axillis nudis; gluma superiore obtusiuscula. Low places, Galisteo, New Mexico; October. Utricle obovate, somewhat coriaceous, closely investing the ripe seed, but easily separated; loose before the seed is mature.

VILFA TRICHOLEPIS (n. sp.): culmo erecto simplici tereti, nodis distantibus, vaginis glabris, ligula truncata; foliis angustis (½ lin. latis) utrinque glabris, panicula oblonga, ramulis flexuosis; glumis subæqualibus acutiusculis valvulas subæquales pilosas ¼ brevioribus. Sandia mountains, New Mexico; October. Culms a foot or 18 inches long, growing in tufts. Branches of the panicle alternate, naked in the axils, when old somewhat open. Pedicels mostly rather longer than the spikelets, which are about a line in length. Glumes smooth and almost hyaline. Paleæ nearly equal, very hairy on the back and margins, particularly on the nerves; the lower palea 3-nerved. This seems to be a genuine Vilfa.

MUHLENBERGIA GRACILLIMA (n. sp.): cæspitosa, glabra; culmo simplici; foliis angustissimis involutis brevissimis (1–1½ poll.), ligula elongata fissa; panicula diffusa capillari, ramis subsolitariis; pedicellis spicula (1½ lin.) subduplolongioribus; glumis muticis lanceolatis, paleis vix duplo brevioribus, palea inferiore glabra apice minute bifido setam ipsa æqualem gerente; callo nudo. Llano Estacado, and near the Antelope hills of the Canadian River; September. Culms (including the panicle) about a foot high, densely cæspitose, erect. Leaves mostly in radical tufts, more or less tortuous. Panicle 5–6 inches long, pyramidal; the branches capillary and widely spreading, alternate, or sometimes opposite. Spikelets lanceolate, mostly purplish. Glumes acute. Inferior palea 3-nerved, slightly 2-toothed at the apex, with a straight awn about the length of the valve, between the teeth of which it is inserted. Superior palea not bicarinate, but rounded on the back. Caryopsis very slender and acute, nearly the length of the palea.

GYMNOPGON RACEMOSUS, *Beauv. Agrost. p.* 41, *t.* 9, *f.* 5. Anthopogon lepturoides, *Nutt. Gen.* 1, *p.* 82. Prairies, on Pecan creek, Indian Territory.

CHLORIS ALBA, *Presl; Kunth, Enum.* 1, *p.* 264. Var. ARISTULATA: aristis valvulæ vix dimidio longioribus. C. alba, *Benth. Bot. Sulph. p.* 56; *Torr. in Emory's Rep. p.* 152. Banks of the Upper Rio Grande; October. This is the same as No. 395 of Drummond's 2d Texan collection. The awns are commonly less than half the length of the valves.

BOUTELOUA ERIOPODA, *Torr. in Emory's Rep. p.* 154, (sub Chondrosium.) Pyramid mountain, near Laguna Colorado, and in deep ravines on the Llano Estacado; September.

BOUTELOUA OLIGOSTACHYA, *Torr.; Gray Man. Bot. ed.* 2, *p.* 553. Atheropogon oligostachyum, *Nutt. Gen.* 1, *p.* 78. Prairies on the Canadian; August.

BOUTELOUA HIRSUTA, *Lagasca Elench. p.* 5. Chondrosium hirtum, *H.B.K.;* Kunth, Enum. 1, p. 276. Atheropogon papillosus, *Engelm.* High sandy prairies, Upper Cross Timbers of the Canadian; September.

PAPPOPHORUM BOREALE, *Ledeb.; Steud. Gram. p.* 200. P. phleoides. *Turcz.* Llano Estacado, in deep ravines. This agrees so well with the authentic specimen of P. phleoides received from Fischer that we can hardly regard it as even a variety. It is not uncommon in New Mexico.

LEPTOCHLOA MUCRONATA, *Kunth, Enum.* 1, *p.* 270. Eleusine mucronata, *Michx. Fl.* 1, *p.* 65. Banks of Boggy creek, Indian Territory; August.

LEPTOCHLOA FASCICULARIS, *Gray, Man. ed.* 2, *p.* 550. L.? polystachya, *Kunth, Enum.* 1, *p.* 270. Diplachne fascicularis, *Torr. Fl. N. York,* 2. *p.* 472. Festuca fasciculatea, *Lam.* Sandy banks of the Canadian River; August.

AIRA ELONGATA, *Hook. Fl. Bor. Bor.-Amer.* 2, *p.* 253, *t.* 138. Plains and hill-sides, Mark West's creek, April 30; Napa Valley, May 5, (a small form.) This is hardly a true Aira. The spikelets are commonly 2-flowered, with a plumose stipitate terminal rudiment. The upper perfect flower is distant from the lower one, on a hairy rachis. Glumes equal, subulate-pointed, obscurely 3-nerved. Paleæ bearded at the base; the inferior one unequally 5-toothed at the summit, awned below the middle; the awn twice the length of the palea, and somewhat geniculate; upper palea hairy at the tip. Stamen solitary. No. 2030 of Hartweg's Californian collection is the same grass as this.

AVENA FATUA, *Linn. Spec. p.* 118; *Kunth, Enum.* 1, *p.* 302. Hills and plains, Feather River; Benicia, &c. April and May. This is the common wild oat of California. It may have been introduced by the Spaniards; but it is now spread over the whole country, many miles from the coast.

TRICUSPIS MUTICA (n. sp.): cæspitosa, glabra; culmo simplicissimo erecto; foliis convoluto-filiformibus; panicula terminali longe exserta racemosa, ramis brevibus oligostachyis; spiculis teretiusculis 5–8 floris; palea inferiore mutica integra vel bifida, margine dorsoque longe ciliata. Laguna Colorado, New Mexico; September. About a foot high, growing in tufts. Root perennial. Culm rigid terete. Leaves 3–6 inches long. Panicle about 3 inches long, the short appressed bearing 3–5 spikelets. Glumes unequal 1-nerved, rather acute, scarcely half the length of the spikelets. Inferior palea (after flowering) usually more or less deeply notched, otherwise entire; or when old slightly toothed or eroded; the midnerve not at all produced into a mucro, and the lateral submarginal nerves scarcely reaching to the summit; the long white hairs confined to the lower half of the nerves. Superior palea one-third shorter than the inferior, notched at the apex, plumose on the margin. Stamens 3; anthers oblong. Styles short, stigmas plumose, purple. Caryopsis oblong, concave on the inner face, finely striated longitudinally.

TRICUSPIS PULCHELLA. Uralepis pulchella, *Kunth, Enum. p.* 108, *and Suppl. p.* 274. Trichodia pulchella *H. B. K. Nov. Gen.* 1, *t.* 47. Gravelly hills, near Albuquerque, New Mexico; October. A beautiful little grass with densely cæspitose culms and few-flowered panicles, which are crowded among the fasciculate leafy branches. It occurs along the Rio Grande, and southward to Mexico. The root appears to be annual, but Kunth says that it is perennial.

TRICUSPIS PURPUREA, *Gray, Man. Bot. ed.* 2, *p.* 556. Uralepis purpurea and U. aristulata, *Nutt. Gen.* 1, *p.* 62. Wet ravines, Elm creek, Indian Territory; August.

ERAGROSTIS PURSHII, *Schrad.; Gray, Man. ed.* 2, *p.* 564. Poa pectinacea, *Pursh, Fl.* 1, *p.* 81, *non Michx.* Sandy soils on the Rio Grande, near Albuquerque; October.

ERAGROSTIS TENUIS, *Gray, l. c.* Poa tenuis, *Ell. Sk.* 1, *p.* 156. Prairies, and along streams, Upper Cross Timbers of the Canadian; August. E. Frankii, *Mey.*, scarcely differs, except in the smaller number of flowers in the spikelets.

ERAGROSTIS OXYLEPIS, *Torr. in Marcy's Rep. p.* 301, *t.* 19, (sub Poa.) Poa interrupta, *Nutt. in Trans. Amer. Phil. Soc. n. ser.* 5, *p.* 146, *non Roth. nec R. Br.* Sandy ravines, near the Canadian river. Spikelets larger than usual, and some of them 30–40 flowered.

POA ANNUA, *Linn. Spec. p.* 99; *Kunth, Enum.* 1, *p.* 349. San Francisco, April. A common grass in the settled parts of California, and doubtless introduced from Europe.

POA TRIVIALIS, *Linn. Spec. l. c.; Kunth, l. c.* Mark West's creek, California; April 30. This also must be an introduced grass.

FESTUCA MICROSTACHYS, *Nutt. Pl. Gamb. in Jour. Acad. Phil.* (*n. ser.*) 1, *p.* 187. Hill-sides, Napa Valley, April 26, (an unusully large form); near San Francisco, April 8, (a dwarf state.) This is a polymorphous species. The sheaths of the leaves are often retrorsely pubescent, but not unfrequently smooth. The panicle, in the humbler form, is strict and spikelike; but in more luxuriant specimens several of the lower branches are somewhat elongated, and at length spreading or diverging and secund. In a variety (as we are inclined to regard it) from Mark West's creek the panicle is very open, and the spikelets are all distant and diverging. The paleæ in some of the specimens from Napa Valley are puncticulate-scabrous, and not hairy. No. 2030 of Hartweg's collection is a variety of this species.

FESTUCA TENELLA, *Willd. Sp.* 1, *p.* 419? var. ARISTULATA. Hill-sides, Napa Valley. Very likely this may prove to be a distinct species from F. tenella of the Eastern States.

FESTUCA PRATENSIS, *Huds.; Kunth, Enum.* 1, *p.* 404. Corte Madera and Tomales Bay, April. Introduced?

Festuca scabrella, *Hook. Fl. Bor.-Amer.* 2, *p.* 252, *t.* 233. Hills near Tomales Bay, California; April 19. A tall glaucous grass (2–3-feet high.) Spikelets 5-flowered and a rudiment. Paleæ scabrous.

Brizopyrum Douglasii, *Hook. & Arn. Bot. Beech. p.* 404. Poa Douglasii, *Steud. Enum. Pl. Glum. p.* 261. Sandy sea shore. Punta de los Reyes. April 17.

Melica poæoides, *Nutt. Pl. Gamb. l. c.* Corte Madera, California; April 20. Spikelets 3–4-flowered, the uppermost abortive (male or neuter.) In depauperate specimens the spikelets are often but 2-flowered, with rudiment.

Melica imperfecta, *Trin. Gram. Suppl. in Act. Petrop. p.* 59, *and Icon. Gram. t.* 355; *Hook. & Arn. Bot. Beech. p.* 403, (sphalm. M. imperforata.) M. clpodioides, *Nees in Tayl. Ann. Nat. Hist.* 1 *p.* 282; *Steud. Syn. Pl. Glum. p.* 291. Red-woods, April 12, (spikelets with two perfect flowers and a capitate rudiment; leaves glabrous;) Mark West's creek, California, April 30, (spikelets with a single perfect flower and a capitate rudiment; leaves pubescent.)

Uniola stricta, *Torr. in Ann. Lyc. N. York*, I, *p.* 153, *& in Marcy's Rep. p.* 301 *&* 20. Dry salt marshes, Indian Territory; August.

Sesleria dactyloides, *Nutt. Gen.* I, *p.* 165; *Torr. in Emory's Rep. p.* 154, *t.* 10. Llano Estacado; September. As usual, with male flowers only. We have now examined specimens of this grass collected in very many places, and from an extensive range of country, but have not yet found it in seed, and very rarely with even abortive pistils.

Bromus carinatus, *Hook. & Arn. Bot. Beech. p.* 403. Mark West's creek, April 30. As Hooker & Arnott truly remark, the grass is intermediate between Bromus & Ceratochloa; but it is nearer the former.

Bromus Kalmii, *Gray, Man. Bot. N. States, p.* 600? Var. aristulatus; glabriusculus; panicula debile, ramulis elongatis divergentibus, spiculis 6–7-floris; paleis minute pubescentibus, inferiore integro, apice brevissime aristata. Mark West's creek, California. April 30.

Bromus ciliatus, *Linn.*, var. purgans, *Gray, Man. ed.* 2, *p.* 567. B. purgans, *Linn.* Mountain ravines, on the Pecos, New Mexico; October.

Arundo Phragmites, *Linn.* Sandy alluvions of the Canadian river, near the Antelope Hills; September.

Elymus villosus, *Muhl. Gram. p.* 175; *β.* glabriusculus: radice repente; culmo foliisque glabriusculis; vaginis inferioribus pubescentibus; spica erecta, spiculis 2–(raro 3;) floris–glumis lanceolato-subulatis scabriusculis breviaristatis; palea superiore scabra arista ipsa 3-plo longiore. Napa Valley, California; May 6. This grass, though apparently only a variety of E. villosus, is also closely related to E. Europæus.

Hordeum pratense, *Huds.; Kunth, Enum.* 1, *p.* 452. H. secalinum, *Schreb.* H. Chilense, *Brongn.* It is also No. 2025 of Hartweg, and No. 756 of Coulter. Corte Madera, California; April. Differs from our Swedish specimens of H. pratense in the lateral flowers being one-valved and neuter; but in this genus the awns of the neuter flowers are variable.

Sitanion elymoides, *Raf. in Jour. de Phys.* 89, *p.* 103; *Steud. Syn. Pl. Glum. p.* 351. Ægilops Hystrix, *Nutt. Gen.* 1, *p.* 86. Elymus? Sitanion, *Schult. Mant.* 2, *p.* 426. Polyantherix Hystrix, *Nees, in Ann. Nat. Hist.* 1, *p.* 284; *Hook. & Arn. Bot. Beech. p.* 404. Elymus v. nov. gen. *Torr. in Nicollet's Rep. p.* 165. River banks, Mokelumne Hill, California; May 17. We restore the name given by Rafinesque to this grass, because it is the earliest. Our California specimens are nearly two feet high. Indeed, we have never seen the plant of so humble a stature as that described by Mr. Nuttall. It is a widely diffused grass, being found from northern Minnesota to Texas, and west of the Pacific. It is often mistaken for an Elymus.

Lepturus paniculatus, *Nutt. Gen.* 1, *p.* 81. Llano Estacado, and plains near Galisteo, New Mexico; September—October. This species is remarkable for its triangular branching rachis and long very slender spikes. There is but a single one-flowered spikelet at each joint of the rachis, without any trace of a rudimentary flower. Glumes 2, opposite, contrary to the rachis, very unequal, lanceolate, sharply carinate, each terminating in a bristle as long as itself. Paleæ somewhat coriaceous, linear-lanceolate, almost terete, long as the upper glume; the inferior acute, rough on the keel; superior pubescent on the back, with two approximate nerves, which are produced into teeth at the summit. Stamens 3; anthers linear. Styles long; stigmas plumose on the inside. Caryopsis linear-fusiform.

MONROA. Nov. Gen.

Spæculæ 2–6-flor; flores sessiles distichi hermaphroditi v. terminali tabescente. Glumæ 2, suboppositæ mucronatæ, flores multobreviores. Paleæ 2 herbaecæ rigidæ, inferior apice mucronata vel brevissime aristata, ecarinata, æquilatera, lateribus in spiculæ superiores versus basim baribatis, in spicula infima plerumpue glabris. Caryopsis glaberrima, palea superiori obtecta. Gramen annuum, repens, ramosissimum, ramis fasciculatis. Spica capitulæformi sæpius foliorum terminalium subspathæformibus suffultæ. Spiculæ 3, 2–6-floræ.

MONROA SQUARROSA. Crypsis squarrosa, *Nutt. Gen.* 1, *p.* 49. Hills and ravines, Anton Chico, New Mexico; September. "On the arid plains of the Upper Missouri, near the Grand Detour, it covers, almost exclusively, thousands of acres."—*Nutt.* This grass is very distinct from Crypsis, and belongs, as we think, to the tribe Hordeaceæ. In the notice of Dr. James' plants, collected in Long's 1st expedition, (Ann. Lyc. Nat. Hist. N. York, 2, p. 254,) it was intimated that it was probably a distinct genus. The culm is prostrate, much branched from the base; the branches 3–8 inches long. Leaves 1–2 inches long, flat, 1–2 lines wide, somewhat pungent, scabrous on the margin; those near the summit of the fasciculate branches with broad sheaths, embracing the small sessile heads, which thus appear involucrate. Spikelets mostly 3, closely approximated, usually 3–4-flowered. Glumes sometimes almost unilateral, linear–lanceolate, carinate. Paleæ 2–3 times longer than the glumes, lanceolate, acute; the lower one often bifid or 2-toothed at the summit, with a cusp or very short rigid bristle between the teeth, 3-nerved; the lateral nerves nearly marginal. In the uppermost spikelet, and often in the middle one, these nerves are bearded with long white hairs towards the base; but the flowers of the lowest spikelet are usually quite naked. Superior palea bicarinate, rather obtuse. Stamens 3; anthers linear. Styles long and slender; stigmas plumose. Achenium compressed, very smooth and even, usually covered with the introflexed margin of the superior palea. We dedicate this singular genus to Major Monro, of the East India Company's service, who has made the grasses an especial study.

TRITICUM (AGROPYRUM) REPENS, *Linn.* Prairies, on the Canadian River; August. An awnless glabrous form, with narrow and somewhat involute leaves.

SETARIA GLAUCA, *Beauv.; Kunth, Enum. p.* 149. Banks of Little River, Indian Territory; August.

SETARIA VIRIDIS, *Beauv.; Kunth, l. c. p.* 151. Laguna Colorado, New Mexico; August.

PANICUM CRUS-GALLI, *Linn.* Oplismenus Crus-Galli, *Kunth, l. c.* 1, *p.* 143· With the last; also on the banks of the Pecos, New Mexico. All the specimens from the latter locality belong to the awnless variety.

PANICUM VIRGATUM, *Linn.; Kunth l. c. p.* 100; *Torr. Fl. N. Y.* 2, *p.* 425. With the last.

PANICUM SANGUINALE, *Linn.; Torr. l. c. p.* 423. Alluvial banks of the Canadian, and near Galisteo, New Mexico; August—October.

PANICUM LATIFOLIUM, *Linn.; Torr. l. c. p.* 425. With the last.

PANICUM OBTUSUM, *H. B. K.? Torr. in Marcy's Rep. p.* 299. Plains, Laguna Colorado, New Mexico; September.

CENCHRUS TRIBULOIDES, *Linn.; Torr. Fl. New York,* 2, *p.* 931. On the Canadian River, and near Galisteo, New Mexico; October.

TRIPSACUM DACTYLOIDES, *Linn.; Michx. Fl.* 1, *p.* 60. Pecan creek, Indian Territory. T.

cylindricum, *Michx.* l. c., is a Rottbollia, (R. cylindrica,) and seems to be the same as R. campestris, *Nutt.* l. c. *p.* 151.

ANDROPOGON NUTANS, *Linn.* A. avenaceus, *Michx. Fl.* 1, *p.* 60. Sorghum nutans, *Gray, Man. ed.* 2, *p.* 584. With the last.

ANDROPOGON SCOPARIUS, *Michx. l. c.; Torr. Fl. New York,* 2, *p.* 478. With the preceding, and on the Llano Estacado; August--September.

ANDROPOGON FURCATUS, *Linn.* Pecan creek and Llano Estacado; August—September. Pedicels of the sterile spikelets clothed with longer and whiter hairs than in the eastern plant.

ANDROPOGON JAMESII, *Torr. in Marcy's Rep. p.* 302. A. glaucus, *Torr. in Ann. Lyc. New York,* 1, *p.* 152. A. Torreyanus, *Steud. Syn. Pl. Glum. p.* 392. Comanche Plains, Indian Territory; August.

LYCOPODIACEÆ.

SELAGINELLA STRUTHIOLOIDES. Lycopodium struthioloides, *Presl, Rel. Haenk.* 1, *p.* 82, (ex. Hook. & Arn.) L. rupestre, *β. Hook. & Arn. Bot. Beech., p.* 267. Wet rocks, mountains of California and New Mexico; March.

SELAGINELLA RUPESTRIS, *Spring; Brackenridge, Fil. U. S. Expl. Exped. p.* 331. Mountains of New Mexico.

EQUISETACEÆ.

EQUISETUM EBURNEUM, *Schreb.; Braun & Engelm. in Sill. Jour.* 46, *p.* 84. E. fluviatile, *J. E. Smith, Eng. Bot. t.* 2022; *Hook. Fl. Bor.-Amer.* 2, *p.* 269. E. Telmateia, *Ehrh.* Redwoods and mountains near Oakland, California; April. Plant sometimes 3–4 feet high. It is very doubtful whether this species grows on the borders of Lakes Erie and Superior. The station given for it long ago by Dr. Beck, in his Botany of the Northern States, was on my authority, and I was led into the error by the incorrect label attached to a specimen which I received from a correspondent.

EQUISETUM ARVENSE, *Linn.; Pursh, Fl.* 2, *p.* 651; *Eng. Bot. t.* 2020; *Braun & Engelm. l. c. Torr. Fl. N. York,* 2, *p.* 480. In overflowed places, Duffield's Ranch, Sierra Nevada; May 11.

EQUISETUM HYEMALE, *Linn.; Pursh, l. c. Eng. Bot. t.* 914; *Braun & Engelm. l. c.; Torr. Fl. N. York, l. c.* Santa Rosa Creek, California; May 1. We can hardly distinguish several of species allied to E. hyemale, described by Braun & Engelmann, l. c., for they seem to pass into each other by imperceptible gradations.

FILICES.

POLYPODIUM VULGARE *β.* OCCIDENTALL, *Hook. Fl. Bor.-Am.* 2, *p.* 258. P. vulgare, Virginianum, *Bong. Veg. Sitcha, p.* 57. Redwoods, California; April 12. This is nearer P. vulgare of Europe than is the plant of the Atlantic States, which we are now inclined to regard as a distinct species.

POLYPODIUM CALIFORNICUM, *Kaulf. Enum. Fil. p.* 102; *Hook. & Arn. Bot. Beech. p.* 161 *&* 405; *Hook. Fl. Bor.-Amer.* 2, *p.* 258. Mountains near San Gabriel; April 5. Differs from the preceding in the membranaceous fronds, shorter and rather obtuse pinnæ. The figure in the Icones Filicum of Hooker and Greville (t. 56, P. Scouleri of that work) represents a dwarf state of this species.

POLYPODIUM INTERMEDIUM, *Hook. & Arn. l. c. p.* 405; *Hook. l. c.* Rocky ravines, Cajon Pass; March. This plant greatly resembles P. Californicum, and is chiefly distinguished from it by the oval sori.

ALLOSORUS ANDROMEDÆFOLIUS, *Kaulf. Enum. Fil. p.* 188. Pteris andromedæfolia, *Hook. & Arn. Bot. Beech., p.* 406. Hill-sides, Cajon Pass, California. This seems to be the plant described by Kaulfuss, although the next species has often been taken for it. Dr. Parry collected it near Monterey. Our specimens more than a foot high. The pinnules vary from 3 to 5-foliolate.

ALLOSORUS MUCRONATUS, *D. C. Eaton, in Sill. Jour.* (*2d ser.*) 22, *p.* 138. Cajon Pass, Sierra Nevada; valley of the Sacramento, *Dr. Stillman;* California, *Douglas.* Our specimens are much larger than the plant described by Mr. Eaton, of which we have duplicates from that promising young botanist. It is often more than a foot high, the pinnæ 10 to 20, and these pinnate, with the pinnules trifoliolate, somewhat verticillate, and crowded. It is much more common than the last species.

ADIANTUM CHILENSE, *Kaulf. Enum. p.* 207; *Hook. Fil.* 2, *p.* 43, *t.* 75, *B.* Deep ravines near Los Angeles; also in Napa Valley and near the Redwoods, California; March.

ADIANTUM PEDATUM, *Linn.; Torr. Fl. N. York,* 2, *p.* 487; *Brack. l. c.* Redwoods; April. This differs somewhat from the plant of the Atlantic States, in being more slender, with the lobes of the frond broader at the base, and more deeply cut, but it can hardly be considered even as a distinct variety.

PTERIS LANUGINOSA, *Kaulf. l. c.; Hook. & Arn. l. c.* Rocks near San Francisco Mountain, Western New Mexico.

ONYCHIUM DENSUM, *Brackenridge, Ferns of the U. S. Expl. Exped.* 1, *p.* 120, *t.* 13. Wet places, Grass Valley, California; May. This neat and rare fern has much the appearance of Allosorus acrostichoides; and Sir William Hooker says it must be removed to that genus or to Pellæa. It is beautifully figured in the work here quoted.

HYPOLEPIS CALIFORNICA, *Hook. Fil.* 2, *p.* 71, *t.* 88, *A.* Mountains near San Gabriel, also near Marysville, California. Mr. Schott found it in Sonora.

CHEILANTHES FENDLERI, *Hook. Fil.* 2, *p.* 103, *t.* 107, *B.* On rocks near the mouth of White Cliff Creek, Western New Mexico.

CHEILANTHES BRADBURII, *Hook. l. c. p.* 97, *t.* 109, *B.* New Mexico, not rare.

CHEILANTHES VESTITA, *Swartz; Hook. l. c. p.* 98, *t.* 108, *B.* On rocks in various parts of New Mexico. Extremely woolly when young.

NOTOCHLÆNA DEALBATA, *Kunze, in Sill. Jour.* (*2d ser.*) 6, *p.* 83. Cheilanthes dealbata, *Pursh, Fl.* 2, *p.* 675. Rocky hills, San Domingo, New Mexico. A beautiful and delicate fern, remarkable for the sharply zigzag branches of the rachis, and the white incrustation on the under surface of the frond.

GYMNOGRAMMA TRIANGULARIS, *Kaulf. Enum. p.* 73; *Hook. & Grev. Ic. Fil. t.* 153; *Hook. Fl. Bor.-Am.* 2, *p.* 259. Hills and rocky places, Cajon Creek, and Redwoods. Young fronds sulphur-yellow underneath, (in dry specimens); the old ones brown. This species occurs also in New Mexico.

WOODWARDIA RADICANS, *Willd. Sp.* 5, *p.* 418; *Hook. & Arn. Bot. Beech. p.* 162 *&* 405. W. Chamissonis, *Brack. l. c. p.* 138. Cajon Pass; March; in fine fruit, probably of the preceding season. Mr. Brackenridge considers this to be distinct from W. radicans. Like W. Virginica, it belongs to the genus Doodia of R. Brown, which is now generally regarded as a section of Woodwardia.

CYSTOPTERIS FRAGILIS, *Bernh.; Hook. l. c. p.* 260. Aspidium tenue, *Willd. Sp.* 5, *p.* 280. Hill-sides, Yuba River, Redwoods, and other parts of California. The indusium at first has a long lacerate apex which lies over the joint, but which finally breaks off, leaving the broad cucullate or cup-shaped base.

ASPDIUIM MUNITUM, *Kaulf. Enum. p.* 230; *Hook. & Arn. Bot. Beech. p.* 162. Polystichum munitum, *Presl.; Brack. l. c. p.* 203. Mountains near Oakland, and on hill-sides along the Yuba, Downieville, California. This species varies greatly in size, and in the length of its pinnæ. It is allied to A. acrostichoides of the Eastern States.

ASPIDIUM (LASTRÆA) ARGUTUM, *Kaulf. l. c. p.* 242; *Hook. & Arn. l. c.* Lastræa arguta, *Brack. l. c. p.* 196. Mountain ravines, Oakland, Cajon Pass, and near San Francisco. This species as a general resemblance to A. rigidum, *Sw.* The sori are as large as in A. marginale. When young, the stipe and rachis are thickly clothed with chaffy scales.

Aspidium aculeatum, *Swartz; Hook. Fl. Bor.-Am.* 2, *p.* 261; *Torr. Fl. N. York*, 2, *p.* 498. Deep ravines, Napa Valley, California. Some of our specimens agree better with A. lobatum than with A. aculeatum; but we fully agree with Hooker, that these and A. angulare constitute but one species. Kutzing thinks that a part, at least, of the North American forms of A. aculeatum should be referred to A. (Polystichum) Braunii, *Spenn. Fl. Frib.*

SALVINIACEÆ.

Azolla Caroliniana, *Willd. Sp.* 5, *p.* 541; *Torr. Fl. N. York*, 2, *p.* 513. A. microphylla, *Kaulf.; Hook. & Arn. Bot. Beech. p.* 162. On the surface of slow-flowing or stagnant waters, Western New Mexico and California.

EXPLANATION OF THE PLATES.

Plate I. CROSSOSOMA CALIFORNICA.—Page 63.

A BRANCH OF THE NATURAL SIZE.

Fig. 1. A branch with the leaves more fully developed, and the carpels half mature.
2. Plan of the flower.
3. A sepal.
4. A petal.
5 and 6. Front and back views of a stamen.
7. A flower, longitudinally divided, to show the insertion of the stamens; all the figures moderately and equally enlarged.
8. Transverse section of an ovary; more enlarged.
9. An ovule; considerably magnified.

Plate II. VIOLA SHELTONII.—Page 67.

AN ENTIRE PLANT OF THE NATURAL SIZE.

Fig. 1. Three of the petals; enlarged.
2–4. Different views of a stamen.
5. An anther divided transversely.
6. The pistil; all the figures magnified.

Plate III. THAMNOSMA MONTANUM.—Page 73.

TWO BRANCHES OF THE NATURAL SIZE—ONE IN FLOWER, THE OTHER IN FRUIT.

Fig. 1. Plan of the flower.
2. A separate flower; moderately enlarged.
3. The same, with the calyx and petals removed.
4. Immature fruit, showing the gynophore or prolongation of the glandular disk.
5. Ovary, with one of the carpels longitudinally divided; and,
6. The same transversely divided; magnified.
7. An ovule; more magnified.
8. The fruit; enlarged.
9. Seed, longitudinally divided; magnified.

Plate IV. HOSACKIA INCANA.—Page 79.

A PLANT OF THE NATURAL SIZE.

Fig. 1. The banner, a wing, and one of the keel-petals; considerably magnified.
2. Stamineal tube, laid open; equally magnified.
3. The pistil, longitudinally divided; also equally magnified.
4. An ovule; highly magnified.

Plate V. SPIRÆA MILLEFOLIUM.—Page 83.

UPPER PART OF THE PLANT OF THE NATURAL SIZE.

Fig. 1. Plan of the flower.
2. A petal; magnified.
3. A stamen; equally magnified.
4. Fructiferous calyx; also equally magnified.
5. A separate carpel.

Plate VI. HORKELIA TRIDENTATA.—Page 84.

AN ENTIRE PLANT OF THE NATURAL SIZE.

Fig. 1. An expanded flower and two buds; enlarged.
2. The flower laid open; a little more enlarged.
3. A petal; magnified.
4. A stamen; more magnified.
5. The head of pistils.
6. An achenium, with its persistent style.

Plate VII. WHIPPLEA MODESTA.—Page 90.

AN ENTIRE PLANT OF THE NATURAL SIZE.

Fig. 1. A separate flower; moderately enlarged.
2. A sepal; and,
3. A petal; both a little more enlarged.
4. Front view of a stamen.
5. Back view of the same; equally magnified.
6. Pistil, transversely divided; more magnified.
7. An ovule; more magnified.
8. A flower, longitudinally divided; considerably magnified.
9. Plan of the flower.

Plate VIII. CORNUS SESSILIS.—Page 94.

A BRANCH OF THE NATURAL SIZE.

Fig. 1. Umbel of flowers and involucre.
2. The involucre; shown separately.
3. An exterior leaf of the same.
4. Interior leaf of the same.
5. A separate flower.
6. The same, with two of the petals and stamens removed to show the teeth of the calyx.
7. The fruit.

Plate IX. HOFMEISTERIA PLURISETA.—Page 96.

A PLANT OF THE NATURAL SIZE.

Fig. 1. A separate flower; enlarged.
2. The corolla of the same laid open; more magnified.
3. A stamen; still more magnified.
4. Two paleæ and a hair of the pappus; more magnified.
5. An achenium, crowned with its pappus; considerably magnified.
6. Involucre and receptacle; moderately magnified.

Plate X. ASTER BIGELOVII.—Page 97.

UPPER PORTION OF THE PLANT OF THE NATURAL SIZE.

Fig. 1. A ray flower.
2. A branch of the style from the same.
3. A disk flower.
4. A separate stamen from the same.
5. Style and its branches, from a disk flower.
6. An achenium.
7. A hair of the pappus; highly magnified.

Plate XI. APHANTOCHÆTA EXILIS.—Page 100.

A PLANT OF THE NATURAL SIZE.

Fig. 1. A head of flowers, moderately enlarged.
2. Involucre and receptacle, from which the flowers have fallen, more enlarged.
3 and 4. Scales of the involucre, equally magnified.
5. A pistillate flower.
6. A perfect flower.
7. A stamen, highly magnified.
8. Summit of the style of a pistillate flower, equally magnified.
9. Style of a perfect flower, equally magnified.
10. An achenium, enlarged.

Plate XI. EVAX CAULESCENS.—Page 101.

Fig. 1. A plant of the natural size.
2. A head of flowers ; vertical section, enlarged.
3. Involucre and receptacle ; more enlarged.
4. Inside view of one of the paleæ from the summit of the receptacle.
5. A male flower.
6. A stamen, from the same.
7. One of the paleæ subtending the female flowers.
8. A female flower.
9. An achenium ; the details all magnified.

Plate XII. LINOSYRIS BIGELOVII.—Page 98.

A BRANCH OF THE NATURAL SIZE.

Fig. 1. A flower ; enlarged.
2. A stamen ; magnified.
3. The style ; more magnified.
4. An achenium, with its pappus ; enlarged.
5. Receptacle ; enlarged.

Plate XIII. STYLOCLINE GRAPHALOIDES.—Page 101.

A PLANT OF THE NATURAL SIZE.

Fig. 1. Involucre and receptacle.
2. Receptacle, with a male flower on its summit, and its subtending palea.
3. A stamen.
4. One of the fertile flowers enclosed in its large palea.
5. Dorsal view of a fertile palea.
6. Vertical view of the same.
7. Transverse section of the same ; to show the way in which the achenium is enclosed in a dorsal fold of the palea.
8. A fertile flower.
9. An achenium ; the details variously magnified.

Plate XIV. QUERCUS ECHINACEA.—Page 137.

A BRANCH OF THE NATURAL SIZE.

Fig. 1. A leaf without serratures.
2. An acorn ; both figures of the natural size.

Plate XV. SYNTRICHOPAPPUS FREMONTII.—Page 106.

AN ENTIRE PLANT OF THE NATURAL SIZE.

Fig. 1. Involucre and receptacle.
2. A ray flower.
3. A disk flower.
4. A separate stamen.
5. Style and its branches.
6. Portion of the syntrichous pappus.
7. One of the leaves of the same ; highly magnified.

Plate XVI. LAYIA PENTACHÆTA.—Page 108.

A FLOWERING BRANCH OF THE NATURAL SIZE.

Fig. 1. Vertical section of part of a head of flowers; enlarged.
2. A ray flower, with its embracing involucral scale.
3. A marginal palea of the receptacle.
4. A disk flower.
5. A stamen of the same; magnified.
6. Style of a ray flower; magnified.
7. Style of a disk flower; equally magnified.
8. Involucre and receptacle; enlarged.
9. Achenium of a ray flower without its scale.
10. Achenium of a disk flower, with its pappus; the details variously magnified.

Plate XVII A. CALAIS BIGELOVII.—Page 113.

A PLANT OF THE NATURAL SIZE.

Fig. 1. A separate flower; magnified.
2. Divisions of the style, showing the stigmatic lines; highly magnified.
3. An exterior achenium, and
4. An interior achenium; both moderately enlarged.
5. A separate palea of the pappus.

Plate XVII, B. CALAIS TENELLA.—Page 114.

Fig. 6. A separate flower; magnified.
7. Divisions of the style; highly magnified.
8. An achenium, destitute of pappus.
9. Another achenium crowned with two awned paleæ.
10. The receptacle. The last three figures equally magnified.

Plate XVIII. CALAIS CYCLOCARPHA.—Page 113.

Fig. 1. A flower; magnified.
2. A stamen; more highly magnified.
3. The style; equally magnified.
4. An achenium crowned with its pappus; magnified.
5. A single palea; equally magnified.
6. Receptacle; enlarged.

Plate XIX. ERIOGONUM LACHNOGYNUM.—Page 132.

AN ENTIRE PLANT OF THE NATURAL SIZE.

Fig. 1. An involucre, from which several flowers protrude; magnified.
2. Perianth laid open; more magnified.
3. A pedicel, with a pair of bracteoles at its base; equally magnified.
3 *a*. A third and broader bracteole, inserted exterior to the others; equally magnified.
4. The pistil; more magnified.
5. A ripe achenium; considerably enlarged.
6. Embryo, from the same.

Plate XX. OBIONE HYMENELYTRA.—Page 129.

Fig. 1. A branch, with male flowers, of the natural size.
2. A branch from a female plant, with fruit, of the natural size.
3. A male flower; magnified.
4. A female flower; also magnified.
5. The same, with one bract removed to show the pistil; more enlarged.
6. Embryo; considerably magnified.

PLATE XXI. DAMASONIUM CALIFORNICUM.—PAGE 142.

AN ENTIRE PLANT OF THE NATURAL SIZE.

Fig. 1. Plan of the flower.
2. A flower; somewhat magnified.
3. One of the sepals; also magnified.
4. An anther; more magnified.
5. A pistil, laid open to show the position of the ovule.
6. A ripe achenium; considerably magnified.
7. Seed; still more magnified.

PLATE XXII. SCOLIOPUS BIGELOVII.—PAGE 145.

A PLANT OF THE NATURAL SIZE.

Fig. 1. A separate flower.
2. A sepal, with a stamen, seen anteriorly.
3. A petal.
4. Anther, with part of the filament, posterior view.
5. Pistil, with the ovary divided transversely; a petal and a stamen.
6. Portion of the ovary divided transversely and vertically.
7. An ovule. The details, except figure 1, more or less magnified.

PLATE XXIII. STROPHOLIRION CALIFORNICUM.—PAGE 149.

AN ENTIRE PLANT OF THE NATURAL SIZE.

Fig. 1. The perianth laid open; moderately enlarged.
2. The pistil; more enlarged.
3. A ripe pod, showing the dehiscence.
4. One of the carpels of the same, laid open and showing the seed.
5. Transverse section of a pod.
6. A seed; considerably magnified.
7 and 8 should be erased.

PLATE XXIV. ODONTOSTOMUM HARTWEGII.—PAGE 150.

AN ENTIRE PLANT (EXCLUSIVE OF THE ROOT) OF THE NATURAL SIZE.

Fig. 1. The unopened perianth; magnified.
2. Flower laid open; equally magnified.
3. A stamen; more magnified.
4. Part of the ovary; longitudinally divided and magnified.
5. An ovule; also magnified.
6. Transverse section of an ovary.
7. Immature fruit.

PLATE XXV. *CORALLORHIZA STRIATA.—PAGE 152.

A PLANT OF THE NATURAL SIZE, IN FLOWER AND FRUIT.

Fig. 1. A flower; moderately enlarged.
2. Lip of the same; magnified.
3. The column; equally magnified.

* Incorrectly named C. Macræi on the plate.

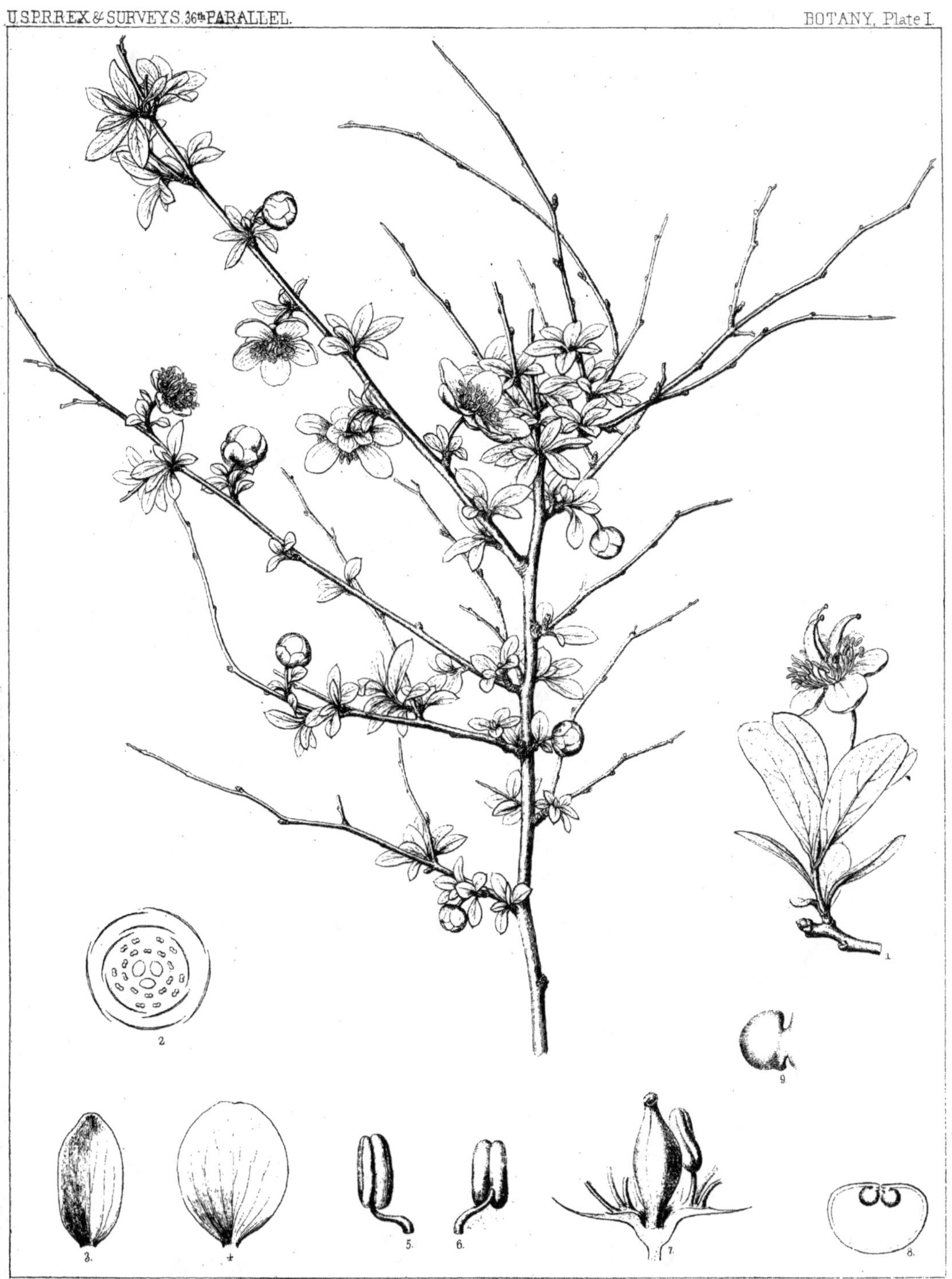

Ackerman Lith 379 Broadway. N.Y.

CROSSOSOMA CALIFORNICA.

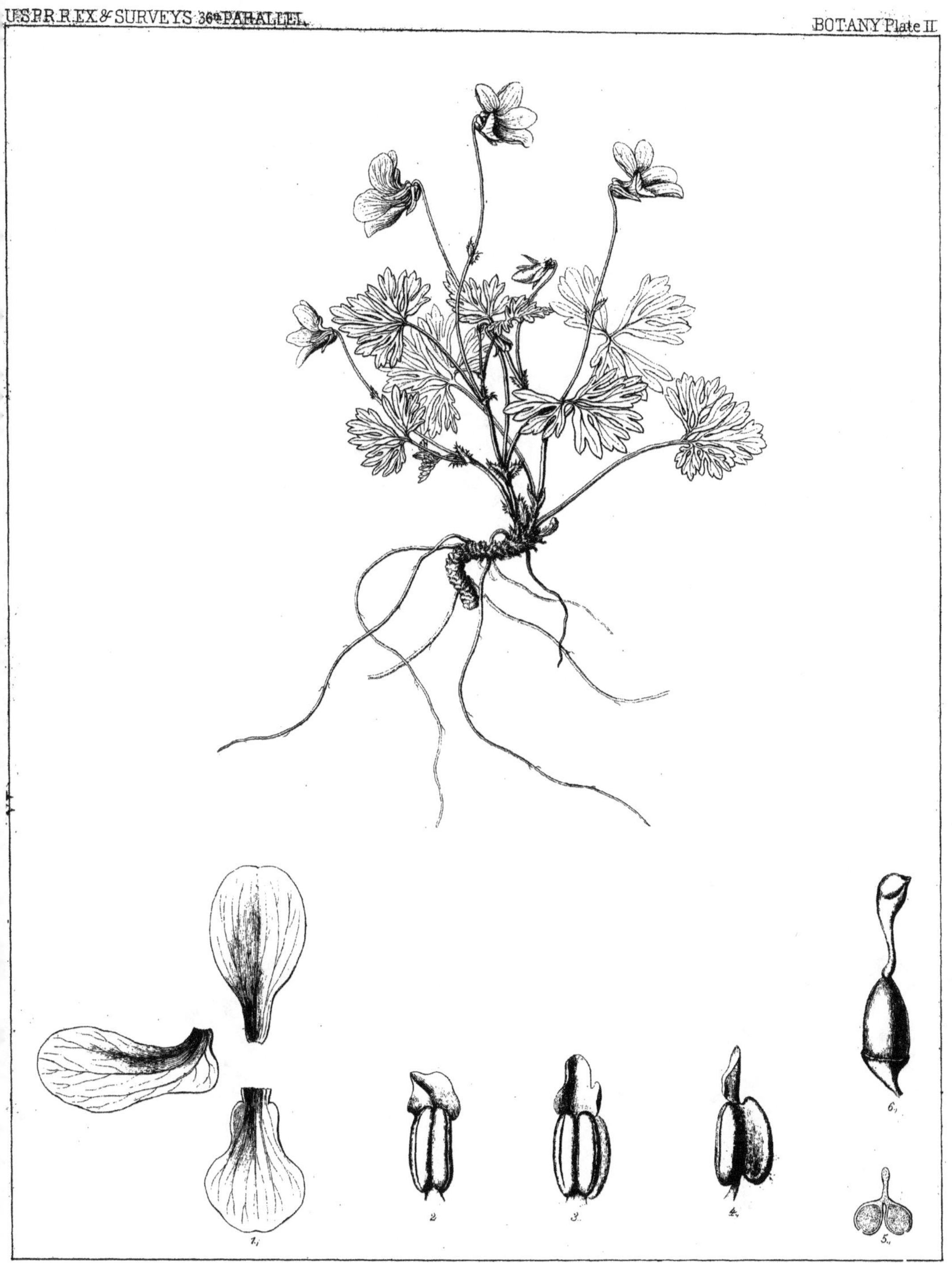

Ackerman Lith 379 Broadway N.Y.

VIOLA SHELTONII.

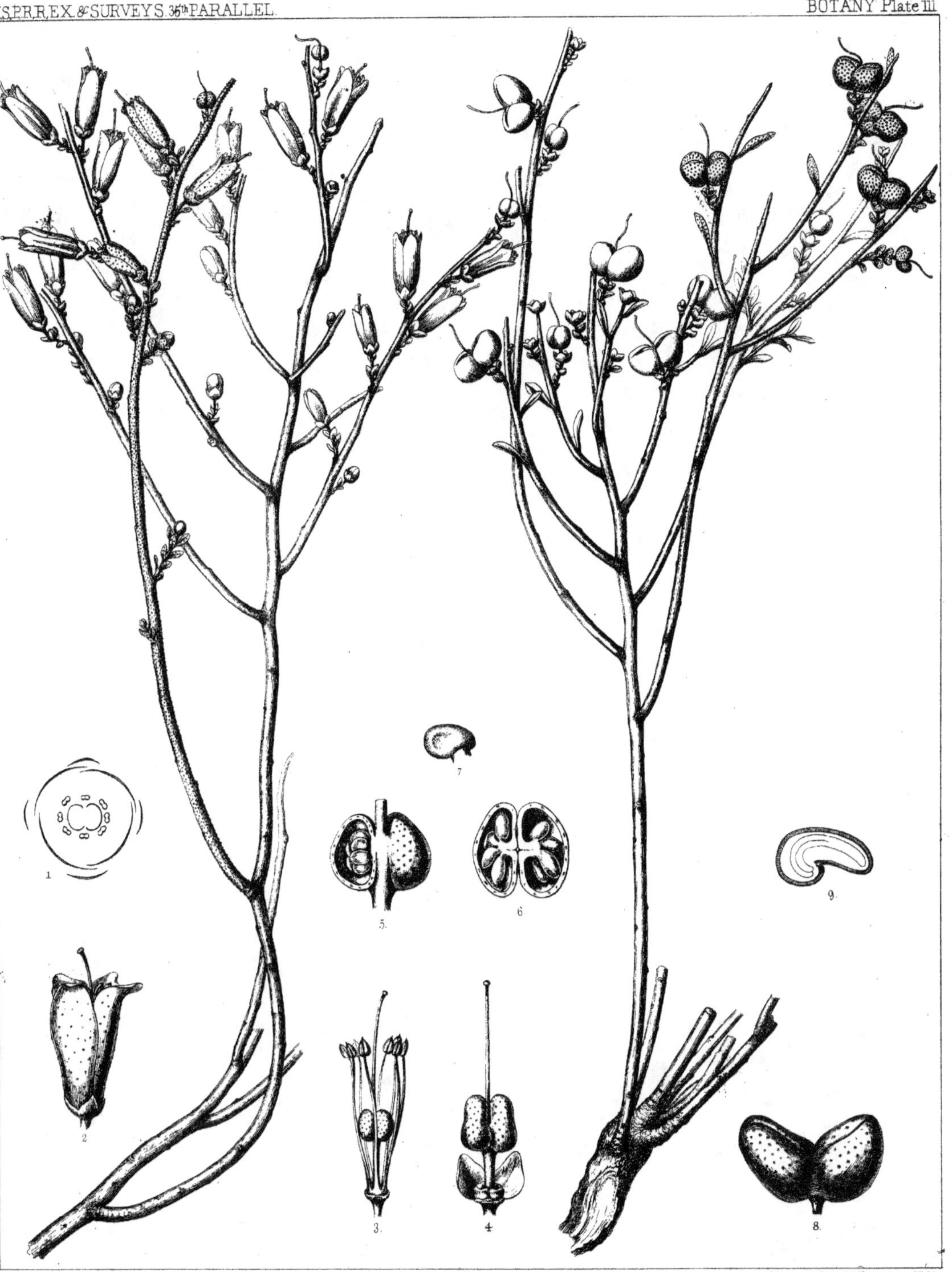

Ackerman Lith. 379 Broadway N.Y.

THAMNOSMA MONTANUM.

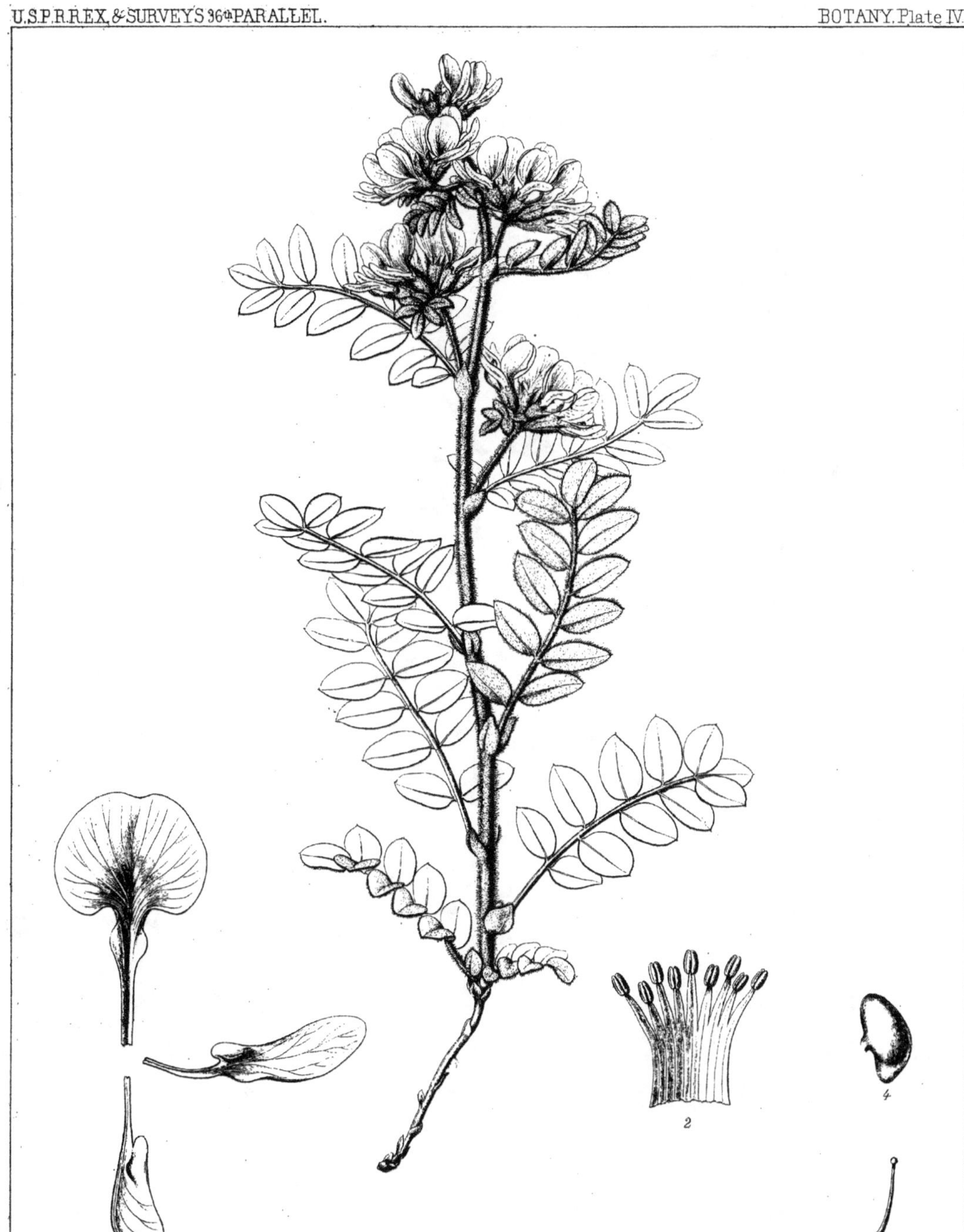

Ackerman Lith. 379 Broadway N.Y.

HOSACKIA INCANA.

SPIRÆA MILLEFOLIUM.

Ackerman Lith 379 Broadway N.Y.

HORKELIA TRIDENTATA.

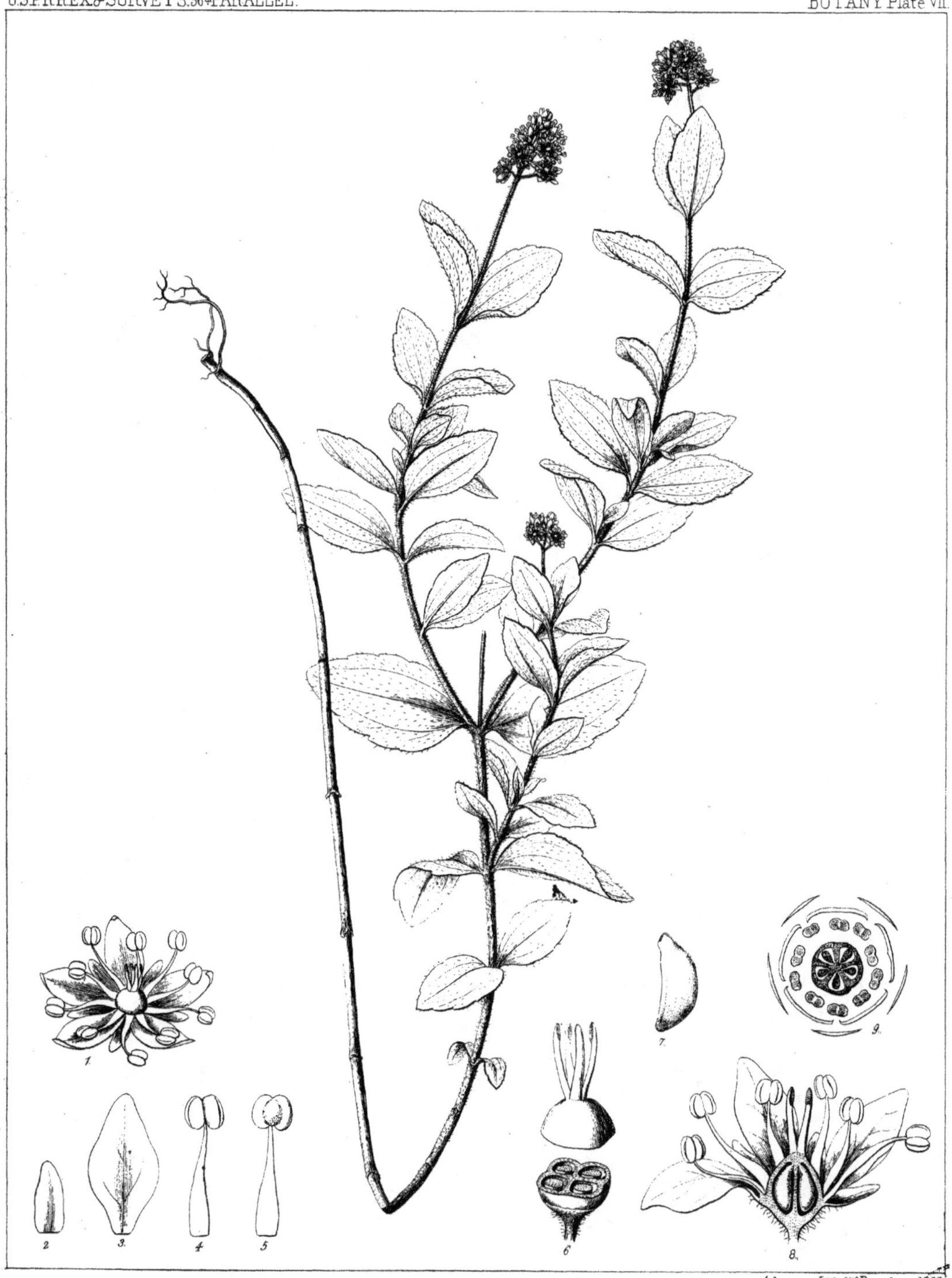

WHIPPLÆA MODESTA.

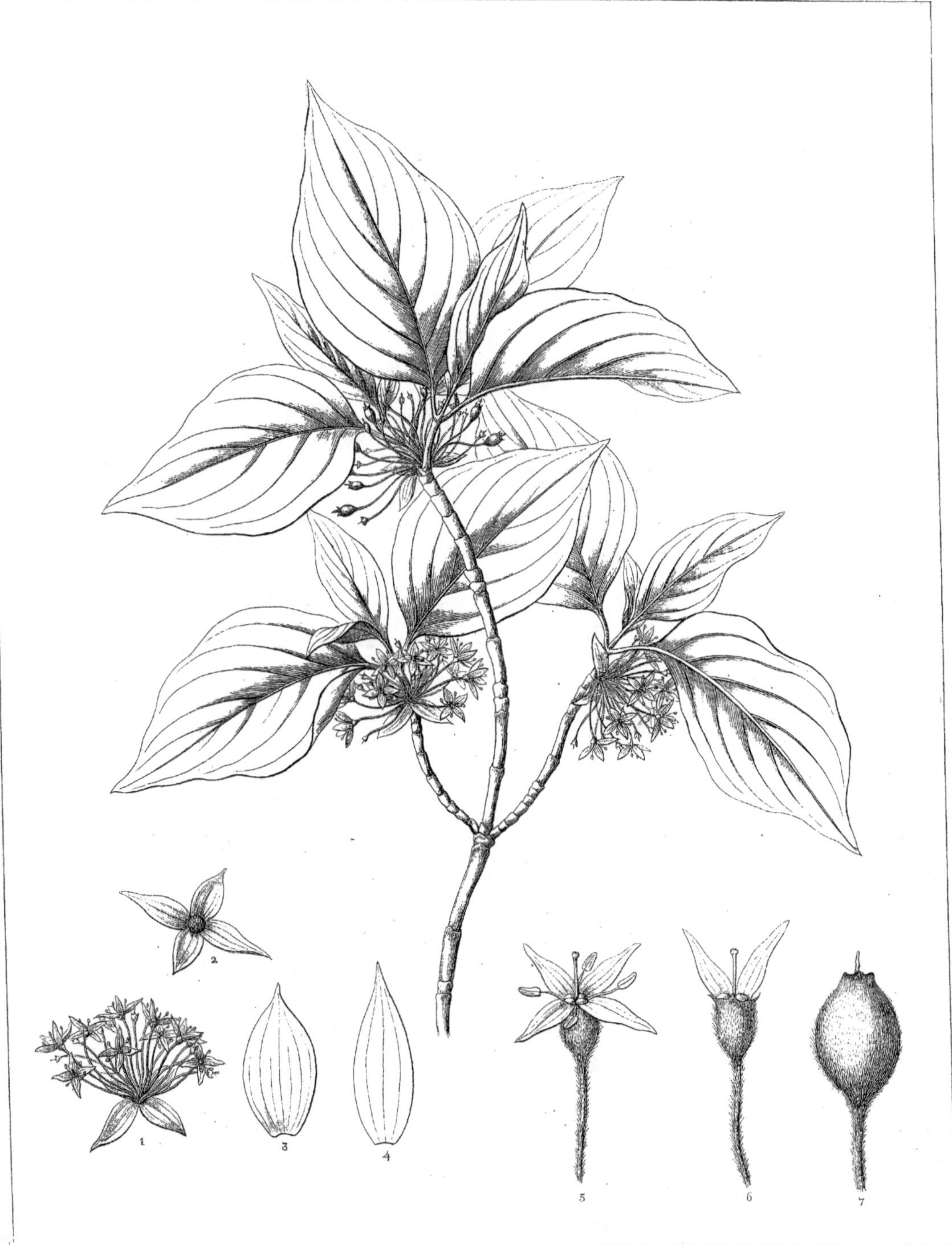

Ackerman Lith. 379 Broadway N.Y.

CORNUS SESSILIS.

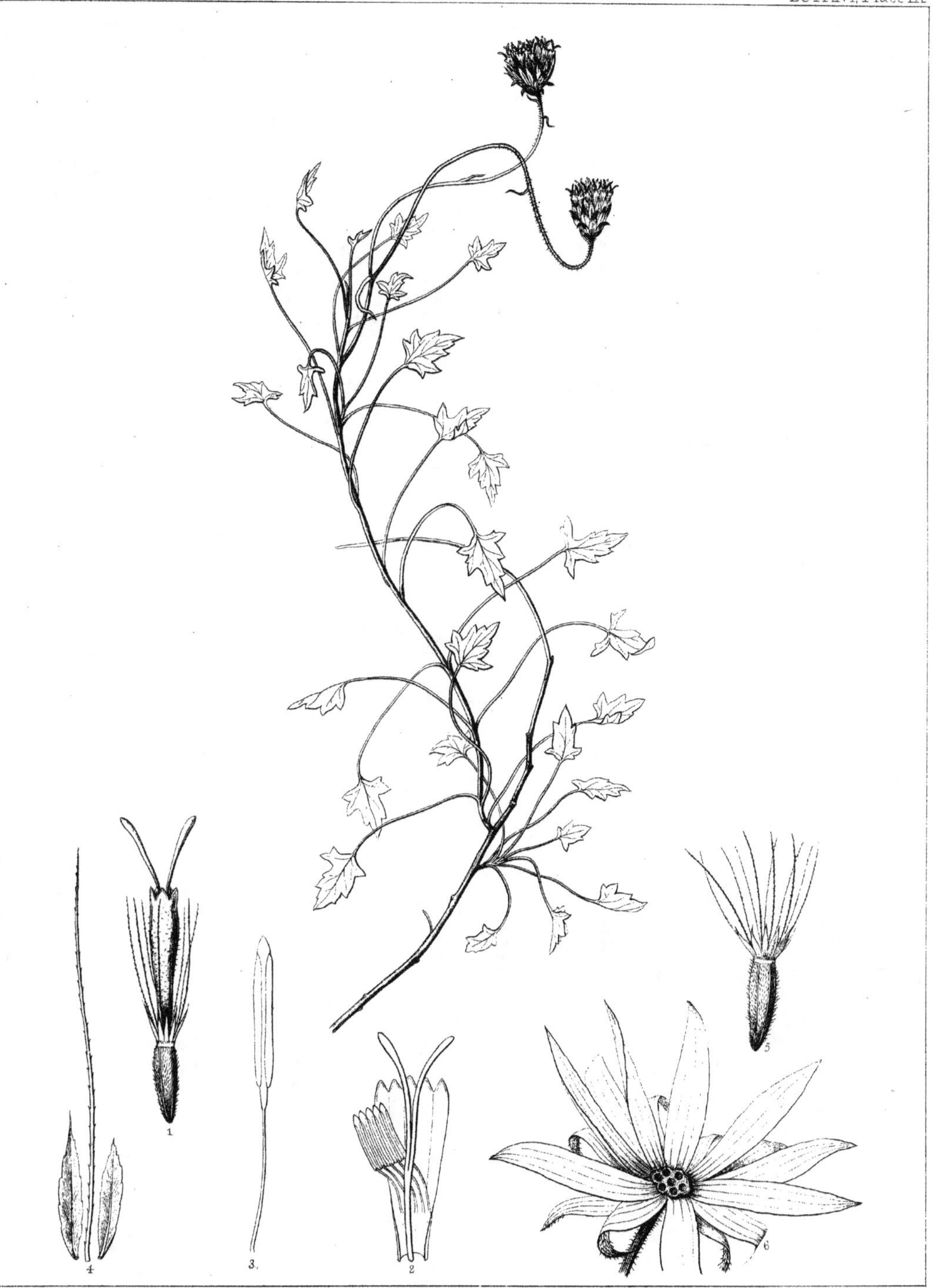

Ackerman Lith. 379 Broadway N.Y.

HOFMEISTERIA PLURISETA.

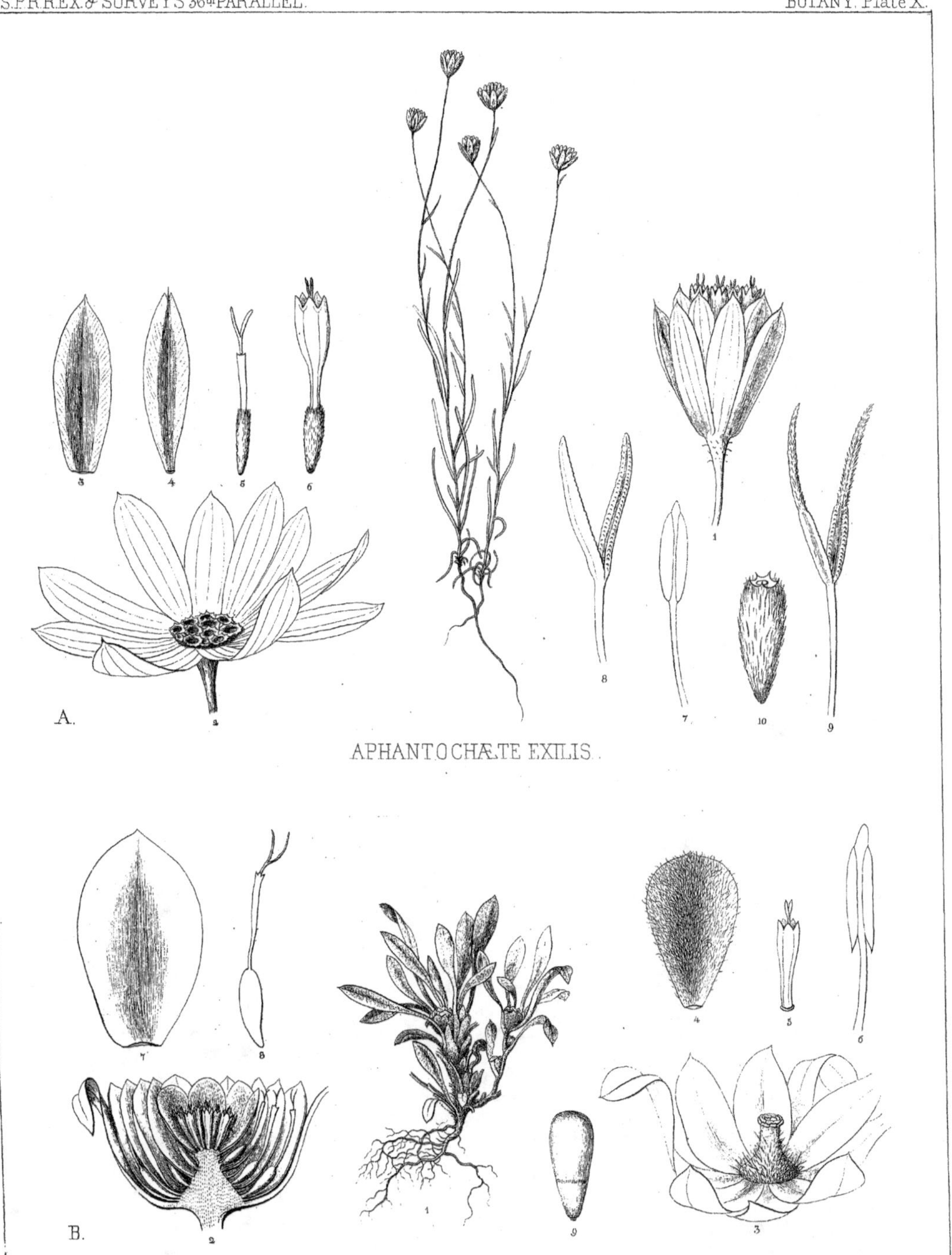

Ackerman Lith. 379 Broadway N.Y.

EVAX CAULESCENS.

Ackerman Lith. 379 Broadway N.Y.

ASTER BIGELOVII.

Ackerman lith 379 Broadway N.Y.

LINOSYRIS BIGELOVII.

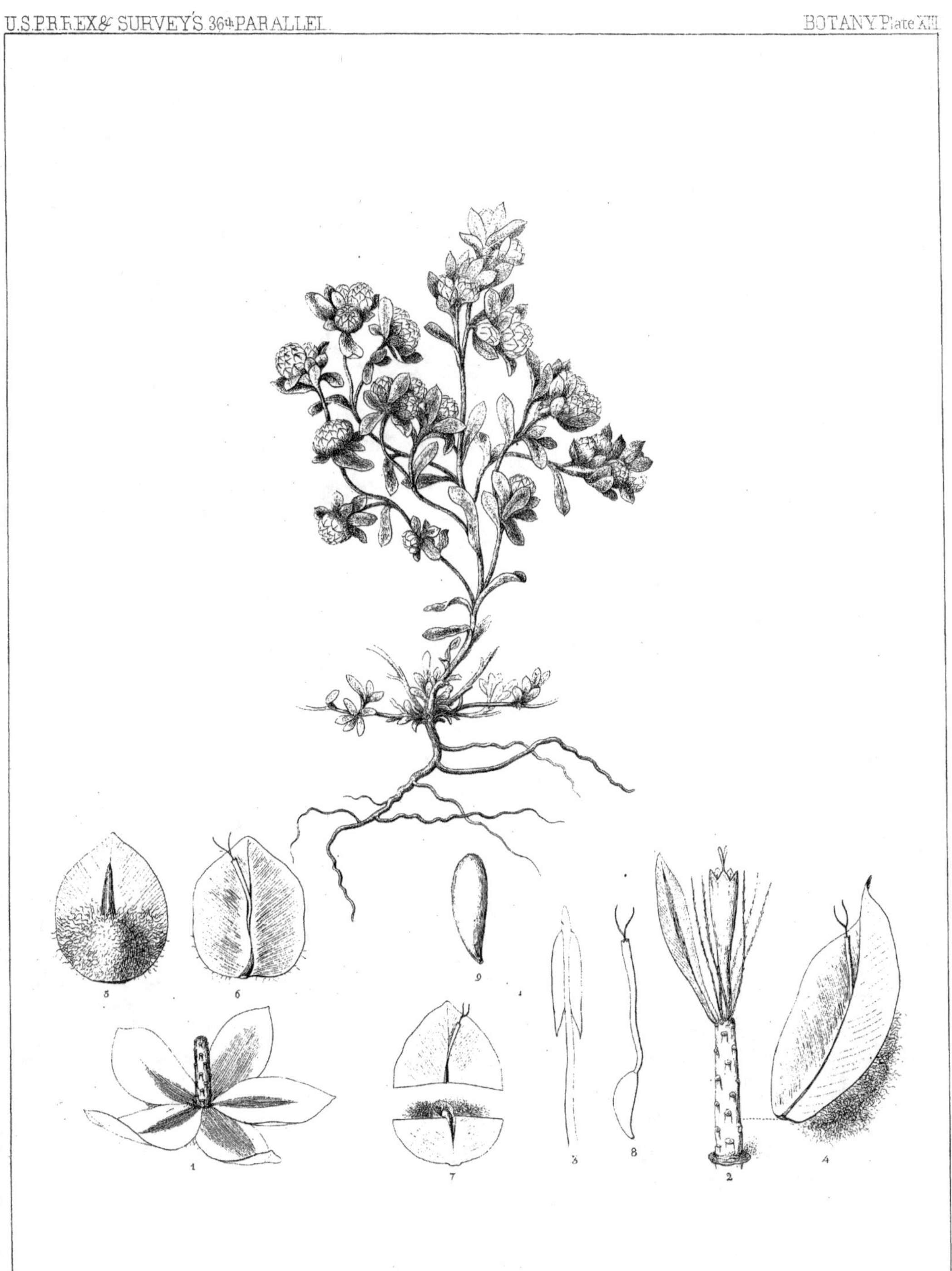

Ackerman, Lith 379 Broadway N.Y.

STYLOCLINE GNAPHALOIDES.

Ackerman Lith. 379 Broadway N.Y.

QUERCUS ECHINACEA.

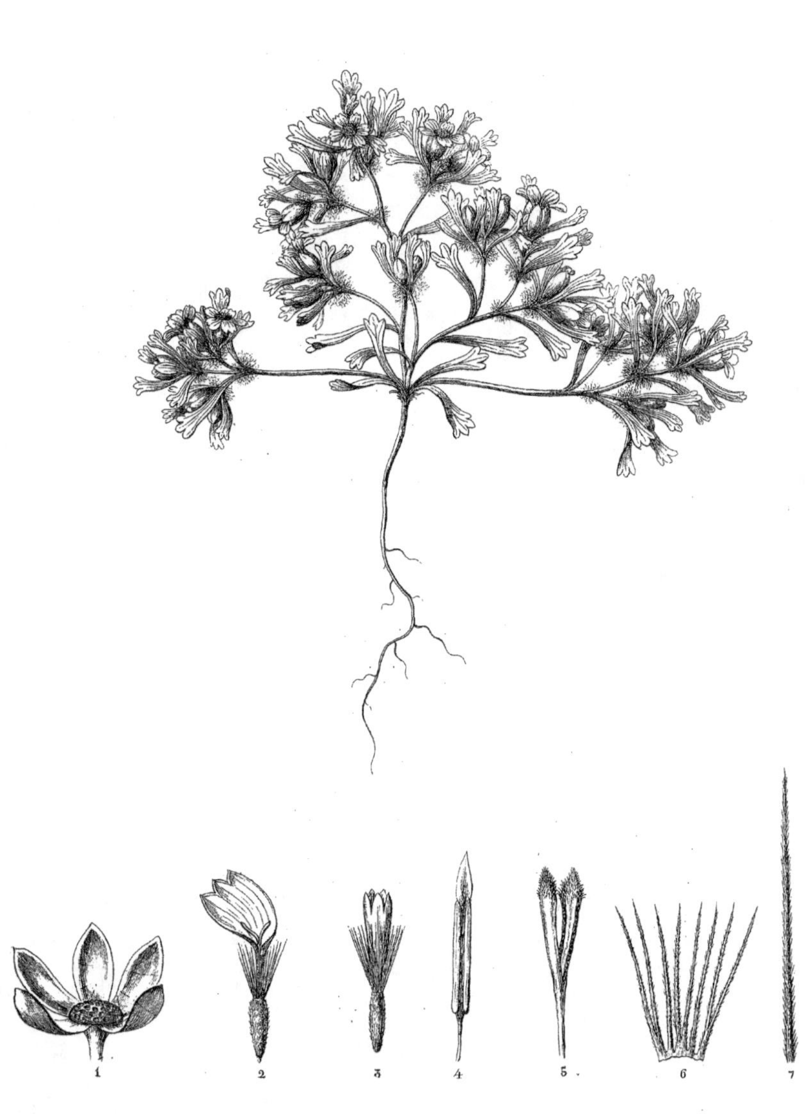

Ackerman Lith 379 Broadway N.Y.

SYNTRICHOPAPPUS FREMONTII.

Ackerman Lith. 379 Broadway N.Y.

LAYIA PENTACHÆTA.

Ackerman Lith 379 Broadway N. Y.

CALAIS BIGELOVII. CALAIS TENELLA.

Ackerman Lith. 379 Broadway N.Y.

CALAIS CYCLOCARPHA.

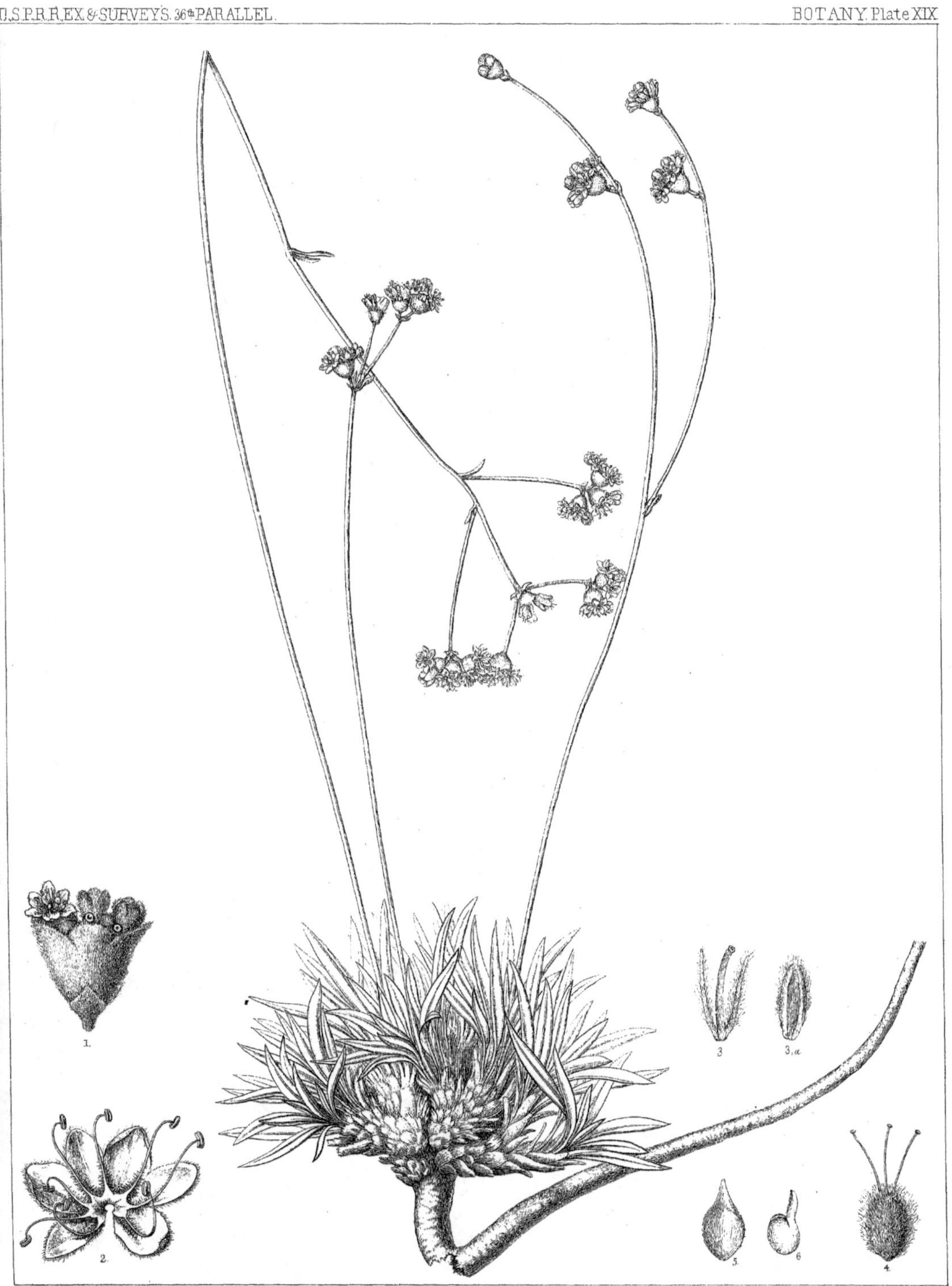

Ackerman Lith. 379 Broadway N.Y.

ERIOGONUM LACHNOGYNUM.

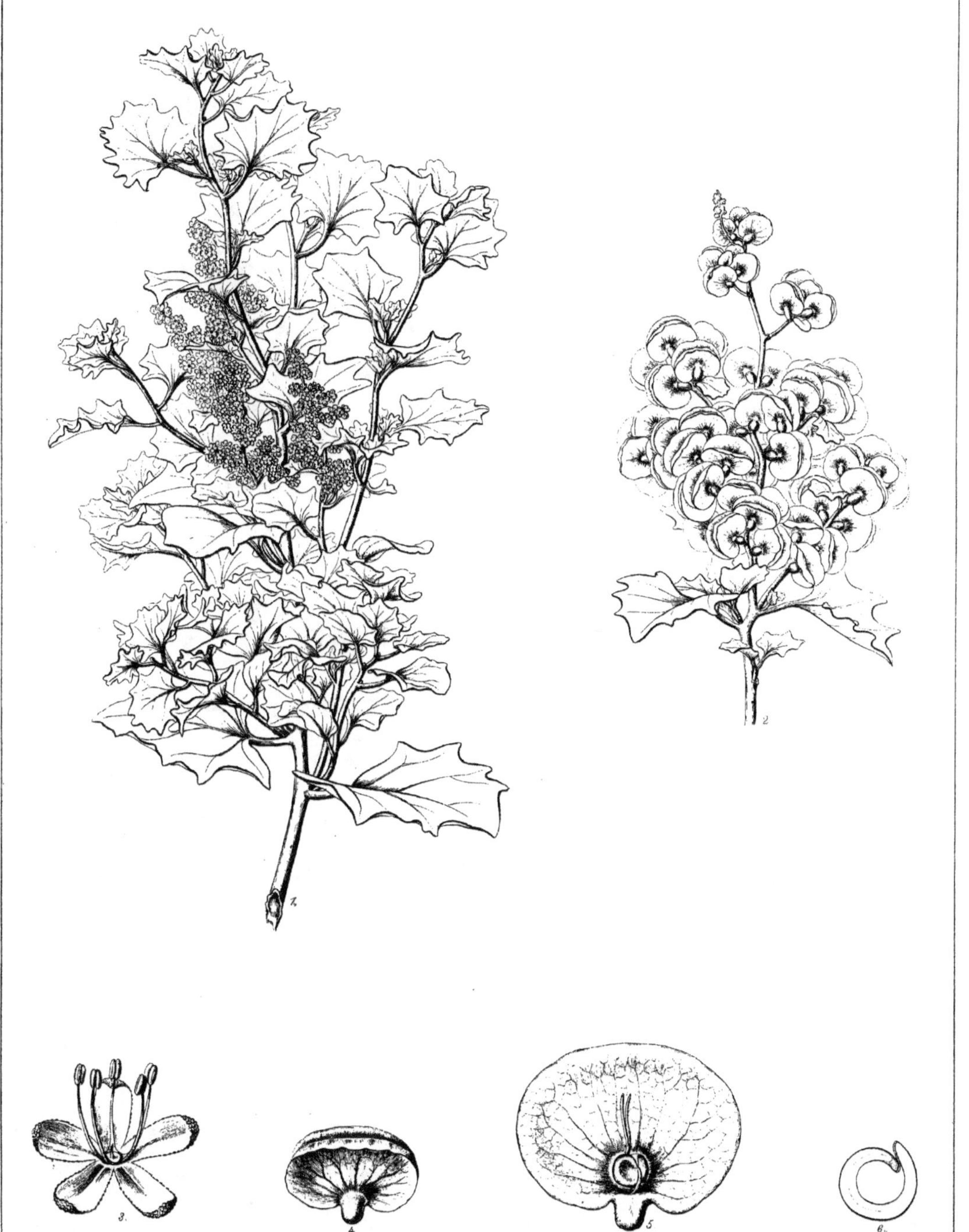

Ackerman Lith. 379 Broadway N.Y.

OBIONE. HYMENELYTRA.

Ackerman Lith. 379 Broadway N.Y.

ALISMA CALIFORNICA.

Ackerman Lith. 379 Broadway N.Y.

SCOLIOPUS BIGELOVII.

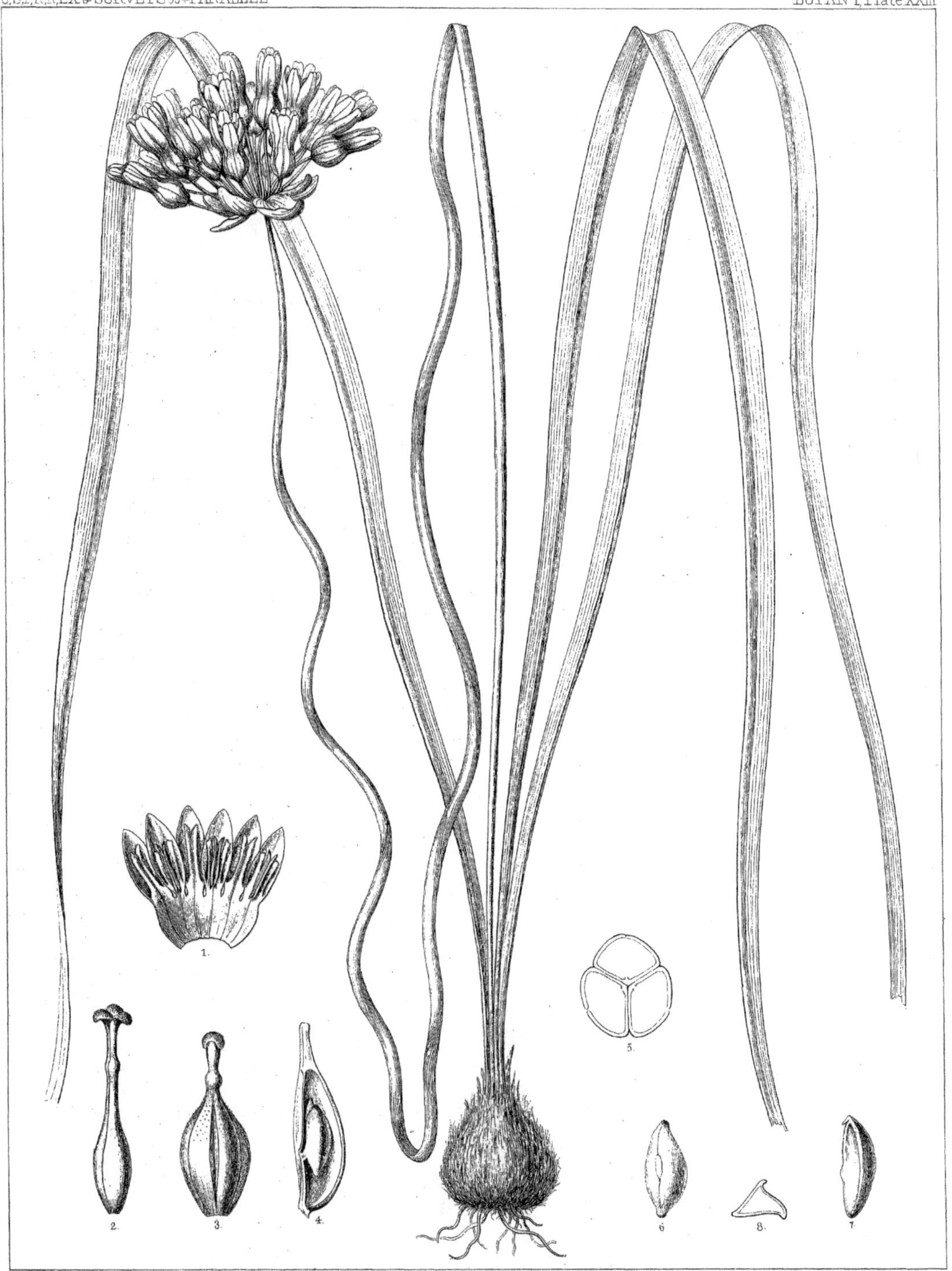

Ackerman Lith. 379 Broadway N.Y.

STROPHOLIRION CALIFORNICUM.

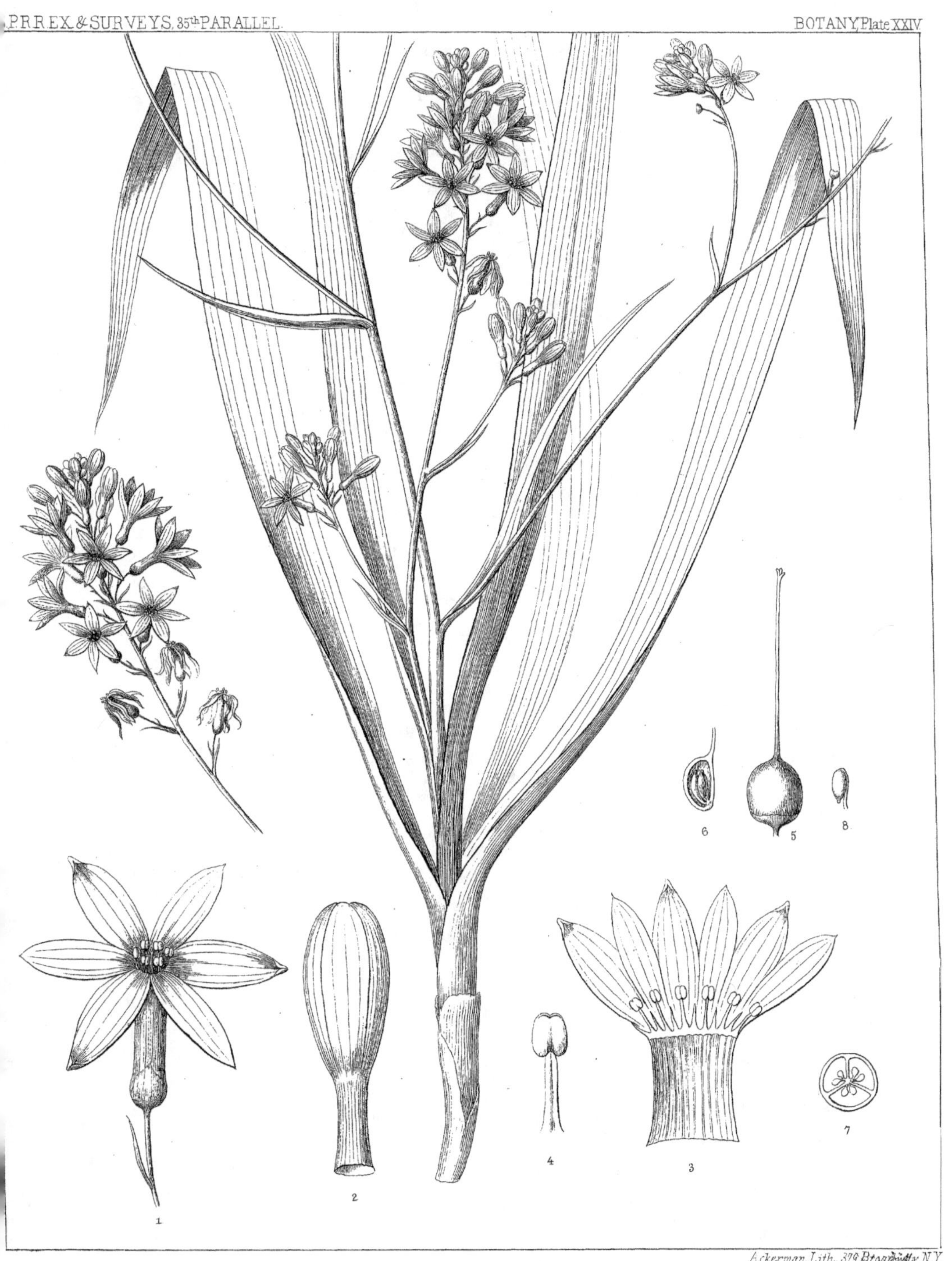

Ackerman Lith. 379 Broadway N.Y.

ODONTOSTOMUM HARTWEGI.

Ackerman Lith. 379 Broadway, N.Y.

CORALLORHIZA MACRÆI.

INDEX TO BOTANY.

[The regular names of Species, Genera, and Natural Orders are in *Italic*. Synonyms and names of plants otherwise noticed are in Roman.*]

*From some misunderstanding, the types have been reversed from their ordinary use in such cases. This was discovered after the index was set up, and it was too late to make the change. The author thinks it is proper to state that, owing to his distance from the press, and the rapidity with which the printing was done, he was not able to revise the proofs.

No. 5.

DESCRIPTION OF THE MOSSES AND LIVERWORTS.

BY W. S. SULLIVANT.

MUSCI.

WEISSIEÆ.

GYMNOSTOMUM CALCAREUM, *Nees & Hornsch.; Bryol. Europ. Gymnost. monogr., p.* 6, *t.* 3 *and* 4: var. perpusilla, foliis erectis ovato-lanceolatis margine crenulatis, capsula pyriformi-ovali. On clayey soil, near San Francisco.

G. CURVIROSTRUM, *Hedw.; Bryol. Europ. Gymnost. monogr., p.* 8, *t.* 7 *and* 8. Wet rocks, Leroux's springs, base of San Francisco mountain, Mogollan range.

WEISSIA VIRIDULA, *Brid.; Bryol. Europ. Weis. monogr., p.* 5, *t.* 2 *and* 3. Various places on the ground.

W. CIRRHATA, *Hedw.; Bryol. Europ. Weis. monogr., p.* 9, *t.* 6. On the prostrate trunk of a Wellingtonia "mammoth tree grove."

DICRANEÆ.

CERATODON PURPUREUS, *Brid.; Bryol. Europ. Cerat. monogr., p.* 5, *t.* 1; var. xanthopus. Near San Francisco; appears to differ from the normal form in nothing but the pale yellow pedicels.

A large Campylopus (?) was found growing with Weissia cirrhata, but not in a fit state for determination.

FESSIDENTEÆ.

FESSIDENS LIMBATUS, (sp. nov.): monoicus pusillus acrocarpus; foliis 8–10 jugis oblongis hyalino-marginatis apice excepto, lamina apiciali duplicaturam inferne latisime marginatam vix æquante; capsula sub ovali inæquali cernua; perist. dentibus maxime introflexis. Near San Francisco; about the size of F. bryoides, from which it is distinguished by its cernuous capsule, the deep insertion of its peristomial teeth, and the denser areolation of its leaves, remarkable for the broad margin of their complicate portion. (Plate I.)

TRICHOSTOMEÆ.

TRICHOSTOMUM TOPHACEUM, *Brid.; Bryol. Europ. Trichost. monogr., p.* 9, *t.* 6. Cajon Pass, Sierra Nevada; also, near San Francisco.

T. FLEXIPES, *Bryol. Europ. Trichost. monogr., p.* 6, *t.* 2. Near San Francisco.

T. CORNICULATUM, *Schwægr. Suppl.* 2, 1, *p.* 75, *t.* 118. With the last.

BARBULA MEMBRANIFOLIA, *Schultz; Bryol. Europ. Barb. monogr., p.* 17, *t.* 3. Dry ravines on Williams' fork of the Great Colorado, near the mouth of Santa Maria Creek.

B. CHLORONOTOS, *Schultz; Bryol. Europ. Barb. monogr., p.* 18, *t.* 4. Hab. same as the last.

B. FALLAX, *Hedw.; Bryol. Europ. Barb. monogr., p.* 23, *t.* 9. Cajon Pass, Sierra Nevada; also near San Francisco.

B. BRACHYPHYLLA, (sp. nov.): dioica; dense cæspitosa; caule fastigiato-ramosa; foliis patentibus ovatis breviter obtuse acuminatis toto margine recurvis usque ad apicem valido-costatis; capsula cylindracea erecta; perist. dentibus vix contortis e membrana basilari perangusta ortis; annulo simplici; operculo longe rostrato; calyptra brevi. Near Benicia. Stems 8–12 lines high, rooting profusely their entire length, and branching from below the floral apex. Leaves dark, brownish green, of a firm, thick texture; cellules minute sub-quadrate. Pedicel 5–7 lines high, red. Teeth of the peristome contorted scarcely half-way round. This species has the habit and aspect of a Trichostomum, particularly of T. rigidum, but each of the 32 teeth of its peristome consists of two conjoined lines of tubular cellules, one placed before the other. (Plate II.)

B. VINEALIS, *Brid.; Bryol. Europ. Barb. monogr., p.* 24, *t.* 10. Oakland, opposite San Francisco; also Sonora.

B. SEMITORTA, (sp. nov.): dioica; laxe cæspitosa; caulibus subsimplicibus basi solum radicantibus apice congesto-foliosis; foliis e basi erecta amplexante horizontalibus lineari-lanceolatis concavis margine planis, costa solida cum apice desinente; capsula cylindracea erecta aciculari-operculata, anguste annulata; perist. dentibus longiusculis semitortis; calyptra vix infra operculum descendente. Growing with the last species, which it resembles, but has a shorter calyptra, longer operculum, and less contorted peristome, with a narrower basal membrane. Its leaves are more tufted at the top of the stems, squarrose-spreading, gradually tapering from near their base, (not suddenly and long acuminated,) with margins nowhere recurved; areolation much larger. (Plate III.)

B. CONVOLUTA, *Hedw.; Bryol. Europ. Barb. monogr., p.* 29, *t.* 16.—Oakland, opposite San Francisco.

B. VAHLIANA, *Schultz; Bryol. Europ. Barb. monogr., p.* 33, *t.* 18.—Cajon Pass, Sierra Nevada; also near Los Angeles.

B. MARGINATA, *Bryol. Europ. Barb. monogr., p.* 33, *t.* 19.—Dry rocky places, common.

B. SUBULATA, *Brid.; Bryol. Europ. Barb. monogr., p.* 36, *t.* 21 and 22.—Dry ravines on Bill Williams' fork of the Rio Colorado, near the mouth of Santa Maria creek.

B. INERMIS, *Mont.; Byrol. Europ. Barb. monogr., Suppl.* 3.—At the base of a mountain fifty miles west of the Rio Colorado in the line of the survey.

B RURALIS, *Hedw.; Bryol. Europ. Barb. monogr., p.* 43, *t.* 27.—Cajon Pass, Sierra Nevada.

B. MULLERI, *Bryol. Europ. Barb. monogr., p.* 44, *t.* 28.—Various localities; appears to be a common species.

POTTIEAE.

POTTIA SUBSESSILIS. *Bryol. Europ. Pott. monogr., p.* 6, *t.* 1.—Los Angeles.

P. MINUTULA, *Bryol. Europ. Pott. monogr., p.* 8, *t.* 3.—Growing with the last.

ORTHOTRICHEAE.

ORTHOTRICHUM LYELLII. *Hook.; Bryol. Europ. Orthot. monogr., p.* 27, *t.* 16.—Growing on trees; not uncommon in California and Oregon. Differs from the European form in its longer and narrower leaves, more undulate on the margins, and more contorted when dry. The articulated gland-like bodies, (Converfa Orthotrichi,) so frequent on the leaves of European specimens, are seldom present on the Californian. It is the var. foliis longioribus siccitate magis crispatis, (*Brid. Bryol. Univ.* 1, *p.* 728.) founded on specimens collected by Menzies at Nootka Sound.

In the collection are imperfect specimens of another Orthotrichum gathered at the crossing of the Colorado, growing with Schistidium apocarpum, and also on rocks at Lereux's spring, near the foot of San Francisco mountain, Mogollan range, which apparently belong to O. cupulatum.

GRIMMIEÆ.

SCHISTIDIUM APOCARPUM, *Bryol. Europ. Schistid. monogr.*, *p.* 7, *t.* 3.—On rocks at the crossing of the Rio Colorado.

GRIMMIA CALIFORNICA, (sp. nov.): dioica ; laxe cæspitosa ; foliis erecto-patentibus elongato-lanceolatis carinoto-concavis margine revolutis, costa in acumen hyalinum denticulatum excurrente ; capsula ovali oblongave, sub-pyriformi pendula, sicca vix costata ; pedicello breviusculo arcuato ; operculo recte longe rostrato ; calyptra dimidiato-mitriformi basi 4—5 fissa ; annulo majusculo triplici ; peristom. dentibus bifidis.—Oakland, opposite San Francisco; also near Sonora. Approaches near to G. trichophylla, *Grev.;* but that has less crowded, longer, more slender, and flexuous leaves, and capsules distinctly and prominently ribbed when dry, with subflexuous and longer pedicels.

G. Olneyi, *Sulliv.*, a more closely related species, is not so robust ; has leaves canaliculate-concave not recurved on the margin ; when flattened, linear-lanceolate from an ovate base, and the teeth of the peristome perforated (not bifid) at their apices.

G. Californica differs from both species in the more or less obovate outline of its capsule, with an evident collum.

In the same habitat occurs a variety differing from the typical form in the strong recurvation of its leaves, an unusual feature in this genus, and which is to be found in only one other published species, the Algerian Grimmia ancistrodes, *Mont.*, which, according to original specimens from Dr. Montagne, is likewise dioecious, not monoecious, as stated in his Sylloge. This variety may prove to be a distinct species. (Plate IV.)

G. TRICHOPHYLLA, *Grev.; Bryol. Europ. Grimm. monogr.*, *p.* 16, *t.* 9.—Shaded rocks, near Benicia.

G. PULVINATA, *Smith ; Bryol. Europ. Grimm. monogr. p.* 12, *t.* 4.—Rocks on Bill Williams' fork, near the mouth of Santa Maria Creek. There occurs in the collection sterile specimens of a Grimmia agreeing very well with G. commutata ; locality not mentioned.

HEDWIGIEÆ.

HEDWIGIA CILIATA, *Ehrh.; Bryol. Europ. Hedwig. monogr.*, *p.* 5, *t.* 1 and 2.—On rocky cliffs, head waters of Bill Williams' fork, near the Aztec Pass.

POLYTRICHEÆ.

POLYTRICHUM JUNIPERINUM, *Hedw.; Bryol. Europ. Polyt. monogr.*, *p.* 12, *t.* 15.—Hillsides near Downieville, on the Yuba river.

P. PILIFERUM, *Bryol. Europ. Polyt. monogr.*, *p.* 11, *t.* 14.—Rocky places above Sonora, base of the Sierra Nevada.

BRYEÆ.

AULACOMNION ANDROGYNUM, *Schwœgr.; Bryol. Europ. Aulacom.*, *monogr.*, *p.* 11, *t.* 4.—On the ground, or on much-decayed logs. A common species in Oregon and California, somewhat larger than the European form, and, unlike it, fruits copiously.

BRYUM TOZZERI, *Grev.; Bryol. Europ. Bry.*, *monogr.*, *p.* 41, *t.* 16.—Coast mountains near Oakland.

B. PYRIFORME, *Hedw.; Bryol. Europ. Bry.*, *monogr.*, *p.* 45, *t.* 18.—Banks of streams, Quiqualmungo Ranch, near the Cajon Pass.

B. BIGELOVII, (sp. nov.): dioicum ; laxe cæspitosum elatum multoties innovando-ramosum ex apice ramulosum ; foliis caulis innovationumque inferne parvis distantibus ascendendo majoribus imbricantibus erecto-patentibus oblongo-ovatis (comalibus lanceolato-acuminatis) concavis margine subintegro vix recurvis, costa valida percurrente vel infra apicem desinente ; capsula alte pedicellata sub pendula pyriformi-elliptica: flore masculo terminali capituliformi. Banks of streams above Sonora, base of the Sierra Nevada. The dark yellowish-green of the foliage; the shorter, more obtuse, and nearly entire leaves, with a closer areolation; the less obovate capsule, and the capituliform male flowers of this species, separate it from B. Wahlenbergii, its nearest congener. (Plate V.)

B. ARGENTEUM, *Linn.; Bryol., Europ., Bry., monogr., p.* 78, *t.* 41.—On rocks, dry ravines, fifty miles west of the Rio Colorado, on the line of the survey.

B. CALIFORNICUM, (sp. nov.): dioicum? dense cæspitosum; caule atque innovationibus brevissimis bulbiformibus; foliis inferne dissitis superne majoribus densissime capituliformi-imbricatis concavis subquadrato-ovatis breviter apiculatis, margine subintegerrimis subplanisque, continuo-costatis; capsula atro-sanguinea oblonga vel oblongo-ovata pendula, collo haud angustiore siccatate rugoso basi obtusato; operculo minuto hemisphærico; peristomii dentibus dilute purpurascentibus profunde insertis remotius articulatis, ciliolis singulis brevibus exappendiculatis; annulo magno revolubili. Near Benicia. This species, compared with B. atropurpureum, has a more compact mode of growth, leaves broader, shorter, less acuminate, and of a subquadrate or obovate-quadrate outline, costa not excurrent, and capsule with a collum as long and as broad as the sporangium.

In B. versicolor, another nearly allied species, the pedicel at the base of the capsule is more suddenly bent, and the branches somewhat julaceous, with leaves longer, more acuminate, and cuspidate by the excurrent costa.

B. Californicum is best distinguished from either of these species by its short bulb-like stems and branches, its very small conic-hemisphærical operculum, and the deep insertion below the rim of the capsule of its peristomial teeth. The inner peristome is seldom well developed.

B. Blindii has a globose-pyriform capsule, with a tapering and much smaller collum; its peristome and the areolation of the leaf are also different. (Plate VI.)

B. OBCONICUM, *Hornsch.; Bryol., Europ., Bry., monogr., p.* 59, *t.* 37.—Near San Francisco and Napa City.

Specimens, partly incomplete, of a Bryum collected in Mammoth Tree Grove, on the decayed trunks of trees, may belong to this species. The capsules, however, are shorter and less clavate, and the comal leaves longer and more gradually acuminate, and the habitat, on decayed wood, unusual.

B. INTERMEDIUM, *Brid.; Bryol., Europ., Bry., monogr., p.* 47, *t.* 19.—Var. foliis elongato-oblongis sensim acuminatis. No locality given. The capsules are in various stages of development, as is common in this species.

B. TORQUESCENS; *Bryol., Europ., Bry., monogr., p.* 49, *t.* 20.—Var. foliis latioribus densius areolatis siccis minus contortis. Oakland, opposite San Francisco.

B. OCCIDENTALE, (sp. nov.): dioicum, brunnescens; caule brevi inferne defoliato tomentoso superne congesto-folioso; innovationibus gracilescentibus in media longitudine incrassatis; foliis ellipticis breviter acuminatis (perichætialibus oblongo-lanceolatis) costa valida excurrente cuspidatis, decurrentibus margine subintegerrimis vix recurvis, reticulo rhombeo-hexagono cellulis inferioribus subquadratis; capsula pendula oblonga vel oblongo-obconica macrostoma; peristomio normali ciliolis ternatim interjectis exappendiculatis; annulo permagno; operculo convexo-apiculato: planta mascula graciliore innovando-continua: flore terminali gemmiformi polyphyllo. Near San Francisco. This species is separated from the nearly related B. cæspiticium by its erect, appressed, decurrent, scarcely margined leaves, not so acuminate nor so long-cuspidate, by their heavier costa, with a denser texture, composed, in their lower half, of quadrate cellules. It has also an oblong and smaller capsule, with but a slight tendency to a pyriform outline, a wider and reddish (not yellowish) operculum, and a larger annulus. (Plate VII.)

MNIUM MENZIESII, *Hook. in Botanic. Miscell.* 1, *p.* 36, *t.* 19; Hypnum acanthoneuron, *Schwægr. Suppl. t.* 258. Common on the coast range of mountains; fruit rare.

FUNARIEÆ.

FUNARIA HYGROMETRICA, *Hedw.; Bryol. Europ. Funar. monogr. p.* 8, *t.* 4. Various places.

F. MUHLENBERGII, *Schwægr.; Bryol. Europ. Funar. monogr. p.* 6, *t.* 1. Near the crossing of the Rio Colorado on the line of the survey.

F. HIBERNICA, *Hook.; Bryol. Europ. l. c. p.* 7, *t.* 2. Cajon Pass, Sierra Nevada.

FONTINALEÆ.

FONTINALIS CALIFORNICA, (sp. nov.): caulibus flaccidissimis multoties divisis ramosis, ubique foliosis; foliis concavis patentibus distantibus late ovalibus laxiuscule areolatis, cellulis utriculo primordiali subsoluto instructis; fructu non viso. Rivulets in the coast range of mountains north of the bay of San Francisco.

Resembles F. Eatoni, *Sulliv.*, but is a somewhat smaller plant, with more distant and spreading, shorter, broader, and less acuminated leaves of a looser areolation, composed of shorter and wider cellules, in which the primordial utricle is more or less conspicuous; color reddish-brown or copperish.

The species of this genus have each a peculiar aspect or facies, (difficult to describe,) which is little liable to variation in consequence of the uniformity of their habitat. Their sporules have a diameter of about $\frac{1}{125}$ of a line, not $\frac{1}{225}$, as erroneously stated in the second edition of Gray's Manual of Botany.

LEUCODONTEÆ.

PTERIGYNANDRUM FILIFORME, *Hedw.; Bryol. Europ. Pterigyn. monogr. p.* 3, *t.* 1. Near San Francisco; on trees.

PTEROGONIUM GRACILE, *Swartz.; Bryol. Europ. Pterogon. monogr. p.* 4, *t.* 1. With the last.

ALSIA CALIFORNICA, *Sulliv. in Proceed. Amer. Acad. of Arts and Sci., Jan.*, 1855; also in *Cryptogam. of the U. S. Exp. Expedition, t. XXV, ined.;* Neckera Californica, *Hook. & Arn. in Beechy's Voy. p.* 162. On trees; not uncommon.

LEPTODON CIRCINATUS, (sp. nov.): dioicus; ramis primariis e rhizomate horizontali oriundis inferne nudiusculis superne dense frondiformi-pinnatis (siccitate circinatis) paraphyllosis; foliis quinquefariam imbricatis erecto-patentibus lanceolatis acuminatis subcarinato-concavis evanidicostatis dorso papillosis margine parum recurvis superne serrulatis, retis pellucidæ areolis minutis chlorophyllosis ovali-rhombeis e costa radiatim seriatis alaribus subquadratis confertioribus; floribus masculis substipitatis axillaribus secus rachim utrinque crebre dispositis; antheridiis numerosis copiose paraphysatis; fructu ignoto. Coast range of mountains south of San Francisco. Grows in dark-green cushion-like masses. The main stem or rhizoma hard, woody, buried in the soft bark of trees, and throwing out at right angles numerous elastic primary branches—1½ to 2 inches long—of which the lower half is simple, the upper expanded into a densely pinnated ovate frond, circinate when dry. The simply pinnate ramification of the primary branches, and the shape of the leaf, separate this species from its cogeners. (Plate I.)

ANTITRICHIA CURTIPENDULA, *Brid.; Bryol. Europ. Antitric. monog. p.* 2, *t.* 1. Oakland, opposite San Francisco. The specimens are without fruit, and differ from the normal form (which has likewise been found in California) in its julaceous branches, and shorter and more crowded leaves, resembling the var. Hispanica, which occurs mostly in the south of Europe.

HYPNEÆ.

HYPNUM BIGELOVII, (sp. nov.): dioicum, subdendroideum; surculis e caule rhizomatoidea arcuato-ascendentibus fasciculato-ramosis, ramis ramulisque complanatis; foliis patentissimis bifariis elongato-oblongis breviter acuminatis apice serratis subplanis, marginibus uno latere inflexis, costa sub apice evanida, areolatione densa superne rhombea inferne oblonga parenchymatosa; perichætialibus lanceolatis lineali-acuminatis serratis evanidicostatis; capsula ovali subæquali inclinata collo distincto instructa; pedicello cygneo crassiusculo; operculo conico-rostrato; calyptra cuculliformi; annulo composito; perist. dentibus lineali-lanceolatis dense articulatis, ciliis e membrana lata plicata lanceolatis carina hiantibus, ciliolis binis nodosis. Valleys of the coast range of mountains north of and near to the bay of San Francisco. Plant 1–1½ inches high, growing in close mats. Stems rather stiff and elastic, with shining bright green leaves, striate when dry. Pedicils aggregated, and arising mostly from near the base of the larger branches. (Plate VIII.)

This species appears to be near Leskea gymnopoda, as proposed by Taylor in London Journal of Botany, 1846, p. 65, but that species is there described as having attenuated branches, ovate-lanceolate, semi-costate leaves, and a Leskeoid peristome.

The description of Hypnum expansum *Tayl.* l. c., p. 65, except in the less dendroid habit subpinnate ramification and gradually acuminated leaves, applies very well to our species; both, however, of the Taylorean species just named are considered by Mr. Wilson, (than whom there is no higher authority,) with authentic specimens before him, one and the same, and identical with Neckera longirostris, *Hook.*, of which we have authentic specimens, clearly showing it to be quite distinct from Hypnum Bigelovii.

Our species is interesting as being the most northern representative of a group of Thamnoid Hypna that appears to abound on the Quitinian Andes.

H. Whippleanum (sp. nov.): dioicum pusillum cæspitans sordide virescens; caule filiformi bis terve diviso, divisionibus arcuato-prostratis pinnatis flagelliformi-attenuatis apice radiculosis; foliis erecto-patentibus caulinis deltoideo-ramulinis ovato-lanceolatis acuminatis minute quadrate oblonge areolatis opacis dorso papillosis toto ambitu dentato-serratis, costa pellucida fere ad apicem attingente; perichætialibus filiformi-acuminatis evanidi-costatis; capsula abrupte horizontali, ovali oblongave, subinæquali, collo conspicuo instructa; peristomii albidi dentibus lineali-lanceolatis crebre articulatis, ciliis carina solutis, ciliolis binatis, omnibus æquilongis; operculo conico in medio constricto; pedicello tuberculato cauligeno. Habitat same as the last. A small species with thread-like stems 1–2 inches long; branches of the same thickness as the stems, 3–5 lines long, numerous and pinnately disposed. Pedicels 5–7 lines in height, cygneus. Perichaetia rooting at the base. Capsule dark chestnut brown, pachydermous; its junction with the pedicel being nearly at right angles: collum blackish, obtuse at base. Male flowers numerous on the main divisions of the stem, slightly stipitate; perigonial leaves broad-ovate long-acuminate ecostate; antheridia 10–15 copiously paraphysated.—(Plate IX.)

Hypnum crispifolium and Leskea laxifolia of Hooker, found on the northwest coast of this continent by Menzies, appear to be nearly related to this species; but from the description and figures of them, given by Hooker and Schwaegrichen, they are both larger plants than H. Wippleanum, particularly the first, which has subfalcate-secund, flexuous leaves much longer acuminated, and when dry crisped: the second has an ovate-globose capsule, a Leskeoid peristome, and leaves of a different areolation.

H. calyptratum, (sp. nov.) monoicum exiguum; caule filiformi repente subsimplici pinnato apice flagelliformi foliis erecto-patentibus late ovatis longe tenuiter acuminatis denticulatis inferne margine recurvis continuo-costatis dorso parce papillosis e cellulis minutis subquadratis dense areolatis; perichætialibus pellucidis striatis lanceolatis filiformi-acuminatis, costa excurrente; capsula cylindracea obliqua curvula exannulata; perist. dentibus lineali-acuminatis, ciliis linearibus foraminulosis, ciliolis singulis brevissimis; operculo conico obtuso; calyptra permagna cuculliformi infra capsulam descendente; pedicello cauligeno gracili longiusculo: flore masculo globoso gemmiformi, perigonialibus orbiculari-ovatis apice tenui recurvo, antheridiis eparaphysatis. Near Los Angeles, on the ground. A very small species belonging to a group constituting the genus Thuiduim of the Bryologia Europæa of Bruch and Schimper. Its distinctive characters consist in its small size, simply pinnate ramification, narrow elongated, inclined slightly, curved and exannulate capsule, conic operculum, slender pedicel and very long, narrow calyptra, descending below the capsule and embracing the pedicel. It resembles small forms of H. scitum, *Beauv.* and H. gracile, *Br. & Sch.*, but differs essentially from both in its calyptra and in not having an annulus.—(Plate X.)

H. NOTEROPHILUM, *Sulliv. et Lesqx. Musc. Bor.-Amer. exsiccat., n.* 348; *Sulliv. in Gray's Manuel of Bot., 2d ed., p.* 478. Margins of small streams.

H. SERPENS, *Linn.;* Amblystegium serpens, *Bryol. Europ. Amblyst. monogr., p.* 9, *t.* 3. Common.

H. RIPARIUM, *Linn.;* Amblystegium riparium, *Bryol. Europ. Amblyst. monogr., p.* 14, *t.* 8. Wet places, frequent.

H. ADUNCUM, *Hedw.; Bryol. Europ. Hyp. monogr., p.* 35, *t.* 24. Grows with the last.

H. MYOSUROIDES, *Linn.;* Isothecium myosuroides, *Brid.; Broyl. Europ. Isothec. monogr., p.* 7, *t.* 2. Near San Francisco, dry woods.

H. NUTTALLII, *Wils.; Bryol. Brit., pp.* 334 *and* 339; *Sulliv. and Lesqx. Musc. Bor.-Amer. exsiccat., n.* 338*b*. On decayed trees, south of San Francisco.

H. OREGANUM, *Sulliv. in Mem. Amer. Acad. of Arts and Sci., v. IV, n. ser., p.* 179; *Cryptogamia of the U. S. Expl. Expd., t. XIII, ined.* In woods, on the ground, mostly in damp localities.

The collection contains five or six other species of hypnum; but the specimens are too imperfect to admit of determination.

HEPATICÆ.

FEGATELLA CONICA, *Corda.; Nees. Hepat. Europ. IV, p.* 181; Conocephalus vulgaris, *Bischoff. de Hepat. in Nov. Act. Acad. Nat. Cur. XVII* 2, *p.* 1001, *t.* 69, *f.* 4. On wet rocks, and on the ground near springs.

FIMBRIARIA TENELLA, *Nees. Hepat. Europ. IV, p.* 271; *Bischoff. de Hepat., l. c. t.* 69, *f.* 11. On dry ground, in shady places.

REBOULIA HEMISPHÆRICA, *Raddi.; Bischoff. de Hepat., l. c. t.* 69, *f.* 1. Dry, shaded rocks.

DUVALIA TENERA, *Gottsche. in G. L. and N. Synop. Hepat., p.* 554; Marchantia tenera, *Hooker in Kunth. Synop. Plant., p.* 45. Moist earth.

ANTHOCEROS LÆVIS, *Linn.; G. L. and N. Synop. Hepat., p.* 586. Springy, gravelly places.

METZGERIA FURCATA, *Nees.;* Jungermannia furcata, *Linn.; Hook. Brit. Junger., t.* 56. Damp, mossy rocks.

FOSSOMBRONIA PUSILLA, *Nees.;* Jungermannia pusilla, *Hook. Brit. Junger., t.* 69. Damp earth, frequent.

EXPLANATION OF THE PLATES.

Plate I.—*Fissidens limbatus.*

Fig. 1, plants of the *natural size;* 2, 2, plants ; 3, 3, stem leaves ; 4, 5, base and apex of stem leaves, showing the areolation ; 6, cross sections of stem leaf ; 7, capsules ; 8, portion of capsule, with the peristome viewed from without ; 9, the same viewed from within ; 10, portion of capsule wall, showing the areolation ; 11, a tooth of the peristome ; *all magnified,* except fig. 1.

Plate I.—*Leptodon circinatus.*

Fig. 1, plant in a moist state ; 2, the same when dry, both of the *natural size ;* 3, portions of primary branch and of a branchlet, the former having sterile flowers in the axils of its leaves ; 4, leaf of a branchlet ; 5, 6, base and apex of a leaf showing the areolation ; 7, 7, cross sections of leaf ; 8, cells of the leaf ; 9, 9, paraphyllia ; 10, sterile flower ; 11, the same without perigonial leaves ; 12, perigonial leaves ; 13, antheridium with paraphysis ; *all enlarged,* except figs. 1 and 2.

Plate II.—*Barbula bachyphylla.*

Fig. 1, a sterile and two fertile plants, *natural size;* 2, a fertile plant ; 3, upper portion of the sterile plant showing the terminal perigonium, with a portion of an innovation ; 4, a perichætium, with an innovation from its base ; 5, 5, leaves from upper part of the stem ; 6, leaf from lower part of stem ; 7, perichætial leaf ; 8, 9, base and apex of a stem leaf, showing the areolation ; 10, cross sections of a stem leaf ; 11, capsule, operculum, and calyptra ; 12, capsule and operculum ; 13, two peristomes ; 14, portions of peristome and annulus ; 15, portion of a tooth of the peristome ; 16, portion of the annulus ; 17, antheridia and paraphyses, perigonial leaves, excepting one, removed ; 18, antheridium, paraphysis, and perigonial leaf ; *all magnified,* except fig. 1.

Plate III.—*Barbula semitorta.*

Fig. 1, plants of the *natural size;* 2, a plant ; 3, 3, 3, 3, 3, stem leaves ; 4, a perichætial leaf ; 5, 6, base and apex of stem leaf, showing the areolation ; 7, 7, cross sections of leaf ; 8, vaginula with archegonia paraphysis and a portion of the pedicel ; 9, archegonium and paraphysis ; 10, 10, capsules with opercula and calyptra ; 11, calyptra ; 12, 12, peristomes ; 13, portions of the peristome and annulus ; 14, 15, portions of the teeth of the peristome ; *all magnified,* except fig. 1.

Plate IV.—*Grimmia Californica.*

Fig. 1, a sterile and three fertile plants, *natural size ;* 2, a fertile plant ; 3, apex of the stem bearing the perichætium vaginula, pedicel, capsule, operculum, and calyptra ; 4, capsule operculum, and calyptra ; 5, capsule and operculum ; 6, capsule ; 7, capsule and portion of the pedicel in a dry state ; 8, calyptra ; 9, portion of peristome with annulus, viewed from without ; 11, vertical section of the same ; 10, two teeth of the peristome with spores ; 12, perichætial leaf ; 13, 14, stem leaves ; 15, 17, base and apex of leaf showing the areolation ; 16, cells of the lower part of the leaf ; 18, apex of the leaf ; 19, cells of the upper part of the leaf ; 20, sterile flower ; 21, perigonial leaf ; 22, antheridium ; *all magnified,* except fig. 1. The var. fig. 1*b*. plant of the *natural size ;* 2*b*. a portion of the stem ; 3*b*. a leaf ; *both magnified.*

Plate V.—*Bryum Bigelovii.*

Fig. 1, two fertile plants ; 2, a sterile plant, *all of the natural size ;* 3, a fertile plant ; 4, 4, stem leaves ; 5, 5, comal leaves ; 6, 7, base and apex of stem leaves, showing the areolation ; 8, cells of the lower part of the leaf; 9, cells of the upper part of the leaf; 10, 10, 10, capsules; 11, operculum; 12, portion of the peristome; 13, vaginula; 14, sterile plant; 15, apex of the same, enclosing the sterile flower; 16, antheridium, paraphyses, and perigonial leaf; 17, 17, cross sections of stem leaf; *all magnified*, except figs. 1 and 2.

Figures 2 and 14 are inverted through a mistake of the engraver.

PLATE VI.—*Bryum Californicum.*

Fig. 1, plants of the *natural size;* 2, a single plant; 3, 3, stems and branches; 4, a branch; 5, 5, 5, 5, 5, leaves; 6, cross sections of leaf; 7, a leaf showing the areolation; 8, portions of peristome and annulus; 9, vertical section of the same; 10, 10, 10, capsules; *all magnified*, except fig. 1.

PLATE VII.—*Bryum Occidentale.*

Figs. 1, 1, fertile plants; 2, sterile plant, *all of the natural size;* 3, a fertile plant; 4, 4, 4, leaves; 5, base of leaf and portion of branch, showing their junction; 6, 6, cross sections of leaf; 7, 8, base and apex of leaf, showing the areolation; 9, cells of the lower part of the leaf; 10, cells of the upper part of the leaf; 11, portions of peristome and annulus, outside view; 12, vertical section of the same; 13, 13, capsules; 14, capsule when dry; 15, vaginula; 16, sterile plant; 17, sterile flower; 18, perigonial leaf, antheridium and paraphyses; 19, perigonial leaf; 20, antheridium and paraphyses; *all magnified*, except figs. 1 and 2.

PLATE VIII.—*Hypnum Bigelovii.*

Figs. 1, 1, fertile plants; 2, a sterile plant, all of the *natural size;* 3, fertile plant; 4, portion of a branch; 5, 5, 5, leaves; 6, apex of leaf showing the areolation; 7, cells of the same; 8, base of leaf showing the areolation; 9, cells of the same; 10, 11, 12, capsules, opercula, and calyptra; 13, portions of the peristome and annulus; 14, a tooth of the peristome, side view; 15, perichætium; 16, 16, perichætial leaves; 17, vaginula with archegonia and paraphyses; 18, sterile flower; 19, antheridium, paraphyses, and perigonial leaf; *all magnified*, except figs. 1 and 2.

PLATE IX.—*Hypnum Whippleanum.*

Figs. 1, 1, 1, fertile plants; 2, sterile plant, all of the *natural size;* 3, fertile plant; 4, portion of sterile plant; 5, portion of a branch; 6, 6, 6, 6, stem and branch leaves; 7, 7, lower portion of leaves showing the areolation; 8, 8, upper portion of same, showing the areolation; 9, 9, 9, 9, 9, capsules; 10, 10, opercula; 11, portion of the peristome; 12, perichætium; 13, vaginula; 14, 15, perichætial leaves; 16, portion of the pedicel; 17, sterile flower; 18, antheridium and paraphyses; 19, perigonial leaf; *all magnified*, except figs. 1 and 2.

PLATE X.—*Hypnum calyptratum.*

Figs. 1, 1, 1, 1, plants of the *natural size;* 2, portion of a plant; 3, portions of a branch; 4, 4, leaves; 5, a leaf showing the areolation; 6, portion of same; 7, cross section of leaf; 8, perichætium; 9, perichætial leaves; 10, 10, capsules with operculums and calyptras; 11, capsule with operculum; 12, capsule; 13, calyptra; 14, portion of peristome; 15, sterile flower and perigonial leaves; 16, antheridium; *all magnified*, except fig. 1.

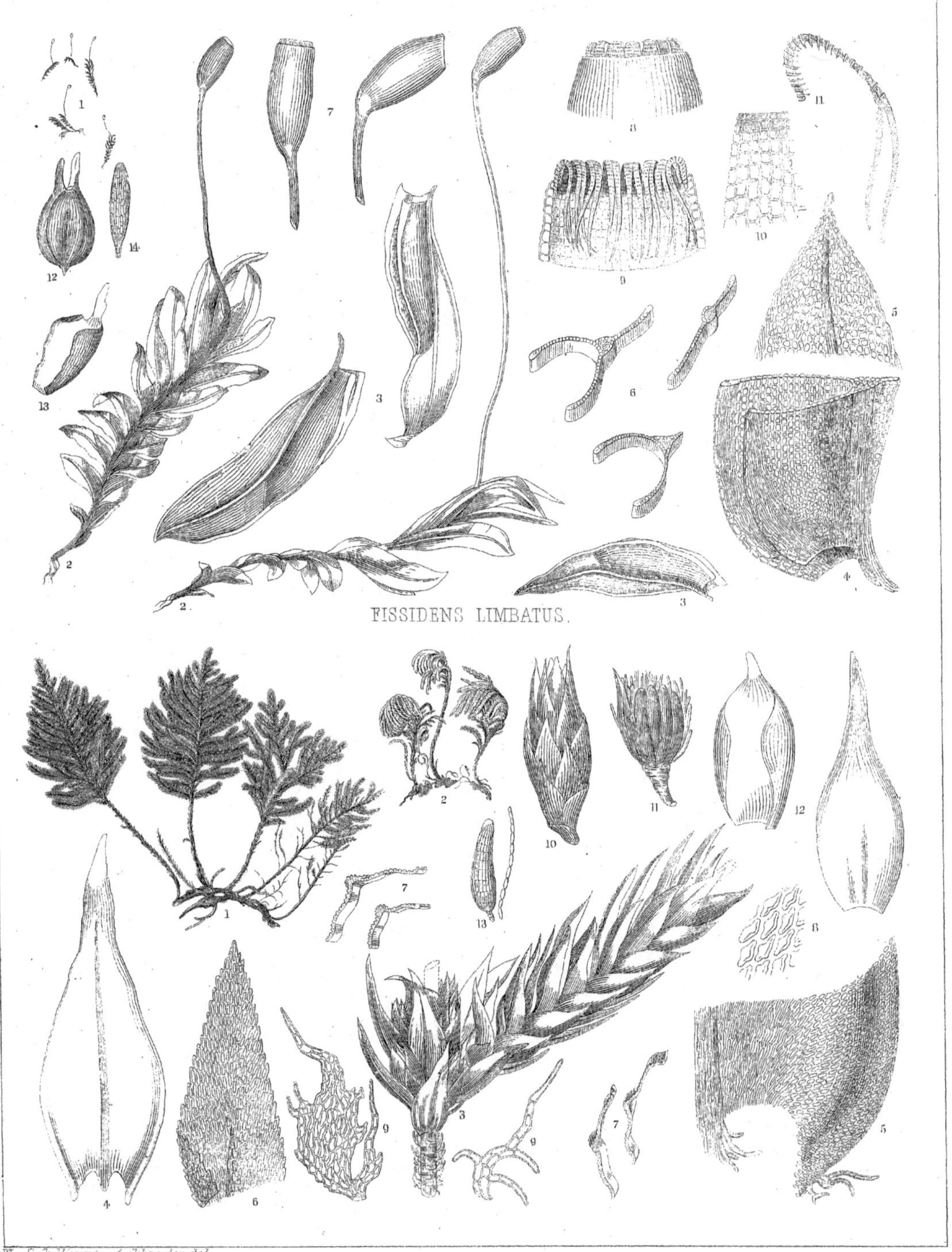

W. S. Sullivant & A. Schrader del.

LEPTODON CIRCINATUS

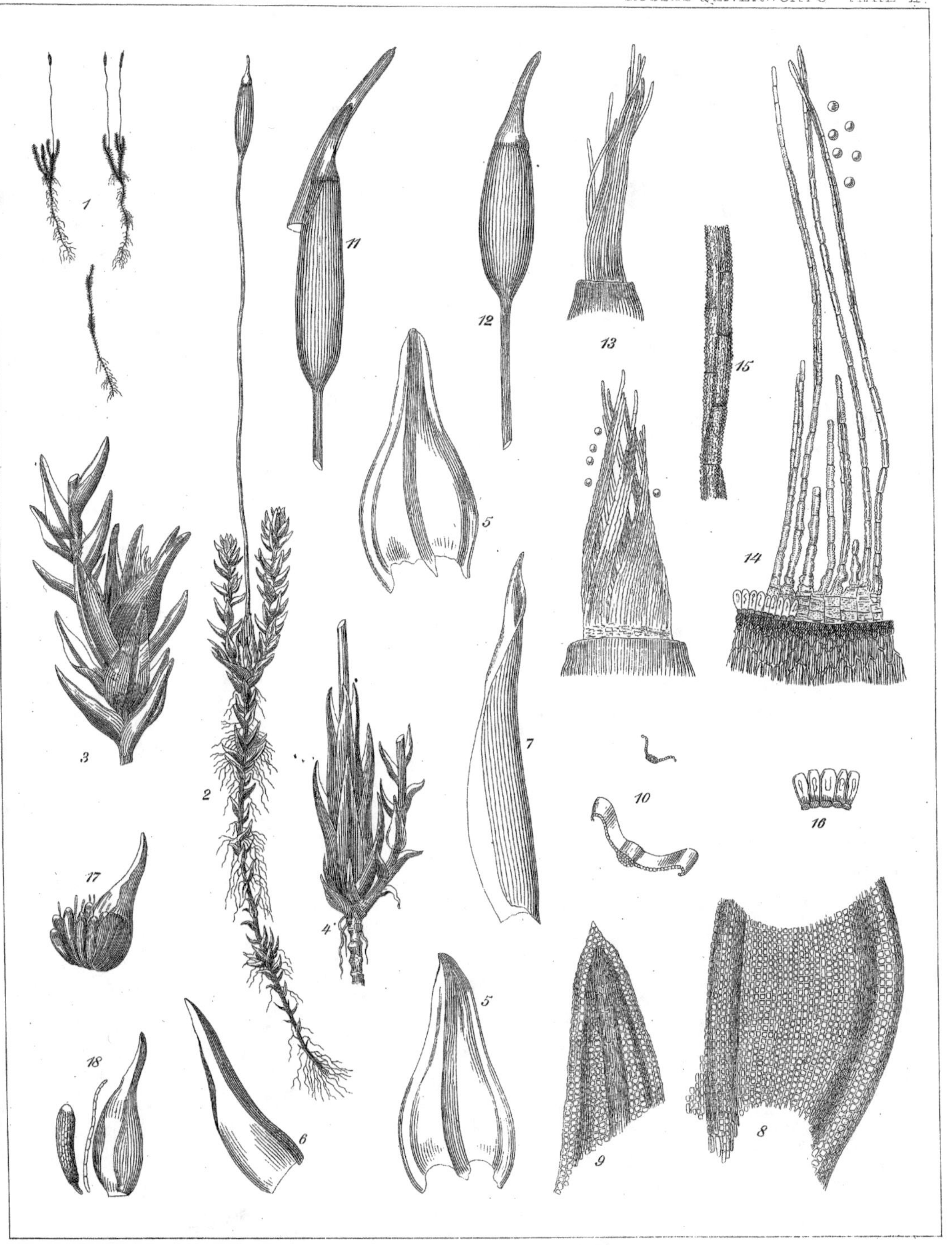

BARBULA BRACHYPHYLLA.

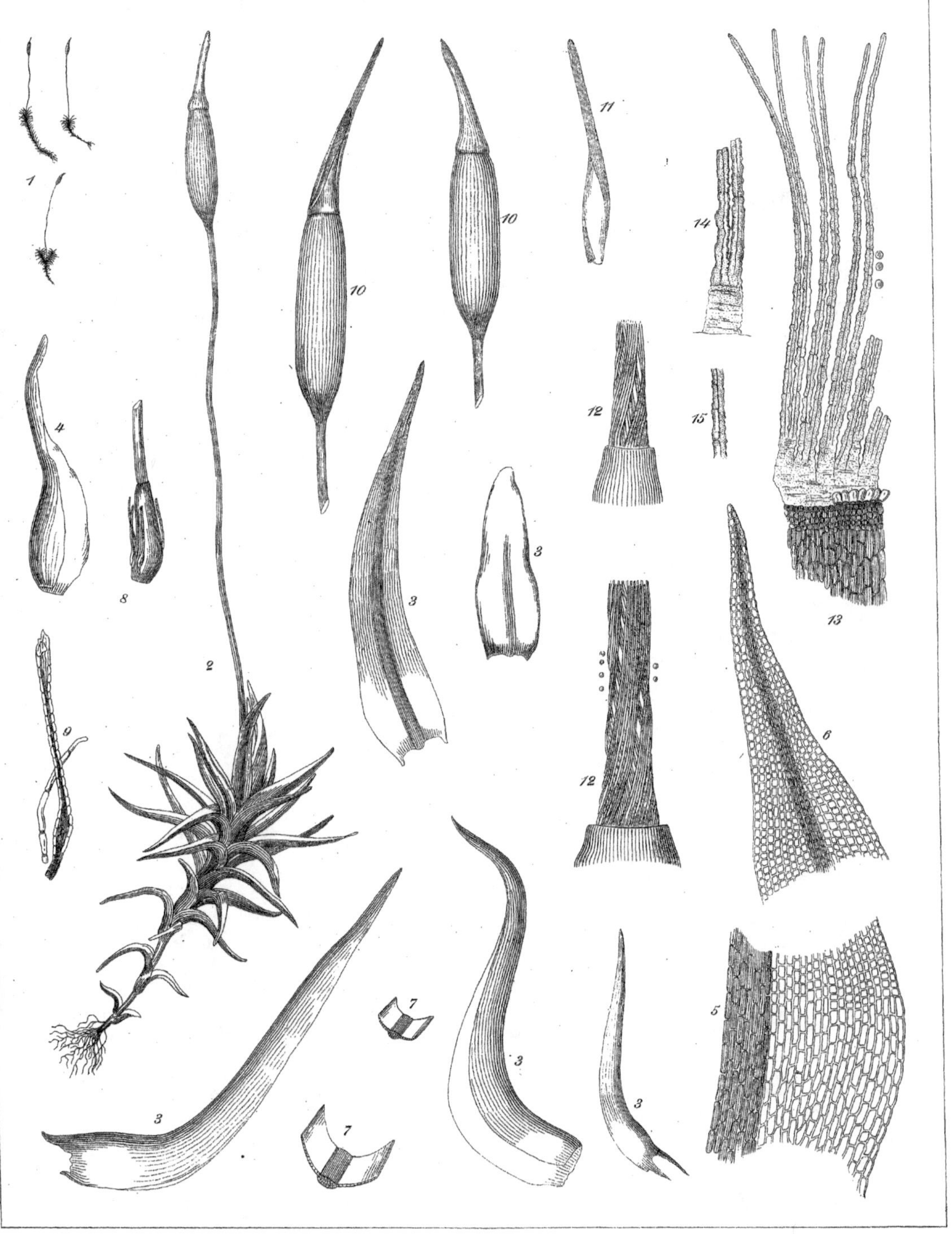

BARBULA SEMITORTA.

GRIMMIA CALIFORNICA.

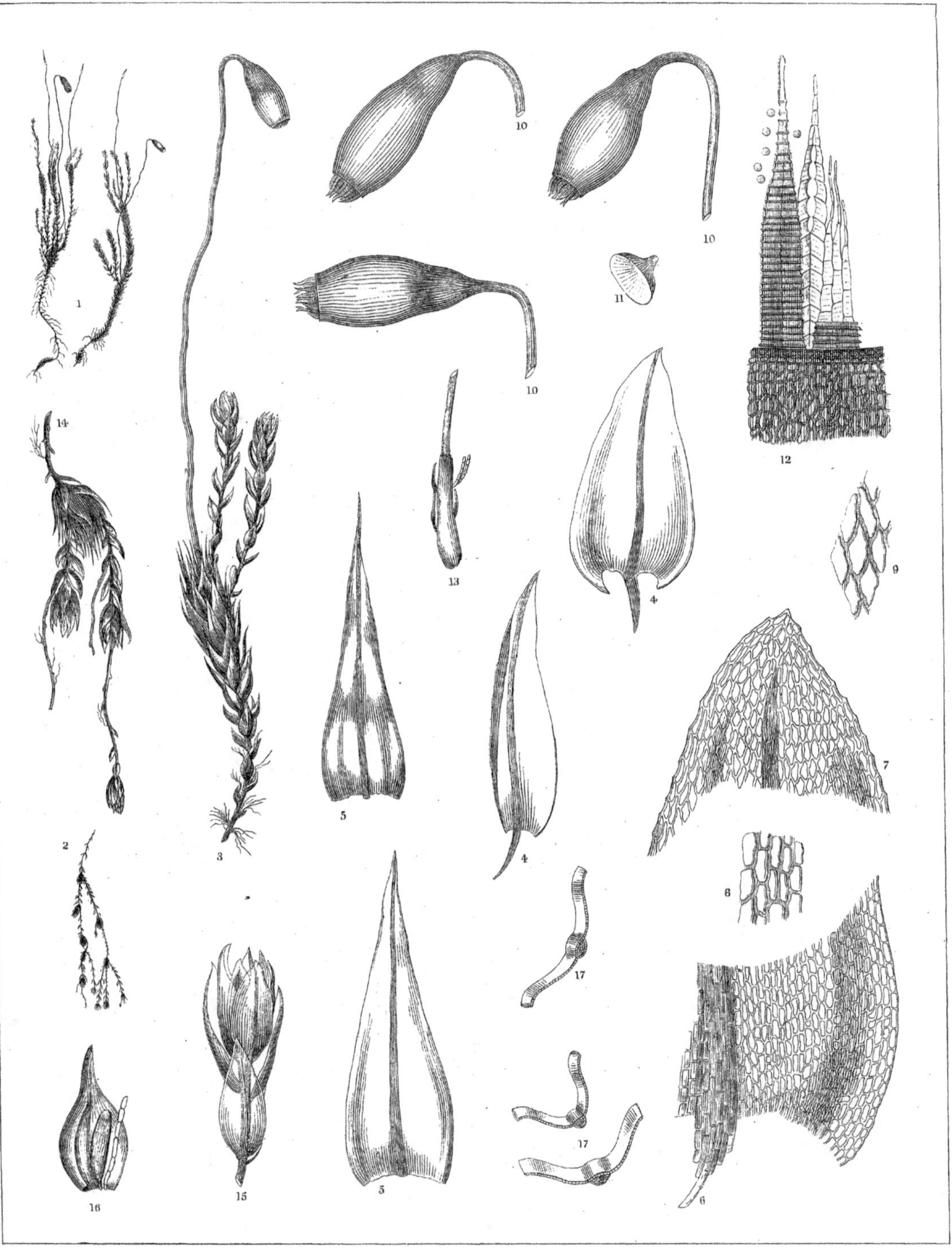

BRYUM BIGELOVII.

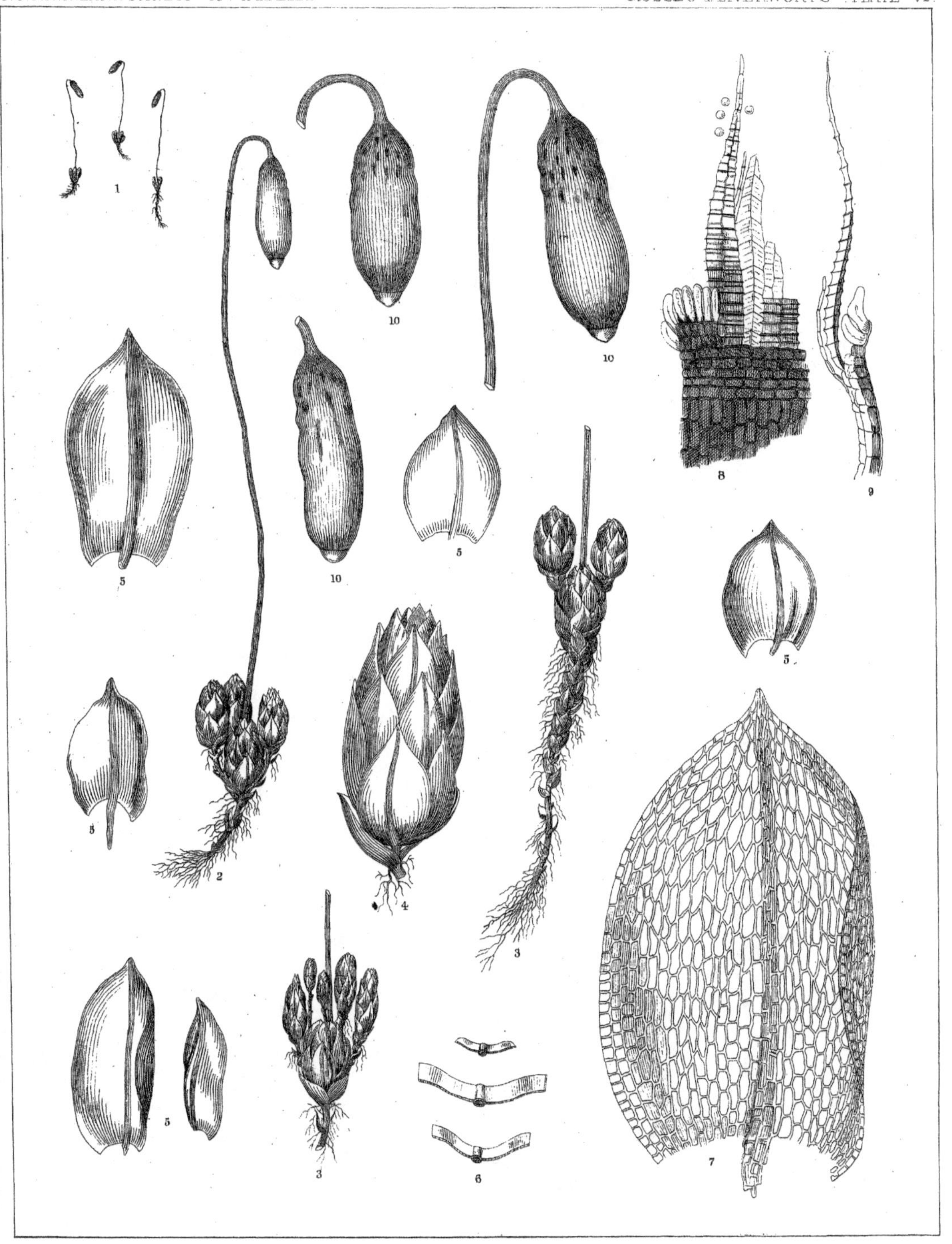

BRYUM CALIFORNICUM.

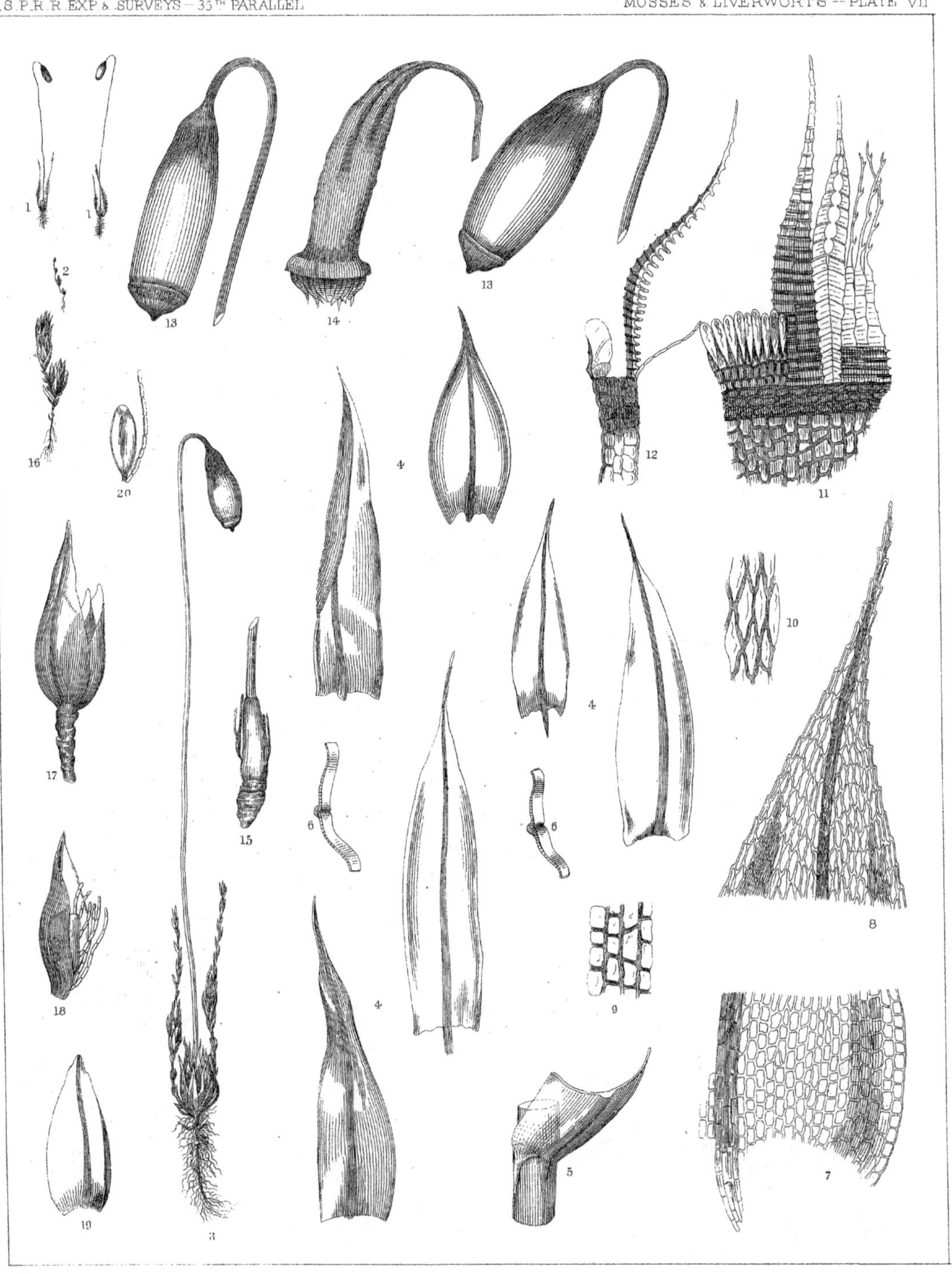

BRYUM OCCIDENTALE.

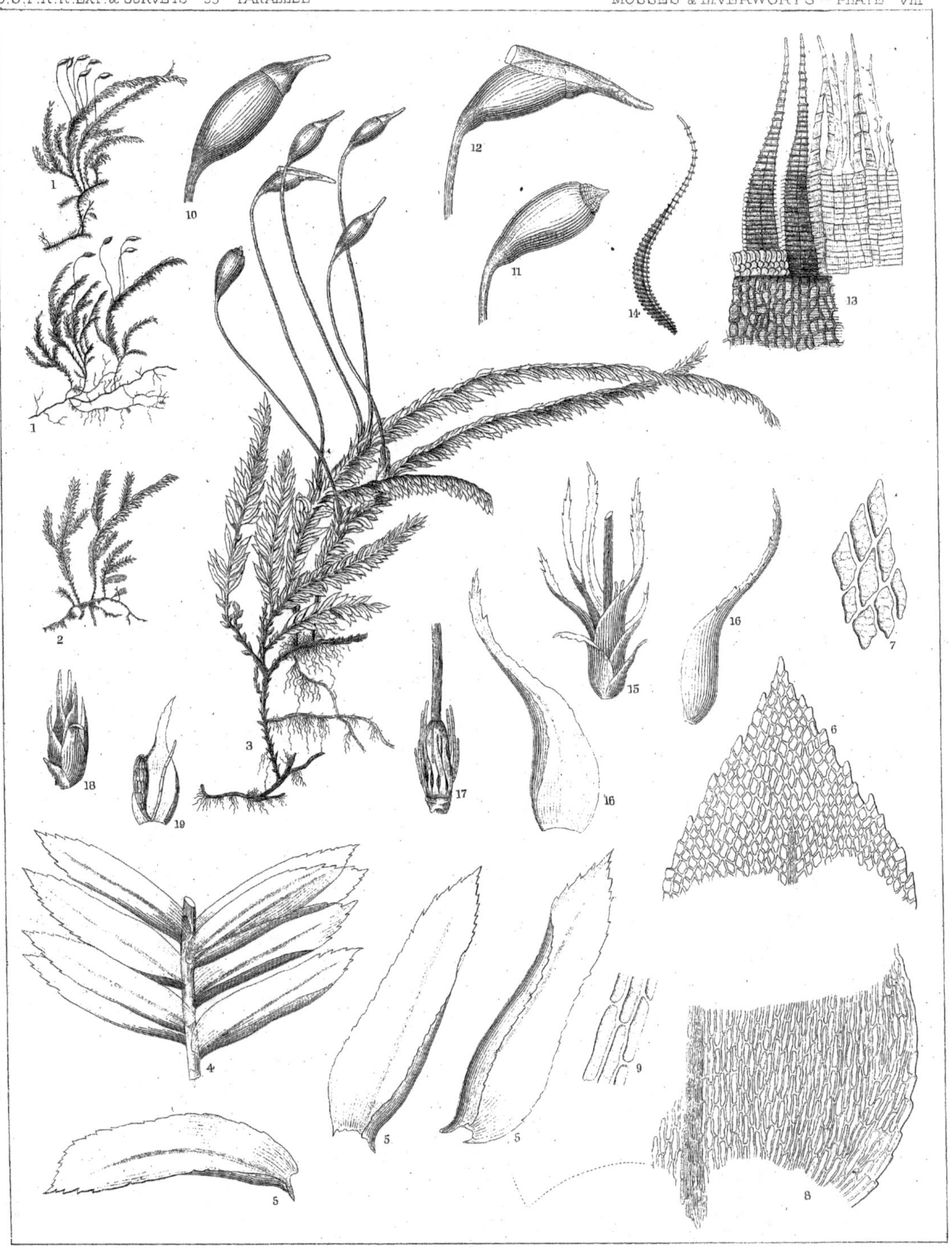

HYPNUM BIGELOVII.

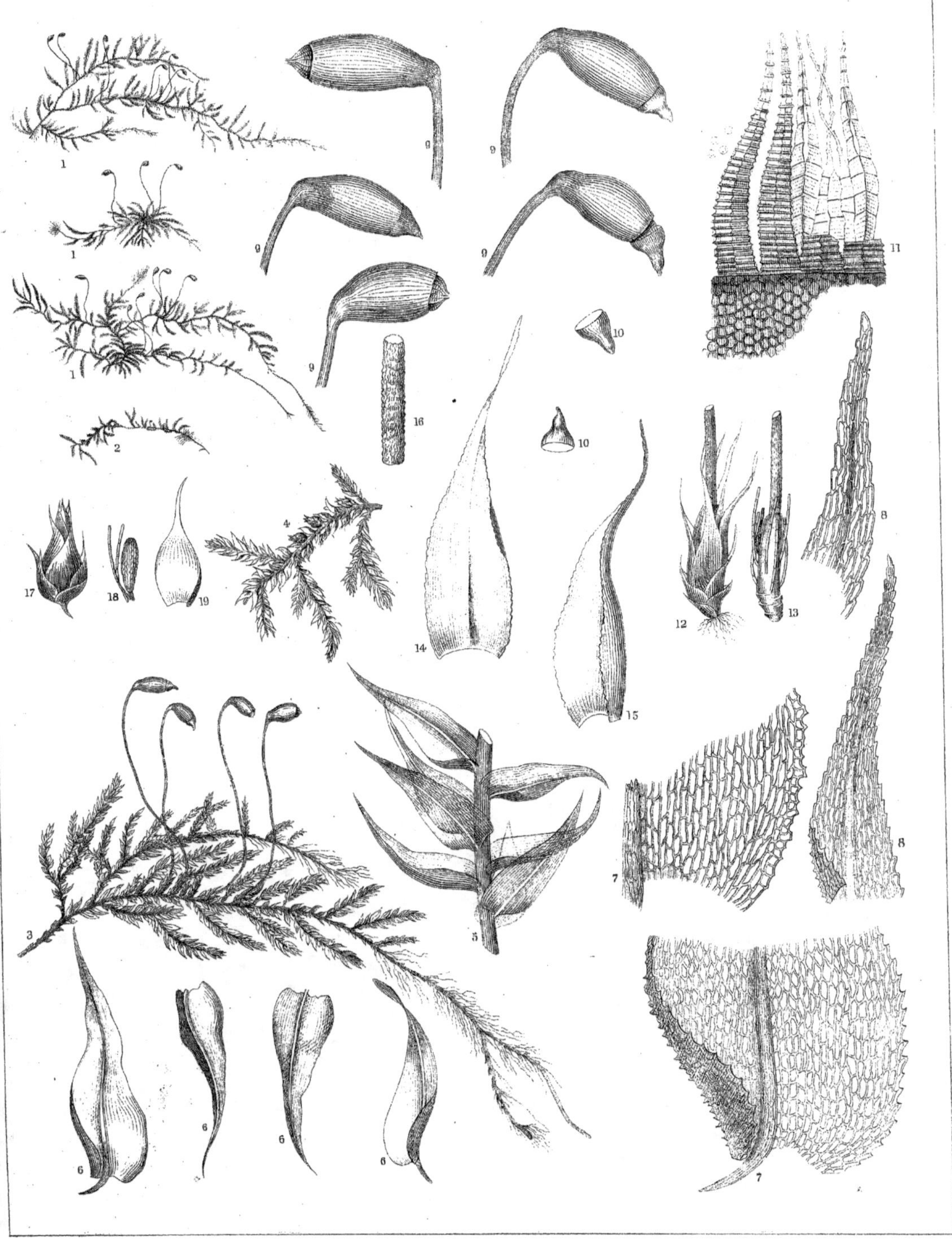

HYPNUM WHIPPLEANUM.

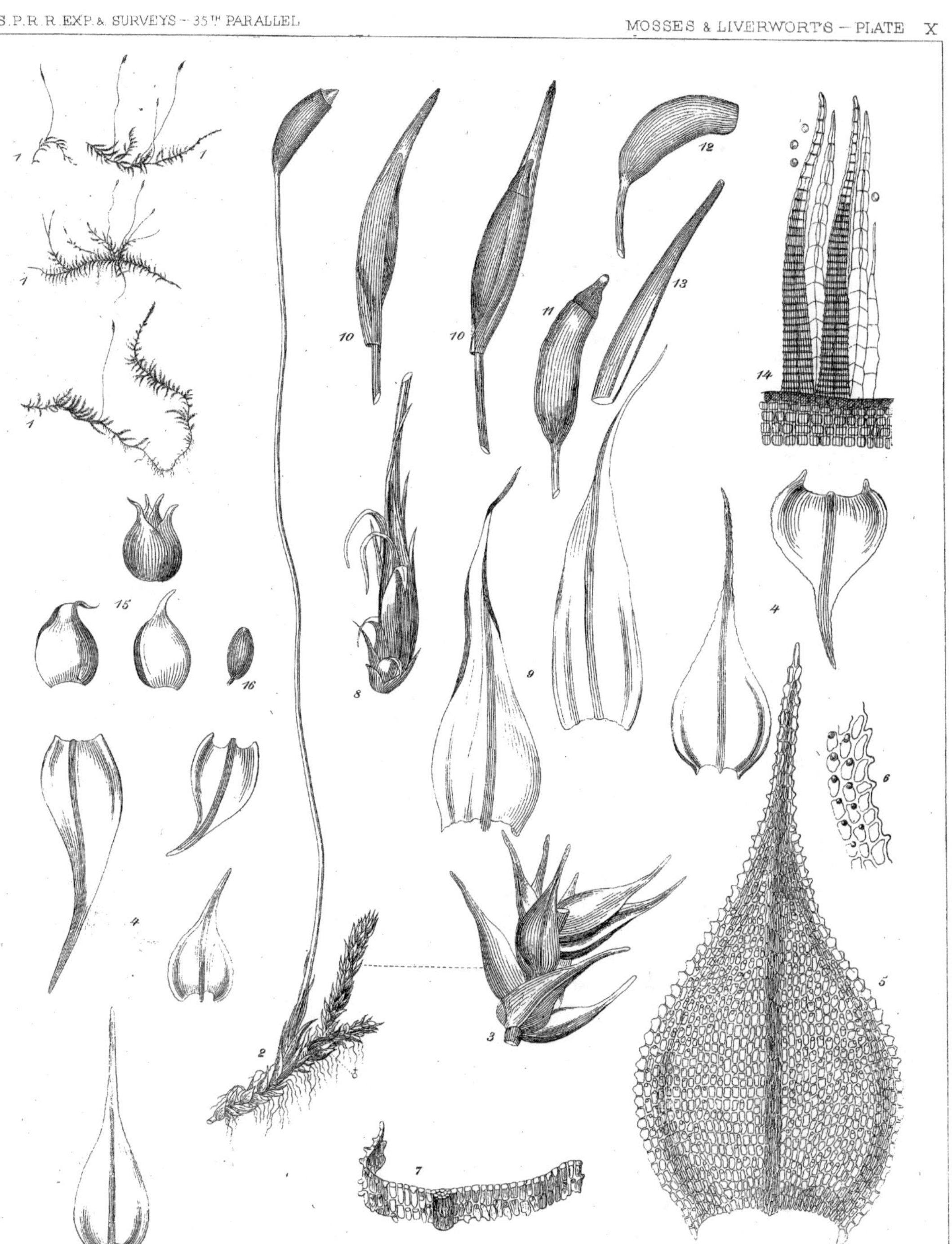

HYPNUM CALYPTRATUM.

www.ingramcontent.com/pod-product-compliance
Lightning Source LLC
LaVergne TN
LVHW020105110826
845151LV00001B/69

* 9 7 8 1 4 2 5 5 4 5 3 2 1 *